The
L/L Research
Channeling Archives

Transcripts of
the Meditation Sessions

Volume 7
June 17, 1984 to October 13, 1985

Don
Elkins

Jim
McCarty

Carla L.
Rueckert

Copyright © 2009 L/L Research

All rights reserved. No part of this book may be reproduced or used in any form or by any means—graphic, electronic or mechanical, including photocopying or information storage and retrieval systems—without written permission from the copyright holder.

ISBN: 978-0-945007-81-4

Published by L/L Research
Box 5195
Louisville, Kentucky 40255-0195

E-mail: contact@llresearch.org
www.llresearch.org

About the cover photo: *This photograph of Jim McCarty and Carla L. Rueckert was taken during an L/L Research channeling session on August 4, 2009, in the living room of their Louisville, Kentucky home. Jim always holds hands with Carla when she channels, following the Ra group's advice on how she can avoid any possibility of astral travel.*

Dedication

These archive volumes are dedicated to Hal and Jo Price, who faithfully and lovingly hosted this group's weekly meditation meetings from 1962 to 1975,

to Walt Rogers, whose work with the research group Man, Consciousness and Understanding of Detroit offered the information needed to begin this ongoing channeling experiment,

and to the Confederation of Angels and Planets in the Service of the Infinite Creator, for sharing their love and wisdom with us so generously through the years.

Table of Contents

Introduction 6
Year 1984 8
    June 17, 1984 9
    June 24, 1984 15
    July 1, 1984 22
    July 8, 1984 28
    July 15, 1984 31
    July 22, 1984 36
    July 29, 1984 41
    August 5, 1984 45
    August 12, 1984 53
    August 19, 1984 58
    August 26, 1984 64
    September 30, 1984 71
    October 7, 1984 75
    October 14, 1984 77
    November 11, 1984 82
    November 18, 1984 91
    November 25, 1984 97
    November 30, 1984 103
    December 2, 1984 109
    December 9, 1984 111
    December 16, 1984 118
    December 23, 1984 124
    December 30, 1984 127
Year 1985 135
    January 6, 1985 136
    January 13, 1985 142
    January 22, 1985 148
    January 27, 1985 153
    January 27, 1985 157
    February 10, 1985 165
    February 17, 1985 173
    February 23, 1985 176
    February 24, 1985 182
    February 26, 1985 187
    March 3, 1985 190
    March 10, 1985 196
    March 17, 1985 199
    March 24, 1985 206

March 26, 1985	212
April 3, 1985	217
April 7, 1985	222
April 9, 1985	229
April 14, 1985	235
April 21, 1985	242
April 28, 1985	252
May 5, 1985	261
May 12, 1985	268
May 19, 1985	273
May 26, 1985	280
June 2, 1985	285
June 9, 1985	292
June 16, 1985	297
June 18, 1985	305
June 23, 1985	311
June 30, 1985	316
July 2, 1985	325
July 7, 1985	332
July 14, 1985	338
July 21, 1985	344
July 28, 1985	350
August 4, 1985	357
August 11, 1985	362
August 18, 1985	369
September 15, 1985	374
September 22, 1985	381
September 29, 1985	385
October 6, 1985	390
October 13, 1985	394

Introduction

Welcome to this volume of the *L/L Research Channeling Archives*. This series of publications represents the collection of channeling sessions recorded by L/L Research during the period from the early seventies to the present day. The sessions are also available on the L/L Research website, www.llresearch.org.

Starting in the mid-1950s, Don Elkins, a professor of physics and engineering at Speed Scientific School, had begun researching the paranormal in general and UFOs in particular. Elkins was a pilot as well as a professor and he flew his small plane to meet with many of the UFO contactees of the period.

Hal Price had been a part of a UFO-contactee channeling circle in Detroit called "The Detroit Group." When Price was transferred from Detroit's Ford plant to its Louisville truck plant, mutual friends discovered that Price also was a UFO researcher and put the two men together. Hal introduced Elkins to material called *The Brown Notebook* which contained instructions on how to create a group and receive UFO contactee information. In January of 1962 they decided to put the instructions to use and began holding silent meditation meetings on Sunday nights just across the Ohio River in the southern Indiana home of Hal and his wife, Jo. This was the beginning of what was called the "Louisville Group."

I was an original member of that group, along with a dozen of Elkins' physics students. However, I did not learn to channel until 1974. Before that date, almost none of our weekly channeling sessions were recorded or transcribed. After I began improving as a channel, Elkins decided for the first time to record all the sessions and transcribe them.

During the first eighteen months or so of my studying channeling and producing material, we tended to reuse the tapes as soon as the transcriptions were finished. Since those were typewriter days, we had no record of the work that could be reopened and used again, as we do now with computers. And I used up the original and the carbon copy of my transcriptions putting together a manuscript, *Voices of the Gods*, which has not yet been published. It remains as almost the only record of Don Elkins' and my channeling of that period.

We learned from this experience to retain the original tapes of all of our sessions, and during the remainder of the seventies and through the eighties, our "Louisville Group" was prolific. The "Louisville Group" became "L/L Research" after Elkins and I published a book in 1976, *Secrets of the UFO*, using that publishing name. At first we met almost every night. In later years, we met gradually less often, and the number of sessions recorded by our group in a year accordingly went down. Eventually, the group began taking three months off from channeling during the summer. And after 2000, we began having channeling meditations only twice a month. The volume of sessions dropped to its present output of eighteen or so each year.

These sessions feature channeling from sources which call themselves members of the Confederation of Planets in the Service of the Infinite Creator. At first we enjoyed hearing from many different voices: Hatonn, Laitos, Oxal, L/Leema and Yadda being just a few of them. As I improved my tuning techniques, and became the sole senior channel in L/L Research, the number of contacts dwindled. When I began asking for "the highest and best contact which I can receive of Jesus the Christ's vibration of unconditional love in a conscious and stable manner," the entity offering its thoughts through our group was almost always Q'uo. This remains true as our group continues to channel on an ongoing basis.

The channelings are always about love and unity, enunciating "The Law of One" in one aspect or another. Seekers who are working with spiritual principles often find the material a good resource. We hope that you will as well. As time has gone on the questions have shifted somewhat, but in general the content of the channeling is metaphysical and focused on helping seekers find the love in the moment and the Creator in the love.

At first, I transcribed our channeling sessions. I got busier, as our little group became more widely known, and got hopelessly behind on transcribing. Two early transcribers who took that job off my hands were Kim

Howard and Judy Dunn, both of whom masterfully transcribed literally hundreds of sessions through the eighties and early nineties.

Then Ian Jaffray volunteered to create a web site for these transcriptions, and single-handedly unified the many different formats that the transcripts were in at that time and made them available online. This additional exposure prompted more volunteers to join the ranks of our transcribers, and now there are a dozen or so who help with this. Our thanks go out to all of these kind volunteers, early and late, who have made it possible for our webguy to make these archives available.

Around the turn of the millennium, I decided to commit to editing each session after it had been transcribed. So the later transcripts have fewer errata than the earlier ones, which are quite imperfect in places. One day, perhaps, those earlier sessions will be revisited and corrections will be made to the transcripts. It would be a large task, since there are well over 1500 channeling sessions as of this date, and counting. We apologize for the imperfections in those transcripts, and trust that you can ascertain the sense of them regardless of a mistake here and there.

Blessings, dear reader! Enjoy these "humble thoughts" from the Confederation of Planets. May they prove good companions to your spiritual seeking. ♣

For all of us at L/L Research,

Carla L. Rueckert

Louisville, Kentucky

July 16, 2009

Year 1984

June 17, 1984 to December 30, 1984

Sunday Meditation
June 17, 1984

(C channeling)

I am Hatonn, and I am now with this instrument. We greet you, my friends, in the love and the light of the one Creator. It is indeed a privilege to speak to you tonight and welcome a new friend to this circle. It is always a privilege to blend our humble words to be spoken to one who seeks. On your journey you will not be alone. Always you will find that as you travel that you will contact kindred spirits. They may not come from where you expect them. If you follow a certain path prescribed by one of your religions, those who may share the journey may not necessarily come to you from those who follow your specific faith To know those with whom you may share, one must open himself, offer meditation of love, for as a small light in a darkened room, you will find that others were drawn as you may be drawn to another life. I am Hatonn.

At this time, if we may, we would transfer this contact to another instrument. I am Hatonn.

(Carla channeling)

I am Hatonn, and I greet you once again, my friends, in the love and the light of our infinite Creator. We shall once again attempt to speak through the one known as S when we have used this instrument for awhile yet. We are giving this instrument word by word communication rather than using the concepts because at times this form of communication is helpful to the group, and this instrument is the only one at present which has experience at using this form of communication. It is somewhat difficult, and therefore there is the need to remain, shall we say, in practice, much as the baseball player must pick up his mitt from time to time or he begins catching too far off the palm and the ball begins to fall on the ground. So it is with word-to-word, or for that matter, concept communication. The catching must be renewed so that the practice will be fresh and the communication therefore clear.

We take you as in a story to a castle. You look at the ruins of a castle. It is gray. No smoke rises now from the once bright turrets. No rushes now adorn great halls. Battle has passed by; centuries have passed also. There is no life within the castle any longer, no nobility, no slave, no joy and sorrow. And yet the life that was is read by one who studies the ruins, by one who sees laid out upon the plain the stone delineation of each wall, the stark skeleton of the battlements, the suggestion of the once great flying buttresses and castellated points of defense, the now heaped moat, dry and full of earth.

Many wonder why there are those who are drawn to ruins, and, yet, my friends, you will be drawn magnetically to your life when once you have lived it. You shall not see each stone of your own castle, each battle, each year, each joy, each sorrow. What you shall see is what you have built. You shall see the floor plan, as it were, of a life that has been lived, that has been created by you within your incarnational experience. You are at this time a'building. You may find yourself tearing out walls, adding sections, adjusting, reshaping, accepting. Above all, we hope that you find yourself loving, for that is what makes your floor plan, your life, that which you may gaze upon in retrospect without feeling that you have wasted the materials and the tools of your illusion.

Some build small lives and some great, just as some prefer the cabin and some the castle. Each fights his own battles, some are fiercely inward, some are quite visible to those about the entity. But the sum total is not supposed to be any shape, any size, any number of rooms, any degree of complexity. The supposition with which you came into this incarnation was simple. You supposed yourself to be a part of the one infinite Creator and as such you supposed yourself to be capable of coming into a new relationship towards yourself. That is, you supposed yourself to be capable of learning. Learning, my friends, begins with the supposition that there is a hope of knowledge. If one believes there is a certainty of knowledge, it may be said that one perhaps is too smug, for this is not an illusion of certainty. But those who hope and seek for knowledge are building well.

Each day there are times, whether those times be infinitesimally small—the ticking of a clock or the wail of a siren—or quite long—an evening period late at night when you may turn in true and pure seeking, regardless of how busy you may be because of those things which you must do to live within the illusion—to that which is sought. What do you seek? And how purely and carefully and lucidly do you pursue it?

We ask you these questions as we ask them of ourselves. We know that we seek service; you may not. We have an advantage; we are not of your density. You have the chance to choose service to others, not in the knowledge but in the hope that it is possible to serve others. You will spend the rest of your incarnation, if so you choose, attempting to untie the Gordian knot of service to others. It is very difficult; it may often seem impossible. It is the way you build your life.

Thus, you see, my friends, there is no time that you must consider lost, for in the beat of your heart, in the striking of the noon whistle, in any moment you may turn fully for that moment to affirm your seeking, and that moment will fill you for hours or for days. If you awaken in the reaches of the night and have no one with whom to speak and yet you seek, you are immediately not alone, for there are countless millions who seek. There is no second of time when one of those upon your sphere seeks alone. Always, as you seek you seek with a mighty company of those within your incarnational experience, those upon your sphere at this time and those in your so-called inner planes, angelic presences and teachers who rush to assist those who seek so that there is no solitude in the negative sense, but a solitary peace which comes from joining your own river to the sea of seeking consciousness, that which waves and waves upon itself, always in motion, never still, always seeking, but always full.

You see, my friends, you were born and you shall die and, therefore, it seems to you that you are much like a building, the castle of which we spoke, that your life has a framework and that you work upon it and look back upon it, and all this is so, and yet, at the same time you are one with that which was before time began. You have never left the great ocean of the one original Thought, the one great Logos, that which we call love.

At this time we would transfer to the instrument known as S. We have been conditioning the one known as R, and would spend some time as we transfer with each of those in the circle, if each desires. You have but to ask mentally and we shall be with you as always. We transfer now. I am Hatonn.

(S channeling)

I am Hatonn, and we greet you, dear friends, once again. We are most pleased to be with this instrument, for it has been some time since she has felt comfortable with our presence. She is most accepting of us this evening and we are grateful to her.

Dear friends, we hope that we are able in some small way to aid you as you travel what may often seem a long and difficult path. The path at times may seem nearly unpassable but we also realize that each is aware that at any moment one may diligently clear those obstacles which may be ahead of you at any particular moment, and often you find that the path is cleared with much less effort than perhaps you had anticipated. And often a boulder that may look very large and very heavy is not what it seems in that the boulder that may look very large and very heavy often is moved aside with a very light touch.

We wished only to exercise this instrument for a short time this evening. She is somewhat distracted by what she feels is an oncoming sneezing attack and is somewhat anxious that she does not disrupt us with this. We would therefore leave, and as we depart we thank each present for the gracious invitation and we also are aware of the unity which your group has shared with us, and we feel especially at one with you this evening. We leave you, dear friends, as always, in the love and in the light of the one infinite Creator. We are known to you as Hatonn. Adonai.

(Jim channeling)

I am Latwii, and I greet you, my friends, in the love and in the light of our infinite Creator. We are most honored to be asked to join your group once again in the attempt to answer those queries which you may have upon your minds. We would preface our service with the reminder that our words are but opinions. We suggest weighing them accordingly, reserving those which have meaning and discarding those which do not. May we then begin with the first query, my friends?

R: Yes, Latwii. First, I'd like to say just "Hello." It's been so long, I feel like a stranger with you. I have to thank you inadvertently for something that happened this week, reading the transcripts from a few Sunday meetings ago and it's had a very interesting effect on just things that have been happening for the last five days or so last week.

I really have a question, but, since, you know, since you were involved basically with what was going on, I wonder if there is any general comment or statement you could make to just confirm or deny the positive/negative/positive/negative/positive/negative problem that I guess not only I have but everyone in this room has from time to time?

I am Latwii, and am aware of your general concern, my brother. We are most honored to greet you once again and attempt some small service. We can affirm that each entity shall encounter those experiences which are most promising, shall we say, in the developing of those biases which each wishes to develop. The experiences will seem to be of a positive or negative nature according to the current attitude of the entity's mind or perceptions, for, indeed, and in truth, each experience is of no, shall we say, particular charge but is of a neutral nature containing the Creator in full. How the experience is perceived is a function of the mind and perception of the one who is within the experience.

One may take the most cruel and harsh experience and find within it the infinite love and light of the one Creator, for, indeed, it resides there as that love and light resides within all experience. We can suggest that the perception of an experience as being of a negative nature is not necessarily less efficient or does not demonstrate less understanding than does the perception of the experience as being positive, for it may be most helpful for an entity to experience what seems quite negative and to use that experience to carve out a great potential, shall we say, within the inner being so that experiences of a wider variety and range may be available then to that entity. This would then increase the eventual positive perceptive ability of that entity.

May we answer you further, my brother?

R: Briefly, Latwii. I wonder if you could comment on an observation that negative being more … I don't know what the … maybe easy or more glittery or something, but that we all have that capability of negative or positive or that energy. Is that perhaps why your initial response to catalyst sometimes, or maybe most times, will be negative, but then, if your second response is allowed to come through, it would be a very balanced level-headed positive type attitude so that you'd go for the quick one for the thrill, but the real basic truth, I guess, is that second response.

I don't know—these are weird questions I'm asking you. I understand and appreciate your putting up with it. Could that be true or false though, that first response/second response to catalyst being negative/positive?

I am Latwii, and feel some grasp of your query, my brother, and shall attempt a response. We may suggest that, indeed, the negative response may seem quite easy at first. By this, we mean it is easy to think of the self before thinking of another. It is easy to make the sharp response to an imagined insult. Yet, upon reflection one might make what is called the magical transformation of the moment and refrain from such sharp response and turn towards the serving of the other self by seeing that other self as the Creator and observing the situation that is shared as an opportunity to share the love of the Creator with the other self which seems a threat.

It is easy to begin the travel upon the negative path and to begin to serve the self, but that path is a most difficult path to continue to the point of harvest. Though it is more difficult to make the response and seek to serve the other self, that path, in truth, is the most easily traveled of the two paths, though its initiatory stages are most difficult.

Might we answer you further, my brother?

R: No, you've answered very clearly, as always. Thanks again, and thanks again for making me laugh this week, reading your words.

I am Latwii, and we thank you, my brother. We are most happy to hear that our words have also provided joy and happiness, for we are of that vibration, and feel great joy with each experience of the Creator, and seek to share that in some small way through our humble words.

May we attempt another query at this time?

Carla: Could I just run down what R said, because I was really interested in how you answered it. I just had a couple of thoughts and wanted to check them. First of all, you answered about the negative/positive by saying that a lot of times your first vision of another person is negative and then you see the other person as the Creator the second time around. When I analyze responses that I've made to people that are what I think are less than great, the person that I've found not recognizable as the Creator actually is myself. I have some lack of self-confidence, some dislike of myself, or some feelings that I'm not worthy or something screws my thinking up enough so that I perceive the other person as not the Creator, whereas, if I were being the way I often am, then I would just see the person as a nice person, and you'd have to work real hard to convince me otherwise, which I suppose can happen.

First of all, is that a distinction worth making, that a lot of times it begins within the self-confidence of the worthy/unworthy portion of the work that's being done spiritually by the person that's having these negative/positive experiences that causes them? It's the attitude of the self before it even gets out towards the other?

I am Latwii, and am aware of your query, my sister. We feel we might be of the most service by affirming that, indeed, the purpose of each experience is to find the Creator. The finding of the Creator may occur in various ways. The beginning for some people is to see that Creator and to find the Creator's love within another being. Yet each being and each experience that one encounters is a mirror. One will finally see the self within that mirror. If one has been able to see the Creator in that mirror, one may then see the Creator in the self. Others, on the other hand, may begin by finding the Creator within the self and then radiating that image onto the entities and experiences that it encounters. The finding of the Creator …

(Side one of tape ends.)

Carla: … Well, that's really neat. That means that they are just two different tools, but the same thing, and depending on your personality you can either start from yourself and work out or start with people and work in.

The other question that I had, sometimes I have heard my friends, well, this hasn't happened lately but I've heard it often enough, complain about the attention that they get from men, women friends complain about the attentions that they get from men, and I've often wondered why that is perceived as an insult when actually it's a normal *(inaudible)* response and that's why they're using the eye makeup and that's why they're brushing their hair and wearing pretty clothes. And I have this feeling that a lot of times probably guys feel guilty about the same thing, you know, "Gee, I shouldn't be thinking that girl's pretty and I'm in a married situation here," when actually its just a normal response, and if you just accept it, it would just fall into place as a part of love and not a part that has to be acted out, just a part that's understood. But it seems like it gets in people's way, and I wonder if that is a real sub-negative/positive class of its own, just sort of a blockage of recognition that those feelings aren't threats, you don't have to do anything about those feelings but accept them? Did I make that too complex?

I am Latwii, and feel that we may pluck from the words the gist of the query. We would suggest that when one is both punished and rewarded for the same action there may be the confusion in the participation in that action. That is so in many realms of your people's experience and is a portion of the confusion which each has the opportunity to wend its way through, for within such confusion one must exercise the inner strength and become strong. If there were no confusion there would then be less opportunity to gain that spiritual strength by which one may evolve in mind, body and spirit.

May we attempt further response, my sister?

Carla: I'll have to read that. I'm not sure what relationship that had to my query. Thank you so much, it's very good hearing you again. Bye.

I am Latwii, and we greet you also, my sister, in great joy and thank you for allowing us to attempt to serve in our small way. May we attempt another query at this time?

S: Yes, just briefly, Latwii. I was wondering if you could comment or give me some advice about fasting. What I mainly want to know is, do you know of any way, first of all, to make this less painful? I thought that any words you gave me I could think over in moments of stress to help get me through it, and also how to get the most out of the experience in a spiritual way?

I am Latwii, and am aware of your query, my sister. To take the last portion of your query first, we might suggest that the greatest harvest can be achieved by making the fast a symbol for some spiritual pursuit. By attempting the gross cleansing of the physical vehicle it is possible for the entity to also cleanse the mind and spirit portions of the complex by which it moves through evolution. If one then can set this purpose in symbolic form for the fast firmly within the mind, then the pains of the fast which accompany the practice may have a purpose which can be understood and used as a strength to propel the entity through the experience. When one undertakes such an experience it is well to use the same type of tuning that is used for these meditations in a periodic fashion in order to reinforce that purpose for which the fast has been undertaken.

May we answer you further, my sister?

S: No, as always, you've been perfect. Thank you.

I am Latwii, and we thank you, my sister. May we attempt another query at this time?

Carla: When one is speaking verbally to a person who for some reason has a diminished mental capacity, is one on any level able to leave a message of any kind, and if so, what's the best way to leave that message?

I am Latwii, and am aware of your query, my sister. Yes, it is quite possible to leave a message to one who is somewhat impaired in the understanding of verbal communication and this method is what we might call the intention. The desire within your being to communicate is that which shall be communicated upon a level which one might call the unconscious, yet it shall reach into those levels of the conscious mind, and take whatever form is understood by the entity with whom you wish to communicate.

Therefore, if you feel that words fail, do not give up the words, but place them upon the firm foundation of a strong and pure desire which you shall communicate by your very being, your presence, your feelings, the movement and motion of your hands and eyes and the love which flows from your heart.

May we answer you further, my sister?

Carla: Yes. When such a person is so devoted to a healthy person that that entity would be perfectly happy to live the entire life through the healthy person, this being part of his mental impairment, is love expressed to that entity by the healthy person on any level by the severe withdrawal from constant company with that person, the intention, of course, being to enable that person's own health to come back?

I am Latwii, and am aware of your query, my sister. Yes, this experience which you describe does contain love, but it is that love which has attempted a balance with wisdom, for to give purely in love might mean the martyring, shall we say, of the self. This would allow certain lessons to be learned and services to be offered yet would end the ability to do such at some point which might be called premature. To balance this great love with that known as wisdom would then offer another type of service and lesson, neither type being what we might call good or bad or better or worse, yet their natures differ. To seek to aid another in such a manner might result in, as you have described it, the regaining of the health of the other self and the continuing of the life pattern in a means which is more balanced, shall we say. To withdraw completely might also provide certain lessons and services again not of a good or bad, better or worse character, yet of a certain nature.

The path which one will follow and needs to follow according to its own choices for serving is a path which is found after great desire has been expended and prayer and contemplation and meditation. We affirm the great underlying nobility of the intention of the desire to serve. The manner of service is a person's choice.

May we answer you further, my sister?

Carla: No, thank you.

I am Latwii, and we thank you, my sister. May we attempt another query at this time?

(Pause)

I am Latwii, and as it appears that we have exhausted the queries for this session we shall take our leave of this instrument and this group. As always, we leave each in the love and light of the one infinite Creator, and remind each that we are available for your meditations upon request, and would be most honored to blend our vibrations with yours at any time you should so request. Again we remind each that we are but humble messengers of the one Creator and our words are as the shifting sands, and support those who travel as we travel. We recommend once again to leave those words which do not travel as you wish and to take those on your journey which are fair companions. We are known to you as those of Latwii. Adonai, my friends. Adonai vasu borragus.

(Carla channeling)

I am Nona, and I come to you in the love and the light of the infinite Creator. We are so happy that we are able to speak through this instrument. It has been some time. Many times we have been called by this group and have not been able to use this instrument, for it did not have the proper tuning, it was not strong within, and we wished to speak only long enough to point that in the healing work the worry, the fretting, is not the praying. The worrying causes a weakening of the truth stirring within so that energies such as that of Nona devoted wholly to healing cannot possibly come through. Therefore, this instrument had then to release the worrying to some extent in order that healing might come through this instrument. This is true of all healing and all prayer to the extent that we are aware. We now respond [to] many weeks of requests for our hearings vibrations and know that we think in love and in light.

(Carla channels a healing vocal melody from Nona.) ♣

L/L Research

L/L Research is a subsidiary of Rock Creek Research & Development Laboratories, Inc.

P.O. Box 5195
Louisville, KY 40255-0195

www.llresearch.org

Rock Creek is a non-profit corporation dedicated to discovering and sharing information which may aid in the spiritual evolution of humankind.

ABOUT THE CONTENTS OF THIS TRANSCRIPT: This telepathic channeling has been taken from transcriptions of the weekly study and meditation meetings of the Rock Creek Research & Development Laboratories and L/L Research. It is offered in the hope that it may be useful to you. As the Confederation entities always make a point of saying, please use your discrimination and judgment in assessing this material. If something rings true to you, fine. If something does not resonate, please leave it behind, for neither we nor those of the Confederation would wish to be a stumbling block for any.

CAVEAT: This transcript is being published by L/L Research in a not yet final form. It has, however, been edited and any obvious errors have been corrected. When it is in a final form, this caveat will be removed.

© 2009 L/L Research

Sunday Meditation
June 24, 1984

(K channeling)

I am Hatonn. This instrument was exceedingly reluctant to begin this evening but we are glad she finally consented. We rejoiced while you were laughing. As we have said before, laughter is good medicine, and as we have indicated also in the past, the peoples of this planet are far too serious. You work at everything too hard instead of living and working freely in the creative mind and spirit of the universe. You will remember that the one you call Christ said, "My yoke is easy and my burden is light." He also said, "I came to give you abundant life, a joyful life." You could benefit, my friends, by being joyful, and we adjure you to think of yourself as walking in the light.

And you were just speaking of magic. And what is magic but the tuning in to the light, the beauty, and the caring of the universe. The universe is indeed rich to all those who trust in its beauty, and even its magic. As some of your seers have demonstrated, one can [lay up] in peace even under dire circumstances because one can tune in to the harmony and the balance and the peace of the universe just as one can tune in to the hate and all the other negative emotions. It is a matter, my friends, of choice, a matter, if you please, of willing, because the power of the universe does indeed work with you.

We wish to thank this instrument for permitting us to speak through her, and we leave you now and transfer to another instrument. I am Hatonn.

(Carla channeling)

I am Hatonn, and I greet you once again in the love and the light of the one infinite Creator. We have passed among each of the other instruments, and have found the request, "Not this time, not this time," and so we come to this instrument. We find this instrument much involved in the challenging of a new entity. Therefore, we are giving this instrument time to tune to us that we may speak of that power which is that in the universe which is always sought in one way or another by those who dwell upon your surface.

Some say they seek money, my friends, and some say they seek truth. Some seek position, and some seek justice, and some search rubble for history, but all are in search of that which is powerful, that which works within your minds, your bodies and your spirits to feed, to clothe, and to inspire. The value of seeing all kinds of power as roughly equal is that it enables [you] to choose more clearly and lucidly the kind of power you wish to pursue. Money is power, and you may pursue the making of it with great vigor. Those without money are certainly powerless in the most fundamental way. Position is power. There are things which position may gain one which money cannot. And you will frequently find that those who have money may yet desire power, the power that they cannot have. The wisdom of knowing what has been is power, for that which has been and that which will be are linear. And except for flashes of lightning, shall we say, which herald the dawning of each new age, human behavior can be predicted and extrapolated and needs can be met humanely.

Truth is the ultimate power, and yet, my friends, it has the least effect upon your illusion. When you seek truth, you must face the fact that you are seeking something that is not eminently practical. We search this instrument's mind to discover the most appropriate analogy and we find that all other kinds of power are polyester but truth is cotton. It will not bend itself to you; it takes care, and it is costly. That which is truth lies beyond space and time. Therefore, that which you know shall always be less than that which there is to know. And yet, with the power of truth, with the mere seeking of this truth, you uncover for yourself a connection beyond space and beyond time with that which was before the world began its stately movement through space and time. In other words, my friends, you gain the advantage of the very wide viewpoint of infinity. Those who seek money, power, prestige or knowledge seek puny things which shall be killed off and which shall rot with the bodies which have sought them. And the world of your third density shall repeat, and repeat again, and repeat once again, the great cycles that teach.

And what do they teach, my friends? They teach finally, for those who pay close attention, that the truly powerful thought, knowledge, power and birthright is the one original Thought, which connects that which is incarnate with that which is infinite. Many and many are the lessons of love which involve the ultimately frustrating fact that all wisdom, money and power are equal to folly, foolishness and ignorance in the handling of a certain situation. To be wise and to be foolish are as one, for some situations are unacceptable and shall remain so, and it is against the hard wall of this fact of the illusion that you must press the mind and your spirit until ultimately all gives way to the understanding that in love, in the original Thought, all things are acceptable. All things have an acceptable time and an acceptable space, for all things that are endured are also outlasted; all teach love.

If you are not learning love against the wall of your illusion, seek within, for we say to you, my friends, that it is there and its power is great enough to remove [you] from your distress. That which you can do with money, with wisdom, or with power you shall do. Those who seek to serve others shall day by day use each tool to do so. But the race is not to the swift nor victory to the wise, for all things are equal: the lesson is love.

We ask you to move in meditation with us now as we ask you to do each day, and yet at this time we shall be with you. We ask that you move far, far away from the domicile, the birdsong, and the pleasant evening air into the deepest reaches of starlit space, until you are beyond the stars, and find yourself clad only in the thick darkness of that which is your mother and your father—the one original Creator, the one Creation, the beating heart of which you are a part. You are no longer isolated, but wrapped in soft darkness, and you feel the rhythm and the movement of timelessness.

Ah, my friends. To say we are one is to repeat ourselves. To spend some time each day within the vastness of infinity, within your own inner quiet, is most highly recommended for those who wish to pursue the least powerful and the most powerful of all powers, the truth. We remind you that that which we give you is our experience and our opinion. In your life and your thoughts, use those things which we have said which may inspire, but quickly discard those things which do not seem proper, for we would not be a stumbling block to you but only an aid as we gain in service by being able to serve you. We thank you for the opportunity to polarize in service to others. It is our great delight. We thank each who did not wish to be instruments and acknowledge the great service each provides. And we thank each who call to those of Hatonn, for it is a great pleasure to share our thoughts with you. We shall be with you if you request our presence mentally. And now, my friends, we must leave this instrument to her challenging. We leave you in the love and the light of the infinite Creator. We are those of Hatonn. Adonai, my friends. Adonai vasu.

(Carla channeling)

I am Yadda. I am requested by this instrument to greet you in the name of love and light of Creator.

We do. We have had some time here challenging. This instrument challenging us in the name of Christ. We say, "Challenge us any way you like. All Creator. How about Buddha?" She say, "No. Christ." We say, "Okay." We greet you [in] love and light of Creator. We Yadda. We come because call. Not usually speak to groups of this kind. Very honored to be called, and only called because request of "Who are you?" That is question: "Who are you?" We say to you, you are not anything like you think you are. You are not what you do. You are not nine o'clock, ten o'clock, eleven o'clock, twelve o'clock. You must remove from yourself ideas this kind. Not help you. There is intense seeking in this group to know who you are. Remove from yourself all your clothing, your name, your nationality, your society, your neighborhood, your wife, your kiddies and your golf cart—all gone. Now who are you? We are not taking away from you, we wait for you to add to yourself the Creator.

You have heard of the masters. Do you think people become masters because they do not know who they are? Do you think you can take course to find out who you are or any kind of teaching? Not so. Not so, my children. Move along to a clearer perception of who you are. This is fundamental question which you must answer in order to do work. If you have machinery, you got to plug it in; you got to know amperage and voltage; you got to have right plug—male/female. You got gasoline engine, you got to know it's gasoline; you got kerosene, you got to know the fuel.

Now, you are a spiritual engine. You were made to do work. What is your fuel? Who are you? We thank you for calling us, and we thank this instrument, and thank the instrument also for the challenging, although we find the insistence upon Christ somewhat naive. We also feel it to be essential, and recommend the practice in some form that is workable to each who does work in channeling. Never receive without the tuning and the challenging. Otherwise you get pretty strange programs. No need to confuse you. I am Yadda. We suggest to this instrument that it do research. There has been this contact before. Not to this group. We leave you in the love and in the light of the One that Is. Adonai. Adonai.

(Jim channeling)

I am Latwii, and greet you, my friends, in love and light. We also are most appreciative of being asked to join your group this evening. As usual, we come in great joy and anticipation at being able to blend our vibrations with yours and attempt answers to your queries. Without further delay then, may we ask for the first query?

C: Latwii. In the last few weeks I'm getting a very depressing type of feeling in the house we now dwell in. Would you comment on whether or not anything—what's going on?

I am Latwii, and am aware of your query, my brother. We scan your recent memory and find that there is the parting of the dwelling and your own selves which produces a type of pain that might be described, as one of your poets has done, as a sweet type of sorrow, for that dwelling in which you have spent a great portion of your being and time is an entity as are you, and there has been much experience shared which shall not again be shared.

May we answer you further my brother?

C: This feeling's anything but sweet.

I am Latwii, and can only make the additional comment in response to your comment that there are other energies of a parting nature apparent and seeking expression.

May we answer you further, my brother?

C: Maybe later.

I am Latwii. We thank you for your patience and great desire. Is there another query?

K: Yes, Latwii. I am, I think, on a mailing list that is referred to as networking. I first read about that concept in Marilyn Ferguson's book, *The Aquarian Conspiracy*, and then I heard it in Chicago a year ago this past April when I was at a seminar. Would you comment on the concept of networking?

I am Latwii, and cannot refuse the pun that that would be the query of the fisherman, but shall, in a more serious vein, attempt response by suggesting that as those entities such as yourselves, which populate your country and your planet, begin to seek the light and love of the one Creator, and begin to radiate that light and love, there then is formed a great series of centers or sources of light. As these continue to seek in service to others, bonds or lines of communication are established, often by the exchange of letters, lectures, books, and in-person contact. As the energies are exchanged from center to center, there is then formed the network formed by light, and the desire to share that light with others.

May we answer you further, my sister?

K: Okay, then, is this light or band of light that we're talking about, is it all over the planet or is it just localized in this country?

I am Latwii, and am aware of your query, my sister. We joyfully …

(Side one of tape ends.)

(Jim channeling)

I am Latwii, and am again with this instrument. You may see each entity, to use an analogy, as a light bulb. Some have not been connected to their energy source in a conscious fashion and some have. The conscious connecting is analogous to screwing in the light bulb so that contact is made and this contact is being made throughout each country, as you call it, of your planet.

May we answer further, my sister?

K: So, then, this is really a raising of consciousness, or these entities are becoming more aware of their mission or more aware of who they are. Is that what we're talking about?

I am Latwii, and am aware of your query, my sister. These are indeed ways or means of describing the process which is occurring and has been occurring upon your planet for a great measure of time, for as each planetary sphere is inhabited with those of the third density form, there is the progress along the evolutionary path at each moment, but there are some points along that path which are of primary interest. These points are then able, because of their potential, to provide a greater radiance to the seeker which has passed the point. One of those points is that of seeking in a conscious fashion the answers to the great questions of your illusion, those questions, "Who am I?" "What is this life that I live?" "Where do I go from here?" and so forth. As the seeking becomes a conscious process, then the bulb is securely connected to its source and begins a radiance which was not previously possible.

May we answer you further, my sister?

K: Yes. Just pursuing the same line of questioning. It seems to me that psychology has tuned in, or at least some psychologists have tuned in to, I guess I could say, a mysticism. And psychology itself seems to me, has made fairly rapid strides or improvement in the last, oh, shall I say, five to ten years. Would you comment on that? Or at least it certainly seems to be—a lot of it seems to be different than what it was when I studied.

I am Latwii, and am aware of your query, my sister. It is correct that the field which you describe as psychology, as well as many other fields, has made great strides within the recent of your time called past. Many upon your planet in each walk of life, as it is called, has done a similar thing, that is to take what has been known in the field of study in which the entity finds itself and add the great desire to know the truth. Then that information which has gone before may either be seen in a new light or may be altered so that it provides a clearer picture, though still perhaps quite distorted, of the entity and its nature, the universe in which it finds itself, and the means by which the entity may move through that universe in an evolutionary manner.

May we answer you further, my sister?

K: No, Latwii. It's all very exciting. Thank you very much.

I am Latwii, and we thank you, my sister. Is there another query at this time?

S: Yes, Latwii. Could you comment on the advisability of channeling what would seem to be local entities or spiritual guides of some sort, whether it be working with the tarot or in working with the Oriental couple that apparently worked with me and R, providing that one's intentions are to seek knowledge and truth and that one is especially careful of tuning?

I am Latwii, and, my sister, we believe that you have answered your own query, for if, indeed, one is desirous in the utmost sense of seeking and serving the one infinite Creator, and wishes to more specifically to seek and to serve in the means of the channeling experience, then it is of little concern whether the entities that are channeled are of distant galaxies or your own neighborhood, shall we say. The primary point of concern is, as you have noted, the tuning of your own reception through your desire, and the refined tuning of whatever means you utilize so that the entities which are then able to channel through you are of the greatest positive polarity possible.

May we answer you further, my sister?

S: No, I just wanted confirmation. Thank you.

I am Latwii, and we thank you, as always. May we answer another query at this time?

Carla: Yeah. I'd sort of like to follow up on C's second answer. Because he kind of suggested that when there have been positive and negative energies put into a house or experienced within the house during the stay there, when you leave, the positive and negative energies are both there. I was wondering if it would be a responsible act on C and D's part to cleanse the house of the negative portion of the energies as they leave, and maybe to dedicate the new house for positive energies as well?

I am Latwii and am aware of your query, my sister. We may suggest looking upon the dwelling place which you call a house the same as one would look upon an entity, a companion, a friend, a loved one, with which one has spent a great deal of time, and with whom one has shared a great many experiences. What would one do if one should part with such an entity? This is the query which we believe the answer must come from those who part. And we provide this query and this perspective in order that that those who leave any entity might express whatever feelings of gratitude and honor, thanksgiving and respect, are truly felt.

May we attempt further response, my sister?

Carla: Yes. Because what C said was, the way he felt in the house was anything but grateful, sweet or any positive word, that he had felt negativity in the house, the energy seemed to be negative in the house. And so what I was wondering was, is this little entity called the house kind of schizoid or is it just a perception or is there another force besides the house itself that is entering into it …

(Sound of cat meowing)

Carla: … not A.

I am Latwii, and are very grateful that we are more easily found than the one known as A.

(Laughter)

Yet the call goes out as well for us, and we hear your call. We would respond to the query which you have asked with great sincerity by suggesting that there are those portions to this query which we have alluded to and may only allude to. We feel that additional comments have been offered in the light of the viewing the house as an entity which indeed it is. There have been experiences within this dwelling which have shaped those who have had the experience and the dwelling which has housed the experience. As the parting of these entities occurs, there is the drawing out of those experiences which have been left, shall we say, undone. We do not mean to make a large point of this particular issue, for there are indeed other factors to consider, but wish to state that it is a natural progress or process of relationship for the unfinished work to be drawn, shall we say, to the surface when the parting is nigh.

This is not always the case, but for those who have developed certain sensitivities there will be noted the experiences which are somewhat unusual in the normal frame of reference. In this particular case, there is the opportunity to resolve certain difficulties which have been experienced, though the opportunity presently seems to be of a negative nature, the digging below the appearance or surface shall uncover the potential for great positivity.

May we respond further, my sister?

Carla: That was really clear. I thank you for that. I would like to ask a couple of other questions, and I hope they're not too frivolous but I've always been curious. Are all houses and cars and things like that that are made by men alive in their own way? I have always felt that they were, and as a matter of fact have gone through life naming and talking to them. But that's just been my own way. Are they?

I am Latwii, and am aware of your query, my sister. As a beginning to this query we may suggest that, indeed, each portion of the one Creation is quite alive and intelligent, for the one Creator is all that there is. With this easily understood, then we may move to the portion of your query which we feel that you deal with here, and that is the individualizing process which occurs most notably within your third density illusion. This process begins as soon as there is a created portion of the universe. Therefore, rocks, dirt, trees, flowers, plants and, indeed, places may become what you call enspirited or invested with an identity as they are able to give and receive that which you call love. This love we would describe as the sharing of experience in an open and harmonious manner. Therefore, any place or thing or even idea may be so enspirited so that it exists as an entity and assumes an identity and continues on the evolutionary path as an individualized portion of the one Creator.

May we answer you further, my sister?

Carla: So what you're saying is that cars and houses aren't necessarily alive, it's just that if they've been invested then they have become entities, and a car or some other piece of machinery—a typewriter which is often talked to—could actually be something that has aliveness to it and can respond. Is that what you're saying?

I am Latwii, and am aware of your query, my sister. We feel that you have a great portion of the gist of our response. We may add that some of these entities which you have named will have what we have loosely termed an identity only for the, shall we say, length of their incarnative type existence. Here we find words are most difficult to use in the description of this process, but we wish to present the concept that, indeed, an entity such as one of your automobiles may exist as an entity for the length of its use as an automobile, and will perhaps, shall we say, dissolve its identity when no longer of an integrated nature, and shall find a new identity in another form.

May we answer you further, my sister?

Carla: Yeah. I've just always wanted to know this. Do houses appreciate being cleaned?

I am Latwii, and can answer in the emphatic affirmative, for, indeed, how does one feel when one is bathed and refreshed after a hard day's work?

May we answer further, my sister?

Carla: Yeah, I have another question, but that closes out that one. I got a tape from a friend who owns some very expensive taping equipment. He bought the taping equipment because he's a hi-fi nut, and he bought an expensive microphone to plug into this expensive equipment so he could tape letters to me some time ago. It seems I have blown not just one but two of his machines, or at least they won't work when I send my tapes and he tries to play my tapes. One of them won't work at all any more, and has to be sent back to the factory. The other one will work as long as my tapes aren't playing through. But if one of my letters which are on tape is inserted into the machine, it will not run. What's going on?

I am Latwii, and am aware of your query, my sister, and feel that you are aware also of the answer to your query, for your effect upon those mechanical devices that are of a electromagnetic nature is well known.

Carla: But Latwii, long distance? He's in Michigan. I don't understand.

I am Latwii, and am aware of your query, my sister. He is, indeed, some distance from you but your tape itself is with his machine and carries the charge in the form which you have given it, and therefore the effect upon his machinery is quite the same as your effect upon your own.

May we answer you further, my sister?

Carla: Is there any way to stop this effect from occurring? I mean while using the machinery?

I am Latwii, and am aware of your query, my sister. We know of no particular means which might provide relief from this bothersome situation other than attempting to send the messages in another form.

May we answer you further, my sister?

Carla: No, thank you.

I am Latwii, and we thank you, my sister. Is there another query at this time?

K: Yeah, there sure is. I don't want to wear you out but I'm really quite confused. I've read Seth from A to Z, and Seth says that we make our own environment, whatever my environment, I have made it myself. And that like attracts like. Like attracts like. So, I take this seriously, and my husband and I don't agree on very many things. And when I am having discord with my husband, I don't blame him any more. I say, well, I've got myself in this jam so I can't blame anybody else. I really have decided that whatever environment I'm in I've made it for myself, and I'm the one to learn from it.

Now, from what—I guess I haven't understood this quite because it sounds contradictory to me about the house affecting me, it seems, anyway. I accept the fact that I'm responsible for whatever environment I'm in. If it's misery, I put myself in misery to learn from it. Now, am I the one who's confused? Oh, yes, and by the way, Seth also says that even a nail in the house has some kind consciousness. I remember the first time I read that I about flipped. But I certainly think my car has some kind of consciousness, and I tell it all the time, you know, how grateful I am that it serves me so well. But let's get back to this environment. Do I create my own environment?

I am Latwii, and am aware of your query, my sister. The one Creator is all that there is. Therefore, each portion creates itself and its environment in cooperation with each other portion. You are a portion and are the one Creator who creates in cooperation with all other portions all that is created.

May we answer you further, my sister?

K: Yes, I understand that, I think.

Carla: I think she meant, if a house is an entity, is she not creating it? Is that right?

K: I guess I've read too many different things. So I guess maybe I've got to live with this a little while and think about it. But I am what I think I am. If I think I'm evil, I'm evil, if I think I'm good, I think—you know, I am what I think. I really can't be anything else, I believe. I think that's what I'm trying to say. If I think I'm in an evil environment, then I'm in an evil environment. Or if I think I'm living in a beautiful environment, then I'm in a beautiful environment. That's what I'm trying to say, I think. Could you comment on that?

I am Latwii, and am aware of your query, my sister. You are not only what you think you are, you are all things. There are no boundaries other than the ones that you choose for the purposes of learning and serving in specific ways.

May we answer you further, my sister?

K: No, I believe I'm going to accept that. Thank you.

I am Latwii, and we thank you. Is there another query at this time?

C: What I have in mind, I'd like to bounce a name off of you, and if you could, could you tell me if it's just a meaningless, made-up word or whether this is some type of entity and if so, what kind? It is called "Cre[t]e" *(The consonant is unclear)*.

I am Latwii, and although we have examined this sound vibration for pertinence in your particular incarnative existence, we can find no collection of meaning which can be transmitted, and are not aware of such.

May we attempt further response, my brother?

C: No, thank you.

I am Latwii, and thank you. Is there another query at this time?

(Pause)

I am Latwii, and would now once again wish to express great appreciation for being able to join with this group this evening. We of Latwii are of a nature which experiences great joy at being asked to speak those concepts which have some aid in another's evolutionary progress. We have, through our humble experience, traveled a significant portion of that path which we share with you. On this journey we have found many things to be of aid in the traveling, but none aids as does the sharing of the love and the light of the one Creator with another seeker. We could tell you of great adventures, astounding experiences, and the most incredible of sights, but we could not compare any of these experiences with the joy and meaning that we find as we attempt to share our humble understanding with this group and those of like minds. We cannot thank you enough, my friends, yet thank you always we will, for we travel with you on this great journey, the journey of the One to the One. On that journey, for the moment, we leave you in the love and the light of the one infinite Creator. We are those of Latwii. Adonai vasu borragus. ✤

Sunday Meditation
July 1, 1984

(Jim channeling)

I am Hatonn, and I greet you, my friends, in the love and in the light of our infinite Creator. We are privileged to be asked to join your group this evening. Though your group is small, we observe a great desire to know more of that which you call the truth. My friends, we share that desire with you, and cannot claim to know all that there is to know of the truth, but our experience has been such that we have gained some knowledge of this truth. And what we have gained thus far indicates in every degree that the greater portion of truth is what you call love. The foundation of all knowing is that quality of being known to your peoples so imperfectly as love. This quality of being is hidden within each portion of your creation and within each entity in order that each might have the opportunity to find it, for it has been our experience that there is nothing but the love of the one Creator with which the Creator has made all that is made, and that each portion of the one Creation seeks at its heart to purely manifest the love of which it is made and by which power it moves and has its being.

Many do not know that they are love and that they seek love. This is to say, many do not know that they seek themselves. Yet at some point, my friends, this great yearning to know love and to seek the self becomes apparent to each person so that a person becomes a seeker, a conscious pilgrim upon the great path of evolution, as you might call it. And when the seeker who consciously seeks that called truth, and that we have described as love, continues for some of what you call time upon this path of seeking, there come the testing, the obstacles, and the seeming difficulties upon the journey.

It is at such times that the seeker is provided an opportunity to demonstrate the degree of its own understanding of love and to assess in some measure for itself the further studies, shall we say, that are necessary in order to continue to more and more purely manifest the love which is its source and destination. The difficulties appear to be of a threatening nature, just as your illusion appears to be many parts, each separate from the other. The illusion in these facets is necessary in order that each seeker be able to gain the spiritual strength from meeting the difficulty that would not be possible were the illusion clearly perceived as an illusion. It must seem very real—that difficulty and those tests—in order that the seeker will participate. For when it is clearly known and experienced by the seeker that all is love, then the testing is no longer necessary, and likewise the illusion is no longer necessary, for the lessons available in that illusion have been taken advantage of, have been learned, and then the seeker passes on to another class, we may say.

And what shall power the seeker through the testings and the difficulties when it seems that there is not love anywhere, not within the self, not with the other, not within the life experience, within any portion. The testings are of what you may call a gradual nature so that no seeker is given more than the seeker can bear, and as the experience is gained, there develops those qualities that we might call the faith and the will that serve to power the seeker when all seems lost and love seems no more.

The faith, my friends, is that which cannot be adequately defined, yet it is a kind of knowing, for the roots of the being of each entity are one root in truth and feed each entity as the entity travels the path of the seeker. This knowing takes the form of what we might call faith, the knowing that somehow, in some way and in some degree all is well and shall be well. This we may call the faith. And as the experience continues for each seeker, growing with the faith is another concept which we may call the power of the will. As the experience is gathered, then the will is given the opportunity to be strengthened in order that the journey might continue. The desire of the seeker is most important to guide the will as it is exercised; then the faith holds that seeker's focus firmly upon the path of love.

Therefore, my friends, as you journey upon your own individual path, know that you do not journey alone, though you are unique. There is a great company of seekers, both seen and unseen, who travel with you, so that your faith and your will are shared by many and each encourages each as you continue those experiences which so adeptly hide the love implicit in each, yet make it available to those whose desire is on nothing else.

My friends, these are humble words which we share with you, and words which may at a glance seem but common sense, and, indeed, we feel that is so. We feel that the most common of senses is that sense of being which seeks love, seeks to give and to receive that known as love. Therefore, we give this simple message as a reminder that your journeys and your experiences, though seemingly of a very complex nature, are at their heart quite, quite simple. You stand upon the foundation of love. You are that love. You seek that love. And all about you is some form of that love made manifest and hidden within that illusion in order that you might have the opportunity of finding it.

We thank you, my friends, for calling for our humble assistance, and we remind each that we are available in your meditations at your request, and would be most happy to join you should you so request. We leave you now in the love and in the light of our infinite Creator. I am Hatonn. Adonai, my friends.

(Jim channeling)

I am Latwii, and I greet you, my friends, in the love and the light of our infinite Creator. We are also very privileged to be able to join this group this evening. We see that our brothers and sisters of Hatonn have already put one of your group to sleep by their didactic method, and we hope that we are not fated to put the other members to sleep, and shall ask if there might be a query with which we might attempt a response, and hope that we might keep this one awake.

J: May I ask a question about my dogs, Latwii?

I am Latwii, and we would be happy to attempt a query, my friend.

J: I am having problems with my female wanting to breed. Can you tell me what is wrong?

I am Latwii, and am aware of your query, my friend. We hope that we can transmit some information which might be helpful through this instrument, though information of a specific nature of this type is somewhat difficult to transmit with the telepathic contact, for we utilize a portion of this instrument's knowledge and blend it with our own in order to transmit concepts with which [he] or any instrument might be familiar. There might be those concepts which we are unable to transmit, but we shall attempt to do at this time what we can.

The entity of which you speak, that entity being your dog as you call it, is an entity which has an identity which is quite unique, as you well know. It is often the case with such an entity that it will desire certain, shall we say, non-instinctual qualities or preparations before it will accomplish that which you call the mating process. This is not so with many of this creature's type, for they operate primarily from that level which you may call instinctual and do not have these requirements. But this particular entity has been endowed, or shall we say, inspirited by your loving kindness, and has picked up, shall we say, certain desires of its own in relation to the mating process. This entity requires a certain kind of sensitivity on the part of the male, as you call it, a sensitivity which is somewhat like that of its own, and is, as you might say, finicky, if we might use that term when it comes to the mate with which it is presented. We cannot give you direct information as to precisely what to do, but we might suggest providing another mate of a more sensitive nature for this entity to mate.

May we answer you further my brother?

J: Thank you. That was very interesting. I would like to ask you a question about my male dog. We've been having lots of trouble with ear infections and we just can't seem to cure it. Can you give me any information about that?

I am Latwii, and am aware of your query, my brother. Here we find that our ability to give information is even more reduced, but we shall make our meager attempt.

In most entities of your own kind, that being the human type of being, the disease serves as a reminder that certain lessons have not been well learned. However, there is less of this quality in those of what you might call the second-density plant and animal kingdom. However, this particular male entity is experiencing a difficulty in the otic portions or the ear as you call it, which are a result of the infestation of [an] even more minute form of animal of what you might call the microscopic nature. It is often the case that such creatures as this male dog entity will serve as a host for the microscopic creatures of second density which seek to perform their service in a manner which is somewhat irritating to the dog entity, and is somewhat difficult to eradicate, if we might use that pun. We feel that it might be helpful for this creature to be included in your meditative circle of healing energy, for we feel that it is responsive to such energies due also to the enspiriting of this entity with those vibrations of love. Other than these suggestions we are afraid that we are of little aid in this area.

May we attempt another response my brother?

J: Thank you. I would like to do automatic writing. Do you have any suggestions as to how I may go about this?

I am Latwii, and am aware of your query, my brother. This area of seeking is one which requires a great deal of the, shall we say, purity of seeking, and that which this group has come to call the tuning. The area of seeking information from levels of being which are not your ordinary conscious levels of experience is a type of seeking which can be most helpful to the sincere seeker. Yet to one whose desires are tainted with less than the highest desire to serve others, this type of experience can be difficult and, shall we say, misleading.

We suggest when the desire is for this type of experience that the one with such desire find some form of what we have described as tuning mechanism to begin the session. We suggest that any song, prayer, chant or visualization which has a personally inspiring connotation to the seeker be utilized in order to focus as finely as possible that desire to seek truth in order to be of service to others. Then, that some form of meditation be entered into in order to open the channels between the conscious and unconscious minds, that any impression which is felt be allowed to find expression. Then, with the, in this particular case, automatic writing, that all judgment be set aside for the moment, the moment during which this experience occurs. Do not analyze that which comes through these channels while it is attempting to come through. Allow it to flow freely, and when the experience is over, then utilize the powers of conscious analysis in order to discern as to the nature of that which was received.

Again, we shall summarize by suggesting the tuning is the most important ingredient in this type of seeking. To utilize it before it begins, and then as the contact is made, to make the challenge to whatever entity attempts to transmit information in order that you are assured that the most positive type of entity and information possible is, shall we say, on the line. And then to open the self completely to all impressions which are received, reserving analysis until the experience has ended.

May we answer you further, my brother?

J: Thank you. I'd like to ask you about my fifteen-year-old son. We're having a lot of problems with him. I can't figure out what's going on with him. Can you tell me anything about him?

I am Latwii, and am aware of your query, my brother. We in this particular case can only speak in general terms, for if we laid this particular case out plain, then there would not be that challenge which exists at present and provides the opportunity for growth by its very existence. We can speak in general terms, however.

This entity is at that particular stage which those among your species, and most especially the male of your species, finds most challenging for the entity is no longer the child but is not yet the man. In your particular culture there is no opportunity that is culturally presented in order that this entity might prove itself to be worthy of the state of manhood which it is about to enter. This entity, as others of its kind, finds a great deal of what we may loosely term its energy of being available to it at this time, seeking expression in some fashion, seeking the great challenge that will provide the identity for the entity which it seeks. It is seeking the nature of its human being, and it would be helpful if it had some, as you might call it, trial or test in order that it might be able to exercise this great reservoir of energy in a useful fashion, for without such test, the entity is, shall we say, on its own, and must fashion its own type of testing which is not always approved by the culture or by the family unit.

May we answer you further, my brother?

J: Thank you.

We thank you. Is there another query at this time?

C: Latwii, it seems I'm not used to being around … It seems that all of a sudden there's a rash of people that I know that are either hurting at home or in the hospital *(inaudible)* different sicknesses during the last several months. I … Tell me, is there anything in particular going on at this time?

I am Latwii, and am aware of your query, my brother. We can speak of that which is occurring by describing in brief the great cycle of evolution which is now ending upon your planet. During this great span of what you call time each entity upon your planet has had many of what you call incarnations in order to learn those lessons of love which it seeks to learn. As the cycle begins to draw to its close, the remaining few years which you have before you are those which are filled with what becomes the last chance to learn those lessons, and to provide those services which each has come to do. The opportunities, though limited, are greatly intensified in order that the time which remains might be utilized most efficiently and the graduation, as you might call it, might occur.

To offer such an opportunity to be graduated, it is, shall we say, a great honor to accept, but the brow weighs heavy, for such opportunities are usually not recognized as opportunities, for they come as the difficulty in some form. The opportunity to find love may come when one becomes what you call divorced and seemingly without that called love. Yet such an experience may cause one to seek even more fervently that known as love. When the health becomes less than functional or normal, then it may be that certain experiences are symbolized by the illness and provide the entity which is ill the opportunity to see how to focus its own desire more finely towards that seeking of love.

Most opportunities of this nature are not well-observed or taken advantage of, shall we say. Only in some portion is the opportunity accepted. Therefore, the opportunity continues to allow the full acceptance by the entity however the entity is able to do so. Yet, as we mentioned before, the opportunity may be the difficulty which is in truth the disguise of love.

May we answer you further, my brother?

C: Something popped into my mind, something that I heard … some information years ago when I first started coming on psychotronic weaponry being used on the planet. Could you comment about what is occurring with these devices these days?

I am Latwii, and am aware of your query, my brother. We may comment by suggesting that the use of these and other devices is of small concern, not because they do not have great effect upon your physical illusion, but because they are merely one of many, many sources of catalyst, sources of experience which provide opportunities for those of your peoples to learn that which we have called love. The difficulties that might come from such devices' use provide the opportunities—again the disguise—of love.

May we answer you further, my brother?

C: The current weather patterns we've been experiencing over the last three or four years, is there a correlation [of] this particular cycle and the use of those devices?

I am Latwii, and am aware of your query, my brother. We can suggest that these devices are altering that which the peoples of your planet have sown as seed, and is now producing the harvest. This is to say that throughout the great cycle of your planet's evolution there has been enough of that which we might call disharmony that this disharmony has permeated the crust of your planet, and is now having its effect upon your planet and its weather systems as the heat of anger and disharmony is released in a fashion which is more intense than has been known for many, many of your planet's years and evolutionary cycles around your sun. This release of heat is having its effect on its own, shall we say, and it is this effect that is being somewhat manipulated by those who have access to the technology with which to do such.

May we answer you further, my brother?

C: Is anyone deriving anything positive from such devices at this time?

I am Latwii, and am aware of your query, my brother. We might state in short that such is quite so. All experience, or as you might call it, catalyst, provides the opportunity for the seeker to find the infinite love and light of the one Creator. An entity may also ignore such catalyst. An entity may also use such catalyst to become more separated from others, and more distrustful, and, as you might call it, self-centered and seeking.

It might be, for instance, that in a certain location there is that known as the drought. The crops do not grow, food is short. One entity may use this situation in order to share what it has with all who ask and are around it, and in such a manner share the love and light which initiates such action. Another however, may utilize the same …

(Side one of tape ends.)

(Jim channeling)

I am Latwii, and am again with this instrument. To continue. The same situation then, my brother, has provided catalyst of the same nature to two different entities, and these entities have expressed the polar opposite responses. So it is with all the seeming difficulties that the seeker encounters. The heart of the seeking, then, is the most important ingredient which determines how the seeker shall utilize the catalyst, the situation, the difficulty. If the heart has chosen to serve others, and to share always that love and light which is found in each moment, then each moment, no matter what its disguise, will be yet another opportunity to share the love and light that exists in infinite amount in each moment that it encounters. If, on the other hand, the choice has been made to serve only the self, then the catalyst may be used to do just that. It may also be the case that a choice has not been made, and an entity may swing from serving others to serving self back and forth and remain confused upon its path. Yet all respond to the same catalyst, the same opportunities are presented to each. It is the desire of each which determines that benefit which shall be derived.

May we answer you further, my brother?

C: No, thank you.

I am Latwii, and we thank you, my brother. Is there another query at this time?

J: Yes, Latwii. I would like to ask you about incarnation, some of mine?

I am Latwii, and am aware of your query, my brother, and though we readily acknowledge the great desire to know in order to serve others, we are unable to provide information which deals with what you call the previous incarnations, for it is our humble understanding that to do so may be to infringe upon your own free will, for it is the case with each upon your planet that the greater portion of your being which is loosely called the higher self or oversoul has, with your assistance, placed you where you are in each incarnation in order that certain lessons and services might be learned and provided, and to be most purely learned and provided it is most helpful if they remain untainted by knowledge of previous experience which could guide one on a slightly deviant path. Yet we know there are many who give information of this kind and it is, as we know, quite possible to use it to benefit the evolutionary process. We do not feel it appropriate for our service to include such information, and we humbly beg your forgiveness for not being able to give this kind of information.

May we attempt another query, my brother?

J: Thank you.

I am Latwii, and we thank you, my brother. Is there another query at this time?

(Pause)

I am Latwii, and we find that we have exhausted the queries, though we have happily brought one from sleep perhaps less exhausted than before. We thank each of you, my brothers, for asking our humble presence and service. Our attempts to answer your queries bring us great joy, and we hope some small aid to you. We shall now leave this instrument and this group, as always, in the love and in the light of the one infinite Creator which indwells in all. We are those of Latwii. Adonai, my friends. Adonai vasu borragus. ☘

Sunday Meditation
July 8, 1984

(S channeling)

[I am Hatonn,] and we are pleased, as always, to greet you in the love and in the light of the one infinite Creator. We are most honored to be able to join your group this evening, and we are pleased to be able to speak through this instrument. We are filled with joy as we join you this evening, and are filled with the love that is so overflowing this evening. We wish to spend a few moments of your time as we attempt to share a few thoughts with you. We are aware of the abundance of confusion that those upon your planet experience. It seems that when one finds itself in a so-called ball of confusion, the escaping this ball is often difficult, for often the confusion has a tendency to feed itself, and we might suggest that at those times when you find yourselves somewhat enclosed by this bubble, you take a moment of your time to sit down and relax and close your eyes and see yourself rising to the top of the bubble and turning into a form of gaseous light and entirely escaping, and in so escaping, you might see the confusion for what it is. It is not real, it is a—we correct this instrument—it is an illusion, and you may at any moment escape to your meditative state and find yourself in the palm of the Creator where the confusion is no longer apparent.

The ability to look down upon the confusion rather than sitting in the middle of it might aid you in collecting your thoughts and seeking the simple truth, and in seeking the oneness of the Creator, you might find that all that is confusion simply falls away, for the one Thought may not be confused, it is a simple Thought. There is no confusion to this Thought. To put yourself in the palm of the Creator is to seek that which is One, that which is unity, and dwell, my dear friends, in the love of that oneness.

We wish to express our appreciation to this instrument for bearing with us and allowing us to spend a larger amount of time than usual with her. We would transfer this contact at this time. I am Hatonn.

(Carla channeling)

I am Hatonn, and greet you once again through this instrument in love and in light. It is a great privilege to use each instrument, and we do thank each and thank you for calling us and allowing us to share our thoughts with you. Those of you who call us are confused, troubled and disturbed. My friends, it is quite often those who do not call us, and are not yet ready to listen to what we have to say, that are not at all disturbed, confused, or troubled by the mysteries of those things which are evident to anyone with the eyes open. For this reason let us tell you a bit about our own feelings about our mission at this time among your people.

We attempted earlier in what you would call your century to contact individuals, governments, societies, and people of influence because we were quite aware that this particular third-density planet was not only ready for harvest, but was also capable of a great deal of destruction, and by this we refer to the atomic bomb as you have called it. We found our attempts to be far less than satisfactory. We found that those in power among your peoples were not those people whom we indeed needed to contact. We found that our concepts, our very being, had a different meaning for them than for those who are seeking. We found that you have developed within your planetary societal web a system of unfriendly companions, each of which chose to put the heart of the sphere with which he identified above the care of the whole of the sphere with which we identify.

We are those of Hatonn. That is not our home town, or our county as this instrument would call it, nor our state or province or parish or country or nation. We are those of a planetary consciousness. We speak to those who realize that there is one consciousness and that this consciousness is equally available and useful to all those upon your planet. We have chosen to serve in the Confederation of Planets in the Service of the Infinite Creator by sharing our thoughts with groups such as your own who call out to us. This is our service and our pleasure, and our beings thrill with the joy of being able to serve you, for you are ourselves. Just so, my friends, you are we, and we all are the Creator. To put it in quite another way, the unimaginable vastness and complexity of the universe is honed on the sharpness of the one Thought and that is love. That word, love, has been greatly harmed by overuse among your peoples, so that when we say that all is love, it may not mean what we wish it to mean. Therefore, we try to find infinitely various ways of saying that all is light, that all is one, that all is the Creator, that all that you have to do within your illusion is serve each other, for in serving each other you serve the Creator.

We wish to move back now to the confusion of which we spoke earlier. This confusion is a tool much like a saw or a hammer. It is the thing which you may grasp about yourself and about your life at any given moment; normally it is confusion. You use a saw to saw wood; you use a hammer to nail things together. You use your confusion to work upon yourself, for you in the midst of that confusion are waiting to learn from that confusion. You are waiting for that trouble to bubble up until you escape, look back, and learn from your experience. The rapidity with which you learn from this experience, from this confusion, will depend upon your willingness to work with yourself. But at least, my friends, you have the sense to be confused. You are not asleep, you are not dreaming, you are not distracted in the half world in which nothing is very important and no question is truly worth answering. To these people we cannot offer any help whatsoever. These people shall again and again experience this illusion until they become aware of the process that is shaping their destinies.

We do not suggest to you that a, shall we say, "trouble bubble" is an easy thing to completely and utterly solve, to rise above, to understand. We say only to you that the love and the light of the infinite Creator is with you in your attempts to balance your confusions, to gain objectivity and to learn. What a fine tool confusion is, my friends. What a wonderful illusion you have. We are aware that you would prefer the security of simple rules, and there is one simple rule, and that is to love wholly and freely and without reserve. But, my friends, it takes a lifetime for each entity to choose the manner by which it shall show love and to whom it shall be given. Needs are all about you. If you wish to start with the most simple needs, there are the hungry and thirsty and cold upon your planet. Your sphere is full of such confusion, my friends—such a hubbub, such a babble.

What shall you do, where shall you go, what is your discipline to be? We ask you to return to the one original Thought on a daily basis. It does not matter if this returning or meditation be for five minutes or for fifty. What matters is that you have the discipline to turn again and again, day by day, to the Creator. That which will precipitate from your daily meditations shall be unique, for each particle of consciousness is unique. No two people can face the same problem ethically, morally, economically, socially, or in whatever way, and find within himself precisely the same answer.

The universe is indeed confused and the lessons are subjective. When you have found enough truth to tell from the rooftops, you shall not be able to do so by any proof, for proof is the farthest thing from your needs as individuals. Each of you needs to find his own way. Each of you needs to find his own truth. There are some constants, such as confusion, love, charity, compassion, sorrow and weariness. These things each person can understand, and yet how that will be weighed in a person's life, how they will be used to shape a consciousness is a question that must be answered by each. We would not dream of informing you of one overriding absolute truth, which if believed will carry you to some heavenly kingdom. No, my friends. We are in a heavenly kingdom, as we are in the fourth density, that density of love, and from this density we can see the Creator in each of you and in each of us. But we cannot give this vision to you nor would we wish to. We wish only to enspirit you so that you may go forth and seek your own answers. We may promise you that at any time that you wish to meditate we are with you.

As we close, let us bring you in meditation closer to ourselves until we truly feel oneness. Through this instrument's ears we hear the lonely sound of the train going from somewhere to somewhere else, much like you, my friends, on a lonely journey. And yet you are together, held on a straight and narrow track, for your vision is of love and your desire is for mercy. We are one with you. Where is the Creator? Ah, my friends, there is the great question. Shall we say the Creator is you? You shall not be satisfied, for you are not satisfied with yourself. Shall we say that the Creator is in the seeking? You will not be satisfied. Shall we tell you that your journey has no end, and that that endless journey is the Creator? Perhaps, my friends, we come closer to that which you desire to hear this evening. We leave you upon the wind of chance and change. And yet, how solid is your caring for each other and for love and for seeking.

We are known to you as those of Hatonn. We leave you in the love and the light along the endless track of an endless journey of the infinite Creator. We leave you in that which is perfect in all ways. We leave you. Adonai. Adonai vasu borragus. ♣

Sunday Meditation
July 15, 1984

(Carla channeling)

[I am Hatonn,] and I greet you, my friends, in the love and the light of our infinite Creator. We are strengthening our hold upon this instrument in order that we may speak more loudly, for this instrument is used to speaking quietly, and we find that not all were able to hear the previous sentences. We trust this level is appropriate for this portion of your dwelling. We thank you for asking us to share some of our thoughts with you on this very beautiful twilight of your third-density world. How lovely is your habitation, and how gracious are your second-density creatures, your birds singing to the evening in the trees, the trees themselves lifting their fingers to the last rays of the sun as it bids farewell for one more day. How quietly your dwelling place rests and cradles you so that you may have comfort and protection and shelter. And in a way we can see how these things could almost be taken as evidence that the universe is rigid, for the house does not move, it does not get up and dance, nor do the trees seem to clap their hands for joy, nor are the bird's songs construed by your peoples as chantries of happiness. Rather, it is the expected, it is the unnoticed, and in many cases it may seem to be the prison within which you must live, which does not seem to have enough choices nor give you enough freedom.

There was once a young boy who searched for freedom. He felt the restrictions of his parents as they asked him to do many chores and to live up to many expectations, many of which he was unable to fulfill, some of which he was. Yet he did not wish to differentiate between what he could and could not do. He simply wished to be free from all the expectations and from all the responsibility. And so this young man left his home and went out into the world to seek freedom. He quickly discovered that it was wise to furnish oneself with enough of your people's money that he could buy those things which made him happy, and so he began to accumulate the accoutrements of freedom. He had libations that would make him feel very happy. He tried various chemicals that altered his consciousness and made him feel ecstasy. He chose among the pretty young girls and found sexual fulfillment to add to him happiness also. He bought the clothes that he liked, he lived the way that he liked, and for a while he was very happy because he had found his freedom.

There came a time when no libation made him truly happy, when no repetition of mind-altering drugs was enough to fulfill his needs for understanding, and even when no pretty girl could charm him completely, as he gazed only upon the outward portions, knowing nothing of the individual inside. And yet, he had formed his life around the premise that these things constituted freedom, and so he realized that he must reevaluate what freedom is, for one thing he was sure of, and that was that freedom carried with it a side effect, and that was happiness.

Upon reflection he realized that he had bonded himself in slavery to his own desires. Because those desires were not interesting for the maturing soul within, he had begun to get restless, yet still he must work even to eat and to have a place to sleep. He was in bondage, therefore, to a job he did not particularly like, and had even walked into that bondage gladly, finding it preferable to meeting the demands of other human beings. He had given himself all that he wanted and he had lost his freedom.

This man was truly puzzled, and so he began to search within himself for the desires that he might have that would be more interesting, that would make his bondage easier, for, indeed, he was in bondage to his appetite for food and for daily rest, these things he could not do without unless he was willing to risk the life of a person upon the street. This he was not willing to do; this freedom was too chaotic for him, and yet he wanted freedom. He knew that it existed and he was positive of its virtue.

Restless, often angry, this man grew in years, and took long to find his own answers. He began trying to see beneath the surface of things. He began putting down his personal roots out of instinct more than any knowledge. He found and eventually married a woman whose thoughts he preferred, and in time a family grew, the son now becoming the father, the child the husband, and once again he was asked to be responsible for much, far much more than he had been asked to be responsible for as a child. And again there were expectations he could fulfill and there were expectations he could not fulfill.

As the years passed, it became very evident to this man that he had found his freedom, for he had found things to love. He found that it was possible with communication to express the difference between those things he could do and those things he could not, and that he had chosen a woman who was able to release him from those things he could not do and to praise him in gratitude for those things he could do. He found himself asking a great many things of his wife and his children, and in wonderment began to find himself a culprit in expecting too much from others, in failing to differentiate between what they could do and what they could not do.

My friends, each human who incarnates upon your planet will experience a bewildering array of stimuli. To each of you many things are given and from each of you other things are hidden. Each of you is unique, a mystery one to the other, and misunderstandings are inevitable and each person feels the prison walls close in, begins to feel as rooted as a tree, his song as aimless as that of a bird, and in many cases this song becomes still and the person bitter as an oak leaf upon the ground.

We ask you, my friends, to look upon freedom. You have one freedom, and that is that you may choose the manner of your being. The more that your being has to do with love, the more your manifestation will be service, service to those whom you love. This is a reflection of your loving, not the loving itself. Each service that you perform for others is a stride along the road of freedom. Each time that you choose the manner of your beingness you offer yourself a great boon. It is inevitable that there are times when the happenstances of your existence will seem anything but potentially free, when that which you seem to be asked to offer is beyond you.

You each have two capacities; one is human. When you deal from the human capacity—and this is, my friends, often in even the life of a saint—then there are many times when you must say in honesty, "I cannot do what you wish me to. Forgive me, I am not able." There is another capacity within you, and when you call upon it and are able to become a channel for it so that love flows through you, you may become an infinitely efficient instrument that may manifest that which is desired under any circumstances whatsoever. To do this you must put yourself at risk. Before you gain a clear channel you may lose much, for true freedom is a great risk. True freedom, my friends, involves deep choices, and when the choices are made, a clear and lucid accountability to yourself. You often must put your foot upon ground you cannot see because you have been asked to do so either by a spirit within you of love and fellowship, or by a specific request by one who is in relationship to you. You are asked to see love in moments where there seems to be none, and you step out, seeing nothing, and somehow, my friends, the air begins to be solid and you have ground beneath your feet that you could not see before. The risk is in the choice. Each choice must be true, and you must have the patience to wait for the truth of your seeking to manifest.

As we said, during that time you may feel that you have lost much. You change, you grow, you bear fruit, and often, my friends, the fruit that you are asked to bear does not even make sense in one way or another. Those who will harvest what you sow are unknown to you in some way. The virtue of planting a crop of love and thanksgiving is completely hidden, and yet you choose. Freedom, my friends, is a risky business.

We suggest that you aid your own evolution of spirit by daily meditation, by daily contemplation, by daily analysis of your thoughts to the extent that you are able in your environment. What you seek when you seek happiness is an illusion. What you seek when you seek freedom may or may not be an illusion. If you seek freedom from responsibility you have created a dream within a dream, and you shall be a slave and no free man. When the freedom that you seek is the freedom to love and to serve, you stand on firm ground—not safe ground, my friends, for to love is not easy, to serve is most difficult, to communicate is treacherous, to share deeply of yourself is painful, and yet, love abides and draws you to it, for you are that which loves and that which is love. You are both sides of the magnet which is the creation. The great attractive force is the same force that created you, and that force is love.

Do you wish to be free? Then prepare yourself for a bumpy ride through life but a joyous one, for when you give and count not the cost, you purchase that which has no price. It is written in your holy works: "You who sow in tears shall reap in joy." May your tears be blessed, may your joy be great and may your seeking be filled with the love and the light which are the manifestations of the one infinite Creator which speaks through us to you and from you to us, echoing and re-echoing over and over the great rhythms of thanksgiving.

My friends, the trees do clap their hands, and the birds do sing for joy, and this dwelling place is not static but rather a nurturing and living environment, and you within it are also love. You have two things not given to houses and trees and birds. You have movement, and you have self-consciousness. May you find freedom in your movements, may you go in peace to serve and to love in whatever way the day has called forth for you. You do not know what tomorrow will call forth for you, you only know what is asked today. Therefore, we ask you to attempt to serve in the present tense, to bend your motions, your thoughts, intellectual and emotional, to the present moment and the present movement, the present dynamic, the present people, the present situation.

You have self-consciousness. What shall you do with your awareness? We trust that you may find in your adventures much about which to laugh and comrades with whom to share the laughter, and in the darkest moment we ask you to use your self awareness to seek the kingdom of the Father that is within you and that will inform you in a loving and gracious way so that you may indeed manifest that which you wish, so that you may indeed have understanding and knowledge or, in the absence of that, hope and faith. You may depend upon each other and yet always remember, each is limited, each may have trouble communicating his limitations. Depend first upon the Creator, and seek that Creator constantly within yourself in quiet and in confidence, for you seek only to remember, you seek only to return, and just as you give to another's harvest, so others will sow for you that you may reap joy from them. How surprised man is to find joy in the narrow span of life, and how unsurprised he is to find sorrow. May you be surprised constantly, my friends.

We leave you in the love and in the light, in the joy and the laughter and the unity of our infinite creation. Again we thank you for allowing us to share our foolish thoughts with you, and ask you in all humility to never take anyone's word for anything spiritual, least of all ours. Do not depend upon Hatonn or any other spiritual source, but only yourself. You are the evaluator of all that you hear. Much may be nothing to you. There is no promise of sureness to the spiritual path, only the promise of great and continuing risk of an enormous vulnerability, of a sensitivity that will be with you always as you seek to learn. We are with you on that path, vulnerable, foolish and at the same time, perfect, perfected in love and one with the Creator. We are those of Hatonn. Adonai, my friends. Adonai vasu borragus.

(Jim channeling)

I am Latwii, and we greet you, my friends, in the love and in the light of our infinite Creator. We are pleased to be asked to join your group once again and rejoice at the opportunity of providing our humble service. We thank you, as always. Now, to that service. May we attempt a query at this time?

(Side one of tape ends.)

Carla: I have a question generated by the preceding message. On what level does a bird sing for joy or do trees clap their hands? I thought birds just chirped because they were giving signals about being hungry or looking for a mate or something like that?

I am Latwii, and am aware of your query, my sister. We may suggest that those creatures of which you speak sing for joy and clap their hands for joy at the very basic level of their being, at the same level at which each portion of creation sings and claps and dances and rejoices in its beingness. At this level, which you may see as the very nature of the being, the substance of the molecular structure, there is the clear recognition of the One by the One and as this level of being is brought into a more and more conscious being, it becomes more and more, shall we say, comprehensible by your third-density means of comprehension. When the bird sings, it may indeed be acting out that ritualized process of seeking the mate or defending the territory, yet the energy which powers that song and that ritual is the very essence of the entity's being, and in that essence and upon that level the song of life rejoices in life.

May we answer you further, my sister?

Carla: So, for a human being at the nuclear level, the self and the body are in a state of rejoicing? Is that right?

I am Latwii, and you are quite correct, my sister. May we answer you further?

Carla: Illness is so prevalent among human beings. If a human being could contact that level of joy, it seems to me that healing would be self-generated instantly. Is that correct?

I am Latwii, and am aware of your query, my sister. We find again that you have struck at the heart of the matter, for it is the nature of the one Creator to heal when asked by the entity needing healing, and all remedies which we take and seek from outside the being have their effect only insofar as the entity seeking the healing has been able in some degree to contact this level of rejoicing, this level of the one Creator that is contained within the entity's own being.

May we answer you further?

Carla: How does a person contact that portion of his consciousness?

I am Latwii, and am aware of your query, my sister. We see that you are approaching the age-old question of the seeker from yet another angle, for the answer that we give is one which you have heard many times. The journey which each seeker is upon is one which has been described as straight and narrow, yet it is one which is traveled over many a rocky path, a journey which has many twists and turns, a journey across which blow harsh winds and down upon which shines a searing sun. There is the need of each seeker to accomplish that which may be called the crystallization of the being, the balancing of all distortion, the purifying of the desire to serve others and to seek love.

This is an easy statement to make, yet it is a difficult journey and task to undertake. Yet, as love is found in each portion of the being the path is made straighter, another rock is removed, and another step is taken, yet at each moment each seeker has some access to this portion of its being, yet upon what might be called the unconscious level. It is this unconscious connection with the one Creator that rejoices in each cell of being that supports the seeker as it consciously moves in what it sees as darkness. Yet, as love and light are found, the darkness is illumined and the connection becomes more and more conscious, so the seeker is able to heal the self more and more effectively with the love and light that it has found by its own efforts.

May we answer you further, my sister?

Carla: When we stopped the Ra work, we had been concentrating on the archetypes, and I wondered if the archetypical mind was as deep in the mind as this cellular, nuclear, joyous consciousness. In other words, could one use the hints and clues of the archetypes to reach that which was at the same level, or are you using tools when you use the archetypes that are of a level not as deep in the roots of mind as nuclear consciousness?

I am Latwii, and am aware of your query, my sister. This is not an easy query to answer, yet we shall attempt such. That which you have described as the nuclear awareness of the oneness and joy of all creation is ever present within each cell of your being and within each moment of your existence. It permeates all that is and all that is not created. It is the sum and substance of the one Creator. There are various tools which seem separated from this nature of awareness which might be used to reveal and uncover this nature of awareness to the seeker, yet within each tool is also found that same joy and unity of being. You may indeed proceed upon this path by utilizing those concept complexes called archetypes to gain a greater understanding, if we might use this misnomer, of the joy and unity which is within all things and situations, yet do not be confused or misled by mechanics. Seek the heart of all creation and the heart of your own being first and foremost within your thoughts and actions, and utilize any mechanical means of so seeking by focusing always upon the heart of the desire.

May we answer you further, my sister?

Carla: No, thank you.

I am Latwii, and we are most grateful to you, my sister. Is there another query at this time?

(Pause)

I am Latwii, and we find that for the nonce we have exhausted the queries, and would be well advised for the comfort of the instrument to take this opportunity to bid this group farewell for the evening. We thank each of you, as always, for asking our humble service, and remind you that our words are but our opinions and are the result of our journey, a journey which we share with each of you, a journey in joy and a journey in light and love. We thank you, my friends, and shall leave you at this time. We are with you always upon request. We are those of Latwii. Adonai. Adonai vasu borragus.

Sunday Meditation
July 22, 1984

(Carla channeling)

[I am Hatonn,] and I greet you in the love and the light of the infinite Creator. We apologize for the delay but there is one among you who must first make up the mind as to whether the channeling was appropriate at this time. We cannot go where we do not feel that we are called freely, as you know. Therefore, we would gladly wait any amount of your time, and thank you greatly for the pleasure and privilege of speaking with you. Although our thoughts are poor, our hearts are full of gratitude. This instrument is being given a fairly complex concept. However, we wish to make a point this evening which seems to be driven at better this way than any other.

There is a relationship between you and the infinite Creator. This is one of the most general affirmations upon your sphere, spiritually speaking. The only entities who would disagree with this statement are those who believe that there is no Creator, and therefore there is no possible relationship. Your philosophers and theologians have said many things about the relationship of humans to the Creator. We would suggest that you examine what occurs when two bluebirds mate. Is not that tiny entity which breaks through the egg a bluebird? Just so, when an acorn falls from an oak tree and germinates, in good time does not the oak tree duplicate itself so that yet another beautiful oak will wave its leafy fingers through the winds. And so, when among your peoples those who are mated have children, is it not common to say, "Oh, this child takes after the mother and this after the father"? The relationship in all cases is an identity within which uniqueness of each entity is preserved.

And now we have settled your humanity, we shall go on to your relationship with the Creator. There is much to learn from these examples. You may well think of yourselves as children of the Creator, and yet, how are you children of the Creator? Where is your son-ship and what birth have you to show? This is an area which bristles with trouble, my friends, because it is so simple and so straightforward that mankind finds it almost impossible to accept. When we look at the bluebird, we see both the bluebird and the ideal of the bluebird. When we see one acorn, we know that we have seen all acorns in miniature. We trust the identity to continue throughout the species. And we know somehow that the idea and the ideal existed in order to form the first oak tree, the first bluebird, and, for that matter, the first human entity. The source of these ideas and ideals is the Creator of them, and there is a portion of all things that does not come into manifestation in flesh or feather or leaf but, rather, stays with the Creator, so that that which the Creator has made is in the Creator and the Creator in that which He has made. Therefore, you carry with you an identity with the Creator which is most usually not carried into manifestation. Nevertheless, it is within you, and the relationship is identity. You are the Creator and the Creator is you. You are also children of the Creator in that you were enabled to begin your journey of consciousness by the Creator and the one original Thought, which is love.

If then you are children of love, and, indeed, love itself, since this is an acceptable alternative term for the Creator, why cannot your gestures and your beings manifest love? Why is this not the natural? You are identical with the Creator. Why does this nature not prevail? My friends, that which is dear and rare is treasured because it is seldom seen and difficult to find. For most among your peoples it is ever difficult to find the Creator within. The day distracts the eye and the mind, the fingers become busy with petty details. Moment upon moment is lost, and the life wears away, the incarnation coming to a close without the person taking hold of the stream of time and making a conscious effort to manifest love and to express that identity with the Creator. It is for this reason that meditation is so greatly recommended, more especially meditation upon a daily basis, for if you have the habit of silence within, you will the better listen to what one of your holy works has called the still, small voice. The thunder of daily business can drown that still, small voice out very easily if the will of the seeker is not constantly returning to the search for the identity with love which is the true identity of each and which is all that shall outlast the grave.

To meditate often seems rather difficult. We are aware that this so. However, the intention to meditate, the setting aside of time for that purpose, the action of attempting to meditate, all of these things add up to an increasing awareness of the sanctity that you carry within you, even if you consider that you do not meditate well. It is not important to meditate well. It is important to desire to meditate well and to continually seek the truth in your meditations so that you are tuned and carefully aimed at assuming your true personality—that is, love.

Each of you seeks and each of the seekings are in some way flawed at times. We ask you, as you go into meditation, to examine that which you seek, for that which you seek you shall find. If you beckon something it shall come to you. You will get what you want. Therefore, be sure you are asking for what you truly want. Perhaps the greatest disappointment in many incarnations is the realization that one has gotten what one wished, and the harvest is an unhappy one. Wish well and find yourself worthy to continually seek in the direction of that which you desire. Moving into meditation and moving back out can feel like moving in and out of a cleansing waterfall, that which causes health and healing, compassion, forgiveness and understanding. Let these vibrations stream down upon you as a waterfall would. Open yourself after carefully tuning to the benevolent love and light of a universe that is one with you. Yes, my friends, each of you is a fallible, foolish human being, as you call yourselves, and in the light of your own judgment, how cruel you are in your judgment of yourselves, my friends. Love does not so cruelly judge. Therefore, surrender yourselves to the influence of love. Seek your identity. Begin to recognize who you really are.

We have greatly enjoyed speaking with you but would wish at this time to leave this instrument. We hail and bless all in the joy of oneness, and leave you in the love and the light of our infinite Creator. I am known to you as Hatonn. Adonai. Adonai.

(Jim channeling)

I am Latwii, and I greet you, my friends, in the love and in the light of our infinite Creator. We are most happy to be asked to join your group once again and offer our humble service of attempting to answer your queries. May we remind each that our words are but our opinions and our findings which have resulted from our own journey, which we share with you. Take that of value; leave that which has none. May we begin then with the first query?

Carla: Well, I have a question. I've often wondered if the Confederation of Planets and angels were two different ways of saying the same thing. Are they?

I am Latwii, and am aware of your query, my sister. We blush at so being described but may suggest that, indeed, it is a method of describing those of the Confederation of Planets in the Service of the One Infinite Creator to call them angels as well. The term "angel" or "angelic presence" is a term which is usually reserved for those entities who are of your own planetary influence. This would mean that such an entity would have evolved upon your own planet first and would have achieved those levels of, shall we say, harvestability, and would have chosen to remain with this planetary influence and become that known as an angelic presence, guide, or inner plane teacher which would respond to the call, much as we respond to your call though we are not of your planetary influence. The Confederation of Planets is made up of many entities from many planetary influences including your own, my sister.

May we answer you further?

Carla: Yeah. There aren't enough people that have been harvested from this density this time around to fill up heaven, as one tends to think of it being, ranks on ranks, and all that. Are some of these holdovers who have decided to go through a whole other octave on the inner plane?

I am Latwii, and believe that we grasp the gist of your query. Please query further if we have not. These entities of which we have been speaking, those termed the angel or angelic presence, are those entities which have obtained that level of polarity in service to others which would allow them to proceed forward, shall we say, in their own evolutionary progress if they so chose. It is most usually the case with a positively-polarized entity achieving harvest that the entity will choose to remain with those of its own planetary influence until the cycle of third density has been completed and those of its kind have been offered the greatest possible opportunity for achieving harvest as well. In some cases these entities will continue to remain with some portions of the third density of its planet if these entities have not achieved harvest and then remove themselves to another third-density planetary influence for a repetition of those lessons.

May we answer you further, my sister?

Carla: Well, that's what I was driving at, among other things. So, are angels mostly come from places like Mars and all [different places] like that if they were already graduated before they came to this planetary influence?

I am Latwii, and am aware of your query, my sister. And we can asseverate that this is indeed the case with a great portion of those as angelic presences. There are entities which have many planetary influences which have given their populations to your own at the end of their third-density cycle, for their populations were in need of a repetition of that density or grade of experience, and your planetary influence offered that very lesson. Those few who were able to be harvested upon such planets needing a repetition of the cycle have in many cases joined those needing the repetition in order to provide whatever assistance is possible in response to a call for such assistance.

May we answer you further, my sister?

Carla: What's the basic difference between inner planes and outer planes?

I am Latwii, and am aware of your query, my sister. As an entity moves from the, as they have been called, inner plane experiences toward that which is called the outer plane experience, an entity moves from that which might be termed the metaphysical in purity to the physical in purity. This is to say that an entity will be moving from the inner plane of the nonphysical to the outer plane of the physical. The differentiation between these terms and states of being is that of the denseness of light contained within the inner plane and the denseness of matter and illusion contained in the outer plane.

May we answer you further, my sister?

Carla: Then you and angels are both inner plane beings or entities, right?

I am Latwii, and am aware of your query, my sister. For your purposes and according to your perceptions, this is so, yet this is so in a relative manner, for in our own illusion we inhabit a portion of what you may call a higher density, which also has its own so-called outer plane or space/time portion of experience. In your way of perceiving this experience, it would appear that we would be the same as an entity inhabiting the inner planes of your own planetary influence, for both experiences are much more filled with light than is your own, and are much less filled with the manifestation of illusion than is your own.

May we answer you further, my sister?

Carla: Yeah. Angels, then, are third density, able to graduate to fourth density, therefore virtually fourth density. Is there any possibility that angels or angelic presences—I suspect that you must want to say something different because you keep saying "so-called"—can go further than the beginning of fourth density? Is there further learning possible without leaving the inner planes and reincarnating?

I am Latwii, and am aware of your query, my sister. We have prefaced the term, angel and angelic presence, with "so-called" as a modifier for it is quite a large universe that we inhabit and which your planet finds itself in as well. There are many learning opportunities available to those so-called angelic presences within your planetary influence, and there are many types of angelic presences as well. We have spoken to the majority, and have not spoken of the greater variety of entities which may be perceived as angelic presences. Some are of what you would call a higher density, shall we say, having come to this planetary influence in response to a specific call. Some are of your own planetary influence and remain in the, shall we say, role of angelic presence for the greater portion of their beingness. Some chose to reincarnate and apply their beingness to a physical incarnation in order to be of more service in that manner. There are, as you see, more types of angelic presence than can be adequately described by your language system and your sense of comprehension and our ability to so describe.

May we answer you further, my sister?

Carla: No, thank you.

I am Latwii, and we thank you, my sister. Is there another query at this time?

Carla: Just one question, which you probably can't answer. I've been having a lot of trouble [this week.] Do you have any tips? [Do you have] a manifest [ready]?

I am Latwii, and am aware of your query, my sister, though you have not spoken it in detail. We can speak in general. To any seeker which feels the difficulty in manifesting those ideals which each seeker holds dear, and by which each seeker attempts to move the self in service to others and along the path of evolution, it is the intention of your being which is of greatest importance as you attempt to be of any service and as you attempt to match the life with the ideal. Each seeker will find the moments of falling short of the ideal, for it is not within the capability of any seeker to match that which is infinite in a finite illusion. It is instead the honor and the duty of each conscious seeker of truth to make whatever effort is possible, to make it with a whole heart, and to accept that which comes from the effort in joy and in thanksgiving for the opportunity which has been met.

Your illusion is one which works quite well, my sister. The purpose of your illusion is to both hide that which is true and reveal enough of that which is true to cause the seeker to move toward that which is true. As you find those times of difficulty in finding and manifesting that which is true in your own life, retire to those places within your being that are silent, gentle, healing and loving. Whether this be in prayer, meditation or contemplation, find that place where the One resides. Find that place where you have been before, that place of love that has no condition, that place of joy at the very opportunity to be where you are and to do what you do, for, indeed, each situation is full of such love and such joy, for the one Creator resides in full in all at all times, and there is much service to perform, and many lessons to learn in those times of difficulty, these times of testing, that the seeker might then find the greater reserve of strength within its being which it was unaware existed before the seeking and the needing such strength.

What we have taken so long to say, my sister, is that there is great virtue in perseverance, great virtue in the attempt, and great …

(Side one of tape ends.)

(Jim channeling)

I am Latwii, and am once again with this instrument. We thank you, my sister, as always. Is there another query at this time?

(Pause)

I am Latwii, and we are aware that there are yet two or three queries which have not found their final form, and which, therefore, we may have the opportunity of attempting a response to at what you would call a later date. We thank each present for allowing us to join your group this evening. It is always a great honor to join the company of those who so ardently seek the truth of their being and journey. Your journeys are at times quite, quite difficult, for the illusion which you inhabit is a most heavy and dense illusion, where that which is fine and light and true and beautiful is often quite unapparent to those who move within a gross physical existence. Yet we would remind each that the real work and fruit of your labors and journey is stored up within what might be called the metaphysical portion of your existence, and you shall not be directly aware of these fruits for most of your conscious incarnation, yet when the journey in this life is finished, it is with great joy that you will look upon those fruits, and with great amazement recognize the real purpose of the incarnation which has been completed. Rejoice, my friends, and know that each labor, each tear, each agonizing moment produces a fruit that is whole and perfect, sweet and loving, and is a great portion of the one Creator. We thank each of you for every effort which you make as seekers of truth. We are those of Latwii, and we leave you now in the love and in the light of the one infinite Creator. Adonai. Adonai vasu borragus. ✣

L/L Research

Sunday Meditation
July 29, 1984

(Carla channeling)

[I am Hatonn.] It is my privilege and my blessing to share your consciousness with ours. Truly, although we come to serve, we find ourselves served ten times over by the beauty of the vibrations, the vitality and sharp peaks and valleys of your existences. We who refine our choice have a great deal of intensity to our existence and have much to tell of our journey, but those [who] make the choice at this time, as you would call it, have a much more heightened experience, a much sharper illusion. Perhaps it is our way of saying we enjoy memories of the good old days, when the good old days were perhaps not quite as easy as we remember. Perhaps each of you would asseverate that this is true. The illusion that you experience is not easy, though we remember it with great affection. We have made our choice, and you are making yours.

This evening we would speak of a portion of information about the one original Thought, which is love, and your relationship to it that is called gratitude. It has much been studied within the distortions you may call Christian, and we find within this instrument's mind a great familiarity with the story called the prodigal son.

In this parable the teacher known as Jesus described a situation where an unruly and wild young heir to a great fortune demanded his fortune before the death of his father, while his patient and kindly brother demanded nothing but remained in his father's house. The prodigal son took all that he now possessed and squandered it foolishly and quickly, and one day found him eating the same food that he brought to the swine. He thought to himself, "How much better I would have it if I were even a slave in my father's house. I shall be go back and ask to be taken on as a slave." And he walked through several countries until he came again unto his father's house. His father, seeing him afar off, rejoiced and made ready a grand celebration. The patient, kindly brother who had never left home was upset, for he had never had such a party given to him and he had served his father throughout many years.

(The telephone rings.)

We shall pause.

(Pause)

(Carla channeling)

I am again with this instrument. I am Hatonn. We thank you for pausing with us. We shall continue in love and in light. The good son said to his father, "Why, you have never given me such a wonderful party, why is that?" And the father said, "Why son, you have always been here with me, and everything I have is yours. But your brother was lost and now he is found; he was dead and now he is alive."

Let us examine this parable, my friends, for gratitude is not what many find it easy to define. Spiritual gratitude is difficult. However, it is one of the linchpins on which spiritual development rests. The prodigal son was not grateful to his father, either when he left or when he returned. He was in the first instance arrogant, and in the second unknowing of what was about to occur. He had, however, given all hopes up of ever being a member of a family to which he had once belonged. The son who had always been with the father and who shared all that was the father's knew no gratitude either at his father's attitude or at the return of his brother, for he was jealous and wanted more than was his share, more than his father could give. The father alone was filled with gratitude because of a son that had betrayed him and squandered his inheritance. This same father could just as easily have been outraged to see such a foolish son returning. The words could have been hard and bitter. "Go away," he could have said, "Go away, you are no longer my son, and what I owe you I have given you." Yet, to the father the idea of just portions was foreign. The father gave all that he had and then found more to give, grateful simply for the sight of that which he had nurtured, that which was in his keeping.

Within this illusion it is difficult to know how one may see praise in many, many situations. Being grateful for the experience which may just as well hurt as heal is inestimably difficult, and yet if there is gratitude in sufficient amount, gratitude for the challenge, gratitude for the prodigal son offering you that challenge, gratitude for the infinity of love which is your birthright and which manifested through you may be all in all. This gratitude homes the shepherd, the father, the nurturer, in so that all moments eventually ring with praise, and the illusion finally begins to lift. You will notice that the father in this parable saw that for which he was grateful, that for which he could have been distressed, a far way away. His gratitude stepped into a void that would only be filled when the son showed his gratitude for being again acceptable by his family. There are seldom moments within third-density experience when that gratitude which is spiritually based may come easily and after something is accomplished. Spiritually or metaphysically speaking, gratitude calls to itself, that is, the gratitude comes within the void of unknowing. The fatted calf is killed before the prodigal son reaches home, before the nature of this unexpected return is known.

How many experiences, my friends, partake in some way of this vulnerability. Something occurs to you. It, given the nature of your illusion, has a tendency to be more painful than pleasurable, for that is the nature of your experiences. Good experiences and bad experiences there are, all seen through the subjective eye, and yet because of the desolation and confusion of many, far more negative thoughts invite their reflection than positive, and thus the illusion often seems to be full of discord and strife. There is then the chance to be grateful—to be grateful, to give thanks, to shout aloud with praise at nothing, for what seems to be real is disease, disharmony, discomfort or despair. As you express thanks, so the seed will be sown. To whom it manifests is always unknown. Your seed may be sown for another or for yourself. Planting has little to do with harvest. However, if you can be thankful for the simple gift of consciousness, if no more than that, if you can be quiet and peaceful in the face of difficulty, if your heart may shout with joy and ecstasy in the face of discomfort, then that which you manifest to the universe shall be that light, that manifestation of the one original Thought in your own unique expression that brings not just to you, but to those who surround you a reflecting manifestation of thankfulness and gratitude.

One thought as we leave this instrument. We do not intend in any way to describe the nature of the Creator by speaking of this parable. We are not attempting to describe metaphysical geometry in which the Creator has certain characteristics. We would not be so bold nor would we tamper with your own study. We use words for the Creator and in close association with the Creator. Those words are: love, the original Thought, light, oneness, you, I. These are not characteristics, as the Creator is far more deeply personal than to have a personality. The technique of gratitude, rather, is much like that archetype which shows a fool or a wise man stepping off into space.

Give thanks, my friends, not for what you see, not for the kindliness of the Creator, not for the excellence of your circumstance, but, rather, give thanks because you are able to give thanks, because you live and breathe and think. You define the nature of your being; no circumstance ever may as long as this is understood.

We are with you, my friends, and of course at any time you may ask us to be with you mentally during meditation we shall be glad to be there as silent partner to aid your contemplative and quiet moment. I am Hatonn. I leave you in all that there is, the love and the light of the original infinite Creator. Adonai. Adonai, my friends.

(Jim channeling)

I am Latwii, and I greet you, my friends, in the love and in the light of our infinite Creator. It is our privilege and our pleasure to once again be asked to join your group. We thank you, as always, for inviting our humble service which we attempt to provide by means of answering those concerns that you bring with you. May we then ask for the first query at this time?

Carla: I'm really glad to hear your voice, Latwii, but I don't have any questions.

I am Latwii, and, my sister, we are filled with joy to hear your voice as well, and to feel the vibrations of this group. We feel that there are those concerns that are present, and if they can be formed into words at this time, we would be happy to attempt to reply. Is there a query at this time?

Carla: I will ask for a friend of mine. It's a question in general, for I'm sure there are many people that share his difficulties. How may he work to remove his difficulties, and achieve a proper spiritual, emotional, mental and physical balance?

I am Latwii, and am aware of your query, my sister. We find that this query is of a general nature, and has not those specific qualities which would infringe upon the free will, thus we may attempt an answer and shall do our best.

Each seeker within your illusion moves within that which might be called the darkness. Nothing is known except perhaps that the seeker does exist and move within certain boundaries and these boundaries seem quite real. They are that which the seeker has made familiar through the thinking and the experience which are attempts to reflect the true heart of being, and to make the journey known in a conscious fashion.

These boundaries serve to focus the seeker for a portion of the journey, and when they have served their purpose there is the opportunity to release the boundaries, to bid farewell to that which has been familiar to the seeker. Many of your peoples call this transformation, and some such changing of the guard, shall we say, may be called initiation as well, for the old is given away and the new is born. These are new boundaries, my sister, but boundaries which are somewhat widened and offer more freedom. Yet, with the new-found freedom comes the first fear of taking new steps, for that which is new is not known nor is it familiar, yet the seeker, full of the desire to move onward, will take that first step as the fool into space, and with faith and will exercised to the fullest ability will find firm ground on which to step, for that ground shall be a new portion of the seeker, and shall be that which awaits the formation first in, shall we say, desire or mind. The step is thought, and then it is taken, and it is taken because it is thought.

Thus, the journey continues within new boundaries, and the seeker once again moves forward for a portion of what you call time until those difficulties that are a result of the new bias mount to the point where a threshold of resistance, shall we say, is constructed, thereby providing the opportunity for yet another transformation, as what once was a new field of experience becomes too restrictive and must be replaced and transformed by a larger field of experience. The faith and the will are those tools which propel the seeker through such transformations. The rejoicing at such an opportunity is also a concomitant portion of the seeker's own creation that is most helpful in this journey, and most especially during such transformations.

May we attempt further response, my sister?

Carla: That was very complete. Thank you. I had a secondary query, and that was, if a person carries confusion of some kind to the point that most people would call delusional to the close of the incarnation, will that person be, shall I say, caught in that confusion as the next incarnation opens?

I am Latwii, and am aware of your query, my sister. Inasmuch as each entity which inhabits your illusion contains a certain amount of confusion, it is necessary upon the cessation of any incarnation for any such confusion or imbalance to go through the process of healing. Therefore, according to the nature and degree of the difficulty or confusion, the entity shall find within itself the need to heal that which was broken, to make clear that which was confused, and to make whole that which was broken. There are many, many individual situations to consider in the general nature of your query when making reference to the needs of the next incarnation. The entity may be ready for that which is called the harvest, and may find that, though confused during the incarnation, was sufficiently polarized to continue to the next level of lesson, and may find a need to include the first portion of studies as that confusion which was carried forth from the previous incarnation. For an entity not able to harvest itself within your third-density illusion, such confusion then might be a portion of its next third-density incarnation lesson.

There are, as you know, a great variety of entities upon your sphere at this time. Many have come from other densities and planetary influences to be of service, and may find that there are certain difficulties and confusions which would necessitate a particular plan of study to be carried forth, perhaps within any number of situations which would perhaps include another third-density incarnational experience or could take forms which are most difficult to describe to you at this time, for to those of other densities there are various means of relieving and healing the distortions accumulated within a third-density incarnation.

We apologize for not being able to give a specific answer at this time, but are aware that you recognize the difficulty with the infringement upon free will which is potentially within our response.

May we respond in more detail, my sister?

Carla: No, thank you, Latwii.

I am Latwii, and thank you, as always, my sister. Is there another query at this time?

(Pause)

I am Latwii, and we find that we have exhausted the queries. Though few in number, we find that the focus of each query was sufficiently well tuned to provide information which we hope may be of some aid in your quest for truth. We share with you that same quest, and thank you for allowing us to share what humble opinions we have gathered on our journey with you. We shall be with each of you upon your request in your meditations, and shall be honored to join your group at your next gathering, should we be so requested. We are those of Latwii, and we leave you now, my friends, rejoicing in the love and in the light of the one infinite Creator. Adonai. Adonai vasu borragus. ☙

Sunday Meditation
August 5, 1984

(Carla channeling)

I am Hatonn. I greet you in the love and the light of the infinite Creator. We are most grateful to be able to speak with this group this evening and greet with great joy the one known as S. How beautiful is the desire of each heart that seeks a dwelling place in the metaphysical sense. And what beauty within beauty shall that seeking unfold. We greet you in love. At times we feel perhaps we should make more effort to point out the reason for our greeting you and our leaving you in love and in light. We do this because of our opinion that this greeting expresses as well as words can all that there is either knowable or numenal within our experience.

"The love of the one infinite Creator" is indeed a practice in redundancy of phrase for love is the one infinite Creator having been called from the deeps of the universe's infinite rhythm that this creation and all others may be born, coalesce, experience, be flung outward and ultimately recoalesce within the great heart that beats beyond all telling.

That which you know of and think of as the Creator is already one step from the Creator. And yet this is all that we shall be able to tell you of the Creator, that the Creator is one Thought, one powerful, fiery and creative Thought which we call love. This love then acts in infinite variety upon that material which is called light in order to make all the vibrations and rotations which cause the illusion in which you now exist and all other illusions including the one in which we now enjoy experience. What else could we find as words of greeting? The Maker and the material, these are the elements of our greeting, for these are all that there is besides the free will that has caused each of your consciousnesses to be as they are. Whatever you consciousness, whatever your state of mind, whatever your emotions or your spiritual path, your Creator is love and the material of which you are made is light. The vibrations are yours to choose through the act of free will.

We wish to speak through this instrument this evening in such a way that this instrument has no idea of what is coming next. We are continuing to develop this instrument in order that it may be more sensitive to the content of our thoughts once it is assured that we are able to pass the challenge of the tuning which this instrument calls Christ and which others may call Christ consciousness or white light. As always, we encourage each in all cases when the vibration is felt to challenge the entity and to bid goodbye with blessing and love to any about which it feels even doubtful. For those who are of the positive path are those of Christ consciousness as you know it. For Christ consciousness is love and the teacher you know as Jesus was a perfect example of that love. And the incarnation and teachings of this teacher constitute a body which when studied will yield some awareness of the nature of the penetration of the illusion and the understanding of freedom.

We would speak to you now about one who went about hungry for many things. Let us call this entity a woman and let us place this entity in a city. This young woman is hungry for those things which life may teach her, for those foods which life may give to her. And over and over again she pursues one path and then another, physically, mentally, emotionally and spiritually. She looks to the sea, to the sky, to all the pleasures that can be bought with money and the sensations that can be experienced because of the great generosity of your creation. This woman becomes older and chooses to herself a true love. She experiences the pain and the joy of loving another and in time the even more painful and joyful experience of children.

In each pleasure, she reflects to herself in her old age, she has seen pain. If the sky was lovely, soon it would rain, if the earth bore her footprints lightly, soon she would get a blister. All that she loved caused more pain and joy and at the end of her life she was still hungry for experiences, experiences which she felt instinctively were hers. Many people there are that come to illness, older years, and even the deathbed knowing nothing but dissatisfaction and hunger. And yet they do not know that for which they hunger nor can they. For they have been separated by a belief in outer pleasure.

What we wish to share with you this evening, my friends, in part is that there is no separation between this woman and love nor is there separation between anyone and that same love. It is not easy to find unity with mankind when mankind is so dissatisfactory. And yet it is this mankind, person by person, which wears your face and which thinks your thoughts and seeks with your hunger. The teacher known to you as Jesus offered peace. But immediately following this offering he said very clearly, "This peace is not what the world thinks of as peace." He spoke of a journey and one of those whom he taught said," We do not understand what journey upon which you go." To which the teacher replied, "Each of us is the journey. The journey is not outside yourself. You do not seek for something as if you were grabbing at the ring at a carnival ride. You are seeking within yourself and this then will bring you peace."

We would say to you, my friends, that it is a kind of peace that the world often finds suspect and sometimes even dangerous. The smile of joy in the face of apparent trouble seems not a victory, but an inappropriate reaction. The heart and the courage to lift oneself up in the face of a daunting situation seems to a dark world the action of a fool or at least one who is not paying sufficient attention.

My friends, have you ever wondered why in various holy works high places are considered holy? You must know that all things are holographs for all other structures. The structure of yourselves, the structure of the earth, the structure of the universe—study one, you begin to understand the others. Yes, the high, the mountainous, the peak is holy and not because your thinking causes it to be so but because of the nature of height. As one looks down from a height, one sees many more than things than one may see when one is in the valley, on the surface, unable to see over the next ridge or knoll, past the next tree or rock. Within yourself, each of you has the opportunity to experience the deep surfaces, the crevices, the rocks, the valleys, the vales, and the forests of existence. Each has ample opportunity to choose to be misled, to be unhappy, to feel darkness. Each of you also has within you the birthright and the opportunity at all times to seek the high places. Walk then in meditation up your own mountain. Picture yourself cleansing yourself at a clear, cool and refreshing mountain stream. And then clad in cleanly garments, visit the most high place of your being in meditation and in peace. Metaphysical peace does not deny the apparent chaos of a boisterous illusion but rather reaffirms and restates for you once again the perfection of the Creator, the Creator that is in you and the you that is in the Creator. You are old, older than rocks and sky and earth and sea. You are consciousness. You have seen and experienced and chosen many things. Today you may choose again. It is only through meditation that your choices will be consistently positive. And by that we mean that your choices will be consistently those of service to others.

When one is upon the rock, how easy it is to feel that there is no one to serve and if there were others to serve, still yet there is no chance of true service. It is easy upon a rock to wonder where you will be fed, when you will be served, and yet you have food in plenty. As you gain in compassion, so you gain in your nearness to time spent and to infinite supply.

Only you know what shall fill your appetite for peace, for love, and for giving of that which you have gained to those about you. We hope you have hearty appetites.

Our hearts are full with gratitude and thanksgiving that you have allowed us to share our thoughts with you. We are quite prone to error and are anything but authoritarian. Never take our word to be absolute, but rather, test it against this illusion on a daily basis over a period of time. If what we say is so, your life shall be considerably simplified and most certainly changed. If the change is towards an inner joy and peace, then we have spoken well. If what we say is not appropriate, toss it aside without a backward glance for there is inspiration everywhere. We are only one of countless sources. Listen, my friends, with inward and with outward ears to the joyous voices of the infinite Creator. Listen always, even when you talk. For you, too, are full of inspiration. Find inspiration in silent sayings as well, for the voice of the Creator is often silent.

We must leave you at this time as we are having difficulty with this contact. I am Hatonn, and I bless and thank and greet each of you and assure you that we are with you at any time you may request us mentally in meditation. We have come to you, for we are love, for you are love, for the creation is love. And we speak to you because all things manifest in light. We leave you in the love and in the light of the infinite Creator. Adonai vasu borragus.

(Jim channeling)

I am Latwii, and I greet you, my friends, in that same love and light that our brothers and sisters of Hatonn have left you in. What a blessing it is to speak to this group this evening. May we also welcome the one known as S, who has in your measure of time been long absent from this group, though not absent from our blessings and our presence. Our service, as always, is that of attempting to answer those queries which each brings as a means of continued seeking. May we then begin with the first query?

J: It's always good to hear your voice, Latwii. I have a query. I have an idea for a product which requires a patent, but I'm just sitting on it, not doing anything about it. Can you tell me anything about it?

I am Latwii, and, my brother, we are most happy to hear your voice as well and to attempt to the best of our ability to respond to your query. In this instance we find that there is a means by which you may pursue certain lessons through this activity that you have devised. We cannot give advice as to whether or not you should or should not proceed in any particular manner with a lesson which has implications for your evolution for it would not be proper for us to point you in any particular direction. Yet, we would suggest that when you find an inspiration which has come to you as a result of your seeking and when this inspiration takes a form which you feel is well, that it is helpful to follow inspirations. For whatever the outward form of any inspiration, it is fulfilling a deeper need and offers the opportunity for the growth of the being, shall we say. In short, we suggest following those inspirations which come from within the being.

May we answer you further, my brother?

J: Thank you.

I am Latwii, and we thank you, my brother. Is there another query at this time?

Carla: Just to follow that up. Is there anything legitimately wrong with making bucks, with money?

I am Latwii, and am aware of your query, my sister. We do not find the wrongness, shall we say, in any action which any of your peoples might contemplate, for all actions are productive of the opportunity to learn and offer each entity an avenue to do so. That which you have called money is one particular item within your illusion which has much controversy gathered about it for there are many of the spiritual path who find the concern with the monetary matters to be quite inappropriate. We suggest that any action or thought may be used efficiently by the seeker of truth.

May we answer you further, my sister?

Carla: Do you want to repeat that last sentence?

I am Latwii, and it was our suggestion that any action or thought could be well used by the seeker of truth. It is the intention that is the factor of most importance.

May we answer you further, my sister?

Carla: I'd always had a kind of a hunch that the only reason that money had such a bad name in spiritual circles was that it tended to become an end in itself, like idolatry of some sort. Is that somewhere close to the way that it really is?

I am Latwii, and am aware of your query, my sister. We might suggest the general principle in this case could be generally stated as that which is of most importance in the life of the seeker is that which continues to provide an avenue for further seeking. That which becomes an end in itself ends the seeking and indeed becomes that which you have called an idol is that which is of less importance for it has limited value and indeed limits the seeking.

May we answer you further, my sister?

Carla: No, that was fine, thank you.

I am Latwii, and we thank you, my sister. Is there another query at this time?

(Pause)

I am Latwii, and we are somewhat surprised that we have exhausted queries so early in the evening with a group which is so full of the inquiring nature of the seeker. We perceive that there are some queries which have yet to reach their final form and would ask once again if there might be any kind of query to which we might attempt reply?

S: Okay, I have one. Why is there always that stumbling block that all of us seem to go through? Where you want to tell people all about what's going on, there always seems to be that large hurdle one has to make. And some people stop there and some people can go ahead, go through and one's progress and search is so much easier when we do. I'm speaking of the *(inaudible)* where everyone wants to wear their spirituality on their sleeve and I speak from experience because I went through it to. But it seems to me that it would be so much easier and so much more enlightened if we didn't have to have that road block in the way.

I am Latwii, and we feel that we have the gist of your query, my sister, and we thank you for asking a query which is of great interest to our own seeking. For we are speaking to this group as a result of a desire to be of service to the one Creator in our way. You speak first of that desire one feels to speak what one has found to be true of a spiritual nature to those with whom one has relationship. The seeker, when first embarking upon the path in a conscious manner, will undergo that experience which is likened unto the fire being set within the heart. The seeker has perceived that which is of great value, yet is somewhat overwhelmed by the nature, the depth, and the potential of that which has been encountered. Whatever the means the seeker has used, whatever the group the seeker has joined, whatever thought the seeker …

(Side one of tape ends.)

(Jim channeling)

I am Latwii, and am once again with this instrument. To continue. Whatever means the seeker has used to begin the conscious search for truth, shall we say, the seeker then finds to be that which it wishes to share with others and to influence the others as the seeker has been influenced. It is a fire which burns most brightly for those beginning the journey. Yet it is a fire which is in need of, shall we say, the gentle touch. For such a fire can burn and singe and sear as well as illumine the darkness. It is not for the seeker to be, shall we say, adeptly able to shine the light in the manner it is needed in each instance. It is more likely that the seeker shall run about with the torch burning brightly, sparks flying, little fires smoldering here and there, quickly extinguished, unless, of course, there is the chance for the lighting of another fire which is possible upon occasion, for there are those who need but a gentle nudge to have their own flames ignited. Yet it is most likely that the seeker shall find great difficulty in using this flame in a manner which is both loving and wise.

Now we move on to that subject of the stumbling block in general. Every so-called stumbling block is most important for any seeker, whatever nature the stumbling block may take. For it is not the purpose of your illusion nor of your incarnation to move smoothly without the jolts and jangles and stumbling from time to time. It is in such upsetting of the journey that all is shifted about so that there needs from time to time to be a reassessment of that which has been gained and that which is sought and the means for doing so by the seeker of truth. It is at such times that whatever spiritual strength that has been gained by the seeker is put into play and is allowed its full reach that the seeker, as the young kitten, may test itself and roll and tumble with life and its catalyst, if we may so pun, and find that new synthesis of being. The continuation of the journey of seeking is that which is most important for it is an infinite journey and each stumbling block does not in truth hinder the journey but truly speeds it by providing the opportunity for that which is old and worn and no longer useful to be discarded and for that which is a new possibility for the seeker's consideration to be placed before the seeker's mind.

May we answer you further, my sister?

S: No. I have another question, though. How much spiritual progress can be done on a subconscious level, as opposed to a combination of consciousness and subconsciousness working together? Can you give me a number level or a … that can be reached on subconscious completely or through a dream state or something like that?

I am Latwii, and am aware of your query, my sister. Here we find that the response to this query may be that which surprises, much as this illusion is that which hides the truth and which surprises the seeker when it finds the truth. Indeed, my sister, we would suggest that the spiritual treasures which may be gained in your illusion are very infrequently gained in a conscious manner. The conscious assessment of spiritual progress is an attempt which is most futile. For within your illusion, the treasures of the one Creator are hidden beneath what may be called the veil of forgetting. And as you move through the illusion and encounter those situations which are yours to encounter, you shall deal with them in one manner or another and shall consciously register the effects within your mind and shall count the gain and note the loss and shall feel satisfaction or dismay. But in truth, that which has been gained of a spiritual nature has eluded the notice of the conscious mind.

It is as though the merchant who buys and sells the goods stores in his vault the gold of trade and measures his success by the gold, its purity and weight, and when the day finally comes that this entity passes from this incarnation and reads his own book of life, he will find that it was not the gold that was stored, not its purity, not its weight that is of importance in his life. Yet it was the manner in which the transactions were conducted with the other selves, the love that was given, the love that was received.

It is so with the life of each. Each counts the spiritual gold by the definition which each provides for the self. Yet, as you move within an illusion, so is the description of spiritual gold most illusory. That which is true value in the metaphysical sense is indeed stored up within your being but is of a nature which is quite beyond description and beyond your comprehension for it is not an illusion of comprehension in which you move. There is nothing which is understood completely or even in a small degree. You move within an illusion which requires faith and the will to move. You move in what might be called a darkness of being, seeking the small slivers of light. And it is within the heart of your being that such seeking is motivated and recorded in its true sense.

May we answer you further, my sister?

S: Yeah. I'm not sure if you answered it or not, but I don't think you did. What I was trying perhaps to get at is, can, by consciousness which is on one path that I am aware of and the troubles in the life that I am going through now and the joys and sorrows that I am consciously aware and I'm consciously aware of the lessons to be learned and the karma to undo and all of that on one level … I also feel that there is another, at least one other part of me that is also on a different spiritual path, moving together or simultaneously with this other outer spiritual path that I'm doing here. And if that is going on at least on two different levels and that they're learning two different lessons or levels of lessons, could there be more, or am I confusing that, and I shouldn't even be thinking about the two different levels? Now I only get very brief glimpses of this other level which is the thing that is the only reason that I'm bring it up.

I am Latwii, and hopefully we are more aware of your query at this time and shall attempt responses. We may affirm that for each seeker there are truly two levels of seeking. One is that which you have described as the conscious seeking during the incarnation. The other level is the level which more nearly approaches that which may be called the metaphysical truth. That level of being and seeking is what might be called the preincarnative choice. The entity before incarnating, having made contact with the higher self and with the aid of those guides and presences which have been called to the entity in service sets out a plan for the incarnation, a blueprint, shall we say. We, for want of a better term, shall call this plan the pursuit of truth and it is set forth in clear terms yet with general guidelines for accomplishment. Then during the incarnation as the entity begins to awaken to its preincarnatively chosen plan, glimpses of this plan will become apparent as the entity indeed pursues that plan, both upon an unconscious and upon a conscious level. Whether the pursuit of the plan is unconscious or conscious, it is imperfectly perceived. Of course, as the journey of the seeker becomes more and more a conscious portion of the incarnation, the perception becomes clearer, yet in our previous response we intended to state that no matter how clearly the conscious mind is able to perceive the plan for the incarnation, it is the nature of your illusion that such [a] plan is never purely perceived. It is not clearly delineated for the conscious mind, but through the unconscious sets a tone and, shall we say, haunts rather than explicates itself.

May we answer further, my sister?

S: No, that's fine.

We thank you, my sister, for your most thoughtful query. Is there another query at this time?

Carla: Yes. Perhaps I'm just being dense, but I'd like to follow up S's first question. She was asking what the purpose was of the constant stumbling blocks you run into when you … people even want perhaps to know about what you're studying or how you feel and yet stumbling blocks do arise and misunderstandings arise and sometimes they seem overwhelming. What I was wondering was, I understand the virtue of this is to the person that's trying to be of service, but to the person who is listening and discovering the stumbling block, what is the gift which is given by this stumbling block?

I am Latwii, and am aware of your query, my sister. We might suggest that the gift of such a stumbling block to the one listening to the seeker of fire is to awaken the ability to question that which is given from any source and to awaken the ability to seek for the self all answers and to, shall we say, develop the ability to filter from any resource any information which is given.

May we answer you further, my sister?

Carla: Just for the heck of it, how would you like to respond to accusations that we get about every once, six months, twice a year, maybe, that we are messengers of Satan and that you are a demonic being? All of you, of course.

I am Latwii, and am aware of your query, my sister. Our response to such a statement would be to recognize the one Creator which speaks and to suggest that such an entity has discovered that which we wish to share is not appropriate for that entity's path of seeking and has so responded as a means of describing not only to others but to the self that another path would be more appropriate than to give any value to information which we might share or to give any value to the possibility of information being shared by such entities in such a manner. It is the right and privilege of each seeker to choose its own path and is indeed the duty of each to do so whether it is done with grace or clumsily, it is yet the one Creator which finds its own expression in its own way and time.

May we answer you further, my sister?

Carla: Why are you such a threat to people such as the Christian fundamentalists that are generally the ones who would say that?

I am Latwii, and am aware of your query, my sister. First we may state that we are truly no threat to any. But there are those whose minds are configured in such and such a manner to whom we may seem a threat by their own thinking. As the viewpoint is widened and as love is seen in those places and beings in which it was not previously seen, there is less and less seen to be a threat, until finally, all is seen as one Being, full of love, and that Being is not only the self and not only a Creator which exists outside the self, but is all things, all thoughts, all experience. Thus, each seeker begins with a narrow point of view and travels the path of truth which then allows the experiences that will aid the seeker in widening the point of view and the point of love.

May we answer you further, my sister?

Carla: Yet, you, yourselves have cautioned us frequently to tune so that we might get a carefully tuned positive love-oriented, service-to-others-oriented message. Is there a point in the development towards the final density and reunion with the Creator at which negative channeling and positive channeling or service-to-self and service-to-others channeling are heard with equal joy?

I am Latwii, and am aware of your query, my sister. This is indeed correct, my sister. At some level of each entity's being this is possible. Yet within your illusion, you move in a darkness and in a manner which requires the careful choosing of polarity, shall we say. For in order to do work of a spiritual nature, the battery of the seeker must be polarized as purely as possible. This polarization process proceeds for much of what you call time through many experiences. And as the seeking becomes more and more refined, the seeker in the positive polarity is able to appreciate more and more the essence of the one Creator which resides in all things, including those entities who have chosen to express the negative polarity of the one infinite Creator. Such a positive entity with this ability to appreciate the one Creator in all is an entity which has refined the process of seeking to a degree where all is seen as one; all is seen as the one infinite Creator and there is no polarity at this point.

May we answer you further, my sister?

Carla: I take it that's quite a ways down the road?

I am Latwii, and we would agree, my sister, that for the seeker of truth in the positive sense this is quite a lengthy journey and reaches its culmination, shall we say, at the mid-sixth density level, at which time for any entity wishing to continue the process of evolution, it is necessary to see all as the one Creator. Yet it is possible from time to time on this journey for any entity to so purify its own thinking that it is able to experience the unity of all the creation for briefer moments.

May we answer you further, my sister?

Carla: No, just an observation that that sounds in some ways like risky business.

I am Latwii, and in one sense, my sister, we would agree. Each seeker of truth finds the path laid before it in a manner which leads inevitably to the one Creator. For in each moment the one Creator is all that is. Yet as the one Creator seeks to know Itself and has portioned Itself throughout the one creation in the positive and negative senses, those entities who travel this path of evolution will find that path, though inevitably leading to the one Creator, can be a path which has many surprises for those whose step is not sure and whose attention has been diverted for the moment. And it may be necessary from time to time for the seeker to learn lessons which may be described as difficult. Yet each lesson teaches love, wisdom and unity for those who are alert to the possibilities within difficulty.

May we answer you further, my sister?

Carla: No, thank you.

I am Latwii, and we thank you, my sister. Is there another query at this time?

S: I have one. And I should know the answer but I don't. If one incarnated on this planet from a different dimension, let's say a higher one, and if that entity didn't do any large boo-boos that would keep him in this density and leave him with this social memory complex, upon completion of this service, does an entity go back to his own social memory complex and kind of jump in where he left off or if he has made great progress in the third density, can he shoot ahead out of his social memory complex into another one, say on a different dimension, if he came from the fourth dimension, did good work, could he shoot ahead to the fifth, or does he jump back into the evolution of the, or the fourth density he came from?

I am Latwii, and am aware of your query, my sister. We must attempt general response to a query which has a great many possible responses. If an entity from a density which is in advance of this third density illusion incarnates for a certain purpose, the incarnations within this illusion may be expected to continue until that purpose has been fulfilled, whether it takes one or many incarnations. There is also the possibility of revaluation of such purposes between the incarnations within this illusion and at this time, shall we say, it is possible for new services to be added or for modifications to be made upon the service which was originally chosen. If an entity is successful in providing the service and learning the lessons which were set before the incarnation or incarnations, it is most usually the case for such a positively polarized entity to remain with the social memory complex, as you have called that it originally began with. For it is not the nature of a positively polarized entity wishing to be of service to leave that group with which it has provided services for great portions of what you call time and experience. It is more likely that such an entity would use those increased abilities gained in the, shall we say, successful incarnation to advance the social memory complex as a whole rather than to take the fruits of his labor and go its, shall we say, merry way.

May we answer further, my sister?

S: No, that was fine. Thank you.

I am Latwii, and we thank you once again, my sister. Is there another query at this time?

(Pause)

I am Latwii, and we thank each within this group for providing those queries and energies which allow us to provide our humble service to each and to the one Creator. We shall follow our brothers and sisters of Hatonn with the same injunction, that whatever message and words that we have provided which you find to be of service, we offer in joy and thanksgiving. Whatever words may not be helpful at this time, we suggest that you leave behind with no thought or regret. That which we have to offer, we offer as our opinions and as our gift with no expectations that what we say shall carry any weight. We speak to the one Creator in each which knows all that can be known and is all that can be. And it is our great honor and privilege to speak with the one Creator gathered this evening in this place. We thank each for allowing us this great privilege. We shall leave you now it would seem, though in truth we are with you always and at your request shall be most happy to join your meditations. We are those of Latwii. We leave you now, my friends, in love and light. Adonai. Adonai vasu borragus.

Sunday Meditation
August 12, 1984

(Carla channeling)

I am Oxal. I greet you in the love and in the light of our infinite Creator. We gratefully acknowledge our opportunity to work with the one known as S. Ours is not an easy contact and we were attempting to practice with this instrument. We thank the one known as S for her cooperation, and will now speak for a few of your moments through this instrument. We thank each of you for calling us this evening. We are those who are more involved in the questions of the mind than the heart. We may suggest to each that our being called does not mean that each here has learned the lessons of the heart. It means only that there is a great call for wisdom, for clarity, and freedom from illusion.

It is perceived among your peoples that the heart cannot give freedom from pain, that the heart cannot see clearly and that the heart is useful only as a means of generating experience, much of which is painful. This perception of your illusion may well be true. That is for each of you to say. For what is the heart? We with our wisdom gaze at compassion and realize that that balance between compassion and wisdom shall be our next lesson. But let us for a moment assume that there is in many of your peoples an excess of compassion which causes pain and then a desire to seek. Very well, my friends, the pain has its first meaning, for seeking is the activity of the deity. It is in some ways the definition of the Creator, the sign of the creation. A tree may appear to be rooted and still, yet, does not each leaf seek the light? So you feel that love is so weak a tool that you must instead seek wisdom.

We shall share that which we feel to be correct with you, admonishing you that our opinions are fallible; therefore take from our statements those things which are helpful and toss away the rest, for are we not all one, and is this knowledge not inside you that you seek now? Is this peace that you seek not also within you? Do you think perhaps that you are like a mountain—at the bottom there are verdant fields of love, at the top, the peak places of wisdom. We say to you, your perceptions of wisdom will be greatly skewed until you learn the lessons of love, and therefore we of Oxal wish to speak to you of love from the standpoint of wisdom.

Let us look at perfect compassion. Let us look at a perfectly smoothly running, perfectly timed universe. Perfect compassion, which we call love, for want of a better word, is power. It is power that has been so disciplined, guided and considered that all things work together in harmony. That which powers the universe is not understood. That which powers the universe is love. Wisdom is the vibration which love uses. It is the material the artist uses to create experience for those who are conscious. Therefore, as you wish to learn the one original Thought, so you wish to learn all that there is.

Wisdom is the refining of love into its shapes, designs, its nuances and its shadows.

There is, shall we say, a ship with its sails furled upon a great sea. It may seem that you who are on the ship are victims of the wind and the waves and you lack of knowledge of navigation and astrogation. However, there is within each of you an innate guide, a rudder, shall we say, that steers you if you will let it. That which steers you is not a wisdom but an association with love, that love which is the original Thought of the one Creator. Your voyage may seem endless, perilous, difficult, pointless and confusing. This, my friends, is the voyage of one who has not yet picked up that association which forms the rudder of experience.

(Pause)

We apologize for the delay. We are feeding this instrument concepts that it is having difficulty enunciating. This in itself is an example of how the wisdom baffles the working of the deeper part. This instrument's intellect does not see any association between the next concept and the previous one. Therefore, the instrument questions the concept and we must pause in order to tune this instrument as we are talking and regain the line of our poor speech.

There is a call in this group this evening that stems from a very deep place, that place before time was or space. It is the call of the soul or spirit to the conscious self. We may take the voyager through space and through time but it is that which is beyond space and time which will yield the simplicity, the peace and the power which is sought. The fruit is single. We are all love and we all distort that love. We are each unique, and yet we are each perfect, both as we are and perfect in the literal sense of being, in part, beyond space and beyond time, a part of the Creator. That is why you already know each answer you seek. If we inspire you, it is but a remembering. And yet, that which you need to remember is buried, and therefore, in meditation, you sit and wait.

Those who seek learn the meaning of the word patience. You seek the same thing over and over again. You seek to find the truth, the love, power within your daily experience which may well seem false, disturbing and powerful only in its ability to cause pain. So many of your peoples, my friends, live in a narrow world, bounded by that which is seen and heard and felt. This group seeks that which is beyond the boundaries of the prison which is called your lifetime. Yet, my friends, we say prison, for you are indeed behind the bars of an illusion, the illusion that you were born and you will die and you will be no more. Within that illusion there are few good reasons for having faith, for behaving ideally, or for holding ideals. Yet, the instinct of those who seek has put them in touch with the awareness that the true self, and, indeed, the majority of the self is outside the prison already.

You have put yourself in this situation and you have within you that which may remove you from the prison. We do not speak of death, although that certainly will remove the bars. We speak of your own ability to seek. What shall you seek? Observe yourself in any situation and let that observer within you ask, "What do you seek?" Do you seek love? Do you seek to become a messenger of love? Or do you perhaps seek that which may be well within the bounds of those who are still asleep and do not even know they are in prison? There are many apparent powers—money, position, relationships, the feeling of being in an appropriate place, and yet what is the true power? Look at each of those subjects and you shall see those things that change are not true but temporal. You seek peace and within this world those same things that give you power are reputed to offer peace, and yet, do they? Ask yourself if any peace of a lasting and infinite nature occurs within the bounds of the temporal world.

We shall say to you once again, there is peace, there is power. Those things are to be sought carefully. You are those who love. You do not love in perfection as your conversation noted previously, and yet you attempt. In each attempt is power and peace. The power of love is unmistakable, healing and radiant. Those who live in light, manifest it. People are attracted to them and enjoy their company. It is not they but the love channeled through them which is attractive. There is a peace in loving that cannot be found by buying and selling, giving and taking. In bargaining there is no peace. In loving, alone, is there peace. If you love yourself completely you are at peace. If you wish to serve others in love completely, you are at peace. Between these two points, in one degree or another, you shall not be at peace.

Therefore, we urge you at least once in your day to say to yourself, "Ah, the bars of my cage shall [not] hold me well, for I shall sit beyond space and time and I shall seek love, I shall seek the truth and I shall do it in silence." For there is, indeed, as one your holy works as said, a still, small voice that enables seeking to continue and flourish within you.

We are those who learn the lessons of wisdom, and we see you as those tossed by the Creator which is yourself into the depths of your prisons, or to move back to our other analogy, those lost upon an endless sea. The point is that you are kept, somehow, apparently, from your freedom. In our seeking towards wisdom we see your peoples as those who now have the opportunity to face once again towards the same Creator that has flung you upon the water and cast you into prison. In meditation you may break forth from prison in contemplation and inspiration, in dreams, in converse with others who are seeking; you will find those things, those coincidences, those sentences which strike you, which tell you where to move your rudder, in which direction to go.

That is the rhythm of each density. You are flung out and you learn to return. It is you, yourself, who has placed you, each of you, as you are now, experiencing what you are now, dealing with what you are dealing at this point. Turn then, to meditation and find out why. Climb the mountain slowly, slowly, my friends and see each step clearly. What you are doing at this point, what you are thinking, how you are seeking, how you are feeling; these are your tools. These are tools that can give you beauty beyond measure, that can make you rejoice, even, perhaps, as you weep. Before your footsteps lies the mountain but you must climb it one step at a time, one day at a time, one moment at a time.

We rejoice now with you as we experience the vibration of this group and share our love with you. We are very blessed to be able to speak this evening, to listen through the ears of this instrument to the cicadas and the murmur of your *(inaudible)*. Such beauty, my friends, in a single moment; it is almost too much to believe for us, for we do not experience your illusion. We seek a different kind of beauty and must learn to become aware differently. The beauty about you now, the beauty within you now, the power, the peace and the love within you now is very striking to us, and we give thanks that we are able to join you.

We would leave you now, having spoken far too long, we fear. We leave you in all that there is, love and light, the love and the light of the One Who is All. I am known to you as Oxal. I leave this instrument. Adonai.

(Jim channeling)

I am Latwii, and I greet you, my friends, in the love and in the light of our infinite Creator. We are most privileged to once again join your group for the purpose of attempting to answer those queries which may be of aid in your seeking. We thank each for so inviting our presence. And we remind each that our humble words are but fallible opinions which we offer in hopes that they might be of some small service to you. May we then begin with the first query?

S: Yes, Latwii, I have a question from R, who will read your answer. He wanted to know if you could make any comment or give information about the faces he's been seeing in his meditations. They're all different and they change, it's not like he's seeing the same faces over and over again. But he wanted your comment.

I am Latwii, and am aware of your query, my sister. We find in this instance that we are once again relegated to the role of speaking in general terms in order that the free will of the one known as R might be preserved as he continues his journey of seeking. Each entity shall find within the meditative state certain experiences that are of significance upon the journey of seeking the truth, as you call it. These particular visions or faces which the one known as R has been experiencing are those portions of a larger process which is underway, shall we say, within this entity. One may look at each experience within your illusion as a symbol of that which is a deeper truth. This is also true within that state which you call meditation, though this state is capable of producing experiences of a greater clarity, shall we say, than your normal waking state. These images might be fruitfully used, we suggest, by the one known as R if they be looked at for a symbolic value, for a certain resonance which each contains. This resonance then may be placed by the entity with certain life experiences or lessons which are seeking expression at this time within this entity.

May we answer you further, my sister?

S: Well, since I'm not really sure, I guess I'll just go with what you've given me because it sounds like it'll be very helpful to him. I did have another question, though, on a different subject. About a month ago, R and I were almost on a daily basis having minor aches and pains back and forth and back and forth to the point where it became comical. We were making jokes about it and I would say, "Is your knee getting better now, because mine's beginning to hurt?" I would like to know if you could give me any information about the possibilities of us maybe subconsciously attempting to heal each other or if there's another explanation?

I am Latwii, and am aware of your query, my sister. Again, to speak in general terms, we may suggest that it has been well said that those who together seek shall far more surely find. It has been your experience which you have shared with the one known as R to intensively seek …

(Side one of tape ends.)

(Jim channeling)

I am Latwii, and am once again with this instrument. To continue our response. You may look at these experiences, as we have suggested before, for their symbolic value. As you proceed in your seeking together you shall find that the catalyst which you use is catalyst which you share. Those aches and pains, as you have called them, are indeed offering opportunities for the healing, as you have suggested. This is the purpose of all catalyst and experience, to speak generally. All distortions, all that is not whole, may be made whole and clear by the successful use of catalyst. Those experiences which you have shared of the physical discomfort are symbolic, and reach deeper into your shared experience and are representative of certain lessons which you share together upon levels other than the physical.

May we answer you further, my sister?

S: Well, if the aches and pains go away, does that mean that we have been successful in using the catalyst?

I am Latwii, and am aware of your query, my sister. In general, we would suggest that this assumption is correct. The catalyst which has not been well used in the mind is then given to the body, that it might be noticed more fully and more fully utilized. This is not to say that should such physical representation of the catalyst disappear that the catalyst has been completely used, but is to say that it has been used to the point of clarity so that further symbolic manifestation in the physical body is not necessary.

May we answer you further, my sister?

S: Well, yes. You could clarify one more thing for me. Are you saying then that because we as a couple have spent a lot of time together there are some lessons that we chose to learn together, and that if both of us are not successful at any particular time … wait, that's not what I mean. Okay, first of all, is what I've just said correct, and second of all, do we then have to work on the catalyst as a unit rather than as individuals?

I am Latwii, and am aware of your query, my sister. To speak to the first portion of your query, it is basically correct that you have chosen to learn certain lessons together and that you have, as you have progressed through your learning process, come not only to see each as a mirror for the other but have come to see the self in the other.

To speak to the second portion of your query, it is a most efficient means of learning for an entity to learn with another in order that this mirroring effect might be utilized to accelerate the learning process. It is quite possible to learn as a solitary being, but without the mirrors of other selves to show the self the intricacies of the self, the self then is more likely to miss the refining ability that mirrors provide.

May we answer you further, my sister?

S: No, that's been very illuminating. Thank you.

I am Latwii, and we thank you, my sister. Is there another query at this time?

Carla: I'd like to follow up on S's *(inaudible)*. It seemed to me that you were intimating, but not saying, that this couple, like many couples, have been not just through this incarnation together but through others and that that way … my question is, then, is the previous experience with each other necessary before you get to the point to where you are really working together and what's catalyst for one becomes catalyst for the other, and they're sympathetic and so forth?

I am Latwii, and am aware of your query, my sister. We can suggest that your assumption is in a great portion correct, for those entities which have had experience as the mated pair before this incarnation shall find that there is a great reservoir or resource which may be called upon by the deeper portions of the entity as the incarnation proceeds and as the mated relationship attempts to refine the process of evolution.

May we answer you further, my sister?

Carla: Yes, just one final thing. In observing certain couples, I cannot see any karmic bonds. These are the couples that seem to be doing the best work together. Certainly R and S strike me as one such. Is the karma free … I guess what I'm really trying to ask is, is there a portion of the third density where mated pairs that have worked through the karma and have become free from karma as we understand it, then come back in order to become what some people have called masters or to find true balance, in other words, is a karma-less state a prerequisite for this particular lesson, that is, working as a couple?

I am Latwii, and am aware of your query, my sister. We may suggest that that state which you have described as karma-free might be more clearly described as balanced karma. That is to say that entities of the mated relationship nature which have chosen to once again incarnate as mated pair are much more able to provide the services and learn the lessons chosen before the incarnation when the karma is what we would call balanced, rather than being out of balance so that one entity would need to assume a role that is more distorted from, shall we say, equality than the other in order that certain lessons left incomplete from previous incarnations might be balanced in the current incarnation.

May we answer you further, my sister?

Carla: Was that an affirmative answer? I get lost in your answers sometimes. Did you basically say, "Yeah"?

I am Latwii, and we beg your forgiveness for being somewhat abstruse from time to time. Yet, as we use this instrument's mind, we find that there are certain concepts that, though helpful, do have certain tendrils of abstractness about them. We have attempted to suggest that your basic assumption was correct, yet we wished to make hopefully more clear the situation of entities that are utilizing the mated relationship efficiently, that is, their karma has been balanced rather than removed. To remove the karma is to remove experience, and is to remove a great reservoir or resource that is a great aid in the incarnation.

We might further suggest that as entities have gained experience as mated pairs in previous incarnations and have balanced their karma, then the portion of the next incarnation devoted to the personal lessons grows smaller and the portion devoted to providing services for others grows larger.

May we answer you further, my sister?

Carla: No, thanks.

I am Latwii, and we thank you, my sister. Is there another query at this time?

(Pause)

I am Latwii, and we find that we have for the moment exhausted the queries, and we are most appreciative for the opportunity to be of whatever service is possible by our humble words. We apologize for seeming to be without our normal humor and for seeming so formal in our replies. We are hopeful that as we continue to utilize this instrument that it shall be able to widen its own perceptive abilities and allow that which is of a lighter nature in our own being to shine through in our responses, for it is a great joy and a pleasure for our group to be able to make contact with your own, and we wish to give this joyful feeling expression whenever possible. We are those of Latwii, and we shall now leave this group and instrument, rejoicing in the love and in the light of the One within all. Adonai, my friends. Adonai vasu borragus. ☙

Sunday Meditation
August 19, 1984

(Carla channeling)

I am Hatonn, and I greet you in the love and in the light of our infinite Creator. What a blessing it is to blend our energies and lives with yours as we blow, flow along the never-ending river of love and light. This evening we would speak with you about that which one might call a kind of reality that is hard to discover within the heavy chemical illusion within which you live, think and act. It has been sometimes called the Kingdom of Heaven. The most apparent condition of this reality which each seeks—as it is more closely aligned with what you would call truth than is your experience—day by day is its harmony.

As we speak to you now, there are millions of life forms about you that are vibrating in harmony with you that have changed slightly in their pitch and tone and *entendre* in order to be in harmony with your vibrations. The very particles of air, furnished as they are with light which is their chief characteristic, and the energy of love which moves that light scintillate in a dazzling display of harmony which ascends and ascends until all is white and light and there is no more for the eye to see. This is occurring about you at this moment. We are aware that you would like to become familiar with this experience and to leave behind experiences of disharmony and banality and folly with which the incarnation you now experience has provided you. The experiences of these energies have been had, and are being had, and will be had by many in these, shall we use the phrase, latter days, due to ingestion of chemicals which alter the rhythms of the mind so that the mind may become aware of that which is more real by one step than your illusion.

These harmonious vibrations are also an illusion, my friends, it is simply that it is a denser illusion, far more filled with light and therefore more pleasing. How wondrous it would be if within your physical bodies, awake and alert, you could still perceive the flowers and the trees nodding and rejoicing in rhythm to your footsteps and your thoughts, feelings, the musical interactions of air and earth and water and sunshine, as these elements adjust themselves to all that is about them and to the one underlying vibration which is the original Logos and from which all harmony stems.

The Kingdom of Heaven is one of harmony. It is fourth density. It is remembered by many. Many yearn for it as they would a home. Beyond harmony is unity, the white light of which we spoke, being far more naturally the experience of one whose true home is within fifth density, and many there are who yearn to abide in that comforting presence always and who lack the awareness in the waking state.

We have spoken to you many times of meditation, and therefore you know that we shall say that these experiences are within you to remember, not to gain, and that meditation is like the key that opens the door. It is a reaching out and turning of the latch. Regardless of how well one meditates, one is still reaching, and therefore these experiences may begin to come. Very often they begin to come in a distorted manner and not in the waking state as much as in the hypnogogic or sleeping state, either in dreams or in half-waking visions. They may be personified by a teacher who is attempting to help you gain what you seek or by a certain symbol which haunts you. Pursue these distortions with the knowledge that they are the road within your own self which will guide you past the blocks that you have set up against yourself to keep you from remembering.

The sleeping experience is not understood among your peoples. We find in this instrument's memory a recently read article on the subject of sleep. In the sense in which we are discussing sleep, the greater percentage of those upon your sphere sleep twenty-four hours a day, as this instrument would say, for they do not use the time within sleep to learn, to seek, and to experience harmony, unity and love. This process may begin within sleep and one may begin seeking because the subconscious and sleeping self has pushed through in dreams those things which cause an entity to begin to question the apparent reality within which there are so many shadows and so many unexplained and unresolved discrepancies.

It may happen the opposite way. There are those whose minds are stronger than their intuition and for these the intellect first becomes curious. For these entities the journey towards total commitment to seeking may be longer, as the intellect is devious by nature and tends to hold a percentage of what you call judgment back. Within the dreaming state, and within the intuitional state while awake, there is no holding back of the judgment, but only the experience. Judgment is done after the fact, not during, thus the experience is undiluted.

We say to you, my friends, you dwell in a universe so beautiful, so harmonious, so unified, so totally full of love, that words are never enough to begin to acquaint you with the character of that which you may call reality. You experience one reality which by its very nature has the potential of transcending space and time. That is the sexual orgasm. If you could imagine this experience as a steady state you would begin to understand the character and the nature of reality. There is a great hunger to experience this in each seeker, and we encourage this hunger, we urge you onward. Once you have experienced one moment of this reality, you will not subjectively doubt the validity of your seeking.

We take you, therefore, to the vast meadows of fragrant existence that lie before you in time and space. We ask you drop those things which you have in your hands, all the worries, the concerns, the qualifications, the distinctions, and the limitations which you think you have and by which you think you should abide. The strength of the universe is one. Its fragrance, its beauty, its joy are one. The experience of this one original Thought will continue to be available, and we urge you to pursue it in meditation, in vision, and by dedication of the self in whatever state and in whatever experience within your illusion, to the seeking of reality, if we may use that term, for truly we speak relatively. We know a bit more than you as we have experienced more, but for us to talk of reality would be foolish, for we have not seen the end and the beginning nor have our teachers. The mystery of the universe remains hidden in the Creator and therefore, hidden in all of us.

Rejoice, then, that you have within you that which you seek. Know that the answers are simple, too simple for the mind. Know, too, that you will often be hard put within your illusion to manifest any awareness of those things which you seek, of those ideals to which you have dedicated yourself. It is the nature of your illusion to block and block and block again every pathway so that you may express love in the removal of blockage. It is the intention of your higher self that the pride within you be humbled, that the humility within you be made proud, that the plain may be made complex and the complex plain. In other words, my friends, your higher self wishes you learn the lessons of love and these lessons are not simple. They are as complex and, if you will excuse the misuse of words, three dimensional as a chair or you yourself, and all of these things you shall not learn by the mind. You may put all that you wish into your mind, you may think and contemplate and guess and worry and fret, and yet you shall not feel harmony unless it is by coincidence alone, for the mind is a servant that is too often the master by default.

What do you have, my friends, that may seek, that you may trust more than your mind? What shall be the master of your mind? As you seek reality, we ask you to ponder this question, for in the seeker the mind is grossly misused very often and the far-seeing vision within is cut off, downplayed and mistrusted.

When we are with you, my friends, we experience a great deal of joy, and we wish to thank each, for we too cast our burdens down as we speak with you. We too are able to inspire more than we are inspired by ourselves. We too find the saying easier than the doing. We find these experiences in different ways than you, for our experiential continuum is different. We see the harmony but we are having our own difficulties in seeing the white light of fusion, and that we seek, refining upon our grasp of the truth in our own incarnational experience. It is greatly helpful to us to share experience with you and to offer service to you. It is very inspiring to us to see those who are making their choice to serve and to love the one Creator and the Creator in each of us, and we offer you courage and encouragement, for truly that which you seek is awaiting you. You have shut the door upon a glowing and vibrant harmony, upon the infinity of light, upon the mysteries that lie beyond all knowing. You have hands, you have a will; reach out, grasp and open. This is not often a quick process, unless, as we said before, experienced by means of the so-called mind-altering substances, and when experienced in such a way, the results are unpredictable, and it is sometimes too much of a vision for the spirit of that particular entity at that particular time to experience, and the equivalent of a spiritual injury is done so that the aura, as you would call it, is not then able to bear the full light without much regrouping, rededication and re-searching.

Therefore, seek ye what may be called the Kingdom of Heaven. Whether it be for moments at a time or for hours, let it be daily, and then seek to share whatever you can of your journey with whomever there may be who comes before you and asks, "What is there, my friends, that shall master the mind? And how shall you go about strengthening that faculty?" Ponder this well and with joy. We shall be with you, as you know, at any time that you may wish to ask for our presence mentally. Indeed, if you are alone and do not create a stumbling block by calling out for unseen presences, it sometimes helps entities who are seeking to invoke names aloud that are able to undergird and strengthen the meditative carrier wave, shall we say.

We have been anxious to use the instrument known as C. However, we find within this instrument's mind a request to be able to listen this evening which we respect. We would, however, like to take a few moments to exercise this channel by means of conditioning and also to make our presence likewise known to each. We shall pause.

(Pause)

I am Hatonn, and am once again with this instrument. This instrument is somewhat overcome by the conditioning which was made stronger for others. We are adjusting the contact. My friends, many are the times that we speak to you of the dragons and the [chimeras] of your illusion, of all the difficulties that you face. There are times when it is best to turn one's back on consideration of the entire spectrum of your incarnational experience and focus instead upon one single thing. You do not exist because you think. You do not exist because of what you have done. You are not a child of the Creator because of who you know, what power you have, what moneys may be yours, what influence you may peddle. You do not belong to the One because of how nice you are, how intelligent, how pleasant, or any other quality or character that you may propose. There is no justification for your existence, nor has there ever been, nor will there ever be. You are a portion of joy which has no reason for being but itself. You experience this joy in a vastly distorted way in your day-to-day experience but never mistake the quality of your life. You are love. You are joy. You are One. Past all the stumbling blocks that [a] human mind can conceive there lies a kingdom whose music is haunting you and whose beauty is just beyond your fingertips. There is mercy within you, mercy that forgives all that is within the human portion of yourself, mercy that is like a pointer saying, "You need no justification. Come and follow joy." We urge you to consider your priorities and seek first …

(Side one of tape ends.)

(Carla channeling)

Then turn back into your world, into space and time as you experience it and be the conditional limited entity that you can be, careful of yourself and loving, insofar as you are able, to others. Be yourself, my friends. Be yourself with that which shall not pass away from you.

In this we leave you, for that which does not pass is that which you are and that which you wish to experience, the love and the light of the One Who Is All and in all. I am Hatonn. I leave this instrument regretfully, realizing that we have been verbose, and yet it has been such a pleasure to speak with you. Our hearts leap with you as you experience the yearning for truth, for joy, comfort and for peace. We can now only say to you, you do not seek that which does not exist; that which you seek is within you and is awaiting the reaching. Adonai, my friends. Adonai vasu borragus.

(Jim channeling)

I am Latwii, and I greet you, my friends, in the love and in the light of our infinite Creator. We are overjoyed to be asked to join your group this evening. Once again it is our privilege and our pleasure to respond to your call. We, as always, hope to impart some bit of assistance in attempting to answer those queries which you have brought with you. May we then, without further delay, ask if we might attempt the first query?

Carla: What was that question we were going to ask?

(Group discussion.)

Carla: We had a question before this meditation that we didn't have any idea about the answer to and at one point we were wondering if you could answer the question, but I'm so absentminded I forgot what we were asking. Could it have been about the coincidence of the 1947 beginning of the modern UFO era, and also of the possible peak of the harvesters or the wanderers? Can you comment on that in any way?

I am Latwii, and am aware of your query, my sister. And though this query is not that which you had at first intended to query upon, we can indeed comment upon this subject. We find that in the observation of your people and your planet that the Confederation of Planets in the Service of the One Infinite Creator has from time to time attempted to provide service in answer to the call of your peoples and this service has taken various forms. In order to provide a service which has, shall we say, endurance and hope of raising those vibrations which are somewhat of a fluctuating nature between the negative and positive, a great portion of the plan of service to your peoples has been for various individualized portions of our Confederation to enter into those manifested planes of your third-density experience as third-density beings, those you know of as wanderers. These entities, with the memory of their heritage forgotten for the length of the incarnation in order that their service might be, shall we say, earned and purely given, have come that they might bring in some form those abilities to seek and serve which are their birthright, and this wave, as you speak of the occurrence which followed your so-called second great war, was undertaken at that time because it was at that time that the call of your peoples was of the proper, shall we say, frequency and strength to enable the great influx of wanderers to incarnate and provide those services which each his sought since to provide.

The calling was affected by that second great war, and was affected in the manner of a great desire sweeping your planet for peace, the second great war having unleashed the destructive powers of separation and control to a great extent upon much of the surface of your planet. Therefore, it was the desire of many of your peoples in a conscious fashion as well as in an unconscious fashion to do whatever could be done to achieve peace and harmony. Therefore, the time and calling, shall we say, were ripe for the response to come in the form of what you have called wanderers.

May we answer you further, my sister?

Carla: Only if it's possible for you to tell me what the question was that we were going to ask and then answer it.

I am Latwii, and am aware of that which you are not, for we have the advantage of this instrument's mind which has the quality of that game which you have recently undertaken, the Trivial Pursuit, and we find in this instrument's mind the remembrance of that query having to do with another instrument which has the incarnational vibration of Jane Roberts. It was given as a portion of information that this entity had been visited and, shall we say, overtaken to some degree by an entity of the negative vibration, and it was upon your mind, shall we remind you, as to whether this information might be correct.

We feel that this is a fair statement of the query. We shall now ask if there is some further elaboration upon the query which you wish to make. Thus we may attempt response to a query which has been asked us, and not respond to that which we have asked for you.

Carla: What you said, could you make a comment, either to verify it or to comment upon it?

(Sound of firecrackers going off nearby.)

Carla: I didn't mean that kind of comment.

(Firecrackers continue for a while longer.)

I am Latwii, and we were waiting for the drum roll but had to settle for a firecracker barrage. We are aware of your query, my sister, and are aware that your concern for such an occurrence is great and sincere. We, however, are not those who specialize in verifying the validity or non-validity of those rumors which may circulate among seekers from time to time. We can state in general that any entity who seeks to be of service to others by means of the vocalized channeling, whether of a telepathic or trance nature is an entity which is undertaking a great responsibility and is somewhat at risk. There is the honor of standing close to light, there is also the responsibility of reflecting and radiating that light as purely as is possible. No negative entity may do anything to another being, but any being may provide an entry into its own being by creating its own negative thoughts which may then be intensified by one of negative polarity.

This is a, shall we say, risk which any instrument assumes either consciously or unconsciously when such a service is begun. It is well for each instrument so choosing to serve to develop those means of protecting the self as the service is given. Such means of protection are available upon your planet, and are found within many, shall we say, esoteric teachings that are available to those who seek to be of service. It is well to so investigate, remembering at all times that the praise and thanksgiving and seeing each entity as the one Creator are the greatest protections.

May we answer you further, my sister?

Carla: Yeah. I just had one more question. I never can predict whether you can answer these or not, but I've been feeling very dizzy lately, and I actually fainted once, and wondered if there was some other than physical cause, or all a part of the dizziness, or whether it was a simple physical complaint?

I am Latwii, and am aware of your query, my sister. We find in this instance that we may speak in general, and note that the dizziness factor which has been a portion of your experience from the new times of your incarnation through your work in trance channeling has reappeared in yet another form or intensity of experience for you. We can suggest that your current situation within this group of working might be examined for those general trends or emotive feelings which then might be symbolized by the dizzying of the perceptive abilities and the momentary loss of control of the physical vehicle.

May we answer you further, my sister?

Carla: I suppose I'll have to read that. I've been looking at it from the standpoint of where I'm blocking in order to create a request for intensification of an already existing dizziness. I haven't been able to determine whether it's blue ray, indigo ray, or even green. Could you give some guidelines on that? I certainly have been blocking some communication because I don't want to discourage Don. I've been blocking indigo because I just feel cruddy sometimes when things get strange, and I've been blocking green simply because I find myself pulled really quickly towards martyrdom if I reach out to Don too much without protecting myself. So it could be any of the three. The guidelines, not just on this particular instance but on how you analyze blockages of this nature.

I am Latwii, and am aware of your query, my sister. We appreciate the multiple-choice selection of colors. We shall do our best to lend the proper hue to our response. We may speak again in general, and suggest that for each entity within your illusion the great lesson from which all lessons spring is the lesson of love. This lesson has as one of its primary features the ability to accept that which is apparently not acceptable, for is not all the Creator? Is there any portion of the one Creator that is not acceptable? As you move through your illusion and see that which is apparently not acceptable, it is then your great opportunity to take that situation or thought and examine it that you might become it and feel it also to be the one Creator, whole and perfect. Thereby do you learn that which you have come to learn, not only to accept but to be that which seems unacceptable and quite alien to the self.

May we answer you further, my sister?

Carla: No, Latwii, you just took all the fun out of dumping on people. That's very helpful. Thank you.

I am Latwii, and we thank you, my sister. We would at some date perhaps share a bit of gossip that we have about various entities, but since you do not know them, we must, for the nonce, refrain. Is there another query which we might attempt to answer?

C: Latwii, would you give comment on the … you see, we've been feeling other presences in the house in which we now live. Do you suppose you could comment on what these are—about their nature?

I am Latwii, and am aware of your query, my brother. We find in this instance that the presences which have become apparent to you within your new dwelling are those which been with this dwelling for a significant portion of what you call time. The entities previously inhabiting your new dwelling, by virtue of their nature of expression, had drawn to them entities of a varied spectrum, shall we say. These entities are basically of a harmless nature, yet are not the kind of entity which one would look to for inspiration of the spirit kind, shall we say. These entities are those which move through their existence in a somewhat random form, not having yet regularized those means of seeking which are available to them. We could suggest that if there is the desire to purify the new dwelling and call to your experience there entities of a more inspirational and positive nature, that you could undertake that type of cleansing which has been used within this particular dwelling, and which is available in written form in material which you may find here.

May we answer you further, my brother?

C: No, thank you.

I am Latwii, and we thank you, as always, my brother. Is there another query at this time?

Carla: I guess I have a question. I've got a newly dead child, and a grandmother who is probably going to die very soon. I was wondering what work I can best do for them spiritually and mentally?

I am Latwii, and am aware of your query, my sister. We can suggest general principles in this kind of situation where the desire to serve is a desire to serve one who is leaving your illusion and is making that transition which you have called the death. First, we would suggest that you work through your own grief for such an entity in a conscious or perhaps a prayerful manner before attempting to provide service to such an entity, for such service is best presented without those heavy feelings of grief which are the first natural response of your peoples to one's leaving of the illusion.

Then we can suggest that within the prayerful state, the contemplative state, or within the meditative state you might, in joy and praise and thanksgiving for the passing, send these feelings of joy and praise and love to the one who passes from your illusion. This will provide a food, shall we say, a milieu or environment in which the entity may be strengthened in its continuing journey of seeking the One.

We might also suggest that as you have sent joy, praise, thanksgiving and love to such an entity, you may also visualize this entity surrounded in the white light of the one Creator and you might send the mental suggestion to this entity that it remain in this white light for as long as is possible, that it might rejoice in this light, that it might find peace in this light, that it might be directed by this light to its next experience as the one Creator.

May we answer you further, my sister?

Carla: No, thank you.

I am Latwii, and we thank you, my sister. Is there another query at this time?

(Pause)

I am Latwii, and we find that we have for the moment completed those queries which were upon the minds of those present, and we are most grateful for such an opportunity to provide a simple service to each of you. We thank you, as always, for inviting our presence. We rejoice with you as you seek what is called truth. We remind each that our words are approximations of that truth. The whole and undistorted truth rests in your being. We hope to have pointed the way for you to find it more clearly there. We shall now take our leave of this instrument and of this group, leaving you always in love, in light, in peace, and in power. We are those of Latwii. Adonai. Adonai vasu borragus. ☙

Sunday Meditation
August 26, 1984

(S channeling)

[I am Hatonn, and I am pleased] to greet you this evening in the love and in the light of the one infinite Creator. We have spent some moments of your time with this instrument as she requested so that we might be prompt in speaking through her this evening. We hope we have not caused alarm to any who were planning on a longer wait this evening. We are grateful for the opportunity to be with this instrument, as she is sometimes hesitant to allow our vibrations to come through her but we feel we have a splendid mixing this evening.

We are often surprised by the amount of confusion that overwhelms some of your peoples at this time, for we sometimes think that it would be so simple if your peoples were able to escape this confusion by simply allowing themselves to enter their own being where the confusion is less apparent. But this is not always the case. We look upon your planet with love and hope in our hearts, and we are so honored when the love from groups such as this is returned to us and we are grateful for the love and light that is shared between us. We are always hopeful and ever looking forward to the next meeting, and we look upon those past meetings with a good feeling in our hearts, and we are humbled by the love expressed at these times.

The anger upon your planet is often very easy to see, the love sometimes more difficult. But for us the feeling of love is very powerful and runs deeply through many of your people. The love is not always expressed openly in an aggressive manner, but be assured, dear friends, that love expands and is felt throughout the universe. The continuous pumping of love, as if from a heart, to the ends of creation is a pulse that is felt by all and there are times when your planet beats strongly.

We realize that that which is printed in your newspapers is not usually of this nature and one must realize that the newspaper is not the place to find this feeling. In your quiet states allow yourself to relax and feel the love as it beats and pulses around and through your very being, for it continues from each entity and it reaches to the ends of creation and it does not become a smaller quantity as it reaches out further. As the love pulses, so does it multiply and so does it become greater, ever moving onward, ever more powerful, and ever making a louder pulse. Become aware of the love that you send and allow it to flow freely for we and all of creation [are grateful] for that which you are generous enough to send.

We would transfer to another instrument at this time. I am Hatonn.

(Carla channeling)

I am Hatonn. We must adjust to this instrument's vibrations, if you will allow us to pause briefly.

(Pause)

We greet you once again in the love and in the light of the infinite Creator. As this heart of love pulses, my friends, so does the entire creation pulse, each Logos, as you would call it, pulsing in its own depth of love and sending forth the slightest variation on the universal signal which is the beat of the universe as it contracts and flows forward. Much has been made of your astrology, but we say to you that the most vital portion of this art is the specific note of the music of the heartbeat which pulses from each of your stars and, in a larger sense, of your galaxy.

Indeed, there are influences upon you from the heavens in that you have rhythms, the beating of your heart, the intake of your breath and all your diurnal and monthly cycles. As you go through these cycles, it is as if there were light beamed upon you, shone through different colored lenses, each color affecting you slightly differently, so that your rhythm sings with a slightly different mellowness or harshness. There is great creativity in the unending variety and equally never-ending predictability of the cycles of these hearts of love, which shine and send their radiations of love and light to the universe, and, as you stand where you may be affected, to you personally.

In your turn, you yourself may affect the universe. Not upon any level that you may understand in a dramatic and mundane way, but you may think of the experience of gazing down at countryside as you fly through the darkness. There is a light here and one there and you know that you are passing through a very uninhabited place. And suddenly, as you cross the crest of a mountain or a hill, you see before you the lights of a great city. So are your light groups. Such is the nature of love that those even two or three, as it says in your holy works, who gather together in order to seek light and to offer light and love to the creation may form a light that is as exciting and visible as one of your great cities.

This is due to the fact that truly a group is not the sum of its parts but is far greater. Each has a vibratory dynamic with each other in a group. Each further has invoked or evoked a principle or a truth. You have evoked that which is truth, that which is love. Yours is what may be called a universal or cosmic invocation. Other groups may invoke persons which have inspired them or forces of nature. When any group meets together in love and invokes or evokes that which is positive, the light is born and it pulsates, throbs, enjoins with other lights, other groups, other centers, other great beings which are not of your space and time but are on other planes of existence and which vibrate in harmony with you as you seek love.

Indeed, my friends, as you seek you present a beautiful and glorious feast for our eyes and for our hearts and we wish to take this opportunity to encourage you, knowing how many times you feel that you have fallen and failed but yet knowing the determination to seek once more, always and ever, that which is love.

The nature of love has been approached in so many ways within your philosophers' works, your so-called religions, your poems, and your books. It has been dismembered and analyzed by those who call themselves psychologists and scientists, and yet we say to you that love is not at all understood. We say this to you, knowing that this, to your sorrow perhaps, you know all too well, for you seek to learn the lessons of love, and the lessons are elusive. We would offer to you this evening only a short tale that may illustrate one way of looking at the manifestation of the original Thought of the Creator, a manifestation that is available to all who seek with no exceptions, for it is within you. It is, shall we say, an over-the-counter commodity, its simplicity so staggering that the mind can hardly deal with the true nature of the manifestation of love. And so we shall begin by saying, "Once upon a time," as you begin your stories.

Once upon a time there was a king. He was not a great king, he was not a cruel king; he was a mediocre king. There were many about him. There was the queen who gave great feasts and parties and entertainments so that her king could make a toast proud of his house and his wealth and his generosity. There were those who counseled him, giving the best advice another could, spending many, many hours and days at a time pondering questions of state and enabling the king to prosper in his kingdom. There were those who went out to collect taxes so that the king's coffers might be full. Sometimes they might take a bit too much, but after all, it was for the king, whom they loved and whom they wished to serve.

And so it went, the many servants of the king excelling and loving the king or begrudging every minute of hard labor because to be a king seems so much better than to be a servant. The least of all in the kingdom was one who had a deformity and was unable to walk without great difficulty. Her back was hunched, and one eye looked east while the other looked west. All reviled her, including the king. She waited at the gates of the great city, which housed the palace, and begged. And she blessed all who went by, those who gave money and those who did not.

This situation is a description of different ways you look at love. It is assumed that there is an object of love, in our story, the king. Some take the object of love and give the best of their hearts, some the best of their minds, some the gifts of their greed, some as little as they can. But the one who truly loves gives love with no object.

We are aware that your minds ask you, "How can I acquire this high-sounding principle? I seek to love and to serve many entities but truly a few special ones. They are the object of love, and I wish to know how to seek to serve with heart, with mind, with gifts, with what I can."

Love is more simple than that, my friends. To love, to serve, involves moving with the heartbeat and being careless of the object. The heart does not always know how to serve, nor does the mind, nor can any gift be predictably correct to reinforce love and to manifest its brightness and its joy. The heartbeat that pulses within each for each, from each and to each, is one original Thought. This Thought lives and has its being in you and each of you and in all that is.

As the quiet of evening settles about you and you feel the love within this group, within this domicile, within the mighty trees and all the many insects that make the night ring within you, we seemingly leave you, although you know, my friends, that we never can be apart from you, for if we are all one and if the universe is the Creator, how could we ever truly be apart? How could any peoples of any relationship ever be apart? Love that which is, whether blessed or cursed by those images of yourself who pass you. We encourage you to love, for the activity of loving is in fact the sharing of the Creator with the Creator.

We leave you in this love and the light which is its manifestation. I am known to you as Hatonn. We ask, as always, that you be aware of our foolishness and seek not either to convince yourself or to convince others of anything which we may say. Allow those things which seem inspirational or helpful to you to sink deep within for there are underground rivers within you which are fed by inspiration. Allow those things which are not helpful to fall away quickly with no second thoughts. Know that we love you and that we thank you for your love for each other and for us and for the truth which is the Creator. Adonai, my friends. Adonai

(Jim channeling)

I am Latwii, and I greet you, my friends, in the love and in the light of our infinite Creator. We are privileged once again to be asked to join your group in our attempt to serve you by attempting to answer those queries which are upon your minds as you seek truth. We are honored to follow those of Hatonn and feel that if we can achieve half the inspiration that our brothers and sisters of Hatonn have achieved that we shall, indeed, have added some measure of inspiration to your journeys. May we begin with the first query at this time?

S: Yes, Latwii, I have a question for you which you may feel free to answer in a general manner. I was wondering about the origin of the children who are being born to [those] who are wanderers at this time. Could you tell me anything about that?

I am Latwii, and am aware of your query, my sister. This query is one which is not easily answered, for there are a great number of sources of these children, for it is the nature of the entity that you call a wanderer to attempt to be of service to others. This attempt may take any form. When children are a portion of this attempt, again there are many ways in which a so-called wanderer may serve. It may be that the child has a special need which the wanderer shall by nature be more able to provide, and therefore an agreement shall be made and the child shall find shelter and nurture within the love and being of the wanderer. One may suppose that such an entity as you have mentioned would have the child which would be of a special vibrational nature, perhaps one readying itself for graduation or perhaps one having been graduated and preparing itself to become the new population of your planet or perhaps even another of what you have called wanderer.

And this is, of course, possible that any or all of these sources may be drawn to such an entity as you have described. But we may also suggest that services are required by a great variety of entities at this time, entities which may need to feel and experience in the incarnation great difficulties in order that difficulties may find balance, and love may become the manifestation of difficulty. It may be that an entity would wish such a parent if the entity were one which had frequently lost track of its incarnational course in that which you have called its past, and would wish to join one or two who may be able to provide a more firm compass bearings, shall we say, through which the incarnation might find its full expression.

As you see, there are, indeed, a number of sources from which those called wanderers may find entities coming into its sphere of influence from. There are, of course, others as well. We have spoken to the general run or way of things, shall we say.

May we answer you further, my sister?

S: Well, I was wondering if I could pin you down enough to say which group that you have previously spoken of would comprise the larger percentage?

I am Latwii, and am aware of your query, my sister. Let us see, as we survey the so-called demographic statistics. We find that the greatest source of the new entities which you call children who are incarnating in those households in which there is an entity which you have called the wanderer is that entity which is nearing the graduation and has a certain kind of lesson or balance that is needed in order that the graduation might be achieved.

May we answer you further, my sister?

S: That research was wonderful. Still along the same lines somewhat, a thought occurred to me that parents are generally loving and very giving towards their children, while children, at a young age especially, tend to be somewhat selfish and self-centered and really do a lot of absorbing because they really need that at that particular time, but I was wondering if it ever happens that a negative entity would choose to be born into a household where there would be positive parents, because it would have such a great potential of absorbing so much love or would … is that the kind of situation where it's kind of an agreement that's made beforehand, so it would be likely to be agreed upon beforehand, I would think? Does that make any sense at all?

I am Latwii, and am aware of your query, my sister. We find the thread of logic in what you say, and can suggest that such a situation is most unlikely, for the entity which you have described as being of a negative polarity is of a nature which would not find the nurturing within such a household as you have described as being that which was helpful to …

(Side one of tape ends.)

(Jim channeling)

I am Latwii, and am with this instrument once again. It would seem that the opportunity to absorb love which is freely given would be the ideal situation for a negative entity. Yet, the negatively-oriented entity would find the harmony and freely given love to be somewhat repugnant to its nature, wishing instead to test its desire for separation and control upon those whose desire was of a similar nature, thereby being a test of, shall we say, so-called equals in which the strength of separation could be gained.

Therefore, the situation in which a negatively-oriented entity would find most desirable for its incarnation would be one in which the polarity of the parents would be either negative or neutral, and disharmony would be possible.

May we answer you further, my sister?

S: No, I think you've worked on my logic very well. Thank you, Latwii.

I am Latwii, and we thank you, my sister, as always. May we attempt another query?

Carla: Well, just following that up. If you had extraordinarily positive parents, wouldn't the entity that wanted to learn one more lesson and therefore—and also you mentioned, had lost track of its incarnational course many times—and was therefore trying for one last shot before graduation, wouldn't such an entity that had a bunch of rough edges seem to such positive entities to be negative, even though it was just kinda blah compared to really rotten kids, just because of the sensitivity of the parents?

I am Latwii, and am aware of your query, my sister. It may be that such an entity would be perceived by its parents, as you call them, to be of such a nature as you have mentioned. It may be that such an entity would be perceived in a variety of ways depending upon the sensitivities of those called parents. We believe this is the gist of your query.

May we answer further, my sister?

Carla: Just a point that I'm curious about. What would you call parents?

I am Latwii, and am aware of your query, my sister. We would call those which you call parents, more according to the sound vibration, teacher.

May we answer you further?

Carla: No. No, thank you.

I am Latwii, and we thank you, my sister, as always. It is a pleasure to hear your voice. May we attempt another query at this time?

S: Well, yes, along the same lines. If these children have come here because there is something that they need to do in order to graduate, are the parents, maybe by preincarnative choice or otherwise, partially responsible for the children becoming aware of this or would you see the parents' main job is to love these children and to … I'm sorry, I'm not making a lot of sense. What I'm trying to say, is are these children mainly on their own, I mean, are they pretty much responsible for their own ability or inability to graduate?

I am Latwii, and am aware of your query, my sister. We may suggest that the answer to this query is both yes and no. We shall attempt to explain. It is true that each entity is, indeed, in charge of its own lessons and pace of learning them. But it is also true that an entity wishing to learn ballet is unlikely to engage in a course in which football is taught. Thus it is that entities will before the incarnation determine the general guidelines, shall we say, or parameters within which the lessons and services shall be learned and provided. When an entity has found, shall we say, a match between its needs and the needs of another, then an agreement can be made and free will can be observed in full sway, for each entity shall find the greater opportunity for its needed catalyst to be provided during the incarnation with entities of a like mind, shall we say, rather than if agreements were to be attempted between entities whose general guidelines were quite dissimilar.

May we answer you further, my sister?

S: Well, yes. Then it's possible that one reason that my children chose me to be a mother was so that they would be exposed to my type of religion rather than being born into a Catholic house. Is that kind of what you're saying?

I am Latwii, and am aware of your query, my sister. This is the gist of our response. It would be perhaps the choice of entities such as your children to enter into a household such as your own which is able to provide a somewhat broader perspective upon that which you have called religion or philosophy than to have joined a household where the perspective was of a more restricted nature and the truth was seen to be of a narrower nature.

May we attempt further response, my sister?

S: No, thank you, Latwii. Somehow you've made it a little easier to be a parent this evening. Thank you.

I am Latwii, and thank you, my sister. We look forward to the next PTA meeting. May we attempt another refreshing answer?

Carla: I just have one follow-up to that whole thing, and that is that when coincidence control has heavily managed the planning of one's family instead of one's own logic, can that same coincidence control be trusted when one thing changes, and that is that the person becomes aware that there is the potential for one more soul out there, or do things change so that the mother and father need to then make a conscious decision instead of letting coincidence control and preincarnative agreements rule the day?

I am Latwii, and am aware of your query, my sister. We might suggest that that quality that you have called coincidence control is a much more personal quality than you might have imagined, for it is the case before incarnation that a most general guideline is laid out for the incarnation by the entity, its, shall we say, guides and its higher self. And during the incarnation there are, shall we say, alternate possibilities that present themselves when another possibility has been chosen or perhaps has not been chosen, so that there is during the incarnation a constant interplay of possibilities which swing into action and appear as the coincidence when the time is right. It may be that a certain lesson can be learned in many ways and that many ways are chosen as possibilities so that should the first, shall we say, bus be missed, there shall be another soon with the same destination.

Sunday Meditation, August 26, 1984

May we answer you further, my sister?

Carla: In other words, *(inaudible)*? No, that's fine. Thank you.

I am Latwii, and we again thank you, my sister. Is there another query at this time?

Carla: Well, if nobody's going to jump right in there, I had a fascinating thing happen to me. In the middle of what seems like a sad thing—my grandmother is very ill with a stroke which just happened this week, and I was sitting with her and she saw things. She saw many, many angels that were flying about the room. She saw something around, just above my head and around it as she described as snowflakes and rectangles that were lit up like neon or something like a movie marquee flashing. She saw something that was of an indigo-blue-green mixed color right around my forehead. She saw lace that was whirling around my neck, and I asked what color it was and she said red. And she saw a twelve or thirteen-year-old boy, dark hair, dark eyes that was standing right beside me.

I was very interested in this and wondered if she was the victim of extremely poor eyesight, hallucinating or seeing those things on other planes that we call chakras and the blocking of chakras which I would interpret the red around the throat to be and perhaps entities that are with me for some reason and with her for obvious reasons, the angels I mean.

I am Latwii, and am aware of your query, my sister, and am aware that it is a query that moves into the concept of the infinity of the universe. Therefore, we find our ability to speak coherently upon the various points of your query somewhat limited by both words and sensibility. We shall attempt general commentary upon those qualities of your query which we feel competent to investigate.

It is the case with entities such as your grandmother who are preparing to leave your plane of existence that they shall find, as the old body and senses are beginning to be shed, that they do not lose as much as they gain. The eyes which once looked upon a world of three dimensions now see that world not only in a different light but see that which you might call another world as well as they begin their transition from one to the other. Those colors and shapes which were noted about your being may be seen as, shall we say—we give this instrument the picture of a Baskin Robbins and quite confuse him.

But you are, indeed, like such an establishment which has many flavors or qualities of being, and during one portion of time or month you may have a variety of them on sale, shall we say. There may be various qualities within your being or nature which at one time are evident to those with eyes to see, and which sparkle in brilliance as their nature is expressed by you. At another time you may find other qualities taking precedence over the ones which had sway at a previous time.

The beings which have been noted by this entity may be likened unto the travelers which join the pilgrim for a portion of its journey. Just as you move through your third-dimensional illusion and gather about you certain friends and acquaintances and spend time with them on occasions, just so, there are those entities of other realms, shall we say, who travel with you in much the same fashion. Though unseen and to most unapparent in any regard, yet do they journey with the seeker and add their portion of being to the seeker's journey. These entities may range from that which is commonly known as the guide or angelic presence to astral souls who have recently been within your third density in a manifested incarnation and who may now find a helpful experience in their own journey to be that of joining you for a portion of yours, and who add their own nature of helpfulness to your journey in a manner which is unseen and quite likely not apparent in any way except to those with certain sensitivities such as your grandmother is now developing as a result of the transition which she is accomplishing.

May we answer you further, my sister?

Carla: Just one question, and I thank you for that answer. Fascinating. When I was thirty-two I almost decided to conceive a child. I came very close to deciding to do that, it would have involved a great deal of personal upheaval, leaving, and so forth. However, I really wanted to have a child, impractical as it was. I decided against it because I really couldn't leave Don, and I couldn't stick him with a kid that wasn't his, so I didn't do it. And I was wondering, because the age was right, if that spirit is the child that was waiting to be born to me and has now decided to stay with me on an astral plane?

I am Latwii, and am aware of your query, my sister. We find in this case that our ability to speak is somewhat limited due to our desire to maintain the free will of your current incarnation.

Carla: Let me put it another way. Does it ever happen?

I am Latwii, and we may respond in the affirmative that such a situation is possible and does occur from time to time, the entity not having been born into the incarnation choosing to remain with the incarnated potential parent in a, as you have mentioned, astral form so that experience may yet be shared with this entity, yet shared in a manner quite unlike the third-dimensional experience which each of you now find yourselves within.

It may be that such an entity could do what you call a double time or experience by not only remaining in an astral form with the first, shall we say, choice of parents but also incarnating with another set of parents and having a dual experience, though the astral experience would not be immediately available to the incarnated portion of the entity's self.

May we answer you further, my sister?

Carla: If one were to have an astral child like that how would one serve the child?

I am Latwii, and am aware of your query, my sister. Well, we might suggest that the food bill would not be increased but there would indeed be that which is called the spiritual food which would be made available to this entity in the form of the world of experience available in thought. The fruit of the mind, then, would be the food upon which such an astral entity would find nourishment, and, indeed, the nourishment there could be of a quite substantial nature, for not all thought finds its way into manifestation and therefore does not become available to those third-dimensional children, whereas it would be much more available to an astral child, shall we say.

May we answer further, my sister?

Carla: Does the astral incarnation end when the parent's physical incarnation ends?

I am Latwii, and am aware of your query, my sister. This is variable according to the choices and agreements which have been made between the entities involved. It is not, shall we say, set such as your third-dimensional incarnation [which] may have more, shall we say, concrete boundaries to the agreement.

May we answer you further, my sister?

Carla: That's really a bad pun. No, thank you.

I am Latwii, and we thank you, my sister, and apologize for bad puns, but at this point in this instrument's development we are happy with any pun that we can get through.

May we attempt another query at this time?

J: I'd like to ask a question, Latwii, and it's good to hear your puns. About my dog's ear. I think it's improving, but I'm not sure. I think it's what I want to see. Can you give me any new information on it?

I am Latwii, and am aware of your query, my brother, and we are quite pleased to hear your voice once again. We can suggest in this particular situation that the healing which is desired for the ear of your dog is a healing which will take a good deal more time, for in the experience of providing the healing for this entity, this entity is gaining more than healing. There is the love and the affection which is naturally shown to one which has this kind of, shall we say, disease or disablement. Therefore, this entity gains a great deal of the investment of your love and caring as you attempt to complete its healing.

May we answer you further, my brother?

J: Thank you.

I am Latwii, and we thank you, my brother. Is there another query at this time?

(Pause)

I am Latwii, and we find that once again we have exhausted those queries which each of you have so generously brought with you this evening. We thank you, as always, for the honor of sharing our humble opinions with you. These opinions are our foolish attempt at service, and we remind each to take that which has value and leave that which has none. We hope that we have provided you with some aid in your seeking, and we shall be most happy to join you at any time during your meditations that you might wish our presence. We also now seem to leave you, yet shall remain with you in that love and light of the one infinite Creator. We are those of Latwii. We are your own selves journeying with you through the One to the One in joy, in peace, and in power. Adonai, my friends. Adonai vasu borragus. ✤

L/L Research

L/L Research is a subsidiary of Rock Creek Research & Development Laboratories, Inc.

P.O. Box 5195
Louisville, KY 40255-0195

www.llresearch.org

Rock Creek is a non-profit corporation dedicated to discovering and sharing information which may aid in the spiritual evolution of humankind.

ABOUT THE CONTENTS OF THIS TRANSCRIPT: This telepathic channeling has been taken from transcriptions of the weekly study and meditation meetings of the Rock Creek Research & Development Laboratories and L/L Research. It is offered in the hope that it may be useful to you. As the Confederation entities always make a point of saying, please use your discrimination and judgment in assessing this material. If something rings true to you, fine. If something does not resonate, please leave it behind, for neither we nor those of the Confederation would wish to be a stumbling block for any.

CAVEAT: This transcript is being published by L/L Research in a not yet final form. It has, however, been edited and any obvious errors have been corrected. When it is in a final form, this caveat will be removed.

© 2009 L/L Research

Sunday Meditation
September 30, 1984

(The tape is inaudible until about one-eighth of the way through the first side. Then the group is heard retuning with the song, "Come to God … ye shall return … like a ray of light turning to the sun.")

(C channeling)

I am Hatonn …

(The channeling is inaudible and continues for several minutes. Then Carla's voice, "(Name) will you call C?" Then Carla's voice continues inaudibly. Then Carla sings an Alleluia chant.)

(Carla channeling)

I am Hatonn. We greet you through this instrument once more. We wish the one known as C to know …

(Most of the following is not sufficiently audible to transcribe. Ellipses indicate inaudible portions.)

… in order that we may remain with this group, for as you know, we come as we are called. The one known as Carla … as we do with this instrument … Nevertheless it is well … that you remain … to those to whom … And truly there is healing for those who seek it … We shall tell you a story about a … who seeks, about … that perhaps we make our statements more … We ask that you … that we are but those who … yet … vulnerable to error … the very best that we can … share joy.

There was once a beautiful young … Before he was even … he had inherited a crown … His progenitors … The prince wore only … He enjoyed … and so did others. He invited his courtiers … He did not stray beyond the gates … Why would he wish … From his window he could see … His days … One day this prince … he found he could leave the castle … winds … Seemingly … And so he set out … for the people were … hard work had … coarse food was scarce and the wood seemed very dark. All knew of the great king and the beautiful castle … He walked … Never did he find wisdom, beauty or leisure. He found only the grinding poverty, the near starvation and the various meanessess with which he had never …

Another beggar … approached … and asked what was … You cannot go in said the prince. You do not belong … the beggar, however, desiring that which he had never before seen walked through the barrier which the prince … One by one people began to … lower the gates … and all … And yet the prince could not … and he raged at the … And yet things remained as they were and the castle was full of all manners of … Finally the prince began to remove his attention from … He began to enjoy the beauty. He took his place by the … and welcomed each happy soul … One day he began to say, "Welcome to you … one day he began to say, "Come all … and so … and on that day … Inside the walls the castle

… both in mind and in spirit full of … and laughing … So, where the great gift … And so when the prince …

(Several more minutes of inaudible channeling of the same story.)

We will pause.

(S channeling)

I am Hatonn, and we are pleased to greet you in the love and in the light of the infinite Creator. We are pleased … that we … delighted to take us up on our offer, so to speak … concerns are many this evening. She is attempting to push them aside momentarily. We are grateful that we have been able to spend some of your time with you this evening and we are honored that you have … We wish to remind each that you are never alone. For we await for your call at any time so that we might allow our vibrations to blend with those … It is indeed a privilege …

(Side one of tape ends.)

(S channeling)

… and we will once again express our gratitude. We shall leave you but our leaving is for the moment only and we shall return at any time we are called. We leave you, dear friends, in the love and in the light that shines ever brightly and gives a warm touch to us all. Adonai. I am Hatonn.

(Jim channeling)

I am Latwii, and I greet you, my friends, in the love and in the light of our infinite Creator. It is our great privilege once again to speak through this instrument to this … We thank you for calling for our humble service and we are eager to share that which we may. As always, we shall attempt to answer those queries with our opinions and we remind you that such is the case.

May we begin then with the first query?

J: Yes, Latwii, I'd like to know … *(Rest of question not transcribed).*

I am Latwii, and am aware of your query, my brother. Now do you think that we have such friends? Well it is not within our providence at this time that part which you have riddled but we shall be happy to inform you of what we may for we are aware of your great desire to know that which has recently occurred in your experience and you know of its nature. We of Latwii are not at this time, as you call it, of the inclination which takes its form in the craft of which you speak. It is our nature to join seekers who call our services to their presence in their meditative states. Many there are that we join unbeknownst to the conscious mind in meditation and in dreams. For this is the kind of contact which we feel most comfortable with even though we treasure the opportunity to speak through instruments such as this one. The entities inhabiting the path of which you speak also seek to join you in love, yet are of another higher density, though we are all one being.

May we answer you further?

J: *(Inaudible).*

I am Latwii, and am aware of your query my brother. We could give a name, but such would be an approximation of these entities' vibratory *(inaudible)* for they have not chosen that which you call the name in their attempt to represent and glorify the one Creator. Therefore a name would not be appropriate.

May we answer you further, my brother?

J: *(Inaudible).*

I am Latwii, and am aware of your query, my brother. It would be possible for us to identify the *(inaudible)* were such an identity not in our humble opinion an infringement on free will. For if the identity of such a vehicle were known, it might persuade your thinking in a certain way which we feel would not be appropriate. It is, as we are aware you know, more appropriate to approach the mystery of this appearance in the meditative state so that those resonances of your deep mind which were touched by this spirit's might be brought by your own seeking to the more conscious portions of your mind and used there as resources that might enrich or *(inaudible)*.

May we answer you further, my brother?

J: *(Inaudible).*

I am Latwii and we thank you, my brother, for allowing us to perform this service. May we attempt another query at this time?

C: *(Inaudible).*

I am Latwii, and am aware of your query, my brother. We find in this experience of this *(inaudible)* that a number of factors lend their color to what has affected your being and we shall attempt clarity if possible. There is within this dwelling the experience of illness which has occurred for a period of time and has become an energy of its own. Your recent experiences are a function of your increased sensitivity and when this increasing sensitivity is toward the vocal channeling without the requisite skill of inner tuning, then you find that whatever energies are present are easily sensed by your increasing ability to enter that which is called sleep trance. We might suggest for this particular type of service as a vocal channel that you determine a means of the tuning and challenging of an energy or entity which you sense in any manner and that you utilize this means of tuning and challenging so that you might express to the channel only those energies and entities that are of a positive and beneficial nature to those about you and to your own being as well. This type of tuning and challenging is also useful in the daily life, shall we say, where one has a time set aside, preferably before the day begins, to set the course, shall we say, that the entity shall attempt to follow for the day. A course that is built upon service and seeking and is illuminated by the light and love of the One dwelling in One. This means a ritualizing of the tuning may enhance your ability to use your increasing sensitivites in ways which shall assure a balance for the mind and the body and the spirit.

May we answer you further my brother?

C: *(Inaudible).*

I am Latwii, and this is *(inaudible)*, my brother.

May we answer you further?

C: *(Inaudible).*

I am Latwii. We are honored by what you bring, to listen to your experience and shall always be available to the ball or to the string. May we attempt another query?

Carla: *(Inaudible).*

I am Latwii, and am aware of your query, my sister. We find that your latter assumption is more nearly correct though there are also those energies which are attempting the healing.

Carla: *(Inaudible).*

I am Latwii, and am aware of *(inaudible)* and would respond by suggesting that in part it is correct, yet there are also other energies drawn to this light that are also within the healing. For there is both the call and the resistance to the call and only so much may be done when there is resistance.

Carla: On this particular subject, is there a way … *(inaudible).*

I am Latwii, and am aware of your query, my sister. We find that the suggestions which we have made to one known as C, if they are utilized, will permit that entity to enjoy the meditative experience within this group and within this dwelling without the discomfort which it has experienced this evening due to the lack of the challenge and tuning which would exclude the more unpleasant of the vibrations. We find within your illusion there is a great mixture of that which might be called the positive and negative, pleasant and unpleasant, light and dark within all portions of your illusion. For the creation which you inhabit is one which contains all these and to move that *(inaudible)* which you enjoy during this *(inaudible)* would be to move it from the One to the One. It is within the ability of each entity to cleanse its own being and the place in which it works and the place to seek and share *(inaudible).*

May we answer you further, my sister?

Carla: Yes. *(Inaudible).*

I am Latwii, and am aware of your query, my sister. We find that this group has utilized these things to be channeled, the visualization, for a great period of what you call time in the meditative meanings and we can only recommend an intensification of this *(inaudible)* so that there is a greater effort made to construct what might be called a wall of light. There could be the selection of inspirational music to be listened to, followed by a short period of singing or chanting, also to be followed by a period of prayer which is now utilized and then the recommendation made that each individual in the group utilize some personal form of tuning to be continued silently as the group tuning has been completed.

May we answer you further, my sister?

Carla: I'm sorry to *(inaudible)* but I was thinking more of the *(inaudible).*

I am Latwii, and am aware of your query, my sister. We find that this dwelling shall be inhabited by the entity of which you speak and shall therefore have a certain coloration of the difficulty that will remain with it as long as the difficulty remains with the entity. We can therefore suggest that this particular room might be cleansed with the cut clove of garlic at each entrance point and this shall remain throughout the week and shall be changed and refreshed with a new clove at each entrance point each week just before the meditation is to begin. This procedure taken in consideration with our previous suggestion should provide a place of working which has the optimum ability to enhance those vibrations of seeking and sharing which characterize this group and serve as its great potential.

May we answer you further, my sister?

Carla: *(Inaudible).*

I am Latwii, and am aware of your query, my sister. This is correct. May we answer you further?

Carla: Only *(inaudible)* question that I *(inaudible).*

I am Latwii, and am aware of your query, my sister. We find that your supposition has the beginning of truth, yet there is more involved. We can suggest that the bond which you share with the one known as Don has ramifications which are most difficult to elucidate but which can in the neophyte attempting magical ritual cause the opposite of that which is desired, that is, in your particular case there can be the removal of vital energy rather than the enhancing of such when the magical ritual is attempted in a situation which has the many layers of, shall we say, discordant characteristics which we find in this particular situation. We cannot speak to each particular characteristic but can suggest that the lack of physical energy on your part and the assault upon the mental/emotional energy of *(inaudible)* is of enough significance that the performing of the banishing ritual of the lesser pentagram is not recommended until those energy complexes have been replenished and the recovery of balance and energy has also occurred within the one known as Don with whom you share a bond that permits the transfer of pain to your *(inaudible).*

May we answer you further, my sister?

Carla: *(Inaudible).*

I am Latwii, and we appreciate the opportunity to be a ghost instrument. May we attempt another query at this time?

(Pause)

I am Latwii, and as it appears that we have exhausted the queries for the evening, we shall leave this group, as always, in joy and shall before leaving remind each that the illusion in which you dance and have your being at this time is an illusion which contains the one Creator in each portion of your experience though it may seem from time to time that you inhabit a portion of the creation which has been unfortunately depleted of any love and light. We know that your experience is one which weighs heavily upon your minds and your hearts from time to time and is an experience which brings the tear and the pain. Know that your work in this illusion is that work which produces a fruit from such pain and from so many, many tears.

You exist within an illusion which has great benefit to such growth and production of fruit of allowing you to move in a darkness, in a forgetting in which it is not easily apparent that you are the one infinite Creator and that you gather the fruit of love with every movement of your mind, your life, and your experience. Yet that great virtue of moving within the darkness allows this fruit of love to be harvested.

It is also the great deterrent to your current enjoyment of the illusion. For it is difficult to feel and [be inspired] by a fruit which you cannot see, which you cannot taste. Yet, my friends, know that such fruit is gathered in each moment of your experience and is enhanced by your continuing desire to give that which you have for that which you cannot see.

We are those of Latwii, and we leave you in the love and in the light that ever lights your path and beams within your heart. Adonai. Adonai vasu borragus. ❧

Sunday Meditation
October 7, 1984

(S channeling)

I am Hatonn, and we are pleased to greet you this evening in the love and in the light of the one infinite Creator. We have been with this instrument for some time as requested and we are grateful for the opportunity to speak a few words through her this evening. We are grateful also for your gracious invitation and we are pleased to be able to offer to your group our service.

We find that we often have difficulty in finding new and more exquisite ways of praising that message which is invariably simple and always the same. We are not always able to speak in a manner that is precise, for the same simple message may seem to some to be tedious or repetitive. However, we assure you, dear friends, that the message is the message of love and no amount of words can ever express that which is so simple than to use the word love. The meaning of the word often gets lost upon your planet and few seldom stop and think about this word when it is heard or spoken.

The immensity in this single simple word is truly overwhelming. The thought or the energy that goes into this word is indeed more powerful than we are able to express. The energy that is received when this word is truly felt is a powerful influence. To picture love as a very small and insignificant four-letter word is to deprive that word of its true and deeper meaning. Take not this word lightly. Take this word to heart and within your own consciousness expand that simple word to its ever-reaching potential. Let not those four small letters get lost in a haze of many letters. Let them stand out and shine with the power that is truly within the thought behind the word. Its immensity is truly beyond comprehension. We shall leave this instrument at this time and once again we thank her for this opportunity. I am Hatonn.

(Carla channeling)

I am Hatonn, and I greet you in the love and the light of our infinite Creator. We shall continue through this instrument. We speak of the one original Thought. The simplicity of our message is deceptive. It deceives in that it is far more difficult to do those things which are simple yet deep than to accomplish those things which may take many steps but which are laid out before you as it were so that each step was well known. We can give you no recipe for grasping, experiencing or manifesting love. We can only offer the tools of inspiration through messages such as this one and the inward silent listening which is called medition(al?) prayer. Sometimes when we speak to a small group we are able to speak more to the heart of individual's needs and that is so this evening.

We would begin the, shall we say, variation upon a theme of the incredible relief of *(inaudible)* by moving backwards in your way of thinking until you reach that you feel is before all other things real. Shall you call this island in space which is to your heart real? It would seem to be real. Shall we call the steady progression of seasons and your time real? The progression would seem to be quite real and dependable. Yet you are not seeking because you wish to find the real things that you can hold. You are seeking as do all because of the firm suspicion if not downright believed that behind that which is touchable there lies that which is more real which created that which you see and experience. It is the fervent hope of most who ponder such things that this force, principle or other reality have some structure and *(inaudible)* so that each of you is not living in anarchy and chaos, and indeed we believe that that is the case. And we have termed that which is behind all things, that which has created all things, that which is the one original Thought. Of course it beggars the imagination. It is too simple. We shall through this instrument explore one portion of the nature of the Creator [for awhile] for that particular variation has been on the mind of the instrument and has a margin of interest [for the rest].

We would speak to the virtue of a characteristic that is often thought among your peoples to be a hindrance. That characteristic is what you may call weakness. Within your third-density experience, again and again compliments and the regard of others are given to those who are seen to be strong: strong-willed, strong in ambition, strong to endure, strong to wait, strong in the face of adversity, powerful with people, with events, and with the forces of unplanned adversity which often appear to be emergencies. Far too little credit is given to the characteristic known among your peoples as weakness. There is a saying within this instrument's memory, "If you can keep your head when all around you are losing theirs, you may lack awareness of the situation." Weakness is frequently the appearance which an entity gives who has such a firm grasp upon the situation that the entity is aware there is nothing that can be done and that therefore there is nothing to do [about something]. It often may appear that such a person is weak, but in actuality the person is far stronger than the one who thinks, struggles and attempts to control others and forces which are beyond any reasonable control. Let us use as an example that weakest [of all] the elements. For earth is heavy, fire light, and the air whispering. Water, as it rains on the cedars, [bespeaks] of that which does not have strength.

(The remaining channeling becomes increasingly inaudible. Ellipses indicate inaudible portions.)

We do not mean to confuse you by looking at the waters and the wind as peoples. No, my friends, we speak now of water as it goes about the business of gentle rain which soaks into the earth, runs into the ocean, and is evaporated. This has a tremendous … for personal growth. If the ground is … with … or paved with concrete, water attempts no … but is instead attracted without … to one of two things. The living … for … or the force of … to gravity which calls it be lower … Already we have described the incredible Creator-healer … force for he goes …

But let us look … In your imagination … imagine the feeling that … The earth begins … Water … The infinite … Water is without … It is not … it will not … And as it … As you gaze at each … imagine the … the water which moves in streams … There are many changes, shall we say within your illusion … Those who choose to … This entity has for several of … Then slowly … weeks of … to leave … And yet … Whereas the seeming strength of … would have … There is a progression within each … Within this progression there are … The desire to give service to others …

(Inaudible to the end of the tape.) ❧

Sunday Meditation
October 14, 1984

(Carla channeling)

I am Hatonn, and I greet you in the love and in the light of our infinite Creator. It is a great privilege to be with you, to share in your life experience at this time, and to be able to tread your path with you for this brief time as we, in speaking words through this instrument, attempt to do that which is beyond words, that is, to evoke a sense of mystery, of consciousness, so that we may aid you in your curiosity and encourage you in your seeking. Poor indeed is the man who has never asked a question, for riches do not lie in the answers but in the questions themselves. Therefore, we ask you this evening to examine what questions you have concerned yourselves about during this diurnal period. We do not care what conclusions you may have drawn, but wish to focus only upon that which has been in the forefront of the mind this day.

This day are you rich or are you poor? Are your questions those of a petty and mundane nature or have you instead asked this day for that which draws you outside of the world that you know? How rich you are if you have dressed yourself in seeking as if it were a festive garment and gone forth into your environment clad with the desire to know more, with a wonder as to how to serve better and with the rejoicing question: "How can I perceive such loveliness as this day has offered to me?"

We apologize for the pause. The instrument had become distracted by our message and had begun to analyze it—its own experience. This may make for a wiser instrument but not for a longer contact.

My friends, there is a great interest in your culture in what this instrument would call the bottom line, the final answer, the solution. Those who would be powerful within the illusion are those with a talent for creating situations within which their bottom line works, for you see, my friends, each of you has an inborn series of bottom lines. Each of you has ways of dealing with situations, typical solutions, and normal habits of mind. Without meditation, what occurs is that time and again the entity bounces around from situation to situation until it finds a situation where it fits, where its bottom line is the answer for the question implicit in the situation. This is unconscious and not to be scorned, for it is a way of learning. There is a quicker way of learning and that is to focus upon the questions and not upon the answers. My friends, you know the answers. That which we say to you is so utterly simplistic and so repetitious that you can have no doubt that you know what our opinion of the bottom line is. The bottom line is love.

But what is the question? What will you ask? What avenues will you seek? How much of the truth do you want to know within this fragile cage of your physical bodies? What great heart do you wish to realize? What great spirit do you wish to encompass? Will that fragile being that you are, full of earth and breath, be able to contain your deepest and highest hopes? How far can you reach? Meditation is a form of reaching within the vast infinity of your own being with the mute question, the question that has no words, and because it has no words and is not in any way articulated, it is the pure question and you will receive the purest answer with it, for you listen in silence just as you ask in silence, and you shall be answered also in silence but with a power that transcends our ability to express that which is creative, peaceful and energetic.

You here seek for nothing less than the key which shall open to you your universe, your creation, your Creator, and in asking for the light, you ask that which transforms each of you into a source of that light. The principle is simple, and difficult to grasp because of its simplicity. You are what you seek, therefore the choice of what you seek is all-important.

We ask that you remove yourself from the question of what subjects you have sought answers regarding during this day. Take a longer view, each of you, and ask yourself, "With what attitude or point of view did I seek and ask regarding each subject, each situation, each relationship, each seeming difficulty or moment of joy?" That which is within you has an intimate and ultimate power. So seek you well, for you shall be aware of what you now ask. You shall receive that which you seek. Be oh so very careful in your seeking, for we would not guide you upon a tour of many planes and dimensions, many masters and teachers and wise ones, many wanderers and circuses and shows full of spectacular fireworks. It goes without saying that there are techniques by which you can use your seeking in order to experience that which is novel, exciting and seemingly significant. We wish to home you back to the one beacon that lies within yourself that is a pure light and a pure love, that which lies behind all the displays of the journey upon which you have set your foot. We, in fact, offer a sort of surface service ourselves. Our speaking through instruments such as this one is novel. However, it is much less novel and far more open to doubt than our appearing among your peoples and speaking as if we were infallible. Therefore, since we wish to aid you and must needs use communication of some kind, we choose the least showy display, the least gaudy method of sharing a philosophy which is not an end in itself but is only meant to point you to your own senses of discrimination, of determination, of faith and hope.

We share with you one thing—the original Thought of the one Creator. We share with you ways to put yourself more in line with the shadow of that great Thought. We set your feet upon the path that leads from shadow into light. We can direct you no further than yourself. The meditative and gently analytical methods of touching that tangent which you have with the one original Thought and with processing in a useful way your own experiences is our gift to you. It is an answer of sorts. What was your question? Never trust answers, for the only generalizations that work are those so simple and so controlled as to have little metaphysical use. Over and over you may say to yourself as if it were an answer that is infallible, "I am learning a lesson of love. I am learning a lesson of love." This has value. But to the seeker there is far more value in saying, "What am I perceiving, what am I learning, where is love now, right now in this moment?" You cannot tell yourself what you are learning—you must ask. And the answers may well be different than those you would create for yourself. Free yourself from the limitation of your own expectations and ask—with care, with sincerity, and with constancy. All else shall follow.

We leave this instrument, grateful that this instrument has been able to clear its mind that we may use it. This is an ongoing process for each of you and we recommend it, for each of you is a channel, a pipeline, if you will, and that which flows from you is that which has come through you. You share your consciousness with all the energies which you have developed. You develop your energies and attract the principles of those energies by the process of asking—of asking, of reaching, of hope, of beginning again each and every moment that you stumble.

We thank you, my friends, for being yourselves. It is a great and honorable thing to be in company with you. It is now appropriate that we leave, for this instrument is fatigued. We leave you only in the sense that we shall refrain from speaking through an instrument. Ours is one energy, the principle of which you have attracted by your asking. We are with you as comforters, as strengtheners, as comrades, as those who love each of you at any time that you may wish that companionship. We are those of Hatonn, and we leave you now in the love and the light of the one great original Thought that is the Creator, the creation, and the created. Adonai, O Creation. Adonai, O Creator. Adonai, Questioners. So we you greet. Adonai.

(Jim channeling)

I am Latwii, and I greet you, my friends, in the love and in the light of our infinite Creator. We are privileged once again to be asked to join your group, and we thank each of you for so asking. Our service, as you know, is a simple one which we sometimes seem to make complex, and that is the attempt to answer those queries on your minds which you as seekers have interest in. May we begin, then, with the first query for this evening?

J: Latwii, I have a query. I thought my dog's ears were getting better, but I find that they are not. Can you tell me what's going on?

I am Latwii, and am aware of your query, my brother. As we look upon this entity which is described as the dog, we see the ears which have the continuing difficulty of the parasitical infection. For the second-density creature, there is little symbolism in such a difficulty. It is, shall we say, for such a creature, a world in which there are many diseases and physical challenges to overcome by one means or another. This particular difficulty with the ears serves the purpose of allowing this entity to receive the attention from you and other third-density beings which then causes an investment for individualization of this entity, thus increasing its chances of harvest, shall we say. It is often the case that the means by which such a second-density creature chooses to receive the opportunity of investment are means which the third-density entity will find to be discomforting. To the one known as the dog, upon its basic level of awareness, the infection of the ear, then, is a means by which it expands its beingness. To you, the owner of this entity, shall we say, such a means is not apparent and is indeed perplexing. The interaction between the two of you is the dog's purpose fulfilled, that is, to be invested, and also is a portion of your purpose fulfilled, that is, to learn to give love.

May we answer you further, my brother?

J: Does that mean that the ear is never going to be healed?

I am Latwii, and am aware of your query, my brother. We cannot say whether this infectious situation shall be healed, for the future is quite full of possibility. We may say that this second-density creature shall continue in its efforts to gain investment and individualization, whether they be along this line or another.

May we answer you further, my brother?

J: Well, I have done everything possible. I have taken it to veterinarian's schools, I have taken it to veterinarians to have cultures taken, I have bought medicines, and I really want to show this dog, and nothing's happening. Is it the dog himself that doesn't want to get well or cured?

I am Latwii, and am aware of this query, my brother. We may say that this creature has a desire for growth which utilizes that called a disease, and that this desire for its own evolution is the greatest force within its being.

May we answer you further, my brother?

J: Well, I don't understand, but—listen, let me go on to the second query that I have. I had a dream the other night and I dreamed that I was here in meditation. But while I was here in meditation, I was all nude, I didn't have any clothes. Everybody was very gracious and made believe that they didn't see anything, and I cannot understand the dream. I would like to know what it meant.

I am Latwii, and am aware of your query, my brother. We find that our response must be bated under the Law of Confusion, that is, we do not wish to work so much of this riddle for you that your own efforts then will not produce the fruit which is available. We may suggest, however, that one look upon the newborn infant. This entity is not swaddled upon the birthing. It enters the world of its experience without the clothing. It enters pure and fresh without the feeling of shame or guilt and is therefore ready to embark upon a new adventure. As it embarks upon this adventure, it shall learn to wear various kinds of clothing for various purposes. As you look at your experience in this group, look you then to the new portion of your being which seeks to be born.

May we answer you further, my brother?

J: Very good. I have a better perspective now. May I ask you a question about the Christ? I have read four different versions of people who have contacted Christ and each one was different. What can you tell me about this?

I am Latwii, and am aware of your query, my brother. We may say that the one known as Jesus the Christ is an entity which has great bearing and influence upon the peoples of this planet, for its incarnation was completed in a fashion which set a model, shall we say. This entity prepared a way which each may utilize in some fashion, as each is the seeker of that of which the one known as Jesus Christ was also a seeker and he did find that which he sought. As those entities of your planet who have interest in this entity and its particular means of seeking travel their own path of seeking, many are of such strong desire to know the one known as Jesus the Christ and to know this entity's path that they are, indeed, in contact with this entity in some form or manner, for all entities of the nature of the Christed one who are called by the seekers are then responsible for answering in some manner the call. It is an honor to be called, and a duty to respond.

But the difficulty for many of your peoples in understanding such response are the many distortions which each entity holds in regards to the one known as Jesus and the path that a Christed one may follow. Therefore, the response to such a call is filtered through the various beliefs, habits and rituals of the one who calls. In few instances is the response received in its pure form. It is as though one of your sociological experiments is completed upon the metaphysical level, that is, a circle of entities partake in an experiment in which one entity begins to whisper into the ear of another a story, and when the story is completed, then the entity first hearing the story whispers into another ear, until at the end of many translations of this story, the final story has some resemblance and some distortion in respect to the original story.

May we answer you further, my brother?

J: How is one to know the original story, then?

I am Latwii, and am aware of your query, my brother. One may find the closest approximation to the original story by seeking in such a manner that one goes within the self and seeks and calls and waits with patience, for all calls are answered. No seeker is abandoned to seek alone. In this manner may you find your own desire, your own call, and your own answer. Do not be discouraged if your answers seem to differ from those about you. Within your illusion each has distortion. That is not to cause discouragement, but is able …

(Side one of tape ends.)

(Jim channeling)

I am Latwii, and am once again with this instrument. To continue our response. Do not be discouraged by distortion. It is the nature of your illusion, and allows your experiences to occur. If there were no darkness and no distortion, there would be no experience.

May we answer you further, my brother?

J: No, that's very good. I have some other questions, but I think I'll hold them off for awhile because this is too much for me to digest. May I come back some other time with a few more questions, sir?

I am Latwii, and am most honored to attempt response to any query at any time. It is our honor, my brother.

J: Thank you.

Is there another query at this time?

Carla: I have two questions. One is minor, one is I also had an odd bit of a dream stick with me. I dreamt that I had been writing a letter, and translated it at the same time into another language. The translation was in italics. When I got to the end, instead of signing my name, I drew a heart in the original language, and underneath it I drew the same heart in italics. And I wondered what it is that I am attempting to translate.

I am Latwii, and am aware of your query, my sister. Again we give that which does not infringe. You may look at that which is the translation, see the words upon the page, grasp the feeling from the words. It is not the individual word or words which carries the point, but the feeling of the entire message, for you have italicized the complete message, and therefore have placed emphasis or weight upon its total being. Look then to your own being, and see what feelings arise as you scan the message. Look there to your heart, and see what is the feeling that grows as you continue to look upon the message. Then take that which you have found by this investigation and see where in your own waking life there is a feeling of this nature, and see then how it might be translated into the action which is the fabric of your experience.

May we answer you further, my sister?

Carla: Not on that point, thank you. The question that was not trivial but which you probably can't answer any more than you already have, is how can I be of any more service than I already am to Don?

I am Latwii, and am aware of your query, my sister. We see in such a situation the great desire to serve. We see the difficulty in knowing what is the best service. This is the difficulty for each entity inhabiting your illusion, for nothing is plain and the darkness of knowing that all is the Creator is that which promotes the Creator's experience. As you find one who has long sought the one Creator now seems to sit upon a rock along the trail and seeks no further, one would then ask the self if there might be some way in which this entity was falling short of its seeking and could then be aided by another to rejoin the path of the seeker. This assumes that one can err and that one can fall short, and in one sense we can assure that such is true at all times for all seekers, for your illusion is so well constructed that all shall fall short of their goals. Yet each in some fashion continues to seek, for each is still the one Creator, and in this regard can commit no error, for even sitting upon a stone, the one Creator experiences sitting upon a stone. Yet another may still wish to aid an entity who not only sits upon a stone, but may seem to another to be wounded. How to aid the one who is wounded and sitting upon a stone, not seeming to tend its own wound? We may suggest that the offers be made, that service as best as one can describe it be offered, that all offers be made without dedication to any particular result, for who can say what path another should travel? One can only be and offer being to another, and then trust that all is well if it is truly so that all is one.

The greatest difficulty that an entity who wishes to aid another will face is the difficulty of accepting whatever depends from the situation, for many are the desires for another's well-being, and many are the attempts to fashion that well-being for another, yet it is not possible to learn for another. One may only present the self in service without dedication, for this is love. There are no conditions and no guarantees in your illusion, my sister.

May we answer you further?

Carla: No.

I am Latwii, and we thank you, my sister. Is there another query at this time?

J: Latwii, may I please ask you one more question about my dog's ears? Is there anything that I can put into the ear that would help to eliminate the parasite?

I am Latwii, and am aware of your query, my brother. We are quite without degree when it comes to the field of veterinary medicine. We feel that those efforts which have been made by those of this profession are, within our limited scope of knowledge, the most that can be done. In many cases you will find the disease which lingers past all treatment; then it is that one must look to the deeper nature of the disease, its symbol and potential. To this particular topic we have previously spoken. We ask your forgiveness for not being able to prescribe any effective treatment.

May we answer you further, my brother?

J: No, thank you. It's just that I'm obsessed with this, and I want to get all of it. Thank you very much, sir.

I am Latwii, and we thank you, my brother, sir. May we attempt another query?

(Pause)

I am Latwii, and we find that for the nonce we have exhausted those queries at the precise moment that the feline creatures are gathering their own energies for action. We thank each for allowing our humble service to be rendered within this group once again. It is our great joy and privilege to join you upon these occasions, and we treasure each. We shall leave this group as is our custom, in the love and in the light of the One Which Is All. We are those of Latwii, and we leave you at this time in that love and light. Adonai, my friends. Adonai vasu borragus. ✣

L/L Research

L/L Research is a subsidiary of Rock Creek Research & Development Laboratories, Inc.

P.O. Box 5195
Louisville, KY 40255-0195

www.llresearch.org

Rock Creek is a non-profit corporation dedicated to discovering and sharing information which may aid in the spiritual evolution of humankind.

ABOUT THE CONTENTS OF THIS TRANSCRIPT: This telepathic channeling has been taken from transcriptions of the weekly study and meditation meetings of the Rock Creek Research & Development Laboratories and L/L Research. It is offered in the hope that it may be useful to you. As the Confederation entities always make a point of saying, please use your discrimination and judgment in assessing this material. If something rings true to you, fine. If something does not resonate, please leave it behind, for neither we nor those of the Confederation would wish to be a stumbling block for any.

CAVEAT: This transcript is being published by L/L Research in a not yet final form. It has, however, been edited and any obvious errors have been corrected. When it is in a final form, this caveat will be removed.

© 2009 L/L Research

Sunday Meditation
November 11, 1984

(Carla channeling)

I am Hatonn. I greet you in the love and in the light of our infinite Creator, Whom we serve with all of our being. It is an immense privilege to be called to this group this evening. We ourselves have never had anything to tell you, for we in our turn are channels for that which is beyond our own frail understanding. That which we offer to you is offered through us, and only then through this channel. We can speak from no certainty nor do we wish you to bear our words as a weighty burden, listening to each word and pondering the meanings that may not seem accessible or acceptable to you at this time.

With our thanks and our disclaimer aside, we would speak to you about a fair, a grand and glorious carnival, a bazaar in which all of the merchants display their wares and thousands come to try their luck and to view the excellence that people have made with their hands, and above all to rejoice in the feeling of being part of a happy crowd. In a deep sense, this is part of the motivation for those who incarnate consciously and purposively upon the earth plane of your third density. You may have many lifetimes, but when you are not within a physical vehicle, it is impossible to remember that the carnival flags can flutter dismally, slowly and sadly, that pennants may be marred and broken, and that the machinery that governs the merry-go-rounds, the Ferris wheel and all the rides may not always work. As in many, many things, it looks easier in the mind to live an incarnation and to learn the lessons you set for yourself than it is to accomplish the plan you have made. Many of you are ambitious, and your life's plans have already caused you to experience a great deal of what you would call pain, anguish, suffering, disappointment and confusion.

Let us stroll together out from the fair onto the street. It is a dark night. The fair is held in a poor section of the city. The chill in the air causes those who have no homes to bundle up against the cold in whatever they may have. You may find someone lying upon the sidewalk, lost in his drink or other intoxication. Shall you sit down and talk to the Creator now, or shall you pass him by? Shall you go back into the carnival and ride and wave your pennants and your flags and your prizes? It is a choice you make, my friends, each day in one way or another, for if you are open to hear the cries of those about you, you will rapidly become aware that there is no day in which the poor, the hungry, the homeless, and the spiritually wasted are not crying out to you personally. And so you have a brightly lit carnival, and as you stroll through the gates you find a dark carnival. Instead of *(inaudible)* [fine clothes], you have the hand-fashioned rags of the hobo. Instead of the many rides, you have that liquor which intoxicates, or that medicine which is used for oblivion rather than amusement. And what shall you do to be of service?

There was one among you whom you know as a teacher, Jesus, the Christ. This teacher chose the darker circus. Those to whom he reached for discipleship were poor folk indeed—a prostitute, a tax collector, a persecutor and reviler. And yet he walked into the circus with the bright and shining lights, the gaudy displays, the metaphysical rides. He got upon the merry-go-round and rode the Ferris wheel with those whose lives were bound up in that experience. Nor did he condemn any who so chose to live a life of gratitude and experiential gladness. He spoke in temples. His instructions were based upon a hard rule called the Law and all he did that was different from other teachers within this comfortable world in which the flags flew and waved so prettily was that he pointed out that the heart is more important than the Law. Then he would walk forth into the streets and lift those from the gutter and pavement. Of the many, many stories that are narrated within your holy works, the one to which we would draw your attention is that one wherein the marriage couple awaits the guests for a great feast. When all do not show up, when seats remain empty, this teacher's instructions are simple: Go out into the streets and gather all that you can find, and yet, if they have not wedding garments, they may not come.

We are aware, my friends, that you have been pulled from your carnival, your gaiety, and your joy to witness one who suffered, and to wonder, "Why? What can I do?" We must leave that question with you, for this entity experienced both fairs, the light and the dark. Like most of you, he contributed all that he knew how to contribute. Like most of you, he became faced with a difficulty. Shall we then condemn those who lie in the gutter because they have not legs upon which to stand? Shall we sneer at the hungry because we have not given them bread? Shall we remove courage and dignity from the infinite and eternal spirit of one who joined the darker carnival? It is your choice, my friends, and your polarity will surely be affected because of this choice. Far too much has been said about the virtue of caring for the underprivileged who find themselves in darkness. Far too little has been done. When is a spirit not worthy to be fed? When is nobility cut off from the lovingkindness of the Creator?

You are on a long voyage, my friends. The carnival shall end for you, as it has for others, in your physical death, and yet you as spirit shall be free to move ahead to your next experience. One thing only shall be required of you and that is that you shall review this experience. We ask you both to be easy upon yourselves, and to be honest with yourselves. What has lain before you this day which you have not done to help another? What discipline of learning have you not sought because of pressing considerations that shall not survive your death? How can you be of service? This instrument once composed a short article in which this instrument envisioned the teacher known as Jesus coming back into the inner cities. "He would sit down in the gutter," wrote this instrument, "and take his peanut butter sandwich, and break it, and it would be food enough for all who came to touch his consciousness with their own." Your daily bread is but a symbol, my friends, and we ask you to consider again and again the value of the allegorical and symbolical nature of what seems to be reality. Draw back and take the viewpoint of the eternal present. How can you love each other? How can you listen? How can you accept? How can you offer freedom to those who are you wearing another piece of clothing, another physical vehicle?

We are aware that we tread close to reaching the limits of this instrument's fatigue. We are also aware that the energy in this group this evening is such that we shall only exercise the feelings of contact, for this energy is extremely strong. Therefore, we shall pause at this time and move among you. If you request our conditioning, mentally request such, and as this instrument pauses, this shall be done.

(Pause)

(Carla channeling)

I am Hatonn, and greet you again in love and light. We would close through this instrument at this time. We wish to encourage you to live in the realization that you shall leave this caravan of booths and prizes, rides and thrills, and you shall once again have a larger viewpoint. My friends, this is your chance. You have given it to yourself and you undoubtedly feel at this time that you have perhaps bitten off more than you can chew in terms of processing the catalyst of your life so that you may be a true channel of love and of light and of service. Of course you have, my friends. This is the essence of the learning of the lessons of love: to take more than you can chew, and then to pray your way, to meditate your way, to contemplate, analyze and cling to your way until strength is given you, not from yourself, but through yourself.

There are many kinds of courage. May we say that you have witnessed one kind. In this instance, which is extreme and extraordinary, the one known as Don exhibited a courage most difficult to express. This entity had a wish to protect those about him, and so he did. Many things that you do will also be misunderstood, though less drastic. We urge you to do that which you feel to do, asking only that you center yourself daily in meditation and ground yourself in service to others. Let the flags fly; cheer the band on; ride your rides. Be exhilarated and share the joy of consciousness, and when you walk out into the darkness of a cold and rainy street, know that this too is a carnival full of joy and mystery, and find yourself behind the carnival masks that you may see in the gutter, just as you please yourself by seeing yourself as the graceful participants of a circus.

If all things can become one to you, then you can become one with all things, and you shall have learned the greatest lesson, and you may turn to all those whom you meet and say, "I shall meet you in paradise," for the realization of that oneness is the most powerful realization in third density.

Rejoice, therefore, and love one another. Celebrate with one another. Share that which you have and that which you feel, and look when you walk out into the sleet, the cold, the frost, and the stench of a hobo's fire on a bad weather night. Offer your jacket, your hat, your food, your substance insofar as you are able, with gladness at heart and a singleness of mind. See the Creator, and so shall the Creator see you.

We drench you in our love as if it were a waterfall. It is our great, great joy to have spoken with you, and we now leave this instrument, thanking each who responded to our conditioning and assuring each that each may or may not choose to channel as does this instrument, that each is equally able and equally valued. This instrument merely has more time, as you call it, to have learned the tuning mechanisms, the challenging mechanisms, and the trick of emptying the mind so that we may fill it when this instrument does not know what we are to say. No sentence this instrument has said this evening has been known to her beforehand. There are many, many, many other services just as important. We are here only to inspire, never to instruct. Your instructions shall come from within you. We ask you to join us in the kingdom which you call heaven daily, to listen to that universal self which is you and to experience and come to know that which is yours, that which has been given to you to do—for one man, and for one man, then for all men.

I am known to you as Hatonn. We thank Latwii and Laitos for aiding us in the conditioning. We thank a great teacher known to us as Amira for lending an energy that feeds into this particularly powerful group this evening. We give thanksgiving, and we praise each of you. May your hearts rejoice and be merry, for you are yet able to love and be loved, to care and to accept nurturing, to reach out and to enfold, to experience, in short, the carnival of third-density illusion—that grand illusion with many, many mirrors, all of which give you a distorted picture of the one original Thought. Meditate, my, friends, and allow the distortions to fall away.

I am Hatonn. I leave you in the love and the light of our infinite Creator. Remember always that your peanut butter sandwiches, like fishes and loaves, are in infinite supply for those who wish never to hunger again. Break them and give them, for it is an infinite universe. Adonai, my friends. Adonai. Adonai. I am Hatonn.

(Jim channeling)

I am Latwii …

(Side one of tape ends.)

(Jim channeling)

… by giving our humble responses to your queries. Without further ado, may we then begin with the first query.

R: Yes, Latwii. Hatonn mentioned courage in relation to what happened, and Don's wanting to protect those around him. Can you perhaps elaborate on that?

I am Latwii, and am aware of your query, my brother. We are working with this instrument and attempting to channel the concepts in a narrower band than is our usual wont, for this entity feels that it may not be able to serve well in giving information without distortion. Therefore, please bear with us as we bear with this instrument.

The courage which our brothers and sisters of Hatonn spoke of is a courage which may not be apparent to many, but we can assure you that when one is faced with what appears to be a precipice, and when one leads a group on this path—we must pause momentarily.

(The tape was turned over and the recorder restarted.)

(Jim channeling)

I am Latwii, and am once again with this instrument. To continue. When one leads a group and faces what appears to be the precipice, the choice must be made as to whether the group might tumble over the edge and all be lost, it would seem, or whether the one leading shall go first, and by going first, indicate to the rest that the precipice is there and can be stepped back from, for one has gone.

We shall attempt further clarification. The one known as Don saw what has been described this evening as the dark carnival, and saw the difficulties that awaited should this experience be continued which had begun in the recent of your times as you measure experience. There were those images of destruction which filled the mind of the one known as Don, and this entity wished in his deeper self to reserve as much of that difficulty for himself as possible so that those of his comrades might be spared the added difficulties. The conscious mind made use of this decision in its own distorted fashion, and leapt first from the precipice in order that the others might avoid it.

May we answer you further, my brother?

R: I want to understand correctly. Don's polarity was in the process of being tampered with, is that what you're saying, or was he just being inundated with negative images? I'm not sure I understand.

I am Latwii, and shall attempt, my brother, to shine some light upon this most complex of concepts. Let us begin by reminding each that the honor of standing close to light, shall we say, bears also the responsibility to radiate that light as purely as possible. The honor of the contact which this group experienced with those known as Ra brought with it great responsibility. Each stumbled on this path on numerous occasions, and each then suffered the difficulties. The contact is of a nature which is, shall we say, metaphysically potent. To continue in such a fashion of attempting purity over a long period of what you call time, has the effect of increasing the potential for further stumbling. When stumbling becomes more and more, shall we say, treacherous, it can be then determined that to allow that which has been done to continue in its flowering, there needs be some cessation of the potential for great difficulty. The one known as Don felt the work which had been done would suffice to light the way for many, but could be jeopardized if the entire group fell over the precipice. Therefore, the choice was made to take that step in a distorted fashion.

May we answer you further, my brother?

R: No, Latwii, thank you very much.

I am Latwii, and we are most grateful to you, my brother, for allowing us to perform our humble service. Is there another query at this time?

N: Yeah. Latwii, I would like to ask a question. Don taught me how …

Jim: Hold it, N. Wait a minute.

N: Is something wrong, Jim?

Jim: Yes, hold it a minute.

(Carla faints. Pause.)

Carla: Sorry. Let's retune a bit. Don liked *"Row, Row, Row Your Boat"*, *"Mammy's Little Baby."* Sorry, gang, I fainted.

(The group retunes by singing "Shortnin' Bread.")

(Jim channeling)

I am Latwii, and am once again with this instrument. We appreciate your concern, my friends, for the one known as Carla, and we shall attempt to utilize this instrument in a manner which is not quite so conducive to the trance state by the more rapid repetition of the sound vibration complexes.

Please continue the query, my sister.

N: Latwii, I was wondering about Don and which density he's in now. He was a very smart man who taught me a lot, and I'm wondering since we're third density, if perhaps because of his death was in a negative way, if that would contribute to his going to a higher level or entity form?

I am Latwii, and am aware of your query, my sister. We shall attempt to respond to the query which has many portions. Each in this room attempts the lessons of third-density love. Each learns according to a unique pattern of ability. The one known as Don learned much and taught much in his span of time upon your planet. As his transition from this illusion to the next was of a traumatic and sudden nature, the transition then has been somewhat more difficult. But we may assure each that the transition shall be completed well and there shall be the clear experience of the one known as Don of his being the one Creator. This point of view shall so illumine the beingness of the one known as Don that the experiences of the previous life now ended shall be seen in a way that shall expose those signposts missed and shall offer the one known as Don the opportunity and the privilege of setting those signposts right by renewing the experience at another of what you call time.

Remember always, my sister, that the view from your illusion is most limited in order that experience of a dramatic nature might be gained that is not possible when the view is wide and the self is seen as the one Creator. When, then, that self is known to be the one Creator, then those treasures of experience gained in the illusion you now inhabit become a true nourishing harvest to the being of the one Creator. Nothing, in truth, is lost. All shall be made whole and the one known as Don shall move in time and space to experience again those lessons which shall glorify the one Creator. There is, in truth, no positive or negative act. There is the one Creator which knows Itself, and the one known as Don shall indeed experience that in each of his life patterns which he shall set for himself. All shall be pursued in joy. Those experiences seen now in this tiny illusion as failures shall be seen as great honors and privileges to be filled with the fullness of the joy of the one Creator at another of what you call time.

May we answer you further, my sister?

N: No, thank you, Latwii, very much.

I am Latwii, and am grateful to you, my sister. Is there another query at this time?

T: Yes, I have a question. It's very similar to hers. Then Don's experience with leaving this illusion in a traumatic way, if I understand you correctly, may be easier or different than a person of a lesser consciousness who would do the same sort of thing? In other words, it would be easier for Don to make this transition and to learn from it than it would be for someone who is not nearly as conscious as he was, is that correct? Or could you just speak on that?

I am Latwii, and am aware of your query, my brother. It may be correct that one who has a greater, shall we say, grasp of the nature of evolution may find it easier to proceed from what has been called a traumatic experience in leaving the incarnation. What we have intended by our previous response is to suggest that for each entity leaving this illusion, the greater view which is then available is that which puts all into perspective. Within your illusion a death is seen as a great event. A death which is traumatic and brought to the self by the self is seen as most disastrous. Yet from another point of view, it can be seen as a great opportunity to find love where there was no love, to find light where there was no light, to illuminate the darkness with the presence of the one Creator. This, then, is the opportunity which faces the one known as Don. It may be seen as that which you could call karma, yet it can be seen as that which is a great opportunity and a great honor as well as duty.

May we answer you further, my brother?

T: No, thank you very much.

I am Latwii, and we, as always, thank you, my brother. Is there another query at this time?

S: Latwii, I have a question. Is there anything that we can do to help Don, to aid Don without sending a vibration that would cause him to become earthbound or concerned about us?

I am Latwii, and am aware of your query, my sister. We can suggest that each feel the pain of the loss, for as a brother leaves the journey, there is the inevitable feeling of emptiness. Feel that grief and allow that grief to be fulfilled and finished. See then the one known as Don continuing upon his journey, and send this entity the love and light which springs from your heart and your very being, that he might have a comfort upon his journey. Wish him well, send him joy and allow him to depart without the lingering grief. This shall smooth the journey of the one known as Don, and this entity then may continue with that plan he has set before him, as the one Creator moves through him that It might know Itself through his experience.

May we answer you further, my sister?

S: No, thank you.

I am Latwii, and we thank you, my sister. Is there another query at this time?

Carla: Well, along those same lines, I was thinking, since he did commit suicide—of course, he'd been slowly doing it for a long time, but still the ending was sudden—and I wondered if even though the *American Book of the Dead* had Gnostic qualities about it which certainly isn't to be recommended, that it might serve as a grounding so that Don would know for sure where he was and where he was going. Do you think it might be helpful in this case, or is that treading too close to the Law of Confusion?

I am Latwii, and am aware of your query, my sister. We can suggest that whatever be done for the one known as Don, that aid might be most helpfully given by simply sending a generalized form of love and light in order that there shall be no distraction and no tie to the one known as Don. It is helpful to allow the grieving to find its cessation, then to send the love and the light, the peace and the joy, and to wish the departing entity well and when thinking of this entity, to raise this entity into the light, no matter what experience is remembered, that there shall be no ties which hold this entity to this illusion longer than is necessary.

May we answer you further, my sister?

Carla: Just two things. Alternately I have thought of doing what I would normally do under the circumstances, which would be to go to my own particular Christian denomination's Eucharist daily for a couple of weeks to make a dedication to his passage. The other thing I had considered doing was to send postcards to the people that are in the meditation group or that had been and knew him, letting them know when we were going to plant the juniper tree that will be Don's only memorial. Would either of these things hold him back in any way or would either of them help? Because I would like him to be able to go home if there's anything I can do to help.

I am Latwii, and am aware of your query, my sister. In this case we find that we must bate our response somewhat in order that we do not infringe upon your own choices. As we mentioned previously, it is most helpful to make any gesture that which raises the entity into the love and light of the one Creator which is ever available to each. The rituals which attempt to instruct from, shall we say, a distance are those which have the effect of delaying the passage, for the one so communicated with must process the specific information and must make some response. The love and light sendings in a generalized form do not require any backward looking, and ease the forward journey. The intent to raise the entity into the light of the one Creator is that which is most beneficial, whatever the form of the offering.

May we answer you further, my sister?

Carla: No, I think I get the gist of it. The first of my three suggestions would hold him back while he went through the thing, the Gnostic thing. The other two are general and I'll keep it in mind and I sure do thank you.

I am Latwii, and we are most grateful to you, my sister. Is there another query at this time?

J: Latwii, could you say anything more about the nature of the precipice which Don perceived and into which he committed himself so that we would stay back from it?

I am Latwii, and am aware of your query, my sister. This is a concept which is not easy to enunciate but we shall give it our best shot, shall we say, you will excuse the pun. We do not wish to keep our responses in the somber vibration, and shall attempt to lighten them if possible. The precipice which faced the one known as Don is that responsibility which may be too great to fulfill. The work which had been ongoing for some time was that which required in this entity's mind more than could be offered and have in this entity's mind, and perhaps, in truth, have resulted in a greater burden than could be borne, so that the fruits which had been harvested would not then be available to those which sought the harvest. This entity then assured that the fruits thus harvested would be available for a greater portion of what you call time.

May we answer you further, my sister?

J: No, I guess not, although I don't quite understand it all yet.

Carla: Then what you're saying is, he saw a way that perhaps all of us here in the room who were solidly behind the Ra material might be sucked into a situation that would discredit us in some way or make us unable to function to disseminate the material, and he chose not to do that, not to put it that far along. Is that what you're saying? More or less?

I am Latwii, and am aware of your query, my sister. We shall once again attempt to utilize this instrument in a way which this instrument finds difficult to accept. We are attempting to move within the bounds of the Law of Free Will and give information which is sought to those which are of great concern and to those who wish to understand that which is beyond the understanding …

Carla: Well, may I interrupt you long enough to say that I think it's general knowledge in this room that in the last session we had with Ra, Ra said that unless there was a great deal of praise and thanksgiving, I myself might take this opportunity to have a kidney problem and leave the incarnation. So that's what I meant by saying that it would be impossible to disseminate the information, because I wouldn't be here. Go ahead. That's what I meant. Maybe that gets you away from the Law of Confusion a little bit.

I am Latwii, and am grateful for your added comments, my sister. We find that the one known as Don was aware that great difficulties awaited his traveling and the potential for difficulty for each of this group—that is, those involved in what had come to be known as the Ra contact—and foresaw not only his own what you call death, but the death of each of the others within the group when his condition lingered overly long, and therefore wished to avoid that outcome.

May we answer you further, my sister?

Carla: No, thank you.

I am Latwii, and we thank you, my sister. May we attempt another query at this time?

Carla: I've got just a little nitty-gritty. I didn't think I could go in trance as long as I was holding onto somebody's hand; I thought I could just faint, sort of. It's not the same thing, is it?

I am Latwii, and am aware of your query, my sister. It is quite correct that the trance is not possible when the physical vehicle is touched, for the mind/body/spirit complex is called to remain with the vehicle, for there is infringement upon the aura which does not allow the exit. The vertigo effect which you have just experienced is that which renders unconsciousness for a short period of time.

May we answer you further, my sister?

Carla: Why the hands? I know other parts of the body won't work. Or do any other parts of the body work? The feet, the face—I mean, is it something about the hands?

I am Latwii, and am aware of your query, my sister, and we are most pleased that you have asked this query. Consider the difficulties in holding knees or shoulders. Though these perhaps will suffice, they are most difficult to continue.

Carla: So, it's not just because you have nerve endings in your hands, it's just that hands grasp and shoulders don't. Is that what you're saying?

I am Latwii, and again am aware of your query, my sister. This is basically correct, although the hands do have more of an ability to receive and send the vibrations which might intercept the aura and therefore impede the exit of the mind/body/spirit complex.

May we answer you further, my sister?

Carla: No. As I used to say, "Groovy."

I am Latwii. We thank you, my sister. Is there another query at this time?

N: Yes, Latwii, I have another question. It's concerning the—it appears to me that the people who are close to me who kill themselves are very, very intelligent, and I was worried and wondering. It seems like a lot of people lately who are very intelligent have killed themselves that have been troubled before, and I'm wondering if they maybe see things that we don't or know things we don't. Is [it] that the Earth [is] in trouble or are things going downhill quick or is that just circumstance that happens to be around me a lot?

I am Latwii, and am aware of your query, my sister. Those who have the aptitude for mental analysis are those who seek with a fine-pointed pen, shall we say. Each experience is written with the most minute of detail. Each portion, whether of the positive or the negative experience, is recorded and observed and felt with great depth. This is the potential of those with what you have called the mental acuity and intelligence. It is easy with such an ability to focus upon the difficulties, for it is difficulty which seems so apparent in your illusion. Though each difficulty has its solution, solutions do not seem so easily apparent and must be striven for with great dedication.

The propensity to remain with the view of difficulty, then, can be increased for one who has the ability to see the details which may escape another. If one cannot match the great ability to see the difficulty with an equal ability to see the faith and the praise and the thanksgiving and the solution to such difficulty, then the difficulties may grow for such an entity, and if allowed to continue without the praise and the thanksgiving, without the finding of the love and the light of the one Creator within that situation, then it is possible for the effect to build an energy of itself which would not be as possible for one who did not observe so carefully and so minutely with the mental acuity.

May we answer you further, my sister?

N: It seems to me that there seems to be so much more killing and suicide, that it seems so hopeless, that, you know, people are just giving up easier and being angrier easier. Is that—are things getting worse or am I just around it more often?

I am Latwii, and am aware of your query, my sister. It is a correct observation that as your planet nears that called the harvest, the experiences of many shall be intensified, for as time for harvest grows short, the work in order to achieve harvest must be accomplished in a shorter time. When time is short, then intensity must replace the time that is no longer available. Great work in consciousness can be done in this short time that remains before the harvest of souls from your planet. There is, of course, the risk that the work shall be more difficult, yet there is the great opportunity to move forward in the process of evolution as has never been possible before upon this planet.

May we answer you further, my sister?

N: No, thank you.

I am Latwii, and we thank you, my sister. Is there another query at this time?

Carla: I'd like to ask you to—as to the instrument's fatigue, and discover whether or not the instrument should continue channeling.

I am Latwii, and am aware of your query, my sister. As we scan this instrument, we find that there is increasing fatigue and concern upon the instrument's part that it is not functioning in a clear fashion or it …

(Side two of tape ends.)

(Jim channeling)

… has found the necessity to divide its attention in order that the hand pressure may be increased at the same time that concepts are received and transmitted. We do however, find that this instrument may continue for another query.

Questioner: I have a query that I would really like to ask. The one known as Jim has been the one that has been pretty much taken for granted in all of this. Everyone has been concerned about Carla. I would like to know if there is anything that we as a support group can do for Jim, and if there is a way that we can do it that would be acceptable to Jim. *(Inaudible)* Can you give me any suggestion? Prayer is understood, of course.

I am Latwii, and am aware of your query, my sister. We shall ask the one known as Jim to step aside so that the opportunity for Christmas presents at this time do not overcome him. Now to continue. This entity appreciates …

(Laughter.)

I am Latwii, and we shall continue in appreciation of your appreciation. This entity appreciates as well all offerings of service, and can be aided by the one— we struggle for a word that is acceptable to this instrument—heartfelt and sincere sympathy for the one known as Don, and for this entity known as Jim, there is available by simply sending a light and reminding this entity that all does not have to be done overnight.

May we answer you further?

Questioner: No, thank you, Latwii. Thank you.

I am Latwii, and we thank you and each in this group. We find that it is the appropriate time to take our leave of this instrument and of this group. We thank this instrument for allowing us to speak to subjects which it had great difficulty in allowing the concepts concerning which to be a portion of its experience this evening. This instrument will yet learn humor and we commend his continued attempt at it. Hard heads are often good heads in the end, with a simple whack or two.

We leave each in the appreciation of the difficulties each feels for the one that has departed. When brothers and sisters travel upon a difficult path, there is great support in the unity each provides, and the joy and laughter which each provides each. When one has departed, there is often the overwhelming grief that fills the vacuum. We hope that we have been able to inspire joy that can follow grief, for within your illusion it is necessary to forget that each and all is the one Creator in order that the one Creator might gain the greatest experiences with the greatest intensity, variety and depth of possibilities. Thus is the one Creator known to Itself, and glorified by each portion of Itself. No matter what experience is gained, each is a treasure in this great journey of the One through the One to the One, and remember, my friends, that in truth, all is well. The journeys may turn and become seemingly difficult at each turn. Yet, the difficulties themselves are glories to the one Creator, for without them the Creator would be poorer in knowledge of Itself. What, then, can one offer to the one Creator but experience? Be of great joy and cheer in your journeys. Gather your experiences with the confidence that there can be no error too great to balance, no experience too traumatic to give joy for, and no life too short to be an infinite remembrance and glorification to the one Creator.

We are those known to you as Latwii. We leave you now in the everlasting love and infinite light of the one Creator which dwells in each entity and each portion of all experience. Adonai. Adonai vasu borragus.

(Carla channeling)

I am Nona, and spend only a few moments. We have been called to offer healing in love and in light for the sake of our infinite Creator, and in His service we serve, and therefore we pray that you with us vibrate and heal the entity for whom this healing has been requested over and over again. We thank you and we thank this instrument and we thank the universe that is such a place as *(inaudible)* the beauty and *(inaudible)* of love. I am Nona.

Sunday Meditation
November 18, 1984

(Carla channeling)

[I am Hatonn, and I] greet you in the love and in the light of our infinite Creator. We thank you and give you many hopes of blessing for the opportunity to speak with you this evening, for the opportunity to share our lives with yours through these few precious vibratory inconstants which you call moments of time.

We would like to tell you a story, my friends, of a princess. The heroine could just as easily have been a prince upon some levels of storytelling, but for our parable it is quite necessary that this entity be female. As is the custom in fairy tales about princesses, she was awaiting one man who could stir her heart, a heart that was hard-bitten by many, many years of power and lonely beyond words because of that power. Courtier after courtier, peasant after peasant filed by with their best gifts, hoping to win her favor. She had offers of everything from livestock to pearls to kingdoms, new realms to govern. In none of these things was she at all interested and sadly at the end of each feast day she would close audience, still powerful and still lonely.

One day an ill-garbed man came to her court. He was not a courtier or a peasant. He was a stranger. His home was the road. He did not understand why his journey had brought him to this place but when he saw what lay before him, there grew within his heart a great desire to speak his mind and his heart, as all were allowed to do on this great feast day. Having no cap for his head, he tugged at his hair in order to make respect and bowed his knees and in rough words made his plea. "Milady," he said, "I can give you nothing but my days, my nights, my love, and my road. My feeling for you is such that I am blinded. I cannot see any other and so you shall have to help me if we are to be together, for the blind need guides, and I offer you my need as well as my love, for I shall be confused. To share my road is a strange thing indeed. Milady," he continued, "I do not know where I shall be tomorrow, next week, or next year. I have nothing but my flesh and my heart, my mind and my honor, and I give these into your hands. Whether you accept them or not, you are and will always have been my love."

The princess, who for years had turned down treasure upon treasure, came slowly from her high throne and reached her hand to the stranger who stood below her. "You must help me, too," she said, "For I do not know that I have a road; I only know that I wish to find one. I do not that I love; I only wish to find love." He took her and placed her upon the earth and looked down upon her, as he was taller than she. "Milady," he said, "that is the way of all love. Each gives, each takes. I have not loved but I know this to be so." "I have not loved either," she said, "but I know that I am no longer lonely."

The ill-paired couple did not stop for retainers or for chairs to carry them or for any of the panoply or pomp of her circumstance, for that was not his road. They began to walk, and within the hour they were out of sight even to the keenest eye of those in the kingdom at the great fair. Strangely enough, this princess and this stranger were never seen again. Though many told of her years of coldness and haughtiness, there were none to sing the praises of her love, for as she became open to love, just so she became invisible to a great deal of that which mortals may see and mortal ears may hear.

My friends, it is a great folly, or so it seems to be, encased in such flesh as you experience in your density. You feel clumsy and awkward, and so you are, compared to higher density bodies. You feel numb and unable to see the larger picture, and this is so compared to the awareness available at other levels of vibration. Yet yours is the splendor of giving the true generosity that only comes when you truly cannot see and cannot hear the divine but only have faith that there is such a thing as divine love.

In your illusion, may we say that you tend to undervalue your contributions to others. The least of those among you contributes in a vital way. It is not a conscious contribution in many cases, but the contribution of flesh within which a consciousness has been placed, so precious that to think it could be broken as the human body is broken is almost not to be thought, not to be accepted, not to be tolerated. This precious consciousness, you say to yourself, cannot possibly be part or parcel of this flesh. Yes, my friends, you are inextricably bound about the cells of your third-density chemical body. All your acts will be those of men incarnate, men who pour out the blood of heart or mind or will or body without knowing the truth. The chances for courage, for polarizing, for serving, for allowing your flesh to become bread for others, are enormous. How little you value yourselves or your circumstances compared to the reality as we see it. If someone gave you a perfect stone—this instrument's mind does not know precious stones well; we see in her mind diamonds, rubies, emeralds—someone gave you a perfect emerald, and then told you to swallow it and wear it within your body, you would think that man to be mad. And yet that is your consciousness—perfect jewel, a jewel of perfect shape. Not tossed thoughtlessly into a body, but placed with care, with love, with wisdom, into flesh that you may pour out your life beautifully if you wish, having nothing more to go on than deep-felt feeling that this is your road.

You see, my friends, we must many times use females for those who receive and males for those who offer, for that is the archetypical nature of your sexuality. In actuality, each of you is both receptor and giver, taker and nurturer. Never doubt your worth to those about you. Never doubt that your nurturing is questionable any more than you doubt that there is a land in which princes and princesses have grand fairs.

Where did these thoughts come from if there is not a level of knowledge which tells you about yourself? We offer this teaching to you in humility and are so grateful for the opportunity to speak with you. That is all. We can only repeat again and again: O what treasure lies within your bones, what beauty of spirit shines from loin far up into the heavens. There is no distinction, there is no being cut off. The illusion seems to cut you off, but you are a treasure indeed, each of you, just as you are. And in the flesh you shall learn twenty, nay one hundred times better to serve, to love, to give and to accept, to take, to receive. Love is completing circuits; it is not necessarily giving.

We close this circuit and relinquish this instrument at this time. Please be aware that our use of the word love especially is inaccurate, and our sayings, as always, are only as important to you as they are helpful. We are those of mortal opinion who know nothing for sure. We have only walked the road a bit ahead of you. What road is that, my friends? Keep walking, my friends. You shall see and it shall be a joyful thing. I am Hatonn. I leave you in the love and in the light of our infinite Creator. Adonai, my friends. Adonai vasu borragus.

(Jim channeling)

I am Latwii, and I greet you, my friends, in the name of the one infinite Creator. We greet you in love and light. We are privileged to speak to you once again, and offer our humble service. Our attempts to answer your queries are but meager efforts but the one Creator resides in each and makes itself known in such a manner. May we attempt the first query, my friends?

L: Latwii, the intensity of the spirit of power tonight seems to be unusually high. Is there a reason for this?

I am Latwii, and am aware of your query, my brother. This evening this small group has purified its desire to seek what you call the truth in a way which is galvanized, shall we say, by the passing of a brother. It is often the case in such a traumatic situation that those left behind will seek with ever more dedication the riddles and mysteries of the life which seems to have ended for one close. Yet each knows that the life continues and therefore redoubles the effort to make, shall we say, sense of it all.

May we answer you further, my brother?

L: Yes. One further question. When Christ was crucified, he made the statement, "My God, my God, why hast Thou forsaken me?" To whom did he speak and what did he mean by this?

I am Latwii, and am aware of your query, my brother. The one known as Jesus the Christ was a mortal, as are all who walk your planet, yet this mortal was the one Creator which had uncovered levels of its being that few upon your planet have approached. As its life pattern reflected more and more that indwelling power and beingness of the one Creator, the path laid out for this entity became clear to it, and this entity then followed that path with great dedication. The path ended in this incarnation for this entity upon that cross, and it spoke as a mortal those words asking the one Creator why it needed to fulfill that destiny, shall we say. For even unto this entity who had realized much of its beingness there remained a mystery as to why the story needed an ending of such a nature that would require it to be nailed to a piece of wood to hang upon and be mocked by many as it gasped its last breaths in physical pain. Yet this entity was lifted up by its own faith in that one Creator which it had found within its being and had attempted to reveal to those who had eyes to see and ears to hear.

May we answer you further, my brother?

L: No, you have given me food for thought, I thank you.

I am Latwii. We thank you, my brother, as always. Is there another query at this time?

Carla: I have a question, but first I would like to challenge you in the name of Christ, not because I think you aren't great, but because I have an important question to ask you. I challenge you in the name of Christ. Do you come in the name of Christ, Jesus Christ, my Savior?

I am Latwii, and, my sister, we come in the name of Jesus the Christ, the entity of whom we have just spoken. We come in the name of the Christ consciousness, and all those great masters who have sought the one Creator in the positive sense. We appreciate your challenge and applaud your devotion to the one known as Jehoshua.

May we attempt your query, my sister?

Carla: Yes. It's been on my mind that the Ra work may not be finished. I have in mind two people which after what I would consider a rather long period of training together would be able to function with questioning. My questions, therefore, will be split up. First of all, is it possible for you to give any information of this kind?

I am Latwii, and am aware, my sister, of the nature of your queries. We may say that we can speak in general terms, for in this instance the query about that which most definitely affects your future.

Carla: All right, one thing at a time. Is it possible that the two entities that I have in mind, the one known as Jim and I, could reach, sustain and thrive, all except for me, with the level of harmony, health, tranquility and unity that Don, Jim and I experienced that was the basis for the Ra contact? I realize that the instrument knows absolutely nothing about this. This was on purpose, and I would like to say to the instrument, I'm sorry, but I didn't think it would be wise to tell you what I was thinking. I wanted to go into it on a more general point of view.

I am Latwii, and am aware of your query, my sister, and it is fortunate that this instrument was not notified beforehand of these queries, for we are sure that it would have been most difficult for it to stand aside should it [have] had previous warning. We can suggest that the level of harmony that is possible for you and this instrument to achieve is a level which can easily approach that experienced by you and the one known as Don, for it is easier to harmonize fewer energies than many energies. Yet there is a certain level or number of entities necessary to do the kind of work of which you speak.

May we answer you further, my sister?

Carla: Yes. The question was, could these four people sustain that level of harmony and thrive both physically, mentally and emotionally? And the reason I said forget me was that I come in with so many physical handicaps that it would skew the answer. Everybody else is healthy.

I am Latwii, and we fear that we are not aware of salient portions of your query. We are unaware of entities other than the one known as Jim and yourself. May we ask for clarification, my sister?

Carla: I do not wish to say these names out loud. Is it acceptable if I think them?

I am Latwii. This is quite acceptable, my sister.

Carla: I shall do so now.

I am Latwii, and we are grateful that you mentioned that you were going to think of these entities. We appreciate hints. Now to your query, my sister. We see that these entities which you have spoken of before are entities which indeed generate and sustain great amounts of harmonic resonance, and are entities which could with great effort and dedication achieve the level of harmony which would approach that previously experienced in the contact with those of Ra. Whether this harmony would be of the proper pitch is not that which we can either affirm or predict, for the future is most unknown even to those who can see its possibilities.

May we attempt further response, my sister?

Carla: Can you say whether the higher selves of these four beings made agreements to do Ra work before incarnation if necessary?

I am Latwii, and am aware of your query, my sister. We find that there have been agreements made by each of these entities to work in this particular type of contact. The agreements provided for various, shall we say, alternatives or backup probabilities. Whether these can be instituted and manifested is the mystery which lies before you.

Carla: Okay. So, let me see. I've gotten so far that I have identified the proper people as far as agreements made before birth, and that part of our agreements were that we would be free to attempt to reach a level of harmony necessary to sustain the Ra workings. Am I correct up to this point?

I am Latwii, and am aware of your query, my sister. We can correct it only by inserting the modifier "some" of these people, rather than "the" people.

Carla: Okay. Now that brings me to my next deep hunch in a series of deep hunches I've been working with all this weekend. I have a deep hunch that one of these people is absolutely necessary to the group as a battery for the questioner, for the questioner could not do the work without the battery, without the life energy of this person being involved, I guess, in terms of what Hatonn just said, without the circuit being closed between those two people, so that in essence you would have three people and a battery for that third person.

I am Latwii, and am aware of your query, my sister. We can suggest that though there may be a specific entity that is capable of serving in the capacity of what you have called a battery, there may be others who, in a joined fashion, may be able to serve in the same capacity.

May we answer you further?

Carla: Well, that surprises me. I would think there would only be one battery for this particular person. Okay. I would think that the training period would probably be …

(Side one of tape ends.)

(Jim channeling)

I am Latwii, and we shall attempt the answer to your query at this time, my sister. We can suggest that the period known to you as a year is a relatively sufficient amount of time during which the energies of each entity may find the ability to harmonize in a manner which then readies the path and the work. We can suggest that this period of time is not fixed but needs to be prolonged enough that the honest and clear communication is effected. There is great politeness and concern among even the gentlest and most eccentric of entities. This veneer needs to be penetrated in order that even at the lowest ebb of compassion and wisdom the entities are able to maintain a stable harmony.

May we answer further, my sister?

Carla: Yes, sorry you guys, I hope I'm not going … I would assume that although at the beginning it would actually aid us to use mild mind-altering drugs—I'm speaking of marijuana—that a month before we began work we would have to swear off and stay off. Is that correct?

I am Latwii, and am aware of your query, my sister. In this instance we cannot serve as the doctor making a prescription, even in the negative sense. We find that the information which can provide answer to this query is known to this group.

Carla: Okay.

May we attempt another query, my sister?

Carla: Okay. Well, this is the biggie, all right? Is it, in your opinion, at all important that there be more Ra work done? Or is it instead better for us to realize that there are other things to do that we have not yet done. I'm thinking specifically of the fact that we got a new contact from Yadda recently that alerted me to the knowledge that, of course, it is a crowded universe, which I say a lot, but sometimes I don't pay attention to what I say, and it's possible that the Ra work is finished. If it is possible for you to give me your human opinion, I would be interested in anything you had to say on that point.

I am Latwii, and am aware of your query, my sister. Well, now. In our best human opinion may we suggest that the future has within it a great panoply of possibilities. May we suggest that the most important ingredient for realizing any possibility is the simple desire to be of service without a dedication to what that service shall be and how that service shall result.

We can see a future in which you begin again that which has become known as the Ra contact.

We can see a future in which there is no such contact, yet there is great work possible in furthering the information which has been gathered and continuing the meetings which have been ongoing for a great portion of your time.

We see possibilities in which new contacts are achieved and information therefrom disseminated.

We see a future in which each touches many individuals and speaks with compassion and inspiration of the One which indwells in all.

We see a future in which the being of each shines brightly as a beacon and illumines the darkness by its very being with no movement required at all.

We see a future in which each walks a path which is most appropriate, which is to say, that as one places a foot upon the ground and does so in a thoughtful manner centered upon the one Creator, it will therefore be as natural as breathing to place the foot upon the path, one foot after another, until the journey is traveled one step at a time.

We see a future in which all these things are possible, made possible by the firm desire to serve and the free desire for no particular outcome, for as the one Creator moves through each, the will of the one Creator shall be made known, and if each can remove its small self's will, then the will of the great One shall move through each as a channel, and shall carve its own pattern and write upon your third-density creation the words of illumination that inspire and provoke the seeking of those who dwell in darkness.

May we answer you further, my sister?

Carla: Yes. One last question. Can you weight without emotion the value of each of these paths as one being the most valuable or do you see them as equal?

I am Latwii, and am aware of your query, my sister. We see the equality of each path, yet we see the uniqueness and the power associated with each path as well. It cannot be said with certainty that to serve a few in a powerful manner is greater or lesser in service than to serve many in a lesser powerful manner. We see the one Creator in each entity awaiting that entity's seeking of it. We see many ways in which many entities may be inspired to begin that seeking. We see that a great variety of ways is available to each in this group to serve as shepherd, to radiate the love and light to those who hunger for this nourishment. We can only ask each to seek in meditation the answers which have been provided for each of you by your greater self, by your very own self as you planned this incarnation and as you hid various signposts along your various possible journeys. Know that each path contains in whole all that you hope to accomplish. If one tool is removed then another will take its place. Know that all is well. No turn will cause the seeker to be lost from that which is sought, for the one Creator waits not only at the end of each path but along each portion of each path, for it is the One who seeks Itself within Itself. There is none else.

May we answer you further, my sister?

Carla: No, Latwii. Thank you very much, and thank the instrument.

I am Latwii, and we thank you, my sister, for allowing us to provide our humble service. May we attempt another query at this time?

L: Latwii, excluding yourself, how many entities are in this room?

I am Latwii, and am aware of your query, my brother, and we shall not take offense at being excluded, but shall suggest that there is a great choir of entities which has joined this group this evening. Though all may not be, shall we say, contained by this room, there are endless entities listening and speaking and lending vibration to the great symphony of seeking that has arisen from this group this evening.

May we attempt further response, my brother?

L: No, that answers my question. Thank you very much.

I am Latwii, and we thank you, my brother. Is there another query at this time?

(Pause)

I am Latwii. We see that we have exhausted the queries for the evening. We are most appreciative to each present for allowing us a beingness within your group, and for allowing us to put into the poor and inadequate vessels—words—those feelings and concepts which are without bound and can only be understood at the heart of the being. We speak to you in words which we hope will also penetrate the essence of the love which binds each to each. We cannot speak without distortion, but we hope that the heart of our speaking may be known in your hearts. We thank you in a way which we cannot speak at all for allowing our humble service, and we travel with you on the journey. We ask with you the questions of how to travel that journey. We teach and we learn. We are with you always in your meditations, in your contemplations and in your machinations we join you in joy and in praise for the One Which Is All. We are those of Latwii. Adonai, my brothers. Adonai vasu borragus. ❧

Sunday Meditation
November 25, 1984

(Carla channeling)

[I am Hatonn.] I greet you, my friends, in the love and in the light of our infinite Creator. We are so thankful to have this group together this evening. Because of the nature of the atmosphere this evening, in that there are many channels and but one message, the message of love and gratitude and service, the message of the one original Thought, we are using this meeting, if we may, to tell a story using each instrument who would be willing to speak. We shall move about the room and tell our story, giving each of those instruments the exercise of the gift which each offers to the Creator, and through each allowing us to give our poor gift to each of you. We shall begin our small story.

There was once a young boy that was not like the other boys. This young boy sought like other boys. He had the instincts of other boys, he laughed as other boys do and in every respect was like all his classmates. But this little boy had been born with a terrible birth defect. It changed his appearance greatly and therefore he was an outcast.

We shall transfer. We shall not say "I am Hatonn," except when the channeler is challenging the contact. If it becomes necessary, we shall be happy to give our identification, but we would wish the story to flow as smoothly as is possible given each channel's desires. We now transfer.

(S channeling)

This small boy was often looked upon by many to be different, to be other than themselves. Many were unable to penetrate the illusion that was in some people's eyes not beautiful. Few made a real effort to look beyond the illusion, to look deep within the eyes that sparkled brightly with the love and light of the Creator. Many perceived this child as though his eyes were closed, as though the light did not shine so brilliantly from his inner being. We shall transfer.

(Jim channeling)

The boy knew that most of those about him were not able to see beyond his physical deformation. This had its effect upon the young boy, for he could see also that there was a difference in appearance between those who he observed and himself. He thought upon this difference. He thought upon reactions of others to him. And he began to look about him in the world of trees and flowers, of small animals and the creatures that inhabited his neighborhood and beyond. He saw that there was in such a creation great beauty and much variation of form, yet within this, shall we say, second density creation there was no shunning of one creature by another. He pondered long this phenomenon that the people about him would treat him in a manner other than they treated each other. We shall transfer.

(Carla channeling)

One day he came upon his mother sobbing bitterly in the privacy of her room. "Mother, mother," he cried, "what is the matter?" His mother sobbed that she was angry with the Creator, for the Creator had been cruel to her. "How, Mommy, how?" said the little boy, looking at his mother with adoring eyes. "He gave us your disease to bear before the world," said the mother. "Oh, no, Mommy," said the little boy, "that's not right. This is only a birthmark, but I think that many people have a disease in their hearts because they can't see me."

I shall transfer.

(C channeling)

The mother raised her head and looked into the eyes of her son, looked in a way she had not before. She gazed. She began to realize that there was beauty beyond the physical. She took her son into her arms, and felt his form.

We transfer.

(Jim channeling)

As she embraced her young, small son she felt the love of his arms, and she looked into his eyes and saw love there as well. Remembering the bitter words that she had been speaking as he entered the room a short time before, she felt great remorse within her own heart and realized at that instant that the deformation that she had felt such a burden was of no consequence when compared with the love that her son was able to give as freely as rain falling from the sky. It was her own heart and her own eyes that had not been able to perceive, that within this young child was more beauty than she had known in her life before now.

We shall transfer.

(Carla channeling)

The mother smiled into her son's eyes. "What a beautiful thing to say," she said. "Oh mother, thank you," said the little boy, "I thought about it in the woods because I noticed that none of the leaves blames another leaf for being different, and all the squirrels playing together, even if one is browner than the others, all sorts of cats play together. It's only humans, Mommy, that see in a funny way, and they just can't see me."

The mother nodded firmly. "Well, son, you'll have to help the world out a little bit. More and more people will see you because you are beautiful to me and you are beautiful to yourself." "Oh, yes," said the little boy. "Isn't everyone?"

My friends, how many defects have you seen today? How many masks have you been unable to penetrate in your relationships? How many bright and adoring eyes have you missed because of your judgment, because of the disease of your eyes, because of your lack of the loving and open heart? We might suggest to you that since you are here to learn the lessons of love, it would be surprising if anyone were able to say that each person throughout a crowded day had been met with the eyes of love, and with this we begin with you yourself.

Do you see yourself with love's kind vision? Are you aware that the Creator shines within you, a candle you cannot quench and a light which you need not hide? Yet how often do your own defects keep you from appreciating yourself and thereby letting others appreciate you. We do not intend to encourage you to be egotistical, but only to suggest that that greater self which is most truly you is very beautiful, and the touches, the details, the experiences, the uniqueness that you have brought to this particular aspect of the creation that is you are most lovable and most beautiful.

With whom have you had a difficult conversation today? Who, even briefly, caused you to gaze upon an imagined defect? That instance was a mirror which read out clearly and rightly the measure of your disease, or your dis-ease of heart. It has been [said] in your holy works, "To the pure, all things are pure." My friends, to the Creator, all things are the Creator.

We shall leave this group at this time, pausing only to thank each and to acknowledge the work which we most rightfully have done with the one known as A and the one known as H. We appreciate the opportunity to touch consciousnesses, and are aware that there are times when it is better to listen than to channel. In fact, there are times when it is most important. We appreciate the sensitive natures involved and are full of joy to be with each. We also wish to thank the one known as J1, as we have been attempting to make this entity also aware of our presence and have succeeded perhaps in a small degree.

You may ask us if we who speak think that we are so perfect and wonderful. Why is it then that you still help us as if we were quite in need of thoughts to inspire? Well, my friends, there are paradoxes, are there not? We shall leave this instrument at this time, which apparently is somewhat of a relief to her, for we have been giving her word-by-word instead of concept-by-concept practice for most of the evening, a type of channeling that is excellent for our uses but somewhat demanding of the channel in the areas of the faith to speak without knowing the end of the sentence and in the faith that the task is important enough to keep the level of concentration such that a sentence will indeed be ended appropriately. We thank this instrument for this practice period and we thank each instrument. We take this opportunity to thank the angelic presences that dwell and have dwelt within this precinct for many of your years. It is truly a light dwelling, and we very much enjoy being part of your group's consciousness at this time. I am known to you as Hatonn and I leave you in the utmost light and love of our infinite Creator. Adonai.

(Jim channeling)

I am Latwii, and I greet you, my friends, in the love and the light of our one infinite Creator. We are most privileged, as always, to be asked to join your group during your meditation. We thank you for this honor. We hope that our humble service of attempting to answer your queries may have some small use in that journey which you as pilgrims travel together with us. May we then attempt the first query for this evening?

Carla: Well, since nobody's jumping right out, just out of curiosity, is Oxal in the room because H's here? Specific group?

I am Latwii, and am aware of your query, my sister. We find that our brothers and sisters of those known to you as Oxal have indeed joined this group this evening in part due to the presence of the one you have called H and in part due to the remaining configuration of this group which seeks that kind of love which has been blended somewhat with wisdom.

May we answer you further, my sister?

Carla: No. I just wanted to check my person-finding equipment to make sure that I was feeling Oxal, and H has always gotten Oxal the easiest and I figured that might be it. And if I called him J2, he probably would deck me, so I'll be *(inaudible)* and let him be known as H. Thank you very much.

I am Latwii, and we thank you, my sister. May we attempt another query at this time?

A: Latwii, how does the ego serve the person?

I am Latwii, and am aware of your query, my sister. We find that this term, that is, the ego, is one which we have difficulty in utilizing, for it does not describe a portion of one's being which is easy to encompass with a definition. We can utilize the "conscious acting self" in a manner similar to the use of the word "ego." As you in your conscious awareness move through your illusion, you develop various biases and what you may call distortions of perception. These, taken together, are the result of preincarnative programming, if you will, in many cases and are somewhat altered by your experience and constant use of free will. These distortions may be likened unto the white light which passes through the prism and then is broken into the colors of your spectrum.

The distortions of perception are each colored in a certain way so that yet another means is presented to you by which you may learn the lesson of love, for as you examine each distortion each in its turn will yield the opposite response: for patience, you will find impatience; for anger, you will find acceptance; for the various kinds of distortions you will discover that when the balance is achieved, the yield of this process will be an increase in the ability to love.

Therefore, that which you have called the ego and which we have called the conscious acting self will have provided you with a lens or a prism which breaks the unity of all creation into various portions so that you may in each portion reap the harvest of love that would not be possible should the perception not be broken into particles.

May we answer you further, my sister?

A: Not right now, thank you.

We thank you, my sister. Is there another query at this time?

Carla: Well, you said a lot of things about how the ego works, but you didn't say anything that would suggest that it were better to be strong or better that it would be less puffed up or proud or full of itself. I mean, the term "egotistical" is probably what got A started on it, and that just means a person who's just too full of himself and not aware of other people. Could you comment on that, the fact that you didn't judge whether its better to have a strong ego or a weak one?

I am Latwii, and am aware of your query, my sister. We, as we mentioned in attempting to answer the previous query, have difficulty utilizing the term, ego, for it has many, many meanings which many different individuals might utilize. We have no desire to judge whether one's ego might better be strong or weak, or strong at one time and weak at another, or have any particular characteristic, for all characteristics are distortions or biases which allow the entity to discover love in yet another mode of behavior or portion of the self. That is the lesson of your density, my sister, and that faculty which has been called the ego is but one means by which this lesson might be learned.

May we answer you further, my sister?

Carla: I'm going to have to go back and read the Ra material before I ask anything more. I think there's some mention about the ego equaling parts of each chakra. I don't really remember but I believe there may be, so I'll look. The only other question that I had was, I've noticed lately when I get into a really deep meditation, my head vibrates. Noticeably. Why?

I am Latwii, and am aware of your query, my sister. In the meditative state, one is reaching the deeper levels of the self. To be more specific, the deeper mind then is able to yield its resources more freely to the entity which meditates. As you enter the deeper and deeper states of meditation, there is a certain vibration that accompanies this experience. It may be likened unto the harmonic resonance of the various portions of your deeper mind through which you have passed. It is necessary to experience such resonances in a harmonized fashion as one reaches the deeper levels of meditation in order that the resources of these deeper levels of mind might then find a means by which to reach the conscious mind. These vibrations might be likened unto a river and the resources might be likened unto a boat which floats upon that river.

The vibrations, therefore, provide an entry into the conscious mind for those resources traveling from the deeper mind. The shaking of the head portion of your body is simply a harmonic resonance that is set in motion as this energy travels from your lower to your higher chakras and then sets the antenna-like portion of your body into a harmonic motion.

May we answer you further, my sister?

Carla: Just one more question. It's kind of exciting …

(Side one of tape ends.)

Carla: It seems to be that if somebody could measure the vibrations which alter continuously, you could get an actual musical tune that would be the tune of opening up into a deeper level of light. If this is true, would it be universal or is it just for me, my tuning?

I am Latwii, and am aware or your query, my sister. We find that each entity would have a unique vibrational pattern, just as each's voice is unique and each fingerprint is unique. It would be necessary, therefore, for an entity to know the vibrational pattern before being able to set it to, shall we say, music. To clarify, let us say that if one knew one's vibrational pattern, this knowledge would have come from experience, and if the experience is present, there would be no need for the musical reproduction to induce what already exists.

May we answer you further, my sister?

Carla: No, thank you.

I am Latwii, and we thank you, as always, my sister. Is there another query at this time?

S: Yes, Latwii, I have a question that's of a somewhat personal nature, so I know you'll have to be general, but I was wondering if you could kind of give me a multiple choice answer. It seems in the recent past that any major or semi-major steps that I've tried to take have either been thwarted or just have really not gotten off of the ground. And because it's happened so many times in such a short period of time, I'm confused about it. I feel right now like I'm just kind of hanging around. Can you give me any input about this situation?

I am Latwii, and am aware of your query, my sister. Well, here we find that we must either be general or private, and we shall attempt an answer to your query which does not infringe upon your free will, for we do not wish to be a hindrance to that process which you have described which is a portion of your evolutionary pattern.

When you as a conscious, acting being decide upon a certain course of action, each course of action is evaluated by what you may call your higher self and is in many cases planted as a seed by that same portion of your beingness in order that you might travel a path which is rich in potential for your evolution and its progress to the One. When you find that known as the difficulty or the obstacle which blocks this path, you may look at it in many ways.

For instance, one may see simply that the obstacle exists and determine that no further progress can be made upon this path, and there is then the choosing of another path. One may also see the obstacle, and, yet, seeing the obstacle, determine that there is still the desire to travel this path. With such desire doubled and redoubled, then the obstacle may be confronted, may be utilized for learning, and progress upon the path may then continue. Having used the obstacle in such a manner, the entity then may find that there is a lesson which has been profitably learned. However, if you have chosen to travel another path or perhaps have chosen to rest for the moment, there may be the lesson in the resting or the lesson in another path.

One cannot determine with certainty whether an obstacle is meant to test the desire or to stop the movement. We, as always, can only suggest that within your own being you may find these hints and clues. The meditative state is one which is most fruitfully used in the seeking of such clues. There shall not likely be the plain stating of the situation in any event, for it is most necessary that each entity moves or rests according to its own use of faith and that faculty known as the will or the power to move.

May we answer you further, my sister?

S: Well, yeah. Could you explain a little bit what you mean by that? If the instance were the resting and what part faith would play in that resting?

I am Latwii, and am aware of your query, my sister. When one has desire to travel a path and finds the obstacle blocking that path and has further determined that there shall be a rest instead of a movement through or around the obstacle, there then must be the faith that for this moment resting provides the greater lesson in comparison to that provided by attempting to remove or circumnavigate the obstacle.

May we answer you further, my sister?

S: Well, then, the resting could provide a lesson in patience. Is that what you mean?

I am Latwii, and this is our meaning, my sister. May we answer you further?

S: No, thank you, Latwii.

I am Latwii, and we thank you, my sister. Is there another query at this time?

A: I've got a medical question for you. I have a basic understanding that in some illnesses there are viruses and there are bacteria. And with bacteria they can be cured by antibiotics, but usually a virus is allowed to go its own way and either will recess forever, but usually it will stick around and kind of show up whenever it feels like it, or at certain periods of time. I'm seeking an understanding of the purpose and the service that viruses are giving to the body. Can you help a little?

I am Latwii, and am aware of your query, my sister. These second-density creatures, the bacteria and virae, are those entities which provide a service to the host third-density entity by, shall we say, taking that catalyst which has not been well used by the mind or spirit complexes and allowing it to take its symbolic form when needed within the physical vehicle in what you call the form of a disease of one nature or another which may then be noticed by the entity in a manner which it had not noticed before when the catalyst was available only to the mind and spirit complexes. When there is what you call a healing, whether by the use of that [which] you have called medicine and the antibiotics, or by any other means, this healing occurs when the entity has been able to process the catalyst to such an extent that the disease is no longer necessary to point out that which was not observed and well used before.

May we answer you further, my sister?

A: Hopefully. I'm going to ask one from a personal side of helping me understand a little better so that I might be able to deal with the catalyst that I'm receiving of why a virus has taken up house in my right arm so that it … I've been meditating on it but I'm still kind of at a loss of why it will always reoccur and is not one that will be going away. One I can understand, that is, something that is causing great interruptions when I try to use my right arm. Can you help me to understand this a little better?

I am Latwii, and am aware of your query, my sister. We can, as always, speak only in general terms in this instance. When one is experiencing the physical difficulty or disease of any nature, one may begin to trace the roots of such a disease or disjunction by observing the effects that such disjunction has upon one's being and one's movement. Then one may take this analyzed discovery and meditate upon the further ramifications of such. This is to say, that as you are able to discover the effect of the disease or disjunction upon your physical vehicle and are then able to further discover your mental reaction or response to such effects, then you might from these observations gather the clues necessary to provide the balance to a distortion which has found an imbalance within your being and thereby heal that distortion.

May we answer you further, my sister?

A: Well, I gave it my best shot, and I knew you had to stay general, so I'll let it go at that. Thank you.

I am Latwii, and we thank you, my sister. Is there another query at this time?

(Pause)

I am Latwii, and we find that we have for the nonce exhausted the queries which have been so graciously presented to us this evening. We thank each for those queries. Each has been most helpful in allowing us to perform our humble service. As we speak to you concerning those questions upon your mind, we are speaking to the one Creator which has chosen a great variety of means of expressing Itself, and from this one Creator we learn to serve the one Creator.

We thank you with words that are most inadequate for the great feeling of gratitude which we have for each of you this evening. We are those known to you as Latwii. We shall leave this group at this time reminding each that a simple request is all that is necessary in order for our presence to be felt in your meditations. We humbly and joyfully join you there. We are those of Latwii, and we leave you now in the love and in the light of the one infinite Creator. Adonai, my friends. Adonai vasu borragus.

(Carla channeling)

I Yadda. I greet you in love and light of infinite Creator. I give this instrument no peace so she give me no peace either, so I speak what I have to say. I come in the name of Christ. At least I do not have to believe in Santa Claus. For this I am grateful. We come because question, "Who am I?" We always come to that call. What is "you"? Are "you" the here and now? Why are you here and now? Why have you decided to become a bird only to clip your wings and never fly? Why do you make of yourself the great mountain, only to bulldoze yourself to a small hill? Why do you make of yourself the sky and by act of meditation become the earth? Why are things so? There is a wedding of earth and sky. When you have chosen your here and now, your earth, then it is that you must decide how much of heaven you will allow yourself. Meditate, and you are in the kingdom of heaven. You fly like the bird. You stand tall as a mountain. You are not limited. Why do you wish to be so completely here and now when you can be free to be everywhere and everything? Who are you? Meditate, my friends, and give yourself to yourself.

I am Yadda. I leave you as I come. In dark and light. In the unity of all that there is, all that there will be and all that there has been. In the silent unity of forever that is your present moment. Adonai.

Intensive Meditation
November 30, 1984

(Carla channeling)

[I am Latwii, and] I greet you in the love and the light of the one infinite Creator. It is a privilege to speak to this group and to be able to use this instrument, as we seldom are able to channel through this instrument. We wish to work with the one known as L first, as we are aware of the pressing concerns, which though transient in the larger view, loom large within your daily routine. So we say over to you, L, we will exercise you if you will relax. We are aware you are rusty about the edges, but it is like falling off of the bicycle—one never forgets. We now transfer. I am Latwii.

(L channeling)

I am Latwii, and I greet you once again in the love and the light of the infinite Creator. We are pleased to have the opportunity to speak once again through this instrument, and ask that those present be patient as we polish the rougher edges on the equipment. It has been some time since this instrument has been exercised, and the neural paths are responding well. We do not anticipate any long delay until the instrument is once again functional to the level achieved previously during its period of service as instrument. We desire to maintain use of this instrument for as long a period as possible within the realms of comfort for the instrument so as to reacquaint the instrument with our vibration and the subtleties of our signal. We find that the instrument is progressing nicely and look forward to offers of service by this instrument in the field of channeling in the near future.

At this time we will rest the instrument and transfer our contact to another. Again we thank those presence—correction—present for their patience during this period of maintenance, so to speak. I am Latwii.

(Carla channeling)

I am Latwii, and am once again with this instrument. We greet you once again in love and light. We wish to work now with the one known as R, and we would have a few prefacing comments. Firstly, we work with this instrument due to this instrument's native tuning. It is more closely aligned with our tuning than any others, and we make use of this happy coincidence and greet a comrade with love and with *(inaudible)*.

The questions upon the mind of all new channels are the same. It is difficult to know illusion from reality, falsity from truth. It is possible to convince oneself to a certain extent of an untruth. The one known as R has this duty and honor each day as he does his work of unknotting the painful charley horses of life, causing laughter by satire and untruth. It is a good service and it is provided with a heart of hope, and in these things we commend the one known as R.

The length of, shall we say, time during which this has been done has engendered within this particular instrument lack of respect for illusion which borders upon the unbalanced.

We shall explain in order that we may aid the channeling process' beginning. When one is so aware of the gullibility of others, one's own gullibility comes into question. If others are easy to fool, is not the self? Therefore, the channeling process is aborted, for it is impossible to progress while feeling that one has basically been had, as this instrument would put it. We may not break through the mysteries of time, space and silence. That which you receive, you shall receive subjectively. Each gives of himself in order that those things might come through which will feel like nothing more than one's own thoughts. This is a part of the process of learning to channel.

Therefore, we ask this instrument as he attempts to begin this service this instrument not expect proof but only an urge, indistinguishable from any other urge to speak. We ask the instrument to relax, to empty the mind as far as possible, and above all to retain memory and reality and presence of the all-important tuning as evidenced in this particular instrument by white light of which it is aware. Never stray from that white light. Challenge all urges to speak [by] the white light and all will be well. Above all, please do not attempt to analyze. After the challenging has been done, move as you feel; speak as you are moved.

We shall begin in silence by allowing the instrument to experience our conditioning and also allowing us to do some checking out of the tuning which we must do to fit more comfortably into the channeling mode with this particular instrument. We shall condition the one known as R at this time. If you will please be patient, we shall pause at this time. I am Latwii.

(Pause)

(Carla channeling)

I am Latwii. We are once again with this instrument, and we are happy to say that [we have been having] good contact. We shall now simply repeat, "I am Latwii." We shall say nothing but that phrase, and we shall wait for the instrument to inwardly hear this phrase not with the ears but with a deep feeling in order that it may without analyzing speak this one phrase. We shall then come back to this instrument. I am Latwii.

(Pause)

(Carla channeling)

I am Latwii. We must ask the one known as R to avoid going too deeply into meditation. This is a very light state of meditation in which the concentration is completely upon the voice within. To go too deep causes the adjustments to be difficult. We bid farewell to the one known as L.

(Leonard leaves the room.)

We thank you, my friends. We also apologize to this instrument, for in the process of conditioning the one known as R we have been attempting to re-take out her tonsils which she does not appreciate. However, that is the way it has to be for us to be able to make good contact the first time with this particular instrument. We shall work with the tuning process and adjust ourselves more while we exercise the instrument known as S. We shall transfer to the one known as S, thanking this instrument very much for its service. I am Latwii.

(S channeling)

I am Latwii, and we are pleased to greet you in the love and in the light of our infinite Creator. We are grateful for the opportunity to work with this instrument who is quite fond of our vibrations. We wish to attempt to make our words perceivable to the one known as R. We shall attempt to send the phrase, "I am Latwii," to him, and we would hope that as this phrase is perceived he attempt to verbalize that which comes to mind. We shall repeat the phrase, "I am Latwii," to the one known as R several times so that he might choose when he is ready to speak. We shall transfer at this time. I am Latwii.

(Pause)

(Carla channeling)

I am once again with this instrument. I am Latwii. We are so pleased to be making the progress which we are making with the one known as R, and without meaning to put this instrument on the spot, as it were, we would attempt one more time to make a breakthrough. There is sometimes a breakthrough to be made, sometimes not. It is those who speak the most easily when, shall we say, living the illusion that often are the most difficult to train as channels of what we all hope to be truth. There is tremendous care and honor given this and therefore it becomes too important to screw up. We must encourage that side by side with this all-important respect for the service that it is truly *(inaudible)* to perform there be a sense of foolishness, a sense of throwing oneself over the cliff into thin air, a sense of being a clown. You do not know what the next word will be, you do not know what the next thought will be when you channel. That is the way channeling works. When more than one concept is known, it is usually due to the fact that we are mining the sometimes very rich experiences and reading that the instrument has done so that we may give our single message in yet one more variety so as to meet the needs of a particular group at a particular time.

Since the first word is the most difficult, we shall do as we have done many times before in training the new channel and begin with one word only. That word is "I." Who is "I," and can you tell a lie when you say "I"? Shall you channel "I" not in truth? Shall you channel "I" alone? Is there more than one "I"? [Most beloved] portion of the creation to whom we speak, "I" is all that there is. There is no untruth. There is no possibility of miscalculation in this channeling. Therefore, we offer it to you, and once again transfer to you for the purpose of your repetition of that simple word until you become more comfortable in the feeling that goes with speaking as a channel of the one great "I." We transfer now. We are Latwii.

(Pause)

(Carla channeling)

I am Latwii. We give many thanks for the opportunity to work with the one known as R this day. It is exhausting work, and we apologize to the one known as R. There are stiffnesses in the muscles we have been attempting to use in the conditioning, most especially those in the neck. This will not be necessary once the initial exercising of the channel has been achieved. Although we have not been able to speak through the instrument, we have made good contact with the instrument. We give great thanks for each of you.

We are most fond of the one known as S, may we say, far more fond of her than she is of us. We would challenge in a pleasant way, not in a competitive way. But truly, each is most blessed to us, and we have the utmost of joy in sharing in the stream of patterns of your moments of living as we cross them with our own. I am a voice. I am light. I am love. I do not need a name for I am older than *(inaudible)*, and yet I rejoice in each unique and beautiful being that aids who I am, to experience myself. How lovely is each who dwells in the creation. We shall leave this instrument and transfer to another. I am Latwii.

(Jim channeling)

I am Latwii, and am with this instrument. We greet you again in love and light and apologize for the delay in making this contact but we were having some difficulty reaching this instrument, for it was receding into those lower levels of meditation in unconscious anticipation of sleep. May we attempt to answer the queries which may be upon the minds of those present?

R: Yes, Latwii. I'd like to understand if possible the difference in conditioning you would use for a channel and just conditioning, the conditioning that you and I have talked of before that I receive sometimes from you during group meditations, because I was expecting that. I guess I was waiting for that and didn't feel it.

I am Latwii, and am aware of your query, my brother. The conditioning which we have utilized with you in the past has been a generalized form of making our presence known by means of activating certain areas within the head and neck complex. The type of conditioning which we utilize for the vocal channel is a refinement of this conditioning in that the conditioning is somewhat less physically perceivable. That allows, shall we say, a smoother carrier wave and the appearance of our thoughts upon it then is your signal to repeat those thoughts. Of course it is quite difficult to discern whether or not it is our thought or yours which is appearing within your mind at the moment at which you expect the thought to appear. May we assure you that our thoughts are quite like your own, and by simply speaking those thoughts, you will develop your ability to discern our thoughts and to speak them.

May we answer you further, my brother?

R: No, Latwii, thank you.

We thank you, my brother. Is there another query at this time?

Carla: Why was I getting so much heavy-duty channeling? I couldn't understand that.

I am Latwii, and am aware of your query, my sister. Well, my sister, we would think that we after all these years would be aware of the delicacy of your particular instrument and would tone down our conditioning, but, alas, we seem to have once again forgotten that your instrument is one which does not need the heavy hand. We may take some solace in knowing also that your instrument is of an increasing sensitivity as the time as you call it has passed from the last opportunity we had to speak through your instrument.

May we answer you further, my sister?

Carla: No, thank you.

We thank you as well. Is there another query at this time?

Carla: Could you in general speak to the ways of doing what Jim and are trying to do in the intensive meditation, sharing this technique of channeling?

I am Latwii, and we can suggest that the desire to do that which you do is the greatest portion of that which you do. We cannot make any further refinements upon what is being done, not because we do not wish to infringe upon your free will, but because we see what is being done as being well done. To offer the opportunity to learn this particular service at a time separate from the regular meetings of your group is an effort which we applaud with all our being. We shall be with you and shall set, shall we say, the format for such opportunities to share this service as we have done today. The offering of this service is much like performing the service, that is, to have the desire, to be open to the opportunity, and then to move with the energy as it is presented to you.

May we answer you further, my sister?

Carla: No, thank you.

I am Latwii, and again we thank you, my sister. Is there another query at this time?

S: Yes, Latwii. The other night when we were meditating with M and I was channeling you, I seemed to lose thoughts, like I got a few sentences out and then it seemed like it was blank and there was nothing else coming and I sensed myself sort of groping. And then with a little bit of difficulty you signed off. I was wondering if the reason that you had to do that was because …

(Side one of tape ends.)

(Jim channeling)

I am Latwii, and am aware of your query, my sister. Please forgive our delay. This instrument had its duty to perform. We, on the occasion of which you speak, were aware that there was the potential for the entering of the upper levels of that which you have called the trance and were attempting to generate thoughts which might aid in the recovery of an, shall we say, alert state of consciousness. We were somewhat hindered in our ability to accomplish this feat, for there was some confusion upon your part as to whether or not we were indeed maintaining a contact and whether the thoughts which were then barely perceivable to you were ours or yours as you became somewhat concerned and confused. But we were then able to grasp the channel, shall we say, and give our normal ending while attempting to aid your recovery of the conscious state. This condition which you have on a couple of other occasions experienced is one which is an ability that is growing at its own pace, shall we say. The ability to relax the mind to the degree necessary to enter the trance levels of consciousness is an ability which can be useful to an entity in retrieving certain information which lies beneath the normal levels of consciousness, whether this be in the sleeping or preconscious state or within the meditative state, and this ability is also helpful in certain kinds of transmission of thought.

Yet at this time it appears to be developing within your own being at a pace which is, shall we say, somewhat unpredictable because of the lack of conscious attempts in a formalized manner to aid its development. We can suggest that as you determine the use which you wish to make of this ability, and further then exercise this ability under, shall we say, supervised conditions, that it would be well in the meditative state when you are attempting to serve as vocal channel to monitor your own level of awareness, and perhaps periodically open the eyes and turn the head in order to awaken those portions of the body which are first affected by this state.

May we answer you further, my sister?

S: Well, I don't like to stop the meditation because of this happening, because then I, well, because then it comes to an end, and nobody gets to ask any more questions. So I was wondering if when that happens or if I should feel like I've lost you, should I just relax and kind of start all over again and see if I can get you back?

I am Latwii, and am aware of your query, my sister. We can suggest that this which you have suggested is, shall we be redundant, a good suggestion. We can also suggest that the holding of the hand by another might prevent those levels of consciousness which approach the trance state so that perhaps it would not be as possible to lose our contact, shall we say.

May we answer you further, my sister?

S: No, thank you, Latwii.

We thank you, as always. Is there another query at this time?

Carla: Well, it just seems to me that I've known so few people that can do trance and I've known so many people that lose contact for awhile and then get it back, and usually it's just a lack of the holding of the concentration. It's hard to do something that's that fine tuned. Couldn't an improving of the one point of attention be prt of that [which] helps, as well as the avoiding [of the] trance state?

I am Latwii, and am aware of your query, my sister. This is indeed a portion, both of maintaining the contact and in avoiding those levels of meditation which approach the trance, for it is a portion of achieving the trance level of meditation to …

We shall pause.

(Pause)

I am Latwii. Please forgive our pause. This instrument was distracted. It is a necessary portion of entering the trance levels of meditation for the entity to release the fine, one-pointed focus upon the, shall we say, sensory input. In the case of the vocal channel this would be the contact as that focused [on] is lost, there is the drifting down into those levels of consciousness which then enter the entity into trance.

May we answer you further, my sister?

Carla: No.

I am Latwii, and may we ask if we have interrupted, my sister?

Carla: No.

I am Latwii, and we would ask if there might be another query which we could attempt at this time?

S: Well, yes, Latwii. If I decided to work on achieving a trance state in a conscious manner, would that speed up the progress?

I am Latwii, and am aware of your query, my sister. We find that this would indeed speed the process of achieving the trance state—to work upon that ability would indeed speed it in its manifestation within your being. We would suggest that as a preliminary portion of this exercise that it be determined by yourself as to the use this ability shall find within your experience and then to use that as your foundation for further practicing of the skill.

May we answer you further, my sister?

S: Well, only if there are any safeguards that are necessary or that you would recommend.

I am Latwii, and shall attempt this query which is of necessity to those who would practice the ability of entering the trance level of consciousness. It is necessary first as one begins the practice of entering trance to also tune as the tuning is accomplished for the meditations in order that the effort might be of the highest quality in its purpose and direction. Then it is also advisable to surround your own place of working with a wall of light which may be visualized or constructed through the use of established ritual. We then can suggest that the actual attempt at trance be undertaken with great joy and desire for the purpose which has been laid out by your own design. It is advisable to have another entity with whom you share the harmony in your presence in order that any aid which should become necessary upon reviving, shall we say, or returning from the trance then able to be given, whether this simply be the massaging of stiff body parts or the talking that then provides a point of focus that you may use as a crutch or handle in returning to your normal conscious state.

May we answer you further, my sister?

S: No. Thank you, Latwii.

We thank you, as always, my sister. Is there another query?

(Pause)

I am Latwii, and we thank each for allowing and calling for our presence during this meditative time.

We are most happy to join you and are thrilled at the opportunity to exercise new instruments, and applaud your efforts. We can suggest to the one known as R that there has been great progress made during this initial attempt. Even though that progress has not yet taken a recognizable form within your being, the initial connections are well set and we look forward to any future opportunity which we may be given to further exercise your instrument. We shall leave this group at this time, as you call it, as always, in the love and in the light of our one infinite Creator. We are those of Latwii. Adonai. Adonai. Adonai, my friends.

Sunday Meditation
December 2, 1984

(L channeling)

I am Hatonn, and I greet you, my brothers and sisters, in the love and the light of the infinite Creator. My friends, it is a great pleasure to be with you this night for we sense within your vibration a dedication to the service of your brothers and sisters that is an object of beauty, so to speak, to behold. My friends, we of Hatonn seek to encourage those who choose the path of service to others, for it is our desire to be of service in the manner of sharing our own experiences in hope that they might benefit those whose path is similar to our own. To this end, my friends, we strive not to lecture or to teach but rather, as loving friends accompanying you upon your path, to simply share the nourishment of our blended harmonies of spirit and experience.

We of Hatonn desire to share with you this night a simple tale concerning a young child who chose to travel among others of his nation. The child of whom we speak was young, yet not afraid, for the child in truth had yet to learn to fear his other selves, as we know this is an acquired trait. The child then was able to wander fearlessly through forest, through city, to experience many new sensations, for in being young and without fear, the child perceived no distinction between himself and the other occupants of his world, both of second and third dimension. To the child, with untrained mind, the blessings of this world were shared equally by both second and third density creatures, although to the child, those of the second density seemed much less resistant to accepting that bounty which was their own. The child then was peacefully able to extend and receive that love which is available to and from all things and was able to travel peacefully and unendangered through the expanses referred to as wilderness.

Eventually, the child sought in loneliness the company of his own kind, for it is of the nature of entities to interact with those of common inheritance so as to develop the social memory complex. The child in seeking such interaction found instead bafflement, for those to whom the child extended love eyed the child with suspicion and returned only that which you call distrust or hatred. The child persisted, for being familiar with the fact that patience was enough to overwhelm and gain the trust of other creatures, felt confident that in time the rapport would be established and the sharing would occur. The child unfortunately had a patience of the soul that exceeded the patience of the physical vehicle, and eventually the child's physical body died.

At this point, my brothers and sisters, one might look upon the experiences of this child as a wasted incarnation, for the child was unable to establish any apparent communication or receive any apparent acceptance from others of his social memory complex, and in the passing of the physical vehicle one might be tempted to observe that the potential value passed also. But, my brothers and my sisters, consider if you will the blessings imparted upon a confused whole by the small part of the whole which had, however briefly, obtained a sense of inner balance. Consider, if you will, the effect of one such individual, however young, upon those about him. Is it not true, my brothers and my sisters, that the plant, however unaware of the source of its light will nonetheless thrive and grow in its presence? My brothers and sisters, if your awareness extends truthfully beyond that of your green accomplices on your planet, how then can your lives be unaffected by the presence of one of such beauty within your world or your lives however fleetingly?

We would suggest, my friends, that those who have ears may perceive those among you who serve in the role of guides or pathfinders for the rest, but we would remind you also that those who fail to hear or have not the eyes to see are nonetheless served quite magnificently by those who break the trail, marking the signposts for those who would eventually choose to follow. My friends, remember with pleasure and with love those who may have gone before seemingly unheard, for in truth the echoes of their efforts still resound throughout your spheres of existence.

At this time we shall cease to speak so that our brothers and sisters of Latwii might be able to perform their service, if such is your desire and request. We are known to you as Hatonn. Adonai, my friends.

(L channeling)

I am Latwii, and I greet you, my friends, in the love and the light of the infinite Creator. And we extend our thanks to the instrument for being willing to be nudged somewhat faster than usual and to be of service again as an instrument, for we are aware that our usual mouthpieces are overdue for some rest, and would like the opportunity to be the providers of questions rather than answers. So, without further ado, h-e-r-e'-s Latwii. Are there any questions we may be of service in answering tonight?

A: Well, Latwii, do you want to share any good stories with us?

I am Latwii, and am aware of your question, my sister. We are grateful for the opportunity which you provide us, yet fear we must decline, for our brothers and sisters of Hatonn work quite diligently to provide the parables that they generously share, and in this respect we have done no homework. However, we thank you for the opportunity and will consider developing some backups.

Is there another question?

(Pause)

I am Latwii. As it is apparent that no questions are forthcoming, we shall relinquish our use of this instrument, and look forward to opportunities in the future to be of service to those present. Adonai, my friends. Vasu borragus. We are known to you as Latwii. ☥

L/L Research

Sunday Meditation
December 9, 1984

(Carla channeling)

I am Oxal. I greet you in the love and in the light of the one infinite Creator, that light whose glory you celebrate in story and song in the darkness of your winter on your planet, that love to which you bear witness by word and thought as you light your candle and sing your song for the good, for the true, and for the beautiful. That is the glory, the destiny and the employment of your density, to learn this song, to learn it well and to sing it with all your heart. We are most grateful to be with each of you, and thank you for asking for us to be here with you this evening. It has been some time since we worked with this instrument. However, we find the contact to be efficient.

We would speak to you this evening about that which has been upon the minds of several, that is, the manner in which one uses one's memory. We see how easy it is to gaze back into the misty and distorted realms of memory in order to chastise oneself for what one has done or for what one has not done. We find this to be a significant preoccupation of third-density entities who have reached the level of attempting to account each for his own actions so that each is responsible for himself. In many cases there is a further distortion which is laid as inappropriately as a stone upon a rabbit. That distortion is judgment, the judgment of whatever deity you may profess as yours.

The first suggestion that we would make is that you realize, consider, and find, if you deem it proper, that you shall judge yourself just as you are now judging yourself. The deity implied in judgment, that is, the higher authority, is and will be nothing more than light. There are some thoughts which set up a vibratory pattern which causes an entity to be unable to withstand more than a certain amount of the light in which we greet you. There are other thoughts and actions which set up a vibratory pattern about the individual who is thinking and acting in this way so that a far greater portion of light can be enjoyed. That, my friends, is judgment. It is completely and utterly objective. The question that you may ask yourself is as simple as the question you may ask of your light bulb. Can the electricity generate thirty watts, forty watts, fifty or a hundred? You are an instrument, and you are to some extent tuned.

As you gaze back upon your memory, you burden yourself unnecessarily when you consider what you could have done, what you should have done, and what you might have done. We are aware that this is an easy exercise. However, we must inform you that it does not generate light. Well, my friends, you are aware that you have a memory, and that the Creator has formed you with a memory both shallow and deep for a reason. If it is not to judge yourself by hindsight, what then might it be? Have you considered that it is the present to which your memory may best speak?

There are too many things in most entities' experience of daily life. These things clutter the mind and cause it to work extremely inefficiently. Each decision that must be made in the course of such a busy day can best be made in the light of all the experience held in your memory and judged to a certain distorted extent within your incarnational patterns. Here is the use of judgment at its best. In order to use it you must slow down the tempo of your living. It may not be necessary to remove things, experiences, tasks, chores, relationships or commitments. It, however, is of extreme centrality that you remove the distractedness which you have allowed to come over you. You have the power of analysis, you have a great deal of experience. You know that you are now a seeker and that you wish to offer service, love and light. You can feel the light go on within you many times when you are allowing whatever wattage of which you are capable to flow freely through you to other entities, and yet you allow yourself to be distracted. This is not wise. It is for this reason that we must suggest again and again meditation on a daily basis in order that you may pace the tempo of your mind so that you create your day rather than reacting to its events.

Let us be stronger in our language. When you meditate, you are seeking the truth, each in his own way. That which you seek is like fire. It is powerful beyond your imagination. He who realizes light will heal. He who realizes love will bless. The gifts of meditation are far more powerful than the equivalent terms within your language. Many times in your holy works you have seen fire used as that which is holy. Those inspired to write those words felt the power of the gift of your self, your greater self that will come to you in meditation. The power which is potentially yours is such that you could indeed move mountains. You could indeed change your own life. The phrase "moving mountains" seems to be a cliché, and is used within your culture to describe just how powerful the energy which the Creator is, is. Bring it into life, bring it into your experience. Bring it into the circle between your heart and your mind, the circle your spirit makes for you, the circle which encompasses the universe. You can change your life. You can do it in a twinkling of an eye by changing the use of memory from hindsight to sightfulness of the present moment.

There is no need to repeat one single thing which you have felt to be an error. You are not a victim of your own behavior. You are not nailed to the cross of your own previous thinking. The original Thought of the one infinite Creator has the power to give you the peace of the present moment, the fullness of the present joy, and the discipline of one who creates.

In a tempestuous, bewildered and often appalling environment it is especially important that you know who you are, what you seek, and how you shall use your assets. If you believe that you are a spiritual being, if you believe that you are seeking the truth, then your assets are spiritual also and connected to the truth. How close to the fire of truth do you wish your life to come? In the ebb and flow of existence let that question goad you if necessary into the right use of your considerable powers of analysis, memory and will.

Oh, to have the faith that you to whom we speak now have. What a blessing you have, for to you all that is essential is shrouded in mystery. Only through faith do you understand that you are a spiritual being. Only through faith do you seek the truth and only through faith can you come alive and burn with an unquenchable flame. It is within your will and your power. It is not within ours. We refine. But you, my friends, you are mining. You are mining for your own precious heart. We wish you the right use of intellect, will, and faith as you search and dig and search again for the heart that lies beautiful and secret within you in the midst of this disheveled world which is third density.

I leave this instrument now, offering you our gladness and our blessing and our love. I am known to you as Oxal. Again we thank you and we leave you within the flame of truth, of light, of love, within the Creation that is One, within the Creator that Is All that there is. Adonai.

(Jim channeling)

I am Latwii, and I greet you, my friends, in the love and in the light of our infinite Creator. We thank you once again for allowing us to join you this evening during your meditation. We would hope that our humble service might be of some aid if there are queries which we might attempt this evening. May we begin with the first query?

L: Well, since no one's rushing for first place. Latwii, with the understanding that you do not want to prejudice our actions in any direction, could you give an estimate of what the likely future courses are for this group, particularly in areas of shared work, living arrangements, something along that nature, including the meditations and the Ra material?

I am Latwii, and am aware of your query, my brother. We find that this group has before it a great variety of possibilities. We see that within the heart of this particular group there is the great desire to continue with these meditations which have been ongoing for a large portion of what you call time. We can see a great weaving of entities in and out, delivering and taking many blessings. The tapestry which is the potential completed masterpiece is one of great beauty. The attempt to seek truth and to share that truth, that journey, is the binding force of this group. How precisely this force shall manifest within your experiential illusion is a function of many variables, shall we say. Each entity has within its being the desire to serve. Each entity has those lessons and abilities which are the resources upon which it shall draw. Each entity also has those, shall we say, limitations which shall line the environment in which it is able to provide its services and is able to share its abilities.

As you have correctly surmised, we cannot describe in too precise a detail the possibilities which this group may follow or investigate as a group, for this group has such a desire to serve that it might take our words and add too heavy a burden of weight to them. We can see that whether this group functions in a shared living arrangement or in the arrangement which now is in existence, the possibilities for enhancing individual and group awareness and union with all are quite, quite pronounced.

May we answer you further, my brother?

L: No, thank you. You've given me quite a bit to ponder. I appreciate that.

I am Latwii, and we thank you, my brother, for the attempt to shine a light into a future which seems somewhat murky and undefined.

May we attempt another query at this time?

Carla: I've noticed that spiritual communities are almost always in community, that is, when people gather for spiritual reason, often they also come into community. Is there an intrinsic reason for that other than the practical reason for living closely enough together to share goods?

I am Latwii, and am aware of your query, my sister. We find that to generalize as to the reasons why various groups become groups is an exercise which has limitations as to accuracy. We can see that many groups join in order that the resources which are available might be enhanced for the use of each within the group. It is much easier, for example, to utilize one vehicle for transportation among many entities than it is for each entity to find the means whereby it shall have its own vehicle. There are entities which thrive within the environment shared by many. Such entities are of a nature which is outgoing and of a, shall we say, gregarious bent. These entities find it quite natural and a quite happy means of sharing whereby many come together for a purpose. This purpose, when of a spiritual nature, then, is enhanced in its dissemination, shall we say. There are entities which are less able to function within such an environment and are more likely to find means of shining a light by, shall we say, offering as individual entities. The sharing within a larger group then becomes that which is more periodic than continual.

There are many, many groups upon your sphere at this time which have gathered in order that the, shall we say, lessons and missions of the incarnation might be accomplished in a fashion which is in accordance with preincarnative agreements, as we see you have come to call such arrangements. These entities, therefore, follow a path which has been somewhat laid out before them and follow this path as individuals, and find themselves within an environment in which others have also come, though by individual paths now find themselves within a shared community of ideas. It would seem to many such entities that the concept of joining within a group has suddenly sprung upon them, whereas in actuality, each portion of the journey has been carefully planned, and each portion then unfolds as planned.

We, as we began this query, feel that our description of the means whereby groups become groups is a description which cannot include the great varieties of intentions and designs which the individuals comprising such groups bring as the motivation for such formations. Therefore, we beg your forgiveness for our inability to complete a survey of such a great gathering of souls as now is in progress upon your particular sphere.

May we attempt further response, my sister?

Carla: Yes, because you didn't get at what I really intended, although it was interesting. Are you familiar with groups like that of Gethsemane or a cloistered religious community? I'll take it that you are because the instrument is. What I'm interested in, what's interested me before this, is the laying aside of the life entirely for the purpose of prayer, meditation, worship, adoration of the Creator, which is basically what cloistered people do, and what the people down at Gethsemane do, the difference between them being that they have various means of making a livelihood for themselves, and I think Gethsemane supports itself by making cheeses and other agricultural products. I think the cloistered nuns here in Louisville make their living by doing needlework and things for churches. That has always interested me, and since L asked the question, I just thought that I'd ask it, you know, what is it? Is there something in that situation that is more efficient a way to worship or to seek than the individual path? Do you see what I'm asking now? More a general principle than a survey of possibilities for us. I was off into abstractions there, still am.

I am Latwii, and feel that we have a better grasp of your query now, my sister. Within the field of the abstract, we do not believe that we can improve upon two sayings which are somewhat familiar to this group, the first being that "Birds of a feather do indeed flock together," that when the desire is present to glorify the one Creator with each portion of one's existence, then there is a power within the entity which brings it together with those of a similar vibration of seeking. The second quotation, shall we say, is of those known to this group as Ra and is a, shall we say, somewhat more noble statement of the first query, that being, "When those of like mind together seek they shall far more surely find."

There is a great motivating force within each portion of the Creator to know that self as the Creator and the Creator as the self. When the conscious seeking entity has brought itself in touch with this force in a sufficient degree, then it is as though the entity were moved by the power of its own seeking, and moved within the realm which shall be the most, shall we say, nurturing for the nature of the entity. When an entity desires to give its entire being to the glorification of the one Creator, it is difficult to continue those daily practices which …

(Side one of tape ends.)

(Jim channeling)

I am Latwii, and we shall continue. It is, therefore, easier for many entities of such a great desire to seek and glorify the one Creator to come together and provide each with the ability to physically survive within your illusion by making a portion of the day available to the, shall we say, mundane pursuits, thereby freeing the greater portion of the day of each for that purpose which each has joined to realize.

May we answer you further, my sister?

Carla: No, thank you.

I am Latwii, and we thank you, my sister. Is there another query at this time?

L: Yes, of a very vague sort of nature. Generally speaking, each situation has either a good side or bad side, strong side or weak side, depending on your personal viewpoint. We tend, I believe, to regard living together in a group as being an advantageous situation due to our own bias in believing that our greatest advancement could possibly occur in living and serving in a group, and we all, being scattered around this area, find some disadvantage in that situation, be it extra travel time, the inconvenience, whatever, but it would seem to me that there is probably a good side to that too, a strong point that I'm overlooking somehow. Could you speak of this area please?

I am Latwii, and am aware of your query, my brother. We, in examining this area of discussion, feel that there are those points which are quite obvious to those seeking a group experience, that being that each entity within such a group brings a unique set of perceptions, abilities, desires and outlook for the future, shall we say. Within such a richness of resources, the possibilities for group and individual experience and enhancement of awareness are quite propitious. However, each situation, as you have noted, is colored with the light and the dark. Whether one portion will be seen by any entity as light or dark is a function of that entity's own unique perception. For example, the great variety of resources that many entities would bring to a group experience might be seen by one particular entity as being the most happy of circumstances, in which a great force of creativity was in motion and merely needed to be focused in order that great work might be done. Upon the other side of the coin, another entity may see that such a great variety of resources might be the greatest stumbling block standing in the way of such a great work, for how could focus be achieved with so many wishing to go in so many directions?

The experience which results from such an interaction is the great virtue of your illusion, for it is the mingling and acceptance of many diverse points of view which allows the perception of the one Creator to expand that is more important than the supposed products or great works achieved. In the attempt at reconciling those differences which seem to separate one from another the greatest work of all is accomplished. The portions of the Creator come to see that the One exists in each and in all, and thereby there is the movement of the mind from the lesser to the greater point of view where acceptance now reaches with a wider span of awareness than previously it was able to reach.

May we attempt another query or respond in greater detail, my brother?

L: No, let me sit on that one for awhile and look at it. Thank you for your help.

I am Latwii, and we thank you, my brother. Is there another query at this time?

Carla: Just a confirmation. Just listening to everything that's gone on it seems to me that what you're saying is we have our choice of how to serve others and how to proceed in our own spiritual evolution, and the times when a community instead of a family, a smaller unit, are better, are those times when there is an overriding common goal like the worship of Jesus or study under a guru or something of that type, where everyone who comes into the community is coming into the community for very many of the same reasons, at least consciously. Isn't that what you're saying?

I am Latwii, and we believe that you have found the heart of our response, our sister. It is most important that the entities joining a community have a shared purpose. There must be some force which binds. There must be agreement upon how, when, where, and so forth, the nuts and bolts of the everyday existence as well as the underlying purpose must be agreed upon. There are many ways for entities to be of service and to learn those lessons which they have incarnated to learn. However the course is pursued, it is most helpful that it be pursued within a certain degree of harmony, each with the other, therefore the shared purpose and means of attaining such is most necessary.

May we answer you further, my sister?

Carla: No. I think I understand now. Basically what you're saying is people who bond well into a community are doing it basically as a career, as a life focus, and not as part of a lifestyle but as the focus of the lifestyle, and the reason for it is never anything less than overriding, usually having to do with the faculties of faith, belief and seeking in a very mutually agreed upon way.

I am Latwii, and we feel that your comment is quite sufficient unto itself, my sister. May we attempt another response?

Carla: No.

I am Latwii, and we thank you, my sister. Is there another query at this time?

L: Latwii, it would seem to me that the greatest weaknesses in the idea of communal living for this group or any group would fall into two areas. The first, facing inwardly, would be the inability to maintain harmony as a result of the fact that the nuts and bolts, as you put it, of everyday living tend to be a stimulus toward the direction of failing to appreciate one another, the idea that the constant abrasion of people of similar intent with people that you never really chose to live shoulder to shoulder with as you would in a marriage or a family, and that there's a certain grating there [which] would tend to produce a lot of internal pressures and friction. And, facing outward, it would seem to be that there would be a tendency to fall into the trap of the we/they type of perception, a situation where we are the enlightened, the elite, whatever you would have it, and they are the sheep to be saved, the lesser group, perceptions of that nature. Is there a third area that you would suggest that would bear examination? Or a fourth or fifth, for that matter, in evaluating each for ourselves the possibility of communal living at some point?

I am Latwii, and am aware of your query, my brother. We can make a generalization which hopefully has an application, no matter which direction is looked upon. As the ideals of a group are put into action, shall we say, then the test comes for each entity and for the group as a whole as to whether or not these ideals will truly be the governing force of such a group or whether individual preferences will from time to time make the entity blind to ideal, and then allow a movement from the ideal to a personal satisfaction. Each entity which has a lofty ideal also contains feet of clay. If such clay feet can also remember the ideals which formed the nucleus of the group, then there is greater harmony, whether one is dealing with the self, another self or many other selves. The ideals begin a group, the feet of clay continue a group. The feet of clay will then experience the mirroring effect from each entity, and when clay feet can continually become transformed by the ideals which are reborn moment to moment and experience to experience, then you shall see the continuation of such a group.

May we answer you further, my brother?

L: My final area, and then I'll let you rest for the night. An area I'd like to broach is in reference to the Ra material and the potential future for the Ra communications. The communications that have arrived up 'til now have been the result of the communal living situation. The implications that I believe I have perceived, some of the communications in this group since the death of Don have led me to believe that there is a possibility that more Ra material might be available at some future point. My interest lies in exploring the potential for furthering those communications and trying to understand what would be required, how far any or all of us would have to go to get to the point where we could be of some assistance in that area.

I realize this is a very general type of question with a lot of range to cover, but could you just give us some insight into what would be necessary or advantageous with that as an end product that we desire?

I am Latwii, and am aware of your query, my brother. We find some difficulty in successfully transmitting a response to this query, for not only are there great and complex matters to be considered, but there is as well a great desire that we have not to be of undue influence in any particular direction, whether to seek the reestablishment of communications with those known as Ra or whether to cease such efforts. We in our response must be most general though we have upon a previous occasion spoken to some length concerning the efforts which would be necessary should the decision be made to attempt to reestablish such contact.

We find that the nature of that particular contact is one which is most delicate and most powerful. It is not a type of experience or sharing which one can enter into lightly. It is one which requires the most dedicated of efforts, a dedication yet with a lightness of dedication which does not require certain outcomes. We find that this particular group, though great in desire to be of service, would have a most delicate and lengthy journey to travel should such efforts be made in this attempt, and each entity then must look within its own being in order to find that purity of dedication which would be necessary. The most rigorous honesty is recommended, and we can see that each entity begins with such.

We beg the forgiveness of each present for seeming to speak in riddles, but at this time that is our lot, for this is not a simple matter and we would not wish to guide overly much in any particular direction.

May we attempt further response, my brother?

L: Yes. I can understand your reluctance to speak in a manner which may be construed as instruction or influencing. At the same time, each of us who would be interested in stepping upon the path you have discussed is going to have to make a decision every day with every step on that path as to whether or not to continue to follow it. Is it possible for you without undue influence to anyone to simply suggest a first step along that path so that in knowing where we're going and knowing where the path leads, those who would choose to set a first step on it might at least know where to step so as to determine whether they want to continue to follow the path or not get on it at all at this point?

I am Latwii, and am aware of your query, my brother. We may suggest that the first step of any such path is the consideration of that step. Look ye to your own being that ye might see what motivations are within, what possibilities lie before. We cannot be more specific. This is a journey which is of necessity chosen step-by-step and fashioned by the free will of the traveler.

May we answer you further, my brother?

L: No, you've given me enough to work with there. I'd like to speak to more of this in the future but for now that'll suffice for me. Thank you.

I am Latwii, and we thank you, my brother. Is there another query at this time?

(Pause)

I am Latwii, and we find that for the moment we have exhausted those queries which each has so generously offered for our humble attempt at service this evening. We cannot thank each enough for allowing us to share our beingness with your group this evening. It is an honor which we of Latwii value more than words can speak. We shall leave you at this time upon the winds of change but as well on the sureness of the stepping of the foot within those realms of love and light which create all that is and undergird each step upon each path.

We are known to you as Latwii, and we leave you, my friends, in that love and light. Adonai. Adonai vasu borragus.

L/L Research

L/L Research is a subsidiary of Rock Creek Research & Development Laboratories, Inc.

P.O. Box 5195
Louisville, KY 40255-0195

www.llresearch.org

Rock Creek is a non-profit corporation dedicated to discovering and sharing information which may aid in the spiritual evolution of humankind.

ABOUT THE CONTENTS OF THIS TRANSCRIPT: This telepathic channeling has been taken from transcriptions of the weekly study and meditation meetings of the Rock Creek Research & Development Laboratories and L/L Research. It is offered in the hope that it may be useful to you. As the Confederation entities always make a point of saying, please use your discrimination and judgment in assessing this material. If something rings true to you, fine. If something does not resonate, please leave it behind, for neither we nor those of the Confederation would wish to be a stumbling block for any.

CAVEAT: This transcript is being published by L/L Research in a not yet final form. It has, however, been edited and any obvious errors have been corrected. When it is in a final form, this caveat will be removed.

© 2009 L/L Research

Sunday Meditation
December 16, 1984

(Carla channeling)

I am Hatonn. I greet you in the love and in the light of our infinite Creator. My heart is glad that my brothers and sisters and I are able to spend this time with you once again; to be called to your presence is something for which we can only thank you again and again, for it is our nature to come only when called and to serve only when asked. In your turn you do us enormous service, for it is in working with groups such as yours that we ourselves at this particular point in our own development continue our evolution by refining the compassion we feel for you and insofar as we have wisdom, the wisdom that we share with you. We are those who attempt to learn the lessons of wisdom. You are those who are attempting to learn the lessons of love, of compassion, of mercy, and so we would retell an old story. This instrument does not know the story, however it is written among your older works.

It is a story we would very much like for you to hear at this particular evening with this particular group. We ask you, before we even begin, to discount all those things which you may hear that do not ring true to your experience and your own inner knowing, but to use those things which do ring true, take them within and use them, as we offer them in love.

Once upon a time there was a young man. He was determined to learn the truth. He had spent his childhood and his young manhood studying both the natural world and the world within books, and nowhere could he find the metaphysical base for existence that took into account all of his experience and all of his thinking. Nevertheless, this young man was positive that such a work existed, for in his reading he had found traces of others upon the same journey as he, footsteps before him, footprints wearing down the stones of time, so many were those of the number of those who sought the truth of existence. He sold all that he had, and he was a wealthy man. He took his fortune and bought a large ocean-going ship and hired a crew, and he began an odyssey attempting to find the one teacher with the one body of teaching that would contain all that he needed to know about who he was and where he was going.

He sailed all the seven seas and many an ocean. He left his ship and walked toilsomely up many mountains on many continents, and one lined face after another told him a story. It was always and ever the same story, and that was that although he had a ship and they did not, that they were on a journey together and that they had not found what he was seeking. He had not discovered the final solution, he had not plucked the perfect flower.

Ultimately, he put his ship to anchor and started up what was considered to be a holy mountain in South America. He walked and walked and walked. After weeks of walking and many near escapes with dangerous animals and those who lived in the area and were not pleased with white men, he came to a simple, beautiful mountain tarn, a lake so placid that one could not see that it was not glass. How he had thirsted for such clean and pure water during his dusty trek. He took off his clothing and bathed, thanking the Creator for such a gift, for the water, indeed, seemed somehow blessed and blessing to him.

When he came out of the water, his clothing had disappeared. All the colors had changed before his eyes. There were gems in everything—the grass was now emeralds, the sky, the blue of an amethyst, the very far mountains, opals and the lavender and the purple amethyst, and brilliant and deep with color he had never before seen. Instead of his clothing, there was a simple white garment. He put it on and began to walk up a trail which he had not previously noticed. The trail led ever upward. It was dangerous and there were many times that the young man did not know if he was going to be able to continue upwards. But there was the trail. Someone had made that trail; someone had gone before him, and he continued, inching along bare edges, hanging to the sheer cliff, and finally he had reached the mesa, atop the beautiful mountain.

Upon the top of the mountain was a castle made of stone hewed from the mountain itself. Large portions of it were open to the sky. It was of intricate and beautiful design, arched and groined. The man he met there was so ancient that he almost seemed to be held up by his robes as he sat in the lotus position. He held what seemed to be a large leather book in his hand. The young man knelt and assumed the lotus position before the old man. "Sire, I am a seeker of that which I do not know," he said. "I have come to find the one teaching that will inform me on every matter, give me surety and understanding in all particulars of the truth, for I wish to know the complete truth of who I am and where I am going."

The young man gazed hopefully at the ancient who sat before him. The elderly man laughed. "You are not the first who has come looking for such a book," he said, "and you shall not be the last. I have it," he said. "Here it is, and take it away with you if you wish." And he laughed and laughed. The young man's heart was in his throat. Finally he was to be able to have authority, to speak with authority, to know and to understand all the mysteries that had confounded him for his whole life long. He scrabbled hastily with the fastenings of the old leather binder. It seemed to take forever to get them free. The binder opened. The young man looked in it. It was an intricately set mirror that he beheld, bound within the leather. For a few seconds he just gazed dumbly at his own image. The he became angry and threw the binder back to the old teacher. "You told me that you had all that I wanted to know, and then you give me a mirror." The old man was still laughing. He slipped the leather thongs that held the mirror in its binding most securely, and he looked up at the young man as they were seated. "Young man," he said, "I have never known a single seeker who did not throw that one total and complete authority back in my face. However," he said, with a laugh, "I believe you can get those books almost anywhere."

My friends, it is not always easy to accept your own nature. Most of those who wish to be all that they can be and to seek all that they can seek are disappointed in themselves and find things past and present weighing heavily upon their hearts. Never does it occur that perfection lies within the very eyes that meet each of yours each time that you gaze in the mirror. It is a great study—the self. The eyes are windows to a most complex entity. And yet it is as simple as we have said, to the best of our own understanding. The final authority is yourself. You may find things which illumine, which enspirit, which enliven, which heal, which bind up that which hurts. But you will not find the unalloyed truth except in the wordless depth of your inner silence.

We ask for this reason that you meditate, and enter into that silence as much as possible daily. This is not a hobby, an avocation, or a means of relaxation, although it can be all of those things too. First and foremost it is settling down in front of your mirror. To gaze within the self is to behold the universe. The galaxies go on forever within the mind, the heart, and the spirit. We acknowledge the heart and the spirit that brings you together and wish you good hunting with that one original Thought which, although it may be hard to believe, is indeed most clearly and undistortedly scriven within yourselves.

This evening we have not talked about those things which are outer. We have not talked about relationships, we have not talked about service, for there is a foundation which we wish to emphasize and that is meditation. You will note that in the story there was a cleansing, a purification, the bathing in the mountain lake, the donning of white and unblemished garments. My friends, you must be able to accept the portion of yourself which has been cleansed, or to put it another way, which is perpetually cleansed, and allow that self the higher seat within yourself in meditation, for surely there are many small and unimportant details which will flit through your minds, many irrelevant matters. All of these things are acceptable. See them and let them go. There is a portion of you, however, that must abide in what we would call the kingdom of heaven, for such this instrument calls it.

Within this kingdom all things are true, all things are cleansed and part of you has never left that reality, or should we say, that far less murky illusion. Do not satisfy yourself with the casual surface self as you go into meditation. Call upon the self which abides with the most high. Call upon the self which is cleansed, which dwells forever in a place of utmost beauty and peace.

I am with those of Hatonn and I find the energy within the group somewhat low. Therefore, we shall terminate this contact but not without thanking you once again for the opportunity to speak with you and to share our thoughts with you. We are always available. Request us mentally and we shall be with you in meditation. We leave you in the love and in the light of our infinite Creator. Adonai. Adonai.

(Jim channeling)

I am Latwii, and I greet you, my friends, in the love and the light of our infinite Creator. We are once again most privileged and honored to be asked to join your group this evening. We thank you with a full heart of joy for requesting our presence that we might humbly offer that simple service that is ours to offer. We shall attempt to answer those queries which have importance for your seeking this evening. We, as our brothers and sisters of Hatonn, remind each of you that our words are but our opinions. Please take that which has value and use it as you will and leave that which has no value to you. We wish only to serve where asked and can only give that which is within our grasp to give. With that disclaimer aside, may we then begin with the first query of the evening?

J: Latwii, it's good to hear your voice. But the story that Hatonn told about a ship and traveling and seeking. This takes a great deal of money. Where would one acquire this kind of money and time to seek the truth?

I am Latwii, and am aware of your query, my brother. May we say we are also most happy to hear your voice as well. My brother, as one looks upon the journey of the seeker, one may see that there are limitless ways to seek the one Creator and to seek that which is called truth. One may, as the hero of the story of which you speak, spend a great deal of time and money, learn many rituals, speak with many sages, climb to the top of many remote mountains, and in general make a great deal of commotion in the process of seeking, and yet until an entity looks within the mirror of the self, the seeking has not begun. There is no amount of money that can purchase the sincere desire to look within the self for that which resides therein. There is no ship, plane or means of conveyance that can take one where one does not wish to go as a result of one's own efforts. You may speak with many wise and loving beings, and hear many words of inspiration. Yet, if within your own heart of hearts there is not the desire to look within your own being for that which you seek, all else is as nothing.

So, my brother, you need not worry about the expense or the time required to seek the truth. If you have the desire to seek the truth, you may do so each moment of your existence as you see yourself in each entity that you meet, as you see yourself as the Creator in each situation in which you find yourself. There is no end to the opportunities for seeking the truth, the Creator, and your self, for all are one thing. You live in that one thing as that one thing.

May we answer you further, my brother?

J: Thank you, sir. From what you said then, the self comes first, it is that you seek what you need for your self first, and then and only then can you give to another human being. You have to first seek self-esteem, and then you can only relate that to another human being, and that is what takes up so much time. Am I being clear?

I am Latwii, and we feel you have been clear, my brother, and we feel we have a grasp of your query.

You must begin with what you have in order to seek. That is, you will begin with yourself, and you will begin with that which is of concern to you. This usually entails, just as you have spoken, the fulfilling of the needs of the entity. Your young beings, those you have called children, are good examples of this process. There are stages of development which they pass through which require that they be given a great deal from those about them in order that they might be nurtured in their continued growth. As they mature in their years, they do not need as much from others, but are in fact able to give, perhaps to their own children.

You, in your spiritual seeking, begin as the child. You need much in the way of finding out who you are in this illusion, what are your abilities, what are your desires, what opportunities await you. As these, shall we say, more mundane concerns are met by your own seeking, then your seeking becomes refined through your own efforts so that you begin to concern yourself with what might be called the deeper concerns, the nature of life, the meaning of life, and how you shall serve and how you shall learn. Thus, you proceed as does the child which you have been in each portion of your life, continuing as an upward spiraling line of light to return to that source from which you sprang.

May we answer you further, my brother?

J: Thank you, sir. Are you saying that we should have rational values such as being an objectivist rather than being an altruist?

I am Latwii, and am aware of your query, my brother. We have not specifically said that one "should" do such and such, such as have rational values. We have suggested that in the process of your growth as an entity within this illusion, you will begin with such values, beliefs and standards. From these you shall refine your seeking.

May we answer you further, my brother?

J: But I'm trying to get rid of all my old habits and all my old beliefs, and you're saying that I have to begin again, start all over?

I am Latwii, and am aware of your query, my brother. We have suggested that you have undergone this process, and now as you continue your seeking, you shall perhaps get rid of certain values and standards or perhaps you shall transmute them so that what once [was] a value that had certain discrete limitations is now a higher standard that has widened its perspective to include that which was not included before.

May we answer you further, my brother?

J: No, that's very good sir. Thank you very much.

I am Latwii, and we thank you, my brother, as always. Is there another query at this time?

Carla: Well, I just had the … I fastened on the same thing that J did, only differently. I heard—I think I heard it—that he sold all that he had, and I was thinking to myself that maybe it's a sliding scale, what people pay for seeking is a sliding scale, depending on what you have. Because what you do is, you give it all, I mean, you surrender all of it, whatever it is, so if it's everything, then it doesn't matter whether it's a widow's mite, like it said in the Bible, or whether it's millions and millions of bucks. It's everything, so it's really the same amount for all of us that seek. That's the price of seeking, is that we, not necessarily, you know, give up our homes or our creature comforts or anything, but we give up putting them first. Is that right? Did I get that inference from the story?

I am Latwii, and am aware of your query, my sister. This is quite correct, for whatever an entity has in this illusion is but a pittance in comparison to that which the seeker seeks. The pearl of great price is indeed priceless. There is no treasure upon your planet that can match that truth which resides in the heart of each seeker and which is the goal of each seeker.

May we answer you further, my sister?

Carla: Well, now in the Bible when the pearl of great price was mentioned, the man buried it in a field and went and sold all that he had and bought the field, and that was a parable for the kingdom of heaven …

(Side one of tape ends.)

(Jim channeling)

I am Latwii, and am once again with this instrument. We apologize for the delay. We shall attempt comment upon the query which you have so graciously asked, my sister. The pearl which is symbolized in this story recorded in your holy work and that treasure which was buried within the field is that truth which is buried within the heart of each entity, for each is a portion of the one Creator and each seeks that source, that Creator from which each has sprung. In the seeking within your illusion there is much which is placed before the seeker to test and challenge the seeker's desire to seek the truth before all else. What treasures can lure the seeker from this journey? What promises of wealth can lure the seeker away from pursuing that pearl of great price which lies buried within its own being? The field is the entity. The price is the continued seeking for that pearl. All which is sold in order that the field of the self might be redeemed is the great variety of temptations that each seeker will encounter upon the journey. It is a journey which seems quite endless and arduous, yet to the devout that makes the journey, a straight and narrow path. It ends in a moment when that pearl is found and the entity finds that it is one with all things, that it has traveled a great distance and has found itself within itself and within all beings and things.

May we answer you further, my sister?

Carla: Just one question. Are you talking about things like despair and the feelings that we get that aren't helpful at all? Is that the kind of temptation you're talking about?

I am Latwii, and am aware of your query, my sister. These of which you speak indeed can be great temptations to lure an entity away from the faith that its journey will have an end. Temptations may be any lure away from that journey. Perhaps great wealth shall for a while, as you measure time, cause an entity to forget that which it seeks. Perhaps a talent that an entity has will become the focus of that entity's efforts, and it shall forget that it seeks the truth.

Carla: Now you're talking about regular old temptations like power and money, and I never have really related too much to those.

I am Latwii, and we believe that you now grasp the thrust and the breadth and the field of temptations, my sister.

Carla: Thank you.

Is there another query at this time?

J: Latwii, what's wrong with power and money, if used in the right way—as long as you don't control another human being?

I am Latwii, and am aware of your query, my brother. There is nothing wrong with any thing, whether the thing be power, money, friends, position, opportunity and so forth. The seeker shall find its path to be most efficiently traveled when there is one focus upon the traveling. That is what we have metaphorically called the pearl of great price. Although the aforementioned temptations or things are helpful insofar as they are means towards achieving that goal, if, however, they or any one of them should become the focus or the goal so that the goal is forgotten, there is nothing wrong with this situation, however, the seeker shall be, shall we say, somewhat delayed in its journey of seeking until it once again find its focus. We hasten to add, however, that even in the delay there is the great opportunity to learn, so that each experience an entity encounters might be utilized by that entity to enhance the process of seeking.

May we answer you further, my brother?

J: Well, can't one seek power and money and still be on the right journey?

I am Latwii, and am aware of your query, my brother. We do indeed suggest that such is possible. It is possible that one might forget what purpose one intends to use such for. We mentioned this possibility, for within your illusion such *accoutrement*s are usually sought as means and goals in themselves so that the deeper truths are ignored. This is the nature of your illusion. However, this need not be so. An entity which seeks to be of service to others in the positive sense and who seeks [first] and foremost that which we have called the pearl of great price may use any of these items which we have mentioned to further that seeking and that service.

May we answer you further, my brother?

J: Oh, you just blew my thunder, but I … I don't want to. Thank you. I don't want to go on with this any more 'cause you're, uh, having difficulty with this. Thank you, sir.

I am Latwii, and we are most grateful to you, my brother. Is there another query at this time?

Carla: Let me see if I can restate what you said so that J will hear it differently, cause I think I know where the hang-up is, because it says in the Bible, "The love of money is the root of all evil." And it doesn't say that "Money is the root of all evil," at all. It doesn't say that. It's the "love" of it. And what you're trying to say is that when you have a love of position or a love of possessions or a love of money or power or influence, those things, that means that you basically, you've stopped seeking spiritually and you've started seeking a god that is temporal, that is going to die with you; you're not going to be able to take it with you. And that's the delay that you're talking about, is that you're—because of your love of this money or position, you're just putting off seeking spiritually. Whereas a spiritual seeker might well have money, but if there isn't an emotional load on it, if it's considered as a tool, like a carpenter would use a saw or something, if it's considered simply a means to the end of paying the bills and getting on with things, that's not a problem, spiritually. It's the love of it that causes the problem. Is that what you're trying to say?

I am Latwii, and am aware of your query, my sister. This is the gist of our attempt to speak to this subject. May we hasten to add that we do not judge or condemn any entity which loves the money, the power, or the position, for each entity in each action is the one Creator seeking to know Itself. However long this process may take is quite appropriate to each entity, and we would not suggest that if one seeks these items that one is not a spiritual being. One is at all times the one Creator, perfect and whole in each portion of Its being.

May we answer you further, my sister?

Carla: No, thank you.

J: Latwii, sir, thank you for that answer, because I disagree with Carla. I do love money and do love power, but I'm also seeking the Creator; I'm also seeking knowledge, and I agree with your last statement. Thank you. No offense, Carla.

I am Latwii, and we thank you, my brother and my sister. May we attempt another query at this time?

Carla: I'm out.

I am Latwii, and we find that for the time being we have exhausted those queries which are available this evening for the asking. We thank each present for allowing us to speak and to join our vibrations with yours. It is a great honor to serve in our humble way, and we thank you with a heart full of joy at this opportunity. We are with each of you whenever requested in your meditations, and we look forward to each opportunity to speak as we have this evening. We shall leave this group at this time. We are those of Latwii, and we leave you in the love and in the light of the one infinite Creator. Go forth, my friends, rejoicing in this love and light. I am Latwii. Adonai. Adonai vasu borragus. ☘

L/L Research

Sunday Meditation
December 23, 1984

(Carla channeling)

I am Hatonn, and I greet you in the love and the light of our infinite Creator. What a privilege it is to be with you, to catch the source of light which your group is. This evening we would speak to you about light.

From the beginning there has been darkness; from the beginning there has been light. Side-by-side were these two created. Darkness does not comprehend light. So it is written in your holy works. Neither does light comprehend darkness. You live upon the hairline shadow which lies between light and darkness. Your illusion is that of twilight. It is especially noticeable when you spend more of your time with outside darkness that you are indeed an inhabitant of a shadowland. Yet on the brightest summer day, as the butterflies dance and the flowers move in the trees, yet still you are in shadow. This is your density, that density which chooses between the efforts to comprehend the light and the efforts to comprehend the darkness. From this point of view, many discussions which you have may be seen to become simple. In each situation there is darkness and there is light. Your choice is your own. In the darkest and most difficult of situations there is light. You yourself are a brightly burning fire, created and creating consciousness. You may create darkness; you may create light, and each thought and action will reflect your choice.

We would transfer this contact. I am Hatonn.

(L channeling)

I am Hatonn, and I great you once again, my brothers and sisters, in the love and the light of the infinite Creator. My friends, have you wondered at our greeting when we are privileged to speak to those who desire our words? It is through the light which you celebrate on these nights to come that such efforts are made possible, for it is the piercing beam of illumination that drives forth through all obstacles. But, my friends, just as that light must have its source, so also it must have its object. It is your calling that draws the light unto you, that bridges the void which you call darkness. The love, the light of our infinite Creator is quite literally, my friends, at your beck and call, for it is your calling that causes the light to spring forth, and it is the intensity and the faithfulness of your calling that sustains that bridge between your Creator and yourself. It is quite literally that sustenance toward which we strive, the sustaining of the connection between the Creator and His infinite parts on their journey toward reunification with one another within the totality of the Creator.

My friends, in your world you are taught to fear many things. It is not the most fearful of all, the inability to attain this contact with your Creator. Is it not for this reason that your legends which deal with fears and depressions deal solely with those facets of yourself which lead one simply to fail to call? My friends, the one whose birth you celebrate once said, "I am with you always." Therefore, my friends, recognize that your fears are groundless, for the light is indeed with you always. Your birthright is the right of choice, and your road homeward, my friends, is simply to choose to follow the light home.

At this time, we shall relinquish our use of the instrument, that our brothers and sisters of Latwii might have the opportunity to perform their services. But we ask also, my friends, that you remember that in our small way we also are with you always in the love and the light of the infinite Creator. We are known to you as Hatonn.

(L channeling)

I am Latwii, and I greet you, my friends, in the love and the light of the infinite Creator, and am quite happy to be here to share your Christmas cheer as we find that the intensity of light and good will on your sphere increase substantially at this time of year, and are always pleased to be asked to join you. At this time, are there any questions we might attempt to muddle our way through?

S: Well, okay, Latwii, just out of curiosity. I'm a little confused about where you speak to us from. Can you tell your location?

I am Latwii, and am aware of your question. My sister, the temptation is to respond in a flippant fashion, both due to the nature of the instrument and our own joy at being present. However, we will refrain from such and will attempt to answer more clearly. The location of Latwii might be described as a state of mind, in that our consciousness is our true location. At this time, as you are quite aware, our consciousness is very much with you, my sister.

May we answer you further?

S: No, thank you, Latwii.

Is there another question?

N: Is there an approximate age level in our years of your social memory complex?

I am Latwii. My brother, the passage of thousands of your years could be cited, but we do not feel this to be an accurate method of measurement simply because the scale against which one measures oneself, be it as an individual or as a social memory complex, consists primarily of a scale of experiences and growth rather than the passage of time, which is in many ways quite fluid and misleading. For example, the child in your world scarcely perceives the passage of time from one day to the next during the blissfully warm days of your late spring and summer, yet finds time forcibly brought to his attention when the prospect of formal education looms near on the horizon. As the child ages chronologically, he is more frequently confronted with time-significant or time-accurate data. In short, the young child learns to equate growth and experience with time rather than perceiving the fact that such an association is coincidental.

We would therefore answer your question in two ways. Chronologically our age could be described as thousands of your years, however, on our own scale, our experiences as a social memory complex lead us to believe our age as such to be approximate to that of a young adulthood or recently attained maturity as a social memory complex.

May we answer you further, my brother?

N: Thank you very much. Have you contacted other groups such as this in the last hundred of our years?

I am Latwii. The people of your planet often extend a calling that is of an erratic nature in that the understanding rarely coincides with the calling. However, the awareness of the nature or the identity of the respondent is in truth incidental, so we might answer with the statement that we frequently have contact but quite rarely are able to carry on a decent conversation.

May we answer you further, my brother?

N: Thank you.

We thank you. Is there another question?

(Pause)

I am Latwii. As there seem to be no further questions, we shall take our leave at this time, wishing each of you a lasting and conscious contact with your Creator. Adonai, my friends. We are known to you as Latwii.

(Carla channeling)

(Chanted, each repetition one tone higher on the scale, the last two times on the same tone.)

A-mi-ra, A-mi-ra, A-mi-ra, A-mi-ra, A-mi-ra.

I am Amira. I am with you in the love and the light of the Father. O, precious the moment, all glorious the hour, when first you are born. All that is old, my children, may now be put away. The manger of your light is ready for the babe. Now you are new. My children, my children, this is always true. Do not forget, but turn and rejoice. Peace.

(Chanted all on the same tone.)

A-mi-ra, A-mi-ra, A-mi-ra. ☥

L/L Research

L/L Research is a subsidiary of Rock Creek Research & Development Laboratories, Inc.

P.O. Box 5195
Louisville, KY 40255-0195

www.llresearch.org

Rock Creek is a non-profit corporation dedicated to discovering and sharing information which may aid in the spiritual evolution of humankind.

ABOUT THE CONTENTS OF THIS TRANSCRIPT: This telepathic channeling has been taken from transcriptions of the weekly study and meditation meetings of the Rock Creek Research & Development Laboratories and L/L Research. It is offered in the hope that it may be useful to you. As the Confederation entities always make a point of saying, please use your discrimination and judgment in assessing this material. If something rings true to you, fine. If something does not resonate, please leave it behind, for neither we nor those of the Confederation would wish to be a stumbling block for any.

CAVEAT: This transcript is being published by L/L Research in a not yet final form. It has, however, been edited and any obvious errors have been corrected. When it is in a final form, this caveat will be removed.

© 2009 L/L Research

Sunday Meditation
December 30, 1984

(Carla channeling)

I am Hatonn. I greet you all, my friends, in the love and in the light of our infinite Creator. It is a great blessing to be with you this evening and to blend our thoughts with yours. We especially greet those who have not sat within this domicile before seeking the truth, yet know you that no one is new within a circle of light. Just as a chain is as strong as its weakest link, so the entire whole is new and untried each time of the attempting to seek, as you seek this evening. This shall be the new attempt, and the untried attempt, not that which is stale or old, for you are not who you were yesterday, and so each who comes to this meeting is new. Nevertheless, we greet those who travel to sit and seek truth.

We are most apologetic that we are so fallible, for we know that each values our opinions. We ask you to remember that all that is said is opinion and not fact. We have traveled a bit longer on a long path, but the path still wends its way into the far distance for us and we do not say what we say because we know that we are infallible; we say what we have come to say to be of service, much as you would be of service to a neighbor who asked you for a measure of flour or salt. We offer you the gifts we have in humility, and we thank you for the gifts you heap upon us, for in serving you, we serve ourselves, and through serving you, we learn and progress far more than we could otherwise within the structure of our own experiences.

We would like to tell you a story. If there are pauses, please forgive us. We are working with this instrument word by word and therefore this instrument does not have any inkling as to how we shall proceed. It is somewhat more difficult than receiving concepts but each who attempts this type of service in vocal channeling must needs continue to press towards the goal of becoming a better channel for love and light or that which has been given will be lost. There is no point in a vocal channel's development, or indeed anyone's development, when one can say, "Now I may rest; now I may have peace." When you chose to seek the truth, you forsook peace, each of you. But you gained. What have you gained, my friends? This is for you to answer and to know, for each of you has gained something somewhat different.

And to the story …

The clouds had been gathering for a day, and the electric tension of the storm was in the air. A man and a woman stood and watched and questioned, "Shall I stay upon this outcropping of land that is so exposed to the weather? Shall I go safely inland where storm and hurricane can never touch me?"

We shall now transfer this contact. As is our custom when shifting rapidly among channels, we shall not salute you, however, we ask, as always, that the channels challenge us in whatever manner is best for each.

(Jim channeling)

Much thought was given as to whether the journey inland should be made, for it was known that storms of this nature carried great destructive winds and there could be great risk to life for those who remained in the path of the storm. Yet, within the heart there was the desire to face that fury which was fast approaching, for there was adventure and the zest of life within every fiber of the being, and, indeed, within the very air itself.

When the time for choice, then, came it was decided that it would be best for the nonce to retire a short distance inland in order that perhaps the best of both worlds could be enjoyed. Perhaps the storm would pass close enough to allow the feeling of excitement and the thrill of participating in such an event to be enjoyed without a threat to life and limb.

We shall transfer.

(Carla channeling)

And so came the storm, waves thrashing the beaches and winds whipping and flattening those frightful objects of nature or man which rear themselves from the plane of the earth. All that the couple owned was destroyed. Much else was also destroyed. The damage was everywhere and the storm laughed, for it was a wind that carried the cruel and merciless order to extinguish, to cleanse, and to remove. The laughter finally died down to become a reedy, slender whine, as winds fell and rains began to fill the swollen ocean.

We will transfer.

(Jim channeling)

As the rains fell, the couple in the chosen place of safety pondered the fate of that which had been left behind. There was much which could not be carried, for it was too bulky for transport and many of these items were cherished by this couple, having served long and well in the making of a home. As the storm began to lift and the rains also subsided, this couple made plans to return and to gather that which could be gathered, and survey the scene in order to make the home once again. In the pondering by the couple of what they might find, there was time taken to consider that which was truly valued, each by each, and throughout the experience of the storm it was brought to the attention of each that the love which bound them together was the most cherished thing in their lives, yet they also knew or supposed that they knew that even a life filled with love would need some material support.

We now transfer.

(Carla channeling)

Both became very excited as the planning began. There seemed to be so many choices. When their marriage was very young, that which purchases, that which you call money, had been dear and difficult to obtain, and they had felt fortunate to find anything. Now, times had rolled on as the wagon wheel moves in perfect circles along its rutted way, and they could do what they pleased, or so they thought. At each turning there was a discovery that the knitted fabric of their lives was not such that it held unlimited possibility. All building materials, all amounts of space, all whims and fancies could not be afforded. Choices again had to be made.

And so another storm grew, this time within. The energy of the storm revolved around how to disburse that of which each who earns their money is a steward. The couple had been tranquil, and yet now it was argumentative, for in the light of the spurious freedom, a freedom from all lack and all limitation, it seemed to each that all that was desired should be able to be obtained, that there should be no hindrance, yet this was not so, for even with only two of the Creator's entities, only two children of the one Father, there were numerous irreconcilable differences of opinion. And the storm laughed.

We now transfer.

(Jim channeling)

As this couple's life pattern had progressed through these many cycles of change, there came these times of difficulty, decision and disagreement which then required the balance of reconciliation in order that the love which bound each to each might be strengthened and ennobled. Once again, as the couple surveyed the damage of the most recent and most devastating storm yet experienced, it became apparent that another beginning would be necessary, starting from scratch, shall we say, and requiring that all which had been the portion of the couple's relationship be examined in order that the relationship be built step-by-step out of the strongest of materials in much the same fashion required to replace the dwelling and possessions which had been erased by the hurricane.

We shall transfer.

(Carla channeling)

"What did I ever see in him?" thought the woman. "What can we possibly have in common if we disagree so much?" thought the man. And they looked upon each other and did not behold love.

We could finish this story, my friends, in the way of fairy tales, by explaining that all was made whole and all was healed as each reached out to the other with the open hand of peace and sympathy. But it is more important to ask you, "What was the greater loss, the loss of every possession or the loss of one human relationship?" My friends, things are never what they seem. We realize this is an old and worn out statement. The reason is it is so worn is that it is, insofar as we know, the absolute truth. Your third-density experience is made of whole cloth an illusion. No part of it is real. Only that which comes from beyond it and manifests through it has a more lasting reality. All that you can touch and see and taste and hear and catch with the nose's keen scent is an illusion.

What has delighted you this day? What has discouraged you? What do you think you need that you do not have? Examine the questions pertaining to loss and transformation. You are about to lose that which you call your year. And yet you know, as moon follows upon moon, or you seem to know, that this year will be replaced with yet another cycle. You know, or believe you know, that your island home will rotate in the move upon its axis as it roams the heavens one more time, flying outward and held tightly from and by the great sun body which is the center of your celestial neighborhood. Yet when there are losses, when there is difficulty, do you see the difficulty with the automatic reaction of "auld lang syne"? Do you celebrate knowing the dawning of another chapter? We would be surprised if you were able to accomplish this state of mind on a steady state basis. It is highly unlikely that you could penetrate the illusion to that extent, and so we suggest to you time spent in meditation on a daily basis, for those things which you may count as lost are only those things which are yet again to be found.

The one original Thought of the Creator is expressed perfectly in your being. Not in an idealistic sense, but in the sense of here and now. Bitterness, wrangling, disputes, argument, debate and disharmony are all a part of the rough and ready perfection which the Creator praises with all of Its being in you and you and you. Each of you is perfect, yet each seeks the one original Thought. Each seeks the harmony, the peace, the joy that it has not or seems to have not.

We sit high and dry on a spiritual plane, for all has been made straight for us. All is harmonized in our experience. We seek the Creator in each entity. That is part of the dimension in which we live. Yet we are not uplifted thereby any more than you are uplifted by your inhalations and your exhalations. To you falls the drama of wresting the one original Thought from each storm. Yours is the privilege of becoming. The one original Thought presumes a choice, and each of you makes that choice in each moment. Does the storm toss you away or shall you find the center of that storm? When difficulty laughs raucously, shall you cower? Do you think your circumstances are more than you are? We praise the storm and we praise the calm, but we assure you that those who seek shall not be calm, shall not be unchanged.

We leave you in that one original Thought. That Thought is your birthright, and is your very being. You are love and light. There is nothing else. The love is expressed in your consciousness. The light is the material which your consciousness uses to create a body, a continuing set of circumstances and a created power that may use circumstances instead of circumstances using you. You cannot stop the laughter of the storm. Its cruel and mocking tongues will follow all who seek the truth, and, indeed, those who are deep asleep. But your nature, your birthright, your power is in that which cannot be denied, that which is from everlasting to everlasting. Choose, my friends, choose with joy, and learn to laugh ever more deeply, resting in arms polished smooth by trust.

I am known to you as Hatonn. I leave you in the love and the light of our infinite Creator. Adonai vasu borragus.

(Side one of tape ends.)

(Jim channeling)

I am Latwii, and I greet you, my friends, in the love and in the light of our infinite Creator. We are most privileged to be able to join you this evening in your meditation, and, as always, we humbly offer to you our service of attempting to answer those queries which each has upon the mind. We also echo the words of our brothers and sisters of Hatonn in saying that we have no infallible opinions to offer, for what we have to offer is indeed our opinions. We have also traveled somewhat further upon this road which we share with you as seekers of truth, and we offer that which it has been our joy to gather as our experience and expression of the one Creator. May we begin, then, with the first query?

J: Latwii, can you give me your definition of relationship?

I am Latwii, and am aware of your query, my brother. We see that which you call relationship as the interaction of portions of the one Creator toward a purpose, that purpose being that each should aid the other in realizing the one Creator dwells in both.

May we answer you further, my brother?

J: Does one—in a relationship does one person have to be stronger than the other or weaker? How do relationships balance out in that situation?

I am Latwii, and am aware of your query, my brother. We can suggest that there are, shall we say, no hard and fast rules in a relationship regarding whether one shall be stronger in some sense than another, for within any relationship of two or more entities one must realize that there are many, many factors and characteristics to be considered. Strength and weakness within any factor may be had by either or any party. Those within the relationship shall bring that which they have and that which they are, and share that with each other in the relationship. If one has more of what is called strength in one area or another, then there is the opportunity for the balance to be achieved by another or the other entity in another area.

May we attempt further response, my brother?

J: Thank you, sir.

I am Latwii, and we thank you, my brother. Is there another query?

N: Latwii, other than meditation and *(inaudible)* time, is there any, in your opinion, method of removing our own individual blocks?

I am Latwii, and am aware of your query, my brother. We can suggest that any means which one may devise for such removal of, as you have called them, blockages, is quite acceptable and useful to the entity, for the greatest, shall we say, magic that an entity may use in creating changes in its own consciousness is that which the entity creates as its own tool.

Let us attempt clarification. That which you feel within your being needs removal as a blockage may best be balanced or removed in the means which feels right to you. Meditation is a means which is most helpful, for it seats or registers the learning within the deeper portions of the mind of the entity. You may also utilize analysis in a conscious manner; you may also utilize moment-by-moment observation of your experience; you may utilize dreams and hypnosis; you may utilize the criticism of friends and peers; you may utilize the movement within the nature, as you call it, in order that the peace of your second-density creation may cause the more balanced alignment of your energy centers to become apparent to you. Each method and many others may prove useful in the removal or balancing of blockages, yet that means which you have mentioned yourself, that being meditation, is the means by which the learning which you gather as a fruit of any effort becomes ingrained and truly takes hold as a seed planted in fertile soil within your being.

May we answer you further, my brother?

N: The second density you refer to, is this the balancing of the chakras?

I am Latwii, and am aware of your query, my brother. We ask your forgiveness for the use of terms which may not be familiar to you. In our reference to the second density, we spoke of that portion of your creation which you might notice as plants and animals and the surroundings which are part of your natural environment as yet untouched by the human hand.

May we answer you further, my brother?

N: Can crystals be utilized to increase the power of healing?

I am Latwii, and am aware of your query, my brother, and we find the answer to this is in the affirmative. May we answer you further, my brother?

N: Can you explain what would be the best method, in your opinion, to utilize these crystals?

I am Latwii, and am aware of your query, my brother. You have asked a question which enters this discussion into a large field of study. There is much practice required in the part of utilizing the crystal for healing purposes. We shall give a very simple synopsis. An entity must develop some ability to sense the configuration of the various energy centers of another who wishes some form of healing. This may be attempted by the use of any type of swinging weight or pendulum, not necessarily a crystal, in order to determine the configuration of an energy center, whether it be blocked in normal configuration or be under or over-activated. The blockage then being discerned, there are means by which the blockage may be attended to. The crystal, when it is chosen by the one who would serve as healer, needs be that which is free enough of flaws that the light which the one serving as healer shall focus through the crystal will reach the one to be healed in as pure a reflection or refraction of the spectrum as possible. The crystal may be swung upon a chain held in the hand by those who are more adept at the art; the crystal may also be worn around the neck upon a chain so that it rests upon the healer at a point which corresponds to the heart chakra, so that as the healer does its own inner work of balancing its own energy centers, it itself becomes as the crystal and radiates that light within its being through the crystal to the one to be healed in a manner which manipulates or adjusts the auric field of the one to be healed.

We ask your forgiveness for moving into this particular area in some degree that is complex and does not do justice to the topic.

May we answer you further, my brother?

N: Are there any current written references that you could recommend for further delineation?

I am Latwii, and am aware of your query, my brother. We find that such a request lies beyond what we are able to do, for we do not wish to infringe upon your own free will and ability to seek and choose such references. For us to suggest such a source would perhaps be seen as giving this source a special kind of weight, and we do not wish to bias your choice in this area.

May we answer you further, my brother?

N: Is there any direction you can suggest for increased learning?

I am Latwii, and am aware of your query, my brother. We can suggest that you follow that idea or inspiration which comes to you as a result of your own analysis, contemplation and meditation, for you have those knowledges within your own being awaiting your own seeking.

May we answer you further, my brother?

N: Thank you.

I am Latwii, and we thank you, my brother. May we attempt another query?

N: Latwii, can you tell us something about the chakras? Do they play an important part in our spiritual growth?

I am Latwii, and am aware of your query, my brother. We may speak briefly upon this topic in hopes that we may clarify rather than confuse. You may look at your being, including your physical vehicle, as a crystal. Each of your energy centers, or chakras, as they are called by your peoples, are as a facet of a crystal which contains more or less blockage at each center. These blockages are your lessons, shall we say, in coded form. As you work upon your own thinking and perceiving and widen the viewpoint, you remove blockages so that which has been called the prana or the cosmic influx of love and light which enters your being at the lower chakra may pass through your various energy centers in a more and more pure manner. That is to say, as you remove blockages or balance distortion, you allow the light, the prana, the cosmic energy of the one Creator to enter and move through your being in a manner which promotes or allows the white light to remain white and allows your beingness to be infused with the fullness of the one Creator. When this process has occurred through each chakra or energy center, beginning at the base and moving through the crown of the head, that experience which many in your mystical traditions of seeking have called by various names—enlightenment, nirvana, samadhi—then occurs as the entity comes to know itself as that which it has been from before time began, the one Creator.

May we answer you further, my brother?

N: No, thank you.

I am Latwii, and we thank you. Is there another query at this time?

B: Latwii, if a vehicle realizes that they are possibly working on a fifth chakra, such as the throat, can it also be possible that they have missed the second or third chakra in the process of evolvement?

I am Latwii, and am aware of your query, my sister. This is indeed quite possible, my sister. Many of those who are consciously seekers upon the path of enlightenment desire with such great strength to proceed along this path that often that which seems lesser or more mundane in the work of balancing chakras is ignored for the moment in order to, shall we say, quickly pass to the more interesting and seemingly enlightening pursuit of balancing the higher chakra or energy centers. When this occurs in a manner which is unbalanced, shall we say, it is much as though an entity would attempt to build a roof upon a house which had only two walls. The foundation of each entity's process of evolution must be built firmly. This means that each entity must take care that each energy center or chakra is given the appropriate attention so that the structure is firmly placed upon solid ground and is constructed in a balanced fashion, each energy center or chakra being attended to as the daily experience dictates, shall we say.

May we answer you further, my sister?

B: Then your suggestion, Latwii, would be that this vehicle should return to first chakra and start again?

I am Latwii, and am aware of your query, my sister. We cannot say that any entity, having omitted any lower chakra, should then return to the first, the second, the third, and so forth. We can suggest that each entity may observe the daily experience, can analyze those moments wherein catalyst has not been well used, may note the difficulties, may note the disharmonies, may note any moment in which there was not love, may then take that observation and analyze the chakra to which it belongs, and focus work then according to this analysis.

May we answer you further, my sister?

B: Thank you very much, Latwii.

I am Latwii, and we thank you, my sister. Is there another query at this time?

P: Latwii, I've been recently studying a little bit about angels, and came upon the theory that we are, those of us who are humans now, are fallen angels working our way back to, I suppose we could say, the original Thought, and that angels or guardians, perhaps, such as you are helping us get there. With so many things for us to work on, I'm always looking for the ultimate goal. Well, I guess the main question, is there any truth to that about us being fallen angels working towards an angel realm and then another one beyond that?

I am Latwii, and am aware of your query, my sister. May we say that there is some truth in each theory, for no thing or theory exists without some support of truth. In this instance, we may suggest that what is true depends upon one's point of view. To many upon your plane and planet it would seem that the world you inhabit is indeed full of those who have fallen from the grace of the one Creator, for sorrow and suffering abound and ignorance as well, ignorance of what the source of all experience is. From our point of view, humble and limited as it is, we do not see fallen angels when we look upon your peoples. We see the one Creator in each. Specifically, we see the greatest of opportunities existing in each incarnation [for] the one Creator which each of you is to gather those experiences that would not be possible should you not exist as you do. You have forgotten that you are the one Creator in order that you can gain these experiences and thereby glorify the one Creator by experiences which are richer, deeper, more intense, and of greater variety should you not have forgotten that you are the one Creator.

We ourselves have, shall we say, a certain sort of envy for you that we share with all of those beings which you would call angelic, for in our experience of the one Creator, we do not forget that we are the one Creator, that each entity we encounter is thusly the same. Therefore, our experiences are somewhat more pallid, somewhat more etiolated and, shall we say, watered down. Progress of a spiritual nature, shall we say, in our realms of experience is much slower than it is in yours, for you exist and create love in a darkness, in a forgetting. This allows much greater evolutionary progress, for it is done without the benefit of the sure knowledge of your connection with all that is.

Therefore, we look upon you as those who have not fallen, but who have moved in realms not before possible because you have that forgetting which seems in your illusion to be such a great hindrance, but from our point of view is seen as such a great treasure.

May we answer you further, my sister?

P: Yes, please. Is it possible for you, Latwii, to enter our realm, since it seems that you think it is such a great adventure?

I am Latwii, and am aware of your query, my sister. We had portions of our social memory complex within your illusion in the capacity of that which has come to be called wanderer, those beings of other densities who seek to enter yours in order to aid your own evolution by their presence and to aid their own evolution by experiencing the great illusion in which you now move. They also must go through the forgetting process which is the great characteristic of your third-density illusion.

May we answer you further, my sister?

P: Just one more, please. Would it be infringing on our development for you to tell one of us or any of us if we were in fact wanderers, or are we supposed to struggle to find this out on our own?

I am Latwii, and am aware of your query, my sister, and we see that you have answered your own query. May we attempt further response, my sister?

P: No, thank you. I guess I'll carry on.

I am Latwii, and we shall carry on as well. Is there another query?

B: Latwii, we come from another state. We have traveled, as you are aware, I am sure. Is there—how shall I say this? Can you direct us to some place closer that has another entity from your density that we might speak with again closer to home?

I am Latwii, and am aware of your query, my sister. We must apologize for seeming so short of information of this nature, but to direct one's choosing in such a manner we see as an infringement upon your own free will. You as a seeker will seek and find that which is of the most helpful nature for your current needs. This seeking shall carry the power of your own desire, and, as the magnet, shall attract to you that which is helpful. Have the faith, my sister, that as you have found that which was necessary for your own growth in that which you call your past, so your future shall be populated with the same.

May we answer you further, my sister?

B: No. Thank you very much, Latwii.

I am Latwii, and we thank you, my sister. Is there another query at this time?

Carla: Well, if everyone else is taking a rest, I'd just like to sort of follow up on what J was—It was a neat bit of stepping that you did there, talking about how we find each other and accept each other for what each of us is. However, I was wandering if there was an ideal towards which any couple might strive together if each, I should say, both of the couple were intent upon spiritual evolution?

I am Latwii, and am aware of your query, my sister. The ideal which each entity upon your planet strives for, whether in relationship or in solitude, is the ideal of love. This is the lesson of your particular illusion, a state of being which words cannot describe, yet which includes an unconditional acceptance and forgiveness of all. This could be called an approximation of love. As you move within your illusion and within your relationships, you will encounter that which seems unlovable, unforgivable, unacceptable. When you can love and forgive and accept each portion of each entity which you encounter, then you shall be approaching the ideal of unconditional love.

May we answer you further, my sister?

Carla: Yes, just in my attempt to understand that what you're saying, is there is no ideal relationship? There is only an ideal attitude of each person towards himself or anyone else, is that correct?

Is that correct. I am Latwii, and we applaud your eloquent statement of that which we have attempted to share.

Carla: Very cute.

I am Latwii, and we are happy that you have appreciated our sense of humor which we have some difficulty in transmitting through this somewhat somber instrument.

May we attempt further response?

Carla: No, that takes care of that one. Another question sparked up out of my mind about healing, and I was reviewing in my mind all the healers that

I've heard of. There are female healers but the largest majority of the ones that I know of are men. Is there some archetypical reason for that? Is there a type of energy which healing demands which women are prone to be low in biologically?

I am Latwii, and am aware of your query, my sister. We may answer in two parts, the first of which may be a simple suggestion that your particular observation of healers has been somewhat biased towards those of the male nature, yet there is some substance to the assumption which you have made. This substance would then be seen as an archetypical reflection, shall we say, for it is to the biological male given the ability to store and transfer energy of …

(Tape ends.) ❧

Year 1985

January 6 to October 13, 1985

L/L Research

Sunday Meditation
January 6, 1985

(Carla channeling)

I am Oxal. I greet you in the love and in the light of the one infinite Creator. It is our pleasure to speak with you this evening. We ask your patience as we work with this instrument, as this instrument is receiving one word at a time, a method of channeling that is new to her, and thus she must learn to trust more and more completely to her own tuning and to our goodwill. Indeed, we ask each of you to become more and more reliant upon your own tuning, your own sense of how things are and how you wish them to be, for as you seek, so you shall, of course, find. The more finesse used in the seeking, the more pleased you will be with what you find, and the more fruit you may distill from the experiences which make up your life's patterns and tapestries.

Within your minds there is always the question, "Is there a Creator?" It might surprise you to experience the reversal of that question, "Is there anything which is created?" We say to you that there is that which is created. The next question is, "Why should the Creator of all that there is create that which is thrown apart from the Creator, divided by illusion upon illusion upon illusion, separated by dreams and fantasies and phantasmagoria of all kinds?" The answer to that question may be important for you to consider, for within it lies the reason for your being. The ethics of your being lie within other questions.

The reason for your being is very simple. You are experiencing, as we are experiencing, as if we were separate from the Creator. If you look out upon a vast bleak landscape, the skeletons of trees without their leaves standing proudly against the winter sky, the dead leaves scurrying along, blown by a bitter wind, you may have some idea of the creation without the created. All is potential; nothing experiences.

The Creator could have simply created beauty according to a pattern of Its own choice. This the Creator did not do. It is our understanding that our Creator is hungry for that which It cannot Itself will, and that is the fruit that you bear in your experiences. Each day as you go through your life within this density and this experience, you bloom a little, you send out petals of anger, forgiveness, love, kindness, jealousy, and a hunger and thirst for that which is physical and that which is metaphysical. And all these things are to the Creator as flowers, delicate and beautiful, too insubstantial to pluck, but to be watched with great joy. You feel joy and the Creator feels joy; you feel hope and the Creator hopes again. All things that you feel are gifts, are your gifts to the one infinite Creator. Do you wish to give good gifts? Then decide in your mind that which is good, but never doubt that to the Creator you are beautiful, for all experience is beautiful for it is done in freedom, experienced in freedom and given freely back to the creation.

Do you feel that you have made many errors today, that you have somehow gone astray, that your energies were scattered or low? Now you shall not judge, not in this moment, for in this moment we ask you to realize that that too is a gift which the Creator treasures, for all the colors of emotion and feeling, all the distortions of the one original Thought which can be developed by an independent consciousness are as blooming flowers against the bleak winter landscape of the uncreated. Gaze into the face of the deep, gaze at that which you might call darkness and that which is uncreated and chaotic, inchoate and about to be, and you shall see nothing. And then see yourselves—vivid, beautiful and lovely, as the vibrant colors of your personal feelings, your highest hopes and your deepest sorrows all brighten the deep. O, waters of the deep, we salute you, for you tread upon the rim of that which is a void, a void which is full of the uncreated perfection of the one original Thought of love. Yet, love cannot speak to itself, react to itself or even feel. That is reserved for those like you, my friends, and like me who are as yet partially unaware that we are the Creator. Therefore, we feel and we sense; we do, we think, we act, and those gifts are priceless.

Again we thank you that we may speak with you, and we now leave you in the love and in the light of the One Who Is All in All. We are known to you as Oxal. Adonai.

(Jim channeling)

I am Latwii, and I greet you, my friends, in the love and the light of our infinite Creator. We are most privileged to be asked to join your group this evening, and we thank you for this honor. As always, we hope that our humble service may provide you with some small aid in your journey of seeking the truth. Please remember that out opinions are but that, our fallible opinions. With that disclaimer aside, may we begin with the first query of the evening?

M: Sherlock, we have missed your good, sound advice. We'd be interested in any words of wisdom about, oh, some pending decisions—not on what to do, but how to prepare for those decisions.

I am Latwii, and we thank you, my brother, for your query, and we greet you and those others who have been, shall we say, absent from this group for some time.

As you prepare yourself for those decisions which shall determine the outer parameters of your illusion, we may suggest that as you seek to follow the path which is most appropriate for you at this time that you seek with a joyful heart and an open mind. This is to say if you attempt to analyze past the point of being able to assimilate that which has been analyzed, you may further confuse your ability—not to make a decision, but to listen to your own inner voice. We can suggest that you do that which can be done, however much or little that may [be] in the way of attempting to consciously discern how best to be of service to those whom you wish to serve, and how to provide this service most efficiently. Then we suggest that you give over your own will to the greater will of the one Creator which moves through you and seeks through your experience to know Itself. Realize that you cannot make what you call a mistake, but that each path which lies before you offers the opportunity to learn and to serve. To find that path which offers the greatest abundance of these treasures, you must, in the final, shall we say, analysis, give over any dedication to any particular outcome, for as you have sown your seeds as conscientious gardeners, there is a time during which other forces must have the opportunity to work with those seeds which you have sown. As this process occurs, you will notice in your life patterns those signs of the first sprouts. Begin then your watering with your attention and follow those sprouts and they shall lead you to that table which has been prepared for you.

May we answer you further, my brother?

M: Not at all. Very eloquently said. Thank you.

I am Latwii, and we thank you, my brother. Is there another query at this time?

Carla: I have one if no one else does. I wondered if you could give me any words of wisdom about teaching how to channel better because I know—tonight for instance, Hatonn was here and Oxal was here, and I was hoping that Hatonn would speak but the other channels in the group didn't pick it up. I mean, I think they picked it up, they just didn't channel. And I wondered what I could do in terms of encouraging the people that were in this group? Do you know what I'm asking exactly?

I am Latwii, and we feel we have a grasp of your query, my sister. We may suggest that you have done that which can be done. One cannot cause another entity to manufacture a desire which is not present, for whatever reason it may not be present. You, as one who wishes to serve in a certain way, may note certain dedications to how a situation may progress. It may, for example, be your desire at certain times to see the new instruments be exercised, and this of course is most helpful to those learning the vocal channeling technique, but it must first have a desire to motivate. The new instrument must work its way through the process of hesitation and even the process of fatigue. This, my sister, shall, as it has in the past, happen in its own time. As we have previously spoken to the one known as M, when the seeds of effort have been sown there comes a time during which the gardener must simply exercise patience. One cannot shove the water into the seed, cause the seed to absorb it, then cause the seed to push the sprout through the ground. There are others who have their tasks to perform. May we suggest yours has been well done.

May we answer further, my sister?

Carla: No, I feel silly enough already. Thank you very much.

I am Latwii. We thank you, my sister, and join you in a wonder-filled silliness. May we attempt another query at this time?

L: Yes, Latwii. Would you give me a numerical evaluation of the accuracy of my channeling lately?

I am Latwii, and we are aware of your query, my brother. We shall pause for a moment while we consult our panel of judges. We see the cards are held high. On the scale of 10, we see a 6.2, a 7.1 and a 7.5. My brother, fractiousness aside, this a very good rating, for we of the Confederation of Planets in Service to the One Infinite Creator wish to utilize instruments such as yourself to the degree which allows your own experience and means of expressing it to have a, shall we say, balanced sway in the message we provide and the means by which it is expressed, whether an instrument approaches this goal of, shall we say, roughly sixty to seventy percent of our, shall we say, input and thirty to forty percent of the instrument's own input. Whether an instrument approaches this from one angle or another, may we suggest the progress is ever onward to that fine point of balance. Your journey is one of retracing steps which have previously been taken and have been well-learned. Your current experience and expression of the vocal channeling is one which continues to approach this, shall we say, ideal balance.

May we answer you further, my brother?

L: Yes. I have in the past and still today experience some qualms about the idea of channeling, partly because of my suspicion that I was not channeling one hundred percent accurately, which I realize you don't strive to produce, but nonetheless would be an ideal to reach toward for a person attempting to channel accurately. The other is that since a mixture is desirable, there is an amount of responsibility inherent in adding my own salt to the pot. The fact that your own—I should say, my own personal dilution of your message or another entity's message to me has an amount of responsibility involved, in that things that I inject could potentially have a bearing on another individual's—their life, their perception of reality. Could you speak on this subject because I find that I'm uneasy with channeling because of it.

I am Latwii, and am aware of your query, my brother. We are most happy to be able to speak upon this topic, for it is one which is of major concern to all who seek to serve in the means of being vocal channels. We again repeat the theme which we have discovered this evening, that is that to give service the most effectively, one must eventually give up the dedication as to how it shall be given, and simply be that which may be called the fool, the one who becomes so open in the attempt to serve that one takes no thought as to how the service shall occur.

To attempt clarification, may we suggest that as you provide the service of vocal channeling, you cannot make an error which another entity shall use to that entity's detriment, for, in truth, there are no errors, and any word which you speak will have to, shall we say, meet a rigorous standard of excellence which is unique for each who hears the words. No entity will listen with total acceptance; no entity will listen with total rejection. Each entity present in such a circle brings with it a desire to seek the truth and an openness to listen, else we could not speak. Yet each also brings the filter, the biases, and the preferences for one or another means of providing information, and, indeed, a preference for the kind of information provided. You will speak those words which are most appropriate for those gathered about you.

You are a part of a larger pattern of beingness. Many have called it a synchronistic function. It would seem that by chance you have gathered this evening those about you. This is not so, my brother. You are here with each other entity because of a certain desire to serve and a certain desire to learn. As the magnet attracts the iron filing, each of you have attracted the other for this evening, and have attracted these very words which are now being vibrated within your presence.

As you proceed through your own attempt to be of service as a vocal channel, release when possible the fears and doubts which beset you and simply serve as best you can, realizing that your words will simply be seen and taken as guideposts, and will have an effect which is appropriate for each entity. You shall not be able to do irreparable damage, nor shall you be able to lead another along the path faster than that entity is willing and able to journey.

May we answer you further, my brother?

L: No, thank you. The answer's been very good for me. I appreciate it.

I am Latwii, and we thank you, as always, my brother. Is there another query at this time?

K: I have a question, and it sort of goes along with L's question. I have been involved in a group situation such as we are in now for probably six months to a year and have not been a vocal channel in this situation, and I was concerned earlier about also not having practiced meditation as I should, if I would have an effect on the group tonight. How would you rank my abilities at this for channeling and my meditative level?

I am Latwii, and am aware of your query, my brother. We may suggest that the desire to serve as an instrument or vocal channel is that which is most crucial in an entity's ability to perform that service. Likewise, it is true that one who has the desire to seek the truth has the heart of the purpose of meditation. Whether meditation has been regularly engaged in or not, it is true that meditation is a most helpful and recommended means of preparing oneself for seeking in the manner which each in this group this evening seeks. We might suggest that the very fact we are able to speak to this group this evening suggests that each entity within this circle of meeting has prepared itself to a degree sufficient to allow this meeting to occur.

May we answer you further, my brother?

K: Yes. You answered part of my question, for which I thank you, and I probably should have realized that because, as you put it, everything's working. If I were to channel tonight, let's say, what do you think my accuracy would be as compared to in the past?

I am Latwii, and am aware of your query, my brother. We see little virtue in attempting to give a precise equivalent of your accuracy, but may suggest that when one has not performed a certain task or discipline for a period of time, one may expect a diminishing of the ability to perform that task or disciplining. Yet, if one has in the past performed such a discipline, it will be easier for this entity to learn again that skill, for the pathways of recognition are in place even though not frequently used.

May we answer you further, my brother?

K: One last thing that I've been wanting to verify for some time—I hope you can—is that quite often I feel myself talking to a representative of the Confederation, normally Hatonn, and we can carry on a conversation such as, for example, driving over tonight, I expressed my concern to Hatonn as to my meditative ability for tonight, and Hatonn said that he was making certain adjustments so that I would be more in tune with the group. I hope you can—can you verify that this really—that I am communicating with a representative of the Confederation when I do this?

I am Latwii, and am aware of your query, my brother. We do, indeed, wish to be of the greatest service possible at all times, and during this particular time we may suggest that for us to give you a positive or negative answer in this case would not be helpful, for the kind of experience which you describe we note has emotional impact upon you—it is that which you value as a means of seeking. Therefore, we cannot say what the nature or source of your communication is but can leave this determination to your own good nature of seeking, that is to say, the answers which you seek in this regard are within your own grasp and await your own seeking.

May we answer you further, my brother?

K: No. I understand what you're saying, that I need to challenge the source as I have always done in the past, and if the information gained goes along with my current learning and assists that in a positive manner, then I should accept it to be the genuine article. Thank you.

I am Latwii, and we thank you, my brother. Is there another query at this time?

Carla: Yeah. I'd like to ask about my meditations recently. I've been grieving, and it seems that I'm more vulnerable to feeling badly suddenly when I'm meditating or when I'm sleeping. And I wondered if there was a tool that I could use, a metaphysical tool instead of the medicine …

(Side one of tape ends.)

(Jim channeling)

I am Latwii, and am aware of your query, my sister. We can suggest that which you have already begun, that is that some form of not only tuning but protection be utilized during these periods of more sensitive experience of your illusion. This would be useful as you meditate and before the sleeping.

May we answer you further, my sister?

Carla: Are you referring to Psalm 91?

I am Latwii, and am aware of your query, my sister. This, in general, is correct. There are many such readings and rituals which you might utilize in this process. That which has been chosen is a quite effective one.

May we answer you further, my sister?

Carla: I just want to button that down. What you're saying is that that and other inspirational passages, those being read just before meditation and just before sleep, that that would be a beneficial tool?

I am Latwii, and am aware of your query, my sister. This is correct. Such inspirational passages and rituals focus the inner being upon the light which exists in every experience and moment. When one is undergoing a process of the nature which you describe as the grieving process, it is far too easy to focus upon the darker side of the illusion which also exists in every experience and every moment. This focus then serves as a doorway or opening to the more negative portions of the creation which then allows your experience to be of a darker and a heavier nature. The inspirational readings and rituals, therefore, do not allow such openings and focus one's attention upon the light which is ever present.

May we answer you further, my sister?

Carla: Yes. Just on the meaning of one word: ritual. The ritual that we have been doing, the calling of the archangels and the drawing of the star, that was a ritual. And the only other ritual that I know of personally is the ritual involved with my church, morning prayer, evening prayer, some sort of service like that. To which were you referring? The former? That would be my guess.

I am Latwii, and am aware of your query, my sister. Our use of the word "ritual" was more general than you suppose. Our use of the word was intended to convey the concept of repeating certain words and actions for the purpose of inspiration. The ritual could simply be the reading of the words, could also include any of the activities or patterns of behavior which you have mentioned and could include those which you create yourself which are of a personally inspiring [nature] or nature which is light or jovial.

May we answer you further, my sister?

Carla: *(Inaudible)*.

I am Latwii, and we thank you, my sister. Is there another query at this time?

S: Yes, Latwii. I have a question. I was wondering if the magical nature of rituals—like that are done at church—do they get their power from the intensity of so many people putting that power into the ritual or is it more or less done by the individual?

I am Latwii, and am aware of your query, my sister. Any ritual performed by an entity or group of entities derives its power, as you call it, from the purity of intention or desire on the part or parts of those performing the ritual. This purity of desire is built over the span of a life as an entity pursues either consciously or unconsciously the search for truth. As the desire to pursue this search for truth intensifies within an entity, this entity then builds what you have called the magical personality, the manifestation of inner seeking. When this magical personality expresses itself in ritualized form, then there is the metaphysical creation of that desire in accordance with the purity of desire.

May we answer you further, my sister?

S: Well, you could just clarify something for me. In other words, if, say, a person had no real religious ties according to a recognized religion, and this person had a high degree of purity, and were to sit down and make up their own ritual for whatever reasons, using whatever they wanted to use, and it wouldn't make sense to anyone else, is it the purity and intention that would give this validity? Does this make any sense?

I am Latwii, and am aware of your query, my sister. This, in general, is correct. We may also suggest that the rituals which have been long-established, whether by those institutions you have called the churches of various denomination or whether established by more mystical orders of seeking, have described or created in the metaphysical realms a certain substance or reservoir, a resource which may be called upon when the ritual is utilized. This is useful to those who are new to the magical pursuits. The adept shall over a period of time use not only those long-established and recognized rituals, but shall develop its own ritual which shall eventually be the most powerful for that adept, for it shall be most purely infused with that adept's own magical personality.

May we answer you further, my sister?

S: No, I think you answered me pretty well. Thank you.

I am Latwii, and we thank you, my sister. Is there another query at this time?

(Pause)

I am Latwii, and we see that we have gathered the harvest of queries for the evening. It has been a bountiful harvest, my friends, and we thank you for producing such luscious fruit. We shall at this time leave this instrument and this group for the nonce. We are with you at your request in your meditations and our joyful thanks goes to each for allowing our presence this evening. It is a pleasure which we cannot thank you enough for. We are those of Latwii and we leave you, my brothers and sisters, in the love and in the light of our infinite Creator. Adonai vasu borragus. ✤

Sunday Meditation
January 13, 1985

(Carla channeling)

I am Hatonn. I greet you in the love and in the light of our infinite Creator. We paused for some few moments as there are two energies wishing to speak and called by this group this evening. The ones known to you as Oxal have bowed to us, so we shall speak with you for a while. We thank you for the great honor of being called, and, as always, feel very blessed in that we are sharing with your life patterns at this time. We find this group very beautiful, and we are most thankful to be able to share our humble thoughts. We shall tell you a small story this evening. We must thank the instrument known as Carla for the opportunity to continue to work with one word at a time in the way of transmission. It is a more difficult kind of channeling, but we feel it will aid in this instrument's service to the one infinite Creator and be a way of clarifying that which is to be said.

Once upon a time there was a tavern by the side of an old muddied road. Those who frequented this tavern came to it by horseback or walked, never rode in a carriage, for it was not a wealthy tavern but the tavern of those who work hard and long for the little pittance that enables all for whom they are responsible to live. Through the years, the farmers, the herdsmen, and those who ran the toll upon the toll road came to be in such a habit of coming to this tavern that it became something other than a tavern, it became a haven. We now transfer.

(Jim channeling)

Many would come to this tavern, not just for the drink and food which were available, but for the certain kind of comradeship which those who labor long and hard for their living enjoy after a day's laboring has been finished. The means of joining in this companionship were such that those who came enjoyed the journey there, whether on foot or on horseback, with a certain kind of childlike anticipation, for this time and place of gathering was as a reward for the labors of the day. To meet with friends at such a time and place became a cherished portion of many in this area. There was a certain vibration which grew about this tavern as a result of those who came often and found a relief within the walls of this humble structure. We shall transfer.

(C channeling)

The vibration was such that soon the tavern became known to others who, though not a part of the local peoples, needed a time, a place to relieve the hardships in which they lived. These people sought to be one with those who were gathered. They made the tavern such a place of good feeling that the peoples of the tavern always welcomed those who felt the need to be a part of the tavern. We would transfer.

(Carla channeling)

One steady customer had a wife who was legendary for her scolding and her nagging, but at the tavern the man was never scolded nor nagged. He became someone other than the person that worked so hard in the fields only to be scolded upon his return. One person who came to the tavern had no knack for keeping his money, as he gambled and lost over and over again, spending what would be food for his wife and his children at the gaming tables. But at the tavern his friends bought him rounds, and he was no longer without money. Another one who came was ugly in countenance and yet to his friends he looked hearty, healthy and fine. Every trouble that one can imagine was spread among the common people, and as they worked all the day long they did not have the leisure to work out any grand plan for reform, any grand way to fix what was broken, to heal that which needed healing. Their only answer was to go to the tavern. We shall transfer.

(Jim channeling)

As the progression of entities continued to pour in and out of the tavern hall, there was much of good cheer which was shared within the walls so that those who joined there could drink not only of the drinks at the bar, but of the accumulated good cheer which was found within those walls. Each person there was aware that there was amongst them a power or force which each was a part of. It was not directly spoken of, yet within the heart of each there was the recognition that this place and these people were of special nature. Each there cherished this experience and looked forward to its transformative effect, whether consciously or without thought, for the magnetic effect that was born of this gathering in this place was such that it did indeed take on a form, an energy of its own. We shall transfer.

(C channeling)

My friends, those who gathered in the tavern were able to leave the masks that they wore outside of it within the flowing of energies as each saw the other without the appearance that each had manufactured to cope with the hardships that were outside. Within the tavern, each saw the other's essence, the love that was each and flowed between each.

My friends, as they gathered in the tavern, so do you gather together for … We are experiencing some difficulty in our contact with this instrument as he has not done this for some time. We ask the instrument to relax and let the channeling flow, and not to reach out for it. My friends, as you gather together and focus your energies together …

We would transfer as this instrument is feeling anxious and asks that we would relinquish the contact. We transfer.

(Carla channeling)

We are Hatonn, and greet you again in love and light. We ask your patience as we continue to adjust our contact with the one known as C. This instrument may experience more comfort as we slowly relinquish the vocal portion of the contact, offering of course, as always, the basic carrier wave of our vibration that it may aid in the deepening of the meditative state and in the alertness and focus of the meditation. We shall continue.

My friends, as those who glean and reap and labor long came to the tavern, just so do you come to such a group as this. You know that it has been written in your holy works that when two or three are gathered that which is asked will be given. The whole is always greater than the sum of its parts, and each of you being a portion of the group are healers of yourselves and of each other, for the light which can be offered from a group gathered in search of the one original Thought is that of very great intensity compared to the strength of one who seeks in solitude. The polarization is very much greater, which causes the light to develop a color, a bloom, even a song, a melody that enhances the wisdom for which each seeks.

Each of you, my friends, is that which is purely magical. Each of you has to some extent because of your work, your labors, your occupations, and your preoccupations hidden from yourself the magic of your own being. However, in a group such as this that magic is seen, each by the other, so that each may be healer for each, each may care for each, each may love each. And so a spiral of energy begins, glowing golden and white, and by the ending of such a group, whether it be a tavern, a meditation meeting, or any other place where those of good cheer gather with those for whom they care, it matters not the nature of the group, it is the fruit of such a group that is so healing. It is from such experiences that you may begin to consider your own magical nature. How could you without your masks be the people that you are at this moment, loving and loved, deeply one with each other? How could this be except that it is a deeper portion of your nature than your masks.

My friends, as we watch your people use the daylight hours in endless work and then use the evening hours in distraction, we become aware that most of your peoples do not know and do not care that they are magical and that they are capable of seeking truth. Yet it is so deep a part of the nature of each entity that consciously or unconsciously each entity will seek for groups which are magical to which each may lend his own energy, his own brilliance and fire and power and peace. Never be self-conscious or analyze too much the magic of such groups. It is only important that you know that you are at this very moment each a healing force to each other, each supporting each other, and at the same time as you sit in the darkness, there is a radiation which is a source of light for those whom you will never know, never see, of whom you will never be aware, but who are being healed in some way by the change in vibration that resonates in some way with these strangers. You are larger than you think. You are better than you think. Seek and know the truth. Look at yourself through the eyes of your friends and discover your purity, your beauty, your delightfulness. Never trust yourself until you are secure and comfortable with the sense of your own magical, pure, lovable and beautiful nature. Whatever else you are, you are these things too and these things most profoundly. In your meditations rejoin this group. The energy will still be there, the feeling, support, and the love will still be there. The truth will be yours alone, for each shall find his own truth with help from friends.

We leave you in the magic of eternity. We are a breath upon the winds and we sigh onward now. How blessed we have been to spend time with you. We leave you in the love and in the light, in the magic of the awareness of the one infinite Creator in you that each of your friends has. We leave you in infinity. We leave you in all that there is and yet we leave you within the small, small circle of your body as you sit in meditation. You are the universe. It is magic because you perceive it. We are known to you as those of Hatonn. Adonai. Adonai.

(Jim channeling)

I am Latwii, and I greet you, my friends, in the love and the light of the our infinite Creator. We are honored to be with you again and have been looking forward to this evening for some of your time. We are privileged to be able to offer the service of attempting to answer your queries, and we now offer that service with a glad and joyful heart. May we attempt your first query?

Carla: I have a question that someone who was reading Light/Lines sent in and which I couldn't answer, and so I thought it might be interesting to ask it. I understand that most of the contacts that we receive are from the Confederation of Planets in the Service of the Infinite Creator. Is Yadda, who we've heard from a couple of times recently, a member of the Confederation, and why does he speak with an accent? Did he have a—did someone from that social memory complex, if it is a social memory complex, choose to incarnate as an Oriental?

I am Latwii, and am aware of your query, my sister. We find that those known to this group as Yadda are a somewhat unusual gathering of souls. This entity is a group of beings which has achieved the nature of what you have called the social memory complex, the mind of each having become one with each other and the seeking, therefore, for truth also having become one-pointed. Therefore, these entities are of the Confederation as you have described it, and are desirous to be of service wherever possible. The nature of these entities, few in number, is that they have within your planetary influence enjoyed their incarnational experiences in those regions which are of the Oriental affiliation, and therefore when speaking to the very few groups that they speak to, utilize that most recent portion of their incarnation experience since it is most fresh within their beingness.

May we answer you further, my sister?

Carla: Yeah. Would these be those who came from Lemuria?

I am Latwii, and am aware of your query, my sister. These known as Yadda are entities old in your planet's measure of time, and their experience stretches back into your history before yet including that time which you have described as Lemuria. Their origins are other than this particular planetary sphere but due to the necessity for repeating the third-density cycle of evolution, they found themselves able to do this …

(Side one of tape ends.)

Carla: Okay. I'm trying to remember the history as Ra gave it. We're talking either Mars or Maldek then, right? I assume Mars, since the Maldek people are just now coming into third density proper. Is that correct?

I am Latwii, and am aware of your query, my sister. This is incorrect.

Carla: Incorrect. Okay. Well, the only other connection that I know of is the Sirius influence. Would this be they?

I am Latwii, and am aware of your query, my sister. We are afraid that once again you are incorrect.

Carla: Aha. Well, let me try Maldek.

I am Latwii, and we may aid you, we feel, by suggesting that the influence which you attempt to discover is that of Deneb.

Carla: Deneb. I don't know my Ra well enough. Thank you. What I'm interested in actually though is, then these fledglings have perhaps put in for membership, I mean, they're Earth's just beginning social memory complex, right? Or part of that?

I am Latwii, and am aware of your query, my sister. There are those individuals and small groupings of entities within your own planetary influence who have achieved the level of, shall we use the misnomer, understanding necessary for inclusion within the Confederation of Planets in the Service of the One Infinite Creator over the great span of what you call time and history of your planet. Few there have been who have achieved this level of vibrational understanding. Those of which you speak who have called themselves Yadda are a small group of such entities.

May we answer you further, my sister?

Carla: Yes. Do they have a seat on the Council of Saturn?

I am Latwii, and am aware of your query, my sister. These entities are as you have described but newly admitted to the Confederation and are not those who are of the Council. Those of this Council are beings of what you may call the eighth density or octave completion level, and are quite old in the, shall we say, membership within the Confederation.

May we answer you further, my sister?

Carla: No, thank you. That's very interesting. There are various sources that have channeled Yadda and various speculations about its nature and that is very clear. Thank you.

I am Latwii, and we thank you, my sister. Is there another query?

N: Although I have not experienced Yadda, I would wonder if they had not been reincarnated on Earth during the last 50,000 years if they retained, or have they just retained this Oriental accent?

I am Latwii, and am aware of your query, my brother. These entities when speaking to those such as this group tend to utilize the incarnational experience most recent within their shared experience, for it allows them a, shall we say, firmer grasp of the nature of your illusion and enhances their ability to utilize instruments who yet reside within this illusion. Their true nature is one which cannot be expressed in the language, yet when speaking they attempt to approximate this nature.

May we answer you further, my brother?

N: Is Latwii made up of millions of souls or hundreds or thousands or is there some sort of approximation in the total computation of the social memory complex?

I am Latwii, and am aware of your query, my brother. We of Latwii are composed of a great number of beings which have been able to blend the conscious seeking so that it is as one. We number in what you would call the millions of entities, this number approaching twenty-three million entities.

May we answer you further, my brother?

N: Are all the twenty-three approximate millions of the same density, and what density is that, and are they able to focus a single thought pattern?

I am Latwii, and am aware of your query, my brother. We of Latwii are of the density of light, the density numbering five, being two octave, shall we say, jumps or evolutionary cycles beyond your own third-density illusion. We are one in our seeking and are, shall we say, focused as to our desire to be of service to others, though each entity within our social memory complex is able to function as an individualized portion of this complex as well.

May we answer you further, my brother?

N: Are there any specific recommendations that you can make as to further our progress or remove our blocks or whatever seems to keep some of us from progressing at a rate that we might like to achieve?

I am Latwii, and am aware of your query, my brother. We look upon your peoples, each of which moves in a darkness, unaware that it is the Creator, unaware that each whom it meets is also the Creator. The lessons which have been set before your population are lessons which are rooted in the concept of love. There have been many what you call masters who have given you various disciplines, exercises and rituals, each designed to enhance this learning of love. The greatest tool which we are aware of is the tool of meditation which might be utilized by each seeker to look within in order that the source of all Creation might become known as residing there, full of love and light, unity and joy.

Therefore, we can simply say as many have said, that if you love without condition, you shall progress as a natural process of evolution.

May we answer you further, my brother?

N: For those of us who are trying and have tried meditation but haven't seemed to achieve that particular goal, is there any specific or generalized suggestion?

I am Latwii, and am aware of your query, my brother. We can only suggest that as you attempt this lesson of love and utilize the various means of learning it, that your success cannot be known to you, for as we mentioned, you move within a darkness of knowing. The true nature of your illusion, of your very being, and of the fiber of creation is almost totally unknown to even the most, shall we say, enlightened of your beings. Therefore, all that can be done is to seek with a full and whole heart and to accept that effort as the best one can give, and to look about the self whenever possible and to see not this and that but the one Creator. You must have what you have called faith to continue within an illusion which offers so little that is obviously the one Creator and so much that is, it would seem as obvious, not the one Creator.

May we answer you further, my brother?

N: Is there any way to hasten the removal of the so-called illusion other than meditation?

I am Latwii, and am aware of your query, my brother. The removal of the illusion from one's perception is a function of one's ability to utilize the daily round of activities as a catalyst for this removal. If one can look upon these activities as opportunities to remove yet one more veil, then the entity is most efficiently utilizing the illusion in which it moves, for your illusion exists in order to provide you with the opportunity to penetrate the illusion. In order for spiritual strength to be gained, there must be a force or illusion to push against, shall we say.

May we answer you further, my brother?

N: We spoke about crystals and their use in healing. I think that crystals have many other uses. How can we focus the power of the crystal for better healing?

I am Latwii, and am aware of your query, my brother. The crystal, as is true for any tool of the healer, is useful only to the extent that the one who serves as healer has healed the self. As you progress in your own evolutionary pattern, you in your energy centers become as the crystal, regularized and able to traduce light in order that it might provide the opportunity for one who seeks healing to be healed.

May we answer you further, my brother?

N: There have been many so-called healers who really haven't evolved as far as their illusions but in whom the power to heal seems to occur on a natural basis. Are these people more aware or is it just some particular power that they've been able to focus through an unknown source?

I am Latwii, and am aware of your query, my brother. This is a query which must be understood not to have but one or two simple answers. There are many reasons to explain why this or that entity may have what is called the ability to heal. For example, many entities have through previous incarnative work become able to do that called healing and have carried over this ability into the present incarnation, yet are consciously unaware of how the ability works and how it might be refined, yet if they studied this art, they would quickly gain in efficacy.

There are others who from time to time are able to clear, shall we say, their energy centers and provide the healing catalyst as a result of a great desire to be of service to a friend or loved one. There are others who are able to provide the healing catalyst as a result of work done in the, what you would call, sleep and dreaming states where it is possible to heal those injuries of previous experience upon a level which is not consciously remembered.

May we answer you further, my brother?

N: Is it possible for your social memory complex to channel healing to members of the group such as C and Carla at this time?

I am Latwii, and am aware of your query, my brother. We of the Latwii are, shall we say, not as able to do this as others of the Confederation. There is the entity known to this group as Nona who is quite capable of doing this, and is awaiting the call should this be desired.

May we answer you further, my brother?

N: How do we call Nona for this channeling, healing, whatever?

I am Latwii, and your call has been heard. May we answer you further, my brother?

N: Thank you very much.

I am Latwii, and we thank you, my brother. Is there another query at this time?

(Pause)

I am Latwii, and we see that we have exhausted the queries, and would now, shall we say, step aside in order that our brothers and sisters of those known as Nona might perform that which they have been asked to perform. We thank each for allowing our group to join you this evening. It has been our great honor and privilege to blend our vibrations with yours. We are with you at your request, and leave you now in the love and in the light of our one infinite Creator. We are those of Latwii. Adonai vasu borragus.

(Carla channeling)

I am Nona. We thank those of Latwii for giving us the opportunity to advertise. We have been waiting in the wings, and indeed are here as called. We greet you in the love and in the light of our infinite Creator whom we serve with our whole heart. There is no wound that shall not be made whole. There is no broken thing that shall not be mended, for we are one.

(Carla channels a vigorous vocal melody of healing from Nona.) ❦

Intensive Meditation
January 22, 1985

(Carla channeling)

[I am Laitos.] I greet you in the love and in the light of the infinite Creator. We thank you that you have called us that we may be with you and are most eager to work you at this time. We would at this time begin working with the one known as N. While we speak through this instrument we shall be attempting adjustments in order that we may bring our carrier wave into synchronicity with this instrument's own so that the instrument, N, may become aware of our presence in some way which will be unique to him as always.

Meanwhile, we would like to speak a bit about channeling and about being an instrument. There is a saying among your peoples, "Nothing ventured, nothing gained." This is extraordinarily true of metaphysical work of all kinds. The one who takes no risk is the one who will not advance. The more carefully one guards one's gifts, the less that gift will come to mean and the less good that gift will come to offer. It is as though as there were inflation in spiritual gifts so that it is necessary always to attempt more and more regardless of what has gone before. Therefore, one which has little must attempt enough that that little may become a bit more. One which has already had much must attempt a great deal. The responsibility for spiritual seeking is that eternal upward spiral. Seeking does not end. The road does not end. The journey goes on and on, as far we know, forever.

During that journey you shall meet those who are your companions along the way, those who wish as you do to serve, and with them you seek not only the truths that undergird and strengthen your life but also the application of those truths in an ethical manner so that the life experience may be productive, not in the physical sense, but in the spiritual sense, for when we speak of giving of the spiritual gifts, the greatest gift which you give may well be your personality, your character, the way that you are without any effort except that of continually repeating the search for a refinement of the truth. However, there are those who seek to serve in the manner which you call vocal channeling, and for this we are grateful for without such voices ours would be still except to the very few who are able to hear words that are not spoken.

And that is why you are here this evening, and therefore we shall attempt to continue with the one known as N. May we say to our brother, we thank you and we bless you in your efforts on behalf of your brothers and sisters of third density. Whatever the results of these efforts, your own intention will be bright and will shine so that those who see you may see through you to the source of that light that is your greater self, perhaps a self that you wish that you were but feel that you are not. This is always incorrect. All are perfect and all is perfect at this moment. That which seems uncontrolled, biased and quarrelsome among nations is indeed only that which gives balance to the angelic, lovely, kind, compassionate and saintly actions of other nations and other men. Things are not in need of fixing. Each entity is in need of finding and sharing the love of the infinite Creator. It is for this reason that all have incarnated. It is for a more specialized type of service that we now gather, and yet the goals are always and ever the same, to be one with the Creator and to be one with your fellow man. Underpinning all of this is the goal of being one with yourself, of affirming yourself, loving yourself, and preparing yourself for the discipline of service to others.

We shall now transfer to the one known as N, cautioning the instrument not to analyze. When a thought comes into the mind, the thought is felt precisely as if it were your thought. It is a matter of subjective concern for all new instruments that your thought and our thought feel the same. You must, therefore, challenge the contact, and if it stays, go ahead with it, meanwhile remaining in a tuned and disciplined focus of concentration, very much conscious, not at all in trance. Let your body relax and let your mind rest, but let the consciousness be one-pointed, as if you were attempting to catch a long thrown baseball. You catch the baseball and you pitch it again as accurately as possible. Only when you have pitched it and your glove is empty can you catch another baseball.

So it is with the channeling. When you receive a concept, say the concept that you receive. At that point you will be available for another concept to be let forth within your mind. It is this technique which we use with almost all channels, this entity being somewhat of an anomaly, as it wishes to have a more advanced type of contact after much experience. The type of contact which the new instrument wishes to experience is completely adequate to the delivery, explanation and exploration of the one message that we have come to bring, a message that can be said in countless ways, and each new spirit which dedicates itself to offering these messages thus gives the one message of love and light a new voice that is very precious. Again we ask you to stop analyzing, my brother, and simply speak those words which you hear. We shall now transfer. I am Laitos.

(Pause)

(Carla channeling)

I am once again with this instrument. I am Laitos. We greet you once again in love and light. May we ask the one known as N to relax and cease analyzing. This instrument has come a good way since our last time of working. The defenses, however, which a characteristically analytical mind has against the speaking of things not already known is most naturally a stumbling block. We ask that the one known as N continue to attempt to remove that stumbling block by relaxing, and studiously refrain from analyzing again. We now transfer to the one known as N. I am Laitos.

(Pause)

(Carla channeling)

I am Laitos. I am again with this instrument. We feel we are making progress with the one known as N, and would try once more to say one phrase. We wish to say our identification through this instrument. We shall attempt to do so now. I am Laitos.

N: I think I hear, "I am Laitos," but I don't know.

Carla: Okay.

(Carla channeling)

I am Laitos. May we say to the one known as N that one who channels is a fool stepping off the cliff into thin air. It is necessary for the preservation of free will that our contact not be unmistakable but be subtle. Once the first step is taken, subjective proof may begin to come forth. At first, however, it is usually the case that there is a great deal of faith involved in speaking the first few words and messages. We shall attempt once again to speak through the new instrument, emphasizing we wish only to speak the one phrase, and that there is no absolute proof that this is coming to the instrument. Once the experiment has been made, there may be much more upon which the instrument may wish to ponder. Again, we shall transfer to the one known as N. I am Laitos.

(N channeling)

I am Laitos. I greet you in the love and light of the one infinite Creator.

(Carla channeling)

I am Laitos, and am once again with this instrument. We are having to share this instrument's consciousness with the playful second-density creatures which you call cats that frolic about your feet. Theirs is a happy vibration and we are grateful for it. We are grateful also to the one known as N, who has made great progress this evening. Our humble thanks and our promise to continue working at any time that may be possible. We shall pause at this time before the question and answer period so that this instrument's mind may be put to rest concerning the rustling of various papers of unknown origin. I am Laitos.

(Pause)

(Carla channeling)

I am Laitos. We apologize for the inconveniences. However, my friends, those who speak in love and light must needs do so in a dark world where there are many distractions. Such distractions as those of the playful kittens, therefore, are welcome in that they are good teaching tools for circumstances are not always the very best. Indeed, they are usually far from the best. And yet, somehow, there are heroes and saints, healers and those who love with purity everywhere one turns, even in this dark world.

We shall transfer now to the one known as Jim. I am Laitos.

(Jim channeling)

I am Laitos, and greet you once again in love and light. We would now open this session to any questions which those present might wish to ask. May we attempt any queries at this time?

N: Are there others that take many sessions before they can adequately channel?

I am Laitos, and am aware of your query, my brother. We might say that your progress is quite good. We have worked with many instruments over a long period of what you call time and have noted that your experience is quite normal, and we are most pleased that you have been able to receive our vibration and speak our identification. Many there are who take a good deal longer to accomplish these feats.

May we answer you further, my brother?

N: The message just seems to be there, but I'm not really sure that it's there or whether I'm repeating the introduction that I'm expected to be repeating. It's sort of an unusual consideration for me.

I am Laitos, and we feel that within your comment there is a query which we might also comment upon. Your perception of our introduction and our vibration is quite accurate, for though we are indeed quite real, the reality of the metaphysical realm is a reality which is not tangible or provable within your own manifested material reality. Your senses, your perceptions, and your thoughts are all focused upon a world which might be held and touched and seen and tasted and smelled. Our reality, on the other hand, is that which requires a sense quite beyond any of your five common senses, but we must operate as best we can through those means of perception which are at your disposal.

The most effective manner in which we might contact those of your peoples is in this manner now being utilized, that is the mind-to-mind thought transfer. In this manner of communication we speak our thoughts, we send our concepts, and they are received in your mind in much the same manner as your own thoughts become apparent to you. If you will take but a moment to consider the phenomenon of your own thinking and speaking, you will discover that at each moment in which you partake of speech you are channeling from some portion of your being thoughts of a nebulous nature which you attempt to translate into words in order to communicate with another entity. You are not consciously aware of the source of these thoughts. You do not know the next complete sentence which you will speak. In much the same manner, we contact your mind and transfer our thoughts. You will not be able to discern a great difference between our thoughts and yours, thus the concept of the fool who steps into space, unknowing of whether there shall be a place to put the foot, unknowing as to whether the next word shall make sense when viewed with those words previously spoken, thus the necessity for faith that such can occur. This faith balances the will, the desire which you have expressed to learn this service.

May we answer you further, my brother?

N: Thank you very much. Then, as I take it, I am more or less focused on the five physical senses to such a fairly great extent that I have trouble with other considerations such as clairaudience, or at least this seems to be one of the big thoughts, is eliminating the five physical senses in my particular case. Is that sort of what the situation is or is it all thought?

I am Laitos, and we appreciate your query, my brother, and comment by suggesting that you are not alone in this particular way of experiencing your illusion, for if your peoples were aware of all the life-forms about them and the constant communication between these forms, there would be a great difficulty in functioning in a practical manner within your illusion, and a great difficulty in learning those lessons which are your opportunity to learn. The, as you call it, human being upon your planet must be able to screen out this great symphony of communication that is ever-present about it, and be very finely focused through its five senses in order to utilize your illusion.

The development of senses beyond the five is a practice which allows an entity to carefully open its field of perception in order that the one Creation in its joyful singing and experiencing might then be revealed to the entity in ways which enhance the evolutionary progress of each entity. Your particular means of perception and utilization of the five senses is not unique only unto you, therefore, my brother. You share it with your kind for a particular purpose, and as you now attempt to expand your ability to perceive and serve, you shall find there is a great deal of perception that awaits your adventurous seeking.

May we answer you further, my brother?

N: Thank you very much. Yes. Are there ways to expand my ability to perceive in terms other than channeling? I ask this for several reasons. I have meditated for quite some time but still I have not seemed to realize anything more than what might be considered nebulous results. The other thing is that when I go to sleep at night, I hear nothing. I do not dream as other people do. It seems I go into oblivion. Would you care to comment at all as to an analysis of this consideration?

I am Laitos, and we shall attempt this, my brother. You may utilize any means which you desire to utilize in expanding your own sensory perceptions, and, as they are called, extrasensory perceptions. The means of such utilization is not the important factor in what you would call a success. The most important factor is the desire and discipline in using whatever means is chosen. For, indeed, the initial results shall be quite nebulous, and in order to make the results more formed and apparent, one must constantly seek in a disciplined manner to do this. Many fall short of the desire and discipline necessary and move quickly from one technique to another shortly to convince themselves that either the techniques do not work or their own mind is too dense. Yet both assumptions are false, for any entity with the proper desire and discipline may utilize any means of awakening those senses which wait within each portion of the one Creator.

As to your concern that your sleep is without dreams and carries you to that portion of existence you have described as oblivion, we might suggest that your experience during sleep is not necessarily without the dreaming, for many such as yourself experience the dream yet do not remember it. The failure or lack of remembering may have many, shall we say, causes or reasons. In this area we may speak only in general, for your own particular reasons for not remembering the dreams are a portion of your means of evolving in mind, body and spirit. If again your desire to remember your dreams and your discipline in attempting such remembering were focused enough, you would indeed remember that work which is accomplished in your sleep and which does take the form of dream.

May we answer you further, my brother?

N: Thank you very much. I take it that perhaps I am trying to do too much, I am not focusing, I am, as you say, going helter-skelter rather than pursuing one particular single line. The other thing is about the dream. I have told myself to remember the dreams, and have tried to concentrate on this, and occasionally I will, but it's very seldom. Do you have any comment in that respect?

I am Laitos, and we may comment by suggesting that your summation and estimation of your abilities to remember your own dreams is fairly accurate.

May we answer further, my brother?

N: The only other query was the fact that am I perhaps going too much helter-skelter and trying to read too many different articles at one time or listen to too many different tapes, and what might be the best course without influencing free will?

I am Laitos, and we shall attempt this most difficult balance between making a suggestion and avoiding the influencing of your own free will. As the seeker which you are moves through its life experience there shall be many sources of illumination and inspiration brought before its attention by the power of its seeking. You are as the magnet, and your seeking draws close to you those sources of information which may be of value to you. As the seeker views the resources which are about it, the book, as you have called them, and tapes, the entities, the concepts, from whatever sources available, let then the seeker use these catalysts as beginning points from which its own uniquely fashioned journey shall move.

We view, then, a tapestry of your own making according to your own understanding, shall we say, and unto that understanding be faithful and true in your pursuit of that which you seek, the one Creator, full and balanced within your life experience. You are able not only to gather information but to weave it into an unified whole, a pattern which is of your own making and which to you makes, shall we say, sense.

May we answer you further, my brother?

N: Thank you very much. I don't wish to tire the instrument. Perhaps we can discuss this further at a later date. Thank you very much.

(Side one of tape ends.)

(Jim channeling)

I am Laitos, and we greet you once again in love and light. As we see that we have exhausted the queries for this evening, we shall at this time take our leave of this instrument and this group, thanking each for the great honor which you bestow upon us by allowing us to blend our vibrations with yours. It is with great joy that we exercise the new instrument known as N, and we look forward to future exercising of this instrument, and can once again remind this entity that its desire to perform this service is as a great light within the metaphysical realms. Though it cannot be seen with any of your sensory apparatus, we can assure that it does shine quite, quite brightly. We leave you now in the love and in the light of the one infinite Creator. I am Laitos. Adonai, my friends. Adonai. ☥

Intensive Meditation
January 27, 1985

(Carla channeling)

[I am] Hatonn. I greet you in the love and the light of our infinite Creator. We are having some difficulty due to the noise of the dishwasher; there may be pauses on that account. However, it is a good contact and so in love and light do we come. We thank you for calling us. Our brothers and sisters of Laitos are working with the one known as J and the one known as S to make adjustments so that our vibrations might more comfortably enter into the vibratory pattern of each instrument. We come to you as an experiment. The one known as S is a new channel, yet this instrument is not a new channel—it is merely that this instrument has not used these vibrations previously. Therefore, there is a great deal that we can, shall we say, pick up as we go, rather than having to go step by step by careful step mechanically. We do of course need to go step by step with the tuning and the general relationship which the entity has to its own instrument. We are very glad to do this. However, we who are of Hatonn wish to perform an experiment, as we wish to indicate to the one known as S how the actual channeling of concepts occurs, and we wish to do this in a quicker fashion that we would with others because this instrument is capable of it and comfortable with it, mechanically speaking. By this, we mean that this instrument is able to pick up our thoughts, and is able to do so with an acceptable degree of accuracy.

Therefore, we shall tell a story. This instrument has no idea what the story shall be. Needless to say, neither do any of you here. Therefore, all will be a surprise; all will be new, and there will be no right or wrong. You are simply telling a story and you shall discover for yourselves what spiritual or metaphysical meaning we may have intended. We shall now begin with your thanks for this long discussion of our techniques. We did, however, feel that it was not only a good idea, because by explaining first, we eliminated discomfort with the notion of telling a story but also because this instrument had some difficulty at first with the noise, and by using the instrument we were able to ground ourselves within this instrument's energy much more capably.

Once there was a horse. It was a young horse with a wild mane and a flying tail that roamed free across a plain where no people lived. Untrammeled and bridleless, the horse went its way and it thought many things. It would sip water and eat its grass and roll in the Sweet Timothy fields. Trees nodded serenely and the sun shone in summer and in winter. However, the horse, though free, and though unknowing, was unwittingly very lonely.

We shall transfer.

(S channeling)

I am Hatonn, and am with this instrument. The horse wandered through the pasture seeking it knew not what.

The instrument is nervous and trying to think and analyze the thought before she speaks instead of letting the words flow as if they were her own thoughts.

The horse wandered and traveled seeking oneness, for although alone, it had inner feeling and it had inner knowing that it was not alone.

The instrument feels a blockage and is uncomfortable. We are going to transfer and allow our friends of Laitos to aid us in tuning down our vibrations. I am Hatonn.

(Jim channeling)

In its wanderings, the horse was able to experience many things. It roamed the high mountain pastures, found itself descending lush green valleys, and was frequently within the forest regions between. It ate what it could find here and there and was satisfied by the food of the grasses, the waters of the streams, and the sights of its surroundings. Yet within this creature existed this yearning for a greater kind of experience. This simple creature was in its own way aware that it did not exist only of itself but that it was a portion of something else. This creature as it traveled wondered in its own way whether this new environment was what it sought. Each new adventure then became a possible answer to the simple seeking which manifested in this horse.

We shall transfer.

(Carla channeling)

One day it came upon a new being, one which it had not seen before. This being was a man, a young man, a pioneer. The man wished to capture the horse, for that was truly a prize. He laid a trap for the horse and was able to rope it. The horse was furious. It reared and kicked. Its high whinnies echoed to the heavens. It wanted nothing more than to be released and to be alone once again. The young man persevered. He grew to love the horse. He named the horse Daedalus, and told the horse that his name was Luke. Slowly the horse stopped thinking, when called Daedalus, "I am not Daedalus," and began answering to the name. He discovered that this man asked him to do work but in return he was always given good food for which he did not have to hunt. The horse understood that relationship and was grateful. Even more than that, the horse began to feel that which he had never felt before.

We shall transfer.

(S channeling)

The horse began to feel affection for Luke and looked forward to the opportunity to serve in his work and looked forward to the times that they would ride in the mountains and in the forest surrounding their place of dwelling. He looked forward to those moments that Luke would talk with him, for he understood in his way that these moments were special between them. He did not mind the work.

The instrument is trying to see where the story is taking her and is finding it difficult at this moment to allow the flow of our thoughts, for she found herself expressing our thoughts before she realized it and as she realized what was happening, planted her feet like a horse. We will transfer this instrument and allow the one known as S to again regain her composure.

(Carla channeling)

It was not long as horses measure time before the horse had discovered the true secret answer to its loneliness and to its seeking, for the horse was no longer alone. The horse was one in love and service with another entity, each giving of itself to the other, each caring and each being the nature that each was intended to be. Horses are strong, and Daedalus enjoyed his work more than he had enjoyed playing. Luke needed to farm and he enjoyed the outdoors and the beauty that lay all around him, and each was company to the other. Most of all Daedalus could now look at the trees and the mountains and the beautiful water and the rustling grasses and for the first time feel truly at one with them.

My friends, it is impossible to be friends with all that there is unless there is another one to be one with. Many of your sages have sought their own counsel. Their wisdom has been great; their polarity has suffered. When people's paths include others it may often seem that all is scattered and amiss, awry and out of tune. However, in this way does the Creator know Itself and in no other. Consciousness is, but consciousness only becomes with the other to mirror, watch, speak.

We apologize to the one known as S in a way for this is truly a crash course in channeling. Where others fear to speak two sentences this instrument has channeled a substantial portion of a story that it did not know. The discomfort is inevitable at the beginning, for there are the symptoms of nervousness and concern. These are healthy. However the symptoms shall become less and less as the subjective confidence of the entity as an instrument grows. This confidence is made by subjective happenings such as those about you saying after a certain channeling that the channeling had already answered a question with which it had come in.

We shall leave this instrument now and allow for the one known as Laitos to do its most in *(inaudible)* work. We thank each for being patient with us and allowing us to work with the new instrument. We thank the one known as J. We hope we were able to make our presence felt, as do those of Laitos. We do not truly leave you for there is nowhere to go, for it is one universe and we are with you always. We shall, however, remove our manifestation from the lips of this channel. We bid you blessed farewell in love and in the light of the Creator Which knows Itself. We are those of Hatonn. Adonai. Adonai.

(S channeling)

I am Laitos, and we greet you, my friends, in the love and in the light of the one infinite Creator. We were attempting to open through this instrument, which gave her some surprise, and she continuously challenged us in every way she could think. We thank that challenge, and we want the instrument to note that any time she is being greeted or anyone is being greeted, to take the time and to challenge in whatever way is important to them. It need not be speedy. This new instrument feels that she must have a quick sentence in which to accomplish this. It need not be a one or two word phrase for we, too, like welcome, like the warm, loving greetings.

As you note, our greeting to you is not, "Hello." We welcome this opportunity to exercise the nervous one known as S, and we do appreciate her desire to be a channel as a way of serving. We do realize that she puts both a lot of expectations upon herself as well is a lot of feelings of, "I can't do it." Both are true. The important thing for this instrument to remember is that she is but the telephone. We have given her a picture of a very old telephone. She is not sure if she appreciates that, but the old telephone is still useable although it may not have been used or spoken through for a very long time. The wires may be a little tattered and the connection somewhat weak, but the operator is on duty.

We thank you for this opportunity to aid not only the new instrument, S, but also to open some new opportunities for meditation and thought for the one known as J. We realize that the one known as S has felt this most difficult and has had many fears. We hope that this experience today will lend her some confidence. We transfer, but we also thank you. I am Laitos.

(Jim channeling)

I am Laitos, and greet you again in love and light through this instrument. We at this time would like to open this meeting to any queries which those present might find value in the asking. May we attempt any queries at this time?

S: Laitos, can you give me any help or suggestions as to how I can remain more calm and stop jumping in, waving red flags?

I am Laitos. My sister, we are in the position of observing a student who has run the good race and is, shall we say, out of breath. We may suggest that the service you are learning is one which includes as a natural portion of it the characteristics which you find somewhat disquieting. Your desire to be of service in this manner is of great proportion and purity and shall be your primary concern. That you express a portion of this desire in the form of anxiety and intellectual analysis of the process as it occurs is natural to new instruments. Yet, you can utilize this anxiety and let it fuel your desire without the need for the intellectual analysis. Allow the analysis to remain dormant until the process has been completed and you look back upon it in your own discrimination to see how it has worked and how it might continue its working through you. Do not be overly concerned with your nervousness, but as with all learning, observe those anxious moments within your being and allow them to move at their own pace without holding onto them, shall we say. You are undergoing a process which is not common among your peoples and your nervousness is quite natural. Allow this process its natural movement within your being. You are progressing quite well, my sister.

May we answer you further?

S: Laitos, last week Latwii said that those of Latwii and those of Laitos were available to me and to the others in our times of meditation, and I think I need to have some of that clarified a little bit more. I also realize that not to call upon your services in the way of channeling without the aid and the support and the tuning of others. How can I call you in meditation and still have that tuning? I don't know if you understand. I felt a mental conversation in my meditation and later wondered how was that different from channeling, other than it wasn't spoken out loud. Can you speak on this?

I am Laitos and we shall do our best, our sister, to speak on this concern. When we join you in your meditation, it is for the purpose of blending our vibrations of seeking the truth with your own vibrations of seeking the truth. This …

(Side one of tape ends.)

(Jim channeling)

I am Laitos, and we greet you again, my friends, in love and light. This deepening of your meditation, then, has the hoped for result of allowing your inner seeking to find more and more of that which it seeks, in whatever forms or feelings have meaning to you and are therefore perceptible to you. We seldom partake in any type of verbalized contact in these blendings of our vibrations with yours and those of this group on an individual basis, yet there are some such as yourself who are so dedicated to the service of vocal channeling that our offering of our vibrations is then filtered through the desire to feel a contact and frequently takes the form of the mental thought.

We can suggest that this is not necessary, for it may be confusing to the new instrument. Our vibration in its basic carrier wave form is intended in these cases to simply enhance your own seeking, much as the joining of a seeker with another seeker upon a long, mountainous journey provides a comfort to both. Though words are never spoken, the hearts know each other.

May we answer you further, my sister?

S: No, thank you. That was very clear. Thank you.

I am Laitos, and we thank you, my sister. Is there another query which we may attempt?

S: Not from me at this time, thank you.

Carla: I'll wait until tonight, too. Thank you, Laitos.

J: I'm tongue-tied.

I am Laitos, and though our tongue is somewhat looser and roams the worded worlds, we also stand speechless before the One in All. We thank you, my friends, for allowing our presence to be known among you in this meeting. We are with you always and are honored at your request that we use words to reflect that which is quite beyond words. We shall leave you at this time in the love and the light of our infinite Creator. Adonai. Adonai.

Sunday Meditation
January 27, 1985

Evening

(Carla channeling)

I am Hatonn. I greet you in the love and in the light of our infinite Creator. We are most blessed to be asked to share our thoughts with you and we most especially greet those who have come from afar to sit in love and light as we all seek for that which is the one original Thought that we may define ourselves and the Creator and the creation by our growing grasp of infinity and unity. We shall be working with this instrument word by word this evening for awhile as this instrument wishes further refining of its abilities, so we ask your forgiveness if there are pauses.

This evening we would speak to you about that which is called love among your peoples. We would speak to you of what that may mean and what you may hope from its pursuit. More especially we wish to speak about being channels for the one original Thought which created all that there is and is known among your peoples as love. My friends, the meanings associated with that word are multitudinous and yet not one of the many meanings of love can begin to describe that which is truly beyond words, the powerful creative energy which has formed consciousness and through whose eyes we do see and in whose memory all our thoughts and actions are. If we establish that all of us are not only seeking love but are to some extent manifesting love, then we must begin to ask ourselves what we may hope to achieve from the sometimes seemingly fruitless task of seeking the Creator. That which you may hope for is no apparent award or pleasure at all, for the single most clear manifestation in an entity's life is the surrender of a small self in order that a larger self may overshadow and guide in a way which ideally shall touch the heart of each moment, find the love in …

(Page two of the original transcript is missing.)

… questions which our brothers and sisters of Latwii would be delighted to attempt to answer. Yet we wish to leave you with the strong and stern and cautionary love of the words that encourage yet warn. Those who do not think that they are seeking are only seeking very slowly. They will eventually have to make their choice between loving others above the self and loving the self above all others. You who sit in this circle are making the choice at each moment in a conscious manner, therefore your evolution in spirit may be more healthy, more rapid, and much more difficult. Because as you ask, so it shall be given you and when you ask to learn lessons about love, you get lessons about love, and in those lessons you are required to find love in moments of anger, distress, frustration, pain—even agony.

Yet we say to you, there is joy, there is love, there is peace in each moment. You may not be able to express it in words but if you can find it, if you can but intend to find it, your light shall be so bright that kings would bow before you and all nations turn to such a great light. And yet it is precisely because you have put yourself out of the way that this would be so. Kings shall never turn to other men but only to the one original Thought. That is what we seek to express; that is what you seek to learn and to manifest.

How we love each of you, for you are beautiful to us. Yet that is easy for us, for in our density we see all those things which are more difficult within the confines of your third-density illusion. We have the key. You too have the key, my friends. For us the key is that we have already passed your grade, shall we say. For you the key is meditation, for in your meditations you will touch base with the infinite. You shall abide with that which is eternal. You shall find joy and peace and those about you shall find it through you, never in you, my friends, but through you. You are all channels. What shall you channel?

We would wish to say two things before leaving this instrument. The first, as always, is the request that our words be taken as opinion and not doctrine. We do not know the truth; we are seekers of the truth. We have been your way and gone on. Take that which is helpful, leave behind that which is not. We hope only to inspire your own thoughts, your own meditations, your own seeking.

This instrument is fatigued and we are going to leave this instrument early. We leave you insofar as speaking through this instrument in the love and the light of the one infinite Creator. Know that you may call us in meditation mentally and we shall be with you, not as words but only but as an aid to a more powerful meditation. We will tabernacle with you, abide with you in the desert or in the oasis wherever you may happen to be. We are those of Hatonn. We leave you in the great created love and the manifested light of the One Who Is All. Adonai. Adonai vasu borragus.

(Jim channeling)

I am Latwii, and I greet you, my friends, in the love and in the light of our infinite Creator. It is our great honor and privilege to be asked to join your group this evening. We thank you, my friends, for asking us. Our service is a humble one, which we offer in joy. We shall attempt to answer those queries which those present may find the value in asking. As our brothers and sisters of Hatonn, we also suggest that our answers and words are but opinion. We seek as you seek to know the one Creator, to radiate that love and light to all as the one Creator. Yet, though we have sought diligently, what we have to share with you is our opinion and is no hard and fast doctrine. May we then, with that understood, begin our service by asking if there might be a query with which we might begin?

L: Yes, I have a question. Sometime back I had a relationship with another person which was disrupted in a very painful and vicious manner on the part of both concerned. I perceive a healing process going on at this point, what seems to me a chance to what you might refer to as clean up mistakes of the soul. Could you in general discuss that subject—not my relationship—but just the possibilities of repairing mistakes made previously?

I am Latwii, and am aware of your query, my brother. As we look on this situation of which you speak, we do not see mistakes, as you have described them. We see that there has been two portions of the one Creator that have been in a relationship with each other and have through that relationship sought to know the one Creator. Each has had an opportunity to serve the Creator through the other self. Each has had lessons that were hoped would be learned and utilized as means by which love could be multiplied.

When difficulties occur in such a relationship it is not so much a mistake that has occurred, but tests and opportunities of a more intensive nature which have for the moment exceeded the limits of those within the relationship so that love has been more difficult to discover. In such a situation where love has remained hidden, shall we say, and those difficulties and opportunities to show love have not borne fruit, then it is that the entities so involved may, shall we say, drift apart. Yet the thought remains within the mind and the hope remains within the heart of each that love may yet be found, for each is a whole and perfect portion of the one Creator and it is the Creator's wish in all portions that It might know love even in those dark and hidden places which seem so secret and so barren of love, yet there it is as well, my brother.

As you begin that which you have called the healing, you begin to find that love which always was there, which needed more attention in order to be discovered. Often the gift of time and the fond remembrance of the better times between a couple which has parted will bring about the opportunity to rediscover love where it was not found before. The intention to heal and find that love is of primary importance. To attempt that which is difficult is more important than to accomplish that which is easy.

May we answer you further, my brother?

L: Yes, a request for some information I'm not sure you'll be able to give me without interfering. I have had some perceptions recently as to—I could best describe it as the intentions of this other person. Could you give me an idea of how accurately I am perceiving this other person's intentions?

I am Latwii, and am aware of your query, my brother. We may comment by suggesting that it is the nature of perception that what you see is what you are. You have the creative ability to form the experiences in which you partake. As you focus upon one portion or another of another entity's behavior, you shall be as the gardener watering that seed. Choose then carefully, my brother, how you perceive and what seeds you water.

May we answer you further, my brother?

L: No. That was excellent advice. I'll take it to heart. Thank you very much.

I am Latwii, and we thank you, my brother. Is there another query at this time?

Questioner: Yes. There is an entity, the Sixteenth Street Baptist Church, which seems at this time to be disintegrating. I am watching the two sides as they struggle, one against the other. It is my firm belief that each of these sides is truly in love with this entity, the church, the Sixteenth Street Baptist Church. Can you give me some help in the advice that I should give, or that I am called upon at different times to give, to these sides that might bring them together?

I am Latwii, and am aware of your query, my sister. We shall do our best to be of service in this instance, and can suggest that as you view that which is the conflict between those who truly serve and seek to serve the one Creator in differing ways, that as you perceive them, you see them indeed as the one Creator, each and every one. Though there may be differences that seem great at times and though there may be disputes that seem sharp and divided at times, that what is occurring within this situation is also the seeking of love by many portions of the one Creator, and those who would seek to serve as the peacemakers will find a most difficult challenge before them, yet one which has great rewards, for it has been written in your holy works that blessed are the peacemakers, that indeed the meek shall inherit the Earth.

As you move within this experience that these portions of the one Creator have between them, find within yourself first the strong and sure power of the love of the one Creator. Open yourself to that love that you might be a vessel through which it moves. When possible, remove your own will that the greater will of the one Creator might move through you and seek to share the heart of the teachings that these entities revere, that of the master known as Jesus, that we each should love one another. If entities suffering what you may call discord and strife may remember that the heart of each being is love and the face of each being is the one Creator, then there is the calling by each to the underlying unity and harmony which binds each to each even through the illusion of strife and discord.

May we answer you further, my sister?

Questioner: Thank you. I shall do what you have suggested. I agree with all that you have said.

I am Latwii, and we thank you, my sister and remind you that our words are but our expressions of love. We offer them freely and suggest to each that the value that might be there be used where possible and where value is not seen, that those words be forgotten. Is there another query at this time?

Carla: I have one, just right on the heels of that one because I was thinking, and I went through the same thing, and I listened really carefully to what you said but I still didn't find my way out of the maze within my own mind. The church that I grew up in and therefore I was so close to, 'cause I had friends that were in the congregation, were fighting over an organ. Some of them wanted a new organ and some of them did not want a new organ, and about twenty-five people left the church over that organ—that was the choir, the whole choir. Now the weird thing was that within the year they got a new organ, but in the meantime there had been this terrible breakage of people that had been going to that church all their lives. And we all tried to act as peacemakers and give good advice and we failed. And that's just the truth, and I wonder what … Can you speak to the apparent failures of our good intentions, the sometimes heartbreaking reality that occurs?

I am Latwii, and am aware of your query, my sister. As each seeker and, indeed, each group of seekers moves through the pattern of life set before the incarnation began, these seekers shall find the times of seeming difficulty where the belief, the faith, the love, and the wisdom of each is tested. For how can one know what is the heart of one's being unless there is the test? When one has moved upon the path of the seeker for a great portion of time, then the tests become somewhat more severe, shall we say, and the seeker is faced on many occasions with what you have called the failure, and yet this is a matter of perspective, my sister, for as one has attempted to love and to give of the self without thought for the self but only with thought for others, then one has expressed the heart of love. And if love has been expressed, how can there be failure in truth?

Though your illusion may not bear fruits as you feel it should, yet is any within your illusion wise enough to know how the fruits of the one Creator shall be formed and shall be born? All you can do, my sister, is love and continue to love through all seeming failures, through all difficulties, and let that love bind you with others and all others and let that love be the shining star which lights your way, however difficult the journey, however winding the road.

Within your illusion you shall not see the world about you respond as you think it should for it exists as an illusion that when love is born it might be tested. The times that are tranquil and full of peace are indeed restful, yet they do not test love. Love is strengthened in those times of turbulence.

May we answer you further, my sister?

Carla: No, thank you.

I am Latwii, and we thank you, my sister. Is there another query?

Questioner: I have a daughter, twelve years old. The father of my daughter, A, I'm very concerned as to why he never wanted to see her. I had to force the issue for him to see her when she was two, and before she was born we had a very good relationship. But after the birth of my daughter, the relationship turned into bitterness. I have tried communicating with him to see if there is anything that I have done that we could talk about to iron out whatever bad feelings there might be so my daughter can have a communication with him. But he refuses to talk with her, to see her. What can I do about that?

I am Latwii, and am aware of your query, my sister. We can comment in a general fashion upon this subject but cannot give specific advice, for the pattern of service which is presented to each of the three of you is most sacred and holds treasures that are for your discovery. We may comment by suggesting that if one is able to …

(Side one of tape ends.)

(Jim channeling)

I am Latwii, and am once again with this instrument. To continue. If one can see within such a situation that there is love, even though it might be difficult to find, and if one can see that the one Creator in full moves in each, then one can begin with this faith in the perfection of that which seems imperfect. For each there is the opportunity to share love. The test may be difficult, yet is there and love is with it. Perhaps for one there is the great opportunity to forgive and express the compassionate aspect of love. Perhaps for another there is the opportunity to accept responsibility and to love through that aspect. Perhaps for another there is the opportunity to find love where there seems to be rejection. In each life pattern there is what seems to be a lack of love. Yet, my sister, this is but an illusion which each has helped to create in order that love might eventually be found, to accept each within this situation. To forgive each and to see each as the Creator is to lay the groundwork, shall we say, for the nurturing of love so that when possible it might make itself known as each seeks within the self for the solution to solve what seems a most difficult problem.

May we answer you further, my sister?

Questioner: Is there anything that I can do or say to him to create this feeling of love to come forth for *(inaudible)*?

I am Latwii, and am aware of your query, my sister. To simply love and accept another as he is is the most that can be done when another does not wish to communicate with yourself. To keep the door open and the heart open is all that can be done until that entity walks through that door and finds the love within your heart.

May we answer you further, my sister?

Questioner: Thank you.

I am Latwii, and we thank you, my sister. Is there another query at this time?

K: Yeah, I have a question about the people who are starving to death in Africa. Where is the love of the Creator in that? It seems to me it would be an overly harsh and severe test to put these people through.

I am Latwii, and am aware of your query, my brother. Indeed, my brother, upon your planet at this time there are multitudes of entities who suffer daily the greatest of difficulties and degradations, the sicknesses, diseases, hunger, oppression, separation from those that are loved. This is the lot of many within your illusion, and each in some way partakes of what seems a most unloving life and pattern of living. Yet, within your illusion there is the restriction of the viewpoint. Within your illusion you cannot see with the wide-ranging eye that sees the patterns not only of this life but of those lives and lessons which stretch far back into what you call time. It is not possible for your entities and peoples to see in such a manner or else the love of the Creator would be much more easily discovered and expressed. Yet even within the situation within which you have described, there is not only the love of the one Creator, but the one Creator moving in portions of Itself, finding the balance within this illusion for other lessons not well learned in another illusion.

As you see one portion of the Creator suffering the great difficulty, you with your limited perspective are not able to see that from which this situation sprang. As we look upon those entities who inhabit your planet, we see that there has been a great migration of souls from many portions of your universe. This planet upon which you dwell is one which houses those who have had difficulties within the third-density experience which attempts to learn the lessons of love. These entities have migrated to your planet in order to once again attempt the great lesson of choosing to love the self or to love other selves. Many are the lives, cycles and sagas that each entity upon your planet has undertaken. The journeys have not been easy; many have been the difficulties.

Those difficulties now apparent are those which are hoped by the entity suffering that will balance the previous difficulties in order that the harvest and graduation into what you have called the density of love might be accomplished, for each upon your planet at this time is old in experience and each has the opportunity to learn these lessons of love and to move from this density of forgetting into the experience of remembering once again that the one Creator dwells in all. These great difficulties are the tests which provide the opportunities for graduation.

May we answer you further, my brother?

K: Yeah, I'm still a little bit confused in that I can accept a percentage that has probably been with any segment of society since the dawn of creation on this planet, but why so many souls together numerically in one place at one time are going through this? I have a tough time rationalizing the overwhelming massive numbers of people that are dying right now.

I am Latwii, and am aware of your query, my brother. As we spoke previously, many are the sources of planetary influences which have contributed their populations to your own planet in order that these entities might once again be exposed to the illusion of forgetting. Great numbers in your estimation have come from these planetary influences and have together as seekers of truth experienced those conditions which created the distortions and imbalances within their life patterns that they now find the necessity and opportunity of balancing once again. Once again together they journey, once again together they provide themselves the opportunity to learn, once again they find that love supports their every moment of existence even though it seems that there is no love.

May we answer you further, my brother?

K: Are you saying that they're knocking a time line against the harvest and that's why they're doing what they're doing now? The time grows short in this particular cycle?

I am Latwii, and am aware of your query, my brother. Indeed, as what you call time grows shorter and the harvest grows near, the opportunities for covering a certain distance must be intensified in order to do more work in consciousness. Were there more time, as you call it, the lessons might be attempted in a less intensive manner. Yet these entities, as each upon your planet, are greatly desirous of completing this illusion and learning indeed how to love, and have therefore determined that the remaining period of time might best be utilized in this intensive manner.

May we answer you further, my brother?

K: No, thank you.

I am Latwii, and we thank you, my brother. Is there another query at this time?

S: Latwii, it would appear to me that this would be an opportunity to serve those in those portions of the world that are suffering, be it money or would it be more effective to send love and light to help them on their way? Can you speak to that?

I am Latwii, and am aware of your query, my sister. There are many ways to be of service to such entities. To those who are starving, indeed, it is quite fit that food be given, that medicine be given, that the physical needs be tended to in order that the mind might find the rest in which to contemplate the mystery of life and that consciousness then might move more freely through a vehicle which is supported in its barest needs. These entities then provide those other populations of your planet with the opportunity to be of service. Thus you see various portions of the one Creator offering opportunities to other portions of the one Creator to know Itself through love.

May we answer you further, my sister?

S: Thank you.

[I am Latwii.] Is there another query at this time?

Carla: Well, I'd like to follow up on that one because it seems to me that the news is kind of managed. There are people starving to death here in this town tonight, for one reason or another, people that live on the streets. Any big city has them. One can give food, one can send light. I guess my question basically is, is there more starving and misery now because of the nearness of the end of the cycle or has it always been like this in the world? History would have us believe that there has been a lot of this sort of thing through the generations.

I am Latwii, and am aware of your query, my sister. That which you have called history as it has been recorded by your peoples is but a very short span of the entire length of your planet's third-density cycle. Indeed, within the last five thousand years, a period of time which seems great in length within this circle, you are speaking of a period that is but a small fraction of your planet's entire cycle of seventy-five thousand years. Thus, within this small fraction of time, the intensification of catalyst and experience has continued so that those entities of what you may call seniority of vibration who have the possibility of being graduated from your illusion may accomplish these tasks and lessons within the shortening period of what you call time. Thus, you are correct in your assumptions, my sister.

May we answer you further?

Carla: No … So you're saying that all of recorded history is basically that of the end times? As we know it.

I am Latwii, and this is correct, my sister. We find that this instrument is rapidly growing fatigued and would suggest that if it were possible for another to assume the channeling of our attempts to answer your queries that this would be appropriate at this time. If this is not possible, then we shall take our leave of this group. We shall attempt to transfer this contact at this time. I am Latwii.

(L channeling)

I am Latwii. I am now with this instrument, and I greet you in the love and the light of the infinite Creator. At this time we shall be happy to continue our efforts to be of service to those present in offering our opinions and what meager wisdom we possess to those who desire to pose questions. Are there any questions?

Carla: Well, I'm kind of curious as to what starving to death is the balance for. What behavior or what error, what bias had to be balanced by starving to death?

I am Latwii, and I am aware of your question. My sister, in your world at this time there are many who find themselves to be possessed of that which potentially could be shared with other selves. This, in essence, is an opportunity for service. There are many who, upon experiencing that which you call death, are given an opportunity to reflect upon their lessons in the previous life and perceive overlooked opportunities to be of service and sharing that which they felt they possessed. As you are aware, the rapid approach of harvest allows little time in which to provide oneself repeated opportunities for sharing through the experiencing of multiple lifetimes. Therefore, certain entities choose to incarnate under conditions which have a high probability of …

We shall pause.

(Side two of tape ends.)

(L channeling)

Certain entities choose to incarnate under conditions with a high probability of deprivation. This has a two-fold potential for learning. The first is quite obvious—an increased perception of the effects resultant from an entity's failure to be of service through sharing with other selves. Second, an opportunity to be of service to other selves by sharing what meager resources are available to the entity with his or her other selves, a prospect which is quite difficult, yet reaps much reward in the development of the entity. The entity in essence thus provides himself with what might be termed a crash course in brotherhood in hopes to maximize his or her growth on the path of service to others in a minimal amount of time, that is, the time remaining prior to harvest.

May we answer you further, my sister?

Carla: No, thank you.

We thank you. Is there another question.

K: Yeah, I have question, probably the same question but from a different perspective. What is it within the nature of man that makes him make war on his fellow man on a repetitive basis?

I am Latwii. My brother, what is it in man that enables him to perceive both himself and his other selves as separate entities, both from one another and from their Creator? It is that lack of perception, my brother, which is both a lesson in your density and an opportunity to progress along either the line of service to others or service to self. If one chooses the path of service to self, then one is not deterred by the awareness that the pain is inflicted upon oneself. However, if one chooses the path of service to others, one is greatly benefited in that the awareness must be perceived by intention, an intention in analogy to the knight who in seeking the holy grail never allows his glance to waver for a moment from the miraculous image. My brother, this failing is intentional, this lack of automatic perception enables you as an entity to seek either grail: the grail of self-service or the grail of service to others.

May we answer you further?

K: Yeah. The Christian community has a concept of original sin, and I've often thought that it's possible that if in fact that exists, that what it is is the inability of man to get along with his fellow man. Could you speak to that, please?

I am Latwii. I am aware of your question. My brother, the concept of sin is the result of a contamination of information by those who would seek the path of service to self. There is no sin, my brother. There simply is a set of conditions within which the entity exists and is provided with the opportunities to make choices—ideally, choices leading to further polarization in one direction or the other.

May we answer you further, my brother?

K: No, thank you.

We thank you, my brother. Is there another question?

J: Greetings, Latwii. May I ask if the death camps in Germany during World War II, as well as the current famine, is this not consideration to increase the total awareness of all entities?

I am Latwii, and I am aware of your question. My brother, the situations which you describe are the result of choices made by entities incarnate at the times in which these situations exist or did exist. It would not be accurate to describe them as conditions established for the enhancement of awareness of other entities, for in truth, they are the ongoing lessons of both the recipients of the unpleasant influences and those performing those acts. It is not common, to our knowledge, for such intensive experiences to be established for the enhancement of others present in a manner similar to that of a football team performing for the crowd. This, to our knowledge, is not an effective path toward self-development of the audience.

May we answer you further, my brother?

J: Thank you very much. Then you're saying that the increased awareness is only involving those who are involved per se individually, and not a general heightening awareness such as was mentioned concerning the UFO's.

My brother, the enhanced awareness is the increase of opportunity to be of service for those who are not direct participants. The opportunity to be of service which is provided by these situations is a benefit for those made aware and given an opportunity to serve. However, the situations you describe were not established solely for that purpose. Rather, the opportunity for service among those such as are present is more aptly described as a ramification of the situation rather than the focal point of its existence. The focal point, my brother, is for those who in your words are on the scene.

May we answer you further?

J: Yes. Then eliminating the consideration for physical conflict in the area of the famine, from what we're told, it's almost impossible to get food in and get it to the people that need it. That is, just donating food would not be an adequate consideration or money for food, whatever, other than the resultant possible physical conflict. Is that true or not?

My brother, all things are possible. Therefore, it would not be accurate to state that the situation as you describe it is fixed. We would suggest that you examine the possibility that those who seek to be of service to themselves by withholding or preventing the distribution of physical sustenance might waver in their dedication to service to self and distribute these items. This possibility, although low in probability, still exists. Other possibilities would include the determination by those in the seats of power to distribute the food to those in need despite the artificial boundaries of nations. This possibility, although fraught with danger, also exists.

May we answer you further, my brother?

J: May I diverge just a bit to ask you if there was some major catastrophe, oh, prior to five, six thousand years ago, such as the rotation of the poles of the Earth, that caused all prior information to be eliminated?

I am Latwii, and would ask that your question be phrased more clearly in that we are not certain as to the time locus of your question.

J: Approximately five to six thousand years ago our first recorded, present recorded written knowledge became somewhat available. There seems to be some lack of information that preceded approximately five to six thousand years ago. And I was just wondering if there was a major catastrophe that might have occurred—or perhaps it was not a catastrophe, perhaps it was a harvest—but some major physical condition involving the Earth that eliminated most of the prerecorded material that may have existed prior to five …

(Tape ends.) ✣

Sunday Meditation
February 10, 1985

(Carla channeling)

I am Hatonn. I greet you in the love and the light of our infinite Creator. It is a great pleasure to be with you this evening, to share in your lives for this period of what you call time, to embrace with you seeking for the truth.

This evening we would speak to you about that portion of seeking which is involved in manifestation. To put it another way, we would speak with you about service to others. When each individual embarks upon the spiritual journey, there is a time when the seeds of seeking are tender and young and need to be guarded carefully and in private. This is usually known instinctively by seekers. They feel fragile and indeed they are fragile as very small children are fragile, unable to defend themselves within the new life and environment of seeking. As the seeker pursues the journey, however, there is another stage which might be called that of adolescence, spiritually speaking. The seeker has become excited by the power and mystery of the excellence of the path and is often on fire with the desire to share with others the awakening which he may have had.

To put this in a more general context, regardless of the desire and its nature, any desire to serve another is prone to the folly of spiritual adolescence. There is a great disillusionment involved furthermore and an ensuing bitterness which we would at all costs urge each to remove from the being if possible by nipping the adolescent spiritual self in the bud and studying and then living those portions of what we have to say that seem worthwhile to you this evening. Each individual is a mystery, for the Creator is a mystery. Could the co-creator then be less? Further, each individual is unique, and thus each mystery is unique. Within the well-intentioned there is such a desire to be of service, such a desire to polarize and to learn a better way of being that it is easy to find oneself deciding what is needed for another. The excitement of the spiritual path is relayed and there is often puzzlement and sad feeling when the attempt to serve is not accepted but is, rather, rebuffed.

Again, in the more general sense, how often does each individual feel that he knows what is best for another and with a willing and glad heart would do anything to serve another person by making the desired outcome possible? Service to others is one of the great paradoxes, for one is of service to another to the extent that one ceases to attempt to give to another. One is, after all, dealing with a co-creator, an infinite and mystery-filled being. Thus, service to another begins often with the conscious or unconscious decision to attempt to see the creation through the eyes of the one who is to be aided. This is not the end of service but the means. The end is to see the Creator in another, for by seeing the Creator you reflect that which may be the mirror to that person whom you wish to help. That person is then able to discover himself. The gift that you can give is the vision of the Creator.

How many times have you considered that another entity was less than perfect, was troublesome, difficult, or in some way in need of help? When thoughts of this nature come to you and you do wish to serve, begin by the centering of your own disciplined attention upon that part of yourself which is the Creator. Then, with eyes which behold that which is not apparent but only seen through grace, you may aid another, for you may see the Creator.

You will notice that in all that we have said, we have said nothing about doing but only about your manner of being. It is an enormously selfless thing to listen and see with eyes and ears that are centered upon the Creator, for there are so many opinions, judgments and feelings which one has due to the lack of freedom from the illusion that each is separated from each. Once the technique has been learned, it is fairly common for one to be able to be of service. If this technique is not learned, no matter how great your enthusiasm, how beautiful your message, how inspiring your words, that which you give another is part of your own energy and it will not last past your leaving. When you give another self himself in a new vision, consequences are far more lasting and there is no infringement of free will, for all you are doing is acting as a channel.

We are sorry for the delay but there is less energy than there sometimes is in the circle. We shall continue.

The beginning, for yourself and for others, is your decision to serve. If service is not free then you are not free, for your actions reflect your state of mind and your being. Remember always that even though you may aim as high as your imagination can take you and then fail, it is far better to have aimed so high, for it is your intention that draws you upon the spiritual path ever onward. The concept of failure is foreign to the seeker and is best left behind along with other of your cherished possessions such as a feeling of unworthiness, a feeling of being less than one appears to be, a feeling of being too much with the world. You see, my friends, you begin by judging yourself, so stop judging yourself; be of service to yourself. You are, after all, a self; there is that within you which is infinite and it may be of service to you. We do not mean to sound as if we are splitting your personality, but there is within you a greater self that you may call upon and use in order that your mind and your emotions may serve you instead of your being a slave to them. Service to others is the next step for those who seek to love. Spend yourself freely in order to be, not in order to convince. Do not even attempt to convince yourself but merely allow [the] flow of your incarnational experience to teach you and to draw you toward your next challenge.

We find within this instrument's mind a portion of a conversation earlier. We feel that we are not those who should speak to this and therefore we shall leave this instrument, for there is another called by this question. We are those of Hatonn, and we are most grateful to you for calling us to your presence and to the joy of your company. We leave you in the love and the light of our infinite Creator. Adonai vasu borragus.

(Carla channeling)

I am Oxal. We greet you in the love and in the light of the one infinite Creator and thank you that you called us to you at this time. We are adjusting the energy which we use with this instrument. It has been some time since we used this instrument and we are adjusting to this instrument's comfort.

We would speak to you upon [a] subject which, as our brothers and sisters of Hatonn observed, has been raised in discussion. The practice of meditation is central and, indeed, for most an absolute necessity for spiritual evolution. Yet it is inevitably painful in that it is a tool whereby realizations occur. One learns about oneself; one then turns to the self and begins picking at the self, at the past experiences which have been, shall we say, less than perfectly resolved. One becomes tangled within one's own incarnational experiences and judgments about experiences which do not square with those things which meditation is bringing you.

Therefore, you may find bitter fruit cropping up among those fruits of meditation. This is an excellent sign and we encourage each to rejoice when a past misalliance of some kind comes to mind as an unbalanced and unfinished piece of business. It is now time to finish the business. Those who live the life of one who is asleep become increasingly bowed down by the weight of experience. That which is childlike begins to leave and the being becomes heavier and heavier, for in truth nothing is ever resolved to the complete and total satisfaction of a judging entity.

The appropriate action when one is faced with one's own past is to take the past from the shoulders, to refuse to carry it further but rather put it down and gaze at it until all is well, until there is no emotional pull or push to this experience. You are then lighter, more childlike, more spontaneous, more open, more joyful and more ready to be yourself. The great treasure of being that you are must wait for you to unload the package of burdens of your past from you. In the seeker there will be again and again those confrontations with the self in which one judges the self to have fallen short. We may say that when one adds two plus two and writes down the number five, one has made an error. Later one may erase the error because of new and life-giving knowledge. The problem is then solved correctly, two plus two being four. That is all that your past is.

My friends, you are carrying around a collection of unsolved but simple arithmetic problems. The answers usually have to do with forgiveness of the self, and a willingness to use the eraser. You do not have to live your past. You are responsible for the new life of the present moment. If you have not made amends to another, by all means do so. Usually, however, it is the self that is the great scapegoat. Remove this identity from yourself. You will have to be patient, for you cannot find all that you have done badly by meditating once, twice or a hundred times. The fully realized self is a long time, shall we say, in arriving; especially within your illusion. We ask you simply to remain unflustered and use your eraser, loving your mistakes, loving your perfection and being willing to be accountable for that which you are now, not in the past and not in the future.

To be light of heart, to be joyful and gullible and free is the sign of the child and it is that small one within you that is the best learner, the best student. You will gain the best perceptions with your child-self, for your child-self is open and trusting and the universe gives back that which it feels. We encourage you in your meditations. We encourage you in their deliberate discipline. Daily meditation is most central. We hope that we have been able to speak to the concern of the meditation which brings seeming difficulty. It is giving you good fruit, not bitter. It is only the conscious self which may choose to be bitter rather than to pluck the fruit and cast it aside so that new fruit may be born in its time.

I am Oxal. I leave you secure in the infinite unity of all that there is. Therefore, my friends, we cannot leave you for there is only one creation. We shall, however, cease speaking through this instrument, asking you, as always, to cast aside any thought which does not have merit in your own opinion. We leave you basking in the love and in the light of the One Who Is All. Adonai, my friends. Adonai.

(Jim channeling)

I am Latwii, and I greet you, my friends, in the love and the light of the one Creator. We are most privileged to be asked to join your group this evening. We follow our brothers and sisters of Hatonn and Oxal in giving praise for the ability to share our thoughts with you. Our service, as you know, is that of attempting to [give] answers from our philosophical point of view. Therefore, may we begin with the first query for this evening.

J: Latwii, I'd like to ask you an historical question, please. I was reading an article about the Cro-Magnon man in the caves at La Tuc d'Audoubert. I'd like to know how did they learn how to draw, where did they get their colors from, and how did they draw on the ceilings of the cave?

I am Latwii, and am aware of your query, my brother. We are not very good at giving answers to queries that are beyond the bounds of our philosophical reach. To attempt to look upon the historical past of your planet is somewhat of a difficult task for us. We shall, in our humble way, make a small attempt in this instance, focusing as we can upon those portions of the query which are within our grasp.

We find that entities who have partaken in the evolutionary chain of your species' development have from time to time developed those means of self-expression which have been recorded in various ways. The entities of which you speak were of a level of development which enabled them to utilize various substances of the plant and mineral world that surrounded them in the making of those dye and paint pigments that allowed for the recording of their way of being upon the walls of those cave structures in which they found shelter, an environment which was relatively safe in which to dwell. These entities were able to make drawings upon the walls and what you have referred to as the ceilings as a result of utilizing structures which no longer exist within those cave areas. There has been much, shall we say, erosion of the structures and geographical placement of, shall we say, earthen mounds which were then available for such paintings.

May we answer you further, my brother?

J: You did very well, Latwii. Can I still keep on the same subject?

I am Latwii, and we shall do our best, my brother, to accommodate you although we are not skilled in this area.

J: Thank you. Can you tell me, when did the Neanderthal man change into the Cro-Magnon man? And why?

I am Latwii, and am aware of your query, my brother. As we attempt to trace the evolutionary pattern of your particular species, we find that there have been a variety of transitions from one form to another. Many of these transitions did not continue but found an ending in their evolutionary pattern. Your particular lineage is one which does include this entity of which you speak, the so-called Neanderthal man. The transition which this entity partook in with others of a similar configuration was not a transition which can easily be delineated to a specific portion of what you call time, for the transition was the kind in which the, shall we say, donor race or original race of entities died out, giving birth to the successors but a transition in which there was mutual cohabitation for a portion …

(Side one of tape ends.)

(Jim channeling)

I am Latwii, and am with this instrument once again. To complete our attempt to answer your query, my brother, we may suggest that it is most difficult for us to be more precise in giving a date for this transition, for the transition was one that occurred over a great portion of what you call time, and was one in which there were, shall we say, parallel transitions being undertaken at the same time.

May we answer you further, my brother?

J: Thank you, yes. In this cave of La Tuc d'Audoubert there is an ibex which is indigenous of Asia Minor, and also they drew a sorcerer. Can you tell me how did they acquired that knowledge?

I am Latwii, and am aware of your query, my brother. We find that there has been in many cases of entities such as these of whom you speak a greater level of civilization and cultural abilities than has been supposed by those of your scientific community. There have been in your distant past those entities who were able to venture out and observe various phenomena and who then were able to communicate this observation upon the return by the recording of these phenomena in the manner of the drawings of which you speak.

May we answer you further, my brother?

J: You mean they traveled from France to Asia Minor and back?

I am Latwii, and am aware of your query, my brother. We did not mean to intend that these entities were quite this skilled in the traveling, but that in their travels they encountered the phenomena which were at that time more widely spread than is supposed at your current time.

May we answer you further, my brother?

J: No, but I'm perplexed about that. Where did the knowledge come from? This is what I don't understand. They drew perfect bison, perfect horses. There had to be some kind of intelligence. Did they communicate in a language?

I am Latwii, and am aware of your query, my brother. Again, my brother, we must ask your forgiveness for our inability to be more precise and thereby reduce the perplexity which we feel that we have been responsible for. We are attempting to retrieve this information but must apologize once again, for these queries are quite beyond a scope which is a rather limited one when you consider the great amount of information that one may find an interest in. We focus our abilities upon the philosophical aspects of the nature of one's being and the progress of one's own evolutionary trail, shall we say.

As we attempt to trace the physical evolution, we find that our abilities are at a very low level according to what one might expect from entities who are specialized in a type of communication which seems quite advanced to many upon your planet. Though we can do some things well that may surprise various of your peoples, we can do other things quite poorly that will equally surprise many of your peoples. Therefore, we must beg your forgiveness in this, my brother, and ask if there might be a query that you could locate within the very narrow parameters of our abilities to be of service?

J: Please don't ask my forgiveness, and I'm sorry if my questions sounded or were asked in the imperative tense. I'll get off that. I'd like to ask you a question about Jesus. During the trial, he was sent to the Pharisees, and then he was sent to Pilate, and then Pilate sent him to Caesar. Does that mean that Jesus went to Rome?

I am Latwii, and am aware of your query, my brother. Again we are faced with the situation in which we must attempt to look within your planet's historical records and attempt to retrieve this information which is by its very nature quite confused, for there are varieties of thought forms created by various groups and individuals over the centuries which have passed since this entity's, as you call it, death. Many have revered this entity, and have looked at this entity in a great variety of ways, and have therefore created forms of thought which are of themselves energy pools and sources that tend to confuse and hide that occurrence which was indeed the pattern of this entity's incarnational experience.

That this entity was required to appear before those which you have mentioned supposes that this entity was indeed in their native homeland, shall we say, yet it is to our humblest and barest ability of retrieving information not clear as to whether this is completely true or as to whether perhaps there might have been the visiting of these entities in another location to which the one known as Jesus was also required to visit.

We again must apologize for our lack of specific information in this case. We are quite without our usual ability to give information.

May we attempt a further query, my brother?

J: No, thank you. We're not getting along tonight. I think I'll just be quiet. But you did do very well.

I am Latwii, and we appreciate your patience with us, my brother. We, of course, are in great need of such patience when we are beyond our abilities to serve. We attempt in these contacts to offer a philosophical point of view which works with the mental evolution of one's being. We are not historians by nature but philosophers, and in some instances that which you might call a scientist, in that we are greatly interested in the formation of light and its expression by entities such as yourselves.

May we attempt another query at this time?

J: Thank you, sir, but I was not impatient at all. I'm very appreciative of your answers and I hope I didn't give you that impression.

I am Latwii, and our attempt was to thank you for your patience. May we attempt another query at this time?

N: Yes, Latwii. Has the philosophical or evolutional aspects of our thought form patterns been changed by rotation of the north and south pole or rearrangement of our poles very many times in our past?

I am Latwii, and am aware of your query, my brother. We find that the pattern of thought of an entity is responsive only to that entity's influence. It is, however, true that any entity may use any outside stimulus in order to change its own pattern of thinking. Those experiences which one encounters—and this may include those of which you speak—may therefore be utilized in the changing of the pattern of thought. Upon your own particular planet there have been many, shall we say, geothermal changes over your cycle of evolution in the third density. There, to our knowledge, however, have not been any of the changes of which you speak during this 75,000 year cycle.

May we answer you further, my brother?

N: Well, of course the dinosaurs existed many, many eons years ago and they have found fresh flowers in frozen mammoths in Siberia which would indicate probably a polar shift which may have exceeded the time span of the last 75,000 years. However, it just seems that there was much intelligent life before, particularly with the Atlanteans, which seem to have been eliminated some ten thousand, one hundred and some odd years ago. Why is it that our method of counting days and months and years is only five to six thousand years old?

I am Latwii, and am aware of your query, my brother. We find that there are two portions which we may address. Firstly, the great changes in your Earth's structure which were responsible for the down-sinking of the continent known to you as Atlantis were changes not of the polar shift variety, but of the results of what you may call nuclear and crystal warfare, which so affected the tectonic plates underlying the continent of Atlantis that there were generated what might be called artificial earthquakes that were therefore responsible for this great change.

In response to the second portion of your query, the numbering of days, months and years which you now use is a system which has survived for the portion of time which you have mentioned but is not the necessary, shall we say, system of time which has been in effect over the entire cycle of your planet. However, it is a system of measuring time which has its basis upon the revolution of your planet about your sun and the revolution of your moon about your planet. There have been many other means of reckoning time but all have been distortions of these rhythms of revolution which are a natural portion of the creation within which you exist.

May we answer you further, my brother?

N: In our illusion, did not other individuals, perhaps even the Neanderthal man, utilize the distortion of the earth's rotation for accumulating time sequences?

I am Latwii, and am aware of your query, my brother. We find that throughout the historical past of your planet there has been the varying abilities of races and groups of entities to reckon time. There have been many attempts to count the passage of seasons as a means of reckoning time. These attempts were not always based upon the knowledge of your Earth's revolution about your sun body but were attempts to reckon time as a means of utilizing the, shall we say, outgrowth of this revolution of your planet about its sun body, that is to say, the seasons in their passing were recognized as that which seemed to repeat upon a regular and measurable scale.

May we answer you further, my brother?

N: Thank you very much. Back to the Atlanteans. Was that an internal strife of civil war or was that a war between other factions? And in the area that the Atlanteans were located, could it be possible to recover some of the fifteen-foot crystals that existed at the time of the holocaust?

I am Latwii, and am aware of your query, my brother. Again we move somewhat outside of our boundaries of ability and shall ask that you appreciate our lack of ability in this area. We can suggest that at some point there will be those who shall discover the remnants of this culture and perhaps there shall be the discovery of the kinds of crystals of which you speak. The entities known to you as the Atlanteans were in their own culture quite divided, and there were those struggles for power at the latter portion of this culture's existence, for the ability to use the technology at that time had grown quite rapidly toward this culture's end time and there were those within the culture who wished for themselves the use of this technology and found the need to vie with others within this great culture for the utilization of the technology which had a great variety of uses.

May we answer you further, my brother?

N: The Koran—the Indian—several of the Indian reports—the country we know as India report what appears to have been nuclear wars at other times. Have there been other civilizations advanced to the point that they devastated themselves with nuclear devices?

I am Latwii, and am aware of your query, my brother. We, in our knowledge of your planet's third-density cycle, are unaware of any cultures besides those known to you as the Atlanteans who were of the technological advancement necessary to utilize the power of the atom. Therefore, we may suggest that the recording of any such nuclear holocaust might be a recording of this very culture's own destruction.

May we answer you further, my brother?

N: No, I think we're probably tiring the instrument and I want to thank you very much. I have some other questions I want to ask later. I thank you.

I am Latwii, and we thank you, my brother, for your patience as well in bearing with us as we must give information which is not that in our usual grasp or reach.

May we attempt another query at this time?

J: Yes, Latwii. Well, then did the Neanderthal man come after the Atlanteans? Before?

I am Latwii, and am aware of your query, my brother, and we dance with joy to be able to answer this particular query. We are aware that those that [are] called the Neanderthal entities were preceding those called the Atlanteans by a great portion of what you call time.

May we answer you further, my brother?

J: Well, were there any Atlanteans left over after the wars?

I am Latwii, and am aware of your query, my brother. The strife and variety of conflicts which wracked this culture were known to many within the culture for a great portion of what you call time. Over a period of two to three centuries there were those entities within this great culture who traveled out from the doomed culture and created bases of survival in various portions of your planet that were located far enough away from the continent of Atlantis that survival was possible.

May we answer you further, my brother?

J: You mean like Spain and France?

I am Latwii, and am aware of your query, my brother. Due to this instrument's familiarity with the information transmitted from our brothers and sisters of Ra we are able to suggest that these locations are in what you now call Tibet, what you now call Turkey, and what you now call Peru.

May we answer you further, my brother?

J: How could they miss the continent, the European continent. I don't understand, was the European continent existing at that time?

I am Latwii, and am aware of your query, my brother. We can answer in the affirmative that the continent that you now call Europe was indeed in existence at that time. As to whether these entities considered such a journey to be desirable or as to whether these entities did indeed undertake a journey in that direction we are unable to say. Who can account for tastes?

May we answer you further, my brother?

J: No, thank you.

I am Latwii, and we feel that we [have] enough energy available in this instrument for one final query. May we then ask for that query?

J: Latwii, when you answer, you say "your planet." What exactly do you mean by that? Where are you in regards to this planet?

I am Latwii, and am aware of your query, my brother. We are within your planetary influence at this time, though it is not our native planet. We are what you might call visitors observing the opportunity that your planet now accepts for the harvest.

May we answer you further, my brother?

J: I don't understand that.

N: Are you on a space ship?

I am Latwii, and am aware of your query, my brother. We, ourselves do not utilize the craft which you might call a space ship for our current observation and transmission of information. We are, however, existing within what you might call your planet's inner planes, those metaphysical realms which are the, as you might call it, spiritual foundation of your planet.

May we answer you further, my brother?

J: I still don't understand. Do you fly over Anchorage very much?

I am Latwii, and am aware of your query, my brother. We are not of the nature to take excursions over your particular area or any particular area upon your planetary surface but choose instead to allow our thoughts to do the traveling.

May we answer you further, my brother?

J: Oh, this is confusing. No. Maybe another time I can …

N: May I ask if the inner planes are those of the astral or ethereal planes or the subcrust areas?

I am Latwii, and am aware of your query, my brother. It is the former portion of your query, that is, as you have called them, the astral and devachanic planes that we choose to inhabit. We choose more specifically to inhabit those planes that are, shall we say, somewhat removed from the astral planes and are of the devachanic or etheric description, depending upon the terms which you might choose.

May we answer you further, my brother?

N: Thank you. No.

J: Is astral travel like out-of-the-body journeys?

I am Latwii, and am aware of your query, my brother. This is a rough analogy, and is somewhat similar to the type of travel which we are suggesting. However, it is for us not an out-of-the-body experience but is a, shall we say—we must correct this instrument and suggest that it is an experience which is in our body, a body which is more filled with light than the third-density body which you inhabit, is indeed a body of fifth density, that being the density of light.

May we answer you further, my brother?

J: Oh, this is confusing, Latwii, very confusing.

Carla: I want to break in here. How's the instrument doing?

I am Latwii, and we thank you, my sister, for asking as to the energy level of this instrument. We feel that we are able to complete our channeling, shall we say, at this particular time, for the instrument is somewhat fatigued, and is concerned as to the level of questioning for the evening. This concern is further fatiguing the instrument. Therefore, we thank you for your concern and shall at this time take our leave of this group and this instrument.

We thank each present for allowing our presence and for asking for humble service this evening. Indeed, this evening our service has been quite humble, for we feel that our inability to respond to the kinds of queries which were offered us has lent a certain amount of confusion to this group which we feel responsible for. We do not mean in any respect to confuse. It is indeed our hope that our service might remove some confusion. We therefore are most able to provide this service in the philosophical type of discussion which focuses upon areas of the evolution of mind, of body, of spirit. We leave the historical and other areas that lie outside the philosophical to those of your peoples, for these areas are those which are well used for catalyst and as one moves through these areas in one's existence, then arises the philosophical questions as to the meaning of the life, the purpose of its movement, and the process of its evolution in one's own experience.

We at this time thank each again and shall take our leave, leaving each in the love and in the light of the one infinite Creator. We are known to you as those of Latwii. Adonai, my friends. Adonai vasu borragus.

Sunday Meditation
February 17, 1985

(C channeling)

I am Hatonn. I am now with this instrument. We greet you in the love and the light of the one infinite Creator. Tonight we would like to relate a tale, a story concerning a small elfin creature. It has found itself alone and in doubt as it leaves its home searching for what it is not sure it is searching. For it came to pass as the elfin creature what for it was the age when the urge to leave the security and warmth of the family is felt. The elfin creature knew that for it there was something it must find, something that lay beyond its home and so, though it loved its family, it proceeded into a world unknown.

We would now transfer this contact.

(L channeling)

I am Hatonn, and I am now with this instrument. To continue our story. The small creature arrived at a point in its life where it realized the necessity for leaving the comfort and security of its home. As with many who face such a realization, this entity had no clear awareness of the reason or reasons behind this realization but was simply aware that the time had come and it must go. The creature, like many of us faced with departure, first sought the security of a destination, for in your world, does not one who dives from the springboard immediately seek the reassurance of an arrival in the pool rather than the interim where one is suspended in midair?

The entity to whom we refer selected a distant point of which it had some secondhand knowledge and proceeded to travel to that objective, unaware like many of us that the travel was the objective rather than the arrival. The trip was a long one, especially for one so young and away from the nest for the first time. Indeed, the distractions of the trip, the dangers, the need to seek for food, the uncomfortable climate, often drove from the creature's mind the destination entirely. The creature at night, in its loneliness and discomfort, would envision ways in which that travel could be accomplished without the stress and discomforts associated with travel.

My friends, many of us are like that creature. We have all at some point set our feet upon a path, a road that leads us through immense valleys of distraction, of hardship, of disquiet and often, my friends, we sit and wonder what led us to this choice. We envision paths of learning for ourselves which are devoid of hardship, which allow us machine-like to simply record the knowledge we seek, and then we simply envision alighting from our vehicle with our hair unmussed, our clothing unwrinkled, and our growth complete.

My friends, we will not attempt to tell you that the hardships of the path determine the value of the education, for that must be decided within the heart of each, and those answers, with complete honesty, may differ. What we can offer, my friends, is but the observation that each of us, like the creature in our tale, made certain choices, often from reasons dimly understood or perhaps not understood, but choices which lead each of us to a path of perfection which impeccably suits but one individual. My friends, accept with serenity the knowledge that the choices you have made lead you upon a path of your own making, a path leading to your own perfection, a path which within your soul you know is the only path you may follow.

At this time we will relinquish our use of this instrument that our brothers and sisters of Latwii might perform their service. Adonai, my friends. We are known to you as Hatonn.

(L channeling)

I am Latwii, and I greet you in the love and the light of the infinite Creator. At this time are there any questions that we may attempt to answer?

C: Latwii, we found out several years ago that in cases where blood or an organ from one individual is introduced into another one, there is a need of rebalancing because the part of that original person has gone into another. What happens in the case where something artificial is put in? The plastic heart that they're using now?

I am Latwii, and I am aware of your question. My brother, if we might answer your question with a question, what value or sensation do you experience upon receiving an object which was valued by another entity for which you possess a great affection? Is it not true that the object itself becomes imbued with what might be termed the essence of that individual? Is it not often a pleasant experience to enter a space occupied by one for whom you feel respect or affection? An individual imbues those objects around himself with his own atmosphere. Therefore, my brother, we would suggest you consider the quality of the energies directed toward the creation and assembly of the object you describe and consider the effects upon its recipient to receive an object born of benevolence, one might say.

May we answer you further?

C: No, I'll think on that for awhile.

I am Latwii. Is there another question?

Jim: Latwii, last week there were some questions asked that were hard for you to give answers to because they were of a historical nature rather than a philosophical nature. Could you give us an idea of the importance of the kinds of questions we ask as it affects our tuning and the kinds of answers then you are able to give?

I am Latwii. I am aware of your question. My brothers, in respect to the maintenance of attunement within the group, we would observe that a fine line must be tread for maximum efficiency in maintaining group attunement, yet that broad deviation from that line is requisite for the purpose of our service. To elucidate, the ideal question for the maximized maintenance of attunement would be a question which has similar emotional and intellectual impact among all participants within the group, thereby achieving a uniform state of arousal within the interest level of the group when the question is verbalized. Obviously, the terrain that can be covered in this manner is substantially limited. One might therefore observe that the maximum efficiency in maintenance of attunement for the group minimizes the efficiency of that service we attempt to perform. Therefore, a wide range of questions which correspond to the sincere interests of the individuals within the group would be much more valuable in satisfying those interests.

A consideration should be given when one desires to keep the attention of other entities from flagging to limiting the number of questions in areas of limited interest so as to avoid the effect of minds wandering from disinterest over an extended span of questions for which most participants have little interest. However, questions on any subject matter, however limited our ability to answer, are always appropriate and we would emphasize that limiting the subject matter entirely would not be of maximum benefit to any concerned.

May we answer you further?

Jim: Not at this time, thank you, Latwii.

We thank you. Is there another question?

Jim: On another topic, Latwii, I'm interested in why the telepathic level of communication differs so markedly from the trance level, where it seems in trance the type of information can be much more specific as compared to the information that is usually delivered in meetings such as this in the telepathic sense. Could you give me some insight into why telepathic contacts are less able, it seems, to deliver precise information as compared to trance contacts?

I am Latwii. My brother, we ask you to consider the natures of the two contacts in relation to the instruments involved. In the trance contact the instrument has relinquished control to hopefully a benevolent entity to the extent that the physical instrument itself might be considered newly occupied, its original occupant having temporarily abandoned the facility. Within this framework, the new, temporary occupant is capable of unfettered expression, the ability to communicate without the restraints imposed by the non-trance instrument. The information, therefore, is allowed to be communicated without distortion of any significance.

In the non-trance communication by instrument, however, the instrument remains under the control of its rightful occupant and is used in a two-stage manner, that is, the information is transmitted to the occupant of the instrument who assimilates the information, and by necessity must interpret that information to translate it into a useable form which is that uttered verbally. As you are aware, my brother, the communications in this manner often arrive in the form of non-verbalized concepts which must be first comprehended by the instrument, then dismantled into the appropriate verbal symbols which are then communicated by the instrument's voice and hopefully reassembled into some semblance of what was intended by those listening.

The difficulty in the transmission of factual information in this manner resides partially in the emotional status of the instrument and partially in the instrument's capacity to clearly comprehend such data. For example, the conceptualization of numbers beyond the number five is quite difficult, which one might discover if one attempts to picture within one's mind five of the same object simultaneously, each completely distinct from the other four. For this reason, the communication of a picture, so to speak, of any but the smallest numbers would be beyond the capacity of the receiver.

In addition, my brother, the instrument entity performs a necessary screening, or if you will, tainting of information to bring the desired percentage of involvement to the right level. One facet of this performance is that the instrument's emotions frequently allow the instrument to be sufficiently unsure of the accuracy of data transmitted …

(Side one of tape ends.)

(L channeling)

… as to request repeated retransmission of that same data without gaining confidence in its accuracy. The resultant lack of confidence and increasing emotional distress resultant tend to further weaken the link between the transmitter and the instrument receiving, thereby garbling the attempt even further.

Have we expressed this concept with sufficient clarity, my brother?

Jim: I believe you have, Latwii. Thank you very much.

We thank you, my brother. Is there another question?

(Pause)

I am Latwii. We have been asked to communicate an expression of love from the area known as Colorado to this group. Having done so, and with the awareness that there are no further questions, we shall take our leave. In the love and the light of the infinite Creator, we are known to you as Latwii. ☙

Intensive Meditation
February 23, 1985

(Carla channeling)

I am Hatonn. I greet you, my friends, in the love and in the light of our infinite Creator. It is a great pleasure to speak with you this evening. We especially welcome the opportunity to continue the training of the new instrument known as S. You may notice that we almost always refer to entities respecting the fact that the name of the entity is not the entity but merely an artificial label by which your peoples categorize each other. One of the greatest differences betwixt third density and that kingdom which many are about to inherit which we call fourth density is that the labeling on an artificial level becomes unnecessary, thereby freeing entities from the many false vibrations which are thrown out about each entity which is misnamed.

We wish to tell you a parable, a little story. Once upon a time there was an old man who with his trusty walking stick was making his way through the cobblestones of the village in which he had lived and his father before him and his father before him. This man had married and yet his wife had died, and in dying had lost their only unborn child. More than years bent the old man's back as he picked his way along the cobblestones.

We shall transfer.

(S channeling)

The instrument is feeling our vibration but is extremely nervous this evening due to a thought process that she has been going through, one in which she does not feel that she is able to actually serve as an instrument, is afraid to be wrong. Let us assure her that these doubts are a normal process that each new instrument goes through, not to analyze or try to sense ahead in the story or be afraid that it is her imagination and not our words.

The old man felt very lonely and desolate. He wandered through the town and saw many familiar faces, for as he grew up in that town, it was a small town, a small village in which he knew each and every person, their children by name. In the past he had always attained great comfort in this village but today he felt alone. He felt he had lost his only life in the loss of his great love, his wife and the baby he had yet to meet but yet loved with all his heart.

We transfer to allow this instrument the opportunity to relax.

(Jim channeling)

On this day as the old man wandered through the village, his burden of grief and concern brought into his mind a new idea. And upon this idea, this inspiration, he decided to act. With but a few possessions and his trusted walking stick, he set out of the village and began to make a journey over a nearby pass of mountains and wandered for as far as his legs would carry him for the first day. As he journeyed, he felt a certain peace within, and though he knew not his final destination, there was a small measure of comfort that he took as he journeyed.

We shall now transfer.

(Carla channeling)

Soon the sun grew low in the west and he made camp and rested. And is *(inaudible)* a procession of days and nights the old man journeyed far until he was so many miles from his village that no one ever had heard of him. No one knew the man with the walking stick, and at first the old man was lonelier than ever and wished that he had not forsaken his home. Here he felt no one would love him. Here he felt no one would pick him up should he fall, tend him if he grew ill, wipe away his tears, and though love whispered in the trees, murmured along the grasses, his ear did not hear nor did his eyes see until the day when he indeed did become very ill as his heart failed him, and he went to his knees upon the dusty trail just outside another small and unknown village.

(S channeling)

He lay on the ground feeling very much alone, though surrounded by trees and the sky and the flowers nearby. He felt that he was alone in the universe. As the old man lay there with his walking stick nearby, some children passing came upon him. One knelt down to wipe the hair from his brow while another ran home for help. The man lay there wondering, "How can these children help me?" and yet received tremendous love and comfort in the light, cool touch of this little child's caring hand. Before long, he awoke to find himself in a bed in a room full of people who, though [they] had strange faces, had very familiar eyes. The eyes of these people in this small town were the same eyes that he had loved in the town behind. Women served him broth, a man built a fire, children laughed in the other room. Although he knew not their names, nor where he was, he recognized the same sounds, the sameness of people and the caring in these people in this new village.

We transfer.

(Jim channeling)

As he lay upon the bed, many thoughts passed through the old man's mind. He began to think on the times that he had spent in his home village with his wife and how they had hoped for such a long time to have a family of their own. He treasured these memories and thought much about the feelings that he and his wife had shared. Now as he looked about him, he saw many new faces, yet the eyes and the caring were old and familiar as friends, and he thought to himself that there must be some meaning here, for he had just undertaken a long journey through unfamiliar terrain and had nearly seen his life pass before his eyes. And now there was about him a great expression of love and compassion. The old man knew that there was here a caring which was like unto that that he had known with his wife and friends, that could not be changed by location or time and somehow this gave him hope. He looked then into other portions of his life and those things that he desired and had felt would never be his to see if there was perhaps a wider opportunity for these to also be a portion of his new discoveries.

We shall transfer.

(Carla channeling)

As he pondered and as he recovered, he found himself quite often in the company of one particular young man. This young man was drawn to the traveler, and together they spoke of many things and shared many thoughts. The old man discovered that his young friend was only six months younger than his own child would have been had his wife borne him and the young man became more and more enamored of the traveler. They spoke of his falling and the miracle the old man felt had happened when small children were able to mobilize a village in aid of a stranger.

We shall transfer.

(S channeling)

The young man had been dissatisfied with his life in a small town, had been dreaming of traveling to a new and exciting larger village in which to find the happiness that he was seeking. By sharing and talking with this traveler he began to realize the experiences of this old traveler were ones where he could learn from, that the larger town that he had been dreaming of did not have the answer, was no different, would hold the same eyes as the town in which he was presently living. And through the eyes of his friend, the old traveler, he began to see his own village, though tiny, with a new sense, a new awareness. He felt the kindness and the love that had banded together to help the old man. He heard the laughter of the children through new ears. He saw the young girls through a new heart and realized the happiness that he was seeking could be found in the small village in which he lived. He need not venture on a long journey as the traveler had done, for he took that long journey through his sharing in the awarenesses gained through his friend.

This story is one that applies everywhere. Though you may travel from city to city, from mountains to sea looking and searching as the old traveler did for the answers to your loneliness, you may wish before venturing out to choose to listen to the children outside your window, to see the eyes of your neighbors and feel the hearts of your friends. The answers, my brothers and sisters, may be in your own back yard.

We transfer.

(Jim channeling)

Your journeys, whether you ever move in the geographical sense or not, shall be long, and shall have included the great heights that one attains from time to time and the ability to see in the distant past as from the top of the mountain and to discern those portions of your learning which have been well done. You may look into what you call your future and see many possibilities for continuing this journey. And as you continue it, you will find from time to time that there are valleys and vales and turns in your trail which take you in places that are not so easily discerned. You will have your doubts as to which fork in the road to take. You will feel the gains and the losses and a burden with memory, yet still you shall push on, for within the heart of each of you, my friends, is the strong and thirsty seeker which yearns for that which it does not have, or so it seems.

And though you shall move within your mind to many points of viewing, when you sum your journey at any point, you will find that within it is contained the whole of that which you have sought. You are that which you seek; you are the trail that you travel; you are the seeker that yearns; and you hide from yourself the mysteries of your being that you may unfold them when the time of your journey is right.

Like the old man, you have your trusted walking stick, those cherished beliefs that carry you onward and steady you from time to time as the trail becomes treacherous. And yet as the walking stick serves well for a time, it frequently must be replaced for the wear and tear of the journey beats hard upon the seeker and its beliefs. Yet that heart of the seeker remains strong in seeking and is that which sustains the seeker's journey.

We shall transfer.

(Carla channeling)

And whenever that heart fails because of overwhelming circumstances, and you, like the old man, find yourself upon the ground, never fear, for the wind shall tell the sky; the sky shall whisper it to the trees; the trees shall murmur to the birds, the raven, the hawk, the sparrow. And one special bird shall bespeak a small child, a child who prattles as he plays, yet the child shall run to see that of which the bird speaks, and shall then go and receive the aid abundant, running over that [which] is needed. Therefore, be ye of light heart amidst the complexities of the dark world. There is no moment which does not contain all that is needed, all that is good, all that is beautiful, and all that is true. Even if you cry, let your tears be a benediction as you acknowledge the frailty of this illusion and the enormous power of love that shall lift up all that is broken. And if you so desire, make all whole.

Should we ask then for names? Or shall we use one name for all the eyes in all the entities which we see …

(Side one of tape ends.)

(Carla channeling)

We shall leave this instrument at this time, with many thanks to each instrument for the privilege of working with each. We leave you in love and in the light of One Who Is beyond name, beyond identification, in the love and in the light of One Who Is all that there is. We leave you in the infinite love and the omnipresent light of the one Creator. We are known to you by the name Hatonn. Adonai. Adonai.

(Jim channeling)

I am Latwii, and we greet you, my friends, in the love and the light of that same Creator. We wear our name quite proudly in your little group, and are happy to offer our humble service if we may attempt to answer your queries at this time. May we then begin?

S: Latwii, do you have any suggestions as to how I could be a better servant in this process as an instrument?

I am Latwii, and am aware of your query, my sister. Well, now, the subject is one which we could speak at length on but we feel that there is a short [answer] which is most appropriate. That is to persevere, my sister. It is not that difficult to become an instrument, as you are well aware. What is most difficult is to become a foolish instrument, that is, one which is willing to step out upon the limb not knowing whether there shall be another portion to support the stepping again. If you can in your own mind and heart, then, learn to step fearlessly out with no assurance that there shall be support, you shall be developing that ability of surrender which is most helpful in this type of service.

May we answer you further, my sister?

S: Latwii, I live very far from here, and it is very difficult to come here in which to train. I have support and love where I come from but I do want to do the right way and the right tuning to receive your messages of love and light. Is there anything that I can do to speed this process? I have very little patience.

I am Latwii, and am aware of your query, my sister. Well, this is the usual case for the seeker. Seekers begin with a great desire and very little patience, and when the seeker is the adept it has then great patience and very little desire. Upon this journey and this balancing we can continually recommend a healthy dose of patience but can also suggest that as your abilities in this area proceed, you may be able to find those very close and trusted friends in your own geographical location with which you may practice this particular skill after a certain amount of its refinement has occurred to your own satisfaction.

May we answer you further, my sister?

S: Thank you, Latwii. I have a question on another subject, and that is the level or density of what is referred to as personal guides, our spirit guides, those inner plane teachers. Can you speak to that?

I am Latwii, and am aware of your query, my sister. Ah yes, indeed, we may speak to this subject, for again it is one which has a great range of possibilities. One's seeking in one's incarnation is that which attracts to the self those friends and, as you have called them, guides and angelic presences which attempt to serve as a result of the call or seeking of the entity involved. This call or seeking, therefore, can be of an infinite variety of possibility. There are many entities who can and do respond to such seeking. They may be of your own planetary influence, and may be those who have as yourself incarnated a number times upon a certain planetary influence and who between the, shall we say, incarnations, serve as the guide now with a wider perspective. There are guides and friends also attracted from influences and density levels, thus you have at your disposal, according to your seeking, entities of a great variety of sources, yet all are the one Creator in certain distortions or frequencies, seeking to be of service to the One.

May we answer you further, my sister?

S: I think you covered it. I was specifically asking for those guides that are with us from birth until death, knowing that we have the ability also to access higher teachers. It is a question that has come up many times in my work as sharing information under a course of Free Soul. Thank you.

I am Latwii, and we thank you, my sister. Is there another question?

S: How am I doing as a beginner? Is there anything that you can—a fine point that you can give me, a help to better this process?

I am Latwii, and am aware of your query, my sister. At this point we feel that your progress is that which is to be commended. We cannot suggest fine points at this time, for at this time the basic process of becoming the fool, the one who opens the self to another with the tuning completed is that process which you have undertaken and undertaken well.

May we answer you further, my sister?

S: I guess it's the old story of practice, practice, practice. Thank you.

I am Latwii, and we thank you, my sister. May we attempt another query?

S: When Hatonn first came in I felt that Hatonn, those of Hatonn, were trying to open through me. And yet I was struggling with calling it my imagination. Can you speak to that?

I am Latwii and am aware of your query, my sister. And we note that you are correct upon both assumptions.

May we answer you further?

S: No. Thanks.

I am Latwii, and we again thank you. May we attempt another query at this time?

S: There was a dizziness that both Carla and I experienced upon landing in Atlanta, a lightheartedness, a nausea, and a dizziness. Can you give us information on that?

I am Latwii, and am aware of your query, my sister. Upon this particular topic we feel there is no need to discuss in great detail those transient phenomena which can frequently assail the traveler who has moved a great distance in a confined space, and which has felt the accompanying discomfort.

May we attempt further response, my sister?

Carla: Then you're ruling out all possibility of negative entities' energizing the problem?

I am Latwii, and am aware of your query, my sister. We have not ruled out such a possibility, for indeed it always exists but at this point we feel that each of you, my sisters, have enough experience with such that there need not be any over-concentration upon these phenomena.

May we attempt further response, my sister?

Carla: My hand got very bad very fast some short time after that, and S virtually burned her own skin trying to help me get through that pain. Is it important to judge whether there is a negative entity energizing in such an occurrence?

I am Latwii, and am aware of your query, my sister. We feel that the importance in such a case after the recognition of the possibility of what is occurring lies more in the loving of the entity and the finding of the perfection in the moment, no matter what the moment.

May we attempt further response, my sister?

Carla: Yes, just one more. S and I both felt that what we needed to do was to interpret the pain, and when I thought back over the day, the only thing that I'd done during the day was to move a rolling cart that only took the pressure of one finger to move. Nevertheless, had anyone been with me I would not have been willing to do it. I therefore took it as a sign and a warning that I needed to continue to limit myself and accept my limitations, and, indeed, limit myself more than I had been. Can you verify this process of thinking?

I am Latwii, and am aware of your query, my sister. We feel that your ability to analyze such a situation is quite well refined and is of the utmost importance in this particular situation. Therefore, we cannot speak specifically, for your own choices are of paramount importance as you consider the ramifications of your limitations and what is the most appropriate response to them.

May we attempt further response, my sister?

Carla: *(Inaudible).*

I am Latwii, and we thank you, my sister. Is there another query at this time?

S: In attempting to help dissipate the pain, I had an intense burning of my palm. Was I holding too long or too close?

I am Latwii, and am aware of your query, my sister. We may suggest in general when one attempts to serve as that known as the healer that the most efficient kind of, shall we say, healing catalyst is that which moves through the healer and does not use the healer's own energies, for each entity within your illusion is of a finite nature and that which available to each entity is of an infinite nature, and is therefore more able to serve as the healing catalyst.

May we answer you further, my sister?

S: I attempted to visualize a healing energy passing from the spiritual universe through me and actively trying to not give of my energy but just to be an instrument in which to focus energy through. I guess I failed if I'm interpreting what you said correctly. I was giving my energy rather than passing the energy through which was my intent. Although I did not feel drained.

I am Latwii, and we feel that within your comment there is the query. If we have mistaken the query, please re-question. We may suggest that your great caring for the one known as Carla created a concern that your were responsible for this entity, and the desire to aid the entity in the healing of the hand then did carry a portion of this personal desire.

May we answer you further, my sister?

S: No, thank you.

I am Latwii, and we thank you, my sister, and may make final comment in the respect of those who would serve as healers, and that is that the healer asks that the will of the one Creator be done. The healer then has no will.

May we attempt another query at this time?

S: Thank you, Latwii. A question came up the other night of sending healing love or healing energy to another person. I have been sending to those what you call guides of that person, who I feel are far better at—able to discern how much should be passed through to the person. Others have said they send it directly to the person in need. Can you speak on the two?

I am Latwii, and am aware of your query, my sister, and we can speak by asking if you write a letter to a friend, you may give it to the friend or give it to a friend of the friend who will give it to the friend, and when the letter is read by the friend, the friend will take from the letter what it will. Therefore, the message delivered is the same message—that which the friend receives is what the friend chooses. Therefore, we may suggest that it matters not.

May we answer you further, my sister?

S: I guess I was concerned with infringing, sending energy not requested even though I was aware of someone being ill. But I think the previous statement of the will of the Creator being the utmost and just offering light is the true bottom line. Thank you.

I am Latwii, and we thank you again, my sister. Is there another query at this time?

Carla: Just a check, a little reality check. Basically, then, the metaphysics of the situation are that the incarnational personality is the boss of the higher self. The higher self does not protect the self, it is rather a resource of the self, and is used by intention. Is that what you're intimating?

I am Latwii, and am aware of your query, my sister. We have a somewhat new facet to this query, now we have introduced the higher self. Now this portion of the small self, shall we say, does indeed guide and protect when possible, yet at most times is that which is the resource for the entity within the incarnation. The entity's free will is that which is of paramount importance at all times, and is that which will determine whether the entity accepts guidance and protection from any other source, be it the higher self, inner plane guides, or earthly friends who may attempt assistance in any of an infinite number of forms.

This free will is frequently exercised upon a subconscious basis, we may add, therefore the entity may seek healing for a situation which has still some lesson to teach which has not been consciously learned. Therefore, the entity will consciously see the healing yet its subconscious mind shall continue the configuration of the disease until the lesson has been learned. Therefore, the free will is exercised subconsciously in part and in part consciously. The free will in its total exercise will be that factor which determines how much the entity shall accept from whatever source.

May we answer you further, my sister?

S: No, thank you, I'm through. It's nice to talk to you.

I am Latwii, and we thank you, my sister. It is a joy to hear your voice as well. May we attempt another query at this time?

(Pause)

I am Latwii, and we are very privileged to have been able to join this group this evening. It has been a great thrill for us to speak, and we thank each of you. We at this time shall leave this group and shall be happy to join each in meditations upon request. We are those of Latwii and we leave you now in the love and in the light of our infinite Creator. Adonai. Adonai, my friends. ☙

Sunday Meditation
February 24, 1985

(Carla channeling)

I am Hatonn, and I greet you in the love and in the light of our infinite Creator. We thank you for allowing us to speak with you this evening and we use this time to tell a story and to test a point or two that may aid you in your thinking at this time.

Once there was a man who wished to build a fence of bricks. This man was a proud man and he wished his wall to be perfect. It was with exquisite care that he laid the plumb line and found the perfect horizontal level. The man was happy as he took fastidious care to begin his task rightly. The sun shone down upon him until he was very warm, yet he welcomed the sun. Indeed, the entity welcomed the chance to do the work that was necessary in order to begin to build his wall.

We shall transfer.

(L channeling)

I am Hatonn. I am now with this instrument. We shall continue. The entity of whom we spoke welcomed the labors necessary for the construction of his wall for he welcomed the opportunity to place his efforts in attunement with the pace of the universe he was able to sense in operation surrounding him, for just as the plumb line was true and the level a perfect one, so also did the universe about him operate with perfection. And as the subject of our tale perceived this state and moved in harmony within it, he felt the joy one feels when one becomes aware of the Godness within one's own efforts. The act of creation in progress constantly about the entity was reflected in his own efforts to create this wall. And as his efforts were directed truly and accurately toward the completion of this perfect wall, so also did his contentment grow and his sense of fulfillment in this manifestation of that force he could feel about himself.

Upon its completion, another entity spoke to him in regards to his efforts, questioning the value of a wall, an object often used to shut other selves out. His contentment remained undisturbed. His reply was that the perfection lay within the object he had created and that it would remain perfect regardless of the efforts another might make to corrupt that perfection through misuse.

My friends, we often perceive about us our brothers and sisters engaged in actions which we may not understand or may preconceive a value for, and it is difficult to avoid attributing our predeveloped prejudices to individuals or the works they originate which remind us of what has occurred or what we have perceived within our own past experiences.

My brothers and my sister, a wall is but a wall. An act of creation is simply an act of creation which may be used as a tool towards selflessness or selfishness, and it is not always easy to perceive the intention which was in the mind of its creator. Be cautious, my friends, that you might avoid misunderstanding the efforts of another through your perceptions of similar efforts on the parts of those who have gone before, for it is within the heart of the builder, not the hands, that the potential value may grow.

At this time we will transfer to another instrument. I am Hatonn.

(Carla channeling)

I am Hatonn. We shall continue. Relationships with others might be likened to walls but even more we draw the simile of the wall to speak about yourselves. An attempt to come into right relationship with another is an attempt to cross walls on many levels of this meaning. The first wall which must be true is the structure of your own being. Perhaps your basic character is excellent, the lines true and straight, yet they have become dilapidated, bricks or stones missing, mortar failing. Therefore, when one is contemplating the experiences which arise within a relationship, it is well to begin the contemplation with an objective gaze inwardly directed at the structure of the self. If the base is not perfectly horizontal, if it is not quite plumb, then all will seem out of tune, out of order, shaky and fraught with difficulty.

Therefore, we suggest that you use meditation and contemplation to build yourself as inspiration gives you one piece of knowledge and then another and another as you move along the pathway of discovery.

When you gaze beyond your own wall of being, beyond your own structure at another, it is well to remember that there is only one builder for each being that exists; that builder is the being itself. Each entity is created uniquely, first male or female, then an incredible variety of other polarities. All these pieces of structure are placed together to build the skeletal being through which consciousness is manifested.

How shall two walls which are fixed relate to each other? My friends, it is time to release the allegory and gaze at an illusion which may illuminate the denser illusion in which you now enjoy existence. The walls that you build within yourself are energy fields. Therefore, they are moveable and must move with you wherever you go. The stance which you take, the wall which you choose to use, behind which you choose to hide within a relationship with another, is that which must be observed, analyzed and balanced in such a way that the wall again becomes an energy field which is permeable so that two walls may …

(Page 4 of the original transcript is missing.)

… this group once again and we do so in joy. We thank you and we ask if we might attempt to answer a query or two this evening?

Carla: Okay. I have a student who has begun to channel very well. She has no experience and yet it is very difficult for her to come here and gain the experience, technically speaking. When she is properly tuned she is perfectly able to channel. She is very concerned about her ability to channel away from the protection of more experienced channels. I wonder if you could speak concerning her concern and where wisdom lies in my helping her in her work.

I am Latwii, and am aware of your query, my sister. The new instrument of which you speak is one which has indeed begun to assimilate the process of becoming a vocal channel to a degree which is gratifying, and yet is at that point which must be tenderly cared for, for as the new instrument begins to utilize his desire to be of service and finds that service broadening, there is the constant tendency to wonder if that which is received is that which is transmitted. This is where the experience is most helpful to one which is in constant need of building the confidence. We feel that the entity of which you speak is one which is well aware of the tuning necessity and the joint necessity of challenging those contacts which it first feels after the tuning has been completed. This entity is one which has a surrounding of friends which can provide the few who would aid in completing the protection and tuning needs of new instruments, yet it might be well for this new instrument to experience further exercising of its expanding abilities before attempting to, shall we say, set out upon its own in this endeavor. Yet this potential is one which grows with this new instrument's continued exercise.

May we answer you further, my sister?

Carla: Specifically, the entity known as S is unsure whether or not to practice with the support group before she comes here again. I'd like any advice you can give me on what to tell her.

I am Latwii, and am aware of your query, my sister. As we have attempted to iterate in our previous response, this is a point in this new instrument's development which is as the tender shoot which has just begun to move from the seed and is now seeking the light of day for the first time. There are potential difficulties for such a tender shoot as it moves into the light of day. We can suggest that this instrument is near the point in its development at which it would indeed be able to practice its abilities as a vocal instrument with those chosen about it in its, as you call it, distant location. We would not wish to rush this instrument's progress, for though there is a great possibility that at this time it could practice upon its own with support, there is also a significant possibility that it could find difficulties which would, shall we say, set it back in its progress. Therefore, we cannot be specific in our suggestion, for the growth of the instrument is at a point that is difficult to accurately estimate.

May we answer you further, my sister?

Carla: Yes. I agree with you completely. That was my feeling, too.

My feeling further was that as S and I had talked of before, perhaps you could spend not just two days but plan ahead, come as on vacation, possibly even with family, and work for a period of five to seven days, and this week—say of two meditations a day—would put her over the edge safely as far as being able to pick up vibrations and so forth. Could you confirm that?

I am Latwii, and am aware of your query, my sister, and we can suggest that this potential plan is one which would be far more liable to present this new instrument with a firm foundation upon which it shall offer its services as a vocal instrument.

May we answer you further, my sister?

Carla: No, thank you.

I am Latwii, and we thank you, my sister, as always. May we attempt another query at this time?

L: Latwii, would you speak some on the nature of competition? I recognize it in some ways as being a very beneficial way of sharing in the nature of the camaraderie involved between those who participate as opposed to those who are destined to be winner or loser. At the same time, there seems to be such an abuse of competition within our world that I'd be interested in hearing whatever you have to say on the subject.

I am Latwii, and am aware of your query, my brother. We may take this topic and look upon it as a means whereby an individual or group of individuals may seek to develop those skills which lie within in order to express a certain potential, shall we say, much as your young kittens roll and tumble about upon the rug as they seek to express that which is within their physical energy systems. The entities who partake in your competitive games and sport activities are those of the, shall we say, childlike nature who seek to discover the limits to which the self can be put and the fruits of putting themselves to those limits. As these discoveries and fruits are harvested, then there is the choice that the individual and the group of individuals can make. This choice is of the basic nature which is, shall we say, the nature of your illusion itself. That is, shall the abilities of an entity be used to aid and enjoy others or shall these abilities be used to aid and bring pleasure to the self?

When entities utilize the abilities in the manner which lends to the enjoyment of many, then it is as if the gift of the one Creator in its unique form for each entity has been radiated out from this entity to those about it, and the general mirth and pleasure and enhanced experience of the group then is the final result of this testing of self. When the entity or group, however, then decides that the abilities of the group shall be pitted against another group or an entity decides this for itself and shall then pit its abilities against another in order to best or defeat that group or other self, then we have the attempt to gather for the self or group those gifts not only given to the self but those abilities and attentions and recognitions of others as well.

This is the beginning of the service-to-self polarity but is seldom, shall we say, pursued in perfect purity, for there is much within your competitive sports which swings to and fro, back and forth between the poles of radiance and magnetism or positivity and negativity. Therefore, my brother, you have the tool of what you have called competition which may be used as may any tool to serve self or serve others.

May we answer you further, my brother?

L: No, that's been a great help. I compliment you on your analogy …

(Side one of tape ends.)

(Jim channeling)

I am Latwii, and am once again with this instrument. May we attempt another query at this time?

Carla: One more and then we'll quit. I understand that anger often produces cancer in people. I was contemplating what brings about the heart trouble? If it can be associated with certain emotions? Is it as simple as heartbreak or sorrow?

I am Latwii, and am aware of your query, my sister. Though generalities are frequently our lot in attempting to answer your queries, they are quite often not specifically accurate in all instances, for there are anomalies in all general rules. As you look to the disease that any entity may be experiencing, one may look to the nature of the disease, the effect of the disease upon the entity. Frequently it is also possible to look to the location of the difficulty within an entity and be able to place this difficulty with its corresponding energy center, then discovering the nature of the energy blockage according to the energy center involved.

In the case of the difficulties with the heart, one of the two primary organs within the human being as you know it, one deals with a portion of the physical vehicle which has analogous and extensive relationships with each of the various energy centers, for this organ does by its functioning provide the entire physical vehicle with the nutrients that are carried by the bloodstream, as it is called. This organ, then, is that which in the physical sense enlivens the entire physical vehicle and circulates the essence of that vehicle throughout its system of transport, shall we say. An entity who feels the difficulty or disease which is located within the heart is an entity who in many cases has blocked the ability of the finer body or energy center's heart in its action of providing a life-sustaining and life-enhancing energy or essence not only to the self but perhaps to other selves as well.

As you look upon the energy center which has the closest correlation to the physical organ of the heart, the green ray energy center then is brought into focus in it's function of providing the unconditional love and support that is the building block, shall we say, or life-sustaining force throughout all of creation. When a portion of this force has been activated within an entity and then upon a subsequent occasion been blocked in some degree, there may be an expression of this blockage within the physical organ of the heart. The variety of kinds of blockages is so great as to be quite beyond our ability to enumerate with any hope of completion. We can suggest that as we have mentioned, the function of the physical heart in providing the entire vehicle sustenance is analogous to the green energy center and its providing of the unconditional love and creative force which underlies all of creation.

May we attempt a further response, my sister?

Carla: No, thank you.

I am Latwii, and we thank you, my sister. We must apologize for our response which was quite lengthy and yet was not able to be as specific as perhaps you had hoped. May we attempt another query at this time?

Carla: Well, since you've said that, I'll tell you the reason I hesitated. It was not because I didn't think that you were very clear; I did. I realized that you have to take all generalizations with a good deal of grains of salt. I was going to go into the somewhat baroque question of the mechanical things that people will tell you will hurt the heart, the cholesterol, the plaque and smoking, various things like that, and decided not to because—I realized when I thought about it that actually those behaviors, the ways of eating, the way one feels about one's body, is probably tied in, just as you said, with a grain of salt, with the feeling one has about oneself as a person who offers love. So I didn't ask the question, but I thought that you were very specific, as specific as I would expect you could be. Thank you.

I am Latwii, and we thank you, my sister. We can make the additional general comment that when an entity is engaging in those patterns of thought which tend to block any of the various energy centers, whatever means is available to that entity that will allow the expression of this blockage when it has not been noticed by the mental process of analysis will then be utilized. Those which are of the scientist's career have noted the similarity of certain of your cultural habits and customs which are closely related to certain dysfunctions, yet in many cases these are not available to an individual, and yet other means must be found to produce the symbolic disease of the physical vehicle in order that the mental complex might then take note and more efficiently use that catalyst which was not well used when first presented to the entity.

May we answer further of this query or another query?

Carla: Thank you.

I am Latwii, and we find that we have for the moment exhausted those queries which have so graciously been placed before us this evening. We thank you each, my friends, for your graciousness in once again extending to us the invitation to join your seeking of the truth this evening. We, as humble messengers and pilgrims upon that one and the same path, are gratified to be able to join you, and remind each of you that it is only because we have traveled a bit further upon that path that we attempt to aid you upon your journey. We have no hard, shall we say, and fast rules which must obeyed or even listened to. Take that then which has the value to you for your own consideration. Leave that then which has no value in your considerations. We shall leave this group at this time and return upon your request. In the love and the light then, we leave you and thank you and bless you. We are those of Latwii. Adonai. Adonai, my friends.

Intensive Meditation
February 26, 1985

(Carla channeling)

I am Laitos. I greet, you my friends, in the love and in the light of the infinite Creator. It is a great pleasure to be here and to be able to use this instrument, and we thank you profoundly for offering us the opportunity to serve you. We ourselves get so much from the sharing of our humble thoughts and gifts that we can never thank you enough for allowing us to walk with you, to be with you and to aid you as you travel along the path of those who venture into unknown territory in search of invisible yet palpable truth. The process of channeling is in some ways simple enough that it confuses those who are attempting to learn the techniques involved. We do not ask you to refrain from discrimination. Indeed, we ask each entity who wishes to learn to become a vocal instrument to tune carefully, to remain surrounded in white light, and to challenge each and every entity each and every time that entity appears.

There are those who become overconfident believing that they recognize the vibratory pattern of a certain contact. This is not the case. There are those who would wish to eliminate yet one more light giver by the simple expedient of mimicking the vibratory patterns of those such as we who wish nothing except to serve you. Paradoxically, we ourselves are greatly served. However, once that is understood, the simplicity of the channeling process is almost stunning. If one has the catcher's mitt and the baseball is thrown, the catcher will catch that ball. However, he will immediately have to throw it again, hopefully with careful direction, in order that his glove is empty once again as the next ball hits the glove. It is difficult to catch ball after ball in the same glove. The contact is lost just as the concepts or the balls are lost [if] they fall upon the ground and the catcher who pitches is no longer able to function either as a catcher or a pitcher.

This is the way of channeling. We work, as this instrument has mentioned, within the levels of the mind which throw off to your conscious minds the concepts which you then clothe consciously with a vocabulary. We do this for two reasons. Firstly, the state of mind in meditation is such that this is the level which is most properly used. The second is that the one who channels must experience the thoughts and then have the responsibility of using his power of visualization, his vocabulary, his experience, and his being to produce a unique communication. We by no means wish to be one hundred percent responsible for the content of the message. We wish approximately twenty-five to thirty percent of the message to be shaped by the instrument who calls upon his vocabulary, his imagination, and his special gifts as a person.

Thus, our very simple message gains a multitude of various conveyances by means of which the person which cannot grasp the poetic will yet have the opportunity to grasp the practical and down-to-earth, and the person who cannot grasp either of those approaches easily still has an opportunity to listen to a scientific or technical mind analyzing and giving forth the same message. This is why vocal channeling is a partnership. Unlike a trance channel, the vocal channel is alert, and though relaxed, quite awake and able to discriminate. This is our chosen method of speaking to those who would wish to hear.

We are most grateful for the opportunity to work with the one known as J. We shall begin with several times of making the conditioning vibration known to the one known as J in order that the entity may feel the presence of us and may then feel when we are gone. We shall pause, speak again through this instrument, then pause again several times. We shall now work with the instrument known as J, and so we do pause. I am Laitos.

(Pause)

(Carla channeling)

I am again with this instrument. I am Laitos. We have made a contact. We are pleased with the initial strength and shall once again move to the one known as J while he rests and experiences our vibrations. I am Laitos.

(Pause)

(Carla channeling)

I am again with this instrument. We are adjusting our vibrations at this time to match the vibratory frequencies of the one known as J. This is normal. We shall attempt to refrain from causing discomfort. We shall one more time silently greet the one known as J. I am Laitos.

(Pause)

(Carla channeling)

I am Laitos. We do apologize to this instrument for the strength of the conditioning. We understand that this instrument is sensitive and do not mean to cause discomfort to this instrument either. However, it is necessary to use other frequencies when dealing with other vibratory patterns. We are aware that this instrument has given us permission to make her a bit uncomfortable, and we now continue by working with the one known as J in the following manner.

After we have transferred the contact from this instrument, we shall continue sending one phrase and one phrase only. That phrase, of course, is "I am Laitos." It will feel as if the new channel has thought that himself. This is the first barrier which must be breached in order to begin the process of becoming an instrument. It will be months before you are convinced that we indeed are not simply a portion of your inner mind. We ask that the new instrument relax, remove any preconceptions, and wait for the concept to come into the mind, the impulse to come into the mind to say, "I am Laitos." The instrument may repeat this phrase as many times as desired in order to calculate the movements of energy when speaking and when pausing. Please do not analyze what is going on at this point, for there is no intellectual substance to that which we are attempting to teach but only heartfelt desire to serve and to learn in order to serve the better.

We shall now transfer to the one known as J. I am Laitos.

(Pause)

(Carla channeling)

I am again with this instrument. I am Laitos. We find the one known as J to have indulged in the analyzing of that simple phrase. We have also made a good deal of progress in adjusting our vibrations towards this entity's needs. We would ask the one known as J to suspend the judgment and play the fool by stepping off the safe ground into the thin air. This is not an exercise in so-called psychic phenomena. This is an exercise in sharing information about metaphysical subjects. There is no phenomenon except the material itself which is being recorded. There are no bent spoons, there is no healing; we are here only to inspire. Therefore, we use always the light touch. However, in order to be a channel, in order to join those who wish to offer light on a non-judgmental or [non-]dogmatic basis, it is necessary to refrain from analyzing and to feel trust in the process itself. This instrument took a good deal of time to develop to the extent which she has and she is still working upon becoming a more finely tuned channel.

However, the process itself will not begin until tuning and challenging having been done satisfactorily, the instrument clears the channel through which thoughts will come, and then speaks the things which come into the mind freely and without thought, using the faith that such information is worthwhile and that our techniques are designed to infringe as little as possible upon the free will of the instrument.

We shall attempt to do something a little different this time as we find that the new instrument is caught upon the one phrase, "I am Laitos." Therefore, we shall send that phrase and we shall be ready to send any other phrases which this instrument succeeds in clearing through the mechanism of speaking so that we may send the next concept to the instrument. Again we transfer to the one known as J. I am Laitos.

(Pause)

(Carla channeling)

I am Laitos. We again ask the instrument to repeat without hesitation that which comes into the mind. The analyzing causes a stoppage in the channeling. Repeat immediately that which comes to the mind. We shall again transfer. I am Laitos.

(Pause)

(Carla channeling)

I am Laitos, and we feel that there has been enough conditioning for one session. We do not wish to weary the instrument before it even begins its work. However, we assure you that work has been done. We are beginning to be able to blend far better with the vibratory pattern of the one known as J and we hope that the back and the neck pain are not as severe as earlier. We have been attempting to adjust. We thank the one known as J for offering us the opportunity to work with this entity. We are most grateful. We find this group to be a most blessed and happy source of light.

We have greatly enjoyed experiencing some time, as you call it, with you and of course are always available when mentally requested, although we do not speak voluntarily except within a group such as this one, for the new instrument may easily be led astray by those who are clever and have messages which are different from ours, and which cause the elitism that has fueled so many of your peoples' wars and other catastrophes made by man.

We leave you, [being within] the same creation as you; therefore we cannot be apart. We leave you in universal love and light, we leave you in the care of the One Who Is All. We are Laitos. Adonai.

(Jim channeling)

I am Latwii, and we greet you, my friends, in the love and the light of the infinite Creator. We are overjoyed to be called again to this group, and we would offer ourselves in the attempt to answer queries which might be in order at this time. May we ask if there is a query with which we might attempt to be of service?

Carla: How could I help new channels more than I am helping them?

I am Latwii, and, my sister, we find that even with one such as yourself who is experienced as an instrument, the process of aiding another is always and ever the same, for you as an instrument wishing to be of service can only do that which is available to you through your own opening of desire. As you attempt to be of service to others there will be the opportunities that you will note. You will, without hesitation, seek these opportunities and offer that which is in you and with you and which can come through you, offering that as the bread cast upon the water without the dedication to any particular outcome, for that which is freely given is the true gift. To worry overmuch about forming the fruit of such a gift then tends to distort that gift in some manner.

May we answer you further, my sister?

Carla: Well, what you said is very true, but what I wondered was if there was something that I could do that I wasn't doing just to do my job better.

I am Latwii, and we find that your efforts are quite sufficient, my sister. May we answer further or perhaps another query?

Carla: Not from me, thank you.

I am Latwii, and we see that our duty this evening is a short one, yet we are overjoyed to be able to serve even for a brief period of what you call time, for as we walk with you upon your journey of seeking the truth, we walk with the one Creator. We thank you, we bless you, and we shall at this time leave this group, rejoicing always in the power and the peace, the love and the light of the one Creator. We are those of Latwii. Adonai, my friends. Adonai vasu. ☥

Sunday Meditation
March 3, 1985

(Carla channeling)

… and we who are of Hatonn greet you in the love and the light of our infinite Creator. We wish to use this instrument for a brief period before working and exercising with all those in the group for this instrument has been under the impression that it is less than adequate. It is always to be remembered that adequacy cannot be discovered within the human condition, as you would call it. If you allow the illusion to become real enough to mask the metaphysical boundaries under which you actually have allegiance you shall therefore become unable to be of service to yourself or to others. Therefore, we urge each as we urge this instrument most of all to dwell as your holy work says, "under the shadow of the most high," to allow the most high, that is infinitely about you, to move within your vibratory field in order that you may then be a true channel.

Without this simple realization that what you see is not what you get, that the invisible is more important to your survival than the visible, metaphysically speaking, each entity's lot for their third-density lot will be increasing bitterness and sourness and the hardening of the mind in order that new thoughts do not find pathways by which to enter. Living in the human condition, my friends, is the easiest way to fall asleep, and with vibrant life all about you, to remain outside the strength of living waters. It is an effort of will to look for hope where there seems to be no end to difficulty, and yet we do not ask you to dedicate more than a single moment. That moment, my friends, is always the present moment. It is the most difficult state of mind within which to remain. It is also the most important in terms of spiritual evolution.

We would this evening, if it is acceptable to all instruments, spin a tale for you through each instrument, that is, each instrument speaking a small portion of a story in what this instrument would call a round-robin fashion. When we do this practice work with each instrument, we refrain from our name in order that the flow of the story may be more simplified. We do, however, encourage each instrument to challenge inwardly before beginning to speak. It is not ever to be taken lightly that you are a contact for those of Hatonn or any other entity whom you wish to hear. It is always well to challenge. And so we shall tell our simple tale.

It was a hot, hot summer day in Mexico. The land was arid and insects filled the air with their buzzing as they ate what little foliage and grass there was. Although the small and humble house was only a mile or so from the gathering place where all the people celebrated on the days of feast days and market days, there were no buildings around it. This was a hard land upon which to live, a land in which water was priceless, land that thinned the blood with its heat and killed the brain with the numbness of hard, repetitious activity which must be done to earn the daily bread. The young boy sitting by the roadside gazed at it and turned to his mother. "Where does the road go?" he asked. "How should I know?" she answered.

We shall transfer.

(L channeling)

"The road leads to places I have not traveled, for as a child I had some interest in the road but soon lost my interest as the details of the adult world became more pressing, more insistent. I can only say, my son, that the road leads from here to another place or places, and the choices are yours to make, for one chooses when traveling the road first whether to travel at all, again in which direction to travel, and finally whether to be satisfied where one has stopped or to continue further."

The child wondered about the road in the ensuing days, for the road existed, yet he could not understand what maintained its existence, for rarely if ever did one see a traveler upon the road proceeding in either direction. It seemed apparent that most of those who inhabited this place on the road chose to remain where they were. And in wondering at this, the child realized that those remaining were much like the lizard which in early morning pauses to sun himself atop a rock, glorying in the pleasure of the light and warmth, yet, in remaining immobile, gradually becomes stupefied by the increasing heat and light, not realizing that he was slowly dying simply from his reluctance to move away further on his own path.

We shall transfer our contact.

(Carla channeling)

The young boy thought about what his mother had said sitting by the side of the road. It was a sparse place but it was pleasant where he sat. The water which was all-important was to be had in a deep well which had been dug at much labor. There were people to play with at the church, there were young women to please the young men. And yet to the little boy who was so quickly growing, he could hear no song within this whole town, no lullaby at night, no anthem in the morning, no psaltery at night. But even above the loud throng of insects as they buzzed about he could hear a song coming from the road. He gazed into the shimmering distance, the heat waves making all things strange, wavy and surrealistic, and could see no one and nothing that would account for the song. When he put his hands over his ears, the song became louder and one day he knew that he must go.

We shall transfer.

(Jim channeling)

As he packed those few things that he wished to take with him upon the journey, his mother looked at him imploringly and asked if this was truly his heart's desire, for she had not herself been upon this road and knew very little about it and would worry over his welfare. He replied that there was nothing else that held any interest for him, and though he did not know what he would find or precisely why he must go, yet he must go. So he set out upon the journey with his small bundle of possessions, and as he journeyed, his uneasiness at the traveling into unknown areas was somewhat abated by the song that he continued to hear within his own inner ears and this did give him comfort.

His first day's travel was uneventful. The heat of the day beginning to grow, he decided that he would nap for awhile and under a lonely tree he found a small patch of shade and rested there.

We shall transfer.

(L channeling)

His rest was brief. It seemed that he had slept but a moment when he gradually realized that the song seemed louder, somehow more insistent. He moved uncomfortably this way and that, trying to drown out the song, but each time that sleep approached it seemed to tug at his sleep, urging him back to awareness.

In despair, he arose, again shouldered his bundle and moved again onto the road, plodding on, tired yet feeling a sense of correctness in again undertaking his journey, for as he progressed, the road seemed to rise to his feet, his bundle seemed lightened and though still tired he felt that the rhythm of his paces in some manner supported him, soothed his aching, and the song seemed to pull him onward.

By nightfall he had traveled a great distance and again sought the comfort of rest. He lay upon the ground seeking sleep. Yet as he dreamed, the road was before him, and as his body rested, he still traveled in his mind further and further, following the endless road.

When morning came, he arose, shouldered his pack and again strode forward. The way seemed easier now, as though somehow he had traveled this road before, and, indeed, many things seemed different. The sun seemed to shine as a friend now rather than beating down fiercely. The air seemed in some manner richer and full of life, so different from the brittle, arid air of his childhood home, and along with the constant companionship of the song within his ears, he was able to hear a gentle murmuring from somewhere before him.

By mid-afternoon the murmuring had become a rhythmic pulse, the voice of eons of tides breaking against a shoreline, and for the first time the boy beheld an enormous quantity of water, so great that he had never dreamed that it could exist. He approached it cautiously and with reverence. From the land of his childhood water was the wealth through which survival was purchased, and before him lay a sea so vast that its shores curved away gently into the distant horizon.

We shall now transfer.

(Carla channeling)

The boy moved towards the vast body of water which lay before him, tentatively touched it with his bare and dusty feet, and with a shout, waded into the breakers upon the shore. His joy, however, was short-lived as he found he could not swallow this water. He looked again for the road but the road ended at the ocean, and he was no longer in the land which he understood. He did not know how to find water. It came to him that he had not seen a single soul in all his journeying. Yet still he heard the song.

And so he knelt upon the sand and held out his arms with their palms upward. He spoke to no one in particular, yet he had to speak and he did so beseechingly, saying, "I know not why I began this journey, and I know not whether it might lead from here as the road disappears. Oh, singer of the song, speak to me and tell me what I must do." All day he prayed thusly and there was no answer, only the continuation of the song. In the deep blue gloaming that lives briefly before the dusk deepens to night, the young man decided to go backwards, to retrace his steps, to live in the home of his mother. But the road had disappeared, and so he knelt once again lost, lonely, confused. "Oh, singer of the song," he said, " I have changed my life because of the beauty of the music. Are you only a siren to lead me astray that I may never again see home or kindred? To what terrible purpose is this song sung that leads to the thirst of death?"

With dawn came the first sight of another being which the young boy had experienced upon the journey. A small ship lay at anchor and a boat had been dispatched to the shore. The man who rowed shipped his oars, beached the small boat and came to where the young man lay, deep in prayer. The young man looked up, astonished. "Are you the singer of the song," he said? The other man only smiled and shook his head, "No. I am a fellow traveler," and that was all he said as he offered the young man a seat in the small boat which he began to row out towards the ship. The young boy said, "If you are a fellow traveler upon my journey, how do you know the path?" The other man shook his head. "I do not know the path. I seek the path." This did not make sense to the young man. He said, "I too seek the path and the singer of the song but when I wished to go back to the home of my mother, I could not even find the path which I had traveled."

The other man smiled as he helped the young boy aboard the ship. "You will learn many things, you will experience great joys and sorrows. And there will be those who are companions along the way when you need them. Water, fresh water …"

(Side one of tape ends.)

(Carla channeling)

"… fresh water when you need it, all things as you need them. Yet," he said, "you will find that your journey has changed you. I cannot give you comfort in offering a road that goes backwards. You will never again be who you were when you first heard the song. You will never visit the home of your mother, for even were you to go there now, you would be a stranger to her. Your ways would be strange and your thinking outlandish, for you hear the song; she hears the insects as they sing their summer's anthem."

I am Hatonn. To all of you who journey upon the path and who hear a song, know that you have comrades, that that which is needed will be provided, but that you cannot go back. You can only refine your ears that they may listen better to the song of faith, hope, love and peace. Each person wishes for personal power—power to control, the power to shape the destiny, and this is your right, my friends, this is your obligation. Yet know that the first and greatest power is given to you in the act of surrender, for the heart that has surrendered can hear the song which will lead you. Those who close and stop their ears and demand that things be thus and so, thus and so, will indeed hear a siren's song. And the manifestation of sorrow in the life of one who controls shall be less and less. These are the ones who are wayward and lost, for they cannot go home yet they are not able to go forward. Surrender, then, and purify your ears to the song of life, that life which is beyond life and death.

We of Hatonn leave you in that omnipresent love, that omniscient light, that infinite life that is the creation of the Father. Wend your way in joy and hope. Farewell, pilgrims. Take what you can use from our poor story, toss the rest away, and join us in the infinite quest for the Infinite. Adonai, my friends. Adonai vasu borragus.

(Jim channeling)

I am Latwii, and we greet you, my friends, in that same love and light which our brothers and sisters have so joyfully left you in. We are again privileged to be with you. As each knows, we attempt to serve by answering those queries which have been placed before us. Without further ado, then let us begin, if there might be a query at this time.

Carla: I have one. For the last several months I've been trying to work my way through the feeling that I should be dead. It seems very irrational, but my feeling for my friend, Don, is such that I feel that I failed him in an attempt to save him. I have sought professional help with the doctors that work with the mind and the body and although my grief or guilt or both are somewhat softened by the medicine that I'm given, I never know when I'll get an attack of such a depth of sadness that it does seem in all honesty quite logical that I should have been dead, and I feel quite guilty at remaining. Now this does not fit with the true facts, so I know that I'm a little bit crazy right now. And I wonder what suggestions you might have that I might link up the crazy self with the one that knows that she did absolutely everything only after a lot of prayer, a lot of thought, and a hundred and ten percent trying. The two simply don't seem want to become one.

I am Latwii, and we feel that we have the grasp of your query, my sister, though the query is one that covers a great deal of ground, shall we say, both within the illusion which you have your present incarnation, and in the metaphysical sense of the greater portion of your being and your relationship to the one known as Don. There are for each pilgrim upon the path, as the story just completed by our brothers and sisters of Hatonn just illustrated, a number of challenges which will be faced. The situation in which you now find yourself is one that indeed could have been ended, shall we say, as an incarnational pattern at an earlier time, for your existence for a significant portion of your life has been that afforded by the exercise of will and faith. These qualities are those which each pilgrim attempts to develop and refine, for within your illusion there is not the possibility of achieving perfect action, that is, providing service that is undeniably service and is not mixed with any lesser quality.

Therefore, the exercise of will and faith is most salient, for as you enter your incarnation and proceed through it, you attempt to serve the one Creator, to know the one Creator, to be the one Creator in some fashion. In your attempt to be of service to others, you move within a darkness of knowing in which true knowing does not exist. Therefore, you must in some degree fashion a framework of faith in a larger, broader, deeper, richer, purer reality or else the life in which you move has no meaning. As you fashion this greater reality within your own mind, and attempt in some means or manner to reflect it in your life, this attempt then generates or is generated by, we should say, the exercise of will. You take that which is unknown and you fashion that which is not apparent. You take the illusion, the manifestations in which you move, and in some way attempt to transmute it by your own will and faith into a greater reality.

These are together woven into the fabric of any seeker's journey. They are as the rod and the staff that comfort the seeker in what has been called the valley of the shadow of death. As you find yourself passing through this valley with shadows of death, know that your own shadow is upon that wall as well as are the shadows of all seekers, for to this life, truly one day each shall die. Yet it is not this life that is the great treasure to be clung to with all the effort and fiber of being. Yet it is that which this life can provide, the learning of the Creator, the serving the Creator, the welcoming of those opportunities to do both, the accepting of the outcome of any opportunity, the praise and thanksgiving to the one Creator for being provided such opportunities, and the moving forward with the will and the faith intact to continue the journey.

For as long as you draw breath within this illusion, you have the treasures that this illusion can offer, these being the opportunity to transmute what is mundane to that which is sacred, to take that which has darkness and to shine upon it a light, to look where there might be sorrow and to offer a gladdened heart and hand. Dwell not overlong within those opportunities which you feel were less than adequately met, for you shall fall short in each opportunity. You are limited beings attempting to reflect the limitless. Yet, each opportunity comes as a gift from the one Creator to a portion of Itself that that portion might be nourished and continue upon its path of gathering experience that will glorify the one Creator thereby.

In short, my sister, we say to you, look not just at a portion of your journey; look to its overall length and breadth and attempt to move as the Creator would move through you, that your will might be given over. Even in your despair give it over to the one Creator. Let it be worked upon, and let it return to you as renewed faith and a renewed will to learn and to serve within this illusion that at times seems tedious and endless but when viewed from without is but a short, brilliant burst of opportunity and light.

May we answer you further, my sister?

Carla: No, thank you very much.

I am Latwii, and we thank you, my sister. Is there another query at this time?

L: Yes, Latwii. I have a friend who has recently become enthralled with Christianity and is troubled at the fact that I attend these sessions, viewing my lifestyle as somehow one which endangers my soul in that it doesn't conform to a strict path of adherence of Christianity, his concept being that that is the only path through which people on Earth can hope to achieve whatever it is he believes we're trying to achieve. I'd like to ask for whatever help you can offer, not in helping me dissuade him, because it's his choice, but simply to assist me in explaining to him that—first of all, that the two beliefs are complimentary rather than in opposition, and second, that it's not necessarily the end of the world for a person not to conceive of Christianity as the only route of development. I realize that's a broad order, but anything you'd have to offer for assistance would be appreciated.

I am Latwii, and am aware of your query, my brother. As we look upon the points of view of each of you, we see that each has the opportunity to express the heart of each point of view, and that is to love and to accept that which seems unlovable and unacceptable, for it is seemingly in opposition in some degree, each to the other. Those who seek the, shall we say, holy grail, the ultimate truth of existence, do so upon a certain path. It has been said that this path is straight and that it is narrow. Many take this to mean that there is only one path, and no matter what the belief or what the entity, the entity is likely to believe that it is upon that path that others are not.

Yet we may suggest to you that this statement is a statement of the necessary focus or discipline, if you will, that any seeker must exercise as it travels whatever path it travels to the one Creator. One cannot travel two paths or three or four or more and hope for the efficiency, shall we say, and the degree of utilization of the will that is necessary in order for any seeker with any viewpoint to reach its goal. Therefore, each of you have the opportunity to demonstrate the heart of any path that seeks the one Creator that is at its heart, love.

We find that within the holy work known as the Bible, in a portion of this work authored by the entity known as Paul, in his description of various gifts that would come unto those seekers in the, shall we say, latter days, there is listed a gift that it described as the ability to discern spirits. This suggests that even within this belief known as Christianity, it was known in earlier days that communication with other entities was possible and that there were communications that were of a positive and acceptable nature to those known in those days as Christians.

Indeed, as those entities known to you as Christians move within these latter days, there shall be, and have been already, the expressions of these gifts becoming more widely experienced and this phenomenon shall continue and the points of view shall continue to widen as the heart of love and acceptance within this philosophy is uncovered.

May we answer you further, my brother?

L: No, that's given me much to go on. I thank you.

I am Latwii, and we thank you, my brother. May we attempt another query at this time?

(Pause)

I am Latwii, and we find that though the queries have been few, there has been a good deal of thought given to each query, and we are honored to be able to focus our humble attention and experience upon these queries. We thank each for presenting these gifts to us and we hope that in some manner our poor responses have been able to point a direction for your own thought.

We at this time shall take our leave of this group and this instrument with the reminder to this instrument that though it is hopeful in a way to be, shall we say, absent and vacant of mind, it might be more helpful to focus more closely upon this contact. We leave you, my friends, in the love and in the light of the one infinite Creator. We are those of Latwii. Adonai. Adonai vasu.

Sunday Meditation
March 10, 1985

(Carla channeling)

I am Hatonn, and I greet you, my friends, in the love and in the light of our infinite Creator. It is a great privilege to be with you this evening. We come to serve and we do our humble best but, as always, we ask you to discard and leave all that may be found unworthy.

Each of you has seen the picture of a drop of water which is then placed under ten times magnification and then fifty times magnification and so on until we are looking at the very nucleus of [it] and [the] surrounding electrons. You know, my friends, that each time you looked something had changed to that drop of water, something that was outside of that drop of water's control. Scientists surrender to their technical informational equipment. It is left to those of the path to surrender in another way and that is to welcome, accept and encourage spiritual growth and change in themselves and others. What one may see as a drop of water, another may see ten times magnified and so forth. Each is looking at the same universe, caught whole and perfect in a microscope's eye.

This is true, also, my friends, of you in your relationship with yourself, with the Creator, and with others. You must first be able to accept and like yourself in order to serve the one Creator with the most efficacious effect. One entity then may need one thing, another another, but it is all the same experience, seen from different points of view. We are all studying, working, learning and teaching. Yes, my friends, even you who are within third density have sometimes volunteered, as apples often do, to be of service in the subconscious of another entity. Getting to know yourself begins with meditation, is challenged by your creative responses to situations, and your future is melded from the manifestations of your inner seeking. Let us say for now that each instrument has found a balance that then he may then go forward to gaze upon the Creator, to experience love for that great Logos which made us, the intimate and personal love of a true father in a true family. In this part of your attempt at self-examination, we urge that time be taken at the end of the day, if possible, to jot down those things which you found profitable and those things which you found difficult or harmful. Soon you will begin to detect a pattern. The pattern is the pattern of your manifestation which comes through your being from the great levels and touches the people about you.

We see that the harsh winds of summer have blown your streets clear of snow and we are aware that each has a somewhat more buoyant attitude towards this incarnation than *(inaudible)* its surprises during a period of this sort of weather than when the weather is dark and gloomy by its very nature …

We should at this point transfer from this contact. I am Hatonn.

(Jim channeling)

I am Hatonn, and greet you through this instrument in love and light. We appreciate the service of the one known as Carla, though her condition is somewhat marginal. We thank her for offering all she has in this service. To continue with our thought.

As your season moves from that which was the cold, windswept, barren and introspected into that season which begins the warming and nourishing of that which was the focus of the introspection, winter, there is a lightening the hearts, a gladdening and a sparkle, shall we say, to the mind's eye. This we see among your people at this time and it is in your experience likened unto a magnification of the life pattern which surrounds you and through which you move at this time. The tendency of the winter season is to turn the eye inward that those portions of the self which have exercised their luxuriant summer's growth, shall we say, might then be observed and considered for their harvest of that season that this harvest then might then be the foundation of yet another season's cycle of growth.

It is always a joy to reap the harvest and then to consider the sowing for the new year, the new year for the growth of the spirit in your manifestation. You will move through this new season of growth, each in your own fashion, watering those planted ideas, thoughts and tendencies that you feel have value in your continued journey. You shall also, according to your own discrimination pluck those growths that seem as weeds and seem to hinder that spiritual journey which now finds a new level of realization within your life. As you use your discrimination to evaluate the experiences which are placed before you and which you find yourself moving within, you must ever keep before your mind's eye the purposes as you understand them for your movement and your growth, for many are the plants and forms of life within your garden of experience.

From one particular point of view, or shall we say power of magnification, a certain experience may seem very difficult and quite undesirable. It may indeed seem as the weed that needs the plucking and the removal from the garden of your experience. And yet, if you look deeper, my friends, and magnify your own perceptions inwardly and outwardly, you discover within that situation which seemed most difficult and undesirable the possibility of a great acceleration in your spiritual journey. For as you move through your illusion, the strength of spirit which is possible for you to gain is most often that which is gained not with the ease of a feast table, plainly and easily set, but oftentimes is that experience which provides the most difficulty in surviving and evaluating for its value. The experiences which of necessity cause you to reach deeper within your own being in order to find means of achieving harmony with self and other self are those experiences which, as the sandpaper to the roughened board, smooth the spiritual journey in a very real and basic sense.

For as you move through your illusion, you shall discover that those times in which there was an ease of being and expression and perhaps a happy contentment to go with them, there was less of that harvested of the spiritual nature, shall we say. Those experiences, on the other hand, which were very difficult at the time they appeared within one's life may have provided one with the spiritual challenge that then yielded the harvest that was unrecognized at the time, yet at a later time, as you call it, became apparent to the inward-seeking eye.

We cannot with any surety describe to you any particular set of circumstances which might be productive of this type of spiritual growth, for within each life pattern there is a unique potential for realizing such growth. Yet we can say to you that things are not always as they seem within one's life. This is especially true for the seeker of what you call truth, for in the metaphysical sense, it is very difficult for one to determine one's own progress and one's own means of achieving this progress. You move within an illusion which …

(Page 5 is missing from the transcript.)

… moving in perfect harmony with the cycles and seasons and the rhythms of being. We shall leave you now, in an illusory sense only, for in truth we are always with you and always one. We are those of Hatonn. Adonai, my friends. Adonai vasu borragus.

(Jim channeling)

I am Latwii, and we greet you also, my friends, in the love and the light of our infinite Creator. We are happy to tread where those of Hatonn have left their footprints as well, and we offer our humble service in the same manner, asking that you take that which we give with, shall we say, your proverbial grain of salt. We are happy to offer ourselves in the attempt of answering your queries and we would ask at this time if there might be a query with which we might begin?

S: Latwii, is there anything that I can do to help R that I have not already attempted?

I am Latwii, and, my sister, we find that your efforts in this matter have been most exemplary. The most important portion of these efforts, as we have mentioned before, is that intention with which you begin and continue your workings. The desire which you manifest in these workings is that motivating force which many have called love and we can find no better word for this facet and function of experience that you now seek to express in order that another might find a greater balance within its own being. We suggest that you continue upon that path which you have firmly planted your feet upon.

May we answer you further, my sister?

S: No, thank you Latwii.

I am Latwii, and we thank you, my sister. Is there another query?

(Pause)

(Carla channeling)

I am Latwii, and we find that each person has taken one step backwards and left this volunteer to end. We do indeed end our stay with you with much reluctance but we glory in each of your beautiful colors, the vibrations of your being and the energy fields that they have created. How beautiful you are, my friends. We are those of Latwii. We bid farewell in the love and the light of the one infinite Creator. We realize that there are some who would wish that we could walk among you, but that is not a safe thing to do, and so we speak to you, and so we are always available to you. We bid you farewell. Adonai. Adonai.

L/L Research

Sunday Meditation
March 17, 1985

(Carla channeling)

I am Hatonn, and I greet you, my friends, in the love and in the light of our infinite Creator. With those of Laitos, we shall, as we use the instrument, be working with each who will desire, especially the one known as J, in order that contact might be adjusted more carefully and our service of the strengthening of the meditative state might be therefore more available. It is a great privilege and you are most gracious to allow us to do this work, for as we share in your life patterns, we experience a great deal of vivid and what we would call raw catalyst for our own growth, catalyst which in our density is no longer present. In our density we have no boundaries as you know it betwixt mind. The boundaries between one's mind and another is the most powerful catalyst that you will ever experience. Are we misunderstanding? Every conversation of any kind, no matter how well realized, is in essence an experience of one soul battering with wings against the semipermeable membrane that lies between two energy fields or, as you would call it, two people.

We would, to exercise each instrument and to offer our humble words in the most clear manner, wish to move about the room so that that which we have to say may be said in a variety of ways as each within the room has the distinct and unique characteristics which make each channel a potentially excellent channel. We, of course, are up against the semi-permeable membrane betwixt even a discarnate entity and another entity. We therefore experience of which we speak, for we are having to use concepts and words to give our meaning clearly just as you would for your conversation. This is a tremendous catalyst for us, and we give praise and thanksgiving that we are able to serve you as you so graciously serve us.

This evening, we would speak of meditation and of love. Let us approach the subject from the standpoint of love being offered as a goal, as some proper name like a town or a city. Within this instrument's mind we find many popular songs which use this term. "All you need is love," is the one we find most firmly etched in this instrument's memory. This is indeed so, my friends, for there is nothing but love, therefore all you need, regardless of what it is, is love. The tremendous danger in looking in love as a goal is that it becomes a kind of deity unto itself, one which is drawn within the imagination of man's mind, not that of the Creator.

We shall transfer. I am Hatonn.

(L channeling)

I am Hatonn and am with this instrument. The difficult of which we spoke is in the conceptualization of that which you call love as a sort of god in and of itself rather than a facet or characteristic of the Creator. In pursuing oneness with this characteristic, the difficulty lies in the willingness to stop short before achieving the final attainment, for one in this situation strives not toward a reunification with the Creator but rather toward the objective of limitless loving, and in such attainment finds difficulty in reconciling the Creator's universe with that which the seeker believes should be apparent to himself as a result of his attainment. His confusion at this point, characterized by his attainment of limitless loving but lack of awareness of that [which] surrounds him is often a failing point for those who strive in this direction, for in seeking not far enough, yet obtaining the objective of their search, they are suddenly stricken with doubt concerning the validity of that which they have attained, and in doubting, find that their attainment begins to tarnish in their own eyes. This in turn frequently results in a turning away, for in truth, when one attains that which is sought, but initially chose to seek the wrong objective, one is likely to be eventually dissatisfied.

My friends, loving frequently is described as a gift of the Creator. Yet, my friends, is not all equally a gift of the same source? We seek not to devalue that which you call loving, but rather to introduce a perspective through which one might see this gift as a tool through which attainment may be attempted rather than an end product which one may settle for and fall short of the Creator's intention.

At this time we shall transfer our contact. We are known to you as Hatonn.

(Carla channeling)

I am Hatonn. We have consulted with the feelings of each other channel and find a desire to listen this evening. We commend this and encourage it. The vocal channeling must never, never be done as a duty but only as an honor. Serving in general must never be a "should" but always a rejoicing in the ability to do what you have to do. Take all of those things which you should do but do not wish to do and discard them. For only in joy will your service be felt, regardless of its effect, as an honest service. We would conclude through this instrument, therefore.

The master whom you know as Jesus broke his body like a loaf of bread and poured out his blood upon the earth, and yet in no way did he wish to be worshipped for himself. He asked his followers to take bread and wine as a remembrance, not as a worship of himself and spoke always of his oneness with the Father. Likewise, the one known as Mohammed spoke not of himself as the one God, as the phrase is, describing the thought complex, Allah. This entity called himself a prophet. When we examine the role of Arjuna in the Bhagavad-Gita, we do not find this entity to be fighting for love, but rather to be fighting for his life, his honor, and those mundane principles which an honorable man has. If there is one message that comes clear as a bell from this sacred work, it is that man is within a temporal clime, a time of living during which many temporal and completely seemingly nonspiritual decisions and actions must be made.

There is so an even more exquisite articulation of this concept as one follows the life of the one known as Gautama Siddhartha who went on the spiritual journey and after many adventures found himself plying the pole of a boat as he took travelers across the water. He gazed always at the water, not at the men, not at their problems. There was in him no idolatry. This entity has lessons for those who practice any form of idolatry. Most of your idols are unwitting. There is no attempt made upon a seeker's behalf for that seeker to become an idolater. And yet, one becomes enamored of an experience or a point of view and clings to it until it becomes hard, dogmatic and rigid.

If your love is not flexible, endless and sweet as fresh water, then the love which you are seeking is a graven image, a dead figurehead which mimics love. Love is not a thing, it is a force, it is a beingness, a consciousness which you share, it is your birthright. You may love but in the beginning and in the end you *are* love and you are a channel for limitless love. You cannot seek limitless love; you can only open the door through which that love may pour.

Hence, we turn again to daily meditation. Regardless of how much the discipline of daily meditation may cost you in worldly terms, may we suggest its central importance in your seeking. Do you wish to be in the fast lane, as this entity would call it, working hard at becoming a more polarized servant? Then meditation must be your meat and your drink. It need not be long, in fact except for one meditation during the day to center you, preferably in the morning or when first you awaken, it is possible to regain the perspective of meditation in a near-instant by suggesting to yourself that you should meditate when you hear the clock or the doorbell or the telephone make its ringing noise. Lift off of your shoulders this great responsibility for finding a limitless love in a world which does not have what you seek, and open yourself to that love through meditation and through watching experiences as if they were water, flowing past you making interesting configurations. Your life is a pattern. May you make it beautiful by surrendering to love itself.

We leave this instrument in that limitless love and infinite light that is the one Creator, and yet we can hardly leave you, for you are the Creator also and so are we. Therefore, we share with you limitless love. As always, take what we have to say, discard all that is not helpful and use what may be. We are known to you as those of Hatonn, and those of Laitos also send you greetings and love. Adonai, my friends. Adonai vasu.

(The group retunes by singing "Row, Row, Row Your Boat" several times.)

(Jim channeling)

I am Latwii, and I greet you, my friends, in the love and the light of the infinite Creator. We thank you for your efforts in upgrading this tuning of this circle. We appreciate the fastidiousness with which you approach the honor of seeking the truth in this particular manner. We also are greatly honored to be asked to join your circle, and we enter it with the anticipation of providing our humble service in whatever way might be available to us. We therefore would ask if there might be a question with which we might begin our service?

S: Yes, Latwii. I read recently that it might be good to in the morning, say after your meditation, to either use a deck of tarot cards or the Bible or runes, and to pick something at random and to meditate—well, not necessarily meditate—but to think about the symbology of that for the rest of the day. And it said that when you do this, your higher self is working with you and helping you to select that which you possibly need to think about. And I wanted to know if you could confirm this for me, and if you can't, can you give me any other ideas?

I am Latwii, and, my sister, we feel that there [are] an infinite number of procedures and concepts and rituals which one may pursue in the attempt to proceed, shall we say, upon the evolutionary path. Indeed, any conscious focusing upon this endeavor will enhance its effects within one's being. The particular procedure to which you have referred is one which is efficacious in allowing the conscious mind to receive a message from the unconscious and perhaps even that source referred to as the higher self. The procedure is one which tends, in general, to focus the attention upon a concept. This is a good, shall we say, effort that can be made, for throughout one's normal round of daily activities, the attention is most frequently dissipated in a variety of directions, then needing the meditation to once again focus the attention and to reap the harvest of the day at the day's end. To begin the day as you have suggested, is a means by which the attention may be focused and reinforced in its focus periodically as the day proceeds. We cannot give more specific instructions in this particular area, for each entity will of necessity be drawn to a special type of focus for the day, since each entity is quite unique in its configuration of potential lessons and services for any particular period of time.

May we answer you further, my sister?

S: Well, just … I'm pretty sure of the answer, but I want to ask anyway. Would you suggest that one uses whatever they find to be the most comfortable to them?

I am Latwii, and we might agree with this supposition, unless, of course, one wishes to work with those techniques that make one uncomfortable, for there are, of course, lessons to be learned in the uncomfortable as well. We do not mean to be facetious, my sister, but we are simply suggesting that any particular technique is of whatever value one feels and desires it to be.

May we answer you further?

S: No, thank you.

I am Latwii, and we thank you, my sister. Is there another query?

Carla: Just another quick one on that. Would you delete from the list of things to use after meditation the ouija board? I've heard many stories that put your hair on end about how the ouija board is misused inadvertently.

I am Latwii and we feel that this particular means of contacting the deeper portions of one's own mind and perhaps portions of other entities' minds as well is a means which is more easily misused than most tools, for there is a great amount of thought form energy that has collected around this particular tool. Its use has been, shall we say, somewhat sloppy in the past of your peoples. The need for the tuning and the challenging of spirits has seldom been recognized within any particular means of seeking, shall we say, discarnate advice, and within this particular tool these means of assuring the positive use have frequently been omitted. If these means are omitted this particular tool, however, provides the same kind of, shall we say, crutch for the seeker as would any other means of contacting the deeper levels of one's own unconscious mind and perhaps those portions of minds that would be drawn to one's seeking.

Shall we attempt further response, my sister?

Carla: I just wanted to make sure. You said, "if these means are omitted," and you meant "if these are not omitted," right? In other words, if you use the challenging of spirits …

I am Latwii, and you are quite correct and we hope that we have not confused you overmuch by our omission of that which we meant. We shall correct this instrument by our omission of that which we wished to include.

May we answer further, my sister?

Carla: *(Inaudible).*

May we attempt another query?

L: Latwii, in the Ra material there are some rather terse sentences [that] might be regarded as a caution or a warning concerning the attainment of certain areas of knowledge without the practice thereof. Could you elaborate on that please? In whatever direction seems most appropriate to you.

I am Latwii, and with such a broad field to take shots in, we feel that we might hit a mark here or there. We are aware of the portions of this material to which you have referred, my brother, and this in general [is] a statement of the balance between the responsibility and the duty that one shoulders and accepts as one attempts to be of service to others in the specific means of providing the healing catalyst. One may see the self as a crystal that is in the process of becoming regularized. There are within each entity various distortions or flaws, shall we say, that cause the instreaming love/light or prana of the one Creator to be detracted in one means or another as the entity utilizes its daily round of activities to express and eventually balance these distortions. If one assumes the responsibility of that known among your peoples as an healer and gathers the knowledge necessary to exercise this responsibility and then fails to complete the practice of this art and simply stores the knowledge without allowing it free flow through the crystallized beingness, one is, shall we say, storing an energy which will eventually in some fashion burn the circuits within the entity so storing this energy. The burn or feedback of this energy is usually along the lines of fracture or distortion within the crystallized entity, therefore the difficulties which would beset one who had failed to, shall we say, put to use that which had been learned would be difficulties that would enhance those distortions previously existing, therefore forcing, shall we say, the entity to practice upon itself that which it had failed to practice with others in service to others.

May we answer you further, my brother?

L: No, that was very clarifying, thank you.

I am Latwii, and we thank you, my brother. May we attempt another query at this time?

S: Yes, Latwii. I'd like you to clarify something along those lines. What if the person makes every effort and every attempt but is unsuccessful?

I am Latwii, and might we ask if the question could be made more specific as to what exactly the attempt would be focused upon? Is this considering the personal balancing or the utilization of the skills in service to another?

S: I knew I was going to clarify that as soon as it was out of my mouth because it didn't make sense. Okay. What I mean is, I realize that the healer does not heal the person. What I'm trying to get at is what if the person is not able to provide the service, the person attempts to act as a catalyst for the one to be healed, but the person acting as the catalyst either, well, I guess the best way to put it would be, does not have the ability to do that. Does that help?

I am Latwii, and we feel that we have now a better grasp of your query, my sister. Well, since there is no AMA upon the metaphysical level, we can suggest that the efforts which you put forth are not able to be measured by your own senses. You will not know in most cases, especially at the first of your practice, how successful you have been. The important point in this regard, therefore, is the intention with which you make your efforts. As each seeker seeks the one Creator and continually falls short of that seeking, so also the healer attempts to provide the catalyst in whatever manner is possible for it to provide. Yet in most cases, it shall also fall short. That the effort is made with the intention to serve is the important point. The variance between the attempt and the achievement is never measured and may be considered unimportant.

May we answer you further, my sister?

S: Well, okay. It seems as though the attempt is the important thing, and I understand that. What if a person attempts this and attempts it every day for fifty years on different people and never has any results? Does that … Okay … Once the person gets the knowledge, do they have to continually attempt, you know, for the rest of their life?

I am Latwii, and we feel that we have a grasp of your query. The attempt is the most important aspect of this endeavor, as we have mentioned. The situation which you have described is one which is most difficult to imagine, for as one attempts to serve others, there is the fruit of this attempt upon some level of one's being and upon the beingness, shall we say, of those …

(Side one of tape ends.)

(Pause)

(Jim channeling)

I am Latwii, and am once again with this instrument, and very happy to be here for this instrument very nearly lost it. To continue our response to your query—the fruits of your labors are not always, and in fact, are seldom noticeable within your third density illusion. That which you see when there is something to see, shall we say, in the way of an healing is the result of work which has been done first upon the metaphysical levels. This work may take a considerable amount of what you call time or it may not. There are many, many factors to consider in the healing process. That you attempt or even desire to attempt when another may not be present is the factor which is of most importance.

May we answer further, my sister?

S: No, Latwii. After many questions I finally was able to pluck the gem. Thank you.

I am Latwii, and we thank you, and are very happy that [somewhere] within all of that there was indeed a gem. May we attempt another query and perhaps another gem?

L: One more shot, Latwii. We talked about the efforts of the would-be healer. I'd be interested in what you'd have to offer on the subject of seeking to help one who either had not requested that help or would be opposed to receiving that type of help if they were aware it existed, for quite frequently there are those who might be in need of assistance, yet do not request or find the source too unusual to request it.

I am Latwii, and we are happy that you have asked this query, my brother, for it is most important that one who would offer itself as the healer not attempt such efforts unless first approached by the one to be healed, for entities shoulder those burdens which are theirs for as long as the burdens are theirs, and to attempt to remove a burden before it is, shall we say, ready to be removed is much like attempting to peel the skin from the snake before it is ready to be shed.

May we answer you further, my brother?

L: That's an excellent response. Thank you.

I am Latwii, and we thank you, my brother. Is there another at this time?

A: Latwii, I have one on the same line, kind of. For the healer, sometimes with one person he can read them like a book for what is ailing and how to possibly aid this person, where with another person the book is not transparent, and there's almost like a lead case around it. What are some of the possible reasons for the healer not being able to read anything? Would it be … well, just expand on that and we'll proceed from there.

I am Latwii, and we feel that we have good deal to expand upon here. There are, of course, as you would imagine and perhaps fear, a great many reasons for such difficulty for reading the one to be healed. First and perhaps foremost upon this list is what might be termed the concept of preincarnative choices. There are many entities upon your planet at this time who have for one reason or another chosen various limitations and, shall we say, diseases in order that a focus of mind might be achieved because of the limitation or disease. In this instance, the healer would find an impenetrable barrier betwixt its perception and the one to be healed in its configuration of disease.

There may also be various metaphysical reasons that do not have a relation to preincarnative choices—directly, at least—that would cause this same kind of barrier. However, it would not be so much a barrier as it would be an incomplete reading of what was within the entity's auric field. Entities frequently have, shall we say, layers of resource information contained within what are called diseases. The one serving as healer is one who attempts to read these various layers of information. These layers of information contain the services and lessons, the patterns of being of an entity. There are for some entities and for some diseases or configurations of the auric body various levels to grasp in order to complete the healing. The one serving as healer, then, must become adept at penetrating these various levels of information in order to perceive the heart of the disease configuration.

May we attempt further response, my sister?

A: Well, in other words, the healer may be very adept at healing, and it's not that person's fault they're goofing up, it's just something that was already set up ahead of time, that the other person chose not to be healed quite yet, you know as you said to the earlier question of it's not time to peel the snake yet? Is that right?

I am Latwii, and, in general, your assumptions are correct. We may make one clarification, that being that the one serving as healer, when it offers itself wholeheartedly with no personal will as to the outcome, but serves as a channel for the Creator's will to move through, cannot, shall we say, "goof up." It is not upon the shoulders of the healer that the healing is carried, but upon the shoulders of the one to be healed in its ability to allow the Creator to move within its being.

May we answer you further, my sister?

A: No, you summed it up nicely. Thank you.

S: Yes, Latwii, just briefly. I'd like to ask you something about R's condition. In looking up in the dictionary, it seemed to me that the lymph nodes are responsible for filtering and I assume collecting different viruses and microorganisms, so I assume that that's basically what R has collected along with, I don't know, chemical pollutants. My question is if it's microorganisms and viruses, one would think that antibiotics or something of that nature would work. I don't know much about antibiotics; I know they work on some things and don't work on other things. But the problem is, R can't go to his doctor and say, well, you know, our friend Latwii says that, you know, that I have a whole bunch of viruses and microorganisms stored here and could you give me some medicine. Would you agree that what has mostly been collected is virus and microorganisms, and if so, shouldn't antibiotics take care of that?

I am Latwii, and we are aware of your query, my sister. As we mentioned in our previous time of sharing with you and the one known as R, these virae are the manifestations of metaphysical or, shall we say, mental origin. The work, therefore, that would be most efficacious in this regard is that which might be approached from the meditational and contemplational standpoint. The work within these realms is that which is the foundation of what is eventually manifested within the third density yellow ray body. The use of the various antibiotic drugs within in this particular case could be that which is as, shall we say, the training aid or audio/visual aid upon which the mind could focus and use as an analog, a symbol of the cleansing that is being undertaken upon the mental and metaphysical levels of the entity.

May we answer you further, my sister?

S: Well, he's taking antibiotics, and I know he's working very hard meditating and trying to sort this out and basically know what's behind it, but these virae seem to be still collecting, and, I ... well, you probably can't tell me anything. I'm just ...*(laughing)* Thanks, anyway.

I am Latwii, and we enjoy your laughter and your correct assumption, my sister. May we attempt another query at this time?

L: I don't have a question, but I'd just like to thank you for the word, "virae." I like that.

I am Latwii, and we rather liked it, too. May we attempt another query, and perhaps add another word to one's vocabulary?

Carla: I'm through.

L: *(Inaudible).*

I am Latwii, as if you didn't know that. We are most honored to …

(Last page of transcript is missing.)

Sunday Meditation
March 24, 1985

(Carla channeling)

I am Hatonn, and I greet you in the love and in the light of our infinite Creator. It is a joy to be with you and to regale you with our few poor thoughts. As always, we ask that as we speak to you, you take what you can use and discard that which is not useful to you at this time. We bear no authority greater than yourself and we ask for you to use your powers of discrimination, for we, like you, are travelers upon a journey, a journey that shall not end as far as our understanding goes, a journey that moves forever through time and space and beyond time and space, through dimensions and beyond dimensions, through creation and beyond this creation into the next. We speak with old souls, and we are old souls, for we were all at the beginning of this creation. And it is all of us and all of you and all those upon your planetary sphere who shall fashion for themselves a way of being, a way of living, a way of adoring and caring and chiding and feeling affection and being afraid, of being sad, a way of living and dying.

All of these things you fashion and shall continue to fashion, each in our own way, for you are co-creators of your mutual destinies, you who walk together upon this road. This road is as a seamless garment, a skin, shall we say. There is no hole or broken place within the fabric of your spirit or your spirit's experiences within this illusion. Many things may seem to be broken and need to be made whole, but in fact, this is illusion, not the reality. It is for this reason that occasionally miracles, so-called, do occur.

We would speak with you this evening about those things that do occur within each of your minds that cause judgment to occur. We would tell you of the small boy who asks to go into the road and play. "Absolutely not," his mother tells him. The boy is too young to understand that her meanness is the means of his survival. "I have just lost my job," wails the young woman. But this causes the young woman to think about what she wishes to do with her life, and in years to come, she has forgotten the pain of being without a future and has begun to enjoy having a past. We would point out to you that the master known to you as Jesus could have judged himself to be in a sorry state indeed, for he was scourged and beaten and nailed upon a cross until he was as inanimate as the wood which bore him. And yet, the great triumph of resurrection could never have taken place had all that passed not occurred.

We see the circle of each of your lives, the circle of judgment, of poor things which turn out to be so helpful and of seemingly excellent things which turn out to be worthless, and we would point out to you that judgment is a good thing to practice upon but is almost never correct, for the balancing between the good and the bad in each thing that occurs will go on within the widening ripples of your life patterns until the pond ripples no more for each.

Let us turn now and see that which is beyond judgment, that which you may do to more carefully polarize yourself and align yourself with that which is the great and limitless light of the one infinite Creator. That, my friends, has to do not with action but with intention. What you intend in a polarized manner when you begin to act or when you think of acting or when you hold someone in your thoughts is that lever by which you polarize your own being in the service-to-others or the service-to-self way. It is your choice. The choice which most of your peoples make—that is, not to choose—is acceptable. It is not, however, a particularly rapid way to work one's way through the lessons of love which are the lessons of your density until you can graduate and go on to another school, another dimension, another set of lessons, those having to do with wisdom. You shall not be wise in third density. This is a given. This is a part of the density which you inhabit. If you work and give of yourself to the effort of being loving, no matter how poorly or how well your actions are realized, you shall have polarized. When one does all that one can do, that is the end of the ripple.

Now, you must understand, shall we say, that this action will inevitably produce in each seeker a veritable melee of judgments. You judge yourself; you judge others; you judge ideas. Most of all you judge whether or not you are polarized. We urge you to look upon these exercises as a type of spiritual inertia which pulls at you, drags you back and is basically counterproductive. Nevertheless, that you have offered—being loving—cannot be taken from you, for it becomes a part of the vibration and the patterns of vibration which form the field of energy which form that which is called you in this density.

Because judgment is never particularly useful and is often a painfully strong deterrent to one's own progress, we urge each to rest the judgmental faculties. Mind you, we are not urging you to cease from discriminating betwixt one thought and another. We simply ask you to ride the mare, not for the mare to ride you.

Let us be more specific. Your intellect and all that goes with your intellect, as opposed to all that goes with your character, is a tool. It was crafted by you through many experiences and is part of that which is manifest and realized in this incarnational experience. It is a tool for you to use and it is a good tool. However, many there are among those who seek spiritually who allow the intellect to ride them. This is not an infrequent thing at all and, indeed, in those who have had some experience in attempting to govern the mind, is certainly not surprising. But we urge you to temper that intellect, to ask yourself, "Am I thinking or am I feeling?" To ask of yourself, "Is my thinking bent upon aiding either myself or another in spiritual growth?" These answers are most important, not just to you but to those lives you touch, for indeed, you can give nothing but yourself.

There are many who would wish to give you gifts; there are many whom you would wish to give gifts. The effective gift is that of yourself. Therefore, the first person to practice your lack of judgment and your acceptance upon is you yourself. Have you allowed yourself to shine forth today? Have you allowed laughter to bubble in your voice, joy to fill your eyes? Have you listened and looked and heard and seen the music and the joyful alleluias of the creation, the nodding flowers that bend toward the uncertain sun of spring, the first willows that wave their greening branches over the road you travel? The dramatic skies that give you rain and offer nurturing to your new crops? Have you allowed yourselves to be ministered unto by the creation? For only in doing this can you then turn and offer yourself in ministry to others. Whatever it is that feeds you, turn to it, allow it to fill you with the love of the Creator and then allow that love to shine through you. We do not need to tell you that of yourself you cannot do this, for human love is short-lived and human expectation tremendously long-lived. Love can never meet expectation.

We would, as we gaze upon your peoples, almost wish that the planet upon which you live could see itself as bitten by a snake so that the people could begin to take restorative action to contain that poison which is judgment and to release into the body the antitoxin, love. Ah, my friends, the flowers shall bloom, the crops shall mature, and you who are the greatest crop, you shall bloom and mature also. How effective do you wish to be today? How would you like to greet tomorrow's sun? The willow has already made up its mind; it will turn towards the light. Shall you?

Before we go further, we would wish at this time to spend a few moments acquainting each in the room with our particular vibration. If there are any untoward effects, mentally request that we adjust the rate at which we are contacting you and we shall do so immediately. We shall pause at this time that we may greet each of you and allow you to feel our presence. I am Hatonn.

(Pause)

I am again with this instrument. I am Hatonn. We have, in contacting others in the group, caused the fine tuning with this instrument to become somewhat more than she can handle. If we may pause again, we shall adjust.

(Pause)

I am again with this instrument. I am Hatonn, and again greet you in love and light. It has been such a privilege to speak with each of you. If we may leave one thought with you, it would be to request that in your priorities for each day, the first priority be meditation. The world about you—that is, the world that seems to be about you—is always astir with the small and large issues of the day. Even the insects, the birds, make their noises and do not go away. Within yourself is the only solitary place where one may go and shut the door and open to that beauty, that power which is the Creator, and that one great original Thought of the Creator, which is love. You shall not find yourself able to escape judgment; you shall not find yourself able to escape folly, and your life and death are but a tiny parenthesis in infinity. And yet within yourself lies the access to that infinite portion of you which is the Creator, which dwells in the Creator, and which indwells within you. Meditate, open inwardly and then, my friends, turn towards the friendly sun or smile at the raindrops that nurture those crops that are working to break the soil.

Nothing is what it seems; all things are what they seem. We offer this as the one paradox that is repeated over and over. Judge all you can, there will always be another side; love all you can and your lives shall be transformed. We leave you, my friends, in the love and the light of our infinite Creator. In the power of that one great original Thought we leave you. We are known to you as those of Hatonn. Adonai. Adonai, my friends.

(Jim channeling)

I am Latwii, and we greet you, my friends, in that same love and light of our one infinite Creator. We are grateful once again to have been asked to join your group and to offer our simple service of attempting to answer those queries which you may have value in the asking. We echo our brothers and sisters of Hatonn in suggesting that you use discrimination as you listen to our words, for we are but fallible pilgrims upon the same journey with you in the seeking of truth. May we begin then with the first query?

Carla: Since nobody's asking anything, I'll ask a throw-away. What vitamin deficiency causes cracked lips, sores at the corners of your mouth? Do you have any idea?

I am Latwii, and, my sister, we must admit to being somewhat unfamiliar with the chemical vehicles which you inhabit and through which you in your minds move. We can look upon that area of your physical vehicle which you have described and make most general recommendations that your intake of certain vitamins may be increased in the area of citrus fruits and the vitamin C. We cannot be more precise, for many entities are unique in their physical makeup and may suffer anomalistic deficiencies which would require a separate diagnosis for each case.

May we attempt another query or further response, my sister?

Carla: Merely my apology for asking such a silly question, but thank you very much.

I am Latwii, and we thank you, my sister, even for your silly questions. May we attempt another query at this time?

N: Latwii, I greet you in the path of love and light and light and love of the one infinite Creator. And I was wondering if you might explain the White Brotherhood?

I am Latwii, and am aware of your query, my brother. There are various distorted perceptions of this group which is loosely called the White Brotherhood or Great White Brotherhood among the peoples of your planet, for it has existed for a great portion of what you call time and through various means has had its expression in the service of the one Creator. There have been many efforts in this expression through the various channels and means presented to those who are of this grouping. There has been upon your planet for a great portion of its third-density experience those of its population who have through their own seeking been able to, shall we say, harvest themselves, and enter that dimension which awaits your population as a whole at this time. Within what you might call the inner planes of your planetary influence these entities then have gathered themselves and have chosen to focus their attempt at serving others in whatever means has been available.

Many of your peoples have been contacted in what you call the dreaming state, others in the meditative state, and others in intuitional attunements or moments of inspiration. The purpose of each contact has been to answer a call. Those who call of your population seek the love of the one Creator. Those of the so-called White Brotherhood then, receiving this call, move to answer in whatever fashion can be understood by the one who calls. Thus, within the inner realms of your planetary influence, this grouping of light beings seeks to share that which has been their privilege to obtain as the understanding of compassion and love, those lessons of your particular illusion.

May we answer you further, my brother?

N: Is the bulk or the majority of the White Brotherhood located on Earth or on other planets or in another dimension?

I am Latwii, and am aware of your query, my brother. Again, in this response we find the possibility of distortion, for, as we have said in our previous response, many are the perceptions of this grouping of entities, and indeed this grouping of entities is joined from time to time by others who also seek to share the light which has been found in the personal evolutionary process. These who join from time to time that grouping called the White Brotherhood may be from a variety of locations and points of experience. To be generally correct, we may suggest that the heart of this White Brotherhood, in its numbers of member entities, is of your planetary influence, and exists within the inner realms or time/space portion of your planetary experience.

May we answer you further, my brother?

N: Is the White Brotherhood primarily … do they utilize themselves as spirit guides? Or are they of a different type of influence?

I am Latwii, and we can in general suggest that those of this group, the White Brotherhood, do not in general serve as what we understand you term the "spirit guide," that is the, shall we say, angelic presence or collection of such which moves with each entity upon your planet for the purpose of providing guidance where possible and protection where possible. These of the White Brotherhood, on the other hand, may be considered as, shall we say, resources which may be called upon by a specific and purified seeking or working of what you may call the adept. These of the White Brotherhood, then, are more general in their effect in that their service moves to, shall we say, blanket your planet but is the result of a more specific and purified calling than an entity would normally make in its daily round of activities, that round which is more properly the sphere of the spirit guides as you have called them.

May we answer you further, my brother?

N: Then, all the White Brotherhood are of at least fourth density or higher?

I am Latwii, and this is basically correct, for these entities have in their own experience been able to utilize the catalyst which is available within your third-density illusion to the extent that now their understanding, shall we say, has reached a critical mass, and has enabled them to welcome a greater portion of the love and light of the one Creator which is available to all.

May we answer you further, my brother?

N: Thank you very much.

I am Latwii, and we thank you, my brother. Is there another query at this time?

(Side one of tape ends.)

Carla: Yeah. I'd like to know that too because I just saw today that Jesus was of the order of Melchizedek; that's what it said in the Bible.

I am Latwii, and am once again with this instrument as it has completed its mechanical duties *(of turning the tape over)*. We are aware of the query and shall do our best to provide a satisfactory response. Those of the Melchizedek thought, shall we say, are those entities who have found a particular philosophy to be of service to them in their own evolutionary process. Many have been the masters, as you call them, who have walked the surface of your planet in third-density vehicles. These entities are of various origins, many without your planetary influence. The one known as Melchizedek was a, as you call it, master who had consciously followed a certain philosophical path which served to discipline the mind and the personality which expressed the mind so that third-density entities could in a conscious fashion accelerate the evolutionary process that each either consciously or unconsciously upon your planet takes part in.

These entities are a grouping which is usually placed within the ancient mystery schools, those places of learning which existed from great and times within various cultures' histories upon your planet, for always there have been the seekers of truth, and from time to time and in various places these seekers have organized themselves in societies and schools which have sought to preserve and pass on those truths, shall we say, that they have honored to gather.

The one known as Jesus was as one who sought from many schools the knowledge and the expression of the one Creator that is called love. Many were the places and schools which this entity visited and at which this entity learned as a portion of its evolutionary process.

May we answer you further, my sister?

Carla: No. Thank you very much.

I am Latwii, and we thank you, my sister. Is there another query at this time?

J: Yes, Latwii. May I ask if there is any sort of differential in awareness or possible harvest into fourth density among the various religions, whether it be Hindu, Buddha, Christianity, Judaism or whatever, or Moslem, whatever, as far as that sort of level of awareness necessary for harvest, et cetera?

I am Latwii, and am aware of your query, my brother. Each vine has its fruits. Each vine has those branches which are pruned or which die from lack of light, shall we say. Each religion, as you have called it, upon your planet offers to the pure seeker of truth a path to the infinite. Upon any path, whether it is organized as a religion or formed as a personal expression, will have the side roads, shall we say, which can in some degree lead one astray. Yet to the persevering and constant seeker who utilizes the will to know and the faith that knowing is possible, the rejoining of the path which is straight and narrow then occurs.

May we answer you further, my brother?

J: No, thank you.

I am Latwii, and we again thank you, my brother. Is there another query at this time?

Carla: Well, before you go, I'd just like to ask a follow-up on the question about the Brotherhood. I've noticed that whether it's in Peru or Tibet or Mount Shasta, that the teachings of the White Brotherhood or the Brotherhood of the Seven Rays or the Ascended Masters always seem to take place in mountains or on mountains. I wonder if that's a third-density fact, in other words, the high altitudes are more spiritual, or if its a concept of the highest and most high that is just personified by mountains?

I am Latwii, and am aware of your query, my sister. We find that in some degree each of your assumptions is correct. There is within the mountains' terrain the symbolic path of the seeker of truth. The seeker who travels the conscious path of attempting to express and experience that known as love is one which shall find itself twisting with a sinuous path, discovering boulders that seem impassable, and shall occasionally find itself tired and worn beyond its belief that it can continue. Yet the upward trail lies before it, and after a rest the seeker then continues this journey, leaving behind it the great expanse of that which is the manifested illusion, moving towards that which is more, shall we say, substantial in the spiritual or metaphysical sense until it finds itself within the rarefied atmosphere which provides the widened point of view.

The perspective possible from the mountaintop is like unto that ability to love with a wider perspective, to accept that which seemed unacceptable, to forgive that which seems unforgivable, to have compassion for that which seems deserving of none.

There is another reason which has brought many seekers to the mountainous region, and that is the solitude which such regions provide, that the entity may, in a sense, withdraw from the world and focus its being and expressions upon the seeking of the one Creator which is more difficult within the more densely populated portions of your planet, for there the distractions are multiplied. This seeming separation of the seeker from those about it is only illusory separation, however, a separation from the husks of the illusion and a true joining with the heart of all those about it, a joining in love.

May we answer you further, my sister?

Carla: No, thank you.

I am Latwii, and we thank you. May we attempt another query?

J: Yes. Earlier at some time I believe we discussed the fact that the Atlanteans sent expeditions to Tibet and Turkey and the mainland to the mountainous areas. Was there some other reason why they chose these mountainous areas or did they actually expect a catastrophic flood that may have occurred when the land mass sunk?

I am Latwii, and we find that the latter portion of your assumptions is more correct, for if you will remember, these entities were those whose homeland, shall we say, was in the process of being inundated by the waters which surrounded it as a result of the warfare, as you call it. Therefore, these entities sought the safest places possible in order that the knowledge which had been their privilege to accumulate might be preserved for the future populations of your planet.

May we answer you further, my brother?

J: No, thank you.

I am Latwii, and we thank you, my brother. Is there another query at this time?

(Pause)

I am Latwii, and we are aware that there are some queries which have not reached their final form at this time and would benefit by a period of time, shall we say, in their gestation. We shall therefore take our leave of this group, leaving, as always, in the illusory manner only, for in truth we are one. In [love] and light then, we leave you as we find you. We are those of Latwii. Adonai, my friends. Adonai vasu borragus.

(Carla channeling)

I am Nona, and we shall not keep you long, but we have been called for the healing vibrations especially for the one known as N. Therefore we shall make our vibratory sounds and leave you in the love and in the light of the One Who Is All. I am Nona.

(Carla channels a beautiful healing melody from Nona.)

Intensive Meditation
March 26, 1985

(Carla channeling)

I am Hatonn. We would speak with you briefly before moving on to the, as this instrument calls it, intensive portion of the meeting, wishing only to greet you in the love and in the light of our infinite Creator and to explain that we aided the instrument somewhat in its choice of tuning. Each entity had a good deal of busyness to the day and there was much relaxation that would be fruitful for the adventure of attempting the vocal channeling. Indeed, the relaxation of the body is most important. It is often the case that one does not know how caught up in one's very physical vehicle they have been in the daily round until one first sits down to relax. It is as if the physical vehicle does not communicate perfectly with the mind of the individual. This is unfortunate, my friends. There is much illness or disease among your peoples that could well be solved if entities were aware of their bodies all the time and responded appropriately when the need arose. We shall leave you at this time in the love and the light of our infinite Creator. We are known to you as those of Hatonn.

(Carla channeling)

I am Laitos, and I greet you, my friends, also in the love and in the light of the Creator Who Is All. We are aware that you seek us, yet we also are aware that in each mind there is the questioning. Therefore, we shall attempt to give a good balance between the working with each new instrument and the desire for answered questions. We would, as always when transferring to another instrument, wish to provide the basic information concerning who we are and in what guise we come. We shall pause.

(Pause)

Carla: Let's visualize all of this inside, the beautiful limitless white light, so that we can retune.

(Carla channeling)

We are those of Hatonn and Laitos. That portion speaking through this instrument is now Laitos but both energies are with this group at this time. Again we greet you in love and in light. We thank the one known as R for the attention to the quieting of the distracting noises. As this instrument would put it, we need all the help we can get. It is a joy to be with you and a joy to be working with each new instrument. We shall transfer now to the one known as J in order to exercise this instrument and say only a few simple thoughts. We ask the instrument not to analyze and to speak freely without attempting to analyze in any way that which is spoken, realizing that our concepts seem a good deal like one's own thoughts. The difference is subtle and as one becomes more and more capable and vocal channeling becomes easier to spot, one is aware that one has not thought something, and yet it is there. That is the channeling as you know it.

We now attempt this process through the one known as J, and we leave this instrument. I am Laitos.

(Carla channeling)

May we comment that it is almost as difficult to get this instrument's attention sometimes as it is to gain the attention of the one known as J, and this instrument has a habit of being a million miles away which is sometimes counterproductive. It is our joy to be working with the one known as J. We feel that we have good contact. However, we have not been able to fasten upon any single way of expressing subjectively to the one known as J that we are with this instrument. We shall be working on that detail. Meanwhile, we thank very much the one known as J and would move on to the one known as R. If this instrument would appreciate or desire the experience of the vocal contact, this is the time, my friends. Now is always the time. Later is almost never the time for what one wishes to do. Therefore, we would at this time transfer to the one known as R.

(Carla channeling)

I am again with this instrument. I am Laitos. We were able to get the feeling of conditioning with this instrument but the conditioning that is desired has not yet, shall we say, peaked. We shall continue working to substantially aid the instrument in feeling our presence and meanwhile we would go on to the one known as N and say to this instrument, you are not expected to do anything, or, if you wish, to say anything. These vocal contacts are services that may be performed for the benefit of others. It is one of an infinite array of ways to help another. There is no extreme rightness or cachet to the ability to channel nor is there any lack of service if one wishes to serve in other areas. To channel is not to be spiritual. There are times when to be spiritual is to desire to channel. We ask all of those who may see or hear these words to keep this in mind. Meanwhile, we shall rush upon our way to the unsuspecting next channel which is latent within the one known as N's bosom and attempt to make some verbal communication such as "I am Laitos" clear to this new instrument. We now transfer. I am Laitos.

N: Laitos promised to turn up the volume but he didn't turn it up.

(N channeling)

I greet you in the love and light and light love of the one infinite Creator. You are … I think I lost it.

(Carla channeling)

I am Laitos. I am again with this instrument, and again greet you in love and light. May we say to the one known as N that we are most exuberant to have made contact and appreciate that success and the dedication which it springs from. When a new instrument begins to speak, may we say to the one known as N, it is very frequently the case that the contact becomes lost because of analysis of the message or because of the distracting "rush," as this instrument would call it, of feelings that accompany the contact.

In order to maintain contact under these conditions, there is a simple trick which one uses and that is to refrain from speaking in the first person. The one losing that fine tuned contact will be instructed as part of the package deal we are offering these days in communications. However, the instructions will be in the third person, as you are channeling about yourself in the third person and not as yourself. This has aided many a new instrument until the confidence is there to stride forward in a more authoritative way.

We would, before we close through this instrument, once again contact the one known as R. We transfer to this instrument at this time. I am Laitos.

(R channeling)

I am Laitos.

(Carla channeling)

I am Laitos, and once again elated to find that our signal is being picked up. We have a way to go in order to make this contact crystal clear. However, the simple knowing of our presence is very elating. We thank the one known as R, and again we would transfer to the one known as J. I am Laitos.

(Carla channeling)

I am Laitos. We had been so close to contact with the one known as J that we were reluctant to cease attempting it. But we feel that our time is about up. We have had a glorious time working with you and sharing incarnational vibrations with you. We thank each of you and as this instrument would say, all our rowdy friends are coming out tonight. *(Sound of a cat meowing.)* There are many of us, but we are as one, and within that love and that oneness you are always included, my friends, never more so than at this moment. It is time for the questioning and so we shall close this instrument. I am Laitos.

(Carla channeling)

We rejoin this communication. We are those of Laitos. We would correct the instrument. We are leaving, not to transfer, but in order that the one known as Latwii may speak. We leave you, therefore, in the love and in the light of the infinite Creator. We thank you and we shall be with you. Adonai, my friends. Adonai.

(Jim channeling)

I am Latwii, and we are most happy to greet you, my friends, as well, in the love and in the light of our infinite Creator. We have joined this merry group this evening, those seen and those unseen to your physical apparatus, and together we make quite a, as the previous instrument said, "rowdy group." We shall at this time, as is our usual custom, open this session to the asking of questions in hopes that we might be of service in this manner. May we begin then with the first query?

R: Yes, Latwii. First off, hello. I wonder if you could comment to me on the conditioning. The conditioning I received from Laitos is very similar to the conditioning I've received from you. A very unique difference, though—I mean it was very obvious that it wasn't you, but yet the sensations were the same. And I remember once long ago you told me that you'd made an agreement with me that that would be the form of my conditioning, and I was wondering if that was the same agreement that Laitos had made and also if maybe times and circumstances had changed since then and can you tell me more about the actual technique that you used to do that [open to higher energies]. It was wonderful; it felt great. I'd like to thank Laitos for that too.

I am Latwii, and am aware of your query, my brother. With each new instrument which we work with in the providing of the conditioning we are able by an unspoken, in most cases, agreement to utilize some portion of the instrument's sensory system in order to become noticed, shall we say. In each instrument this manner or means of making our vibration available is somewhat different, though each new instrument will share much with others in how a conditioning is experienced. In your particular case we have been able to utilize certain anomalistic patterns within your, shall we say, electromagnetic energy field or aura in order to make our presence known to you.

As you or any new instrument proceeds along the path of balancing distortions, there become available finer and clearer means of making our presence known. This is a process which is congruent yet has a separate identity to the instrument's own ability to increasingly perceive with greater clarity those contacts available to it. Therefore, as your own progress upon the evolutionary path proceeds, and as you make additional attempts to perceive our contact, there grow from these two closely intertwined processes an increased ability upon your part to perceive our contact.

May we answer you further, my brother?

R: I feel, I guess, kind of proud because I hadn't been able to receive Laitos conditioning up until now. I guess you are able to reach the blockheads earlier than the rest of the Confederation. I have no question, just thank you for your services again, and Laitos and Hatonn also.

I am Latwii, and we thank you as well, my brother. In many cases it is not so much that we have a greater ability to transmit our thoughts to those who would receive them as it may occasionally be the case of simply using a bigger hammer, hopefully with some skill.

May we attempt another query at this time?

N: Yes, Latwii. I wish to thank Laitos also. I wonder if there's any way that individually we can increase our perception or, as Laitos once said, this group can increase the volume, so to speak. It seems that I know the words are there but I just can't quite pull them out. I don't know … even though I'm not trying to analyze, it just seems as if I'm reaching for the words but can't quite pull it in. Do you have any suggestions in that respect?

I am Latwii, and am aware of your query, my brother, and may suggest that as the newness of the vocalized channeling begins to wear off, then you will discover through your own patient persistence the ability to perceive that which seems at this point just beyond your ability. You are as one who has come in from a brightly lit day and has retreated to the darkness of the meditation room and yet looks with the eyes in a darkened room, attempting to make out the furniture in order that you may recline upon a comfortable piece for your meditation. It takes some, as you would say, of that called time for your eyes to become accustomed to the darker environment, and after a period of time and adjustment, then you perceive the furniture around you, dimly lit as it is. This is the process which you now experience in an analogous form as you attempt to become the vocal channel.

May we answer you further, my brother?

N: Yes, please. This may be somewhat divergent, but would one of my crystals help R?

I am Latwii, and we cannot give a specific answer to this query, for it is most general in its statement, and is therefore not well enough defined in order for us to answer with any hope of clarity. May we ask for a rephrasing of the query?

N: I really don't know how to rephrase. One of the crystals that I carry that I have charged, would it help R's condition? I don't know how to phrase than any way else.

I am Latwii, and we feel we have a better grasp of your query, though by asking if a crystal can help an entity, it is still somewhat of a general query which needs the focus. We feel you are, however, desirous of providing this charged crystal in the capacity of aiding that called disease and in this regard we may suggest that a crystal such as the one which you possess might be of aid to the one known as R if it were used by an entity which itself had become as the crystal, regular in its ability to perceive and transmit the infinite intelligence of the one Creator in a pure and undistorted fashion, that is, in the relative sense.

May we answer you further, my brother?

N: If I understand correctly then, I'm not that pure so the crystal wouldn't really help. Is that the essence of the answer?

I am Latwii, and this is a portion of our response, though we were not being ourselves specific as to any particular entity which might attempt to utilize the crystal. The utilization of the crystal would be helpful if utilized by any entity which had itself become regularized as is the crystal.

May we answer you further, my brother?

N: Without thwarting free will, is there any way that we can become regularized as a crystal, any method, any direction that we can take in that respect?

I am Latwii, and am aware of your query, my brother. Indeed, there are as many ways as there are entities seeking such ways, my brother. There are throughout your history recorded a great many ways of the, as they are called, mystery schools which have been used throughout time and culture to remove those distortions within the entity seeking to become that known as the healer. Indeed, each entity upon your planet, whether it follows a path that has been studied throughout the ages, as you would say, or does not follow any conscious path at all, is pursuing the evolutionary path of mind, body and spirit which will eventually result in the entity becoming that which we have called crystallized, balanced or regularized in its ability to perceive and transmit those finer energies which are available to all. The choice of path is the choice of each seeker.

May we answer you further, my brother?

N: No, thank you very much. I guess I'm confused enough.

I am Latwii, and we do apologize for any confusion which we might have been responsible for. The queries which you have asked are queries which many, many books have been written about and which therefore are most difficult to summarize in a short and understandable manner.

May we attempt another query at this time?

Carla: I guess I have a question. When Don Elkins was alive, he had a fellow once that had a very bad stomach condition. He could only [eat] baby food; he had bleeding ulcers. Don put the person into a more relaxed state, a light hypnotic state, and then talked to this person about perspective and not taking things so seriously. Whether as a coincidence or whether as cause and effect, the ulcer went away. Would this technique be helpful in working with the one known as R?

I am Latwii, and am aware of your query, my sister. We find that there are many techniques that might be of aid to the one known as R or to any entity suffering that imbalance which is called disease among your peoples. Indeed, in many cases, it is not so much the technique that is used, but the intention with which the technique is used. The intention of the one to be healed is paramount in such an experience, for it is the desire and ability of the one to be healed which is the salient feature which then allows the healing to occur.

We find that there are some techniques which can enhance the effect of the intention to be healed and to provide healing catalyst. The technique which you have mentioned is one such technique, for it speaks more directly to the deeper portions of an entity's mind in order that communication might be [enhanced], shall we say, and with less interference of the conscious mind.

May we answer you further, my sister?

Carla: No, thank you.

I am Latwii, and we thank you, my sister. Is there another query at this time?

(Pause)

I am Latwii, and we thank each of you, my friends, for allowing us to join you in your meditation this evening. We hope that we have not confused too many too much, for there is much time for that and there is apparently so little for the removal of confusion. We do not wish to add to your burdens, my friends. We shall at this time take our leave of this group and this instrument. As always, we leave you in that light and in that love which is our joy and privilege to share with you at all times. We are those of Latwii. Adonai, my friends. Adonai vasu borragus. ☙

Intensive Meditation
April 3, 1985

(Carla channeling)

I am Laitos, and great you in the love and in the light of our infinite Creator. We would wish before we begin to energize this group to the best of our poor ability, for each within this circle is weary and the weariness is only partially physical. Thus, we would ask your permission which you may give mentally to receive the energy of the spiritual and the emotional in order that we may have better contact through each instrument. We shall pause and attempt to energize as we have described. We shall pause for just a moment or two. I am Laitos.

(Pause)

I am Laitos and am again with this instrument. We are having to adjust as we often do with this instrument which is very sensitive, more sensitive than the norm, shall we say. We have a fairly good spiral of energy from this group now, and we thank it that it may become available to us that we may do our humble work with you. At this time we would speak through the one known as J. We ask the instrument to relax and to speak what pops into his head without analysis. We shall transfer. I am Laitos.

(Pause)

(Carla channeling)

I am again with this instrument. I am Laitos. We paused for a fairly long period of what you call time due to that fact that we are in good contact with the one known as J and would wish to give this instrument every opportunity to become used to that contact. We shall visit the one known as J again within this session if the instrument gives mental permission.

At this time now we would wish to communicate to the one known as N. We transfer now. I am Laitos.

(N channeling)

I am Laitos. I greet you in the love and light of our one infinite Creator. There is a time element for conditioning which all must observe. This varies with the sensitivity of the individual. Much practice with meditation is needed and many an *(inaudible)* because of this variation. Your time will come. If it's difficult to judge the relative consideration for any entity although the variability is enormous …

I think I started to analyze. I messed it up.

(Carla channeling)

I am Laitos, and greet you once again through this instrument. We are most pleased to be able to begin to speak through the one known as N, and can only urge this instrument to refrain from judging itself. The concepts which we are able to offer through an instrument such as the one known as N are quite unique to this particular entity. This is the great strength of the free will communication. When one is in trance, one is an instrument with only the tuning of the instrument as a measure of the excellence of the message. When one is working with the conscious channeling, one may use far more discrimination, and be able to put into expression those half-formed thoughts which are part of the basic nature of that unique individual. We use the thoughts, the experiences, and the nature of each instrument.

We also encourage the one known as N to remain within the circle of subjective reality, which is broken when the instrument changes from the instrument speaking spiritually to the entity judging itself. It is not advisable nor are any excuses necessary nor is there any apology, for before the channeling began, there was no concept. Regardless of how far the entity which is channeling is able to get, the concept which has been offered is then part of the, shall we say, etheric atmosphere which is ambient within the dwelling and the immediate vicinity of the dwelling. In a larger sense, these thoughts thus become part of what this instrument would call the "zeitgeist" or "the way things are" planet-wide.

We would again transfer the contact to the one known as J. I am Laitos.

(Pause)

(Carla channeling)

I am Laitos, and am again with this instrument. We thank each for waiting while we worked with the new instrument known as J. There is a good deal of internal defense mechanism which has unconsciously been brought into play with this particular instrument. Each instrument has a different personality. Each instrument has therefore a greater or lesser amount of defensiveness and privacy. The one known as J is a most private person, and the ability to remain a private person in such a public world is, as we have mentioned, quite variable. Therefore the amount of effort and time needed to free an instrument from its own defense mechanisms is widely various. The instrument known as J shall certainly be able to channel. There may be more of a time factor, as you would call it, which means only in our point of view that that which is precious is worth the effort.

We thank each of you, and before the questions begin, we would give ourselves over to the one known as Nona as this has been requested this particular evening for the ones known as R, S1, S2 and G. Thus, we take our leave of you, but never take we our leave of our love for you. We are always there if you wish to call upon us for the aid in the meditation. Merely request silently that we be with you and we in our own silence shall be as you ask. We are those of Laitos and would sign off for both Nona and ourselves, leaving each in the love and the light of our infinite Creator. Adonai.

(Carla channels a healing melody from Nona.)

(Jim channeling)

I am Latwii, and greet you, my friends, in love and light, in the love and light of our infinite One. We are honored to join you this evening, and give ourselves over to your potentials in the asking of queries. This is our service which we provide with joy. May we ask for our first query this evening?

Carla: I'd like to ask the question that N wrote out before the meeting, and that was, as the planet Earth, as we call it, spirals into fourth density in space/time and in time/space, does it carry it with it the solar system and the galaxy or is it a local phenomenon?

I am Latwii, and, my sister, we may suggest that the galaxy and the solar system more properly carry with it—we correct this instrument—carry with them your particular planet. There is a great movement in time and space throughout all of creation, for all creation is in motion; there is no portion of creation that is truly at rest, for the light which is the, shall we say, building block of all creation always vibrates at some frequency. Those portions of the creation which you call planets are also in vibration. Each level of vibration is determined by the planet's success, shall we say, in seeking the one Creator. Throughout all creation this seeking continues. It is the force which motivates all action and reaction, for the one Creation seeks the one Creator from which it was made and by Whose hand it was fashioned.

Thus your planet in its seeking of the one Creator moves according to its vibration, and as it moves through one portion of its experience which is your third-density experience, it then …

We must apologize, this instrument was distracted. This movement, then, of your planet is reflected in the increase in vibration of its core atomic particles, as you may call them.

May we attempt further response, my sister?

Carla: No, thank you, my brother.

I am Latwii, and we thank you, as always. Is there another query at this time?

N: Greetings, Latwii. As this core atomic structure starts vibrating at an increased rate, will there by tremendous terrain changes on Earth or shift in poles or any combination?

I am Latwii, and am aware of your query, my brother. We find that though your assumptions are in general correct, that is, that there shall be some geothermal activity during this period of shifting of frequencies of vibration, that these geothermal activities are not necessarily related to the change in vibration from your third to the fourth-density vibrations. These geothermal changes are, however, a result of the relative disharmony that has been experienced by the great majority of the populations of your planet for a large portion of what you call time, for as the bellicose nature of various cultures has been expressed in what might be seen as a basically disharmonious fashion, these vibrations of anger and disharmony then move into the surface of the planet and are stored as what you know as heat. As your planet moves then into a higher frequency of vibration, this heat must find release in some fashion, and this will be seen as various geothermal events which will cause some disturbance upon the surface of your planet's garment.

May we answer you further, my brother?

N: Nostradamus predicted that the area of the San Andreas fault would be involved in 1988. Is this geothermal or just plate rearrangement?

I am Latwii, and am aware of your query, my brother. We find that in all such potential geothermal and realignment of the tectonic plate structure events of your planet that there are a number of factors which may be seen as the cause, shall we say. There are, as we have mentioned, upon the surface of your planet, many areas which have the heat of the bellicose nature stored within the upper regions of your planet's surface. There are as well deeper layers of this heat storage which then can effect the planet's tectonic plates in their alignment and realignment, seeking the balance which has been upset, shall we say. There are also various implements of your technological invention which have accelerated this process, these being of the nature of the nuclear testing and the advanced weaponry systems which have had some effect upon the planet's outer garment and upon its tectonic plates as well.

May we answer you further, my brother?

N: Is it correct then that the higher the terrain, the taller the terrain, the more storage of this warlike energy as well as the effect of nuclear testing and other weaponry? And will this eventually within the next thirty years as predicted cause a rotation of the planet's poles or rearrangement of some sort?

I am Latwii, and am aware of your query, my brother. We find that it is not so much the elevation of a location, but the location of cultures which have engaged in the warlike behavior which is the determining factor in whether a portion of your planet has stored within it the heat of the anger and the disharmony which has accumulated for a portion of your time.

We, as we look upon the possibilities that await your planet in what you call your future, can see a great variety, and it is not possible to sort from these possibilities the one possibility which your planet as a whole shall choose. We can see that there are many possibilities which suggest that there shall be some shifting in your planet's alignment as it moves through space in its orbit about your sun body, and we therefore cannot be specific in describing what changes shall indeed occur, for these changes are a function of your planet's population. This choice can change from moment to moment and indeed has many times changed, and may be expected to continue in its changing course as the population of your planet refines its desire and its ability to seek and express the one infinite Creator.

May we answer you further, my brother?

N: Thank you very much. We were discussing the pyramids also. Are there a number of pyramids in the Atlantic Ocean that we don't … or in the Atlantic area, in the Pacific area that we do not know about, as well as this pyramid in the Bermuda triangle? And is it possible to locate them?

I am Latwii, and am aware of your query, my brother. We look upon your planet and see that the work done by various social memory complexes in portions of what you call your past has frequently taken the form of constructing those structures which you have called the pyramid. These structures have, for the most part, been useful in aligning and balancing the instreaming love and light of the one Creator, that this new configuration of energy presented by the pyramids might then balance the disharmonious effects of your planet's population's tendencies towards the disharmony and warlike behavior.

There are throughout various portions of your planet, then, those structures called pyramids, and many of these have become well known to the population of your planet. There are those which yet remain undiscovered, and which at some future time may be revealed, for there are means of detecting such structures. Their exact locations we cannot reveal, for this would be an infringement, for such structures do exist and have some potential in effecting—we correct this instrument—have some potential in affecting the future of your planet in its seeking of the one Creator.

May we answer you further, my brother?

N: Would it be an infringement to ask how deep the pyramid in the Bermuda triangle is in terms of yards or feet or meters?

I am Latwii, and we would not at this time care to either affirm the existence of such a structure in this location or to be more specific in describing its possible location, for such a structure may indeed affect the future of your population.

May we answer you further, my brother?

N: Would it be possible to build a new ring of pyramids around Earth such as was contemplated previously—contemplated and completed previously—that would more nearly balance our bellicose nature?

I am Latwii, and we find that such is possible yet might be superseded by the continued movement of the various entities towards the resolution of conflicts between nations, between entities. This action would have much more chance of balancing the disharmony that has been present upon your planet for a large portion of your time.

May we answer you further, my brother?

N: I'm afraid I didn't quite understand. Are we saying that we're more close to a nuclear war, or some warlike action, that even with an accumulation of funds from various groups and so forth, that new pyramids could not be completed in time?

I am Latwii, and though your assumption does have some merit, we attempted to describe a more effective means of balancing the bellicose nature of your planet's populations, that is, to intensify those efforts which have been ongoing for a great portion of time and which have generated a momentum and an awareness, shall we say, of the destructive nature of any kind of warlike activity. This movement towards peace is one which has a greater likelihood in the balancing of your planet's bellicose nature than would any construction of mechanical devices which would then take a larger portion of what you call time to, shall we say, render an effect.

May we answer you further, my brother?

N: The pyramid is considered a mechanical device? In your thoughts?

I am Latwii, and we may affirm this supposition, my brother. It has been truly said that the pyramid is as the metaphysical training wheels.

May we answer you further, my brother?

N: Although there may be a significant peace movement in the western hemispheres, how would we stimulate a peaceful movement in the eastern or what might be considered the communistic block?

I am Latwii, and we may suggest that within each nation upon your planet there are those whose love of peace far supersedes the love of war, and within each nation then there are those entities who move towards the resolution of conflicts in the peaceful manner. To these entities one may send the love and light of the one Creator that in the metaphysical sense they might receive the support that then they could, shall we say, channel or manifest within your third-density illusion. Remember, my brother, that all is truly one, and when you send the love and light and thoughts of peace to any entity, that entity is as yourself and receives your message as clearly as if you had sent it to yourself.

May we answer you further, my brother?

N: Thank you very much, my brother.

I am Latwii, and again we thank you, my brother. May we attempt another query at this time?

(Pause)

I am Latwii, and we thank you, my friends, for inviting us this evening to your meditation and for presenting us with the gifts of your queries. We are most honored and shall join you again at your request. We shall leave you now in the love and light of the one infinite Creator. Adonai, my friends. Adonai. ☥

L/L Research

L/L Research is a subsidiary of Rock Creek Research & Development Laboratories, Inc.

P.O. Box 5195
Louisville, KY 40255-0195

www.llresearch.org

Rock Creek is a non-profit corporation dedicated to discovering and sharing information which may aid in the spiritual evolution of humankind.

ABOUT THE CONTENTS OF THIS TRANSCRIPT: This telepathic channeling has been taken from transcriptions of the weekly study and meditation meetings of the Rock Creek Research & Development Laboratories and L/L Research. It is offered in the hope that it may be useful to you. As the Confederation entities always make a point of saying, please use your discrimination and judgment in assessing this material. If something rings true to you, fine. If something does not resonate, please leave it behind, for neither we nor those of the Confederation would wish to be a stumbling block for any.

CAVEAT: This transcript is being published by L/L Research in a not yet final form. It has, however, been edited and any obvious errors have been corrected. When it is in a final form, this caveat will be removed.

© 2009 L/L Research

Sunday Meditation
April 7, 1985

(Carla channeling)

I am Hatonn. I and my people greet you in the love in and the light of our infinite Creator. We most heartily and humbly thank you that you have called to us this night and we bless each within this room in the name of light. May all that you manifest be as true as that which you manifest at this moment. This would be a part of our thoughts to aid you. It is one often missed by your peoples who are always striving for more—more food, more recreation, more freedom, more of everything, and yet more and less are irrelevant for you are who you are and what you are now at this moment, at this crux. You may choose freely and you may do well, for as far as we know, the Creator is kindly and affectionate to those of us who are upon the path and to those who are lost.

We apologize if there are pauses in this transmission. We are attempting to use single word contact which is somewhat more difficult to receive. However, this instrument requests that it may progress in this skill and this is the next step. This day, my friends, that is yours, that you have made, that the Creator and you have co-created, this day I say unto you is that which you are. If you have feasted, you have feasted upon yourself. If you have started, you have made your metaphysical being bones and rubble. This instrument has returned from the church, as you would call it, which is pleasing to her distortions with the wondrous feeling of the near end of the passion of the teacher known to you as Jesus. What this instrument has not realized is that before the one known as Jesus could be transformed, he had to die.

I would at this time transfer to another entity who channels. I am Hatonn.

(L channeling)

I am Hatonn. I am with this instrument. My friends, this day you celebrate a reawakening of a spirit. The one whom you call Jesus, the bearer of the Christ force, is recognized as a teacher among many of your people and rightfully so. But, my friends, you are all teachers, and each of you is but a vessel which may allow itself to accept the triviality which surrounds and permeates it. This reawakening is the object of the path of those who seek opportunities for service to others. In serving your brothers and perceiving the oneness of your self and your other selves, you allow the reality which exists about you to be made manifest through your own creative act. It is your act of creating, of placing your will, your self on this path that reawakens the sleeping world about you, that shatters the stone of confused perceptions which would hold you back, and that leads you forth to perceive the light of that day which dawns.

My friends, when the one known as Jesus stated, "All these things and more you shall do," he foresaw the dawn to which each of you would awaken. My friends, the darkness of confusion can exist in your lives only for those moments you are willing to accept that condition. Therefore, my friends, simply go forward; follow your path and see within its light that which truly exists.

At this time, we shall relinquish our use of this instrument so that our brothers and sisters of Latwii might perform their service in answering questions. In the love and the light of the infinite Creator, we are known to you as Hatonn.

(L channeling)

I am Latwii, and I greet you, my brothers and sisters, in the love and the light of the infinite Creator, and would extend to those present our gratitude at being able to perform our service at this time. So without further ado, are their any questions?

R: Yes, Latwii. The last time we spoke you recommended sweating to me and I've been doing that, and now I'm wondering if there's maybe some kind of pacing that should be done. Is it well to sweat every day or should it be a once a week thing or once every couple of days?

I am Latwii. I am aware of your question. My brother, if you would but reflect for a moment, you would probably conclude that the process which you describe is a tool for the individual to attain growth upon their specific path, be it a path of service to self or service to others. At any rate, one who follows a path does not walk by the hour but by the growth. Therefore, we would suggest that rather than being attentive to a physical time schedule, one might be effectively benefited by a meditative process through which one determines whether it's time yet.

May we answer you further?

R: No, Latwii, thanks.

We thank you, my brother. Is there another question?

Carla: Well, just along those same lines, is there a way that you could abuse your body instead of helping it if you took sweats every day, for instance?

I am Latwii. I am aware of your question. My sister, the physical vehicle is quite adaptable and within a wide range [of] extremes is capable of accepting the stresses described with great frequency. This is not to suggest that such a course would be beneficial, as it is somewhat wearing upon that same physical vehicle. However, when accorded sufficient amounts of rest and nutrient, a high frequency of such experiences would not be damaging to a healthy physical vehicle. In greater specificity, however, we would suggest that one who like yourself [who] has a weakened physical condition should exercise greater caution.

May we answer further?

Carla: Rats. And no thank you.

Is there another question?

D: Yes, Latwii. I'm an astrologer and I've been working on a project and I wonder if you could answer a question about a project I'm working on?

I am Latwii. My brother, as you are aware, there are limitations to the ability to answer specific questions without infringing upon the free will of the recipient of the answer. To do so would be no service and as our path is that of service to others, we would simply observe to you that we would be happy to be of whatever true assistance can be offered with respect to your free will fully observed. Is there a question you would like to present?

D: Yes, this is a technical question more than one specific. I'm working on a way to correlate between the Mayan calendar which I've been studying for a number of years and the Julian calendar concerning a date that will indicate the close of the past 21,060 year cycle and the opening of the next 21,060 year cycle. There have been two dates that have been put forward: one is in 1989 and the other one is 2011, and I've been doing research on the later date, December 24, 2011, and I would wonder if you could comment on that and give me any information that you might have concerning that particular date.

I am Latwii. I am aware of your question. My brother, the moment in time of which you speak is one which could be regarded by many of your planet as quite significant to the physical plane. Beyond that statement, we regret that we must decline to proceed for two reasons, the first being the previously described reluctance to interfere, the second that we recognize a potential for development within the grasp of yourself if you would extend yourself to reliance upon that which you intuit to be correct, for the development of the sense of intuition within yourself is strong while the confidence upon that intuition within the area specific data is somewhat weak.

May we answer you further?

D: Yes. Years ago I made a contact with an alien presence on this planet from the constellation Lyra from the specific star group near the star Vega which is a double star, and I wondered what the significance of that contact was since it hasn't occurred again other than the fact that I've had two UFO experiences which may have been from the same source. I just wondered if you knew anything about the purpose of these particular beings on the Earth plane?

I am Latwii. My brother, you are quite familiar with the statement, "Ask and you shall receive." There is within you a calling for that which is beyond the readily apparent illusion and your desire to receive assistance in determination of a path to follow was responded to in this fashion. This is not the result of an overall directorate, but more correctly a result of a natural law within that which exists. Your calling was made; your calling was answered.

Is there another question?

D: No, thank you.

We thank you for the opportunity to be of service, my brother. Is there another question?

S: Latwii, I have a question about a contact that I made recently that claimed to have been a Confederation source by the name of Shirrah, and I was wondering if you could maybe verify the authenticity of it as being a Confederation source, and maybe give me some assistance on the work that it wishes to sort of cooperate in me doing?

I am Latwii, and I am aware of your question. My brother, the contact which you describe was a contact which grafted the message of a service-to-self entity within the message initiated by an entity seeking to serve others such as yourself. This is not an uncommon effort made on the part of the service-to-self entity to attain greater polarity. For this reason, we would not attempt to describe a specific type of work which this combined entity, if you will, would seek for you to perform, for the divergent philosophies would hardly qualify as a single path or thread of thought or contact.

May we answer you further?

S: No, thank you.

We thank you, my brother. Is there another question?

A: How is the instrument doing?

I am Latwii. The instrument is in good condition, and is grateful for your care. Is there another question?

N: Latwii, I wonder if you'd explain the difference between the Confederation and the Federation of Thirty-Three of Galactic Intent?

I am Latwii. I am aware of your question. My brother, the Confederation is an organization, if you will, of entities seeking to serve others within parameters understood by them as beneficial both toward their own seeking and the seeking of those whom they attempt to serve. The group to which you refer is a somewhat misunderstood group of similar effort whose communications have been confused, or if you will, contaminated by the injection of service-to-self communications within their overall effort.

May we answer you further?

N: Then the members of the Federation of Thirty-Three of Galactic Intent are not necessarily service to others, is that correct?

I am Latwii. That is not correct. The intention of service to others is correct. The messages or communications from this source have been polluted by additional communications claiming falsely to be of that same origin.

May we answer you further?

N: Yes. Is Lavendar a member of service to others or service to self?

I am Latwii. My brother, the information you desire is information that you must seek from within.

May we answer you further?

N: Thank you.

We thank you, my brother. Is there another question?

S: Yes, Latwii. I read a book called *The Treasure of El Dorado* in which it was stated that members of the White Brotherhood worked through spaceships circling our planet. Could you comment on that, please?

I am Latwii. My sister, the organization to which you refer is one which is in essence not an organization but rather a number of entities of similar purity and purpose. Their efforts … We shall pause.

(Sounds of a cat knocking over and spilling a jar of pencils and then the contents being gathered up.)

Their efforts have been highly successful in the direction of service to others and have worked in the manner which you have described.

(A sentence is inaudible due to the continuing sound of the pencils being gathered up and replaced on the table.)

Is there another question?

N: Latwii, may I ask if the White Brotherhood is supposedly on a UFO or a space ship called the Star of Bethlehem which is encircling the Earth?

I am Latwii. My brother, the White Brotherhood, as you call it, is more correctly described as a group of highly developed entities or wanderers who have chosen at specific times to return either singly or in numbers to assist in specific fashions. They are not relegated, therefore, solely to specific physical vehicles or locations, for it is a calling that produces an effect rather than the tools of the trade, so to speak. The necessity does not exist for a specific physical location to contain the entirety of this group.

May we answer you further?

N: Well, may I rephrase that question, and state that a number of the White Brotherhood may be present on such a vehicle as the Star of Bethlehem or TX-11 as well as the Brotherhood of Crystal or the Crystal Brotherhood. Just a number of them, not the entire group.

I am Latwii. My brother, we regret that we are unable to answer as we are not clear as to the content of your question, and respectfully request that it be posed again in simpler form.

N: Are specific members of the White Brotherhood or the Crystal Brotherhood or other of the Thirty-Three Entities of the Federation of Galactic Intent in a space vehicle called the Star of Bethlehem or TX-11 which frequently is in the area and communicating with entities on Earth?

I am Latwii. Yes. Is there another question?

N: No. Thank you.

We thank you. Is there another question?

J: Latwii, I've been aware lately of a number of people who are experiencing back pain. The possibility has occurred to me that the catalyst for this back pain might be a common source rather than individual catalyst. Could you comment generally on that possibility?

I am Latwii. My sister, the perception that you have is accurate to a large extent in that the physical reality, if one might use that term loosely, is the result of the creative efforts of those on the job site. Therefore, it is not at all uncommon for a building, for example, with very low ceilings to produce backaches in those who choose to build it and occupy it.

May we answer you further?

J: Umm. I'll have to sort that answer out later. Could you give me any suggestions as to how people who are experiencing this back pain could use the catalyst more efficiently and not have to suffer the back pain so much?

I am Latwii. My sister, the pains which you describe are the alarm bell tolling, the entities individually informing themselves that their constructions are not up to their own standards. The catalyst is, in that sense …

(Side one of tape ends.)

(L channeling)

The catalyst is self-explanatory. It exists for the purpose of informing the individual that it is time to draw back from the illusion and analyze what mistakes are being made, just as one who attempts to occupy an habitation with four-foot ceilings will find discomfort to the extent that one in such a situation would eventually be driven to leave this habitation and regain the clarity of a perspective more in attunement with the individual's desires. When the irritant ceases, so also will the pains you describe. The similarity within those you describe are the result of similar conditions of which those entities are recognizing a discomfort with.

May we answer you further?

J: Yes, just one more thing. A book I read had an Indian medicine woman saying that when we turn our back on our own power, we experience back pains. I think I'm seeing some congruency between what you're saying and what she said. Can you comment on that?

I am Latwii. My sister, when we turn our back on our own power, our power will eventually turn us back upon that which we should see. The function of the self is frequently that of gaining the attention of the conscious mind, either by stick or carrot, and the stick quite often is applied in the manner you describe.

May we answer you further?

J: Yes, just one more question. If I finally pay attention to the stick, then do I get to have the catalyst some more or does it go away so I know that I'm getting the idea?

I am Latwii. My sister, we regret that we have managed to misplace the device that assigns catalyst for individuals. Therefore, we would suggest that a reduction in catalyst in this case can only be accomplished through the individual's inner self communicating sufficiently to the individual the reason for the pain or attention-getter, and the steps which would be adequate to reduce the cause.

May we answer you further?

J: Thank you, no. You've given me lots to think about. That was really good. Thank you.

We thank you, my sister. Is there another question?

N: Yes, Latwii. There's been a great deal discussed on healing of self by self. There seems to be numerous blocks in many individuals, or some individuals at least. Is part of this block due to a lack of silicon in the diet or is that irrelevant?

I am Latwii. My brother, the major lack would be described as consistency in pursuit of one's path, for the spirit contains the ability to transmute that which is available into that which is needed. However, a lack of attention to the path has no panacea.

May we answer you further, my brother?

N: Well, considering a life of adequate attention to the path itself, is it true that we can communicate with various cells within our body as well with other areas outside of our body if the amount of silicon is at a proper level?

I am Latwii. My brother, we would suggest that one consider for a moment those cells which compose the hand, how with majestic telepathic ability the individual can cause those cells and their members to work in cohesive coordinated effort to raise the hand, extend the finger, and gracefully scratch the nose. Is this not communication, my brother? The difference is in the perception of what is accomplishable and what is unable to be accomplished. The individual who says to himself or herself, "My healing must come not from within but from outside," is the individual who handicaps their own ability to be healed, for the statement, "Ask and you shall receive," is again very evidently in application. He or she who insists that the healing must come from a doctor or healer handicaps their own ability to communicate and extend comfort and healing to the cells in the manner which you describe, and it is this handicap more than any other which retards the healing process.

May we answer you further, my brother?

N: Well, I think I understand, but I was referring to the self within self, not relying on outside sources primarily, and the fact that sometimes with a low silicon level we are unable to communicate with certain non-responsive areas inside our body, and that's what I had primary reference to, not to consideration of an outside healer.

I am Latwii. My brother, we assure you that the extension of your will and your ability to create is not limited by the presence of specific elements.

May we answer you further?

N: Thank you very much.

We thank you, my brother. Is there another question?

S: Yes, Latwii. There is a specific technique for healing of self and others called Reiki. Do you know of this, and could you comment on how the technique works?

I am Latwii. My sister, the techniques of healing are the tools within the tool bag of the builder. One builder might choose to drive a nail where another would choose to insert a screw, both for the purpose of creating a bond. Within the example given, each is sufficient, each is perfect, and each builder has performed admirably to accomplish that which was needed.

The various schools of healing all have the potential for substantial accomplishment and each is a set of tools which specifically serve some healers better than others. The tools themselves have no life, no healing ability, but rather are channels through which the healing occurs, and in truth this is the role of those referred to as the healer. They are the channels of energy through which two things primarily may be accomplished. The first, assisting the patient, if you will, in identifying and healing for themselves the injured areas, and second, extending a controlled vibration to the patient or a specific area of the patient's physical vehicle to produce the desired effect.

The latter is generally of a very temporal nature, for that which occurs may be described as follows. The patient of his or her free will accepts the entry of the healer's vibration within specific parameters. The healer projects his or her vibration and that vibration is accepted and retained by the injured area or the individual. It may be likened to a person within a bed sheet who opens a small hole, allowing the healer to reach through and touch. Once the healing process or extension of energy from the healer has ceased, the patient's original vibration will reassume or reassert its dominance of the area. The rate at which this occurs is dependent upon the patient's willingness to retain the vibration and the intensity of that cause which has resulted in the injury or disease.

May we answer you further, my sister?

S: No. Thank you very much.

We thank you, my sister. Is there another question?

Carla: Yes. I'd like to know how the instrument is.

[I am Latwii.] The instrument is becoming somewhat fatigued and it would be wise to transfer the contact to a more rested instrument if further questions are forthcoming.

Carla: I think you ended up at about the same time they did.

I am Latwii. We thank you for your consideration, my sister, for the instrument's well-being. Are there any more questions?

(Pause)

I am Latwii. As an air of compassion has filled the room, we will take our leave. Adonai, my friends. Vasu borragus. We are known to you as Latwii.

(Carla channeling)

I am Yadda, and I greet you in love and light. "Love and light, love and light," this instrument causes me to go over and over. "Love and light." However, we appreciate the need for the challenging. We come because we are called, and we have little to say. May we say, you are blessed and loved for yourselves. Many, many questions in this meeting about other people, about wise men and teachers, about constellations and galaxies. What do you wish to learn, my friends? What do you wish to know? Do you know yourself? There is that in the desire for knowledge which is a kind of contamination. For only learning is when one does not have. Once one has learned to wish for something, then one occupies one's mind and abilities to getting this new gadget, if it may be a thought, a word, a game, a career, or a challenge. All your little toys, all the blocks that you may build, but you still do not know yourself.

We cannot say enough when we say, "Meditate, meditate, and mediate more." What part of you do wish to have? If you are concentrating on yourself is it then a type of what this instrument calls spiritual pride? We hope not, my friends, for that is a real danger, and it will slow you up, it will cause you to move less fast. Once you have turned your attention to self, learn through self and not from self, for the universe within is such that the physically beheld creation in your density is as nothing. That, you are and more. We ask you not to be so concerned with the thoughts and the ideas and the playthings which are the toys of one who wishes to seek but in easy stages which shall not be too painful. We encourage you to meditate and find the joy and the peace which issues from a true knowledge of the self.

Who are you? Where are you going? And what do you believe the truth to be? Seek these things. Care not for the folly of the squabbles of relationships, the difficulties with making the money, but only view your living as one who has discovered dirt. Then one must automatically make up the soap in order that one may be clean. We are not not saying that before you noticed the dirt you were not dirty. We are only saying that the dirty man that is not aware does not need to discover soap. You have chosen to see the dirt. We encourage you to try to get your ring around the collar very clean. But please, do not puff yourself up as consequential, and do not puff up others. You must use your discrimination as always—on us, on any teacher, or on yourself. But remember: yourself first.

We thank you for allowing us to speak through this instrument. We make good contact. This good group. We blessed to be here and leave you in the love and the light of the One Who Is All. We are Yadda. Adonai. Adonai. ☥

Intensive Meditation
April 9, 1985

(Jim channeling)

I am Laitos, and I greet you, my friends, in the love and the light of our one infinite Creator. We thank each of you for inviting us to join you, and for giving us the opportunity of being of what service we may. It is a joy to be asked, and our privilege is to join you in answering your call. We appreciate the discussion that you have given to this topic previous to the beginning of your meditation, for it is helpful in such discussion to focus one's intention more clearly and purely upon that which is the goal. As each shares each understanding and experience of this service of vocal channeling, each then learn from the other, and together you progress more quickly than if experiences were not shared and examined for their content. This is true, of course, my brothers, in all portions of your life, and is especially true as you set your feet upon this path of serving others by means of providing vocal channeling. We will repeat that which you have come to know in some degree as instructions, those being to simply relax the mind and the body shall follow, and then to speak thoughts that appear within your mind without analysis, become indeed the fool, step out without knowing if thin air or earth awaits.

We shall at this time attempt to speak a few words through the one known as N. We shall now transfer this contact. I am Laitos.

(N channeling)

I am Laitos. I greet you in the love light, light and love of our one infinite Creator. It is sad that we cannot all partake in channeling. It is a light for each individual who seeks it. I thank you for your attention to detail. I think I kinda analyzed now. Transfer back to you, Jim.

(Jim channeling)

I am Laitos, and we again greet you through this instrument. We thank the one known as N for his willingness and his desire to serve as a vocal instrument. We are most pleased that we have been able to speak a few sentences through this new instrument. It is always a joy to be able to express the love and light of the one Creator through a new instrument, no matter how many instruments have previously been utilized, for the unique point of view that each entity has to offer as instrument is as yet another beautiful vessel which holds the nourishing waters and offers them to those who thirst.

As the instrument observed, it was its tendency towards analysis which then caused the contact to be lost for the moment. As each new instrument practices this skill, that tendency will be reduced, for as you build the confidence in this type of service, it becomes more of an automatic or natural skill, shall we say.

At this time we would attempt to speak a word or two through the one known as J. Again we remind the instrument to relax and simply speak those thoughts that appear within the mind. We shall now transfer this contact. I am Laitos.

(J channeling)

I am Laitos. I welcome you to journey with me. I've lost it, I think.

(Jim channeling)

I am Laitos, and am again with this instrument. We are happy to have been able not only to make contact with the one known as J but to have been able to speak a few words through this instrument. It was most well done, shall we say, by the new instrument to be able to reestablish contact after speaking our identification and then momentarily losing the contact. This is the type of skill, shall we say, which usually takes somewhat longer for a new instrument to develop, for the new instrument is more likely to not be able to reestablish contact when losing it for the first time. Therefore, we commend and encourage the one known as J in its endeavors and can continue to recommend that the speaking of the thought without regard as to its source is the point upon which this instrument may focus its attentions at this time.

We shall once more attempt to speak a few words through this new instrument. We shall now transfer this contact. I am Laitos.

(J channeling)

I am Laitos. I greet you in the light and love of the infinite Creator.

(Jim channeling)

I am Laitos, and am again with this instrument. We again appreciate greatly being able to speak through the one known as J, and again commend this new instrument for its progress in this new skill. The speaking of our identification and our greeting is the first major step in becoming the new instrument. The next, of course, is yet another step in this process, that being speaking a thought which is not previously known to be identified with beginning the contact. And if the one known as J will continue in its process of speaking those thoughts which appear within the mind, this next step shall also be taken.

We, at this time, would open this meeting to the queries with which each has joined this group this evening. May we attempt a query at this time?

N: Yes. Is there any way through meditation or focusing that we can amplify the thoughts? They seem so distant, like pulling them out of the ether.

I am Laitos, and, my brother, we can only suggest attention in those areas which have been previously mentioned. You are, of course, correct in assuming that the focus of the attention is of paramount importance in being able to perceive the thoughts which we transmit. We would not suggest any particular technique for attempting to amplify our thoughts, for that is, shall we say, our task, for we are those who send and you are the, as you might say, receiving station. To become the more successful, or shall we say powerful receiver, it is merely necessary to be able to clear the mind to such a degree that its entire field or scope is open to reception. If any portion of this scope or field is concerned with a thought or a sensation or a response to either, then that portion of the field provides, shall we say, a static which makes the perception of our thoughts somewhat more difficult. You become able to increase your ability to perceive or receive our thoughts as you are able to widen the availability, shall we say, of your scope or field of perception. As you clear your mind and relax your thinking, then you are as a still and deep pool which can then become aware of any ripple upon its surface and focus its attention upon describing speaking that ripple.

May we answer you further, my brother?

N: When we meditate, can we contact you, Laitos or Latwii, and if we do contact, do we know that we contact or we just state our purpose? I don't seem to be able to ever get what I would consider an acknowledgeable response that I am in contact in any way whatsoever.

I am Laitos, and concerning your query and its parts, my brother, we may begin by saying to you that you shall not know anything within your incarnation for sure, for yours is not the illusion of knowing with certainty, thus the factors and faculties of will and faith are the sure and steady rod and staff of the seeker of truth, in your vocal channeling, as in all portions of your seeking, as you attempt to discern what is before you and the nature of your reality.

If you in your meditations ask for our presence, we are most happy to join you and will make ourselves known by our conditioning vibration. Yet your perception of that vibration is unique and is also open to any doubts which you may have as you attempt to serve as vocal instruments. Again, if you simply request our presence, it is suggested that no verbal channeling be attempted, but simply the request for our conditioning vibration, for in a group of this size or larger, there is protection that is necessary but is omitted or not possible, shall we say, when you are alone in your meditations. Therefore, it is best simply to ask that we join you in your seeking, and then attempt to feel our presence as the conditioning wave.

May we answer you further, my brother?

N: No, thank you very much, Laitos. I knew that I wasn't even supposed to try and channel, but I thought that perhaps there should be some vibration of recognition, but I guess I'm too thick-headed to interpret it. But thank you very much.

I am Laitos, and we thank you as well, my brother, and did not at all mean to suggest that yours or any head was thick, but that your illusion does not permit sure and, shall we say, undisputed proof of any phenomenon. Yet, you can recognize our vibrations, for in these meditations you have come to know them.

May we attempt another query at this time?

N: Could I ask, Laitos, if there are no other queries, to tell us about the White Brotherhood of Antares—where it's located. Is it a social memory complex or planet?

I am Laitos, and we are aware of your query, my brother. We shall attempt to speak as best we can to this topic with the understanding that many of the so-called brotherhoods, as you have heard of them and spoken of them, are perceived and described not only by others but by various portions of the brotherhood in different ways, for though each brotherhood is a gathering—we correct this instrument—for though it is true that each brotherhood is a grouping of numerous entities, all dedicated to serving in a similar fashion, each is yet unique and sees that service in perhaps a different light, so that as entities of your population become aware of these various brotherhoods through numerous sources, each source is most likely to add yet another facet or dimension or description of the various brotherhoods so that [while] it may, in many cases, seem as though the information describes different brotherhoods, it may indeed be various perspectives of fewer brotherhoods.

Now to the topic which you have phrased. The brotherhood which is generally described in the terms, "The White Brotherhood of Antares," is a grouping of entities or what this group has come to know as social memory complexes. These races of beings are desirous of and committed to serving others within not only your illusion, but other third-density illusions who seek information concerning the love of the one infinite Creator, and, more specifically, how to become aware of this love and experience the reality of loving, shall we say. This grouping of entities, then, has sought to communicate to various instruments upon your planet these general concepts which no matter the source, are always and ever the same, for the love and the light of the one Creator are as they are throughout all creation, yet each entity may become aware of that love and light through any of an infinite number of means. Those of this brotherhood, then, bend their efforts in expressing and sharing their experience and expression of this love and light to those upon your planet who call for this information.

May we answer you further, my brother?

N: What is meant by the word "species" in the Federation of Thirty-three Species of Galactic Intent?

I am Laitos, and to the best of our understanding, my brother, limited though it is, the term "species," in this phrasing refers to that which may be described as this group has done, as social memory complex. The phrase "race of beings" could also be used. In many cases these are planetary populations which have achieved at least the fourth-density level of cooperative or shared consciousness experience.

May we answer you further?

N: Then the word "species" does not refer in any way to the physical, but implies a social memory complex?

I am Laitos, and again, my brother, to the best of our understanding, the physical vehicle utilized by each of these groups or races or species is incidental to their seeking and sharing of love and light, and, indeed, the physical vehicles may be greatly various, yet simply be as the clothing or cloak that is worn, and serve the same purpose of providing a vehicle through which the mind and the spirit may be expressed.

May we answer you further, my brother?

N: Well, these thirty-three species on the starship or UFO or spaceship, are they present in body as well as spirit, or are they a group of spirit complexes floating around within this shell? When we talked the other day, we referred to the Star of Bethlehem or the TX-11 in which the Thirty-three Species of Galactic Intent were, shall we say, sheltered and I was just wondering if it was all a spirit, then would they not commingle to a point that it would be difficult to identity each individual species?

I am Laitos, and we find that you have asked a query which is most difficult to clearly and concisely answer, for there are many points to consider. To begin with, in an effort such as the effort aboard this craft, shall we say, it is frequently the case that representatives of each species or race will be partaking in the effort, whereas other portions of that race or species may be in other locations and serving in other capacities, and perhaps with other missions, shall we say.

In some instances, there is the exchange of entities from the, shall we say, ship or position in what you call time and space with the, shall we say, home density or planetary vibration. Therefore, there may be more entities lending assistance to the ship or specific mission than are actually, shall we say, aboard that craft or in that location. The location is also a point to be considered, for the location can be in various frequencies or densities or realities as you would call them. Your own planetary vibration has its space/time location which you now inhabit, and has its time/space location which may generally be described as the astral through devachanic levels of your so-called inner planes. Your planet has inner planes of each density level.

Therefore, there are numerous potential locations that are not visible to your physical eye and numerous locations in what you call time and various entities in this effort lending assistance from a diversity of sources so that it is not easily described in your language and according to your understanding what, precisely, the nature of this effort is. We have, to our humble abilities attempted to describe a portion of the scope, that you might see the width and the depth that remains to be plumbed.

May we answer you further, my brother?

N: I understood that all the entities of each species were not aboard the ship but that some of them were. May I ask why the craft was named "Star of Bethlehem," and what does the TX-11 mean, and is this craft very often in third density that we might communicate or is it a completely an ethereal consideration?

I am Laitos, and am aware of your query, my brother, and its portions. This ship is seldom within your third-density illusion, and has been given various names by those of your own population at various times, as this grouping of entities has contacted numerous groups and individuals over the span of what you would call time or the history of your planet. The various names have been chosen, most frequently that is, by entities upon your planet according to the information received from this group of entities in regards to previous services. This particular craft was involved, shall we say, in what you would call the birth of the one known as Jesus and has therefore been given the name of that particular teacher's physical birth location. The other naming has come more recently, shall we say, and has been somewhat of a codified distortion of a service which this ship also provides, and this code may be seen as what you would call an acronym, with the [letters] and numerals standing for concepts which are related to the vibratory level of this grouping's service in sharing love and light and making these manifest upon your planet.

May we answer you further, my brother?

N: Thank you very much. I had wondered if the Star of Bethlehem had anything to do with the birth of the Christ child and its naming there. And as far as the TX-11, I wondered if that had to do with whether the craft was a thought formation or whether it was built on one particular planet, and if so, how was the craft constructed?

I am Laitos, and we again reach some difficulties in providing this information, for it, shall we say, lies somewhat outside of our scope of abilities. Each entity or grouping of entities which seeks contact in service to others with those of your planet has certain foci or points of focus that become the channels through which the sharing is made available. By focusing upon these various points of reference, then, we are able to maintain your somewhat difficult vibration in a clear enough manner to be able to send thoughts. When we attempt to stray too far from our purpose or ability to share with your peoples by attempting to retrieve information which lies outside of that ability, then we, shall we say, somewhat lose our focus and are less able to transmit in a clear fashion that which lies outside of our scope. That is true as far as we know with any group that seeks to contact those of your population, that is, any group which is not a portion of your third-density physical experience.

The entities upon the craft which you have described have the purpose of sharing a certain vibratory level of love and light which is theirs to share. When you look at the sources from which this group has been drawn and schematically place this list in what you would call your astronomical charts, then there are terms which have been used throughout the ages, shall we say, to locate various points, and when groupings of points have become known as brotherhoods, shall we say, then frequently these groupings are also labeled in a manner which can be categorized and recalled. That is the nature of the letters and numbers which have been used to identify this group.

May we answer you further, my brother?

N: Well, thank you very much. I did not mean to ask or question outside your scope, it was just that I had wondered about several considerations. May I ask if, when we are reincarnated, if the spirit enters the body at the time prior to birth, at the time of conception, or just at birth?

I am Laitos, and we find that each of your assumptions is potentially correct, for there is no set point at which the spirit, as you call it, enters the physical vehicle which shall carry it through its incarnational experience. Some are present before the moment of conception, and indeed serve as what might be called as somewhat of a guide to those who will soon become its parents. Some spirits enter the soon-to-be-born vehicle at any point thereafter from the conception to the birth. And in some cases, those of a, shall we say, reluctant nature, there is the entrance after the birth, not usually a time exceeding what you would call one revolution of your moon body.

May we answer you further, my brother?

N: Thank you very much. I had wondered if there was a specific time. The Star of Bethlehem was instrumental, the craft or the species of the Federation of Galactic Intent, in, shall we say, guiding the incarnation of the reincarnation of Jesus from another density … lost my train of thought … as a star seed?

I am Laitos, and we feel that we might best describe the relationship of the so-called Star of Bethlehem and others with the one that has come to be known as Jesus of Nazareth as he entered your third-density physical illusion. The occasion can be seen much as the send-off that a great and varied grouping of friends may give one of its own as it goes off upon a long and lonely journey to a distant land that is in, shall we say, great distress and calls with great intensity for the services that all within this family of entities have to offer, and these services then shall be individualized and manifested by one of the group, and in this case, the one was known and is known among your peoples as Jesus of Nazareth, the Christed One.

May we answer you further?

N: Is the instrument getting tired?

J: Exhausted?

I am Laitos, and we find that this instrument has a good reserve of energy, and is happy to lend its services, as are we, if there might be a further query.

N: Thank you very much. I assume then that the Star of Bethlehem was just there, as you say, to send off something that had already been preordained. May I ask just one last question then, and that is the meaning of Antares.

I am Laitos, and am aware of your query, my brother, and feel that we can best respond to this query by suggesting that Antares is a location within your known celestial charts that has been utilized by this grouping of species or races of being as a sort of way station, shall we say, a point chosen in time and space for its particular vibration that serves to nourish those of this co …

(Side one of tape ends.)

(Jim channeling)

I am Laitos, and am once again with this instrument. We had completed the query which was asked, and simply wished to allow this instrument to reposition the recording devices that there might be a recording of any further queries if there might be one at this time.

N: Yes, Laitos, thank you very much for your last answer. This way station, is it like our planet Earth, or is it like an asteroid, and if so, what sort of name do we give to it by our astronomers?

I am Laitos, and am aware of your query, my brother. We find that though this instrument's knowledge of such terms is quite sparse and spare, that the terms Antares and Arcturus might be used most frequently by those who study and describe the heavens. This actual location is a grouping of bodies or entities which you would call stars, planets and asteroid-like orbiting entities, that together provide a field or network of vibrational frequencies that serve as what you might call the battery or nourishment of those entities which are of this same general vibratory level.

May we answer you further, my brother?

N: Thank you very much. I don't want to tire everyone. I appreciate all your answers. Thank you.

I am Laitos, and we are most grateful to you and to each within the group this evening. We also must apologize if we have tired any this evening with our responses. We have found that this instrument was most open this evening, though in some cases was somewhat vacant as well and could be more, shall we say, helpful in the contact if more focus was provided, and the field was somewhat reduced in scope for this endeavor. We are with each upon the quest, as we have mentioned, in your meditations, and would be happy to lend our conditioning vibration there that your meditation might be somewhat deepened and clarified. We shall leave this group at this time. As always, we leave in the love and in the light of the one Creator, for there is nothing else, my friends, in which to leave or be. We are Laitos. Adonai. Adonai vasu borragus. ✤

Sunday Meditation
April 14, 1985

(Jim channeling)

I am Hatonn, and greet you, my friends, in the love and the light of our infinite Creator. We are pleased to be able to speak to this group this evening. As always, we come to share that which as a group you call for this evening. We had some difficulty initiating contact, for each potential instrument was desirous of allowing the other to speak. We are grateful that each instrument makes itself available whenever it is within its ability to do so. Each instrument and each present in seeking our presence allows us to be of service in a manner which would not be possible if such a group did not call in such a fashion.

This evening we would speak a few words upon a subject which is ever and always the focus of our being: that, of course, is love. There is much upon your planet that is written concerning this concept that is described so inadequately by the word "love." Many upon your planet over all portions of time within your past have sought to express the experience of love. These in some fashion or other have been what you would call seekers of truth, those who seek the nature of the reality in which they move and have their being, for the human creature upon your planet is one to which has been given great self awareness, and with such a great gift then it is a natural function of that gift being exercised to seek the nature of the environment in which the entity finds itself.

When you move past the ordinary descriptions of love, you find a concept which becomes difficult to describe in words and most attractive to seek in experience. Beyond that which you know as romantic love or the love of brothers and sisters, parents and children, teacher and student, there is a greater love, or shall we say, greater and greater perceptions and experiences of that called love. Indeed, my friends, as you pursue the path of seeking what you call truth, or the nature of your reality, you will find that within each portion of it is embedded a creative force which is described in many ways by many ways by those who discover it within your physics.

There are those seekers called scientists that attempt to describe the first principle, shall we say, upon which your universe is built. The matter and the energy being two paths presented to such entities soon dissolve into one as all is seen in the clearest sense as a universe of motion in which nothing is static but all changes. Then this energy is seen as a primal force by others who attempt to describe the nature of their reality in the more mystical sense, that which seems to be closer to the heart of that which is the experience of all, and in this means of describing love, love is seen as a focus through which the will of the Creator moves and makes that which is made.

Love, then, in this description, is seen as a force which creates and creates and creates, that the one Creator in many portions might seek Itself, might then experience Itself. Seen in this fashion, love as the energy becomes the container or the vessel in which the Creator places Itself and moves through Its own being in form as well as essence, for before there was anything created, there was that which had no form and was merely what you would call essence. This essence of the one Creator, then, has found its form and seeks its expression through that called love.

Now, my friends, we understand that when seen in such a fashion and described by our poor and meager words, even this description of love can seem to be most mechanical, for it seems to have parts and relationships and it is not as easy to see where this force moves in one's life as it is to see a great landscape and scheme through which this energy called love moves. But we can assure you, my friends, that as you continue your journeys, those journeys of seeking the nature of your reality and the possibility of experiencing this called love, you will find that there is slowly and surely an experience of this energy waiting to move and increasingly so moving through your life pattern, for as you seek so shall you find, as it has been written in your holy works.

That is a statement of what you may call a principle, not only of physics, but of that called metaphysics, for you are as the magnet attracting the iron filing. That which you desire, being a portion of yourself, then is made available to you by a greater portion of yourself. As you are able and as you are willing to open your being, your mind, your heart, and your experience to the unknown of love, then is it brought into your awareness from deeper portions of your own being, those portions which are, shall we say, less distorted and more aware of the connection between all things and your own being. This love, then, that is such a mystery to your peoples and to each of you as seekers reveals itself in your experience as you continue to seek it and as you continue to accept the fact that you know not the fullness or even a brief description of that which you seek, but seek with blind abandon, shall we say, that which is beyond your grasp, it would seem.

At this time we would pause for but a moment that we might pass amongst this group and make our presence known to those who would mentally request it. We shall attempt to adjust our conditioning vibration to each in order that it not only be aware of our presence, but not be made uncomfortable. We shall pause at this time. I am Hatonn.

(Pause)

(Jim channeling)

I am Hatonn, and we are with this instrument once again. We thank you for requesting our presence. We hope that our vibration was of a comfortable level for each. At this time, we would attempt to close this contact through another instrument if this is acceptable. We shall now transfer this contact at this time. I am Hatonn.

(S channeling)

I am Hatonn, and I am with this instrument. We are making necessary adjustments so that this instrument may better vocalize our transmission. We would like to conclude our contact with a thought about the love, the love that we have spoken of. It is within each and is to be strived for in the sharing and of the learning that we will all attempt to do when we are on the path for the truth.

We will at this time take our leave so that our brothers and sisters of Latwii can be with you so that they can perform their service. I am known to you as Hatonn. Adonai.

(Jim channeling)

I am Latwii. We are with this group and we rejoice in our [having] been asked to join you, my friends, and greet you in the love and light of our infinite Creator. We also are humble messengers who have but a single theme, that which we share with all creation, that of love. We present ourselves in the capacity of attempting to answer queries that might fall somewhere within this topic, my friends, for indeed it is that which underlies all that is. Might we begin, then, with the first query?

L: Latwii, I have a couple of questions I'd like to put to you. The prayer that we call the "Our Father," am I correct in my assumption that the wording has been altered somewhat due to translation, transcription, the number of people who verbally relayed the message prior to it being written, other sources? Is that correct?

I am Latwii and, my brother, you have done such a fine job in answering your own query, that we might consider you for a position on our team, shall we say. We may add that indeed, as is the case with this particular prayer, so is the case with almost all teachings, rituals, prayers and procedures which those seekers of truth have codified and attempted to record in verbal written form throughout all of your history, for there are in some languages words which are more expressive of various concepts than are available in other languages. There are those groups, councils and committees that organize themselves from time to time and change those written translations and so forth, as you have mentioned, my brother.

Is there another query?

L: Yes. In meditating upon this particular prayer and its meaning, I have decided to attempt to reword the prayer to reflect my own personal distortion of its true meaning as an effort to more fully understand it, which progressed well until I began, because in trying to correctly interpret and more accurately word what I understood to be meant with them, the opening phrase, "Our Father," I failed to come up with anything less than approximately a dozen words. Would you have any suggestions to offer in a more accurate wording that would more fully capsulate the meaning?

I am Latwii, and am aware of your query, my brother. In your attempt to re-word this prayer, you perhaps can appreciate the difficulty any entity or group would have in attempting to verbalize that concept which lies beyond the boundary of the word. Yet in your attempt, you can find that when you are able to put a phrase or a word in another manner that has meaning to you, you increase, shall we say, the power of the prayer or ritual for yourself, for the words within any prayer or ritual may be seen as the clothing that one would wear to protect the self, shall we say, from the storms and inclement weathers that journeyer would experience. If the cape that covers the shoulders is too small or too large, then, and does not fit in just the precise manner, the journeyer will find that either it has too great a load to carry or is not covered in all areas which are necessary for this particular entity.

As you attempt to fit any particular prayer or ritual to your own needs, you must of necessity look carefully at your own distortions in order that you may not only describe them with preciseness and purity, but perhaps balance where there are those imbalances that have perhaps gone unnoticed. The unique nature of this process makes it most difficult for us or for any to comment concisely as to what word or phrase would best fit any entity. Therefore we must leave this task to you, my brother.

May we answer further, my brother?

L: No, that was very helpful in itself. Thank you.

I am Latwii, and we thank you, as always, my brother. Is there another query?

S: Yes, Latwii, I have a question. Last time I was here, something happened during the meditation, and I was wondering if you could tell me what happened so that I know more or can learn more from that experience? And in particular the experience that I assumed was some type of attack.

I am Latwii, and am aware of your query, my brother. We find that in this area in which you have query there is a perception of that which occurred that has been, shall we say, colored by your own distortions or preferences. As each seeker attempts to be of service in its own fashion, it will develop those ways of looking at its experience which are useful to it, that is, ways in which the experience might be understood and might be perceived and perhaps might then be shared with others. You are aware, my brother, that as one attempts to be of service to others in a purer and purer fashion, there is also the effect that one may notice within one's life pattern those experiences which may be described in various ways, but which you have described as the psychic attack or greeting, for as light shines within darkness, it is noted by those who appreciate light. Those who appreciate light may also be of the negative, as it is called, polarity and an entity in attempting to serve another may from time to time find that it is greeted or "attacked" in the area of its, shall we say, weaker or more pronounced distortions. This is the nature of all such greetings by those of negative polarity, for it is not within their ability nor would it be proper to place within a seeker's path the obstacle which that seeker had not of its own free will chosen. Therefore, those distortions that are less balanced and more distorted within an entity will be those which shall be intensified, shall we say, and will be noted by the seeker in a certain manner that alerts the seeker to the potential difficulty.

We may not comment specifically as to the, shall we say, nuts and bolts description of this particular occurrence for that is within the realm of your own seeking, and is an honor which we would not take from you, for all such attacks, as you my call them, are great opportunities to polarize even more profoundly in the positive sense, for any added catalyst, as you may see it, provides the seeker with a spiritual food that the seeker might utilize, and by processing, shall we say, increase its own spiritual strength. In this type of experience, the welcoming of a negative entity and its sending into one's own heart and seeing this entity as the one Creator and as the other self and bathing this entity in love is that magical, shall we say, expression which transforms what seems negative to that which within your experience is positive.

May we answer you further, my brother?

S: No. As I phrased the question, I wanted to learn from it and you've helped me to learn a great deal. It was a greeting and I do grow from it and gain in confidence in myself, and I responded to it, I believe to be in the proper way of acknowledging that it was there and I returned love and light and thanked it for its service, which I believe is what you just described basically as the appropriate response. Thank you.

I am Latwii, and we thank you, my brother. Is there another query?

L: Latwii, that stimulates a question in itself. If I understood you correctly, there is a value derived from receiving such a greeting and responding to it in a manner that might be regarded as successful for one following a path of service to others. However there seems to be almost a situation where there are points scored, in effect, for doing such a thing, therefore the implication seems to be that one should seek out such contacts so as to gain more points, as it were. This seems somewhat skewed to me. Could you go into that a bit?

I am Latwii, and we would be happy, my brother, to comment to the best of our limited ability. In general you are quite correct. The honor and the opportunity that accrues to one experiencing such an attack or greeting is great. But you need not, my brother, fear that you shall ever fall short in gaining the ability or the opportunity to score the points, for within each seeker's incarnation there are those times of traumatic catalyst, shall we say, during which the entity will have the opportunity to make that same magical response, to see the one Creator before and within the self, no matter what disguise the Creator might be wearing, whether that Creator wears the disguise of anger or hunger, of love, of joy, of jealousy, of war, of poverty, of illness, of dissension. No matter what the disguise, if the seeker can see and experience the one Creator, and love that which has been placed before it as spiritual food for its nourishment, then that entity shall have rung up another few points, my brother.

Within this particular kind of service, that is, the vocal channeling, there is the honor of standing, shall we say, somewhat closer to that which you would call light, and there is the balancing responsibility of reflecting that light as purely as possible. There is the added, shall we say, benefit of that light's attraction of those entities that are called negative so that the seeker in this particular type of serving increases not only its service but the opportunity to continue that service or to detune its service as it finds itself greeted in the manner that each is greeted from time to time as one serves as a vocal instrument.

Therefore, you need not, my brother, seek out more of these types of greetings, for they shall in their own time seek you out, for in your choice to enter this incarnation, you placed before your table, shall we say, a great plenty of catalyst, the spiritual food that you have prepared for yourself in hopes that your service and your learning might be propelled by these catalytic experiences, may we say, "catalytic converters" of another type.

May we attempt further response, my brother?

L: No, that was interesting. Thank you very much.

I am Latwii, and we thank you once again, my brother. Is there another query?

S: Yes, I have another—which is always typical of me. Several weeks ago, I had an experience that I would call a vision. I felt that I had been taken to a place in front of three, as the native Americans would call them, grandfathers, which could be that they were masters of a kind, basically. And they gave me a certain message, and they also called me by a certain name, "Meechi." They said that that was my name before coming into this life that I'm in now. Could you comment on the name and maybe upon the message and whatever else you could add to it, please?

I am Latwii, and am aware of your query, my brother. We may affirm that such experiences do occur for those upon the path of seeking the truth of the experience that one finds oneself in. We may not, however, comment upon this experience which you have described in any specific fashion, for it is, once again, the great honor and the great responsibility of each seeker to interpret those experiences which it finds have been left as gifts upon its doorstep. If we were, for example, to comment as requested in this particular instance, we would be doing that which has great value and holds great treasures for you in your seeking. You may, as you continue your seeking, move from entity to entity or group to group and discover that there are those who will comment and perhaps tell you precisely what each portion of your experience means. But as you review such comments, you must remember that each is expressing an individual and unique and oftimes fallible point of view. In the final analysis, it is still upon your shoulders that this seeking rests, for it is not likely that a conscious seeker of truth shall long accept that which another says without thinking it over and accepting or rejecting for the self that which was said.

This being true, to the best of our knowledge we would rather leave you, in the final analysis, than confuse you by distorting your perceptions and your seeking of the heart of that which has been given as a gift upon your path.

May we answer you further, my brother?

S: No. That helps me a great deal. Basically I had a feeling you were going to say that. I thank you.

I am Latwii, and once again we thank you, my brother. Is there another query?

N: Yes. I have some information about the plains of Nazca. Evidently, somewhere between 1500 and 3000 years ago, the Incas used a balloon to send their dead into the Pacific. They thought they were sending them to the sun, evidently. Can you tell me how they made the fabric that was so well woven at that time that we can't duplicate it today?

I am Latwii, and am aware of your query, my brother. We find however, that in scanning the possibility, shall we say, of this query, that we are unable to answer in any specific fashion, for in queries of this nature we find that we move too far afield from that which is, shall we say, our chosen specialty. We hope that when we are unable to answer to queries that do not lie within our scope that we have not offended any, but have perhaps reminded each that we gather with you to pursue a greater understanding of the process of seeking and sharing the one infinite Creator and its various distortions of love, wisdom and unity. If we answer in a specific fashion questions of this nature on a too frequent basis, we then partake in a moving of the focus or the dial, shall we say, of this group from that which is at its heart's desire and moves, shall we say, too quickly and abruptly into those areas which are of but momentary interest.

May we answer in any further way, my brother?

N: Well, it is said that the Incas thought they were sending the physical remains back to the one infinite Creator or the sun. Can you elaborate on that particular thing?

I am Latwii, and am aware of your query, my brother. The philosophy of those that have been called Incas was, as are all upon your planet, a distortion of a concept of unity. Many have been the entities and cultures upon your planet who have sought the one Creator in a fashion which included the worship of that body which you call the sun. The entity that is in this sun body has from time to time throughout many cultures in your past been seen as the creative force behind all creation, and has therefore been, as you would say, worshipped as such. Those called Incas attempted to join those who had passed the gates of death with the one Creator which they saw as the sun in a symbolic fashion …

(Side one of tape ends.)

(Jim channeling)

I am Latwii, and am once again with this response. Though various physical devices were utilized by those called Incas in this process of attempting to unite those passing the gates of death with the one Creator seen as the sun, this process was in truth symbolic. The devices of a material nature which were used were utilized as are all material devices in what you may call the magic ritual in order that the ritual might be grounded, shall we say, within the third-density reality. In the minds of those called

Incas, then, this ritual and its material accouterment, shall we say, were used in order that a path might be fashioned from this illusion to the next. The entity being so sent off, and having passed those gates of death, then was seen to be carried into the infinity of experience and beingness and to be joined in its higher self sense once again with that entity seen as the sun and as the one Creator.

May we answer you further, my brother?

N: Yes, thank you very much. Then did the Incas formulate this bit of knowledge as to the physical accouterments or was this introduced extraterrestrially, the ability, that is, to fashion a balloon for a flight?

I am Latwii, and am aware of your query, my brother. We feel that though this is a somewhat difficult query to answer that there is value in the attempt, for the process of inspiration and invention, no matter the time period in which it occurs, is one which invites and often includes those resources that may be called extraterrestrial, though this is a gross distortion as a term. To be more specific, let us say that as one seeks in a certain fashion with a great intensity, there is, as our brothers and sisters of Hatonn mentioned, a process that is much like the magnet attracting the filing of iron. As one seeks in the capacity you would call of an inventor, there are inspirations that may come while one sleeps, while one contemplates, while one meditates, while one thinks upon the problem, shall we say. Inspirations are often answers to seeking that are provided by, shall we say, deeper portions of one's own unconscious mind, by entities that may be called guides, by another portion of the self called the higher self, and by various friends and teachers that are attracted to an entity according to the type of seeking or, shall we say, frequency or vibrational displacement of the entity. Therefore, many inventions have been aided, shall we say, by sources unseen and such a process is not relegated to any particular period of your planet's historical experience but has been a constant portion of its process of evolution.

May we answer you further, my brother?

N: Thank you very much. Then what you're actually saying is that the ability to fly may have preceded the Inca's burial rite or flight to the sun?

I am Latwii, and am aware of your query, my brother. We were not specifically aware of having said this particular statement, but of itself, there is some specific correctness in it, for the ability to, as you call it, fly, has been known to various cultures and groups within cultures and entities within groups for a great portion of what you call time. The further one moves backward, as you would say, in your planetary history, the more likely one is to find the knowledge of this ability to have been saved or put aside, shall we say, for the uses of a few. In many cases this few was a portion of what would be called today mystery schools that were able by various individuals within such schools being able to discipline the personality to such a degree that the, shall we say, ability to accomplish that called flight within not only the astral body but within the physical body was recorded and from time to time taught. It is not usually the case that mechanical devices were made as analogs to this discipline of the personality, but from time to time this has also occurred upon your planet.

May we answer you further, my brother?

N: Well, thank you very much. We don't seem to have very much recorded before, say, 1709 or 1783. Is it possible to find any information relative to these mechanical devices as well as their utilization or whether they were only, in other words, used by individuals in our dimension, not extraterrestrials as we think of them or other dimensions?

I am Latwii, and am aware of your query, my brother. Again, as you move further and further back into that called time and the history of your planet, the fewer are the available recorded leavings of your peoples, for much has been lost and misplaced, shall we say, by the various planetary changes that have occurred.

May we answer you further, my brother?

N: Well … No. Thank you very much.

I am Latwii, and we thank you, my brother. Is there another query at this time?

L: I have one more, Latwii, and I promise not to run it very far. There is in our history stories of a great library at Alexandria in Egypt, in very early times of our civilization, that was burned for some reason. What was the reason?

I am Latwii, and am aware of your query, my brother. We may speak in general in the philosophical sense, and suggest that the destruction of this great storehouse of knowledge of your peoples was accomplished by those forces which felt that if such knowledge were generally available to the great masses of the population that such entities then would be more difficult to govern in a coherent, or shall we say, unified manner. Therefore, the forces which wrought this destruction were those who were bent upon conquest and who felt that this conquest would be best aided in the long run, shall we say, if this great storehouse of knowledge were not available to the population which was seen as future subjects.

May we answer you further?

L: No, thank you very much.

I am Latwii, and we thank you, my brother. Is there another query at this time?

S: Hopefully a very short query, talking about libraries that exist with ancient knowledge. I've read of one that is full of gold tablets that is in, I believe, the northern part of South America. Does this exist?

I am Latwii, and am aware of your query, my brother. We find that in the past, as you would call it, of your various planetary cultures that there have been many libraries of the mystical variety that have been constructed in many portions upon your planet's surface. These storehouses or libraries have been constructed for the purpose of saving and secreting those teachings felt to be of a sacred nature, those teachings which would aid the seeker of truth in its process of finding that truth within itself. There are many such libraries with various kinds of materials utilized in the storage of the information deemed sacred. Gold, as you have mentioned, is one of these materials, silver being another, granite another, crystals another. There have also been those less substantial forms of material such as parchment and wood utilized, but for the most part, such insubstantial materials have not been utilized to save those greater secrets, as they are called.

May we answer you further, my brother?

S: I think that's enough. Thank you.

I am Latwii, and we thank you, my brother. Is there another query?

L: What is the condition of the instrument?

I am Latwii, and we find that this instrument is only slightly fatigued at this time and is willing to continue if there are any further queries.

A: Latwii, this is a quicky. How is the tuning of the group by this time of the session?

I am Latwii, and we may suggest, my sister, that as the concert violinist proceeds through the concert from piece to piece, it may be noted that the instrument upon which it plays will by its very exercise suffer that called the detuning, and need the attention for the reaching of the proper notes. Just so is the case within a group such as this one. As the evening grows in length and the meditation and the questions continue, there may be noted the movement of the attention of the group in an unified fashion from its one-pointed focus with which it began the seeking. This is a natural process that each seeker may note within its own meditation, for holding the attention upon a point or a purpose for a prolonged period of time is [more] difficult the longer the period grows. It is a very good exercise, though, my friends, for in such a focus one finds oneself more and more able to discipline the wild and rambunctious mind which is the, shall we say, channel through which the creative energies present themselves.

May we answer you further, my sister?

A: No, thank you.

I am Latwii, and we thank you. Is there another query at this time?

(Pause)

I am Latwii, and we find that we have for the evening exhausted those queries and partaken of that gift which each has presented to us. We thank you, my friends for your gifts of queries, for they are also of the nature of spiritual food for our own being. As you query, you present that which is ours to share, and by this sharing, we ourselves discover more and more the subtle nature of that known as service and that known as love. We continue our journey much enriched by these gifts of queries which you have given us this evening. Upon our journeys and within our seeking, these queries are as treasures, for we would not have thought of them without you. We shall leave you at this time, as always, in the love and in the light of the one Creator Who Is All in All. We are those of Latwii. Adonai, my friends. Adonai vasu borragus.

Sunday Meditation
April 21, 1985

(Jim channeling)

I am Hatonn, and I greet you, my friends, in the love and in the light of our infinite Creator. We are very pleased to be with you this evening. We have enjoyed listening to your conversation and we have enjoyed those questions and comments that each has offered the other.

My friends, when we speak to you through instruments such as this one, we are also offered the opportunity of joining in such a conversation and in your seeking for truth as you call it. We cannot tell you how privileged we feel to be able to speak with you in this manner, for though words are most inadequate to describe those deeper feelings and motivations that the seeker shares with all other seekers, yet words are most direct in the communication of thoughts between two entities. We, through words, may speak those concepts which may have some meaning in your daily experience, whereas if we were not able to utilize words, we would need to wait until you called in a fashion which would allow us to perhaps provide inspirational thought, the vivid dream, or the moment's hunch that affirmed a thought, for in these manners we are frequently able to answer the call of an entity and provide the feeling of inspiration or protection that the entity sought. With words we may attempt in our humble fashion to clothe those concepts in such a way that the message is brought into a somewhat sharper focus.

Again, my friends, we thank you for allowing this phenomenon to occur. Yet we ask, as always, that each take only those words we speak which have value in the personal journey of seeking and that each leave any word or concept that we may speak which does not seem to have that value.

As you spoke this evening, you were manifesting the means by which seekers of truth have from ages long past been able to accelerate their own journey of seeking; that is, you have shared yourselves, your thoughts, your experiences, your opinions in a way which has offered to others the harvest, shall we say, of your lives to this point. When one offers such a gift to another, it is an enhancement of the seeking of each for that gift to be offered, for each of you, being the one Creator and having chosen in this particular incarnation to express some facet or facets of the one Creator in your own way, have therefore a great deal which to offer another.

Often it is felt among seekers that a great deal of time and effort has been spent in a wasted fashion, for the attempt to measure the progress is made again and again and again and seems to come up short. Seekers often become disheartened when they do not see clear and unmistakable markings or milestones upon their paths. It is at some point in each seeker's journey, then, a common phenomenon that the seeker will feel the efforts have failed and have been wasted. At this point it is often easy for the seeker to decide that such a seeking is foolish, for there is no way of knowing what progress has been made.

Yet, when you gather in a group such as this one and others, you can in your own sharing of experience discover that you are much like all others. You seek to know the nature of your reality, the nature of your own being, the purpose for your being in this reality, and your means by which you move and learn in this illusion. You see that no seeker who is honest about his own journey has any surer knowledge than do you, for each moves in the same illusion, the one in which there seems to be great separation and disharmony, and each seeker attempts to learn from that experience which is placed before it. Each seeker also feels that there has been more failure than success, for no seeker has the clear vision to see through the illusion and beyond the illusion for but a short moment, though glimpses of such are offered to many. All who remain within this illusion are subject to its power.

The power of your illusion, my friends, is to provide you with the one Creator in a form which seems to be other than the one Creator, a form which seems to be other than love, other than wisdom, and other than unity, joy, peace and compassion. The power of your illusion is to, shall we say, persuade you that there may be that which is not love, that which is not the Creator, that which is not whole, perfect and balanced. Yet the seeker, as you have discovered in your sharing of experience, can find within any experience the wholeness and love of the one Creator if the effort is made in a sufficient degree and with the purity of will that each is developing.

As you talk amongst yourselves, you discover the one Creator residing in a greater portion of your existence, for you discover that each has had the experiences that might be described as difficult, even traumatic, and yet you will find the inspiration of those who have through their own efforts learned great lessons from such experiences. You then can look within your own experience and discover the same opportunities have been placed there for you and that you have in greater or lesser degree also discovered them in some fashion.

As we observe conversations such as the one you shared before this meditation began, we are pleased to find that each has shared the heart of its own being in a fashion unique to itself. For, my friends, love is always and ever the same; it is one thing. Yet there are many, many ways of perceiving and expressing that love. Each of you in your experiences in your daily round of activities express and experience that same love in a unique fashion. You add another hue to the infinite colors of the experience of the one Creator. You thereby glorify the one Creator in all as you in your own individual fashion move through your daily experience, and as you share those experiences with your fellow seekers you enhance their own journeys as their experiences enhance yours as well.

You are as the many portions or cells of the mind of the one Creator that begin the communication which make many cells one. You gain the knowledge of others and they gain yours. The One comes to know the One in a myriad of fashions. We applaud your incarnations and your experiences, no matter how mundane they may seem at the moment; they are yours, they are unique to you. They hold the wholeness and the perfection of the one Creator, thus through each experience at each opportunity you have before you the wholeness of the one Creator awaiting your discovery. There are layers and levels to each experience: the seeming negative rests upon the outer; the mundane, slightly below; as you continue to move to the deeper levels, you find the nature of the experience approaches that that we have described love. The one Creator awaits at the heart of each experience. How deeply shall you delve, my friends? How carefully shall you search each day's experience? The choice is yours. You may search and dig as deeply as you choose from one moment to the next. There are no requirements that any make upon you for how deeply you shall dig, other than those that you make upon yourself. You do indeed have the complete free will to choose what you shall learn and how well you shall learn it. We salute you in your choices, for they are the choices of the one Creator.

At this time, as we observe those who have gathered this evening, we find that it would be appropriate to attempt to speak through each instrument present, for those present desire to serve by means of providing vocal channels for thoughts such as ours. We would, therefore, remind each new instrument that the analysis of our thoughts is neither necessary nor helpful at this process, and we would suggest the forgetting of the analysis that it might be better saved for later, and that each might then speak whatever thought appears within the mind and speak freely after having provided the challenge to assure the self that the surrender to another source is the surrender to a positive source. We are happy to answer your challenges and we are honored to be invited to speak through each instrument.

We would at this time transfer this contact to the one known as N, if this instrument would relax and speak our thoughts. We now transfer this contact. I am Hatonn.

(N channeling)

I am Hatonn. I greet you in the love and light of the one infinite Creator. It is said that he who travels on a distant journey sometimes must forfeit considerations for a peaceful, nontraumatic existence. It is not for the entity to judge what is correct or incorrect. The entity must decide on its own what is free choice. Free choice is reserved for those entities that are seeking on your plane. It is inconceivable that one on your plane would know all the answers. It appears to be enough that even minute answers are obtained … I thank you Hatonn, but I think I've become too analytical. Please transfer to either Jim or J.

(Jim channeling)

I am Hatonn, and am with this instrument once again. We are overjoyed that we have been able to speak those words through the new instrument known as N. Those concepts which we attempted to express through this new instrument were not particularly easy concepts to perceive, and we congratulate the one known as N in his progress in the vocal channeling. We are greatly honored to be able to utilize a new instrument such as the one known as N. At this time we would attempt to speak a few words through the one known as J. If this instrument would also relax and refrain from the analysis and speak those words and thoughts that it perceives within its mind, we might also then be able to speak through this instrument. We now transfer this contact. I am Hatonn.

(J channeling)

Welcome. I am Hatonn. I greet you in the light and in the love. It … Thank you.

(Jim channeling)

I am Hatonn, and we are with this instrument once again. Welcome indeed to the new instrument known as J. We are most happy to have been able to speak a few words through this new instrument, and we encourage the one known as J in its efforts to refrain from analysis. It is most difficult, we know, to refrain from analyzing that which seems to be originating within one's own mind, yet from another source "without," shall we say. Yet each new instrument will find that as it is able to step aside, shall we say, and to remove the analyzing portion of the mind, that the process of receiving and speaking our thoughts is greatly enhanced. This is a skill which each shall develop with practice. We are honored to be asked to aid you in your practice, and shall be with you again in this capacity.

At this time, we shall take our leave of this group and this instrument that our brothers and sisters of Latwii might provide their service of attempting to answer those queries which each may provide. We, as always, leave you in the love and in the light of the one infinite Creator. We are those of Hatonn. Adonai, my friends. Adonai vasu borragus.

(Jim channeling)

I am Latwii, and we greet you also in the love and in the light of the one infinite Creator. We are honored as well to be asked to join your group this evening. We are always overjoyed to be able to provide voice to thoughts that may communicate with another portion of the Creator in yet another fashion. May we then begin with the first query of the evening?

N: Yes, I have a number of questions, but I've often been wondering, what language "Adonai vasu borragus," or the terminating words that Hatonn and you, Latwii use, what language it is, and what is the interpretation of it, besides "God." I'm sure Adonai is God or the Creator.

I am Latwii, and am aware of your query, my brother. The words of which you speak are words which are taken from what has been called by some upon your planet a solar language, that known as the Solex Mal. These words are those which fellow seekers might leave other seekers, expressing those concepts which each seeks within its life, that is, the one Creator, the love and the light of that one Creator, and the unity which binds all as One. The words may be taken to mean in general, "In the name of the One, Its love and Its light, we leave you, we salute and we are with you."

May we answer you further, my brother?

N: Yes. Thank you very much for that definition. Was the word, "Adonoi" or "Adonai" channeled to the Hebrews as that of the Lord God the Creator?

I am aware of your query, my brother. There have been various cultures upon your planet in your past, as you call it, who have received various, shall we say, words of power in response to their call, shall we say. These vibrations which compose the Hebrew language and the vibrations which compose the Sanskrit language are those vibrations which are quite close in many instances to a more pure and less distorted expression of the concepts of unity of love and of light and these languages, as do others in a lesser degree, contain what may be seen as mathematical relationships that embody certain key concepts within the evolutionary process.

May we answer you further, my brother?

N: Well, then, thank you very much. But, the word "Adonai," then, is many, many eons or multiple centuries older than we have any interpretation or I have any interpretation of, is that correct?

I am Latwii, and this is quite correct, my brother, for this particular language was, shall we say, given upon your planet within the Hebrew race by those which answered the call of this race, therefore the language is from a source other than your own planetary influence.

May we answer you further, my brother?

N: Well, thank you very much again. I had many questions to ask but I have sort of a personal consideration, since Hatonn was so familiar with our discussions earlier in the evening, I had really asked—I hadn't asked anything personal, but in the past life regression that I had, I was on a planet that had several suns, a larger one and a smaller one and four or five moons, as well as no people or plants other than grass. Could you say what kind of catastrophe happened that eliminated them or is this a valid consideration?

I am Latwii, and am aware of your query, my brother. We find that the experience of which you speak was one which was drawn through the roots of your own personal unconsciousness or subconscious mind in a fashion which was meant to be symbolic to your conscious mind. Much, therefore, needs to be seen in another light, shall we say. There might be more to be gained by looking at the symbolic nature of the experience rather than looking too specifically at those images which were presented to the conscious mind.

In this particular experience you have, shall we say, a solitary view of that incarnation, and in that particular view the experience was presented in a fashion to lack fellow beings. We feel that we have extended our response to the limits offered by your own free will.

May we answer you further, my brother?

N: No. I was just a bit disturbed why I was so sad and I was crying during the hypnotic regression, because all the other entities seemed to have been gone and that I was all alone and that there was no one else there and that's primarily the reason why I asked that. I didn't know whether—is there another planet, or is that our choice of free will, the name of the planet?

I am Latwii, and am aware of your query, my brother. There are many within the creation who within the third-density illusion do not utilize the naming concept, for their means of communication has not moved from that which you call telepathic. When one is able to communicate in the so-called telepathic manner, the naming of portions of the experience is not as necessary as when telepathy has been greatly removed from the means available for communication. As words are utilized in the spoken fashion common to your planet at this time, there is the natural tendency, then, towards the naming. Therefore, the experience which you have recalled is one which is difficult to tag, shall we say, with names, for it was not of that nature.

May we answer you further, my brother?

N: Thank you very much. I don't know whether I understood all of the considerations for the telepathic communication, but I assume that you're referring to the fact that I was communicating with a prior life and that I was a third-density individual. Is that so? Or entity?

I am Latwii, and we find that your assumption is correct in its foundation, yet to carry it further within that experience which was recalled, the means of communication was more towards the telepathic and less towards the naming, therefore your planetary influence was not known by name.

May we answer you further, my brother?

N: Only the fact that—are you referring to the fact that I was a third-density individual at that time, and was that the last life? Last incarnation, excuse me.

I am Latwii, and we feel that we are aware of your query. Please requestion if we have not responded in a fashion which is satisfactory. We may suggest that your assumption of the third density as the density of this remembrance is correct. We feel it inappropriate to answer as to whether this remembrance was that immediately preceding your current incarnation, for this would be removing an opportunity which is available presently to you to, shall we say, solve this riddle for yourself, for it contains a greater possibility of providing food for your spiritual journey.

May we answer you further, my brother?

N: Thank you very much. I have many questions about other areas but I think I should allow J an opportunity to ask first.

J: Thank you, N. Is Latwii tired or is he all right to answer more questions?

I am Latwii, and we always are energetically available for answering queries. The instruments through which we speak, though, from time to time do become fatigued, for we tend to use a number of words to express concepts. We find, however, that this instrument is also energetically available for queries. May we attempt your query?

J: Yes. I'd like to know more about you, Latwii. Were you ever in human form?

I am Latwii, and am aware of your query, my brother. We of Latwii, in our evolutionary progress, have experienced the third density which you now inhabit. Our experience of that particular density was one which utilized a vehicle which was in many ways similar to your own as it was also bipedal and erect. We were, however, enough dissimilar in our general bodily configuration, and especially in the area of the, shall we say, cranium, that we would appear quite different from any of your races currently inhabiting your planet.

May we answer you further?

J: Yeah. What did you look like?

I am Latwii, and though we find this information is not, shall we say, very helpful upon your own spiritual path, it is somewhat harmless. We of Latwii were somewhat larger in shape in the area of the frontal lobes, extending to the occipital lobes. This, shall we say, protrusion of the skull area was for the purpose of containing a brain which was of a slightly larger portion than your own. Our eyes were also somewhat larger and darker. We had smaller appendages in the location of your ears, for our ability to …

(Side one of tape ends.)

(Jim channeling)

I am Latwii, and am once again with this instrument. We were lacking most of the appendage that you call the ear, for our utilization of the spoken word was far less than your peoples utilize. Our communication, therefore, was of the telepathic nature. Our arms and legs were, shall we say, somewhat less developed than your own, and were of a thinner and more delicate nature, for we were able to utilize the powers of our mind to a greater proportion than are most of your own populations. Our physical vehicle, therefore, was more frail and delicate.

May we answer you further, my brother?

J: Well, this isn't for my spiritual growth, but I'm fascinated. Can I continue on or would you rather I stopped?

I am Latwii, and we are happy to attempt to answer queries of this nature, but may respond in more general terms than perhaps you would desire, for we do not wish to focus undue attention upon our own selves. We are messengers.

May we answer you further, my brother?

J: Well, okay, I'm fascinated. I'd like to know more, but I'll get off it. Tell me about the aura colors. I've noticed that Hatonn mentioned colors. Would you like to comment something on that?

I am Latwii, and am aware of your query, my brother. We find two concepts within this query. Those of Hatonn spoke of colors in relation to the experiences which each seekers offers that are unique in their nature. This uniqueness was approached in description by those of Hatonn by the expression of colors, unique experiences being then additional colors. The aura of which you speak is, however, another subject and has colors of another nature, yet there is a relation between the experiences of an entity and the colors of the auric energy field which surrounds each entity. As you are aware, each energy center may be correlated to a color of your known spectrum, red through violet, and when an entity is utilizing any particular experience which comes before its notice, it may utilize one or more of these energy centers, thereby causing a more brilliant expression of color to be manifested at those centers being utilized. This expression of color, then, moves within the auric field and may be read by those who can partake in the discerning of these finer energies.

May we answer you further, my brother?

J: Yes. Yes, he also spoke about incarnations. How do we find about our past lives unless we are regressed?

I am Latwii and am aware of your query, my brother. For the most part, it is not the purpose of an entity according to its own choice to remember previous, as you call them, incarnations or patterns of experience during the current incarnation, in order that the current incarnation might be kept pure, shall we say. When an entity attempts to remember a previous incarnation, this then becomes a possibility and may be pursued in a number of fashions.

The regressive hypnosis, as it has been called amongst your peoples, is the most popular means of partially penetrating the veil of forgetting which separates the conscious from the unconscious mind. An entity may also utilize the dreaming state for such remembering, utilizing the brain and the mind which moves through it to program a remembering of previous experiences. Meditation is also a means by which an entity may move itself or its conscious focus to a time previous to its current incarnation. This technique, however, is one which requires a great deal more skill than the two previously mentioned techniques.

Even greater skill is required for the conscious remembering or putting together the memories of previous incarnation, yet there are some few upon your planet who have been able to do this. This faculty is usually one which is aided by the entity's remembering such experiences from an early time within the current incarnation and having them as, shall we say, friends, which have always been with the entity and which move through the veil of forgetting with the entity.

May we answer you further, my brother?

J: No. I think I'll … How's the instrument doing?

I am Latwii, and we find that the instrument still is able to provide the necessary energy for queries. May we answer further?

J: Well, I do have a few more questions, but I'll turn it over to N.

N: Well, now I've got some questions to follow J's. Thank you very much, Latwii. About the aura. The chakras, then, help determine the auric range, and does the aura extend as we have been told, twenty-five feet around a person so that others may see it that have that capability, and did I understand you to say that if certain chakras aren't balanced, then one chakra may add a significant red or yellow or orange glow, when otherwise it … Well, I don't really understand how I'm asking the question. But the chakras do influence the aura?

I am Latwii, and am aware of your queries, my brother. To begin, the thickness, shall we say, of the auric energy field about any entity is variant and unique to each entity. There are various portions of the aura which are discernible to those with the finer sight that extend for even greater distances than the twenty-five feet which you have mentioned. The activity within any chakra or energy center lends a hue or coloration to a certain portion of the auric field. There is a portion of each entity's aura which records and illustrates the entity's unique balance between mind, body and spirit. This portion of an entity's aura, therefore, is that portion which those known as healers may read in order to ascertain the relative health, as you would call it, of any particular entity.

May we answer you further?

N: Do these healers read by sight or by intuition, the chakras?

I am Latwii, and am aware of your query, my brother. A healer who is able to see the auric energy patterns then reads the aura by the sight so that various colors and configurations of colors are translated as representing the balances between the energy centers and these balances being expressed in mind, body and spirit. There are healers who are able to ascertain this same information by the intuitional means which you also have mentioned.

To be able to read an aura in any fashion is a great aid to any who would serve as the healer, for not only may those imbalances which may be in need of the balancing or healing be read, but also the healer may become more aware of the process of balancing and healing as it is occurring, and may be able then to allow the healing process to continue for the appropriate length of what you call time, and may also be able to alter or adjust the energies as they form their new and more balanced configuration.

May we answer you further, my brother?

N: Yes, thank you very much. Can we as individuals balance our chakras within a relatively given limit with simple considerations, or must we have others do it?

I am Latwii, and am aware of your query, my brother. Indeed, each seeker must balance its own energy patterns and chakra configuration. When one known as a healer aids in this process, it is much as though the magnifying glass has been provided to a situation which is always and ever being completed or undertaken, shall we say, by the seeker. In all cases the balancing or the healing is a product of the will and the faith of the one to be healed. The healer lends its abilities to intensify this process to the one to be healed.

May we answer you further, my brother?

N: Well, just one more question that refers to the previous incarnation in which Latwii was in third density form. I seemed to get a mental picture before it was described, and I just wondered if the form of movement that Latwii referred to was psychokinesis rather than muscular energy, and would also like to know if those of third density from which Latwii originated at that particular point are still in existence, and how many years ago it was, in our time sequence.

I am Latwii, and am aware of your query, my brother. We of Latwii have moved from that experience, and though there are others who inhabit vehicles similar to those which we inhabited, they are of their own identity as we are of ours. The portion of time which has removed itself since our experience in that third density is a portion which is great in your measure, and yet is mostly meaningless, for a great portion of our experience since third density has been in realms which are, as you would call them, timeless. Therefore, the interpretation and translation of time is most misleading but can be roughly put at a great many million of your years.

May we answer you further, my brother?

N: Well, only the other question about a method of movement. Was it a form of psychokinesis or the ability to move by brain power?

I am Latwii, and am aware of that portion of the previous query which we had neglected to respond to. We were able to move both by manual appendage motion as you are familiar with, and by a means of levitation which those of the contact known as Sirius were also able to manifest in the contact with those of your planet in the location of Pascagoula, Mississippi, in 1973.

May we answer you further, my brother?

N: Is levitation, or what you might convert to brain power, the same as what we would consider as psychokinesis—were able to move—I understood that you could move manually but that your appendages were very frail and could not do great things. I assume that you're referring to the incident in 1973 where the entities did visit the people on the river or shore by levitation, but is not levitation similar to psychokinesis, or is—I perhaps am referring to the method of our ability to move, but perhaps levitation is an accentuation of psychokinesis, but still by brain power pushing against or holding you up?

I am Latwii, and am aware of your query, my brother. We may define levitation as perhaps being psychokinesis applied to the self. This is a rough definition and lacks the necessary refinement that one would need in order to utilize such a faculty. We may also add that the mind is that portion of the entity which is utilized rather than the brain. The brain is much as the pipe which allows the water to flow through it in such and such a fashion.

May we answer you further, my brother?

N: I'm sorry, I meant the mind—I'm confused. Only one other question, and then I'm sure J has some more. And that is, the entities that visited in Pascagoula, Mississippi, in 1973, were they of the Orion group, and what was their purpose in being here?

I am Latwii, and am aware of your query, my brother. We shall attempt a short response to this query, though there is more information available in the source that has come to be known as the Ra material. These entities of the Sirius influence were third-density entities who had evolved from second-density forms of life that might be likened unto your own trees. These entities, therefore, of this derivation of physical vehicle experienced their lives in a fashion which you would liken to meditation. Therefore, in order to balance this experience that was greatly peaceful and centered, they found the need to explore movement and action of all kinds and chose those known as Charley Hixson and Calvin Parker for their experiences in what you would call bellicose action or war, and viewed their memory banks, shall we say, for such experiences that would serve as a balance to their own more, shall we say, meditational experience.

May we answer you further, my brother?

N: Thank you very much. There are many questions, but I'm sure J has others if the instrument—is the instrument tired or fatigued?

I am Latwii, and we find that this instrument is available for two or three more queries, depending upon their length. May we attempt these queries at this time?

J: Why did you want to know about these two guys in Pascagoula or wherever it was? I thought you had knowledge about us on this Earth? And why did you pick those two guys?

I am Latwii, and if we understand your query correctly, my brother, we feel there has been a misconception. We did not contact the entity; these entities were contacted by those of the Sirius influence, and were contacted in order that these third-density entities might balance their own third-density incarnational experiences.

May we answer you further, my brother?

J: The third density—I really don't understand all that. But listen, can I ask you some questions about Jesus and Christianity?

I am Latwii, and we are quite happy to attempt responses to these queries, my brother.

J: Okay. N gave me a tape by a man name Yadda, and Yadda said that Jesus was crucified for himself, not for the sins of the world, and it was for his own experience. Would you like to comment on that?

I am Latwii, and am aware of your query, my brother, and we would be happy to give you our interpretation of this particular entity's purpose for incarnation. This entity was one of what you might call a group of wanderers, that is, entities from other vibrational frequencies seeking to be of service to your own planetary population by incarnating and moving through the same illusion in the same general fashion, yet in such movement providing a lightening effect, that the light of the one Creator might be made more available in some fashion to all who viewed and interpreted that incarnation for themselves. Yet each entity of a wandering nature which incarnates in such a fashion also has a portion of its own incarnation by which it intends to progress in a, shall we say, more personal manner.

The entity known as Jesus to your peoples was one which attempted to express the lessons of your illusion in as pure a fashion as was possible. The lesson of your illusion, then, being love and compassion, this entity sought to express this love in the total giving of itself including its physical life, that a way might be made more clear or illumined by light. The way was to symbolize the means by which the lesson of love might be learned.

The entity spoke and taught many times during its incarnation. Always its teachings focused about the heart of love. This entity then, after a significant portion of its incarnation had been spent in the teaching fashion, felt that, as you would say, a picture is worth a thousand words. There came to this entity the realization that a certain act or giving of itself would be necessary in order to more vividly create the image in mind and heart, shall we say, within those who would look upon its incarnation, that the giving of the life was then the embodiment of the teachings that the entity spent its life in sharing. The crucifixion, as you call it, of this entity, then, provided the, shall we say, keystone in the building of the structure of the eternal life of which this entity spoke.

The victory over that called death, then, was to illustrate to those who would study this entity's teachings that the teachings allowed an entity not only to move within this incarnation in a pattern which afforded the spiritual evolution but would allow the entity through and beyond this incarnation, and to continue its evolutionary progress in a greater reality, shall we say.

May we answer you further, my brother?

J: Do you mean he's still around?

I am Latwii, and am aware of your query, my brother. This entity in the incarnation of which you are familiar was able in the personal sense by its service to others to expand and promote its own evolutionary progress in such a fashion that it now exists in what you would call a higher vibrational frequency, for as it gave of itself in a pure and undistorted fashion, the bread, as it is called, which was cast upon the waters returned manyfold to the one who gave it freely. Thus is the nature of the service-to-others polarity. As one gives to others, one accelerates one's own progress, thus the self is eventually served, as we might call it, a byproduct of the serving of others. And this entity therefore does indeed yet exist, but upon a vibrational frequency that is not apparent to your own.

May we answer you further, my brother?

J: If one were to ask this entity for help, would he come? Or can he be reached, or what?

I am Latwii, and am aware of your query, my brother. This entity, in its incarnation those two thousand or so years in your past, began a service which did not end with that incarnation, for as it assumed a role as a way-shower, shall we say, it then also assumed the responsibility of answering the calls of those who chose to follow the way which it showed to them. Thus, this entity in some fashion answers all calls. The fashion utilized is unique for each individual so calling. Each individual is able to perceive an answer in some way that is discernible or available, shall we say, according to an entity's unique nature, shall we say.

May we answer you further, my brother?

J: Yeah. But I think N has a question. Is the instrument doing all right? Can we go a little further?

I am Latwii, and we find that this instrument is growing somewhat fatigued but is yet available for another query or two. May we attempt such at this time?

N: The last response to J's question, Latwii, focused upon something I think most interesting. Number one, I imagine, is the entity previously known as Jesus able to answer all the queries, and even if he can answer, can he grant favors or so forth, other than guidance, and something that J mentioned earlier, the result of the—or what happened to the physical body with which Jesus inhabited previously, the entity known as Jesus?

I am Latwii, and am aware of your queries, my brother. To take the last first, this entity's third-density physical chemical vehicle went the way of all such vehicles, and that is ashes to ashes and dust to dust, for as an entity takes off the garment that has served it well and moves on without the garment, the garment then goes the way of all garments. This entity in its attempts to answer those calls which are made to it by those who follow its way may be of service in the same fashion as one's own higher self, shall we say. Each seeker, whether calling upon the entity known as Jesus, upon its own guides, upon its teachers, or upon its higher self may be aided in whatever manner is appropriate to that entity at any specific time. This aid then is variably dependent upon an entity's grasp on the metaphysical level of the lessons and its own desires which are symbolized or contained within the situation for which it prays or for which it calls for assistance.

Therefore, though all calls and prayers are answered, the answers must fit the need of the entity, for often an entity asks for that which would not be truly beneficial in its overall spiritual growth. Yet in the asking, at the heart of the asking, is the desire to be of service or to receive service in a way which is truly service. Thus, the answer to such a call must speak to the heart of the call and entities are not always aware of the heart of their own call, yet each may rest assured that each call and prayer is answered.

May we answer you further?

N: I don't want to over-fatigue the instrument, but I guess I didn't understand part of it in that I think I interpret the fact that the entity known as Jesus' physical vehicle was buried and became dust; it did not rise as stated in the Bible, or did it, or—and the fact that the entity known as Jesus can grant hearings or, well, for whatever, if the entity requests a path or … Could you clarify that just a little bit more, please?

I am Latwii, and am aware of your query, my brother. The physical vehicle of the one known as Jesus was eventually laid down by the one known as

Jesus yet this was done in a private setting after the, shall we say, demonstration of victory over death was made to those who were its followers. The, shall we say, granting of desires is possible only when those desires do not violate one's free will. The free will of an entity is always the focus about the opportunity to learn and to serve. Many entities are not consciously aware of the most appropriate learning and service which is moving through their life pattern. These entities may ask in prayer for that which would not truly serve this process of evolution occurring within them. An entity such as the one known as Jesus would not desire to be of anything but the greatest service to any such entity calling for its aid. Thus, as it answers that called prayer, whatever the nature of the prayer, the answer shall be fashioned in such a way that the one calling or praying is, shall we say, truly served or served in the heart of its call, though its conscious call may be for another manifestation than the one which finally occurs.

May we answer you further, my brother?

N: Thank you. I'm sure the instrument is fatigued. I'd like just a yes or no answer. There have been other entities, I'm sure over the span of many, many, many centuries and cycles and so forth. Can those other entities also answer …

(Tape ends.)

L/L Research

Sunday Meditation
April 28, 1985

(Carla channeling)

I am L/leema *(pronounced "Lahleema")*. I am of the Confederation, and I greet you in the love and light of the infinite Creator in Whose Oneness we dwell. What a circumstance! I know you have not called me. I have never spoken to humans. We are having a good time with this instrument, for we find that as we pick and choose that which we wish to say among the various oddments that she stores in her brain, there are many non-linear connections which cause communication using this instrument to be enjoyable for us.

We shall speak to you but first we wish to give a history of ourselves, for we would not come to speak with those who did not wish us. We are only humble, and if we do not serve we should not come. We are going to use this instrument's vocabulary because it helps us. We are unused to many instruments; we are unused to using any instruments—we can even play four bars of boogie woogie! This instrument's is most enjoyable!

We are in the same line of work as those who call themselves to you Latwii. We are of the density of light, and, therefore, as we have volunteered for this task, we have been in the [color] spectrum or should we say the various densities spectra of your planet. Our concern is somewhat different. We are not quite so much the generalist as was Latwii before this word entity's channel was heard in this group. We work mostly in the area of clarification of belief. We scan …

Clarification of the fastidiousness with which each nexus of each individual which has come through the subterranean days and nights and centuries which separate it from full third density. We note each bias for change in intensity of each mind/body/spirit complex.

We are surprised at this instrument—however, wait, we are not surprised at this instrument. This instrument has been used by one who would use that gift. We must push on for we wish to not just enjoy this instrument but to share our thoughts with you.

We were working in the same vicinity with ones of Latwii who mentioned that this instrument was enjoyable to use and suggested that we launch ourselves into service, for in Latwii's estimation there was service, and as each of us as each of you is unique, each service is unique, though we say the same thing, each of us; we all ask that you turn to the Creator, the one original Thought. However, let us regress amidst the digression.

We asked a selected group of the Confederation for permission to use this instrument as it is necessary to gain special permission to use an instrument which has been in agreement with those which have gone before the Council of Saturn. We were given permission to do what we could with this instrument at this time, and we hope that as we ramble we may move you and fill you with joy and with the intensity of desire that we feel for you.

It is an interesting thing, your language. In this instrument's mind we see roots going deep into the past of your planet's written history. We select two words: vacation/vocation. We ask you to consider one small difference in your rendition of this sound complex. "Vaca," to be open; "voca," to call or be called. "Vacation," to have time, to be free, to be empty; "vocation," to be called, to be selected, to be initiated. We find it unfortunate that those of you in this group come to the group as full of vacation as vocation, not because this is incorrect for third density, but because each of you has vocation and the joy of vocation is such that we would risk annoying you by suggesting that the enjoyment of vacation is on a completely different level of living quality than the soul that seeks vocation.

You all tune with the same tuning, and yet you are not fully a circle, for there is too much of the individual queries which do not have universal meaning. This also is acceptable but it reduces the ability of a positively polarized entity such as ourselves or anyone of the Confederation entities from speaking clearly because of the great desire to not in any [way] tear down but always to build up. Yet there are those things which need examination.

In terms of the workaday world, the need for the empty time, the vacation, is a balance and not a luxury. It is not this vacation of which we speak. At a much deeper level of self, there is the choice between the self that will take itself seriously no matter what the consequences and the self who wishes time off and time out. What you wish you will receive. If you wish vocation you will have life with the moments of joy completely indescribable in any terms except those known to those who have experienced full life in service, full polarization, full use of catalyst, full joy in all that there is. We would urge you to think upon this.

There are things one does to collect the *denaro*. These jobs may be fun or not. This is not vocation. A vocation is that which is so loved that you are called to it, not because you understand or have reason that you should call and go but because you are called and you must go. Each of you is infinite and beautiful Creator stuff. Do you acknowledge the potential seriousness of that statement? You must always remember, it is not the answers you will find most illuminating, for as you learn, you will learn that it is the questions themselves that live, and it is the company of those who seek that may aid you in becoming seekers, serious with laughter, of course, for seriousness should be full of joy. It should be full of all that you are and all that you have. If you wish to be a serious seeker, it is not tomorrow or yesterday that you will be a serious seeker. Take yourself now and acknowledge that you are God stuff. Then ask yourself if you wish to seek the truth. That question alone will fill lives.

We enjoy rambling with you, and yet, though the ones of Hatonn have been most generous, we feel we should stop our talking. We would prefer to answer queries, but we cannot use this instrument and do so. Therefore, if there is any desire for my return, it shall be as is desired. There will, however, be no questions unless there is the question of the group which may be spoken or unspoken but gains great power by its being unified.

We leave you with a merry ditty, and hope that the rest of your experience this evening may enspirit and enliven and fill and that you hear only that which you need, discarding the rest of our foolish talk. We have been beside ourselves to have this experience of working with this instrument and talking with those upon the sphere. We have been working within the sphere, and the mentalities are not as they are in this group and in this group's collective memory in the room.

We wish to leave you on the very pinnacle of all that is true. We are yourselves. This instrument's mind looks as though it thinks of how to spell my name. I thought for at least a week … we cannot know your time. We thought about the name for we had not previously had one which would mean "name" to me. We chose L/leema for subjective reasons known to ourselves. We offer you the spelling: L-slash-L-e-e-m-a. We L-slash leave you in the L-slash love and L-slash light of the infinite Creator. We are one. Do you know what that slash means, my friends: we are one. Think upon the Creator. We leave you in His love. We are L/leema. Adonai. Adonai.

(Jim channeling)

I am L/leema, and we greet you again through this instrument in love and in light. We had some time penetrating this instrument's resistance, shall we say, to initiating a new contact. We have heard about this instrument's resistance. We find it very interesting. We are, as we mentioned, unused to speaking to or through human beings. It is a fascinating experience to look within your minds and discover the means by which you have furnished them. We are also desirous of serving by means of attempting to answer queries. Our brothers and sisters of Latwii have also recommended that this group is a good one with which to begin in this endeavor for it without fail can provide many queries and offer opportunities to serve which are precious indeed. We would then ask if we might attempt a query to begin?

L: L/leema, am I correct in assuming you're willing to answer questions of a general nature in a manner similar to Latwii?

I am L/leema, and you are correct, my brother. Do you have such a query?

L: Yes. I recently completed a book by Shirley McLaine, *Out on a Limb*, in which in part she mentions an extraterrestrial group originating from the area we call the Pleiades who, in her description, are spending some time in an effort to benefit the Earth. Can you give me any information about these individuals or entities as far their polarity and the association they may have with the Confederation, any general information?

I am L/leema. We scan your memory of this information and find that as most efforts of Confederation members, this effort has been initiated in hopes that there could be an inspirational exchange of information that might be used to quicken the evolutionary progress of those upon your planetary surface whose needs are for such information. In each Confederation effort it is hoped that where there is a call, an answer in some form might be provided which then could accelerate the activity of seeking what you call the truth which then quickens the progress of the seeker. As in most such efforts, the effort has had the, shall we say, balancing opportunity of being mixed with some more, shall we say, questionable information, for it is not always known by those who receive such information that care must be taken in the reception lest the reception become garbled in the metaphysical sense, that is, joined with the services of those who seek the darker path.

May we attempt further response, my brother?

L: I'd like to ask a question on another subject. A friend in Cincinnati has—I suppose channeling would be the best description—channeled quite a bit of information which seemed to me it had the feel of great accuracy. I'm curious as to the teachers who provide him information, assist him in his progress. Are they associated with the Confederation or are they operating in some manner independently of the Confederation?

I am L/leema, and in cases such as the one of which you speak, there are often entities who dwell within your inner plane realms who are of your planetary influence and who are, shall we say, in between incarnations and therefore available through agreement with entities who are incarnate upon your planet. They serve, then, as resources and advisors or teachers as you might call them to incarnate entities, and answer calls as do those of the Confederation. Though not in the strict sense members of this Confederation, such entities work conjointly, shall we say, with Confederation entities and principles as they attempt service of another nature than do those who are incarnate.

May we answer further, my brother?

L: No, thank you. You've been of very much assistance. Thank you.

I am L/leema and we are grateful to you, my brother. Is there another query that we might give an attempt to?

A: L/leema, I'm curious. Did you make your presence known and condition individuals in the group before they arrived here in this circle?

I am L/leema, and it was our intent not so much to condition those who would join this circle this evening, as to scan the desires and determine the calling as you have described it of this circle of meditation in order to discover whether or not we might be able to provide a service by initiating a contact.

May we answer you further, my sister?

A: With the contact we're receiving, previously you asked for unified group questions. Could you expand on that?

I am L/leema, and we would be most happy, my sister, to expand upon this most salient of points.

Before joining your group this evening, we made our availability for such service known, and those of Latwii gave us information concerning this group and the potential that we might realize in serving through attempting queries with this group. A portion of the information transferred by those of Latwii concerns the nature of queries which might be expected within any group of beings upon your planetary surface: one can expect queries of any nature. In many cases the queries have but momentary interest and satisfy the curiosity but briefly and add little to an entity's evolutionary opportunities. There are those queries, however, that speak to the point of the incarnation within your illusion. These queries concern the nature of this process, its personal and general application, and the answers to such queries, when well spoken and clearly given, are valuable through all time and hold the interest of the seeker firmly in place, for they are principles describing the nature of one's being, the nature of one's environment, and the nature of one's evolution through the environment of the creation of the one Creator.

Those of Latwii spoke to us in regards to this subject by suggesting that though this group was well focused in general concerning information that does not fade, that there were from time to time those queries which were of little import and had the effect of moving the focus from that which endures to that which dissolves quickly. Thus, we made our suggestion which could be made even to the good and serious student, that queries are most helpful to group understanding, shall we say, and evolutionary progress if they seek to strike to the heart of the mysteries of one's being and the evolutionary progress.

May we answer you further, my sister?

A: No. Thank you for your service.

I am L/leema, and we thank you, my sister, for yours as well. Is there another query, my friends?

C: L/leema, over the past few months I've almost been avoiding any type of meditation because afterwards I've been feeling a weariness, just a physical hurting. I experienced it again the other evening. I was just sitting quietly in another person's house and I started picking up a conditioning, and then shortly thereafter I began picking up a feeling of something or someone hurting. I'm not sure what this is that I'm picking up, but it is causing weariness. It was suggested that maybe I was picking up feelings from the planet. I don't know exactly what's going on but if you can shed any light on it, I'd appreciate it.

I am L/leema, and as we scan your experiential beingness, we find that there are some comments which we may make without infringing upon your own process of discovery. As the seeker encounters the difficult experience, that which stretches the ability to accept, the seeker then finds itself as the drumhead, we find you call it, which has been stretched most tightly across the framework of which it is a part. This stretching within a seeker's being will cause the seeker to become more sensitive to vibrations both within and without its own being. This is a natural portion of the evolution …

(Side one of tape ends.)

(Jim channeling)

I am L/leema, and we again have this instrument's attention. We shall continue. This is a natural portion of the evolutionary process, for it enables the seeker to become sensitive to that which has been placed before it as an opportunity for furthering its own evolution. However, the seeker is also then more sensitive to any experience in which it finds itself. While the more intense portions of one's experience are proceeding, it is often helpful to take more of the time in meditation. This provides the opportunity for utilizing the experience more completely rather than dissipating one's efforts in many directions. This may seem paradoxical that one should increase an experience which seems to be wearying. Yet you will find, my brother, that increased meditative periods will provide you with the ability to utilize that opportunity which has been placed before you and which has caused you for the moment to become a more sensitive instrument.

May we attempt further response, my brother?

C: Just one other thing. Along with something else, a feeling of no longer belonging or no longer a part of things—I feel I've just gotten to a point where wherever I am it's just an act to get along, because I no longer seem to fit anywhere. Can you comment?

I am L/leema. We may comment by again directing your attention to our previous response and that characteristic of the difficulty or traumatic opportunity for learning which renders the seeker more sensitive for its duration. Often another effect which spins off from the primary effort is the seeming distance that the seeker seeks to shield or provide a buffer between it and an environment which is increasingly painful, shall we say. We utilize the word painful in an attempt to describe the sensitivity which the seeker will frequently discover as the difficult experience becomes apparent to it.

May we answer further, my brother?

C: I may have a query later. Thank you.

I am L/leema, and we thank you, my brother. Is there another query that we might attempt?

Carla: L/leema, I would publicly and with the utmost care challenge you as a spirit in the name of my Lord and Savior Jesus Christ. Do you come in his name and for his glory?

I am L/leema, as we have chosen to call ourselves to this group, and at the core of our being we join each of you in that love and light of the one master that is known to you as Jesus. We appreciate your concern and your challenge, my sister. We have spoken to this subject but briefly this evening in mentioning that there are far too few of your peoples aware of the need for such a challenge upon a regular basis for entities unseen who speak through instruments, for as you know, my sister, it is indeed a crowded universe, and many would speak; yet the challenge winnows those with whom you might benefit from the speaking.

May we answer further challenge or speak in any other capacity, my sister?

Carla: Only the latter. I thank you for the appropriate response. It helps to hear it. I thank you. I'd like to ask you two things, and the first one is, how is it, when you came into my mind and the whole time I had the words came easily enough but they didn't always come in sentences because you were bouncing around like a trampoline, and my mind bounces around like a trampoline, and so it was kind of crazy, and you're just talking like the most sober judge in the world there in Mickey [Jim], and I wondered what happened? I mean, he's got a sense of humor that's really good.

I am L/leema, and putting aside the minor amount of improvement or acquiring of skill that we have gained this evening, we are able to utilize this instrument's rather notoriously rigid mental configuration in speaking in a manner which seems more fluid, but if you were in this mind, my sister, you would discover many hard places.

Carla: *(Giggling)* Don't make me laugh. Okay.

We apologize for the discomfort and would complete our query by suggesting that we are yet tumbling about in our abilities to utilize an human instrument, and are somewhat relieved to be able to speak in a seemingly coherent and smooth sense, yet hope that even within this instrument's rigidity that we might enjoy the fluidity which was the characteristic of your own mind, my sister. There is hope.

May we attempt further response?

Carla: Yeah. I really wanted to know. I've heard this before from Latwii and I really would like to know why it is that the fifth density, or at least you two, both seem full of laughter and love and all kinds of good information to share with other people. I get the feeling that it is not appropriate—you said it, you said it never occurred to you to try to communicate with other people, you were … whatever you were doing; I'll have to read it. But then you talked to Latwii or somebody in Latwii, and they're talking about this group and this instrument and so you decided to give it a whirl. But, number one, why is it that that response has come for us, and number two, why did you give us a whirl? And number three, was it worth it?

I am L/leema, and indeed, my sister, it has quite been worth it thus far, and we see great hope for what you call the future of this contact with this group. We sought to serve in the initiation of our contact, and we have sought to serve in a dual capacity, that is, speaking a message of general inspiration and then attempting to lend our point of view and beingness to the capacity of attempting to answer queries. Just as each human instrument is unique and offers an individualized flavor, shall we say, when utilized by any Confederation entity, just so, your group might, we hope, benefit from another flavor of Confederation entity. We have come to this group in hopes that the message which is always and ever the same might find new home within each seeker in a manner which perhaps lends another aspect to that simple message of love.

May we answer you further, my sister?

Carla: No. Thank you.

I am L/leema, and we thank you, my sister. We are gaining somewhat better contact with this instrument and use of its vocabulary and experience and hope that it will bear with us as we move within its mind and search for those concepts which might not only enlighten those who ask the query, but enlighten and enable our own being as well, for we learn much as we share with you that which is ours to share.

May we attempt another query, my friends?

L: I have another one, L/leema. In reference to the sources of information available to those who would be seekers, it appears to me that there are three sources initially available that I'm aware of—the first coming through one's own contact with what might be termed intelligent infinity, one's direct connection with the awareness of the universe; a second one, one's ability on a selective basis to communicate with preincarnate souls, entities who act as teachers; a third source of information, entities such as yourselves. Are there other sources of information as well, that we're not aware of … that I'm not aware of?

I am L/leema, and, my brother, we may say that there is but one source, the One which moves in all, and yet, my brother, we may say there are infinite sources, for this One expressed Itself in infinite variation and your own creation contains infinite resources which any seeker might partake in furthering its own evolution. To look within one's own being is to see all that there is. To look within the eyes of another is to see all that there is through another's eyes. To look at your creation of flowers and trees, of birds and insects, the wind and weather, is to see the Creator moving with a simple elegance yet containing all answers to all queries for those who seek with discerning eyes and ears and yearning hearts. You may look about you at any source, and if you look beyond that which meets the physical eye, you will see the one Creator there in full, whole and perfect, willing to teach all that you seek.

May we answer further, my brother?

L: Yes. I'd like to ask you to clarify whether a statement is correct or not, that among the different, if you will, schools of thought, branches of seeking, the basic information is essentially the same, that which is true and correct. The distinctions between the individual groups lie primarily within either distorted communication of information or a selective bias on the part of the recipient of the information, this being over some minor aspects. For example, the idea some believe that reincarnation exists but that the individual continues as a sentient individual, continually being reborn; other believe that for the individual who does not strive, a regressive type of reincarnation occurs until that individual can regress so far that they can no longer be sentient.

So if I could reclarify my statement for you—I'm thinking out loud, please bear with me. Would I be correct in assuming that among the schools of thought and seeking on our planet, the essential information is correct? The minor information that separates them from one another is the result of distortion through communication or personal bias on the part of the recipients? On that?

I am L/leema …

L: … and patient.

… and we thank you, my brother, for taking the time to phrase a query which has importance to those who seek the many sources of the One. The One is in all. All in some fashion speak of the One. The many voices heard are all the voice of the One. You may liken their method of speaking of the One to accents or colloquial means of description sported in various locations of your own country. All speak your English language, yet the coloration is found in many places. This is the uniqueness which the Creator has sought by making Itself many. To those who dwell within the worlds of the many, these unique colorations may seem confusing in some cases, mutually exclusive, yet if you will look to the heart of all speaking, you will find the One speaking. Therefore, the seeker must take the responsibility of discerning that which is close to the heart and that with—we shall correct this instrument—and that which orbits the far fringes of the heart. All is part of the One. Look for the heart of the One, my brother.

May we attempt further response?

Carla: I get this feeling that you're putting that answer in such a way that L has to think about it and so I want to have a go at it, okay? We're taught generally, at least all three of us, anyway, who have studied all this kind of stuff, that there are a lot of inner plane teachers, that's what L was talking about, people that we listen to … A tape this morning of someone channeling Annie Bresant … Annie

Bresant just wrote about Madame Blavatsky and Madame Blavatsky was just a channel. So you're getting pretty far away there from the source, and Annie didn't have anything really enlightening to say, although it was very lovely and made you feel warm and gooey and soft. And one enjoys listening to warm and soft and cuddly things like that, so I enjoyed that tape very much.

Okay. I think of that—that kind of warmey, gooey, marshmallowey—but love and light, you know, but not real intellectually filling, you know. And then you get the outer densities, densities that don't happen to be involved in the Earth density, and they do really seem to be qualitatively different in the amount of brain power that they can put to the scope, I suppose, with which they answer questions. There's less emphasis on some date, an Earth date, and more emphasis on God's time. So it seems to me that the way things fall, there really do appear to be inner and outer planes of this wisdom relative to, mind you, where we are right now. Is this true?

I am L/leema, and you are quite correct, my sister. There are many travelers on this journey. Some have gone further and seen more sights, shall we say. Each describes what each has seen. All has seen some portion of the one Creator; all seek in some fashion to share that vision. Those who seek also are responsible for what is found. When you seek with a pure heart and a one-pointed mind, you shall find that which is more precisely of value to you. When you seek that of general interest, when you seek to know of some phenomenological occurrence that has little value to your seeking, you shall find that which you seek, and there are those who shall tell you of it. What shall you seek? And what shall you find?

May we answer further, my sister?

Carla: That was a beautiful answer. Helps a lot. Thank you very much.

I am L/leema, and we thank you, my sister. May we share our journey with another query?

N: Yes. L/leema, are you considered a social memory complex?

I am L/leema, and am one of many who are within what you have come to know as a social memory complex, for as the process of evolution occurs within the various densities of this creation, there are those travelers who find comradeship and companionship in the seeking and who join with those who share their experience and their desires. We are those who have joined and to this group have called ourselves L/leema.

May we answer further, my brother?

N: Yes please. Well, are the majority of entities in L/leema of an area grouping or is it quite diverse, and from what area was the origin, as well, a sort of a conversion of time for the group as far as the origin?

I am L/leema. We find within your query some difficulty for us in discerning the gist, shall we say, but we can suggest that our origins are much like your own, for within the creation of the One, it has been found that there is a progress possible from the foundation elements, shall we say, that are those portions of the one Creator with which each octave begin, as earth, wind, fire and water join to form that which shall become matter, as you call it. And as this formation is quickened with the awareness of the One, then the life as you know it proceeds as fruit of that forming and joining. And as this life becomes aware of itself, then it seeks to join in a fashion that is social and is, as you would call, analogous to the human condition. Thus, we have evolved, as have you, through this process of the one becoming many, yet simple; of the many simple portions becoming more complex and having the awareness expanded through a series of exponential jumps or leaps, shall we say.

May we answer you further, my brother?

N: Well, thank you very much. I was sort of interested in an age factor, but that's really kind of irrelevant, I imagine. You said you had spoken only to humans on this Earth occasionally. Are there other entities that you have communicated with who are living on other planets or even within this planet?

I am L/leema. In our introductory remarks we described in a general fashion those entities to which we have offered our service, many within your own planetary influence, and these entities have been more of what you would call the prehuman nature, those entities who seek to move from the group or herd to the individualized conscious natures which is—we correct this instrument—individualized conscious natures which are in general given to the species known as human. We seek to, shall we say, ennoble and enspirit these entities, for they call as a group for such investment, as you may also call it. We have attempted to perform this service upon those within your own planetary influence, and others as well.

May we answer further, my brother?

N: You mentioned just now that—you said that the prehuman groups call as a group, using the present tense rather than the past tense. Could you tell us about these prehuman groups that are calling as a group at this particular moment?

I am L/leema. There are upon your planet and within your planet those entities of what you have come to call the second-density nature who through many cycles of incarnation have gained nearly enough individualization to enter that density that you now are ending. These entities are of many natures and species. There are many who swim your oceans, many who dwell within your tropical regions, some who move within your atmosphere, and others who dwell in deep forests and underground caverns. The variety of species is great.

May we answer further, my brother?

N: Well, thank you. Is … Are you also communicating with third-density individuals on other planets that are not considered human?

I am L/leema. No, my brother, we are not. Yours is the first effort we have made of this nature.

May we attempt further response, my brother?

N: Thank you very much.

Carla: I'd like to know how the instrument's doing, energywise and stuff like that. You really have to take care of them, you know. They'll just conk out on you completely if you run them *(inaudible)*.

I am L/leema, and as we look about this instrument's energy field, we find that it grows thin in some places. We shall have to become more skilled at the utilization of the human brain/mind complex, for our contact is somewhat wearing. This we have discovered upon the scanning of this instrument. We would suggest a final query or two, if they are short.

L: One quick one. In our density we have individuals who have become leaders for the rest of us—forerunners. What about on the second density? Is there such a creature? A porpoise among porpoises?

I am L/leema, and though this phenomenon is not unheard of, it is quite rare, for it is the characteristic of those second-density creatures that they shall express their conscious being in a group form. Each individual entity, then, is closely connected to the group mind, and there is a species type of telepathy which reinforces this natural inclination. Therefore, it is less likely that an individual entity within the second-density illusion will become what you would call the leader. Yet, in some cases, this does occur. Most are found within the relationship that third-density entities have with what you call pets.

May we answer further, my brother?

L: That was sufficient. Thank you very much.

Carla: I'd like to ask you one final quick one, just a confirmation if it's true. When I got the idea that—when you first began speaking, it seemed like these entities were big and shaggy, and I flashed on the Bigfoot type that took on those bodies when Maldek blew up to try to make some sort of entry into third density. And I was just wondering, is this type of being among those that you serve? If you can confirm that?

I am L/leema, and we are happy, my sister, that you have discerned this particular portion of our service, for it is indeed the heart of what our service has been for a great portion of what you call time concerning your own planetary influence. Those of the Maldekian origin, as you have come to know this race, have in great numbers incarnated upon your own planetary sphere from the beginning of its third-density cycle in order that they might make alleviation of their actions upon the planet you have called Maldek. It has been our added opportunity to serve other more truly second-density creatures as an offshoot service of working with those of whom you speak.

My friends, we find that we have reached the safe limits of the use of this particular instrument. We do not wish to overtire any who provide us the opportunity to speak to those who call for our service. We thank you each and every one. We have enjoyed this opportunity. It has been quite a challenge and quite fun, for the mind of the human is concerned with many, many things which we would never think of on our own. We give praise for the variety which we find within your minds and your experience, for each portion speaks of the one Creator which moves Its hand through all our being. We applaud you in your seeking. Go forth, my friends, in that seeking, in the love and the light of the One. We are known to you this evening, and for our time with you, however long or short it shall be …

(Tape ends.)

L/L Research

L/L Research is a subsidiary of Rock Creek Research & Development Laboratories, Inc.

P.O. Box 5195
Louisville, KY 40255-0195

www.llresearch.org

Rock Creek is a non-profit corporation dedicated to discovering and sharing information which may aid in the spiritual evolution of humankind.

ABOUT THE CONTENTS OF THIS TRANSCRIPT: This telepathic channeling has been taken from transcriptions of the weekly study and meditation meetings of the Rock Creek Research & Development Laboratories and L/L Research. It is offered in the hope that it may be useful to you. As the Confederation entities always make a point of saying, please use your discrimination and judgment in assessing this material. If something rings true to you, fine. If something does not resonate, please leave it behind, for neither we nor those of the Confederation would wish to be a stumbling block for any.

CAVEAT: This transcript is being published by L/L Research in a not yet final form. It has, however, been edited and any obvious errors have been corrected. When it is in a final form, this caveat will be removed.

© 2009 L/L Research

Sunday Meditation
May 5, 1985

(L channeling)

I am Hatonn, and I greet you, my brothers and sisters, in the love and the light of the infinite Creator. We are pleased that we were able to make contact so readily through this instrument, for we realize that those whose service includes the initiation of these communications are somewhat fatigued and are less attuned than is their normal state. Therefore, it is pleasant to have the opportunity to use a different instrument, particularly in initiation of this session.

Tonight we desire to share with you a tale of two cities, so to speak. The first was a city of no great size, possessed of no great abilities, neither powerful in war nor in learning, yet a place of calm and of repose for the soul. For it was the nature of these people to seek that which cannot be acquired upon the physical plane. The other city, in contrast, was composed of individuals, of people who sought and fought, who pursued their ambitions, people who attempted much and accomplished less, for in truth, their conflicts interrupted the efforts of each to acquire that which he sought or to gain that which he pursued.

At the time in which these cities existed, for this was within the realm of the physical plane and time was faithfully observed, a struggle arose between those who occupied the city of seekers of the physical realm. For in finding themselves unable to subdue one another, they turned their vision outward and began to plan, to make alliances and truces and treaties so as to turn their energies to the conquest of the city of those who sought within the spiritual realm.

The day came; the banners were unfurled; the marchers went forward; the troops were formed for the assault, and in great excitement they stormed that city, only to find that this city was unoccupied. The treasures they sought were present but seemed somehow tarnished in that no struggle occurred, no fear was sparked, no cowardice displayed, only the treasures of the physical world remained behind in this strangely abandoned city. In their dismay, they scouted throughout the area, attempting to find any of the former occupants of the city that they might question them or perhaps abuse them in some manner so as to make this conquest somehow more appropriate or enjoyable. Yet they found no one.

Finally, they began to argue among themselves. The arguing became more bitter, more angry, and the anger sparked the violence which had been delayed too long. And so they fought and, for the most part, slew one another with pleasure, with satisfaction, and those who remained after the battle, loaded what treasure they could remove from their fallen enemies, their former allies, and returned to their homes.

And, my brothers, each in the story was able to achieve that which he had sought. For those who followed this path of taking and of violence managed to attain the violence which they had sought and to take, each from another in satisfaction. Those of the abandoned city also found fulfillment, for they were able, as was their wont, to peacefully offer what gifts, what possessions they possessed, to their brothers of the more violent city by simply leaving behind that which they themselves no longer could value but knew would be of value to the invaders. And each, my friends, followed their path successfully.

The difference, then, would lie simply in the direction of their paths, for those of that city which might be termed service to self chose a circuitous path which would circle repeatedly back in upon itself, rebounding from its contact with others as they would progress outward, find their pain, acquire their minor treasures and return whence they came, while those of the city which might be termed service to others acquired those gifts which had been provided, made use of those gifts to the extent which they were useful, then left them behind for their brothers and proceeded outward on a path which had no return, only progression.

My brothers, we are of the path of service to others. It is of our choice. It is apparent to those who seek to follow this path that others more readily accept a different path, that of service to self. It is appropriate to be of what assistance one may to our brothers of the service-to-self polarity, for as you know, such service can only be of assistance to both you and they. Yet, it is not necessary for all to lay down their lives for the whims of those who seek pleasure in the taking of life and the destruction of that which we call good.

My brothers, in times ahead, travails will come to each of you and difficult choices will need to be made. In your illusion, there are many examples of what may be termed nobility, common sense, or even "the right thing to do." But, my brothers, remember that confusion might be termed the dominant theme within your illusion and that nobility which stems from confusion may not always be the most beneficial choice for those concerned. Therefore, my friends, look to your heart for guidance and not to conventional wisdom, for it is within your heart and not your mind that the course of your desire will be revealed.

At this time, we will relinquish our use of this instrument that our brothers and sisters of Latwii might perform their service of answering questions. Adonai, my friends. Adonai vasu borragus. I am known to you as Hatonn.

(Carla channeling)

I am L/leema. Glory alleluia, it is good to be with my group. It is good [to be] with each of you and we greet each of you in the love and in the light of the one infinite Creator. Many are the times we have thought that we might be able to contact this group once again, slipping in between other entities. We speak now through this instrument by permission of those of Latwii and we promise not to stay long or to bend your ears overmuch. We are also attempting to learn to speak more roundly and in a dignified manner. We find this instrument is capable of this but the relaxed instrument thinks internally in far less of a stylish manner.

We have been so glad to be with you as we listened to those of Hatonn speak, for there is deep wisdom in this lesson of love. As we are in the density of wisdom, we find it unlikely that we might [repartee] so eloquent upon the subject of compassion as we now learn, tempering and refining by means of what you call wisdom. We find upon this instrument's mind the record which this instrument and each of you in the circle of this blessed group heard as you began your session. We would speak to some small extent upon the concern for the starving.

We might suggest that this has a general implication but we would speak specifically. Since our task as volunteers at this time in your planet's transition is so appropriate to the concern of starvation, we must speak to it and we thank you for the opportunity.

There are—we scan—billions of your peoples whose energy nexi have progressed from the group to the individual. They are very, very confused, still fearful, and yet aware that they are unique. At the same time, their only hope of achieving full third density in their own minds and in the minds of those who comfort them, is to achieve an incarnation of third density which is one dealing totally with privation. This is due to the feeling of tremendous guilt which comes to those who, as Hatonn's story demonstrated, cause the killing, more especially the killing of an entire planet. The balance is long, as you would say, in time, in coming. However, in time many things are healed, and yet always there must be the will of the entity to be healed, and often a great part of being healed is expiation for that for which one feels the guilt.

In this case, the answer is to offer up a third-density existence in full third density, and to die of starvation. There are not enough starving children for our needs.[1] As you might say, the point of view is everything. We, however, appreciate the feeling of this instrument. It is a work of compassion to care for those who are hungry, ill or in any way have lost the harmony of being which is the birthright of those who are fully conscious of the self. Each incarnation is, as this instrument would say, compounded daily so that experiences mount up, one upon another, and a more or less integrated incarnational experience is the result of the incarnational effort.

During the incarnation, which may be short or long, depending upon that which needs to be accomplished within the incarnation, things pleasant and things unpleasant shall occur. Those things which seem terrible and horrible and grotesque will occur to some, most of whom have no reason anyone could say to have deserved these things. Then there are the pleasant times and perhaps again the unpleasant encircling. The end of this experience is, as we have said, a whole in which there is to some extent a pattern or crystallization or regularization of experience.

Each of you has the job not of judging catalyst, but of using it, and in the compounding of use of it as you begin to find your choices of polarity and the speed with which you wish your evolution to proceed. You are looking for something that can be called clarity. Some entities achieve clarity in a soft and lucid manner, the regularization being so subtle and complex that the crystal being is more like water than stone. Others achieve a brilliant clarity which glistens like the gem. Those times when each of you feels muddied in thought are times in which it is well to [repeat] to the self these things which I have told you, in order to achieve the perspective and a balance.

We do not challenge your perceptions of pleasantness and unpleasantness, and we have compassion for the unpleasantness that each of you must experience and that is experienced in such an extreme fashion by those who die in war or starve or freeze. However, remember the goal is to process and balance catalyst.

We are very grateful to this group that we have been allowed to speak, and will now leave with many, many *tekel upharsin*[2]. Actually, that is somewhat appropriate, although there is no ["wall"] directly in the room, there are many thoughts of latter days. It is with many thanks that we leave this beloved group. We thank you for teaching us by your third-density humanity, by all of those things which in each of your hearts we see to be unselfish and positive, those things which others may not know you must struggle to give. Those are the most precious of your treasures. We bow and scrape and thank you, and with enormous joy leave you in the love and the light of the one infinite Creator. Adonai. Adonai. We are known to this group by the name of L/leema.

(Jim channeling)

I am Latwii, and am with this group in joy at the opportunity to present our humble service. We are third on the card tonight, my friends, and so happy to be here. We are pleased that you have been able to meet our brothers and sisters known to you as L/leema. We shall this evening, as always, attempt to answer those queries which you have brought with you and shall ask without further ado if we might begin with a query.

L: I've got one that's not certainly too significant on the surface, but I'd like to hear your thoughts about it. I enjoy fishing, which involves pulling some

---

[1] Carla: This fourth-density contact expresses here an opinion that seems most harsh and unloving in the extreme. However, from the standpoint of unrelieved compassion, which is the heart of fourth-density vibrations, the opportunity to help alleviate the tangle of fear and old error by giving up the self's soul stream to an incarnation in which this imbalance was taken head-on seems a wonderful one. As these souls come into incarnation aimed at the short life and difficult death of one who dies young by starvation, it surely looks completely different and not wonderful at all.

[2] Carla: "Mene, Mene Tekel, Upharsin," is the handwriting on the wall told of in the *Holy Bible*, Daniel 5: 25. He was speaking to the haughty King Balthazar, who had, among other things, lived lasciviously and worshipped clay gods. Its meaning in the Biblical context is "God hath numbered thy kingdom and finished it. Thou art weighed in the balance and found wanting." In the context of the channeling, it simply means the channeling is finished, and that those in the circle had been thinking about ascension.

creatures of this planet out of their natural environment both for sport and for food …

(Side one of tape ends.)

L: … Would you be willing to discuss the morality of fishing for me?

I am Latwii, and am aware of your query, my brother. Well, now, let's see. As we look upon the activities of the peoples of your planet, we see many, many experiences which are undertaken which seem to be of a very difficult and traumatic nature. For a large number of these entities within your illusion, we find that it is not possible to move with the experiences that present themselves to you without the seeming infringement upon the free will of another. As you continue to gather the experiences which are yours to gather, you will find that there comes to your mind, as has been the case in this instance, the considerations of whether one act or another is in the appropriate harmony, that is to say, considering the understanding which you have gathered and the experiences which you have encountered, is one act or another more or less preferable? Within this question, then, falls all potential activities including the one about which you have queried.

My brother, as you know, we cannot make such decisions for you. We look upon all actions of your peoples as the one Creator in search of Itself. We see this search as one of beauty and propriety, yet it is fueled by that which seems most difficult and traumatic, for within your illusion, there is not the clear knowledge of the one Creator existing in all things. Therefore, as you harvest your experiential crop, shall we say, and take within your mind and spirit the nourishment of that harvest, you shall determine for yourself the appropriateness of one action over another or perhaps the appropriateness of one action alone.

With this preface, shall we say, we may simply suggest that that activity of which you speak is one which has the potential of any activity upon your planet, that is, with the proper intention, and to you we leave the definition of "proper," the activity may be most beneficial to all concerned, including those who are the target of your hook and line. Yet with the thoughtless endeavor and motivation, the activity may be as any, that is, somewhat difficult, disturbing and traumatic to all concerned. Within these boundaries, then, you may place yourself according to your own motivations, my brother.

May we answer in any other way?

L: No, that's given me quite a bit to reflect upon. Thank you.

I am Latwii, and we thank you, as always, my brother. May we attempt another query?

Carla: Well, I'd like to follow up on that by asking if consciousness ascends during second density? In other words, I would say that fish had far less consciousness, in other words they are early second density, far less seeking for the light and far less seeking to grow and what not, and those food animals that we eat for the most part seem to be of that kind of dimwitted consciousness which doesn't seem to have much consciousness to it, or at least not much turning to the light or much response when interacting with humans. And in sharp distinction, the animals that are hunted for sport sometimes and not for being eaten, seem to have a beauty which seems to make it far more wrong, in other words, that you're killing much more actual life when you kill, say, a zebra or a magnificent lion—one of the nobler beasts, let's put it that way. Is there … Could you tell me if there is any truth in the idea that there is a gradation in the amount of searching towards the light in second density between animals?

I am Latwii, and am aware of your query, my sister. Though there is the thread of logic in your suppositions, yet we find you have supposed much which would take a great deal of untangling to clarify. We may suggest that in many cases there are those second-density creatures which are quite ennobled by the enspiriting, shall we say, which takes place from third density to second. This enspiriting is a process which can go beyond those boundaries which the domesticated animals and those serving as pets enjoy. There are many noble creatures, as you have called them, within the second density realm which are hunted and killed which then, through that opportunity, return again and continue their progress as third-density aspirants, that is, those of the second density with enhanced opportunity to achieve their own graduation, as we may call it.

We cannot from our point of view describe any particular action or relation of your peoples to these creatures as being right or wrong, for there is much, if not most, of your experience which is more and different than it seems at first glance. If you look at the killing of various animals as being wrong, perhaps it is from a certain point of view that does not see the larger picture. And yet, if one looks at this activity as being only right, then perhaps that is also the result of a limited point of view, for in truth, all of your activities have both the positive and negative potential existing within them. There is no activity that can be described as purely one polarity or another, for it is your intention that is of paramount importance.

We therefore cannot look upon an activity that includes the third-density entity and decide by simply observing the activity whether or not that activity is right or wrong, appropriate or inappropriate. We apologize for being unable to give a clear and concise answer in this area. We do hope, however, that you realize the difficulty of our position in commenting, for your third-density consciousness provides you with the motive for action and we cannot judge that motive in a general sense.

May we answer in any further way, my sister?

Carla: Yes. I appreciate your point of view, although I think our proclivities about fishing are all set and everybody in this room either fishes or doesn't fish already. Anyway. It seemed to me that what went by there was a second-density creature that was being killed was also being enspirited. Could you explain how this takes place?

I am Latwii, and am aware of your query, my sister. The very proximity of one creature to another creates a certain, as you have called it, action at a distance. This is true from the sub-atomic level to the macrocosmic level of galaxies and universes. As the creatures of your planet, both second and third density, co-inhabit your planet and engage in the activities of the hunter and the hunted, there is some small enspiriting that occurs as the second-density creature absorbs the attention that is focused in its direction and becomes in some degree made more aware of its own individuality, for it as an individual creature has attracted your attention, and if your attention reaches its mark then there is the closer interaction, for even a short period, that not only enspirits the creature to a small degree but in most cases gives the creature a chance either to be harvested or more likely to receive another physical vehicle through which it shall continue its journey of evolution. It is no accident, as you call it, that two life patterns cross and one pattern is given a chance to become transformed.

May we answer you further, my sister?

Carla: No, thank you.

I am Latwii, and we thank you, my sister. May we attempt another query?

N: Yes, Latwii. May I ask if the plains of Nazca, with all their diagrams and so forth, in Lima in Peru, were originally devised for religious significance, ceremonial significance, or sports?

I am Latwii, and am aware of your query, my brother. These constructions of a geographical nature were made for the purpose of expressing the spiritual aspirations of the people of their time. They were representations of various aspects of the one Creator which these people worshipped in their individualized form, seeing many gods about them and worshipping them by constructing these lines and hills which to a great degree have become eroded over the passage of time.

May we answer you further, my brother?

N: While they have become eroded in some instances, the majority of them seem to still be intact but can only be observed from the air. They really can't be interpreted at all from the ground. Can I ask what particular significance this was for the people of a spiritual nature?

I am Latwii, and am aware of your query, my brother. It is correct that from the air at this present time, one may make a, shall we say, coherent estimate of the outline of these constructions, and from the ground there is no possibility of ascertaining these coherent relationships. Yet may we suggest that you consider the passage of many thousands of years and the eroding effects that this time and weather have caused. At the time of these lines' construction there were mounds and hills where there are none now and these mounds and hills as a portion of this construction were perceivable from the ground level and were a portion of a coherent pattern from that ground level.

May we answer you further, my brother?

N: Yes, thank you. They also had what seemed to be fire pits at the end of some of the long runways. Were these to light the way or were they to perhaps inflate a balloon or were they for extraterrestrial guidance in any way?

I am Latwii, and am aware of your query, my brother. We find that these entities in their worship of various portions of the one Creator created rituals that were offered as, shall we say, sacrifices to these many god-like portions of the one Creator. In these rituals, various portions of the remaining lines and, as you have called them, pits and runways, then, each played a part. There were various rituals with the season and with the portion of the one Creator being worshipped.

May we answer you further, my brother?

N: No, thank you very much.

I am Latwii, and we thank you, my brother. Is there another query?

L: Yes, Latwii. To return to the subject of the animals for a few moments. If I understood you correctly, the proximity of people to the animals can have an effect upon them. It occurred to me that there some animals such as the wolverine that are regarded as being malevolent in nature, and have a tendency to destroy apparently for the pleasure of destruction. Is it possible for animals to have already developed polarity within their density, and is that polarity a result of contact with humans or is it something they've developed on their own?

I am Latwii, and am aware of your query, my brother. For the most part we must suggest that the second-density creatures are basically unable to develop that you know as the polarized consciousness, for their own consciousness is in the beginning stages of becoming individualized from those of its species—the herd, the school, the flock, and so forth are those types of mental and shared group mind experiences which such second-density creatures are native to. The ability to develop the polarized consciousness in any degree rests upon the foundation of an individualized consciousness to make this choice. Whether this choice is made consciously or unconsciously matters not. What matters is that there is an individualized choice.

The entities of which you speak, those seeming to act in more of an individualized fashion than many of its second-density brothers and sisters, does, however, partake of that same instinctual behavior that is the product of a group consciousness of a, shall we say, less developed nature rather than the kind of group consciousness towards which your own third-density population moves.

May we answer you further, my brother?

L: No, let me work on that one for a while. Thank you.

I am Latwii, and we thank you, my brother. Is there another query at this time?

N: Is the instrument still in good condition?

I am Latwii, and we find that this instrument has been doing his pushups and is in reasonably good shape, and may continue for some queries yet. May we attempt one of those queries?

N: I was just wondering if the Incas who formulated the plains in Nazca and used them for spiritual programs of one sort or another ever committed any of this to some form of writing, and is this form of writing or the program of the spiritual processions available if located?

I am Latwii, and am aware of your query, my brother. We find that these entities attempted in their own fashion to record those portions of their own spiritual seeking which they felt were most important, yet this writing was more of the form of characters or pictures and carvings which do indeed exist until this day. As you inhabit this planet, these drawings are not able to be interpreted by very many upon your planet, and for the most part there would be much lost in the translation by the few who would have any inkling of their meaning.

May we answer you further, my brother?

N: I assume that you mean those who would have the inkling of the meaning as those few remaining Incas or, shall we say, descendants of the Incas, who are presently making some various reed boats and things in the mountains of Peru and adjacent area?

I am Latwii, and this is in part correct, my brother. To this grouping of entities you may add those who have made it their work and purpose to study the cultures of those races of, as you have called them, Incas, that once inhabited that portion of the South American continent.

May we answer you further, my brother?

N: Where would one find the drawings or the carvings, and what kind of substance would they have used?

I am Latwii, and we may suggest that the substances used were primarily those of stone, occasionally those of wood and the by-product, a very crude form of paper. We cannot locate these artifacts, for this would be an infringement which we would not choose to inflict, shall we say.

May we answer you further?

N: *(Inaudible).*

I am Latwii, and we thank you, my brother. Is there another query?

Carla: I had the previous learned opinion that there was a very strong oral tradition among Indians of South America, and *(inaudible)*. Is this true?

I am Latwii, and at aware of your query, my sister. You are correct, and this is one of the difficulties that anyone attempting to study this culture encounters. We were attempting to answer the query concerning what might have been left of the written records, and these indeed are quite few, and, as a ratio, quite small when compared to the tradition of mouth-to-ear teaching, that is, of the oral nature.

May we answer you further, my sister?

Carla: Yes, just very briefly. The geometrical and other designs on the stones which are all over the place, they are just decorative, they're not intended to be code, is that correct?

I am Latwii, and we find that this is both correct and incorrect, for there is some attempt in all such artwork to reveal certain spiritual, as you may call them, principles according to the understanding of those of that culture. There is added to such encoding the design which is of itself merely aesthetic. It is for the, shall we say, researcher into this field to determine the identity of each kind of drawing and this also lends a degree of confusion in this regard.

May we answer you further, my sister?

Carla: But these pottery shards and all of the pottery is not a part of the written artifact left by that civilization, is that correct?

I am Latwii, and am aware of your query, my sister. This, again, is both correct and incorrect, for the culture of this group of people was a culture which was homogeneous, shall we say. Those principles which were considered of great importance, those of the spiritual, as you would call them, nature, permeated the entire culture so that all artifacts in some way or fashion reflected this understanding, yet within each artifact in its construction and design were added those aesthetic portions which did not have a direct, shall we say, coded meaning. Thus the culture was similar to your holograph—one portion could be examined and lend an understanding to the entire culture.

May we answer you further, my sister?

Carla: No. It's an interesting thought that a dress, say, could be part of the written language, any artifact made by man, and I certainly see the point. Thank you very much.

I am Latwii, and am aware that we have in some cases added a bit of confusion to our responses, and we do apologize. It is difficult to give a clear perception of another culture. It is much like speaking another language for the moment, yet in attempting to speak that other language, we must use a language which is not that language but which is understood by yet another culture at another time. We do beg your indulgence for our difficulty.

May we attempt another query at this time?

(Pause)

I am Latwii, and since to the best of our understanding the answer to silence is silence, we shall take our leave of this group, rejoicing in the opportunity to offer our humble service to each present. We thank you, my brothers and sisters, for offering your queries. They are the treasures and the joy of our sharing with you. We are those of Latwii, and we leave you now in the love and in the light which is always and ever the same, of the one Creator. Adonai vasu borragus. ☙

Sunday Meditation
May 12, 1985

(S channeling)

[I am Hatonn,] and we are pleased to greet you this evening in the love and in the light of the one infinite Creator. We are pleased to be with this instrument once again, for it has been some time since we have spoken through her. We are grateful for the opportunity. We come, as always, dear friends, when we hear your call, and we are always grateful for the opportunity to share our simple message.

The thought we send may seem at times complex, but the message all may be brought down to one simple phrase: that you shall love one another is one of the greatest services that you are able to provide to your fellow beings as you inhabit those physical vehicles that have become your temporary home; to look beyond that which is apparent but not always concrete, as this instrument would put it, and to see that essence which lies behind and beyond the physical; to look into each other's eyes and see the love and the light of the Creator reflected and to ignore that which is often a very convincing illusion. Strive to seek that which lies beneath and beyond the illusion, for the essence of the Creator may be seen in all and may be grasped and held and felt, reflected and returned. The wholeness is there, dear friends. Strive for that wholeness in what appears to be a world divided into portions.

We shall transfer at this time. I am Hatonn.

(Carla channeling)

I am Hatonn, and am now with this instrument. We attempted to contact the one known as A and the one known as N and were with the one known as R before we came to this instrument, and hope that you will bear with patience our method of taking an opportunity to attempt to offer our service to you.

We find that this instrument is having some reception trouble, however, we would greet you once again in the love and light of the infinite Creator and request that each in the circle continue to tune that we may have a good level of contact and that we may speak to you.

Have you ever observed, my friends, the younger of your species? The span of attention seems short and yet, for the few moments that something has absorbed a child's interest, it is completely absorbed. When one loves another, it is well to tune that spiritual love with the same intensity and purity with which the child watches the ant crawl over the stick and therefore almost becomes that experience. Each entity that you meet is a portion of the Creator, and yet, of course, many times this is anything but obvious. There is another purity within many children and that is the openness to ask direct questions. There seem to be no limits as to what may be asked, for the young child is completely interested in everything about you or whichever person the child questions.

This is an enormous secret, my friends. When there are difficulties between two entities, the difficulties are normally due to the lack of effort upon the part of the entities to imagine the creativity and accuracy, the actual situation and emotional and mental biases of the young.

To love one another, my friends—how much easier it is to talk about meditation and the discovery of what you may conceive to be creative; how much easier it is to speak of the one original Thought that lies within you within that deep, vast and dark silence. And yet you go through a variety of experiences within your lifetime which puts you in close proximity to a number of other entities. You still look at the Creator. The Creator wears a face as biased and full of self-contradictions as your own. How much more difficult it is to penetrate not only your own confusion but that of another and achieve communication. Yet this is an expression of love.

As the evening rays begin to fall upon your dwelling, you can feel before you the swelling maturity of the earth about you, the weighty roll of the waters onto the earth, and the majesty of the eternal sky. It is a wondrous creation and the silence of the Creator pervades it, deeper, more quiet, more peaceful than can be imagined outside of meditation. And yet, just as much a part of the Creator are all the sounds made by children, colleagues, wives, husbands, children and friends. Each is the voice of the Creator, filtered through many biases. There are times when two recognize each other and for a magical period of the incarnation there seem to be no biases, communication seems clear and life seems ebullient. It is rare that these periods extend throughout the incarnational experience. Nevertheless, we may suggest to each of you that memories of times when closeness had been achieved are very helpful in orienting the self towards the discovery of the biases that separate you from that same harmony at a more difficult time.

To love another is a challenge, and cannot be done without the inner underlying silence, the peace and poise of the powerful forces that unites you not only with each friend and mate and acquaintance, but with all of the creation.

As the light slowly fades from the skies and your sphere turns upon its rotating center into the zone of darkness and the kingdom of the moon and stars, we offer you meditation and love. We are known to you as Hatonn. We leave you, as always, in the love and the magnificent love of the one infinite Creator whom we serve with all of our beings. We find your heart bent toward the same original Thought, your hopes turned to the same star. Adonai, my friends. Adonai.

(Jim channeling)

I am Latwii, and we greet you, my friends, in the love and the light of our infinite Creator. We are once again overjoyed and honored to be asked to join your group. We shall, as is our custom, ask if we may serve by attempting to answer those queries which you have brought with you this evening. May we begin with the first query?

R: Yes, Latwii, I'd like to go back to something Hatonn spoke of earlier, and ask—it seems that our daughters, nine and six-year-olds, are much more—well, they're not really violent, but more aggressive, and it just seems hateful towards each other, and I remember being with my sisters, and the same for S with her brother and sister. I was wondering if you could comment on that?

I am Latwii, and am aware of your query, my brother. To some extent we may comment. We can suggest that as the time moves forward and approaches that which you have come to know as the harvest, there is to those who are sensitive to it an increased opportunity for expressing the energy, shall we say, of the one Creator. In each entity this energy will express in an unique fashion. This will be determined by the entity's, shall we say, distortions or tendencies, those characteristics which make each entity unique and those characteristics which each entity seeks to balance in some fashion in order that it might learn and serve as it has incarnated to do.

The entities of which you speak are most sensitive to any presence or energy, and in their perception of this greater available resource of energy, each has channeled it in a fashion which meets the design of the personality. The design of any personality is that which is the preincarnative choice and pattern. These choices in many cases are made as a result of previous experiences together. These previous incarnational experiences then have a harvest which becomes the seed for the next incarnation. When one observes certain behaviors within an entity, or in this particular case, between two entities, it is possible, though not always the case, that the expression of energy and relationship between these entities is due in some degree to previous incarnational experience and current incarnational balancing.

May we attempt further clarification, my brother?

R: That was most helpful. I wonder, how do we respond when they're at each other's throats? Just keep them from hurting each other, and pull them apart, or is there more going on there that we should know about?

I am Latwii, and am aware of your query, my brother. You speak now of what we may metaphorically call the firing line, the heat of the battle, those portions of the incarnation in which the ideals are tested and in some cases formed. As you look upon your own incarnational pattern of lessons and services, you will see that you have before you a pattern of experience which has the desired result in its foundation to express love, to express and experience acceptance, to express and experience forgiveness, and so forth with the various characteristics of that energy known as love. In any such experience, whether it be with the children of whom you speak, with your friends, with acquaintances, or with strangers, you have the ideal constructed within your inner mind in a fashion which is to the best of your ability whole and perfect. To translate this construction of the ideal into the daily experience and those testings of the ideal we have called the firing line or the heat of the battle, is the challenge before you.

In your particular case, not only do you have this challenge before you, in your response in answering such a challenge [you] set a pattern for those of whom you speak. This pattern is your model or role of excellence. These young entities will learn from you according to what you do. Therefore, it is upon your shoulders, shall we say, to creatively fashion that response which most purely reflects your ideals, those guide posts and high metaphysical standards which you have as your own staff to support you on your journey. You, then, must in your own way construct the response which will in a disciplined fashion teach by repetition that concept of love as you can perceive it and translate it in this case.

May we attempt further response, my brother?

R: No, Latwii, that was most helpful. Thank you very much.

I am Latwii, and we thank you, my brother, for the opportunity to serve. May we attempt another query?

Carla: When a childhood experience is full of harmonious relationships between sister and brother, and the harmony continues throughout the life experience, sometimes bearing fruit, such as my brother's and my singing, could it also be considered to be preincarnative choice of being together?

I am Latwii, and am aware of your query, my sister. This is quite correct. Each entity as it incarnates has those souls with whom it has traveled many journeys through many of what you call incarnational lifetimes. Each entity then will make agreements with a variety of others and these agreements will allow certain relationships to develop certain characteristics to be expressed, certain lessons to be learned and certain services to be offered. Therefore, the relationships between entities upon your planet at this time are many and varied, infinite in variety and full of the opportunity for sharing the love and light of the one Creator.

May we attempt further response, my sister?

Carla: No, thank you.

I am Latwii, and we thank you, as always, my sister. Is there another query?

Carla: Can a plan go wrong?

I am Latwii, and we may respond to this query by saying yes and no. We do not mean to confuse—let us clarify. To begin with, yes, a plan may unfold its outline and its specific experience in a manner other than that which was planned, yet it cannot be said to be wrong, for each entity in each experience may observe the infinite opportunity to learn the lesson of love. In some degree all plans will incorporate this lesson and will reflect this lesson in an unique fashion. When a plan has deviated from the course laid before the incarnation, there are, shall we say, certain fail-safe devices, as we may use this term, which also have been incorporated that have the hoped-for effect of bringing the plan once again back into congruency with that which was determined before the incarnation. There are an infinite number of these devices which are preprogrammed, and there are an infinite number of opportunities for the incarnational entity to utilize these devices or to ignore them, for, indeed, within the incarnation, free will needs that which you may call determinism, and the incarnation then becomes a balance between these two forces.

May we answer you further?

Carla: Is the will of the individual superior to any preincarnatively determined path?

I am Latwii, and am aware of your query, my sister. We may suggest the will can be superior to any preprogrammed plan, yet it must be remembered that the will as it is manifested in each incarnation is colored, shall we say, or influenced by the preplanned pattern of experience, and is unlikely to vary from it in an absolute manner for a very long portion of what you would call time.

May we answer you further, my sister?

Carla: I don't think so, I'll just tell you what was on my mind, and that was I've been pondering whether Don Elkins' death, his leaving this plane of existence, was his plan or his deviation from a plan. There isn't anything in my experience by which I can judge the answer to this. And by what you're saying, I would say the bias would go towards there being at least a portion of Don's dying and going on that was part of the plan. This is the kind of bias you're talking about, is this not correct?

I am Latwii, and am aware of your query, my sister. It is correct that the one known as Don had incorporated within his incarnational experience before it began the opportunity to cease viability within your illusion in a number of ways. It may be that this entity had not precisely planned to exit the incarnation in the manner in which it did indeed find its exit, yet one may rest assured that there are no mistakes, though the surprise may be most disturbing at the time. It is most usual for one to leave a dwelling through a door rather than through a window.

May we answer you further, my sister?

Carla: No. No, thank you very much.

I am Latwii, and we thank you, my sister. Is there another query at this time?

Carla: I have a question that is on a totally different subject, but I've been pondering it off and on. Some people can see auras around people's heads, especially, but [also] around their whole bodies. And I've wondered for a long time whether people were seeing inner dimensional but real in the other dimension colors and the natural force of the body or whether the gift of clairvoyance had its focus in such people in seeing color around a person instead of, say, seeing a reading from a Tarot card throw or from a look into a glass ball or from tea leaves or from whatever other focus that people use? In other words is it an objective or subjective phenomenon?

I am Latwii, and am aware of your query, my sister. This phenomenon of the seeing that which you have called the aura may be a combination of that which you have called a subjective experience and objective observation. We may suggest that to each entity within your illusion is given the opportunity to use the infinite intelligence, the energy of the one Creator. Many will manifest it in a great variety of ways, some in a few ways, and others will attempt perhaps in an unconscious fashion to use this energy in an unmanifested and more metaphysical sense, showing little manifestation of that all-encompassing love and light of the one Creator. When an entity experiences one of the manifested means of channeling this energy, one may see this manifestation as an aside, shall we say, to the primary seeking for truth behind all manifestation.

Within your illusion it has become, shall we say, somewhat the fashion to manifest this channeled energy in some fashion which may be observable. The seeing of the auric force field about your other selves is one such means of manifesting this energy. What is seen is most usually the combination or balance of energy centers which have cooperatively provided coloration or vibratory energy in their channeling of this energy, and the result is that which, in general, is called the auric field. The entity so seeing this auric field sees through eyes which are both inner and outer in their manifested sense. That is to say, the entity sees with a mind which has been conditioned in such and such a fashion, and sees with an inner eye which explores for the first time that which is seen as the aura. Therefore, that which is objectively observed is subjectively interpreted, and those having the aura read then receive this combined objective and subjective interpretation.

May we answer you further, my sister?

Carla: Well, it seems that if perceiving auras is a matter of perceiving various rates of vibration, there would be color surrounding a lot things, notably music. Sometimes I think I can feel the color of music as it varies from piece to piece, from artist to artist, but there are people that go around talking about that sort of aura. Is it because of the fact that there is no personal consciousness in that art form, in that artifact?

I am Latwii, and, my sister, we may suggest that it is indeed a greatly crowded and varied universe including the small portion of it which is your third-dimensional experience. There are, indeed, entities who experience your third-density illusion in just the fashion which you have described. Yet this description is not ordinarily accepted as a representation of that which is. Therefore, one does not hear so much of this kind of description …

(Side one of tape ends.)

(Jim channeling)

I am Latwii, and am once again with this instrument, and we shall continue. There are many, many ways in which the experience of your illusion may be expressed, and if the hearts of all those who experience in an unusual manner were known, one would indeed be surprised at the great variety which is available to your peoples.

May we answer you further, my sister?

Carla: No, thank you Latwii.

I am Latwii, and we thank you once again, my sister. Is there another query?

(Pause)

I am Latwii, and we find that for the evening we have exhausted the queries and perhaps one or two of the listeners. We apologize if any of our words have seemed too long and our sentences too rambling. We do not mean to overburden the listener with a great quantity of verbiage, but we are most privileged and overjoyed to speak to this group, and we thank you each and every one for inviting us this evening. We shall, therefore, take our leave at this time of this instrument and this group, leaving you, as always, in the love and light of our one infinite Creator. We are those of Latwii. Adonai, my friends. Adonai vasu borragus.

(Carla channeling)

I Yadda. I greet you in love and light of infinite Creator. Once again we passed the challenge. Once again we speak to you, for we are called to this meeting. And yet, we tell you something. We are nothing. We are fools. We are full of error and mistake, folly and fun. We are mostly full of a fun which amounts to enlightenment. We pass from folly to joy. Not because we have learned wisdom, steps to take, rituals to practice. No, we find ourselves.

We come to you to make you happy. To show you through our speaking that there is a wonder and a magic and a lightheartedness that causes us to be full of joy. We are aware that we have spoken in groups which were so tuned that we made not so much of the sense, but, oh, we enjoyed the laughter. For you see, you come for inspiration. You come to be lifted up. You come to experience something that you feel that those who speak through instruments such as one may have. You wish to partake in that. And yet, we go away; the meeting ends and you go to your own domicile, to your own joy, to your own fun, or to the denial of this life force that is so great in each. Your joy is hidden in your very nature. Your inspiration is within you. You call us, but we are nothing. Your outside life, it is but nothing. But if your heart can be happy, if you can laugh, if you can find joy, you have flown on the wings of the eagle, and there are no more prison bars in your life and in your experience. All we ask you, do not take the husk so seriously. Find the kernel of infinity which lies within you.

We are sorry that we must sometimes speak to one group, for one group, in a way which does not please another. We assure you this information would not please some, when there are so many spiritual seekers who sure, positive, and without any doubt know that if they can find the right teacher, if they can find the right ritual, the right outward behavior, enlightenment will come. We tell you what come: day come and night and day and night and soon your life is over. You live in love and light. It is your natural habitat. Your darkness is as noon, and above the rain shines the everlasting sun.

We leave you in joy, in light, in love, in possession of your birthright. We Yadda. Farewell. ☥

L/L Research

L/L Research is a subsidiary of Rock Creek Research & Development Laboratories, Inc.

P.O. Box 5195
Louisville, KY 40255-0195

www.llresearch.org

Rock Creek is a non-profit corporation dedicated to discovering and sharing information which may aid in the spiritual evolution of humankind.

ABOUT THE CONTENTS OF THIS TRANSCRIPT: This telepathic channeling has been taken from transcriptions of the weekly study and meditation meetings of the Rock Creek Research & Development Laboratories and L/L Research. It is offered in the hope that it may be useful to you. As the Confederation entities always make a point of saying, please use your discrimination and judgment in assessing this material. If something rings true to you, fine. If something does not resonate, please leave it behind, for neither we nor those of the Confederation would wish to be a stumbling block for any.

CAVEAT: This transcript is being published by L/L Research in a not yet final form. It has, however, been edited and any obvious errors have been corrected. When it is in a final form, this caveat will be removed.

© 2009 L/L Research

Sunday Meditation
May 19, 1985

(Carla channeling)

I am Yadda. I greet you in the love and in light of infinite Creator. We have difficulty deciding how to arrange meeting. Each want another person to speak. We all must speak briefly. I shall not therefore take up much of the time, that priceless commodity. Yet time is what you came here to take up.

Statement made earlier this evening, "Are feelings hurt because of comments about us?" First, no feelings to hurt. We do our best to share with those who have a legitimate metaphysical interest. When one does the best, then one is not apologetic. Moreover, is to be noted in the way the channeling works that the nature of the group vibration and the desires and level of the group together maintain the approach that we use to speak. You come here to spend time, yet each moment you spend time you come here, you spend time seeking the truth. Yet, each moment you can seek the truth. If we are a focus for the truth, that is all that can be hoped. However, never forget that you are the guardians of your own truth. That is why the question, "Who are you?" is so central. Seek well, my friends. We glad to speak with you. We come in the love and the light, in the indwelling nature of all that is the Creator. Adonai.

(Carla channeling)

I am L/Leema. We greet you in the love and in the light of our infinite Creator. We would like to confirm to the one known as A that we were attempting to adjust our vibrations to that instrument's vocal mechanism. However, we are clumsy and new to this and we apologize for the discomfort we may have caused the instrument. We also feel the need for briefness, not because we wish to be the soul of wit, but because there may be substantial questions and we wish to make room for them.

However, there is one point which seems to be worth making at this juncture for those in this group. That, my friends, is that you are all chosen. We work with third-density individuals which are not aware to full extent of their selfhood, of their specialness, of their being chosen, yet they, too, are chosen and have been since before you can imagine, before there was time, before there was any created thing. Older than all the galaxies are the souls that move through levels of consciousness within those galaxies. More experience do you have in yourself than does this planet or the star which warms it. Many, shall we say, consciousness groups inadvertently foster an elitism based upon a truth which is seen but not comprehended logically, and that is that each person who believes in the ideals of love and service is chosen, is special, is anointed or passed by special vows, and that this specialness is a metaphysical and enduring specialness enduring far beyond what you think of on the surface as life. You may see those who have almost no consciousness at all apparently, and those whose consciousnesses, though competent, do not admit metaphysics. Yet these are not those who are lost forever; these are those who are learning a different lesson, taking a different road, going more slowly. There is time enough for all of consciousness which has been created to fully tap the birthright of that consciousness.

There is no elite, my friends. There is in truth only in relative time, as you know it, the so-called remnant. There are no permanent wailers and gnashers of teeth, as this instrument would put it. All shall be made one. For some it will take more cycles of experience than others. Those who speed up their experience speed up both the pain and the joy of that experience, for in using catalyst completely those side effects will occur. We wish you the fullness and richness of that joy and the understanding of pain which it contains.

And we leave you now through this instrument, secure in the knowledge that you shall not judge our words to be perfect or our thoughts to be riveting. We are merely those in converse with you, not those who truly teach. We are comrades of the same road; we are in fact, your own selves. There is no boundary. Take what you wish for inspiration and leave the rest. We shall transfer.

(Jim channeling)

I am L/Leema, and we are pleased to have successfully transferred our contact to this instrument, and we greet you once again in love and light, my friends. We are hopeful that we may be able to answer a few of your queries this evening and with that hope in our hearts, may we ask if we may begin with the first query?

A: L/Leema, I have two questions. The first one, in going through life people deal with fear, and with fear comes in hand worry and also doubt. And I was wondering what some of the opposites of doubt would be. Could you comment on this?

I am L/Leema, and we are happy to give our efforts in the comment, my sister. The doubt which springs from the fear of which you have spoken has as its balancing factor elements which are not contained within your third-density experience when we speak of metaphysical surety and the understanding which erases all doubt. Within your illusion, it is necessary that the seeker move within a darkness of knowing, that is, that the seeker shall move by the motivations of the power of will and faith and shall not have, shall we say, even one small shred of irrefutable proof, for in your illusion the choice of paths must be made as a function of your free will.

To offer proof—for proof to be available to any seeker, then, is to bias that free will and to reduce the potential power of the will and the faith that shall continue to motivate the seeker after it has been, shall we say, graduated from your illusion.

May we attempt a more clarified response, my sister?

A: No, that was fine, that's kind of what I've been thinking; its been a topic of conversation. Another thing that we'd been discussing was the similarities and the contrast between the words transmit and translate. We were kind of interested in your point of view on what the differences were.

I am L/Leema, and we hope that our ability to define these terms may be adequate to your needs. To transmit is, in our perception, to relay a message in the exact form in which it has been given. To translate, then, is an effort which seeks to, shall we say, share a perception which is not understandable in one form by means of placing it in another form and thereby altering or distorting to some degree the message. The former term contains no potential for distortion; the latter, however, contains great potential for such distortion, depending upon the entity's ability at the sharing of perceptions.

May we answer further, my sister?

A: Hmmm. I can't think of the way to word the question I have, so it's going to have to do for right now.

I am L/Leema, and we thank you, my sister, for your queries and your patience with our responses. May we attempt another query?

J1: What kind of a name is L/Leema?

I am for the moment that name, L/Leema, and this is a name which we have chosen for its personalized connotation to this particular group, for within this group there are those who have for a large portion of their incarnation pursued a path of seeking and sharing the love and light of the one Creator, and who have therefore chosen their own name to reflect this service. We, in our choosing of a name to use with this group, sought to harmonize our service to this group with the service that this group has chosen to offer.

May we answer further, my brother?

J1: Thank you.

I am L/Leema, and we shall add one small point, and that is that we are not normally known by name, for the naming concept is not one which many entities utilize. It is quite popular, we find, within your own illusion, thus we use it as well, and have tailored our use of it to this group, the first through which we speak.

May we attempt another query at this time?

N: May I ask if L/Leema will transmit to other groups, will he also use the same name and why was it just particularly adapted for our group?

I am L/Leema. We have chosen this name for this group for the reasons given in our previous response, and should we have the honor of speaking with another group of seekers upon your planet, we shall utilize a name which suits that particular group while offering the information that we have spoken through another group while utilizing another name. Thus we shall hopefully remove confusion amongst those entities through which we speak.

May we answer further, my brother?

N: Well, as stated earlier that we were all chosen for this group, is that because we're a rather homogeneous group or because there is a certain amount of variance within each individual entity?

I am L/Leema. My brother, look at that statement: "You have been chosen." Now—who has done the choosing? That you were chosen is obvious, but we did not state who had done the choosing. We made this statement in hopes that not only would it be asked to us, "Who had been chosen and why?" but that each should ask this of itself. As you have moved into the incarnation, you have set for yourself certain possibilities, certain services and lessons that are the purpose of your incarnation. Much you have chosen, much you have laid in store for yourself. That you shall find yourself within various groups is no accident. This is the primary fact which we wished to illustrate by suggesting that you had been chosen.

May we answer further, my brother?

N: No, thank you very much. Do you mean we all knew each other in another lifetime?

I am L/Leema, and, my brother, may we strike to the heart of this concept and suggest that not only do you know each other on the surface level of incarnational experience, but each is the other.

May we answer further, my brother?

N: Thank you.

I am L/Leema, and we thank you, my brother.

J2: I have a question that was given to me by some friends. They've been experiencing some pain and confusion and asked for some help in dealing with a sense of loss in things like changing life situations—death of a pet, death of a parent, and so on.

I am L/Leema, and we are happy to attempt to respond to this most central experience which each upon your planet experiences at some point within the incarnation. As you gather about you those friends, positions, opportunities, ideas, locations and possessions with which you identify and feel a connection of love and purpose, you gather about you those factors, shall we say, which give you support upon your journey. As you become the conscious seeker of truth, the journey most frequently becomes a lonely process. Friends, family, locations, ideas and so forth are the friendly confines or furnishings of one's mind and experience that give the seeker reassurance when times are difficult and give the seeker joy when times are happy. Yet, at various moments, the seeker will lose, through perhaps a seeming random accident or chance occurrence, a friend, a loved one, a valued possession, a position, a home. These are the tests, shall we say, that all shall face and which shall present the seeker with the inner question of what truly supports and sustains the seeker's life and what is the life that passes so quickly in but a moment when it seemed so solid and sure.

These losses are central motivations, shall we say, provocations indeed, for the seeker to look deeper within its own being for the answers to these questions that become undeniably apparent when loss occurs. Then the seeker must seek with such an intensity and such a desire that the commensurate truth is drawn unto it. Thus, the seeker presents itself through such trauma with the opportunity to see the unity of all things that does not allow true loss in any degree. The seeker also sees the motion of experience that includes the seeming losses and gains of small and great magnitude, that these losses and gains are but the illusion of the One moving in and out of one's life, that indeed, One, as the Creator, is the One as the seeker and this One teaches each of Its portions to yearn for It, to treasure It, to experience It, and through all such experiences of loss and of gain does the seeker then piece together the puzzle of its own existence.

May we answer further, my sister?

J2: Yes, thank you. I want to really thank you for that answer, that will help a lot. I have another question and that is about the feeling and the experience of separation that comes from both separation between people and within a person, feeling a sense of loss of self. Can you speak to dealing with feelings of separation?

I am L/Leema, and we are happy, my sister, to speak to this point. Your illusion in its very basic nature is a fine example of separation or that which seems to be separated, for within your illusion, do not each entity and grouping of entities seem to be quite separate, one from the other? Do you not have the trees and the sky and the ground and the seas and mountains and the valleys and the cities and the cars and the trains and the planes which move, separate, one from the other? Is there any true unity within your illusion? Is there any possibility for finding a unifying purpose within your illusion?

It would seem to many of your peoples that there is only separation, one entity from another, one group from another, one continent from another, one type of this or that from another, and indeed, within an entity, one desire separate from another, one way of thinking at one time separate from another. Throughout your illusion, separation seems the only verifiable fact. Indeed, so powerful is this illusion that many pass an entire incarnation without finding even a small degree of the unity of thought which binds all things within each portion of your illusion. Yet, my sister, the concept of separation is a great opportunity to learn the balancing concept of unity. That portion of your experience which seems separate, quite unaligned with any other portion, is that portion which offers the greatest of opportunities to find the unity which binds together all portions of your experience.

Thus it is so with the concept of separation, where 'ere it may be found. As you see any such concept placed before your notice, you may note within your mind that there is a polar opposite concept awaiting your discovery just, shall we say, behind the one which seems apparent.

May we answer further, my sister?

J2: No, thank you, that was really helpful.

I am L/Leema, and we thank you, my sister. Is there another query?

N: Yes. It has been said that we can keep open all the switches but unless we're plugged into the generator, we're not going to turn on, so to speak. And in that respect, how do we, shall we say, turn on to the fact that there is a complete unity when we are at least separate at this particular moment or how do we become more progressed in the Law of One?

I am L/Leema, and, my brother, may we suggest that each of you is indeed, "plugged in" to the generator. There is no true separation; there is no true removal of your plug from the power source. Each of you has, however, chosen a path of conscious realization of the one Power which generates all creation. You have placed before yourselves a unique means by which you shall, shall we say, "throw your own switch," and illumine your own being. Each is unique, for each of you has had a great many incarnational experiences through which you have gained certain biases, tendencies, characteristics. You have learned a great variety of lessons in a unique manner and in this present incarnation, you seek then to complete lessons which you have left undone and to balance those biases which you have developed previously.

Thus, each has a unique journey that leads to the same point, the same source of power that is found in all portions of creation. Each day you partake in a sacred experience, the experience of your own life. Though mundane it may seem at the time, this is not truly the case. There is great joy imminent in every moment if you will but look deeply enough; there is the unification of all portions of your experience possible if you but search within your own being for the point of viewing which allows this unity to be seen. …

(Side one of tape ends.)

(Jim channeling)

I am L/Leema, and as we have finished our response, may we ask if there is a further response which we may attempt?

N: Well, may I ask if it is the lot, shall we say, of those of us in third density on this particular physical plane to experience difficulty even though we more or less understand the path of love and light and light and love and the Law of One, yet it is more difficult for some of us to follow that path and, not in our thinking or understanding, but in our everyday life—such as when someone who does something deliberately, like, pulls in front of you in a car—you lose this tendency to love, and sometimes, in other instances—it occurs when someone deliberately steps on your toes, figuratively speaking, of course—we can with only great difficulty, and sometimes not even then, follow the path of love and light and light and love of the one infinite Creator. Would you address this particular point or speak to this fact?

I am L/Leema, and we are happy to, my brother. It is true that it is the lot, as you have said, of entities upon your planet and within this illusion to experience that which seems most difficult, for how else shall you test your own ability to express the love and light of the one Creator. The journey that you are upon is one that has no end, thus you must continue in some way to provide yourselves with further opportunities to develop this potential to love all entities and to see light within all experience. If you have no such difficulties, then these abilities would remain at a given level with no further opportunity for enhancement.

Within your illusion that which seems difficult, that which seems unforgivable, that which seems unacceptable, are those experiences which test your strength to love those who seem unlovable and to forgive that which seems unforgivable. Thus, you are as the one who lifts the weight: as the strength is gained, further weight must be added if further strength is desired. When you have passed from this illusion and you look back upon it and thumb through your own book of life, you will have quite a different point of view. You will see those times which seemed most difficult as being of the greatest opportunity to love, and those times then will seem as great treasures, whereas now they seem as they seem as great burdens. It is all a matter of the point of view, my brother. You have the narrower point of view now in order that you may test and strengthen your ability to widen this point of view.

May we answer you further, my brother?

N: Thank you. I understand this particular concept, but even though I understand it, I can't seem to overcome it when it occurs, particularly in driving and so forth when there is some thoughtless gesture, or some deliberate gesture, I should say. Yet I understand what you've expressed. Is some of this a result of some karma from past life or is it, when you understand it, why can you not follow it more easily after repeated experiences?

I am L/Leema, and, my brother, we do not wish to annoy you by suggesting that none upon your planet understands love. We may suggest that there is a great difference between intellectually knowing and being able to explain a concept and actually becoming that concept. Each of you attempts to become that which you believe or feel that you know with your rational minds. Yet, until love has found its roots within the heart of your being, you cannot truly know love. Each of you seeks to know love and you have consciously sought such for a great portion of time and may feel that you understand, yet understanding is not of your illusion; it is that which you seek.

May we answer further, my brother?

N: Well, thank you very much. I can understand what you've said. May I ask a question about—it is said that the Maldekians had a great deal of difficulty in interrelating with our particular third-density physical plane. May I ask what the Maldekians—what their appearance was like, their physical appearance?

I am L/Leema, and, my brother, these entities were much like your own third density in their physical appearance. The choice of this particular sub-logos under whose care you reside for the third-density physical vehicle has been without exception the bipedal erect ape-like form, and those who inhabited the planetary influence of what you have called Maldek had much the same culture and experience as you find now upon your own planet. Indeed, many of these entities now work as third-density entities upon your own planet to alleviate or balance those actions which they set in motion upon their own home planet before its destruction.

May we answer you further, my brother?

N: No, thank you. I'm sure someone else has some questions.

I am L/Leema, and we thank you, my brother. Is there another query?

A: How is the instrument doing?

I am L/Leema, and we find that this instrument is available for another few queries. It has some difficulty in its posture, shall we say, but shall be able to respond through the next few queries. May we attempt such at this time?

A: Well, I had a question that popped in earlier, I don't know where it came from but, but it's just—how is the harvest coming?

I am L/Leema, and we cannot give any definitive response to this query, for upon your planet at this time there are many who are, shall we say, varying in their polarization around the level which is necessary for graduation. There are upon your planet many moves, many directions of energy and choices inherent in these energy movements that can influence great numbers of people. Therefore, we cannot give any definitive response to this query and apologize for our inability.

May we answer in any further capacity?

A: Well, actually you gave a pretty definitive answer to what I was asking. Thanks.

I am L/Leema, and we are grateful to have been able to serve. Is there another query at this time?

N: In relationship to Amy's question. There was a consideration for a thought about the harvest in that before the fifth ecumenical council in Nicaea, called Nicaean, Constantinople, in, I think it was 553 AD, there was much talk about reincarnation and even in Christ's teaching—at the Fifth Ecumenical Council it was deleted from the bible. Has this affected the harvest and how great has been the effect on those who would have considered reincarnation in the Western world?

I am L/Leema, and am aware of your query, my brother. We find that the concept of reincarnation is a concept which allows an entity to view with a greater scope the forces which form one's present experience. Yet, when this concept is absent within an entity's thinking, those forces yet remain in motion and the opportunities that these forces provide an entity are yet viable. Thus, as a concept in itself, it is of small value in the actual process of evolution. Those entities who were of the authority or upper echelon levels of the church at that time felt that entities would work more diligently within a lifetime if it were not known that future lifetimes were available to complete work left undone in the present lifetime. Though this is a choice which is a basic infringement upon the free will of others, it has had some effect in the causing of entities to work with that desired diligence.

May we answer you further, my brother?

N: Well, thank you. I assume at that time … is the instrument still in good shape?

I am L/Leema, and we find that this instrument is more comfortable at this time. May we attempt further queries?

N: At the time that the Council of Nicaea deleted this from the bible, I assume that all bibles were handwritten, and, as such, is there any interpretation in any bible that does have all of Christ's teaching of reincarnation or other teachings of reincarnation?

I am L/Leema. You are correct, my brother, in your assumption that at that time those few bibles which were available were written by hand. It is also to be stated that these bibles were most usually possessed by those elders and priests of the church who were able to read and were, shall we say, in charge of the members of the church and their spiritual teaching which was done orally. Thus, there are very, very few remaining copies of such bibles, and none to be found or available to the current researcher, for it is difficult to preserve those pages upon which such scriptures were recorded over great periods of your time which have passed since that council.

May we answer further, my brother?

N: It has been said that once we have been introduced in whatever way to our spirit guides that we become more and more aware. Is this true, and in what way can we accelerate this introduction?

I am L/Leema, and, my brother, we can state that as you continue to seek the one Creator and unity of all things, you shall become more and more aware, as you have stated. It is not necessary to speak with those unseen or to have communications of this variety in order to become more aware of your process of seeking. To desire such knowledge and experience is all that is necessary, for it has been written in that holy work previously mentioned that as you seek, you shall find; as you ask, it shall be answered; and as you knock, the doors shall be opened, for this is a law of the universe which functions without exception, for that which you seek is within your own being. You are all things.

May we answer further, my brother?

N: Thank you very much.

I am L/Leema, and we thank you, my brother.

J2: Can you say anything about the history of the moon? Did it used to be a planet?

I am L/Leema, and we may say, my sister, that according to one's definition, the moon at this time is a planet. It is not usually described as such within any of your cultures, for there is no known life as you know it upon this sphere and it itself revolves about your own planet, and by so doing, according to most views, then relegates itself to the stature of a lesser body. This body, however, is inhabited from time to time by entities of other dimensions and serves as an entity in its own right that proceeds through its own process of evolution in its close connection with your own Earth influence.

May we answer you further, my sister?

J2: No, thank you.

I am L/Leema, and we thank you, my sister. We find that we have in this instrument the energy left for another query before closing. Is there such a query at this time?

Carla: I'd like to just ask a question about meditation. I noticed that in all of the discussion this evening there wasn't any discussion of meditation—no one was talking about how to speed up the process of manifesting what one intellectually is. I wondered if that was because this particular group was already doing it or because some people are ill-suited to meditation but well-suited to contemplation or what?

I am L/Leema, and, my sister, we are most grateful to you for reminding not only this group but our own humble selves of the great necessity and benefit of meditation, for as you move within your illusion and as we move within ours and as any entity would move within any illusion, the fruit of such movement can only nourish the heart of one's being when one has drunk of it deeply to the core of one's being through the process of meditation. That which the conscious mind has placed within its own boundaries of understanding has value to an entity in the metaphysical or spiritual sense only insofar as the meditative state has incorporated this small understanding into the heart of one's being. Otherwise, one is as the—we find you call it—duck that sheds the water from its back.

Without the meditation, the various concepts and ideas with which one comes in association in the conscious seeking, there are no roots formed and no lasting connections to such concepts, and the entity then must reacquaint itself with that which is consciously sought in order to provide the opportunity once again for meditation to do its work. Meditation is as the watering of the plant which has been set in fertile ground. The plant must be good, it must be strong, it must be consciously formed and analyzed, it must be placed within the fertile ground, the intuition must then serve as the analog to the fertile ground and connect through meditation the concept with the inner being or heart of one's being. This is the watering and the nourishing of the plant that was consciously formed. Thus, in meditation one is as the gardener, plucking those weeds and leaving the flowers and the fruit that shall form the harvest.

May we answer further, my sister?

Carla: No, thank you.

I am L/Leema, and we thank you, my sister. We find that we have, for this particular instrument, reached the limits of our ability to speak without undue fatigue. We are grateful to each for once again requesting our presence. We hope that you will continue to have patience with us as we learn to utilize these instruments without undue fatigue resulting. We are with each of you at your request in your meditations and shall be honored to join you at any time in your futures that you may request our presence. We leave you now in the love and light of our infinite Creator. We are L/Leema. Adonai vasu borragus. ❧

L/L Research

Sunday Meditation
May 26, 1985

(Carla channeling)

I am Hatonn, and I greet you in the love and the light of the one infinite Creator. We thank you most heartily for allowing us to share this meditation with you, and are overwhelmed by the pleasant peacefulness that seems to surround your domicile. We are working with this instrument one word at a time and, therefore, there may be pauses. We apologize for the pauses, but there is some gain in accuracy in working in this manner, although it leaves the instrument without any idea of what is to follow, not even one concept ahead, and therefore it is not often attempted until the instrument has had some experience.

Jupiter or Jove is no longer worshipped. The great interrelationships that held so much meanings in cultures and mythologies other than your own are no more, except in the lasting bounds of literature, poetry and so on. Yet, it is often a good and worthwhile thing to gaze back upon other cultures' seeking for the truth, others' seeking for definition of who they are and what the nature of the world in which they live is. Indeed, it is helpful to gaze at your own culture in this way. You might move ten thousand of your years into the future in your mind and then gaze back at the passion and the majesty of the Jewish and the Christian saga. Much would be put in perspective, both about the nature that the saga teaches that man truly is and about the nature of the world in which man lives.

This is similarly so of any of the other current belief systems. There are those in any culture who have the capacity financially to do precisely what they wish. What many wish to do is to skim the surface of their lives as if the conscious mind were a frozen pond and the waters beneath too dangerous to examine. There are those who do not wish to cook and so they go to restaurants and eat other people's cooking. It is possible that the same food cooked carefully and in small portions, might taste better made at home, but it is not the quality of the food that interests those who go to restaurants as much as the convenience and the lack of personal labor involved in the ingesting of someone else's food. Such is the nature of any dogmatic religion.

The believer chooses to accept a spiritual food which has been prepackaged for convenience. In a dogmatic religion, the questions are ever-fresh, but the answers are often unsatisfying if one wishes to prowl to the extent of looking beneath the surface for the answer. We disclaim any criticism of your religions for it is in the cradle of systematized religious knowledge that those young souls who come into third density thirsting for spiritual truth are given the greatest chance of making contact with themselves in a spiritual sense at a young enough age that the self may eventually use all the knowledge of organized religion to gain courage to take the plunge beneath the surface thought.

Do you long, then, for the Greek mythology? Do you still gaze hopefully at the enchanted glades of yesteryear, awaiting the dryads to peek out from the trees and the nymphs to smile from the waters? It is doubtful. Do you, to some extent, regret loss of Buddhism, Christianity, Confucianism or any so-called organized religion? It is not necessary. It is possible for you to both know of the surface nature of dogma and to know that is also a valuable key which, used by a seeker, may open the door to the self.

During your meditations you can come very close to a door. Even if you do not meditate daily or not at all, it is possible to attain fairly quickly a certain level of awareness of exactly what sort of thing it is that you are seeking, what kind of journey you wish to make, and what equipment you wish to take with you emotionally, mentally and spiritually. The kind of equipment that you look for, the kind of tools, the kind of thoughts that you wish to pack in your bag, are those things which produce fertility or leaven for change, giving good fruit, giving heavenly bread, causing transformation in your journey. It is written in the Christian holy-work that the Kingdom of Heaven is like leaven, and that in time a little leavens the whole loaf. Again, it is like a grain of mustard seed that grows until the birds of the air may nest in its branches.

These similes are not meant to be taken literally, but the feeling of growth, of a more vivid life or a more clarified existence becomes familiar to the seeker, and its lack is a lack that causes an emptiness that cannot be filled by worldly pursuits no matter how enjoyable or how productive they may be, for what each is engaged in is the seeking of the deeper self. If you are choosing the tools to climb a mountain, you would choose carefully, for your life depends upon your equipment. If you chose to go diving, again you would be very careful. Not only would you take care that you had the right equipment, you would work on your skill.

The skill that you need is something which is often called meditation. Meditation has no dogma; it is a form of what this instrument calls prayer. It is a different experience for each person, but in each person it furnishes the skill necessary to use the tools which are given you by your experience and the growing harvest that you have reaped from your experience. If there is not a smile within your heart as you awaken to a new day it may be possible that you have lived upon the surface a day, an hour, a moment too long. It is time to dive within, into yourself, to find that pearl of great price, the self, or, to put it another way, again as it is written in your holy works, the Kingdom of Heaven.

We offer you the caveat, the one that you have already, by your very natures, committed yourselves to change. It may be reluctant change, you may fight against it tooth and nail, for you may not be able to back off for ten thousand years in your mind and view the circumstances which are causing change with a calm mind and cheerful heart. Nevertheless, the change will come.

We encourage you in your growing transformations. Know that all of nature rejoices with you when you have touched upon that central joy that is the Creator within you. Know that it cannot get so deep that you cannot resurface if your seeking be always with the light touch, always with the grain of salt. Your innate seriousness, that is, the innate seriousness of your journey, of your natures, and of your being guarantee that you who have once become aware of terms such as consciousness and love and brotherhood shall not be able to lay those things down but shall carry them in your heart. That heart need not be heavy. The sunshine is within you; the bubbles that sparkle in your mineral waters are within you. The metaphysical humor of consciousness within your clumsy physical vehicles is within you. Circumstance may seem to assail you, but that which can heal and save [with room to spare] is within you.

So let us never bid farewell to Jupiter, nymphs and dryads and satyrs. Let us leave Gautama with his boat and the joys of Christ risen in the kingdom. Let us praise the way with Buddhists and rejoice at truth with the calm stoicism of Confucius. But most of all, let us trust in our own discrimination, in our information.

Each of you, my friends, has a critically unique path. What is extremely valuable for one entity may not inspire another. Therefore, again stepping back, release the rest of the population on your sphere from all judgment, for its spiritual search, for its dogmas, for its conceptions of the divine, and the nature of the self. What matters to you and what shall matter to you long after the physical vehicle which you wear is dust, is the deep self. And how shall you find the deep self? How shall you know yourself, and therefore the universe? One step at a time, my friends.

Be prepared for anything, from years to sudden brilliant revelation. What meditation does in one vibratory system of energy fields may take years, it may take days, it may take instants. Each entity is totally unique. Each entity has its own tools, and it should and it must claim biases, things that seem to the intellect to be crutches, things that you bring to meditation, not things that you keep in meditation.

We leave you to your search. Others wish to speak if they can, and so we would shorten the message tonight to accommodate our brothers and sisters. But we must take this moment to thank you with all of our hearts for sharing the mortal evening with its intimate and personal sounds, the sounds that make a life on the surface, and for sharing the depths of your seeking and your love of the truth with each other with us and with the creation.

We are sorry to counsel patience so often, for we know that it seems from your vantage point to be a real drawback to the spiritual search. Patience is difficult; patience is necessary; and a compassionate acceptance of yourself and your worth while you exercise the patience and wait in faith for that revelation which has not yet come, for that presence of the Creator which you do not yet feel, is a very great and important part of your learning of the lessons of love. We are your brothers and sisters of love and would spend just one moment energizing the heart area of each before we leave this group. We shall pause.

(Pause)

We salute each of your open hearts and trust they may be filled with cheer and the joy of life, both life as you know it now and life in its infinite form which you carry within you as a seed, and for which this mortal life is good rich earth for the flowers that shall bloom an eternity upon your selfhood and your consciousness of the one Creator. We are those of Hatonn. Adonai, my friends. Adonai vasu.

(Jim channeling)

I am Latwii, and we greet you in that same love and light, my friends, as our brothers and sisters of Hatonn have so graciously left you within. It is our privilege again this evening to be asked to join your group. We thank you and we join you with joyful hearts and with the hope that we may in some small way aid your search by answering your queries. May we begin now with the first query of this evening?

Carla: Well, I was going to wait until last because mine isn't very important, but since nobody asked first, I'll begin. Our L/L Research company has never asked for any money and somehow we've always been able to reprint books. Whenever we've done a new project, however, someone has always had to make a sizable contribution, which we've never had to ask for. There's a novel that Don and I wrote in 1968 and 1969 which many people who have read it in the group feel has a lot of spiritual aid in it for people who might read the book. It would cost several thousand dollars to publish for the first time. Would it be metaphysically appropriate to state the above in our newsletter? As I said, we have never asked for money, but would it be appropriate to explain a situation wherein we were attempting to make material available and we're asking for help?

I am Latwii, and am aware of your query, my sister. We may suggest that in the metaphysical sense, one deals with a range of appropriateness which provides you with the opportunity for purity. You may do as you wish in whatever case. Each choice bears a fruit. There is in any situation the opportunity to provide a service and the opportunity to ask others to join in that service. Depending [on] the point of view which is chosen, the correctness, shall we say, will be more or less enhanced. This, of course, you already know and are in this case seeking a more precise declaration or clarification of that which shall be the most efficacious choice.

We cannot make this choice for you. We can suggest, however that you look within the heart of your own being to see what is the basic desire that motivates your actions and your efforts. If you desire to serve with all your heart, then in this choice you cannot be incorrect, for the intention to serve is that which is seen and that which carries weight. We do not mean to seem obscure. We, in this instance, deal with a most delicate matter, for how to serve is the crucial question which each of your peoples who seeks in conscious sense must deal with and in some way reconcile, for to serve is not a case of the black and white easily made choice.

May we answer you further, my sister?

Carla: No, thank you.

I am Latwii, and we thank you, my sister, though we fear that our response was somewhat over-complex, yet we were attempting to transmit, shall we say, the most clear and detailed description which would fit through this instrument's mind.

Carla: Well, I thought it was full and clear—that is, pithy. I was caught up in the realization that it did boil down to how does one serve. Because I had assumed that we serve by making as much information available as possible. Perhaps that needs reexamining. I thank you for the answer, it was not overly complex for me. This time.

I am Latwii, and we thank you, my sister, and are pleased that there was a gist for you to grab within our response. May we attempt another query?

L: Yes. A number of people have experienced what might be referred to as temporary death in the sense that all their body functions stop, their brain stops entirely. Clinical death is a state of being, yet after a period of time they return to their body, having meanwhile experienced a number of, I guess you would call it "other side" experiences. In regard to this and ignoring the difference in time, what is the essential difference between this type of experience and the experience of Jesus Christ in coming back after three days?

I am Latwii, and am aware of your query, my brother. In the basic sense, the difference may be seen as one of purpose, for each entity incarnates with a purpose for the incarnation. There are lessons, there are services. Each decides before the incarnation how the mix between the two shall be made. The one known as Jesus had a purpose which was heavily weighted, shall we say, in the services offered to others, for in its incarnation, it attempted to provide a model by which each entity might provide itself with the means to learn and then to serve others. As the cycle of experience was drawing to a close, this entity, knowing that only a few incarnations for each were left, was providing, shall we say, hints and clues for those still remaining within the testing room, shall we say. Though …

(Side one of tape ends.)

(Jim channeling)

I am Latwii, and am once again with this instrument, and we shall continue, my friends. Those who experience what has come to be called the near-death experience are those who have, in a conscious and unconscious manner, felt that the testing for the incarnation was complete, yet as the papers were handed in, the higher self, which may be seen as the teacher in this instance, asked the entity if perhaps it would care to consider an answer or two which had not quite been completed. Seeing then through the experience that there was more left that could be done in the sense of learning and serving, such entities then return. Having experienced firsthand the realization that, as Jesus taught, death is only a doorway and may be passed through and passed through again, these entities then are experiencing that which was a portion of the master known as Jesus' message to mankind that the lessons may continue apace until they are learned, through however many testings or incarnations are necessary, and for however many so-called deaths may be experienced.

May we answer further, my brother?

L: No, that's given me quite a bit to think about. Thank you very much.

I am Latwii, and we thank you, my brother. Is there another query?

(Pause)

I am Latwii, and, my friends, though the queries were few, we feel a great honor at having been asked these few treasures, and we shall at this time, with the same joy in our hearts that we began this session, leave you, as always, in the love and in the light of our infinite Creator. We are those of Latwii. Adonai, my friends. Adonai vasu borragus.

(Carla channeling)

I am L/Leema, and greet you through this instrument in the love, the light, and the joy and the truth of the one infinite Creator. We have, we confess, been working diligently throughout this session upon the noggin of the one known as L. We hope we have not caused any inconvenience through this. However, we would like to make contact with this instrument as we have not built up familiarity with this instrument yet and would greatly find honor in that possibility. We shall, therefore, attempt to contact the one known as L. We will now transfer. We are those of L/Leema.

Sunday Meditation, May 26, 1985

(L channeling)

I am L/Leema. I greet you in the love and the light of the infinite Creator, and am overjoyed at the prospect of being able to speak so clearly through this instrument, for we have heard our brothers and sisters of Hatonn and Laitos and Latwii through this instrument but until now have not been able to make contact ourselves; so we of L/Leema have been stymied in our efforts to achieve communication through this instrument. We are making adjustments in our signal to facilitate this instrument's ability to identify and process our communications, which of necessity requires a continuous broadcast, so we beg your patience with this seemingly endless run on of communication, for we are refining our signal as rapidly as possible, and would like to do so without overloading the instrument's capacity to receive by accelerating too quickly to keep up with our broadcast. This is achieving the desired objective but we must tune our broadcast to the instrument's speed so we can beg your indulgence as we refine. There. We have it.

We are of L/Leema. We are of the Confederation, and seek to communicate with your group so that we may offer our services in the love and light of the infinite Creator. We of L/Leema have recently begun to communicate with your group, and the desire to offer our services such as they are and in interacting with your group also create the blessings of your service in extending your learning and communicative opportunities to ourselves that we may further progress along our own path of service to others. We of L/Leema are pleased to have been able to communicate through this instrument, and will now relinquish our use of that instrument that it may recover from our efforts to shove it all in one box at one time. In the love and the light of the infinite Creator, we are known to you as L/Leema. Adonai, my friends. Adonai. ☙

L/L Research

L/L Research is a subsidiary of Rock Creek Research & Development Laboratories, Inc.

P.O. Box 5195
Louisville, KY 40255-0195

www.llresearch.org

Rock Creek is a non-profit corporation dedicated to discovering and sharing information which may aid in the spiritual evolution of humankind.

ABOUT THE CONTENTS OF THIS TRANSCRIPT: This telepathic channeling has been taken from transcriptions of the weekly study and meditation meetings of the Rock Creek Research & Development Laboratories and L/L Research. It is offered in the hope that it may be useful to you. As the Confederation entities always make a point of saying, please use your discrimination and judgment in assessing this material. If something rings true to you, fine. If something does not resonate, please leave it behind, for neither we nor those of the Confederation would wish to be a stumbling block for any.

CAVEAT: This transcript is being published by L/L Research in a not yet final form. It has, however, been edited and any obvious errors have been corrected. When it is in a final form, this caveat will be removed.

© 2009 L/L Research

Sunday Meditation
June 2, 1985

(Carla channeling)

I am L/Leema. We greet you in the love and in the light of the one infinite Creator. It is a pure delight to us that you have in your discussion this evening asked for information on a certain subject, that being the only way we may channel answers through this instrument for this instrument is not allowed, nor should she be, to use the question and answer format, lest this instrument move into that which you call the trance state.

We would then speak to you this evening of service. There is a road that always seems to lead upward. To the seeker, perhaps the most burning question of daily living is the question of how to serve those about you. For those who do not seek, the question remains, yet is phrased differently, depending upon the polarity of the entity. To those who are neutral, the question is how to get along with those about you, how to impress those about you, how to live among other people. For those negatively oriented, the question is how to manipulate other people, how to use other people, and how to enslave other people.

In this way we bring you to the questions that one asks if one is of positive polarity. Those of the positive polarity are of service when by action or thought or even intention, another entity or the self is freer to seek his or her own path than before the intended service was performed. The seeker who loves others wishes them to be free. When that seeker is intimately associated with others, that desire can become so far misted and confused by the glassy illusion of societal demands, of shoulds and oughts, that it is often beyond any conscious understanding to reason out how to be of service. Often, in order to grant another freedom, the greatest service is to remain anonymously and impersonally compassionate and supportive. In other words, to pull the point of view backwards, to remove oneself from the microcosm of the relationship to the macrocosm of the perfection of all that is conscious and of the infinity of time that each conscious being has to choose freely, first this path, then this one, and then another.

Let us begin at the beginning of service to others. The beginning is meditation. Many have called this meditation prayer. The overwhelming concept that we wish to instill in you when we speak of meditation and the reason that we use the alternate word, prayer, is that there is a surrender in what this instrument knows as Christian prayer, a surrender that says, "Thy will, not mine, be done." The separation of the self from the Creator is a distortion, for you are co-creators—you and the Creator. Nevertheless, within you, there is a self that is like a clay vessel that deals with mundane things, and that shall not last. Within that clay vessel there is a great treasure. That is your other self—that is, your consciousness. You feed your physical vessel in order that it may supply you with the movement which you need; the surrender in meditation and prayer is the opening of the door to a great dining room, a dining room in which there is a food and a drink that your clay vessel will never know nor need, but without which your consciousness gradually becomes embittered, bowed down, and weary beyond words.

Thus, service to others begins with cleansing the self and sitting down to the feast of silence. In that silence there is a perfection. That perfection is reached first by faith. There is no reasonable or logical way to find or accept perfection within the self, for it is unseen yet never unknown. We listen in silence and are fed and answered in silence. Let us pause for a moment and give an example of one who could not surrender.

It is within this instrument's mind and we take it from her. We find this instrument to be strongly Christian in the contents of the mind, and so we shall use this imagery, asking forgiveness for the limitations of its viewpoint. Remember, there are great truths within any philosophical and spiritual system, and we shall use this example from the holy work which is called the Holy Bible.

The one known as Moses was going about its daily work, and suddenly it looked up and saw the bush that burned but was not consumed. This entity was afraid. A voice called from the bush, identifying Itself as the Creator and calling Moses by name. The one known as Moses in this day and age responded by affirming that he was indeed there, yet he was afraid. The voice informed him that he was on holy ground. The very ground upon which he stood was holy, and yet Moses was afraid. There was not the surrender.

Because of the fact that there is nothing that is not holy, because of the fact that there is nothing that is not of the Creator and that is not the Creator in all of Its perfection and infinity, the seeker will constantly be exposed to stimuli which may be seen to be sanctified. Sorrow, terror and ill negative emotions, feelings and thoughts are sanctified just as much as those positive thoughts that take you very high very quickly. There is nothing that is not holy, that is not the Creator. It is always your choice, each of you, whether or not you shall be afraid, whether or not you shall see, whether or not you shall hear, whether or not you shall understand. This is the work of the self, of the discipline of the self, of the growing love of the self, not on the mundane level, not because of anything that could be considered within the confines of the clay vessel, but because you are upon holy ground, you are sanctified. You are perfect.

This step is so central as the beginning step of service to others and is so difficult compared to action that we emphasize it. You will find that action is far easier than the discipline of the turning of the mind to the Creator, to those things which a child of the Creator may feel as his or her birthright, those things being joy, lightness, power, courage, perseverance, patience and the compassionate forgiveness that is endless. It is as though with the meditation we are focusing upon reality that is far deeper than the clay vessel. That which is your ability to be of service begins to shine as if the clay became more and more transparent and the treasure within became more and more visible to others as well as to the self. Indeed, among those who are of service to others, it is rare that the one who serves is even one-tenth aware of the beauty of the self and could multiply by ten times the amount of service, the quality and the depth of that service in action by expanding knowledge of the nature of the being of self.

We next offer you the image of the shepherd. A shepherd is of service to sheep in very simple ways. A shepherd is not necessarily wise. A shepherd is a simple person, doing a simple job, keeping the sheep safe because the shepherd sees that which the sheep does not. If the sheep is caught, the shepherd can see how to disentangle it; if the sheep has gone astray, the shepherd can find it and bring it back so that it may eat and drink and be comfortable. The sheep, you see, have already been provided for.

The universe in which they live is complete without the shepherd. However, without the shepherd, the quality of the life of the sheep may well be much less, for to be eaten by wolves is not considered to be a good thing, and the shepherd comes to stand on guard. Furthermore, the shepherd helps the sheep to be useful and give its service to others in ways the sheep itself would never imagine. Can you imagine a sheep walking under its own power and will to be sheared so that it might offer its wool to warm a wintry world? How the sheep love being shorn, for in the warm, soft breezes of summer it is well to be without the heavy overcoat. Nothing is lost to the sheep, and the sheep have gained by giving, and this would not have happened without the shepherd.

What we are saying to you is that each of you is shepherd to each other, to each other that you meet, but more especially with whom your lives are more closely entwined. You tell those about you when they have gone astray. You reach a hand to disentangle that which is tangled; you nurse that which is sick. You provide the best of what the natural second density creation has to offer. And because you are dealing with entities such as yourselves and not sheep, the dimension of the shepherd as a cheerful giver arises. Animals such as sheep respond, of course, to a peaceful, cheerful and serene shepherd. So do those about you.

A great deal of what is considered to be a highly complex subject is actually very simple, for those things which are complex are also those things which entities must for themselves do. You may hold the mirror to an experience for one to whom to you wish to be of service. You explain your point of view and offer all of yourself in the situation which you see before you that confronts another. But how and when can you walk for another, can you see for another, can you feel for another?

You cannot be effective if you consider that change is the result of service to others. Surrender—always surrender will give it. Release it and let it go. The shepherd is one who watches, one whose life is dedicated to the care of those entities that have come into its care. And you as shepherds shall more and more vibrate with that compassion. But as you wish to be of service, look always to the freedom of each individual whom you serve. After you have used all of your resources, after you have lifted from the snare that sheep which is caught, after you have fed your friend, your mate, your acquaintance, the stranger who comes to you and says, "Help me," you then remain at peace within your own being, for the choices that shall be made shall be the result and the free will of each individual.

If you have spoken clearly, if you have done the commonplace things and if you have taken difficult situations and given them your best discernment, shown how another can be more peaceful, more harmonious, less antagonistic, or have done whatever you see to do for another, you then step back and realize that you have had the intention to serve, you have formulated the thought as to how to serve and perhaps, if you have been fortunate, you have had the opportunity to put the intention and the thought into action, for that is not only the easiest part but the most naturally joyful part of being of service. Then all is released, all is let go, and you remain aware of the perfection that was and is and shall be.

There is much to be said for the serenity of the one known as Siddhartha, the one who is central to another great philosophical and spiritual system upon your sphere. That serenity is possible because of the surrender of the self to the vicissitudes of the still and the not-still waters of existence and consciousness. You are most of service in and of yourself, and if you can cast your mind towards those who are of service to you, you shall perceive the truth of this statement. Those who are of service to you are as touchstones as much for what they are, who they are, how they are, and why they are as for their actions toward you.

To conclude. In being of service to others, begin with the largest picture, that of infinite, everlasting consciousness, the one original Thought, the Logos. In meditation, in focused silence, fall into the deep ocean of that infinite space, that infinite light, that everlasting love, and lose yourself, lose your small clay vessel. When you come back to this reality as you may call it of the planetary sphere and its day-to-day occurrences, you shall have brought back a treasure—yourself—in the larger sense. Each moment shall seem so much more precious to you, for there are so few of them while you are within this clay vessel, while you are able to interact as you do within the illusion which you enjoy.

Then take upon yourself the cloak of the shepherd. Take up your crook, and do not count the cost of giving nor begrudge any outcome. But within yourself, refine your intentions until they are true, refine and hone your perception until they do not fail you. And when you offer them, give them away. Support, love and set those about you free. With that surrender, you have again entered the Logos, the one original Thought. We wish you well upon your journey. Each of you is of service when you know it and when you do not know it. It does not bear analysis after the fact. Work upon your own powers of discrimination and perception, empathy and sympathy and compassion and most of all, surrender, so that that which is the most positive may shine through regardless of how it is seen by the one whom you wish to serve.

We smile in our hearts as we imagine each of you attempting to picture the perfection of those about you or of yourself. How foreign these thoughts are to you. That is why it is difficult to be of service. Your minds are full of opinions, my friends, your hearts are full of hidden corners, walled-off rooms, and fear. There is nothing to fear. You are free and in the third-density illusion. You can be of the greatest assistance to each other that you shall ever be to anyone. We cannot possibly emphasize enough the height, the breadth and the depth of the possibilities for service in your earthen vessel overbody, for yours is the density of choice. You shall choose your priority or have already chosen, and as you serve, you are aiding the one whom you serve to choose his or her polarity or to increase it. The opportunity will not come again. After the density which you now enjoy, the process of refining begins in earnest and the steps you take become smaller and smaller as they become more and more refined. We share with you our excitement at the very thought at being where you are. We share with you our enormous sympathy and compassion for the pain, disappointment and confusion which you must endure to be where you are now. And we share with you our understanding, such as it is, that you have chosen these moments, these few precious moments of eternity to make your choice and to aid others as they go forth to choose between the light and the dark use of love.

We are those of L/Leema, and again we cannot tell you how grateful we are that you have settled upon this format, for it enables us to use this instrument as we had hoped to. We hope that we have been of some small service to you and wish to …

(Side one of tape ends.)

(Carla channeling)

I am L/Leema, and am again with this instrument. We leave you as we bask together in the glow of your eventide, in the small sounds that we may hear through your ears, sounds of contentment, birdsong, the humming of the domicile about you, the pets that live about you and speak now to each other. There is blessing in the wind, my friends. When it calls your name, do not be afraid. You shall not be consumed by the fire of life. We of L/Leema bid you farewell in the love and in the light of the One Who Is All. Adonai. Adonai. Adonai.

(Jim channeling)

I am Latwii, and we greet you, my friends, in the love and the light of that same Creator. We have been privileged to listen with you as those of L/Leema have spoken of that most difficult service, that is, the experience of your lives, and we join you in seeking to purify our service. Our service is a humble one. We shall attempt to answer any queries which may remain. May we begin, my friends, then with your first query?

Carla: In general is it possible for a service-to-self person living on this planet at this time to appear to be service-to-others oriented, even to close scrutiny?

I am Latwii. My sister, this query is one which requires an understanding which your peoples are frequently without, for to pierce to the heart of service to self, it is as difficult a task as understanding that concept of service to others. For indeed, to serve in a polarized sense, one must be able to perceive the intentions with which an entity enters into its actions and with which it conducts its thoughts. One who is adept at pursuing the path of serving the self first and foremost is one who has for a great portion of its incarnation been what you would call a conscious seeker, and has sought consciously to gather about itself those powers and items which it has determined will best suit its purposes. A portion of the ability to accomplish these tasks is the ability to conceal from others the intentions and the purposes for the actions and the experiences, for few would consciously choose to give over the will to another if they knew that they then in any sense whatsoever would become enslaved by such a choice of action.

Thus, it is indeed possible for an entity to seem quite of the service to others but to be at the heart of its intention of quite the polar opposite polarity. The ability of entities to determine the actions and intentions of another is that factor which makes the recognition of such negatively-oriented *(inaudible)* difficult. Yet if one gives with a whole heart, with a desire to serve and love all about it, one need not fear the meeting of such an entity.

May we answer you further, my sister?

Carla: Well, my motive for asking that question was personal. I had run into a fairly powerful entity over the weekend, a fellow named P, and subsequent experiences that I've had have seemed to me—have had to do with the openness with which I met this entity, due to the fact that I had just had a healing and my taking on of some of the vibrations which he offered which I would not normally have done. I guess there's a lot of fear in the motivation for asking the question, so I suppose the corollary to that is, in what way does one cease to fear that which is hurting one?

I am Latwii. My sister, begin first with the foundation of all creation, that is, unity. From this unity the one Creator, the one original Thought of love, springs all the infinite variety of forms of life and directions for each. Look then to any which seem of a fearful or doubtful nature. See there the Creator that rests as well within your own being. Love that Creator as if It were yourself, for in truth It is. See that which is feared; bathe it in love, see it as self, bless it, bid it travel its journey, and then bathe your own being in the love and the light of the One. In so doing, you have affirmed the unity of all creation, for in truth that is all that there is. To move from that truth and to see any separation is to step upon the grounds which the entities of the negative polarity rule when fear and separation are with the entities there.

May we answer you further, my sister?

Carla: No, thank you.

I am Latwii, and we thank you as well. May we attempt another query at this time?

N: Yes, Latwii, along this same line. I too encountered a number of entities, many of which were very loving and positive and some which were negative. Yet those which seemed to be negative seemed to have a very great psychic awareness, of the ability to interpret past lives of an individual just by sight, perhaps future lives and … Is this psychic awareness the same as service—I meant gleaned through service to others as well as service to self?

I am Latwii, and, my brother, may we suggest that the tools which the one Creator has placed before each of Its portions may be utilized in either the positive or negative sense. An entity may choose to use any ability in either manner.

May we refine our answer in any degree, my brother?

N: Well, perhaps I'm seeking direction for increased psychic awareness, perhaps for myself. I don't know whether that's service to self or service to others. I previously was much more oriented in service to others and would like to redirect myself in that respect again but I'm having trouble.

I am Latwii, and, my friends, we have from that comment perhaps found a point, a comment upon which we may also comment. As one seeks to serve others in the manner which our brothers and sisters of L/Leema have expressed, that is, to allow the entity to be freer, to do that which he chooses, we may make this attempt in one of two basic ways. One which is the most common among your peoples is to attempt to decide with the intellectual mind what one may do to serve, how one may develop one's abilities, and just how these abilities shall be utilized. This is an attempt, shall we say, to fashion and structure the manner and mode in which one serves. It is a noble attempt, one borne of the best of intentions, yet the one most often to fail, for the one Creator moves unseen and quite often unfelt within each entity and each entity has in the deeper portions of its being decided to serve as a channel for the One. How this service shall be manifest is that which is unknown.

To surrender the self, to surrender the decision-making ability in a large degree and to give over the self to the use of the one Creator is the second manner which is most successful and least often chosen among your peoples. To await that which is within is difficult, for you see others seeming to serve very effectively in a manner which is apparent and seems to bear fruit. That you are not first on your block to do so is discouraging, but that you shall eventually do so gives you comfort, and that you shall choose to do so in such and such a manner seems to give more comfort. But, my friends, may we suggest that you give over your desire to do this or to do that in this or that manner and pray that the one Creator moves through you in the way most salubrious, shall we say, for true service to be manifested through being. For each has at least one ability which shall be developed. It may not be showy; it may not be flashy; it may not draw oohs and ahhs from a great crowd. Yet, my friends, the One shall move through you. Know that in your hearts and calm your minds.

May we attempt another query?

N: Then, it is a suggestion that we continue to try to develop this oneness through meditation. And even though the first on the block as you suggest, I would like to be one of those on the block sooner or later, but seemingly with great difficulty at this particular time and place.

I am Latwii, and, my brother, we have perceived an incomplete query upon your part. Yet we do feel that therein lies another point which we might be of service in uncovering. That is that each of you in the heart of your being as you move through your daily experiences is truly of service, for you can do none else but serve. You seek to refine that service in a manner which you may amplify and thereby increase the service. To begin by knowing that you serve is a good beginning. To await that amplification that will point a way that seems more clear is our suggestion. Rather than attempting to, as it has been said, push against the river, move with that river, and in the appropriate moment you shall set sail and call upon many ports and be of service in yet another manner. Do not forget that you serve at all times though, my brother.

May we answer further, my brother?

N: Thank you very much. It's nice to know that we serve at all times. It just seems that sometimes we seem to have more or less direction of service to self. May I ask why the general knowledge of the Council of Nicaea, with reference to the elimination of Christ's teachings and all other teachings concerning reincarnation, is not generally known and, if known, isn't very well accepted?

I am Latwii, and, my brother, many within your organized religious circles are unaware of such information, for who wants to hear bad news? And if such were brought to the attention of these entities, there could be no proof that would be powerful enough to convince them, for one will see what one will see and one will believe what one wishes. Is that not true for each? Let each travel that path that each has chosen, for all paths, as it is said, lead to home, if we may paraphrase.

May we answer further, my brother?

N: Well, yes. In a way it would seem that a deliberate deletion from what was previously the handwritten bibles is an infringement of free will to a certain extent. Why should it be considered "bad news" to such an extent that the news should be shielded or the views should be shielded from the masses? Not that everything is shielded in many of the metaphysical writings, but many of the metaphysical writings are not accepted by the—particularly by the fundamentalists?

I am Latwii, and, my brother, it is not true that those who are willing and able to hear this message of which you speak do indeed hear it. Thus the shield is not complete; it works for those who wish it to work.

May we answer you further?

N: No, thank you very much.

I am Latwii, and we thank you very much. May we attempt another query?

Carla: Just to follow up on that. I have a human opinion, and that was that those at the Council of Nicaea were afraid that the punch would go out of the story of Christ's death on the cross and his resurrection if it were known that you didn't just have this chance to become "saved" but have an infinite number of chances. Could you confirm that?

I am Latwii, and this is in part correct, my sister. To continue, it is also a point which makes what may be called the priestcraft important to the general population, for the one known as Jesus had shown what all could do, and [if] it were generally known that all would live again, then each would have a closer relationship, shall we say, a direct access, not only to the one known as Jesus but to the model and the kind of life and experience and possibilities which that one exemplified, and there would be less need for an intermediary to speak to the great for the lowly, for the lowly and the great would be seen as one.

May we answer further, my sister?

Carla: No, thank you.

I am Latwii, and we thank you. Is there another query at this time?

A: Is the instrument weary?

I am Latwii, and this instrument has a good deal of energy, for it is fresh in the channeling this evening for those of the brothers and sisters had a good deal of the stage for this evening and we are fresh upon it. May we attempt another query?

N: May I ask if there is a method of meditation which will more truly focus our ability to become, shall we say, in macro contact, or shall I say, in contact with the universal mind?

I am Latwii, and, my brother, there are many, many means of meditation which can allow one to experience the unity of all creation. It is, however, not so important the means by which one meditates as it is the desire which fuels the meditation. Whatever path is chosen must needs be chosen with a desire that burns incessantly, for that which you desire is that which you shall gain and that which you shall realize. You shall realize it in a direct proportion to that desire. Choose whatever means you wish, whatever feels right to you, my brother, whatever means you seem to have a natural ability to exemplify in your meditations, whether it be to watch the breath, to focus upon one point, to focus upon a concept, be it love or wisdom, to focus upon a mantra, to do this or to do that. Whichever you do, do with a desire to be one with all.

May we answer you further, my brother?

N: Thank you very much. Would you address, please, a consideration for the fact that whether there is or is not going to be an Armageddon?

I am Latwii, and this is a very humorous question, my brother. We hope that you do not think that we have an unusual sense of humor. But it is as if one at a dance had asked us, "Where was the dance?" My brother, you live within the Armageddon. The times, as it has been said, are indeed a'changing. You live within times that are most uncertain, in which all portions of the life experience change and change with great rapidity. Look about you, my brother. You see the battle of light and dark in all places, in all hearts. You see the doubts and the fears, you see the prophets, the sages; you see all that has been foretold and, yes, you are at the dance.

May we answer you further?

N: Thank you very much. You seem to confirm what I thought, whereas many people feel that it is a future battle rather than a current elevation. Thank you.

I am Latwii, and we thank you, as always, my brother. Is there another query?

(Pause)

I am Latwii. Ahh, my friends, we see that we have quickly exhausted the queries. Yet, we have enjoyed ourselves immensely. This instrument seems to be loosening up somewhat. Perhaps we should subject him to long conversations with discarnate entities more regularly, and tire his overactive mind out. Ah, perhaps this is the formula—we shall remember.

We leave you now. We are those of Latwii. We are with you always upon your requests for the meditation and the deepening of your meditation. We leave you in love and light, for there is nothing else around. I am Latwii. Adonai vasu. ☙

Sunday Meditation
June 9, 1985

(Carla channeling)

I am Hatonn, and I greet you in the love and in the light of our infinite Creator. We feel most privileged to be with you this evening, especially because each instrument is somewhat fatigued and therefore we are most grateful to each instrument who enables us to use the words and the thoughts that go into each life, each experience, and each personality.

We would speak to you this evening concerning that item on the agenda of each seeker which often takes up a great deal of the seeker's time when the problem is first presented. It has been a little while since we dealt with this subject, and periodically it seems necessary to work with our understanding on the subject of earth changes and the progression of your world's sphere into fourth density.

Like most natural happenings, my friends, that are not blessed in people's minds with the love and the light of the infinite Creator, but only with the subconscious hunches of the universal mind speaking in human counterpart, one finds this group of concepts surrounded by mythology and misunderstanding. The heart of the matter is that there is a transition taking place from third to fourth density upon your planet. However, it would be incorrect to think in terms of the time scale which is so often used by your peoples. It is not well to think in terms of days or months or even years. For this, shall we say, transitional period where the Earth is literally in travail on many planes has been occurring for approximately 2300 of your years, if we read this instrument's mind correctly as to time. We apologize for being less than perfectly accurate about time, but it is a difficult concept for us to grasp.

The nature of third density is that of the choice. Consequently, on the subtler planes, the inner planes of your third density, those whom you call angels began the noble quest that still partakes of polarity, the armor of light in battle with the forces of darkness. This has been occurring upon the inner planes for many years, and upon the planes closest to you for approximately 250 years. Again we apologize for any inaccuracies in our time.

The Earth's travail will increase as it has been increasing for the last approximately 40 of your years. The people's travail will increase also as polarity offers its final manifestation within this particular group of conscious entities, this particular group which strives now to make the choice in time for the great harvest. We were sent out to harvest if we possibly could those who wished to make the transition from third to fourth density at this particular opportunity. It is our service, hopefully, to inspire those who wish to be made aware of the situation to seek to graduate from third density, to be able to use the light and the love of the one infinite Creator to an extent which will not impede each of your progresses into the fourth-density quality of light and experience. We have propelled ourselves because you have called. You are now in the valley of the shadow of death, as this instrument would say, steeped as she is within the so-called Christian religion.

Very well, then, my friends. These are the preliminary outlines, the sketches of what shall occur, far more gradually than most expect, far more naturally than most expect, but certainly not without inconvenience, discomfort and what will seem to be enormous tragedy as masses of entities leave their physical bodies during natural catastrophes when they are killed by the forces within the planet, the forces of anger and hostility that have been stored within the Earth itself and which shall come forth.

Many things shall occur. Much has been written about that which shall occur. We ask that you step back from the drama of the illusion and find that within yourself which has two realizations, the first being that you who are infinite shall leave no part of consciousness when you leave this physical body. The second awareness, hopefully, that of a desire to be of service to others. In no event do we wish to encourage you to set up areas of safety, for there is no such thing as safety from the self, and it is within the self that the transition shall truly occur. That which occurs at harvest is within the self; that which occurs within the planet, although interesting, is a separate subject from the one which might well be considered far more interesting to the self. And that is that it is likely that this lifetime or at the very most, for those who die soon from the physical body, one more lifetime, shall be the last opportunity before graduation to refine the polarity of self to the point at which you the seeker might accept the quality of light which is the native light in fourth density.

This is your judgment. It is as simple and straightforward as that. If you can walk into that light within your indigo-ray body, as this entity would call it, you are graduated to fourth density. If you cannot step into that light because of its overbrightness, then you shall have another cycle of third-density illusion during which you may hone even further the choice which you have begun to make. We encourage you on the quest and we encourage [you] to avoid distraction whenever possible. There is much distraction possible when one deals with the unseen and the invisible, and that is that with which we deal exclusively. Attempt in your meditations to remain aware of the simplicity of the original Thought and the corresponding simplicity of the path. When there is great complexity surrounding a subject such as the movement into the so-called Golden Age, that may be a sign to you that there is less to it than meets the eye. When shall this and that happen? We hope that it is not as interesting to you to know that as it is for you to continue to seek the truth. It is that seeking that shall enable you to graduate, not knowledge of when earthquakes shall occur.

We leave this instrument at this time, thanking her most heartily for the opportunity to speak. We are those of Hatonn, who leave you glorying in the love and in the light of the one infinite Creator. We leave you in the thunder and the storm and the serene calm *(inaudible)*. Adonai, my friends. Adonai vasu.

(Jim channeling)

I am Latwii, and I greet you, my friends, in the love and in the light of the infinite Creator. We are honored to be here again, and we hope that we can utilize this instrument effectively this evening in the mode in which we left this group at its last meeting. The joviality was delight and we would hope that we can share again in that fashion. May we begin with a query, my friends?

L: Latwii, I spent some time today with a person that resulted in me feeling psychically drained. Can you give me any information as to what went on, the mechanics of how this occurred, why it occurred, anything along that line?

I am Latwii. We may speak generally, my brother, for when entities group themselves in the pairs in order that the life to which your peoples have been accustomed may be carried on and there may be the order, the livelihood, the rearing of young and the continuation of society, there is presented to each the opportunity to learn much and to teach much, for within such a closely knit relationship, the bonds between two entities grow in many and varied fashions. When the relationship has its difficulty, or we should say, when the entities within the relationship have difficulty maintaining the relationship due to one factor or another, and this difficulty grows to such an extent that the entities find it more beneficial to continue apart than to continue together, there is within each the feeling and perhaps the realization that an opportunity has, shall we say, left, and perhaps each entity feels as though there has been a loss and feels a vacuum or a hole where once there was opportunity, and as you have called it, [a] mirroring effect.

When there is at a future time, as you would call it, any portion of a reconciliation or attempt to complete circuits that were left open and incomplete, one entity may feel this in a greater degree than does the other. This is usually the entity with the, shall we say, larger pull, the greater feeling within that there has been a loss and the renewed desire to complete a previous circuit then is a request from this entity to the other that there be an exchange of energy, a giving, if you will, in order that this hole may be filled somewhat. Thus have you given and thus has what you have given been received. For the moment the feeling is that of being drained, but we can assure you, my brother, that you have given freely to the one Creator.

May we answer further, my brother?

L: No, you've given me quite a bit to look at. Thank you.

I am Latwii, and we thank you, my brother. May we attempt another query?

N: Yes, Latwii. When do we enter the Aquarian Age?

I am Latwii. My brother, if you will look upon the spectrum which you call the rainbow, you shall see each color loses some of its brilliance towards the boundary with the next color and gains some of that coloration as the progression is made from one color to the next. So it is with the ages which pass upon your planet. The age which now leaves and the age which now joins, each have blended with the other so that there is a period of what you may call transition. At the heart of each entity and each atomic cell structure, the beginning of fourth density vibration is apparent. Yet there are many, many third-density vibrational patterns which yet hold sway.

May we answer further, my brother?

N: In other words, we have already begun the Aquarian Age but we're not into it very far?

I am Latwii. This is correct, my brother. May we answer further?

N: No, thank you.

I am Latwii, and again we thank you. May we attempt another query?

Carla: Yeah. I've got a question but I don't know if you can answer it. Is the social memory complex, L/Leema, hoping just to get some experience with a group by working with us or it is hoping to come through regularly?

I am Latwii, and we are aware of your query, my sister. Those of L/Leema wish as do we to be of service in whatever manner possible, yet within the general desire to serve there exists a more specific desire that the service may be more specific, that is, that if this group is able to focus from time to time upon a topic which has great interest in awakening the desire to know the truth, then this group may form the query with the words and the thoughts and hopefully with the meditation [aspect], and those of L/Leema may in turn respond through your instrument, my sister, or perhaps in time through others as well, for all are instruments with the capabilities necessary. The responses that those of L/Leema can make are those which add another flavor, shall we say, to the experience of channeling which each in this group enjoys.

May we answer further, my sister?

Carla: Yes. It has to do with the probable length of such contact. The contact itself is different than any contact that I've experienced before in that I was, as far as I knew, quite conscious and yet I was not at all conscious of the passage of time, and forty-five minutes went by and I was the most surprised person in the world when the tape recorder clicked off. I'd been the one that was channeling; I didn't feel tired, and I had no idea that the channeling had been going on for so long. Is this typical?

I am Latwii, and am aware of your query, my sister. Well, as yet, there is no "typical." We can suggest, however, that those of L/Leema, as each with the Confederation, have some difficulty in reckoning time as you call it. Each attempts to be conscientious in making the responses to queries or the delivery of messages fit within what your peoples would discern as a comfortable period of time, for we do not wish to wear you out with words. Yet those of L/Leema are the least familiar with your means of reckoning time, and [you] may from time to time discover that you have spent a good deal of this time listening. Yet these entities are also desirous of serving in each way possible, and will attempt to make their deliverance more concise.

Your instrument has been utilized for the training that you have been undergoing of late has been that of word-by-word transmission. This type of transmission is more helpful in delivering the more specific type of information. Thus it is likely that your instrument would be the most frequently utilized as the other instruments hone their abilities to partake in the vocal channeling and perhaps also in the word-by-word transmission of this type of channeling.

May we answer you further, my sister?

Carla: Yes. It seemed to me when I thought back over the session—haven't read it yet—that there weren't any excess words, that it was just a matter of systematically going through the subject. Is this a correct perception?

I am Latwii, and this is quite correct, my sister. For when the subject is large, to do such a subject justice one must attempt to cover, shall we say, all the bases, and you may expect variation in the length of deliveries according to the depth and breadth of the subjects you choose.

May we answer further, my sister?

Carla: Okay, so I understand. We need to be specific on our questions to get specific answers. Okay. The only other question was just subjectively interesting to me, what state of mind was I in that erased my awareness of time without erasing my awareness of consciousness?

I am Latwii, and, my sister, the state of which you were is that which is much the child. For the word-by-word transmission mode is that which focuses quite concentratedly upon the present moment and each word which enters that moment. Thus the type of contact which we were utilizing and the message that you were transmitting served to cause your reckoning of time to be put aside in order that you operated in what is your analog of a timeless portion of experience.

May we answer you further, my sister?

Carla: Did others experience the same thing? I mean, is this simply concentration or is it a deeper state of trance than is normal in conscious channeling?

I am Latwii, and we find that your last supposition is more nearly correct. The word-by-word transmission mode of channeling is one which requires both a greater concentration and a deeper state or level of mind to be utilized. It would be more correct, we find, to suggest that the more focused the concentration, the deeper the level of mind that is being utilized.

May we answer further, my sister?

Carla: No, thank you.

I am Latwii, and we thank you, my sister.

A: Out of curiosity, what density is L/Leema?

I am Latwii, and those of L/Leema are of the density of light, which as you number the density is that of five.

May we answer further, my sister?

A: Thanks.

I am Latwii. We appreciate your fill-in-the-blank queries. Is there a fill-in-the-blank, a multiple choice, or perhaps an essay question we may answer further?

(Pause)

I am Latwii. Ahh, my friends, we can't compete with the thunder and the rain. We were considering answering the query of the thunder, but we found that this instrument was unwilling to vocalize our response. Perhaps in time. We thank each of you for requesting our presence, for sharing the love of your hearts, queries of your minds, the pleasure of your company. We are those of Latwii. We shall leave now in the channeling thought sense only. Always are we with you. Adonai, my friends. Adonai vasu borragus.

(Carla channeling)

I am Yom. I greet you in the love and in the light of the infinite Creator Whose number is One. We are called to you by the one known as A, and because there are so few queries which make sense to a group which is not made completely of your scientists which we may answer, we shall be brief. However, the entity known as A wished to experience our presence. Therefore, we shall speak briefly and then dwell with the one known as A, as it is possible our vibration may be comforting.

We would speak briefly of electricity and gravity. The energies involved are spiritual and spiritual integrated with the ratio of space and time. Because this is not understood by your peoples, electricity is not understood by your peoples. It is merely used by your peoples. Because the spiritual nature of gravity is not understood by your peoples, the universe loses the unique cosmology which it deserves, that is, the cosmology of spirit and consciousness. We use a very poor instrument to transfer thoughts of this nature, for this instrument does not have vocabulary or even concept for what we would speak of. However, we give you these few thoughts to provoke further thought within yourself as to the spiritual nature of the physical as well as the metaphysical universe.

You have pondered light, we assume—what light is, how light works, and so forth. You have not come up with any answers yet, we also assume. Remember, we greet you in light. Ask yourself what the attractive power of that which is sent away shall be if all things are indeed one. Ask yourself if children grow up and return to complete a cycle of growth.

We leave this instrument, rejoicing, as do all in the Confederations of Planets in the Service of the Infinite Creator, in the love and in the light of that one Source of all that there is. We are known to this instrument and now to this group as Yom. It has been enjoyable to speak with an engineer once again. We bless you all, even those who are not scientists, and leave you. Adonai, my friends.

Sunday Meditation
June 16, 1985

(Carla channeling)

I am L/Leema, and I greet you in the love and in the light of the one infinite Creator whom we all serve with our gifts in one way or another. It is a great privilege to be with you this evening and we both thank you for your call that we may attempt to be of service to you and assure you that we shall attempt further to be somewhat less prolix than in our discourse previous. We are in the process of adjusting to this instrument. It will be necessary for this instrument to move, so we shall pause.

(Pause)

I am L/Leema, and am again with this instrument. This is a much better position. So that we may refrain from straining this instrument's neck region, it was necessary to encourage the instrument to become more erect in its posture.

When we speak to you of gifts, know that we speak not as your holy book known as the Bible speaks, for the gifts therein mentioned are far too categorized and narrow. Spiritual gifts abound, and there are a variety of spiritual gifts for each entity who seeks to know the truth. The entry into the very gateway of love opens to the seeker a veritable Christmas, shall we say, of gifts. And as the seeker walks a sometimes weary road, the gifts multiply if they are recognized and used, and gradually disappear if the opportunity is not accepted.

Before we speak of gifts themselves, let us speak of the nature of phenomena. We ask you to consider that you are not your body, nor are you those things which your body does. Who you are is barely tangential to the body, the life of the body, and the labor and acts of one who is within your third-density illusion. The actual nature of each entity is one with the one great original Thought, which many have called love, some have called Logos, and others have called any number of names intending to refer to the Godhead or Creator. In this state of consciousness, gifts are available in infinity of supply, yet are unavailable due the fact that there is not an individual with free will which has separated its consciousness from the Creator enough to become a co-creator. So when we address you, we are not addressing entities who shall be known as spiritual due to their works and the apparent display of gifts. We address you as portions of the Creator. Your natures are unchangeable and have been unchanged for an eternity. As you find these words, you are already ancient, ancient in thought, in understanding, and in wisdom.

The concern of the group this evening is not only the nature of gifts, but what methods may be used in order to gain or regain knowledge and use of these gifts. We feel that it is important that we have prefaced this question with the information that the phenomenons about which you ask are not conducive or detrimental to spiritual growth. They are neutral ground against which the biases of your personality will form attitudes towards those gifts. Those attitudes are the most interesting, thought-provoking, informative and important portion of your seeking after phenomenons. All things can be holy and all things can be mundane. Those who approach gifts which are considered spiritual—whether they are in fact spiritual or not—with the desire to serve others are polarizing in a positive direction. This is important and the knowledge that this is important is informative.

It has often been wondered why some are given gifts, seemingly at random, why the large majority who enjoy experience upon third density seem to be either without spiritual gifts or only vaguely aware of the various hypersensitivities that constitute the general concept of the spiritual gift. By this we mean that a hypersensitivity of the ear would produce clairaudience or clear hearing, hypersensitivity of vision producing clear vision or clairvoyance and so forth. Why are some given the gift of seeing that which others cannot, yet that which has substance in the sub-vibration of your inner planes? To understand the answer to this, one may simply gaze at the round upon round of incarnational experiences, the end product of which is each of you. In previous incarnational experiences, some have studied with great earnestness and sincerity and in a future lifetime then have continued that study, either consciously or subconsciously choosing the same area until eventually the entity arrives within the illusion at the beginning of an incarnational experience with a gift. It is a gift that has been earned, my friends, not in one incarnation, but in many. It is the equivalent of one who studies the piano, not in one incarnation but in three. By the third incarnation the human hand guides itself to the keyboard and euphonious harmony ensues therefrom. The singer is a singer, a dancer a dancer of eternity. To each, gifts are given.

We can think of no simpler way to state this simple answer. When a gifted person says to one who is not gifted in the same way, "Why do you not study harder, for this gift is your birthright?" the questioning entity is neglecting to realize that there was no study involved for him or her. It was a gift. The gift may have been refined, indeed, not have been refined by the experiences of the present incarnation; that is the nature of the illusion and it is seldom wasted. Catalyst is used. That which is not needed is burned, that which is deemed appropriate is harvested and the process goes on. To expect to learn a gift within one lifetime is as unreasonable as to expect one who has not danced in previous lifetimes to go through childhood, partaking the lessons of the dance, and then to blossom into a ballerina of the first caliber. It is possible to learn the steps; it is possible to work upon balance, grace, poise and discipline—all of these things a dancer needs. What is not possible to learn in one lifetime is the heart and the soul of the dancer, for the heart and soul of the dancer dances to the one Creator, rejoices and grieves with the one Creator by the movement of arms, torso and legs. The one with the gift of music, be it singing or playing, may feel that the gift has been simply training and a little talent. But the one with the true gift found love in the song, creativity, light and fire in the generation of song. Can these things be taught, my friends? We think not.

We move on to our final thought, and we hope one which one may be helpful in realigning each entity's perception of that which is truly gift. The true gifts are often unremarkable. Seldom does the dramatic incarnational experience involve spiritual gifts, for this is not a third-density world upon which spiritual gifts are greatly appreciated. These gifts are manifestations of love. They seem humble. They are the gifts of unselfishness, of willingness, of enthusiasm, of patience, of courage under distress, of the reached-out hand. These are the gifts which are spiritual and they are the birthright of all of you. Each entity has this birthright. Yes, it is true; you have all knowledge, you have all the answers—these too are your birthright. But how many incarnations shall you go through in order to refine each and every phenomenological gift? And as *(inaudible)* when the treasure, the true gift is a cheerful and willing heart and the mind which is single in its devotion to seeking the truth, to aiding others, and to finding the one infinite Creator in each and every glance, each and every moment, each and every situation.

As you pursue these true gifts we ask you to refrain from judgment whenever possible. And when it is necessary to judge yourself because of your biases, we ask that you forgive yourself each and every time. One attitude and one attitude only shall open to you the gates of the spiritual kingdom and that is the attitude of openness and vulnerability to the Creator. A deck of cards, a set of numbers, designs in the sky, specters and visions in the orb of glass, are interesting for the moment, but as you face the larger perspective, you must at some point choose to turn your face to the Creator, knowing not, but hoping, understanding not, but believing in things unseen. Be clever among men, my friends, but be innocent before the Creator, for as children, you shall learn much from the Father.

I am L/Leema. We are again most humbly grateful to be allowed to be of service in whatever small way we can. We ask you to discard any word or phrase or sentence or thought which we have said amiss or which does not fill a need for you, for we are fallible and humble and what we say to you is our opinion. We too search, and we too find. We leave you, glorying in the love and in the light of the one infinite Creator. May the gifts you seek and the gifts you receive lighten the road upon which you live, and glorify the Creator you seek so diligently. Above all, may you have lightness of heart in your endeavor, and find laughter and joy amongst the cobblestones, the hills and the valleys, the darkness and the noontimes of your search. Adonai. Adonai vasu.

(Jim channeling)

I am Latwii, and we greet you, my friends, in the love and the light of our infinite Creator. We are most happy to be with you again, and we with you have enjoyed the dissertation by our brothers and sisters of L/Leema. We would attempt to offer a similar service, perhaps with more queries. May we begin then with the first query for the evening?

L: I'll jump in. First of all, Latwii, was I being contacted by L/Leema at the beginning of this session?

I am Latwii. My brother, as we scan the time period of which you speak, we find that there was an attempt to condition your instrument by the brothers and sisters of L/Leema, for you have had your initial experience with these entities, and it was their desire that you should also experience the conditioning which you were made aware of in order that your instrument might be able at some point to serve in the transmission of their thoughts.

May we answer you further?

L: Yes. In L/Leema's introductory comments, unless I misunderstood, they referred to themselves as "we both." Is this correct, and if so, could you explain it?

I am Latwii, and we feel that we may explain this comment by suggesting that there are more than two entities within the social memory complex known to you as L/Leema. In that opening comment, these entities meant to both thank you and assure you. If you will look at this transcript when it is complete, you may find the grammatical sense in that reply.

May we answer you further, my brother?

L: No, thank you. I was somewhat … It piqued my interest without … obviously looking deeper than there was depth. Thank you very much.

I am Latwii, and we thank you, my brother. May we have another query?

T: Yes. I have a question. L/Leema said that one of the most important things we can do is to have an open heart and be open to the Creator. Well, if indeed everyone is the Creator and if love of the Creator and an open heart are the most important things, then isn't one of the … I guess I'm looking for an everyday concrete way to work on myself. And it seems to me that if indeed every one is the Creator and love is the most important thing, then the place to start is with love of the self, because when you love yourself, you are indeed loving the Creator which encompasses everything. Could you please comment on that for me?

I am Latwii, and we shall attempt, my brother, to comment upon this most central query in the life of the seeker. Indeed, if it be true that all is One and that one is the one Creator, then you have truly spoken when you have suggested that one may begin with love of the self. In truth, my brother, one may begin at any point, for all points are one. The choice of perspective is that choice which each seeker must arrive at by whatever means has value to the seeker. You may begin at any chosen point, but when you begin at an individualized portion of that one Creator, you first begin with you, for that is all the limited consciousness within your illusion encompasses.

As you first begin your life upon this plane you form the idea of the self first. You then take that self upon many journeys. That self thinks many thoughts about everything that is placed before it, and if that self can feel the security and wholeness of its own being, indeed, if it can love itself, then this love may expand as do the rings of a pond when a stone is thrown within it, and these rings of love then may encompass all that the self touches and all that the self becomes aware of. It would seem that this would be the most efficacious means of knowing love and seeking the one Creator that is in all, yet for many the path is more circuitous, for one or another many selves are given the added opportunity, shall we say—burden, perhaps you will say—of finding difficulties within the self which do not seem lovable. These difficulties or opportunities are for the purpose of enhancing some aspect of love which the entity before the incarnation felt it lacked capability in expressing.

Thus, many entities begin their search and seeking for love and unity partially within and partially without the self. The journey of seeking this love may for some be more efficacious when the love is expressed for another being, perhaps for a place, perhaps for an art, perhaps a thought, perhaps a project and so forth. Then when an entity sees itself reflected in that other self, thought, art or thing, it becomes more able to appreciate and to love self. Thus, it matters not so much where one begins as it matters that one begin to seek love and to find unity with all things. For these basic, what you would call, truths that permeate your entire illusion and all previous and future illusions are similarly built upon the unity of all things and the love which motivates the experience of things, places, universes and entities within them.

May we answer further, my brother?

T: Well, I find many things in what was just said that I can apply to myself personally. I'm just wondering, do you have anything—I don't know if maybe this is not even within the realm of possibility. Do you have anything of a more personal nature, any suggestions for me, I guess I'm saying?

I am Latwii, and, my brother, we may make many suggestions for many entities and yet each shall choose that which has meaning. If we may be most general, we may suggest that each entity you meet and each situation that comes before you be seen as the Creator. Frame the entity or the situation and label it the Creator, and if you fall short in your perception and appreciation of any entity or situation and are unable to feel it as the Creator, unable to love it as the Creator, then use that falling short as your daily meditation, as your meditation for that day, so that whatever keeps you from loving and seeing the Creator in all might then be smoothed, and your journey made more efficient, shall we say.

May we answer further, my brother?

T: No, that's wonderful. Thank you very much.

I am Latwii, and we thank you, my brother. Is there another query?

Carla: I'd kind of like to follow up on that because I'm also seeking intensely at this point. But the conclusion that I'd come to was that what I needed to seek was the Creator Itself, and to stop seeking love of myself or love of others. And I wondered if you could comment on the efficacy of that path?

I am Latwii, and we shall, my sister, attempt to comment upon your observation which is most perceptive in its heart. As the seeker continues upon its journey seeking one portion of truth, and then another portion, and then seeking these various portions in one place or another and then in one way or another, the entity finds a harvest in each place and in each manner of seeking. The entity in its seeking, then, gathers an awareness of love in an expanding and dynamic nature and begins to feel its connection with all that surrounds it. This connection begins to grow and to expand and eventually the entity begins to replace the seeking of love and the seeking of the Creator with that which we may describe as being love and being the Creator. The conscious effort to do gives over to, shall we say, more automatic effort to be that which was previously sought.

May we answer further, my sister.

Carla: I thank you for that general answer, and I don't know if you can answer this specific query or not, but I'm going to be juice-fasting soon, and the doctor that was overseeing this fast was concerned that I would not get enough nutrients, and it came to me as I was contemplating this that what I should do is see if I could arrange for daily holy communion …

(Side one of tape ends.)

Carla: Anyway, my thought was as I started on this path in order to provide a plentiful supply of nutrients, which is hard to do on a juice fast so I understand, that it would be very efficacious for me to take holy communion every day if I could arrange it because that metaphysical food is high in value. Could you comment in general on this thinking, given that the person in general happens to be a Christian?

I am Latwii, and am aware in general of your query, my sister. We find that the preparations which you anticipate for this fast have been carefully considered, and should because of this careful consideration and forceful application of the will, shall we say, be nutritious and supportive to the not only physical but mental and emotional bodies which derive their nourishment from the food which goes into the mouth, and more especially in your case the food which proceeds from the mouth.

May we answer further, my sister?

Carla: I'll have to read that. Thank you.

I am Latwii. We thank you, my sister. Is there another query?

N: Yes, I have a query in that those answers previously derived—I would wonder if we can focus our considerations for all being the Creator in some direct method when it is difficult to accept, shall we say, the transgressions of others. Can we just think it and it's there? Or how can we convince ourselves?

I am Latwii, and am aware of your query, my brother. We find that this is a general query which is specific in application, therefore most difficult to answer specifically, for each entity will find that there are a variety of ways that are useful in, as you have put it, convincing oneself that the Creator is all about one. You must, my brother, make your own choice in this regard. We could give this or that technique, yet no technique would be efficacious without the will and the faith that such technique would be efficacious. You may apply any particular technique. That of importance is the intention of the technique, not so much the technique. If you will also include in this technique the meditation upon your discoveries, you shall then take that which is learned by technique and mechanical application of the technique and seek it within your being, that it might become a functioning part of your perception. Look you first, my brother, to the intention. The technique is basically unimportant.

May we answer further, my brother?

N: Well, in reference to the meditation, when we meditate, many seem to have answers apparent, to those entities that do meditate, although some of us don't seem to have, shall we say, directness of the meditation or answers or however you wish to phrase it. Is there any method of meditation that is better than others or do we just have to wait until we are totally oriented?

I am Latwii, and am aware of your query, my brother. Again, it is not possible to know the true fruits of any entity's meditative efforts. Many speak that which they wish to have occur. Yet, what has occurred? None know, perhaps even the entity itself does not know. Again we revert, shall we say, to our previous response and may suggest that any means of meditation which has value to you will work for you if your desire is pure and strong. If you seek with all your being one facet or another of the Creator, if you seek with all your being the meaning of some experience within your life, you shall find that, for as it has been written it is truly stated that "As you seek you shall find," for if all is one, when one portion seeks, it can only seek another portion of yourself. And you, my brother, shall find you, for you have nothing else to find.

May we answer further, my brother?

N: There is a course called the Silva mind control which teaches that we are all healers if we desire to heal. Can this readily occur as stated?

I am Latwii, and am aware of your query, my brother. We find that it is possible for anything to occur, yes indeed, but we find that it is sometimes not probable. We shall attempt clarification. All entities, being the one Creator, contain at some level of being the ability to do and to be all that may be done and all that can be experienced. Yet within each incarnation there is, shall we say, a plan or a program which each entity wishes to complete in order to balance, shall we say, certain deficiencies or develop certain areas that are seen to need attention within the overall being.

Let us say, for example, that an entity has in a number of previous incarnations been a quite good healer, has had the need to provide this service, and has done so, and before its current incarnation decided that there were other lessons to learn and services to offer and there was no need to, shall we say, pack the provisions for healing, for upon this journey there were other provisions more of importance. Let us say that this entity within its current incarnation decides through one means or another, of reading information, listening to others, that it shall pursue the path of the healer. It may with great difficulty be able to call upon those energies which are within its abilities and develop some potential for the healing. Yet this development would be difficult and in some cases, perhaps, take the center stage away from those areas which the entity decided before the incarnation that it wished to focus upon. Thus it is necessary for the seeker to seek the heart of its purpose or plan for its incarnation and not shop about overlong for one skill and another and another. It is most helpful, therefore, for each seeker to truly know the self, to become aware of those attributes which the self has provided for its learning and its service, to guard and use these attributes well. Each will have a slightly variant selection of such attributes.

May we answer further, my brother?

N: Yes, please. Well, in that respect, we each have a certain amount of karma and we accumulate this, evidently, through prior incarnations. Then as you have just stated, we should seek the purpose or directness…how best can we seek this if we can have the veil of forgetfulness, or how can this veil of forgetfulness be, shall we say, severed to a certain extent so that we can peer into our prior incarnations to sort of direct this present one?

I am Latwii, and am aware of your query, my brother. It is not necessary, my brother, to see the incarnations that have preceded your current one in order to know what the plan, shall we say, for the current incarnation is. If you seek that, shall we say, karmic balancing process that is underway within your own incarnation, there are many quite simple ways in which you may do so. You may simply observe the patterns which continue repeating within your own experience. Where you find difficulties of one nature, strengths of another nature, weaknesses of yet another nature, you may begin then to piece these parts of your incarnational puzzle together and find that as you continue adding, there is indeed a pattern that emerges. Your life is contained in each thought, in each moment; just as the holographic negative contains the entire picture, so does each thought and each experience. Therefore, meditation is the most valuable tool of which we know that can be used to examine the life, the experience, and its purpose and meaning.

May we answer further, my brother?

N: There are other questions, but thank you very much. I'm sure someone else has need for a query.

Carla: I have a follow up on that one because I've wondered this before. It seems almost as though if you know a relationship and the nature of it before, it becomes a mechanical thing to, you know, like homework or something, to just sort of fill in the blanks, you know, and do the right thing to balance the karma. In other words, you're working from the end back to the beginning, and it seems like it might be even more effective if you didn't know, and of your own free you balanced that which was unbalanced simply because it was unbalanced, and you wanted to be of more service than you were in that unbalanced condition. Is that a correct thought?

I am Latwii. Yes, my sister, in general we may agree with your comment, for with the forgetting that each experiences before the incarnation, there is provided a greater opportunity for the finding to carry greater weight within one's total beingness than if one operated without this veil of forgetting. There would be little challenge in solving what you have correctly described as a fill-in-the-blank test. The veil, then, provides the challenge, the weight against which each seeker pushes in order to gain the spiritual strength that is its goal.

May we answer further, my sister?

Carla: Not on that subject, thank you.

I am Latwii, and we find that this instrument is becoming somewhat fatigued, and we would therefore suggest one or two more queries before the ending of this contact.

Carla: Well, I have one I'd really like to ask because I'm like T, I've never had a high opinion of myself; I've always had a pretty low opinion of myself, a real low self image. And I've noticed that in my life I've gotten a whole lot of love; a lot of people really love me. And I've also noticed that it makes absolutely no difference to my self-image. Why is that?

I am Latwii, and am aware of your query, my sister. For one whose lesson is to learn the value of the self and to learn that the one Creator dwells within this self, the acceptance of love from others has little impact when this self does not feel worthy of receiving the love which is so freely offered. Yet this entity can use the fact that others give this love so freely in its attempt to find the value and the worth of the self, for if the question be asked, "What is love when others love me?" and "Why is this loved?" then one can begin to trace that path that leads from the self to the one Creator and back again to the self.

May we answer further, my sister?

Carla: So one can be transparent enough to be a channel for the Creator and give Its love and light while as a human being, being very muddled. Is this correct? I mean, it's got to be correct, because it describes me.

I am Latwii, and this is quite correct, my sister. Indeed, in some cases where an entity has low opinion of the self, there is then seemingly little to get out of the way in order to serve as an effective vessel or channel through which the One may communicate to the One. In the case where an entity has a great opinion of the self, this opinion may be a hindrance in opening such a channel, for there is too great a weight to move from the mouth of the cave.

May we answer further, my sister?

Carla: No, thank you.

I am Latwii, and we shall keep this stand open for one more order. May we attempt one final query?

T: If no one else has a question that they'd really like to ask, I'd like to just follow up a little bit. I don't quite understand how a person—cause I've known Carla long enough to know that very few people that I've known put out more love to other people and at least more empathy and more understanding of other people's situations. And I've not seen too many people indeed who do receive more good feeling from other people, that anyone I've every known, almost, that comes in contact with Carla gives back this to her. How can this interaction be going on, which—I mean I'm fairly certain it is—how can this be going on, and how can Carla or anyone else's, in that situation, own-self image just not automatically improve? You may have answered this and I missed it, but I don't see how it can help but improve when there's such an interaction of love between Carla and people that she meets.

I am Latwii, and am aware of your query, my brother. Ah, perhaps you are addressing the wrong entity, and should address the one known as Carla, yet we shall attempt this query. The opinion that the self has of itself is an opinion that is developed within the confines of the self. Each entity throughout each portion of the incarnation resides within the heart of its being and makes contact with the world about it from the center of the being; the center of the being, then, is that self which is formed moment by moment according to preincarnative design.

An entity such as the one of whom you speak may decide before the incarnation that in order to develop a greater opinion of the self and the corresponding energy which this self-worth corresponds to, that all catalyst which it shall come in contact with shall be seen in a certain light; no matter what the catalyst may appear to another, it shall appear to this self as something other than adds to the self-worth. This then allows a great imbalance to develop. The self-worth is greatly reduced. It has been well stated that it is the nature of such distortion or imbalance that in order to balance this distortion it must first be accentuated. Seeing the catalyst in this manner thus accentuates the distortion so that at some point there is a choice to be made. The entity becomes so aware of its own low opinion of itself that it turns its efforts in seeking the one Creator directly inward that the one Creator might be found more fully even in that lowly center of the self, for indeed therein it does reside.

The patterns and programs of each entity's incarnational patterns are most difficult to easily discern. Your illusion is one which allows the great amount of variety, and an infinite choice of points of attack, shall we say, for any particular lesson or service. Thus, each entity wends its way through each incarnational experience with the coloration of its mind determining how it sees and experiences its illusion, this coloration having been determined before the incarnation in order to add to one facet or another of the overall being of the entity.

May we attempt a short clarification, my brother?

T: Well, I could ask questions all night, but no, thank you. That's fine. Thank you very much.

I am Latwii, and we find that this instrument is somewhat fatigued and is not completely comfortable with the clarity of its abilities at this point. If there are further queries, and if the one known as L is willing and able, we would therefore transfer this contact to the one known as L.

L: I'm willing. Are there more questions?

(Pause)

L: Got out of that one, didn't I?

(No further questions.)

(Jim channeling)

I am Latwii, and we are most grateful to each of you, my friends, for without your heartfelt queries we would have no voice, no service, and no purpose within your illusion at this time. We leave you now in the respect of speaking only, for always we are with you in thought and in service. We are those of Latwii. Adonai, my friends. Adonai vasu borragus. ☙

Intensive Meditation
June 18, 1985

(Carla channeling)

[I am Hatonn.] I greet you, my brothers, in the love and in the light of our infinite Creator. As the calm of the evening settles like fine golden dust about your domicile, we blend our beings with you, and our thoughts, and above all, our blessing of love. We are most grateful that we have been called upon at this time. Our brothers and sisters of Laitos will be working with the one known as N by conditioning the instrument. However, we felt that it was time that we initiated contact with this instrument. Also, as our vibrations are not unlike those of Laitos, the transition should not be difficult to make.

As distant thunder signals the onset of storm and lightning, so those seekers present have heard the harbingers of growth and seeking. Who knows what the lightning holds, my friends? That it shall strike is certain. That it shall strike in the correct place is also extremely probable, for each of you has a plan, my friends, just as each soul of sufficient advancement to choose incarnations does. And according to that plan, a kind of magnetic field is set up which will attract those gifts which you desire, those experiences which are needed and the disciplines which are necessary to achieve your course.

At this time we would like to attempt contact with the one known as N, for this entity has heard the thunder, and its only doubt is as to where the lightning shall strike and what gift shall be opened to this instrument. We ask that this instrument put all such thoughts aside and trust in the plan that this instrument himself has created in concert with the infinite Creator and with those ministering angels which have been attracted by this instrument's needs. Without further ado, we now transfer contact to the one [known as] N.

(N channeling)

I am Hatonn. I greet you in the path of love and light, light and love of the one infinite Creator. There are many considerations for those on the path. If one is to follow, one must leave. There are ways of proceeding which are rather tortuous. One can only do as he feels he should do. It is difficult to outline any specific path as that might impose restrictions on free will. There is a light at the end of the tunnel, for all must proceed eventually toward that light. If one should desire, direction may be obtained. It is a gift, but one should learn to relax and enjoy it. *(Sound of birds are heard.)* It is like the birds singing—it can be beautiful, but you do not focus your attention at this time.

(Long pause.)

N: I don't think I can bring back the focus.

(Carla channeling)

I am Hatonn, and I am again with this instrument. We are most pleased and happy that we have made such good contact with so little difficulty with the one known as N. We hope that this entity will allow us to speak through him in the future.

To continue. The sound of the bird may be but very beautiful, the night sky full of dramatic clouds, the trees may sleep in majestic splendor, and the sounds of wind and rain may [be] before the thunder. All these things are available to the one whose ears are open and whose eyes seek. The situation you face, my friends, is that you are in not a straight tunnel, but a maze, a *(inaudible)*, one tunnel leading to another and then to another, some passages small, some passages large and no rhyme or reason, no man-made logic to the largeness and the smallness that would indicate that either the larger or the small path should be the one for you. Yet the light at the end is always and ever the same.

The path is different for each entity. Each of you is at a different point walking within the cave, and most of you cannot see the light. Therefore, you are motivated only by the blind and fervent desire to seek the truth, to find the light, to know the love of the one infinite Creator and to share, therefore, in that one great original Thought. Even within the tunnel, each entity is free; free to listen or not listen, free to be moved by signs and wonders or to be unmoved by what seem to be irrelevant details. To become sensitized to the seeming coincidences that occur within your daily lives is most helpful, for to the seeker whose ears and eyes are opened, many, many small details of the day speak. Connections are made within which cannot be explained except by saying, "This feels correct."

Many there are who wish to help you, and yet the greatest help is within yourself. As you meditate each day, you cannot help but begin to feel and fathom the extraordinary depth of consciousness that lies within you. You may come back from meditation like a traveler from a long voyage who has lost his luggage, or you may come back burdened with gifts, and yet in both cases you have been in the light. Whatever your consciousness of that light, your seeking of that light has brought you there. Many are the people upon your sphere who do not choose to observe their environments. We speak to those who wish to observe their environments, themselves and thought itself. Trust, therefore, in your intention and in your seeking, in the bone-deep wisdom that knows not in any intellectual way whence its ideas come.

Trust as well your powers of discrimination, for as there are many who wish to aid you, so are there many entities who would wish to desensitize the sensitive soul by furnishing that soul with information which is not correct. This is why we have so often requested that tuning be done, the tuning of entities that join into unity. As we work in this teaching class, we work with a very small group, a group which is rich in friendship and companionship and the tuning is harmonious and unified. You do not play the same note, but you play the euphonious chord. Therefore, we speak with relative ease. The service of those who channel vocally as these instruments have done is simply the extension of personal harmony into what you may call community with others.

The intensity of the group of three is far, far greater than the intensity of one, for you are unified, and each of you has his will turned unblinkingly towards the face of the Creator who moves across the deep. You are co-creator with the One who has been called the Ancient of Days and you shall create your days and nights, your incarnation. We wish you the joy of this adventure and urge you both to take very seriously the choices you must make in order to become more positively polarized, and to take with utmost lightness and delicacy the carrying forth of these experiences. The use of discrimination, the use of humor, the use of the larger point of view, shall all aid the seeker and act as a kind of self-encouragement as you do seek in your part of the tunnel, in your walk towards the light at the end, towards the love that surrounds all, towards the life that is all creation.

Again we thank the one known as N, and assure this entity that at any time this entity wishes [we will] be available to aid in deepening meditations. Meanwhile, our love to each of you. We leave you in love and in the light of the infinite Creator. We are known to you as Hatonn. Adonai. We fly with the evening wind. Adonai.

(Jim channeling)

I am Latwii, and we greet you, my friends, in the love and light of our infinite Creator. We are happy to have been called once again to this group. We fly in on the same wind that our brothers and sisters of Hatonn flew out on, and we hope that we may be of service by attempting to answer a query or two. May we ask if there may be such a query by which we may begin?

Carla: Well, I have a question, but it's transient, but maybe it'll help N be brave. The last two times that L/Leema has come through me, I have had an absolute undeniable desire to sit upright. And I wondered why this was, since with my neck injury, it would normally be most logical for me to be more nearly prone.

I am Latwii. My sister, those of L/Leema have the ability and the desire to focus their service and their energies in the attempt to answer queries in a fashion which is more specific and at the same time more broad than our own efforts are usually. This intensification of the conditioning and overall effect of the contact upon your physical vehicle is more easily absorbed as you are more vertical in your posture of the spine. If you were to engage in this service with those of L/Leema in the reclining position, there would be somewhat more of a chance, shall we say, that you might enter the trance levels or those levels preceding the trance, thus those of L/Leema have encouraged you in subtle ways, shall we say, to assume the more erect posture.

May we answer further, my sister?

Carla: I thought I couldn't go into trance as long as I was holding hands with someone. Is that not so?

I am Latwii. This is correct, my sister. But those of L/Leema are quite conscientious in their efforts to take every precaution that there shall be no misuse of any instrument which they have the honor and the opportunity of utilizing. Thus, they are aware of your tendency toward trance and are further aware of the holding of hands to avoid this state, yet seek the added reassurance of the more vertical posture to avoid that trance state.

May we answer you further, my sister?

Carla: Yes. Would it be to my interest or edification to try to find out more about my trance state or is it better just to let it be?

I am Latwii, and we are not sure, my sister, if we have grasped the gist of your query. We are aware that the occurrence of the trance state within your experience has been shrouded in great mystery, and we assume that you would at this time query concerning lifting that shroud so that there might be a recognition of the steps or procedures that have been internalized in your case and those steps retraced in order that you might consciously understand the phenomenon that you have experienced. Are we correct, my sister?

Carla: Yes, I wish to know only if it would be helpful to pursue that knowledge. And, if so, how?

I am Latwii. We feel that we have the gist of your query at this time, and are examining it for the situation in respect to the Law of Confusion, for we do not wish to speak where words are not appropriate.

Carla: Well, let me help me/you out, then. It's my hunch that I'm a lot better off not asking any questions about it. Can you confirm that?

I am Latwii, and, my sister, we feel that your supposition is one which is appropriate at this time, for the condition of trance is a condition which was carefully guarded and used at a previous time, as you call it, and is a condition which is not so recommended at this time.

May we attempt further response, my sister?

Carla: No, thank you.

I am Latwii, and we thank you, my sister, as always. Is there another query?

N: Yes, Latwii. We were discussing earlier the fact that many children have been deluded by other people, and against their free will, and I was particularly wondering if this sort of query situation could be utilized to locate any specific entities that have their free will deluded, so to speak, such as this A that disappeared in this area a couple of years ago?

I am Latwii, and am aware of your query, my brother. In most instances we would suggest that this type of a query and direction for group energies is a service to those who have been led away and astray. There are some groups that are well-prepared, shall we say, to undertake this endeavor. This group, however, utilizing the instruments at its disposal, and with the contact being of the non-trance variety, would find it most difficult to provide this service, for there must be a great effort put forth in a specific manner and these instruments as they are currently being used would not be able to transmit the information which we could with some effort provide. Ours is a service which is basically philosophical in character, hoping as we do that we may provide some information for each entity's journey of seeking and development of the point of view.

May we answer you further, my brother?

N: Well, yes. You said that was a service that you could provide but not for these instruments, and that you prefer a trance state. Would it not also be a service to others, or should we say, what direction would you suggest so that we might utilize this as a service to others?

I am Latwii, and, my brother, as each entity and each group has the certain talents and skills, we find that in general the service of which you speak is not one which would be possible through this type of contact or utilizing these instruments.

May we answer further?

N: Well, I was just wondering if you could suggest what type of contact or what direction one might take in order to perhaps try to fulfill this service to others?

I am Latwii, and, my brother, we would suggest that one would need to find an entity that were quite gifted in the ability to achieve the level of trance necessary for such specific service and one would have to find this entity also willing to undertake such service and to be knowledgeable enough concerning this service to utilize the proper tuning and challenging techniques with which you are familiar.

May we answer you further, my brother?

N: Well, thank you very much. I was wondering in my particular case, is there any way to amplify the seeming induction of thought phases or thoughts or words in an incident such as myself? I seem to have such difficulty in pulling each word through the purple maze.

My brother, we find that you have proceeded quite rapidly in this endeavor. The vocal channeling is a service which is not always so quickly learned, and we commend your rapid progress and could suggest that you rest your concerns and continue as you are. We can further suggest that the continual refining of this skill is a blend of two characteristics which seem to be mutually exclusive, that is, the increasing of the desire to serve in this manner and the achieving of greater and greater levels of relaxation and opening of the mind in order that concepts may be transmitted without the interference of analysis. To seek strongly such a service and to relax into the level of the, shall we say, out on the limb fool is that recommendation which blends the seeming opposite tendencies or characteristics which allow refinement of your vocal channeling skill.

May we answer further, my brother?

N: I was just wondering if the "out on a limb" came from Shirley MacLaine?

(Side one of tape ends.)

(Jim channeling)

I am Latwii, and we are once again with this instrument. Is there another query?

N: I have for a while wondered, but never really wanted to ask, but now I think that many considerations refer to the light of Christ, and I'm sure that this exists, but what was the phrase used in those who were aware, say with Tutankhamen or the groups that Ra visited, was there such a phrase as—was it the light of the Creator rather than the light of Christ or just what type of, shall we say, phraseology was considered appropriate prior to 2000 years ago?

I am Latwii, and am aware of your query, my brother. We find that throughout the history of the many cultures of your planet there have been many words and phrases used to described this state of awareness. There have been many entities such as the one known as Jesus of Nazareth who attained the awareness that is known [to] your peoples—some portion of them, that is—as the Christ or Christed or Christened consciousness. This term or others like it has been in use for a great portion of time preceding the one known as Jesus as Nazareth. There have been so many ways of describing this state of awareness that we could not list them all nor begin to list them accurately, for in the many languages which describe this state there have been many, many attempts to phrase words which would be succinct and illuminating.

May we answer further, my brother?

N: There was a man in Homestead, Florida, who built a sort of house or castle out of coral, and as we discussed earlier, he would have huge blocks of stones, weighing five tons or so put on a truck overnight. This was before mobile cranes were available for this sort of thing. The only thing that he would say to anyone if they asked him is that he learned the secrets of the pyramids. This man was a Lithuanian who could not speak very good English, so there was a communication barrier. He could not drive, and so forth, and yet he built a very unique edifice using this supposed secret of the pyramids. Was a portion of this secret the ability to lift huge weights or to transmute their location? And if so, could others take such a direction?

I am Latwii, and am aware of your query, my brother. We find in this instance that the information regarding this particular entity has been, shall we say, somewhat distorted in the telling and retelling, and the entity himself was not completely, shall we say, clear and open in his communication of the means by which he did that which he did. We cannot discern the complete story, for there has been a good deal of distortion, and apologize for being unable to provide the answer for which you seek.

May we attempt another query, my brother?

N: Thank you very much. Perhaps Carla has something.

Carla: Yeah, I have a question that kind of disturbs me. The instant that N asked where A was, the following words flashed into my mind, that she was north of the Ohio in Indiana and she was dead. I immediately asked who the person was that gave me this thought, didn't get anything, challenged the entity. The entity successfully answered the challenge. I again asked the entity's name and it simply went away. I don't know whether that was Confederation or whether it only seemed to answer the challenge or what. I also wonder if I'm dangerously near trance just because we've been talking about it.

I am Latwii, and am aware of your query, my sister. We find that the entity of which you speak was one which has no Confederation affiliation and [was] desirous of giving information which would pique the curiosity and perhaps cause your instrument to be utilized in a manner which would be deleterious to your safety and health.

May we answer further, my sister?

Carla: Are you saying that any time I went into trance for any reason it would cost me the same as it cost to do a Ra session?

I am Latwii, and am aware of your query, my sister. We do not mean to be facetious, my sister, but the cost would be far greater. The cost is that of which you are aware.

May we answer further?

Carla: Is there an intensification of the amount of vital energy it takes out of me, trance after trance?

I am Latwii. My sister, we find that you are still seeking that of which we speak. The use of the trance state would have those deleterious effects of which you have been aware for some time. We speak not of the normal wear and tear of any individual trance session but of the more dire results.

May we answer further, my sister?

Carla: Yeah. Let me refine that down a little bit. Would you confirm that any inner plane teacher for whom I went into trance would take a much severer toll on me? And I'm not just speaking of the removal of my mind by a spirit complex if I got hooked up with a negative entity—I know that part. What I'm interested in is just still mechanics, but I noticed during the Ra contact that as much as it took out of me, it did not take as much out of me to do a Ra session as it did when I went into trance for T and let E come through, those two times. That was extreme physical fatigue and pain, and they were very short sessions compared to the Ra sessions. It was a much worse toll on me and I'm wondering if that would be true of any non-Confederation, or really just any contact besides that of Ra which I undoubtedly made agreements with before this incarnation?

I am Latwii, and am aware of your query, my sister. You are in large part correct. The greater toll which a contact in the trance state for the purposes stated would take could somewhat be offset by the more appropriate use of your instrument compared to its use in the two time periods of which you speak. The greater problem, however, is not the greater toll which such trance work would take but is the proper protection being provided, for your work has drawn the attention of those negative entities who are quite willing and able to cause difficulties at any opportunity. Thus the protection must be most exquisitely prepared and is at this time not available.

May we answer further, my sister.

Carla: When you refer to my work, are you referring to my being or to my fruits?

I am Latwii, and, my sister, we refer to whatever fruit might come from the work in trance. May we answer further?

Carla: Then my being by itself does not attract the negative entities. Is this correct?

I am Latwii, and, my sister, any entity who seeks along the path of positivity and service to others will find that its efforts attract the negative attention the purer the efforts become, for such efforts are as a light and such light is as a power, for it may transform others by its being and presence. Thus, those of negative polarity seek to control such power. And if such control cannot be gained, in some instances, then the light is put out, if possible.

May we answer further, my sister?

Carla: If I had never made contact with Ra and I was simply trying to be the best person I know how to be, to attain sainthood in this incarnation, would I have attracted the same negative entity or is it the works themselves that attract the big guns?

I am Latwii, and am aware of your query, my sister. If the case which you hypothesize had been your experience, you would have attracted the minions of such negative entities who would provide as they provide to all such seekers the tests and the temptations that each seeker must discern and put behind.

May we answer further, my sister?

Carla: No, thank you.

I am Latwii, and we find that this instrument has quickly grown fatigued due to its concern that it is somewhat over its head in this particular session. Thus, we shall relinquish our use of this instrument for this evening and we thank each for inviting our presence. We remind each that our words are but our humble opinions and we have no absolute truth to share. Use your salt shaker quite liberally, my friends. We are those of Latwii, and we leave you in the love and the light of our infinite Creator. Adonai, my friends. Adonai. ✣

Sunday Meditation
June 23, 1985

(Carla channeling)

I am Hatonn, and I greet you and bless you in the love and the light of our infinite Creator. We come this evening with great joy to welcome those who are new to this group as well as those who are old in membership, to thank you most humbly for allowing us to be of what small service we can by sharing our thoughts with you. We ask you to remember at all times that we are as you, seekers along a path, seekers who have not found the ending of that path. We are fallible and foolish and know little more than you. That which we know that you do not we are most happy to share. But we ask you to remember at all times that beyond any knowledge that we can share with words, you have within you a discernment, and to that discernment certain things will speak and certain things will not.

We ask you to take those things which are helpful and, without a backward glance, forget anything we have said that is not helpful to you at this particular moment, for we wish to be of service, not to be a stumbling block like so many other spiritual stumbling blocks that ask you to believe this or think that. We offer to you ideals and opinions and we hope that we may be of aid. We are eternally grateful for the opportunity. We are attempting to use this instrument's voice in order to make each word audible to the room, therefore this instrument will be speaking more loudly than usual, and we apologize to those closest to the instrument.

This evening we would tell you a short story about a young man who was seeking and had been seeking for many years to find out what the truth was about himself and about the Creator. Who was he? Where did he fit into the plan, into the scheme that kept the planets and galaxies in place?

This he sought, and at this time he was on a ship which was temporarily harbored off a rocky coast. A terrible storm came up and the young man threw himself into the sea, for it appeared that his ship was breaking up around him. Portions of wood lay all about him in the white and frothy water, and although the water was not deep, as the young man clambered toward the rocky shore, yet it was perhaps the most physically difficult thing he had ever done to climb out of the stormy waters and onto the rocks of land. As he gazed at the land, he found that there was something mysteriously entrancing and magical about it. There were few trees, but there were dark rocky hills which seemed to climb ever upward and which ended in a magnificent castle. Somehow the young man knew that within that castle was the answer to the questions that he had been seeking. The young man studied the mountain very carefully. It seemed almost impossible to achieve the climb and indeed it took him three days and two nights. He was able to find good water but was not knowing enough of plants to find food, and when he finally clambered to the top of what was almost a sheer cliff, he was starving and exhausted.

Now he was faced with more water, water over which a bridge could be put down but there was no bridge; he was not expected. He called out and called out again and no one heard him. And so he plunged into the moat, swam to the other side and again carved his way up the steep bank until he stood at the gate of the castle itself. The front door opened easily. There was no one to welcome him. There were, however, many, many closed doors. Each had a different lock, and so he began to try the doors, knowing somehow that behind one of them lay the answers to the questions that he had been asking for so many years.

He could not get any doors open, not with a battering ram which he made of his shoulder, not with his amateur lock-picking, but he found that a simple knocking at the door would open each one. And so he began knocking upon the doors. The doors opened, one after the other. Some rooms held great gold and silver, some rooms were veritable treasure houses of precious stones, and many rooms held one person or a small group who turned and looked into the eyes of the young man who sought entrance.

The young man attempted to speak with these beings. He had for years worked on the most clever and intellectually precise set of questions that he could formulate about the nature of his being and the nature of his Creator. Each entity or group of entities in each room gazed in love and said nothing in return. The young man mounted the stairs, trying doors, finding no thing that answered his questions, becoming more and more agitated.

Finally, in what appeared to be a kind of dungeon, he came across a double door of beaten copper. He requested entrance from it, and the doors swung outward to greet him. He began to explain to this room which was empty exactly what it was he wished to know. He was interrupted by a voice belonging to someone he could not see.

"Have you been in each room of this dwelling place of the spirit?"

"Yes I have; this is the last," he said desperately.

"Do you still wish to seek the answers to the questions that you have, regardless of the cost?"

The young man looked about him. He did not see implements of torture, he could not imagine the implied threat of what it might mean, but he was quite sincere in his seeking. "Yes," he said, "I wish these answers more than anything in this life which I live."

"Very well, then," came the unseen presence, speaking to him in [a] voice of gold.

Suddenly the room was filled with the same storm-tossed water which he had left at sea. He was caught up in the maelstrom. Somehow, he did not have trouble breathing, but he was moving very quickly and in directions of which he was not at all sure. Darkness had descended upon the face of the ocean and there was no moon, so it came to him after several minutes had passed that he was out at sea being tossed to and fro in the stormy ocean. A sense of despair came over him. He could not see land and he said to no one in particular, as far as he knew, "I surrender. I give my life. I welcome the deep. If there are no answers, that is well. I surrender."

Suddenly, the storm ceased to rage about him, and he was basked in a peculiarly effulgent golden glow. It seemed to take the place of a boat, for he was now dry and he could now rest. So he lay back his head and began to try to come to grips with what had happened to him. He could not. After what seemed to be an infinity of time thinking to himself, he spoke to the light about him.

"Who are you or what power do you represent?" he asked the light. Into his mind came a concept: "I am love," it said.

"Who is 'I'?" asked the young man. Suddenly, the young man was again in the stormy waters.

"Love, come back," he called. And again he was safe.

The young man was dumbfounded. He did not know what to ask; he could not formulate any questions any longer. And so he simply spoke to the light that was around him.

"I have sought long to know the truth about myself and about the Creator. I do not understand what has happened to me, what the meaning was of my shipwreck and of this craft of light that keeps me from the storm." He was back in the water immediately, the storm raging about him.

"Love, come back," he called, and again he was in the craft, safe and dry.

Love then spoke to him, briefly. "My child," spoke the glowing light, "I am love. You are love and all is love. This is the truth about who you are, this is the truth about who the Creator is, and this is the truth about your connection with the Creator. If you wish the storm, so you may learn of the Creator; if you wish peace, so better you may learn of the Creator. But love speaks only to love and tempest to tempest."

Each of you may make that choice at any time—the tempest or the peace. Both are equally full of love; one is intellectually distorted, the other distorted by the biases of compassion and unity. If you accept tempest into your mind or your heart, then you shall learn by the tempest, and it shall be a good learning, though hectic. If you accept the calm within the storm, then love shall speak to you plain and clear. We urge you, my friends, to seek the calm within through the quiet of meditation and contemplation. What inspires you may not inspire another, what aids you in meditation may not aid another. Each is unique, and it does not matter how you attain those few moments each day of quiet. What matters is that you intend to rest in the love and in the light of the one infinite Creator.

All of you move across the face of the deep. All of you are ocean voyagers, and a long, long way from home. We bid you a fair voyage and a craft built with love. And when you are in the midst of tempest, we bid you rejoice that you learn from the storm.

We shall leave this instrument, again thanking you for allowing us to blend our vibrations with you and to share these few moments. We are those known to you as Hatonn. We leave you in deep waters and golden light. We leave you in the creation—where else is there to go, my friends? How far can you search to find one thing? We leave you in the love and the light of the one infinite Creator. And if you should wish us to be with you to aid you in deepening your meditation at any time, please mentally request our presence and we shall be glad to be with you. Adonai, my friends. Adonai vasu borragus.

(Jim channeling)

I am Latwii, and I greet you, my friends, in the love and light of the one infinite Creator. It is also our great joy and privilege to be asked to join you this evening. We come, as always, in hopes that our simple service of attempting to answer your queries might have value in your seeking. We are as those of Hatonn, and like yourselves seekers of truth, quite fallible and wishing each to know that we give our opinions but have no final words as to the truth. Take those words that are of value to you. May we begin with the first query?

L: I'd like to ask a question, Latwii. In the Ra material, mention is made of the fact that there is a sort of seniority system established for entities who wish to incarnate on this planet at this time. Being that the lines are long and the time is short, would it not be an act of service to those entities desiring to incarnate for one who had already incarnated to simply kill themselves, thus making room for another incarnation? I was reflecting on this and it seemed to me to be about as far as a person could go towards service to others. Could you comment on that, please?

I am Latwii, and am aware of your query, my brother. This is a query which has many ramifications which would be quite lengthy in giving of the complete insights. We shall attempt to make comment which shall be brief and hopefully clear. The intentions of any entity are the most salient or important feature of any thought or action. The intentions determine then one's polarity, one's service, and one's, as it has come to be called, harvestability. Each entity in proceeding through an incarnation then will color or charge or empower each thought and action by its intention. If one should then decide that to be of the greatest service possible to another, that it should take its own life that another might live, this then would be well. This is the path of what has been come to be called the martyr. Yet it is not a path which is easily chosen. Nor is it one that is suggested, for as one attempts to be of service to others, one cannot know the final or total outcome of any thought or action. One must move then through the incarnation in accordance with an inner voice for assurance which is the product of long and dedicated service, for the intellect cannot know these things.

Thus, an entity in the position of which you have described would be well advised to seek clearly, calmly and with great intention for that inner voice, that its own will might be given over, that the will of the Creator might move through it. When such has been accomplished, then no matter what action it is that is being contemplated, one may move in the greatest assurance that one moves appropriately according to the plan of the one Creator and the plan that each entity in its higher self forms, constructs before the incarnation, having at that time the greater view of purpose, service and lessons to be offered.

May we answer you further, my brother?

L: No, that was a good response. Thank you.

I am Latwii, and we thank you, my brother. Is there another query?

Questioner: I have a question of sorts—really, I'm just asking for a comment. I've had some thoughts recently about patience sort of being the basis for forming our attitudes and our ability to like and accept other people and ourselves, and I would just like some comment on that. Just on patience in general in our spiritual development.

I am Latwii, and we are aware of your query, my brother. The patience of which you speak may be likened unto the peace or the love which our brothers and sisters of Hatonn began with this evening as their topic. As each seeker moves through the illusion that is your reality, there are many storms of seeming difficulty which beset each seeker along the path. There is much to sway one's attention, much to seemingly detain the progress. Yet, if one can maintain an attitude of patience, of tolerance, and of developing what we might call the light touch, then one might rest where others flail madly about, and in this resting a greater view might become apparent to the patient eye, for it looks keenly and evenly at that which is about it and that which is within it, and reserves judgment, motion and action until a later time, as you would call it.

During this time, a greater view is made available to the patient eye. More, shall we say, pieces of the puzzle come before the attention, that the thoughts and actions which shall be this entity's response to the storm shall carry the consideration that has been carefully determined. Thus, patience is a great virtue, my friends, but one which is most usually preceded by a great deal of flailing about, and making the rash and quick judgments which in their own way teach quite well, yet may leave some bruises here and there.

May we answer further, my brother?

Questioner: No, that's fine. Thank you.

I am Latwii, and we thank you, my brother. Is there another query?

N: I have one query. Is it better to leave the veil of forgetfulness in place, or can some entities benefit by lifting the veil, by whatever means?

I am Latwii, and am aware of your query, my brother. Each of you, my brother, every instant of your incarnation removes yet another small portion of that veil of forgetting, as you have called it, which seems to separate you from the one Creator and all creation. The conscious attempt to penetrate this veil is the path of the adept. Each who seeks in a conscious manner, therefore, is an adept of one degree or another. To penetrate this veil through whatever means is available to you is what we might call an enhancement upon your journey, for within the illusion created by the veil, there is much which seems confused, much which seems broken, much which seems evil, much which seems other than one's own self if you remain within this illusion with no effort to shine the light upon the confusion and to make whole that which is broken. To see the Creator in that which seems evil, and to see the self in all things is the purpose of your incarnation.

May we answer further, my brother?

N: Thank you.

I am Latwii, and we thank you, my brother. Is there another query?

(Side one of tape ends.)

(Jim channeling)

I am Latwii, and we are again with this instrument. We thank you each for inviting our presence this evening. We hope that our humble words have had some small value in your own journey in seeking the truth. Know that your queries and your presence and your invitation for our presence have been of great service to us in our own seeking of the truth, for in each of you we see the Creator in yet another expression, and we rejoice in your uniqueness and in the unity of all. We thank you again. We are with you at your request in your meditations, and we shall leave you at this time in the love and in the light of our infinite Creator. Adonai, my friends. Adonai vasu borragus.

(Carla channeling)

I am Yadda. I greet you in the love and in the light of our infinite Creator. We have, as you see, we come when we call and are called, then, that makes sense, so we are here with you. Is that not so? Hello. And good evening. We talk a little bit, and then we go, for we know it is a long meeting when we hear the tape flip over.

We talk to you of light, for we speak to you in love and we speak to you in light, and yet how often do we concentrate on the light? The light—what is the light that we welcome you in and leave you in? Perhaps you may think that you know what love is. It is doubtful that you know; you may know. But it is difficult or more difficult to think of what light is. But we say to you that light is all that you can see, and all that you cannot that is manifest to any consciousness on any level so that all that is builded that is not with the original Thought of love is builded with light.

Let us take examples: the air is light, both physical light and metaphysical light, that is, light that feeds the eye and glows between; metaphysical light that nourishes your being, that being which is far beyond any physical manifestation at all, for you have been, and you will be, and you are now, but your body is only now—it will go away, and you will probably be glad to get rid of it! What you will have left is another kind of light.

(Background sound of chuckling, presumably at Yadda's accent.)

We are doing better with our "L's." We are proud.

Therefore, what you see is always the same thing. It is not even lightness, brightness or heat only; it is chairs and swimming pools and air conditioners and popsicles and people and thoughts and ideas. You name it—it's light. That's all, it isn't anything else. Light is a vibration and this vibration is infinite in variety. Through the process of free will moving in love, those things which are created are created, some by the infinite Creator of which you are all a part, some by co-creators such as yourself.

Therefore, make your light shine, for you are beautiful. And you can become more beautiful as you stop worrying about how beautiful your light is. The less you worry and the more you rejoice, the more light with metaphysical light your global sphere shall be and the more watchtowers you will find lighting up a dark planet.

So you see, we speak to you of light, and we speak to you of our accent. We would leave you by answering a totally ridiculous question, and that is, why do we speak with this accent? We will tell you why we speak with this accent through this instrument who is bending its wittle tongue in many funny directions. We were on the planet in several capacities with those in what you would now call China. This was a few years ago—many, many years ago, many of your centuries ago. We were very fond, fond in the extreme, of the possibilities, the adequacy and the excellence of the Chinese language, and of its written precision. Now we speak English, because to speak Chinese to this group would be a little silly. So we won't do that, but we have just begun learning the English about—wait a minute, we must work with this instrument a moment, for time is difficult for us to tell.

Twenty-seven years we speak English. That is not very long for us, and we hope that you can understand us. But we also hope that you know that though we love and though we are with you because you are part of us, because you are part of the one Creator, because you are all light and all love, we still cannot be for you the teacher that will give you all the answers; we have no reputation, we are fools. And as serious fools who step blindly forward, we step with you.

We thank you. And we greet you as we leave, in the love and in the omnipresent light of the One. We leave you in that unity. Adonai. We are those of Yadda.

L/L Research

Sunday Meditation
June 30, 1985

(Carla channeling)

I am Yadda. I greet you in love and light of our infinite Creator. We are so grateful to be with you this evening and we have no words of wisdom for you, but only wish to say, "Hi"—is that how you say? Or "Hello" or "Howdy." To the one known as J especially we wish also to make very clear … that was good; did you hear that? We said "c*l*ear" … that we at any time can be called upon with the internal mechanisms of your mind and we shall be with you. We are always happy to be with you in meditation or at any time you may call us that we may deepen your meditation or just hang out, as this instrument would say. We leave you now in the love and in the light of the One. We wish to leave quickly. Adonai, my friends. We are those of Yadda and it is in joy that we have been able to come to speak briefly with you. Adonai. Adonai.

(Carla channeling)

I am L/Leema, and I greet you in the love and in the light of our infinite Creator. It is indeed a privilege for us to blend our life energies with your own as we both walk, one thought, one foot, one idea ahead of the other through a long path, a long life, and one long question that has many ramifications. At this minute, this instrument does not know which of the two group questions we have been privileged to choose as we are using the word-by-word method of communication with this instrument, and so the instrument is concentrating too much on the next word to be aware of the next concept.

It is because of the makeup of the group this evening that we choose the question concerning communication within the so-called spirit worlds. Many of the concepts which work into the answer we would like to give to the question concerning your "day of wrath" or the "beginning of the golden age"—depending upon your state of mind towards this grand event—are simply not available to some of those present, and without these concepts the answer would be basically an exercise in futility, not a kind of exercise which we wish to let you appreciate at this time since it is rather tedious to be bored. Therefore, we would like to take the question and look at it very carefully because there are many, many entities in a very crowded universe that wish to talk to entities upon your sphere and indeed do talk to entities upon and within your sphere.

The most prevalent channeling which you shall experience in your incarnation is the channeling of the self. Although you are consciousness and simplicity itself, your own simplicity is hidden from you in a geometrically precise and somewhat penetrable manner. Therefore, in order to understand and manifest those portions of yourself which lie beneath the surface of the personality, in order to perceive [how] that change of the outer self might be made to conform to the inner self and so forth, avenues are set up within your mind, body and spirit so that information can be passed from your deep self to your surface self. It is seldom that you speak your own words; it is usual that you channel a portion of your complete self.

Almost all human communication is both made possible, and greatly hindered, by the fact that entities do not communicate with their entire selves but communicate with the portion of the self which is available to the self at that particular moment. The amount of the self which is available for self-knowledge is dependent upon the amount of the self that was available to the entity at birth, the amount of aid that the entity may have had by those teachers which aided the entity through childhood, and by the entity's own will to learn and to know.

As always, we recommend daily meditation, for though you may think you are listening to the silence, that silence is a link just as one of your long distance numbers. This one is very long distance, my friends; this is your link with something called infinity. It is also your link with an infinite thing called yourself. It is a most helpful type of learning and will most decidedly aid the most important channeling you will ever do, that is, yourself, communicating with a whole heart and a single mind with another entity so as to offer the most loving responses, create the most loving atmosphere, and manifest to the other self that part of the other self which is also infinite.

We shall not bore you with the details of inner and outer dimensions. That is a question in and of itself, and we need say only that there are some entities connected with the planet itself, some connected with your star system, which are called angels by many in this particular cultural subgroup of your sphere, and in the outer planes, one finds that that particular dimension is also gravid and full of those who have come to this planetary influence from elsewhere as a choice in order that they may be of service.

Let us look at the way there are no differences between them. They all have the basic message. They all seem with the same degree of authority, that is, the same as ours, that is to say, we are all fallible; we make mistakes, we are foolish, and we are not to be depended upon for the ultimate truth. We do not have a corner on that market, not the outer planes and not the inner planes. That which is infinite is also unknowable. The universe begins in mystery; it also, as far we know, resolves into mystery. In between is where you are and where we are and we observe and watch and make our observations known to you in hopes that we may be of service in inspiring you or nagging you or urging you to accelerate the rate of your own growth spiritually, emotionally, mentally and mentally/emotionally, perhaps most importantly by seeking and ever more seriously seeking something called the one original Thought.

Some have called it the Truth. In this instrument's mind, there is a pedestal: TRVTH is written upon it. That is what we attempt to bring you, the ersatz truth with a bit of sawdust in it, so that you may go within to seek the one source that is without fallibility and that is within yourself. So please use your discrimination when listening to any psychic, paranormal or whatever you wish to call it, channeling of any kind. There is something within you that will resonate with what you need to hear and what you need to know and what you need to do. Throw the rest away.

The main question remains: "Why cannot Kuthumi talk to Djwhal Khul who can then talk to Yogananda who can then talk with Ra who could then talk with L/Leema who could then talk with this instrument?" so that you could find out what Kuthumi *et al* were attempting to say.

One of your group members came in tonight explaining that the cassette tape recorder which this particular entity uses cannot be made compatible with any other tape recorder which this person owns. Therefore, this soul is somewhat distressed because it cannot dub off, as this instrument would say, a particular recording which is of value to the entity. This is the greatest reason for the lack of communication between middle-man, in the outer dimension especially. We say that due to the fact that ego plays a far lesser role in the outer dimension since we are all here for one specific general job. Therefore we have fewer loyalties to any one entity. We simply do not have a patch cord that will connect an energy which demands the trance state equivalent in an instrument to that which does not demand a trance state to be given to the same instrument. They simply do not make the fittings, shall we say. It is a mechanical difficulty based upon the tuning that is necessary to receive the entity.

This evening you tuned until a very disparate group of entities became, in general, cautiously and tentatively fond enough of each other to relax into a metaphysical actuality called a circle. That is, a circle of light in which each gives the other the spiritual love, the impersonal love that it would give all mankind if it could. It is a trusting and resting into universal light and love, and you have done so and it is good. It is exceptionally good for this type of channeling, and we are enjoying this energy very much and appreciate the continuation of your tuning, for the group energy remains fairly high. In the inner planes the difficulties are not precisely the same, for the differences between teachers is less, vibrationally speaking. Therefore, in one fairly broad tuning a receptive channel could get a variety of entities.

First of all, inner plane entities usually wish to teach one particular people, group, culture or even entity. Therefore, the messages which they have are highly individualized compared to those of the outer dimensions, although, vibrationally speaking, we are talking about the same octave or sub-octave, shall we say, of coloration or speed of vibration, to use a more precise term.

There is also the individuality of many of those upon the inner planes, meaning that they wish to be teachers and do not wish to teach through another discarnate entity. Normally, one discarnate entity will form a so-called control, thereby allowing other discarnate entities to speak through the same instrument. It is to be noted that those who use inner plane teachers almost always must work in trance which is a type of channeling that is both easy to do as fakery and is very difficult upon the instrument's physical health if done in earnest and with sincerity. That is why we do not choose to use trance channeling. Our message does not need the trance, for the degree of specificity which we feel comfortable with is one of which this instrument is capable without a deep trance.

This is the rapid run-through, shall we say, of the inner and outer plane teachers. There is no teacher that does not have a lesson that will be good for you to hear. There are none to be scorned. Each will prefer one teacher or one type of information that is totally acceptable. It is not for you as those who come and hear this meditation to go forth and then say, "You must come and think of the spiritual in this way which has helped me so much." Indeed, it is then your job as a manifesting conscious spiritual entity to listen ever more sharply and see ever more keenly and understand with ever more compassion that each person's trail is highly individualistic and may well not parallel, become congruent, or even stay in sight of your own.

Listen to what those about you need and do not press your ideas upon them. You may drop your seeds; after that, let them germinate. They may well not germinate; that is also good because this universe is absolutely shouting the one single message that is channeled by trance, light trance, yourself, and every single type of channeling that we could mention. That one single message is: joy. If you look at the trees you can almost see them clap their hands when the sun streams down upon them and lifts up the dew and they turn their fingers to catch all the light they can. The grasses wave and the breeze blows and those of you with your allergies are most aware of this. The song of birds permeates the air, and there is great joy available to you. It is the unconditional joy of an infinity of supply, an infinity of knowledge, an infinity of peace, an infinity of growth.

An infinity, my friends—no limits. You don't have until tomorrow, you don't have until next week. You have all the time you need to decide what you wish to do concerning the Creator's love for you. Do you love yourself, for you know you are the Creator? Can you love the Creator in other people? It is probably easier for you to see it in others than in yourself. The one patch cord you all have, the one channeling that is available to all of you is the channeling between your deep self and your thinking self. Don't think first; meditate first. There are inspirations and intuitions that no logic, no rhetoric, and no persuasion can give you. Let those inspirations come to you. It may take a good deal of what you call time. You have time. If you are waiting—wait. Continue waiting and continue. Just because something is unseen does not mean it is not there. You shall learn. And whatever comes before you, whether it be inner plane, outer plane, higher, lower, upper, downer, all of the supermarket words that you may have heard—drink it in! But if it does not taste for you as you would wish it, do not swallow it, have nothing more to do with it, discreetly spit it out.

Parenthetically, we offer sympathy that we cannot use an intermediary to offer you information from the social memory complex, Ra. Without saying any more to prejudice opinion within the group as to the future of this contact, let us say that a second-hand contact would not be possible. The energy of the three that collected those sessions with Ra was of a certain type and the entity which now channels in light trance was then channeling in deep trance.

A second parenthesis, and that is simply to note that what information has been given is excellent but that it is never wise to depend upon any source but yourself. The wisest among us has the same birthright as do you and that is that shuttle of spirit with all that is infinite and invisible and unknowable, in a word, noumenal. Never despair because you have not got the right contact. And as you go looking for other contacts, if indeed you do so, do so with a merry laugh on your lips for you shall have great adventures and feel a great deal of warm air, just as you are now perceiving especially from the location of this instrument's mouth. Rely upon the self, knowing that there are those in the inner planes assigned to you personally and as a group and on the outer planes who have come because you called and are sensitive to you personally so that we may be with you at any time that you wish.

We thank you for the ability to speak through this instrument. It is always a joy to use an instrument such as this one and to speak with entities who are seeking the truth, whether spelled with a U or a V. We urge you to come off the pedestal, remove the V, and begin opening your ears, your eyes, and your heart to the little, the simple, and the unexpected that occur all about you all the time and which you may miss if you are looking for the big sign that will tell you whither you are to go, what path you shall take. Most of the subjective proof which you will gather in your search for your own self is made up of small, seemingly synchronistic events. Watch for them. The universe itself, in the persona of your higher self, can use all of nature to speak to you, all of mankind's artifacts to trigger memories that will speak to you and to trigger feelings that will inspire.

Our channeling is done, my friends, but the blessing of your presence endures. We bid you adieu. We are those of L/Leema. Adonai, my friends. We leave you in love and in light.

(Jim channeling)

I am Latwii, and we greet you, my friends, in the love and light of our infinite Creator, and we are privileged to be with you as well. We thank you for asking for our presence. We also suggest that you remember that we too are fallible and speak opinion, though it has been our pleasure and our joy and our privilege to gather this experience which is our shared opinion. We would, as always, hope to be of service by attempting to answer those queries which have value to you. May we begin then with the first query?

C: Yes. This is my first experience tonight with the concept of using a group question. It seemed that before, if I understood correctly, that the various entities channeled for the message picked up on whatever the corporal thought was within the group at the time. What's the difference between that and the setting down of the formulation of the question? Or group question?

I am Latwii, and am aware of your query, my brother. The difference between the two techniques discussed is that in the technique which you have used this evening, you are consciously focusing your attention and your desire upon one point. The technique which has been used by this group almost to a majority of experience previous to the last few meetings is one which recognizes an unconscious blending of desire and matching of this desire. When you consciously focus your attention upon a point, you amplify your ability to receive information within the scope of that point. You in effect increase the power of your group receiver.

May we answer further, my brother?

C: So, it's just a matter of by using the group question, we simply amplify our energies to achieve a clearer answer?

I am Latwii, and this is, in general, correct, my brother.

May we answer further?

C: No, thank you.

I am Latwii, and we thank you, my brother. Is there another query?

Carla: Are you suggesting by that that L/Leema and Latwii, being fifth density, that there is an amount of energy that will draw fourth-density and early fifth-density entities to give cosmic sermonettes and tell little stories, and then there's this big sort of quantum leap into the amount of energy needed to answer specific questions? Is that what you're saying?

I thought the reason was because I couldn't answer questions, and so the question had to be asked beforehand. So—but what you're saying is that there needs to be the group energy [that] pushes the energy of the channel, so it's just like it pushes it over a line. Could you confirm that? I'll stop now.

I am Latwii, and we thank you for your query, my sister. To respond, let us suggest that there are two portions to your query. Firstly, the response which we gave to the one known as C was in consideration of a technique, that is, the conscious blending of group energy to form a query or focus for response. The second portion of your query concerns through which instrument this technique can be used most efficiently. Because of your experience with the contact with those of Ra, it is not only possible but recommended that queries be answered through your instrument in the manner which we have seen used this evening. This technique could also be used with other instruments. However, queries through your instrument are best achieved through that technique and that technique alone.

May we answer further, my sister?

Carla: No, thank you.

We are Latwii, and we thank you, my sister.

(Side one of tape ends.)

(Jim channeling)

I am Latwii …

Carla: Hang on. Hang on, Latwii.

… and we are with this instrument once again. We apologize for the delay; this instrument was in the process of rechallenging our contact. May we then reopen this session to queries?

Carla: Latwii, could I have your permission to ask a question from someone who is not in this group?

I am Latwii, and we are most happy to attempt response to any query placed before us.

Carla: Okay. I'll pick one at random. Question number four: "The law of karma is said to be transcended only by reunion between the 'deviltry' and God, yet gestures of grace appear to surface in profusion within every era and in every region. Can further light be shed upon this interplay between karmic law and transcendent grace?"

I am Latwii, and am aware of your query, my sister. The karmic law, as it has been called, is a very simply stated law. It may be seen as inertia. When an action, a thought, or an energy has been set into motion in order to gather experience, this energy will continue in motion until an equal energy in the opposite direction has been generated. At this point there is the balancing of energies. Each entity within any incarnation is subject to this so-called law. This is how experience is gained and variety is achieved in the experience. The grace which has been described is the environment in which this law operates. This so-called grace is that support within all of creation which each entity stands upon and breathes within its being as it sets into motion the various distortions or experiential patterns that are set before the incarnation for such and such a purpose. The grace that supports each entity then is available as the very fabric of the creation through which an entity moves. It assures each entity that no matter what experience it may entertain, it shall not truly move from love, shall not truly move [from] light, from joy or from unity. No entity can travel a distance so far that there is the lack of love. This grace, so-called, therefore, assures this infinite and eternal support.

May we answer further, my sister?

Carla: Yes, a personal question. First, let me just ask you, is this an example of the law of karma which happened to be mitigated by grace? Someone in my church—I'm the head of a prayer group in my church—somebody in my church had this big old cancer and asked us to pray for him when he went in for tests. I wrote him a letter telling him that we were praying for him every day. He had already had one ultrasound and he had a bad lump. He took the letter in his hand and read it, and something jumped from the letter to his hand and he felt something go through him. He's a big man, and so I can't imagine this happening to him, because he's not one of these imaginative people; he has sort of a football player mentality. They took another picture and it was gone. The cancer was gone completely. Somehow in the letter that I sent him, did something—was it, did it turn out to be an instrument of grace? And if so, is there any way to help other people besides just randomly, seemingly? Does there have to be an instrument for grace or can grace hit you, person to person?

I am Latwii, and am aware of your query, my sister. The event of which you speak may be described as one manifestation of grace. There can be any variety or number of ways through which grace can move into one's life in a form which one may understand according to the beliefs that one has built one's philosophy, shall we say, or point of viewing upon. Therefore, it is not always necessary that a physical thing or manifestation be used as an intermediary between an entity and this nebulous state of what has been called grace. Each entity will avail itself of this essence of grace according to its own unique configuration of thought.

May we answer further, my sister?

Carla: No, thank you.

I am Latwii, and we thank you, my sister. Is there another query?

N: I have a question. I would like to know if it is possible to understand what is known as the Tourette syndrome in which there seems to be either a form of possession or is this merely a short-circuiting of the synaptic junctions that create the behavioral pattern, in an otherwise normal individual, that is totally irrational for a momentary time span?

I am Latwii, and am aware of your query, my brother. This particular syndrome, you may be surprised to hear, is also a manifestation of grace, for all about each entity are the infinite opportunities for learning and for service that may be termed grace. And each opportunity is, shall we say, taken advantage of or perceived in a unique fashion by each entity. At some point in an entity's incarnational progress, in this kind of case, there is the turning of the mind in such a fashion that the grace or infinite energy in such and such a pattern is perceived in a slightly different fashion so that the entity begins seeing, in general, a somewhat darker image than is available to the entity. All entities see a combination of light and dark, for that is the nature of your illusion. Yet by choice, each sees a greater portion of one than of the other.

Therefore, any mental configuration, whether described as sane or insane, balanced or unbalanced, or any description which you may choose, is a point of view that has been chosen through a series of choices. The regaining of balance is most generally accomplished by any technique which takes the entity back through the series of steps in order that the choices may be made again in another fashion or distortion.

May we answer further, my brother?

N: Yes, please. Is this extreme form of negativistic, irrational, many times socially unacceptable oral behavior a form of karmic balancing? Since it does occur in young children as well as adults?

I am Latwii, and am aware of your query, my brother. Any point of view, including the one of which you have spoken, is a distortion of preincarnative choices made in response to experience gained in previous incarnations, and forms what you have loosely called a karmic debt or burden. It is not so much a debt, however, as an opportunity. Any point of view, therefore, is some form or intensity or distortion of a preincarnative choice which is hoped will either be a lesson or a service or a combination of the two during an entity's incarnational experience.

May we answer further, my brother?

N: Yes. Is there any way we can accelerate this preincarnative consideration or is it something that must be an individual's situation and worked out only by that individual without external service to other type of assistance?

I am Latwii, and am aware of your query, my brother. Let us use an analogy. Picture yourself and all other selves within what you may call a locomotive. Each entity rides his or her own locomotive. It moves without any seeming energy or effort upon your part. Your life moves on, time moves on, events have their own momentum. Yet, if you look about you within this locomotive, if you consciously seek to know the nature of your being and your surroundings, you see there are switches, letters and dials, each according to your own description and formation of belief. When you know yourself more and more clearly, it is as though you discover another switch that opens yet more circuits and allows more energy to move the locomotive of your being. As you become more and more aware of the switches and the nature of your own being you, shall we say, shed light upon the switches and dials, that you may then cause to function in such a way that your path of progress moves according to your will as it is harmonized with your, as you have called it, sub[conscious] or unconscious mind which contains your preincarnative program or karmic burden as it has been called.

May we answer further, my brother?

N: Well, since this is a preincarnative consideration, it may be in many instances difficult to assist. Is that correct? Because many of us or probably all of us have tried to talk to some of our friends about reincarnation or other considerations, and have of course been more or less slapped in the face with a blank stare and, "where are you coming from" sort of situation. Then I take it that we would have difficulty in directing many individuals in any sort of consideration of service to others? Is that generally incorrect or correct?

I am Latwii, and am aware of your query, my brother. As has been stated previously this evening, you may sow your seeds where you will and as you will. That is according to your life pattern and nature. Whether these seeds grow or are received in any fashion whatsoever is a result of the life pattern of the one in whose mind you have sown the seeds. The response of any entity to your efforts is that entity's pattern. Each will perceive according to a unique configuration of thought.

May we answer further, my brother?

N: Thank you very much. I just wonder how the instrument is doing?

I am Latwii, and we are happy to report that this instrument is available for a number of further queries if there are such.

Carla: I'd sort of like to retune right now if you'll all just hang out with "Row Your Boat." I'd like to get more energy going.

(The group sings together, three times through.)

Carla: Thank you. I'd just like to finish up on his question by saying, is the switch for the tracks inside the train or is that part of the preincarnative choice or is it a mixture? I mean, you have power over the comfort of the ride and the velocity, the getting from here to there, maybe the niceness with which you finish up whatever it is that you're doing on the track, but do you choose the track within this incarnation or is the track pretty well set as to where you're going, preincarnationally?

I am Latwii, and am once again with this instrument, and am aware of your query, my sister. The density in which you dance your own illusion provides the countryside, shall we say, through which your track and train move. The countryside through which you move in your illusion is one of love, is one of the self which has become individualized, making a choice in its use of the energy which gives its life as a gift to it. The choice is to share this energy with others in service to others or to keep and hoard the energy for the self in service to self. The subconscious mind, which allows an entity contact with the higher self, most predominantly before the incarnation, allows the entity and the entire self and guides and friends to describe the general framework or series of tracks available to an entity during its incarnation. During the incarnation, therefore, it is usually the case that an entity, having become consciously aware of some portion of this process, will be able to gain, shall we say, a control, to use a poor term, of the rate of progress of the locomotive over the tracks. However, it is possible for an entity to consciously alter the tracks to be traveled. This, however, continues always and ever within an illusion of love and the opportunity to learn any lesson of love chosen before or during the incarnation.

May we answer you further, my sister?

Carla: Only one question: If we switch tracks, do we end up at the same place we would have if we hadn't? I mean, do we get the same lessons?

I am Latwii, and am aware of your query, my sister. In one sense this is so, for all points are within love and are within some distance or distortion of the choice made before the incarnation. However, as all choices change outcomes when compared to alternate choices, the end point, though quite similar, will be somewhat different yet will remain within the context of love and of preincarnational design to a greater or lesser degree.

May we answer further, my sister?

Carla: No, thank you.

We thank you, my sister. Is there another query?

N: Yes, I have one. Earlier Latwii confirmed or stated that if we lift the veil of forgetfulness, we generally will accelerate our learning, if I interpret it correctly. Is there any suggested method of lifting this veil if you've perhaps had it for a long time, or must we each find our own way?

I am Latwii, and am aware of your query, my brother. We believe that we have heard a variant of this query in previous sessions, and shall say that each entity will provide itself with a variety of means of penetrating this veil of forgetting. During your incarnation, you will be drawn by an inner resonance to one or more techniques for so penetrating this veil. The technique, as we have mentioned before, is not as important as the desire to use the technique. The development of the will to persevere and the faith that there is reason to persevere are those qualities that are most important in the actual penetration of this veil.

May we answer further, my brother?

N: But you do confirm that it is best to try to remove the veil if possible?

I am Latwii, and am aware of your query, my brother. We cannot say what is best, for all experience teaches and each entity learns by a unique set of experiences. However, in general it may be assumed that the lifting of this veil in some portion will aid an entity's evolutionary progress. However, it must be remembered that the veil exists because it has a service to offer. And it may be that for certain entities, and in some degree for all entities, the veil's remaining for such and such a period of your time is the most helpful portion or characteristic of the evolutionary progress. To say this another way, the snake shall shed its skin in its own time.

May we answer further, my brother?

N: Is the religion known as the Sufi religion which in many instances has caused the veil, or in some instances, has caused the veil to be placed for reincarnation after reincarnation when the—one of the disciples did not conform to perhaps the utilization of his or her clairvoyance or whatever, in defiance of the Sufi master? Is this a general consideration or does this occur sporadically or is it only possible for the veil to be continued for one incarnation?

I am Latwii, and believe that we have the gist of your query. Please query further if our response is not indicative of that hope. There is no belief or group of entities that can decide for another that the veil of forgetting shall remain in any degree that may be described for any particular number of incarnations. It is the entity itself, between the incarnational experiences, which decides the lessons to be learned, the services to be offered and the means and manner of penetrating this veil in any incarnation.

May we answer further, my brother?

N: Thank you very much. I'm sure someone else has a question, if the instrument is not tired.

I am Latwii, and we thank you, my brother, for your queries and your concerns. This instrument is available for a few more queries. May we ask if there might be another query?

Questioner: Yes, I have a question. I've noticed lots of times that these meditation sessions will have some people who will fall asleep or whatever, due to whatever reason. My question is though, do your responses to questions talk to a particular entity's subconscious as well as their conscious mind? I guess I want to extend that to a lot of different meditations or even different types of cassette tapes, learnings that are recorded on cassette tapes and you listen to in one or another state of awareness. Do things go through to your subconscious as well as your conscious mind? Can you fall asleep and still get it, is what I'm asking, I suppose?

I am Latwii, and am aware of your query, my brother. Though there is some benefit to one who is in the sleeping state to spend that time within a circle of seeking such as this one, the benefit is decidedly less than if that entity were in the conscious mode of experience, for though there are portions of any message that can penetrate the corked bottle, it is easier to pour into a bottle without the cork. The conscious mind is as the cork which opens the entity to reception of information. However, we must remind each that all information and all sources of information are the one Creator speaking to the one Creator. That which is heard by any portion of the Creator is a function of that portion's point of view and openness to expanding that point of view. Other teachers have described this state as the readiness of the student, for all messages contain the one Creator in whole, perfect and balanced within some portion of the message. The discerning ear can hear the One speaking to it and through it.

May we answer further, my brother?

Questioner: No, that's fine. Thank you.

I am Latwii, and we thank you, my brother. Is there another query?

(Pause)

I am Latwii, and we perceive the silence as the One speaking an unspoken word and each heart knows that word. It is love. In that love and in the light which is its manifestation of creation, we leave you. We are those of Latwii. Adonai, my friends. Adonai vasu borragus.

(Carla channeling)

(Carla channels a lovely vocal melody—a song without words.)

I am Nona. Love and light to you and to the one known as R, to the one as known as D, to the one known as Jim, to the one known as Carla. ❧

Intensive Meditation
July 2, 1985

(Carla channeling)

I am Hatonn, and I great you in the love and in the light of our infinite Creator. We wish to confirm to the instrument known as N that we were attempting to contact that instrument prior to contacting this one, for in the practice of vocal channeling the time comes when the vocal channel is ready to initiate contact, having become sufficiently proficient at the challenging process once the discernment is secure and fixed within the heart chakra. Then the instrument becomes, as it is written in your holy work, the Holy Bible, "wily as a serpent, yet innocent as a dove." The wiliness has most of all to do with discernment and the challenging of spirits as well as the thoughts and everyday actions of yourself in particular and those around you in lesser degree.

What we would like to do this evening is tell a story, using all three instruments. We believe that the one known as N is at this point advanced enough to enjoy this storytelling, for with three entities telling the story, none of the three knows how it shall end or what its meaning or moral shall be, thus illustrating the spontaneity and richness of the vocal channeling process when one is able to use the biases, experiences and thoughts of various entities while telling a story or parable.

The mist rose from the lake. It was almost red in color and looked very eerie through the few lights that were still on. The dim glow of distant kerosene lanterns and the dimmer glow of glow worms and fireflies were the only intrusions into the mist. There came a rider dressed all in black. The horse, too, was as black as the midnight, and his bridle flashed, even in the dim light, of jewels and gold. The horseman slowed; he was looking for tracks in the sand. He was travel-stained and weary and had come a long way.

We shall transfer to the one known as N and continue the story. I am Hatonn.

(N channeling)

I am Hatonn, and greet you in the love and light of the one infinite Creator. The man on the dark horse rode for many hours, or so it seemed, to deliver a message that concerned many individuals in the area. The people did not always receive the message with open arms but nevertheless, the message was delivered. …

N: Can't seem to get anymore.

Carla: When you get to a sticking point like that, N, don't pull yourself out by saying, "I can't get any more," just say, "Transfer," and then you'll have another shot at it next time around.

N: Transfer.

(Jim channeling)

I am Hatonn. The man came with messages, delivered them where they were accepted and then left as quickly as he had come. Because he was such an unusual figure, many looked only at him and paid little attention to the message which was there from him. They became concerned that he was a dark figure upon a dark horse, and many spread rumors about him that their concerns might take precedence in their own minds over the message, which they ignored. Each wished in some way to penetrate the mystery which was with this dark figure, most assuredly with each message he delivered, but many stopped short of the penetration of the mystery and many concerned themselves with promoting the rumors to discredit the figure and his messages and to relieve themselves of their responsibilities in discerning the meaning of the messages.

We shall now transfer.

(Carla channeling)

I am Hatonn. The message was slightly different for each person to whom the saturnine figure spoke. There was about his face and his very air a brilliance of personality that pierced, a coldness of reasoning that frightened, and an accuracy in each message that was often unwelcome. This entity had chosen to pass through the valley of death which each of his countrymen shared because of their actions. This entity knew that the red mist meant more than an unusual light or an unnatural phenomenon. The dark entity knew more than he could and more than he desired to say. His messages, indeed, were distillations of an urging to meditation, couched in the language each person could understand, and undergirded by the certainty that each entity was to have a very shortened life span and therefore needed to become aware of the necessity of gazing at death while there was still the time to do that which was the most compassionate, the most loving, the most life-giving thing in each spiritual circumstance.

He puzzled people because he was dressed so well, because his horse was so fine, because the trappings of saddle and bridle were so splendid. Each looked to his own resources and felt both the pangs of envy and the fear that that which the messenger had come to share was true.

We shall now transfer.

(N channeling)

I am Hatonn. And while the man was exquisitely and splendidly attired, as was his horse, he seemed to present to each a simple message. This was a source of bewilderment for the individuals. And yet few did heed them, the urgency of the situation, although the majority did not. The way of men is at times a puzzlement.

Transfer.

(Jim channeling)

I am Hatonn. Though men often seek the truth in a conscious fashion and speak to others of their seeking, yet it is often difficult for any to discern the heart of truth in any message. When a message is delivered from a mysterious part of one's own being or from an unknown part of one's outer environment or through any means available to one who listens and seeks for truth, the discernment is a unique function for each, and each will take from any message that meaning which matches the seeking for that entity.

So it was for those whom the dark figure visited. For some, there was almost no increase in knowledge or gain from this visit, for the message was ignored. For others there was a small amount of understanding that was the fruit of their seeking within this mystery, for their efforts were soon dissipated and their attention wandered until it found easier ground to dig within. But for a few there was a realization that the message from the dark figure contained a wealth of information and could be studied time and again with added meaning discovered in each study.

We shall transfer.

(Carla channeling)

I am Hatonn. The few who believed and heeded the message began also to travel, though they found the journey rigorous and almost unbearably difficult from time to time and they asked the man many questions. Since he spoke of death and the valley of death, it was often the case that one who believed would ask if the rumors were true, if the man was indeed a messenger from the creature of death.

We shall transfer.

(N channeling)

I am Hatonn. And the wilder man stated that he was not a messenger of death, but rather that of life, for those who heeded when the tumultuous turmoil occurred would certainly enter reality, or—correction—to reality while the others would be allowed to reexperience the lessons they heeded not. The difficulty of the journey was merely a proving point for the evaluation of the true seeker of the truth and light. Confusion abounds within the entity on the physical plane when reality, of which light is a type, or is the type, seems so remote or non-discernible. Transfer.

(Jim channeling)

I am Hatonn. Thus, each seeker must rely upon the inner knowing, or as it has been called, the still, small voice within in order to determine what is of truth for that seeker. All is a portion of the one Creator, thus all things and all ideas are a portion of truth. Yet upon each seeker's path, there will come a time or a season for various portions of truth to have their turn in the focus of seeking and attention. Thus, what might be helpful to one at one time may not be as helpful at another. And what might be helpful to one seeker at this time may not be as helpful to another seeker at the same time.

Thus, each seeks according to the unique nature of one's own being. Any message, any experience from any source is then a message of truth in some degree for any who witness it. It matters not what one's so-called advancement might be, for within any experience there is an infinity of message, yet all unites as a portion of one Creator and the truth of its creation.

We shall attempt to close this contact through the one known as N. We shall transfer.

(N channeling)

I am Hatonn. It is hoped that the gist of the message can be evaluated by each seeker for All Is One and One Is All. And we leave you in the path of light and love, of love and light of the one infinite Creator. Adonai vasu borragus.

(Jim channeling)

I am Latwii, and we greet you in that same love and light, my friends. It is our honor and pleasure to join you again in this evening's meditation. We would ask if we may be of service to any present by attempting to answer a query?

N: I didn't really understand Latwii's total definition or total consideration for the Tourette syndrome. If Latwii would care to enlarge upon it, or I can wait until I have a chance to read it.

I am Latwii, and we would be happy to attempt to expand upon our, shall we say, description of that syndrome which we shared with this group and others previously. It was our hope that we could build a foundation of understanding, shall we say, for any bias of mind by suggesting that any condition one might find a mind to exist within is a condition that that mind or that entity has chosen through, in many cases, a long series of choices. At some point within an entity's life pattern—perhaps it is better stated, at every point within an entity's life pattern, there is the choice to view any experience in the light or in the dark or in some mixture of both. According to each entity's unique blending and innate biases, combined with the moment by moment exercise of free will, there develops such and such a bias of mind.

In the syndrome of which you speak, it is at some point observable to those who see what is unseen and who demonstrate those abilities you may call of the psychic nature, [it is] apparent that an entity has taken a certain road. After some distance traveling upon that road of choice, the entity may find itself in a situation which is described as the Tourette syndrome or any other syndrome or currently definable mental state of health or disease. Because many entities share many roads, there have arisen amongst those of your culture who study the psyche, as it is called, or the function of the mind, many descriptions or diseases which in general describe a certain configuration of mind which has been systematically chosen by the entity.

May we answer further, my brother?

N: Let's see, then, the multiple tics and barking, and uttering of obscenities is so that the entity through this incarnation will learn, perhaps, humility? Or what is the ultimate lesson?

I am Latwii, and am aware of your query, my brother. The ultimate lesson within your illusion is that called love, the unconditional compassion that one feels for another simply because another exists, not because of any feature or characteristic or achievement of an entity but simply because an entity exists and is seen as a portion of the one Creator. An entity experiencing the condition of which you speak may have arrived at that condition in a somewhat distorted fashion, yet in that condition is able to learn the lesson of love in its specific nature as set by this entity before the incarnation, and for each it may be somewhat different. Yet for one who finds the self or perhaps more specifically, the mind, operating in a seemingly diminished capacity, the learning of love is undertaken on a more basic, and, shall we say, simpler level of experience, for the mind is not operating in what you call the normal or smoothly running fashion. It examines those grosser qualities of life and attempts in that examination to discover even in such dark and dingy corners the quality of love that may be given and received from one portion of the Creator to another portion of the Creator no matter what the outer manifestation of either portion of the Creation.

May we answer you further, my brother?

N: I can understand this consideration, your consideration, or our consideration in some aspects but not in a totality because while many of us would try to project love and understanding and an entity would, of course, be receptive to this sort of situation, there would be many individuals on this physical plane who would return the obscenities, would fail to return the understanding in love and would thus seem to confuse and confound the individual to a greater degree so that … Is it only those who will return the love, or the learning of love and humility by the individual or is it a totality? Because I can't—as our physical plane now exists, I do not think that even a majority would return love and understanding. Am I incorrect?

I am Latwii, and am aware of your query, my brother. In this situation, those with whom this entity would come in contact would be given the opportunity to express love under somewhat more difficult situations, shall we say. Thus, the challenge increases the opportunity and further seats the love for those who can experience and express it. For the entity uttering the seeming obscenities and acting in a manner which is seemingly quite unlovable, it may be that in its, shall we say, karmic past, it has neglected easier opportunities for experiencing and expressing love and thus has chosen at a deeper portion of its being, to, shall we say, "up the ante" or provide for itself a more difficult challenge, thus increasing also the opportunity for itself if it [is] able under such extreme conditions to experience and express love. Thus, one may see the situation both for the entity experiencing the seeming mental dysfunction and those with whom it may come in contact that a greater opportunity for experiencing and expressing love is presented to all. Not all, however, shall take advantage of the opportunity in equal degree. …

(Side one of tape ends.)

(Jim channeling)

I am Latwii. May we ask if there might be further queries?

N: I'd just like to say that I understand what you have said but in instances like this, not only would many situations be of variant degree, as you have stated, but there … Would some instances be a totally negative approach? And I was just wondering if this would not, even though while the situation is presented to all, wonder if it would not have a sometime deleterious effect on the entity so involved?

I am Latwii, and am aware of your query, my brother. It cannot be stated or ascertained with certainty how any entity shall respond in any situation, whether difficult or seemingly ease-filled. Yet, when an entity in this particular situation experiences the catalyst which seems heavy-laden with the negative aspect, the entity yet has the opportunity to find the light within the darkness, for within all portions of all experience, there is light. It is there for each. It is the fabric of your experience and your creation.

In one particular portion of an incarnation, it may be that an entity becomes quite confused because of its inability to process the catalyst which it finds in its daily round of activities. Yet, at some point within the incarnation or perhaps incarnations, the experiences gained will prove valuable and will allow the entity to tip the scales, shall we say, and to move further along the path of its evolution. The road may be difficult, there may be distractions, there may be times when progress seems, oh, so slow. There may be times when one seems to be moving backwards. Yet, all experience provides the opportunity to learn and the opportunity to serve, whether the opportunity is taken advantage of within the incarnation during which the experience is gained or is taken advantage of within the next incarnational experience.

May we answer further, my brother?

N: Well, I think I understand, at least a portion. Perhaps the reason I have so much trouble with all the people who I deal with who are—well, most all of the people—with service is that I must learn to love them. That is very difficult to do, even though I'm trying to forgive them … or I have forgiven—in most instances—well, I'm trying to forgive them all the way. But I must learn to love them more as being a portion of the one Creator, and this must be a lesson in that respect? Is that correct?

I am Latwii, and, my brother, this is quite correct for each upon your planet and within your illusion. The experiences of the daily activities are merely the laboratory within which the concept of love is planted. Those activities which allow it to manifest in some form are most difficult to clearly penetrate by even the most astute students of their own evolution. The mysteries and the paradoxes within your illusion are most important, for they draw the seeker forward into unknown territory, and thus require the strengthening of the will and the faith that progress of a lasting quality, of a metaphysical quality, is actually possible within a material world which seems so out of tune so often.

May we answer further, my brother?

N: Carla may have a question, but thank you very much.

I am Latwii, and we thank you, my brother. Is there another query?

Carla: I am feeling the vibrations of Hatonn who have … The vibrations haven't left and I'm wondering if I should pick that channeling up?

I am Latwii, and am aware of your query, my sister. We find that those of Hatonn have remained with your instrument for this length of what you call time in order that you may, shall we say, absorb the healing nature of the conditioning vibration and may, if you wish, also channel that vibration. It is your choice, my sister.

May we answer further?

Carla: No, thank you.

I am Latwii, and we thank you, my sister. Is there another query?

N: If the instrument is not too tired, I have another question.

I am Latwii, and we are happy to entertain another query, my brother.

N: In the method of mind control which is a form of alpha meditation, it is stated that through meditation that we can visit other planetary systems, galaxies, that we can go inside our animals and metals and so forth. Although I've practiced the meditations, I've been unable to experience any of these considerations, although we were told over and over that this is possible. May I ask how it is possible for me?

I am Latwii, and am aware of your query, my brother. Any technique offers the possibility to the seeker of truth that the seeker may take a certain road and manifest in a certain way. Each technique has been devised by the one who has found it of use, and for this one it has worked quite well, shall we say. The success of such an entity, then, often compels it, it would seem, to multiply the technique and its beneficial aspects for other seekers of truth. Thus, you find many such techniques offered to seekers who may try this and that and yet another technique with variant results. The results are of a range from no result to most splendid results for seekers, because each, as you know, is quite unique.

Thus, some will find more attraction to one technique than another. In your own case, my brother, we find that you are given to exploring a variety of techniques, and find within them much of value that you utilize in your own fashion. For you to expect your experience to match that which others have had may not be, shall we say, the wisest possible choice, for as you are quite unique, your experience is also quite unique and much of it is not apparent to your mind. The desire which you enter each experience with is that portion of the experience which shall produce its fruit in a certain fashion. Yet, the fruit may not be the same as the expectation. Yet the fruit exists. The work is done. The benefits are at some level of your being appreciated.

May we answer you further, my brother?

N: Well, I guess the answer is to just keep watering the garden and hoping for the lightning to strike. Thank you.

I am Latwii, and we thank you, my brother, and would remind each that lightning strikes in a certain fashion that is unique to each, and often is not apparent, yet each in great degree fulfills the purpose of the incarnation though it might seem mundane.

May we ask if there might be another query at this time?

(Pause)

I am Latwii, and we are most pleased to have been able to join you this evening and we thank you for your queries and for your invitation. We are with you at your request in your meditations. It is our honor to join you at any time. We shall leave this group at this time, as always, in the love and in the light of our infinite Creator. We are those of Latwii. Adonai, my friends. Adonai vasu borragus.

(Pause)

(Carla channeling)

I am Hatonn, and we greet you through this instrument once again in the love and the light of our infinite Creator. We apologize for the short pause, but this instrument was taking even more care than usual to challenge our vibration, doubting its own sensitivities. We appreciate these opportunities to place ourselves with all the children of the Creator in Christ consciousness, or as this instrument would call it, in the peace and the love of the one known as Jesus, the perfect pattern and therefore the perfect savior for this density.

We have two subjects to cover and we will attempt not to speak too lengthily upon either, but feel that the first is of especial importance as this is meditation intended to concentrate the attention of all present upon the development of new channels.

Each within this domicile was to a certain extent less than completely aware of our intentions during part of our exercise. To be specific, the one known as N accepted the final communication while in an internal state of, shall we may, spiritual exhaustion, and was thus unable to achieve a recommended balance between our thoughts and his own. For the great majority of the channeling this instrument was doing excellent work and we ask that the instrument not become at all discouraged because after some length of your time it grows weary with the concentration required for vocal channeling. Actually, the progress of this instrument has been rapid and this form of channeling is challenging for the most advanced instrument. We choose to push this instrument, knowing that this instrument has a great deal of ability and knowing also that due to this instrument's personality, the instrument would not be satisfied with less in the way of a teaching/learning experience, if we may borrow succinct phraseology from this instrument's mind.

The instrument known as Jim made no errors in transmission except for the one desire for an outcome which so biased the instrument that it transferred to the one known as N. This was not our intent. It is, however, understandable that this should be desired. And again we ask the instrument who is quite advanced not to be discouraged because it personally wishes to offer to the new instrument the experience of closing as well as opening a meeting.

This instrument made no substantial errors in transmission, yet it too had a desire for an outcome, and that was to complete the story. Since this instrument was channeling in concept form, it was able to see a bit more ahead. This is very common for a more advanced instrument, and is very helpful when working with a new instrument due to the fact that the more experienced instrument is able to confirm the accuracy of transmission, not word by word, but concept by concept. We bow to the less than perfectly balanced desire of this instrument to make an ending to our little story which we attempted to transmit but were unable to complete. If you will bear with us, we shall finish the story of the dark horse and its dark rider.

Because that which is said to one may penetrate outer misunderstanding at one time and not at another and because one can say the same message to two entities, one of whom will seize upon it and use it, the other of which will not understand it, those who follow or work with whatever teacher or messenger or message have variable chances of sustaining the interest in pursuing the message. This is why the band that followed this unusual man was so very small.

One of the most faithful, upon noticing that the entity did not eat and did not seem to require sleep asked him what kind of teacher he was. The dark man replied that he was not a teacher, but a messenger, that that which was spoken was spoken through him, not from him, and that indeed he did not, in the understanding of the questioner, exist, but rather had produced himself in a certain form and had produced the magical steed upon which he rode and all that he carried for specific reasons so that he could be a silent messenger as well as a messenger with words.

"Why then, Messenger," asked the faithful one, "have you appeared in black only and why is your face so dark if you are a messenger of life?"

"Life begins and ends in the deepest darkness of earth," replied the messenger, "and because it was necessary for me to be one of you, I wished to proclaim my humanity."

"Well, why then, does your face shine like the sun?" asked the student.

"I leave that to your discretion," replied the messenger.

"I have one final question, Messenger. Of all that you have, although all of it is fine and well-made, only your horse's bridle and saddle are encrusted with precious gems. Why is that?"

The messenger smiled. "My son," he said, "it is not the speed of a horse which marks its value to the rider, but rather two very important aspects which a horse must learn. The first aspect is the taking up of burden. Some call it service to others; some call it responsibility; others call it duty. But a horse that cannot be ridden is not a useful riding animal, thus the value of the saddle. And as for the bridle, it is so magnificent I had hoped that someone would notice the heart and the courage of my steed and the fact that above all, it obeyed my rein and followed my commands. Not just one day or for two days, but for as long as I ask. And so you too, my son, may find your service, find your way and then take the reins of your own impatience in both hands and learn the freedom of discipline."

I am Hatonn. We cannot thank you enough for having allowed us to do our job, for we would not be doing our job in teaching new instruments if we did not help each instrument keep tabs, as this instrument would say, upon its own progress. Learn from each mistake and never become discouraged, for there is no mistake that cannot be adjusted and balanced. There is no error from which one does not learn, for all of these things are alternate biases, distortions of the one love and the light of the infinite Creator in which we leave you. We rejoice with you that you are together, and we are so very grateful that we are able to be with your group at this time. Please call upon us at any time. If you mentally request our presence, we shall be there. We are those of Hatonn. Adonai. Adonai. ✣

Sunday Meditation
July 7, 1985

(Carla channeling)

[I am Yadda.] I greet you in love and light [and] send you blessings in the name of infinite Creator. We thank you for calling us to your meeting and to the pleasant environment of your joined consciousness. We speak while our brothers and sisters of Hatonn work with each instrument.

We ask you a question: Why do you think that the interest is so great in the physical changes of your culture or your planet? We are puzzled by this, my friends. We do not know why you spend so much time out of your precious moments in this density puzzling your mind over the inevitable. You know on the cosmic scale that worlds are born and worlds die, that they go through changes, and that some of the changes may make it difficult for those of you who wish to breathe the air and to be able to stand the temperature to continue to exist.

In the larger picture, this is true. However, you have so few moments while you are in your body, while you are dealing with each other, and you have so much work to do, for within you there is that which is far more than your "Armageddon"; you have your egos to deal with. You have all the structures that are not helping you to live as you wish to live, to think as you wish to think. You are working toward a spontaneity of love that will allow you to become more and more aware of the universal presence of the one original Thought. And what is your work here, but inner work? What does it matter when the ice age comes or when the trees must die or when the rains come and there is a flood or when the poles shift? These are things that will happen to your outer self, and it will go away. You probably knew that before you came here—Hah! Is that not so? You knew that before you came here: you are going to die. But there is a you that is not going to die; that is the one you must life with, if we may use the term, my friends. Put your mind on that which lasts, on the questions that matter.

What questions do you think matter at this moment? We speak to imperishable beings on a perishable sphere in space that is moving and changing. There is that that will not move and that will not change except by your will. It has nothing to do with the planet and its changes. It has to do with your will to do, to seek, to find. What shall you seek?

We leave you with this question. I am Yadda. I leave you in the love and in the light of our infinite Creator. Adonai. Adonai.

(Group retunes by singing.)

(Carla channeling)

I am Hatonn. We have been attempting to use the one known as L, but we find that this instrument is quite fatigued, and therefore we start through this instrument with many thanks. We greet you in the love and the light of our infinite Creator.

We apologize for the pause, but the image which we gave this instrument in order to start the channeling was muddied by the instrument's attempt to analyze. Therefore we shall attempt again.

The stone lies in the forest, unearthed eons ago when mountains were being made, moved closer and closer to sea level through the centuries. Finally it has found a temporary home beneath ferns in the deep forest. The stone rests, travel weary, worn; moss grows upon it. Friendly insects sit upon it. The stone watches heat and cold, wetness and dryness, change of the cycles of the seasons. The heavens gaze upon the stone and upon the planet upon which it lies. In the swirling of the effortless dance of the galaxies, the ethereal heavens are provided with infinite amounts of life and light. And vast as the heavens are, yet the stone touches the heavens and the heavens, the stone.

We shall transfer.

(L channeling)

I am Hatonn. I am now with this instrument. The stone may be seen as that which lies beyond a veil, for, in truth, because of its covering, the life of ferns which lie atop it, one might liken the stone to that which is present, yet unseen, just as in yourselves there is a very substantial portion as real as that stone which is present, yet lies unseen behind the veil. And just as the stone continues to exist and to fulfill its function unnoticed by those who travel through the forest, unmindful of that beneath the veil of foliage, so also does a larger reality exist which most of those who travel your world do not perceive. The stone moves, ever so slowly, but then, what is time? The stone is aware; it experiences, it grows, it changes. Like yourselves, it is acted upon by that which is about it, the weather, the earth, the occasional by-passer. All interact with the stone, and by the interaction, the stone experiences itself, its awareness ever so gently increases, becomes enlarged, more aware of the complexities available for perception, for the world within which the stone lies is a school or a training ground for those who would be aware, and the stone is no exception.

At this point we will transfer our contact.

(N channeling)

I am Hatonn. We will try to be with this instrument one time. Transfer.

(L channeling)

I am Hatonn. I am now with this instrument. The stone is aware of that which occurs beyond the moss, beyond the ferns, and continues to learn while it lies unseen. In like manner, that part of yourselves which exists unseen to those present and to your brothers and sisters of your planet continues to learn and grow, assimilating their experiences, producing order from the confusion, storing it carefully within its stone-like memory, so that upon your return, that which is presently your consciousness on your planet might be allowed to see through the same glass, clearly. But that which exists on the other side of your veil is itself in many ways unaware of that of which it is simply a small facet. For that portion of yourself is also the learner, the perceiver within a larger universe, and is not aware of but a fraction of that Creator which encompasses us all.

We will now transfer.

(Carla channeling)

So you see, my friends, that the external and surface personality that is quick moving and quick to assimilate new experiences is missing the deeper undertones and resonances of learning if the seeker does not adventure into the forest of his own deep mind. That deep mind is the ancient part of the self, the storehouse of that which has occurred since before this sphere existed. It may sometimes be less than easy to deal with the type of learning that the deep self has to offer, for like the stone, the deep self thinks and moves very, very slowly and often accretes to it that which it needs rather than intellectualizing or analyzing; it merely makes itself that which it touches. But it is that part of yourself, my friends, which touches the heavens at all times, and not simply when the will and the faith are turned towards that kingdom which you seek.

We urge you to be explorers. We ask that you prepare yourself for your journey with some care, each and every day, preparing in meditation the fineness, single pointedness, and keenness of your desire to know the universe and to know yourself. These two are one and the same thing. Your journey may take you in many strange directions, speaking metaphysically, for your journey exists within your mind and your consciousness. But this deep and almost completely unknown territory which lies within you is that which touches the kingdom.

You, consciously, live within an illusion. The deep mind stores knowledge that is not of this illusion, as well as many prior biases which you have collected from other portions of the illusion, and hopes, aspirations and ambitions which have not yet been made a part of the manifestation of your experience within this density. If there is that which nags at you and you do not know what it is, if there is an ambition that you do not know what it is, that information will lie within the slow and stone-like portions of your deep mind, geometrically regular, built slowly, moving slowly, thinking slowly.

The deep mind is steady and firm and stable and remembers. Ask and your ambition shall be told you—perhaps not once for the rest of your incarnation, perhaps you must ask once each day. But do not waste this resource, my friends—the heavens touch the stone and the stone the heavens. All the moss and the fern must deal with the cycles of nature, life and death, and all the illusion that goes with those concepts.

We would close at this time, my friends, leaving you only with our hope that you may hope to discover that kingdom within you and without you, for the kingdom is all about you as well as within you. And as you begin to feel this truth within yourself about yourself, you can then see more and more constant and unremitting manifestation of the kingdom of what this instrument would call heaven all about you. May the Creator whisper to you, inspire you and be with you. We leave you in the love and the light of that which you are and that which all are, the one infinite Creator. We are known to you as those of Hatonn. Adonai, my friends. Adonai vasu borragus.

(L1 channeling)

I am Latwii, and I greet you, my brothers and sisters, in the love and the light of the infinite Creator, and am quite pleased at the opportunity to be here and to perform our service of attempting to respond to your queries in some orderly, informative fashion, perhaps with a grain of truth, as well. To this end, are there any questions?

Carla: Since nobody's asked one, I'll ask one that L2 sent in. He entitles the question: "Some ad hoc questions addressed toward the ether." I'll read you the whole thing; tell me which part you want to concentrate on and I'll read it again.

The question goes: "In one sense, all those realms of creation are as an illusion contrasted with the one reality. Yet, to the conditioned mind, it all appears so real, so myriad, a daunting maze, this maze which can neither add nor take anything away from the one reality. A) What really were its reasons for seeming to come into being, that is, made, aside from the obvious one, that it doesn't really exist, and B) How is it best to explicate this relation between that perspective wherein all creations don't really exist and those myriad perspectives wherein this assertion seems defeated by the "real-"ness of transiencies?"

N: That's a question?

Carla: You want me to move on to another one?

(L channeling)

I am Latwii, and we will attempt to respond to these questions in an orderly fashion.

A) That creation which is described as, in part, transiency, unreal, *et cetera*, is actually quite real, my friend, for should one examine the chair within which one sits, one will find it to be quite substantial and capable of resisting the impact of one's appendage to the extent of producing that artifact known as pain. Within one's reality, the conditions are quite real, for those who are a portion of the Creator are made in both the image and likeness of that Creator, that is, possess the same creative abilities as the original Creator, no matter how befuddled those awarenesses and abilities have become through the confused environment. Therefore, my friend, we would suggest that you regard that about you as quite real, for as the saying goes, "Thou sayest it." What one creates one does so for the purpose of experiencing within his own individual reality.

B) The purpose of this environment is that of an area—arena, if you would prefer—within which the interactions may occur which allow the individual entity to accomplish sufficient awareness of dual polarity to develop a preference for one of the two poles therein. As your created reality in this density is one in which dual polarity, that is, positive and negative or service to others and service to self exist, the purpose of the illusion, as you might term it, is to provide sufficient incentive … We shall pause.

(One of the tapes ends.)

(L channeling)

We continue … is to provide sufficient incentive for the entity to choose one of the two polarities as a chosen path, and successfully adhere to that path.

May we answer you further?

Carla: In my judgment, that was a remarkably …

(Side one of tape ends.)

(L channeling)

We thank you for reading the question slowly. Is there another question?

Carla: Since everyone seems to be pretty passive tonight, perhaps we'll make this L2 night. This one's even worse, Latwii, so you can deal with it by again asking me to repeat. Question number two: "Could you afford some connective commentary regarding how the perspectives of the following great explicators mesh into the same central truths? Swedenborg; Michael, in Yarbro's *Messages from Michael*; Seth; Franklin Merrell-Wolff; the Cayce trance testator; Orobindo; Meister Eckhart; anonymous authors; the Bhagavad-Gita; Gautama Buddha; Jesus of Nazareth; Mohammet; Krishna; Babaji; Socrates"—well, that's a starter.

I am Latwii. I am aware of your question. My brother, consider your own situation. You exist within a reality in which many claim to have a perception of that which is real, that which is factual, that which is existent, yet many seem to be in contradiction with one another in their description. Would it be true to say that each is wrong or each is right? We would offer then the following commentary for your examination.

Each of those which you have described, including, we might add, the anonymous writers, has been able to perceive with a varying degree of clarity that which exists beyond your realm of confusion, and in their perception have attempted to relay that image to their other selves in such a manner as to reproduce that perception. However, as you are aware, the reproduction of concept into words is quite difficult and often of poor result. We would therefore observe initially that the translation on each of the source's part has been severely hampered by the inability to translate perception into words. As a further example, we would suggest that one consider the possibility of translating into words a robin's song so that the reader, upon reading the words, could successfully reproduce the musical notes.

The further difficulty arrives at the determination of subsequent readers or translators to correct that which they do not understand or alter that with which they do not agree. This has happened quite frequently in the history of your people, both through accident and intention, for much of your historic religious and philosophical texts have been reproduced a number of times in writing after being handed down on the basis of word of mouth for numbers of years, resulting in quite radical deviations from the original source.

Finally, we would observe that those who perceived the original awareness of that which exists beyond the realm of confusion have themselves often been the recipients of much communication, some of which was distorted intentionally by those who would seek to sincerely follow a path of service to self, therefore, quite literally negating much of that which may have been intended.

May we answer you further?

Carla: I think so. I think the question is, "What connective commentary could you give regarding the central truths if any, which all of these people are trying to explicate?"

My sister, the central truths are of themselves the connective tissue which unite the perceptions of each listed, for it was their perception of that reality, that awareness of both the Creator and the orderly universe which was created, that sparked the imagination of those listed and inspired each to attempt to communicate their awareness to their other selves.

May we answer you further?

Carla: No. I feel that there is some reason that you are angling your answer the way you are, and having met L2, we'll just say, that's fine. And thank you.

We thank you, my sister.

A: How is the instrument doing?

The instrument is tiring but capable of answering to a further extent if there are more questions.

N: I have a query. The Sufis used in former times a nine foot high pole of lapis lazuli which was two feet in diameter. The ritual, I think, has been discontinued for initiates. Why did they use this nine foot object which was two feet in diameter for initiation and why did they stop using it?

I am Latwii. My brother, the object of which you speak was actually not composed in its entirety of the substance which you describe but rather was an object of those dimensions decorated with that same substance. The purpose of this device was to act as a focal point during ceremonies much as the apex of a pyramid would have the effect of a focal point for down-funneling energies. Consider if you will the effect of a conical arrangement of individuals with a single individual at the apex of the cone atop the device which you have described. It was an effort to produce in a simplistic form a pyramidal-type device for the purpose of initiation which was not particularly successful due to the lack of understanding of those performing this attempt.

May we answer you further?

N: If the instrument is not too tired, is this cone of energy an attempt to communicate with what the Sufis consider their home planet?

I am Latwii. My brother, this may be in some way correct, as those individuals whom you describe believe themselves to have come from a single source other than the planet and were attempting to reunite themselves with that source. They, as you may have guessed, were attempting to reunite themselves with the Creator rather than return to or communicate with a physical object such as another planetary object.

May we answer you further?

N: If the instrument is still not too tired, is this form of being united what they called the *barraca* or the spiritual force?

I am Latwii. Would you please repeat the question?

N: Is this form of becoming united used by the Sufis what they consider the *barraca* or the spiritual force?

I am Latwii. The spiritual force which you describe was viewed as a connective energy which would allow the individual in conjunction with his other selves to unite with one another and the Creator.

May we answer you further?

N: Thank you very much.

We thank you. Is there another question?

Carla: Yeah, just a … The Sufis also have the old rope trick, and it strikes me, the similarity of the two strikes me, and it's almost … I'm wondering if that lapis lazuli and what not is not just a further embellishment on the basic lesson of that which does not seem to be and yet is, which is an illusion-piercing thing which the Sufis do practice by supposedly climbing a rope which actually isn't there, which they actually don't climb. However they are able to make it seem so. Can you find a question in there?

I am Latwii. My sister, we view your brief commentary as seeking the correctness of the statement or an observation of the incorrectness of the statement, and in answering we would reply that we are in agreement with that somewhat wordy statement.

May we answer you further?

Carla: A succinct, "No." Thank you.

N: May I ask, if the instrument's not too tired, what did they replace the initiation with when they discontinued the lapis lazuli because the others couldn't understand it?

My brother, the device which you describe was not widely used and eventually fell into a state of disuse and disrepair, having been overturned and shattered by itinerant tribesmen intent upon a path of service to self. The device, however, was rarely in use by this time, as the individuals which you describe had arrived at the realization that the device itself was not essential to their strivings.

May we answer you further?

N: Was it replaced with another device or how was the initiation ceremony changed because of disuse?

My brother, the device was not replaced because it was found to be an unnecessary artifact for the seeker, and was therefore abandoned. The desire to seek the Creator through unity with one's other selves was found to be equally accomplishable through that which you call meditation, though their meditation was in a more active form. The device which you describe was the result of information which may be traced back to that point in time when the pyramids which surrounded your planet were once functional. The device was a very primitive effort to replace one of those devices, and was not particularly useful for that purpose.

May we answer you further?

N: What kind of active meditation did they use?

I am Latwii. The form of meditation was one in which regularized motions were undertaken by the individual in an effort to isolate the mind from the body by, in effect, training the body to perform a particular function which required little or no mental supervision, thus allowing the body to, in effect, be put on what one might call autopilot, freeing the mind for meditation while supplying a high degree of oxygen flow to the brain to produce an exhilarative state. This in some instances may be likened to a dance.

May we answer you further?

N: Would you consider this form of meditation better than our going into the silence or stillness?

My brother, there is no better or worse form for that which you call meditation. Rather, we would suggest that the individual finds one state of conditions more conducive or less conducive to that end.

May we answer you further?

N: Well, if the instrument's not tired, I just wondered, well, that if we're told that one type of meditation is better than another then we think that such an active meditation might be good, but you did state that there was an increased flow of oxygen to the brain.

I am Latwii. I perceive your question as one in which the awareness of that statement prompts curiosity as to the benefits in comparison to the stationary meditation which is currently in use by this group. We would simply observe that the increase in oxygen described earlier produced an effect not unlike that of a drunkenness which was construed to be a proof of attaining an ethereal contact or unity, and is not particularly suitable for this type of work.

May we answer you further, my brother?

N: I think the instrument is getting very tired, but I was not referring to this type of work, I was just referring to our own individual meditation at home. We can discuss it later, and thank you very much.

We thank you, my brother. Is there another question?

(Pause)

I am Latwii. As there are no further questions, we shall, "A," bid those present adieu, and, "B," take our leave in the love and light of the infinite Creator. Adonai, my friends. ☥

L/L Research

L/L Research is a subsidiary of Rock Creek Research & Development Laboratories, Inc.

P.O. Box 5195
Louisville, KY 40255-0195

www.llresearch.org

Rock Creek is a non-profit corporation dedicated to discovering and sharing information which may aid in the spiritual evolution of humankind.

ABOUT THE CONTENTS OF THIS TRANSCRIPT: This telepathic channeling has been taken from transcriptions of the weekly study and meditation meetings of the Rock Creek Research & Development Laboratories and L/L Research. It is offered in the hope that it may be useful to you. As the Confederation entities always make a point of saying, please use your discrimination and judgment in assessing this material. If something rings true to you, fine. If something does not resonate, please leave it behind, for neither we nor those of the Confederation would wish to be a stumbling block for any.

CAVEAT: This transcript is being published by L/L Research in a not yet final form. It has, however, been edited and any obvious errors have been corrected. When it is in a final form, this caveat will be removed.

© 2009 L/L Research

Sunday Meditation
July 14, 1985

(Carla channeling)

I am Yadda. I great you in love and light of infinite Creator. We argue with this instrument. We say, "We want to come and say 'Hi' to our friend, J," and we could not do it at first because this instrument say, "Oh, but the big one is yet to come, don't do this now," and we say, "No, no; we just want to say 'Hello.'" So the instrument say, "Okay," and here we are.

The expression of joy that takes place when souls band together in love, not of earthly things but of metaphysical, is tremendous and this expression of joy is with us now. Our gratitude knows no bounds, and we thank you for allowing us to be a part of session today. We shall be silent now, silent but joyful, and so very, very much blessed to share this time with you. We are not blessed because you are such wonderful characters, because of your amazing personalities or your reputations; we are not interested in that part of you. This is not the local train here; we are talking about long-distance traveling. We are joyful because of the long-distance traveler that is your consciousness. How beautiful it is; how beautiful and perfect you are and how much joy there is to share in an infinitely joyful creation.

We leave this instrument now, full of the love and the light of infinite Creator. I Yadda. Farewell. Farewell.

(Carla channeling)

I am L/Leema, and I greet you, my friends, in the love and in the infinite light of the one Creator. We apologize for the delay in our speaking with you. However, we ran into what we consider to be a noteworthy problem which we wish to share with you, for it bears upon each of your spiritual endeavors at this time to a certain extent.

When this instrument challenged us, we responded by saying, "Yes, my child, we do come in the name of Christ." This is the same answer that this instrument is used to receiving from the one known to you as Hatonn. Therefore, the instrument repeated the challenge, and hearing the answer once again, asked who we were. We projected the vibration that is our signature for name. You would think of it more as a musical tone, with overtones and undertones, than a word. As you may have noticed from our need to scan the instrument from time to time to select an appropriate word, we do not use words. Therefore, there was some delay while we established that we were indeed known to this group as L/Leema. These and other spiritual metaphysical and religious names are for the most part intended to convey some small idea of the vibration that is who we are. However, those of the Confederation of Planets in the Service of the Infinite Creator do not actually have names as you know them, as they are not necessary unless one is unable to speak mind to mind and to recognize musical tones.

We shall now address the question at hand which has to do with values and virtues, what they are, what effect they have upon you, what effect you have practicing that which you come to, shall we say, understand. Perhaps the strongest desire within the mundane world is the desire to live and be loved, to appreciate and to be appreciated. You will find two things to be true about this characteristic of your peoples. Firstly, those who use their lives pleasing others to the exclusion of knowing the self have gained in the eyes of your world, but have lost the power to make the choice. The second thing that is true about the need to love and the need to be appreciated is that the societal values change, and therefore the actual polarity of your intended action is various. Sometimes you polarize well and sometimes there is a negative polarization as you move away from the seeking of truth.

Now, we know what values are not, that is, values are not imposed from without. It is your birthright and as a conscious seeker your responsibility to seek in every way possible to know yourself. To put it another way, it is your responsibility to seek the Creator in yourself and in all things. Values, then, come from within. However, as a mundane personality, the seeking student is precisely as fallible as the person who previously told the seeker what to do in order to be loved. Therefore, we eliminate also from value the mundane considerations of the self for the self.

The question is, what is left to form value? That is a question worth asking. If you have been impressed with feelings, energies and disciplines that seem to you to be of aid in a metaphysical manner, then you have been given the gift of learning. In the process of being given this gift, you have given something up. In fact, the only way that we know of—and remember we are fallible also—to have access to a more clear knowledge of what has value is to lose the self. The more of yourself that you lose, the more of the selfhood that may be overtaken and imbued with that greater self that some call the higher self and others call the Creator within.

Thusly, that which has value is that which comes from within, that which has been paid for by the surrender of the smaller self, and that which is let loose from you in a manner completely free to the world about you, whether it be one person, many people, or simply the environment in which you have your being. Your state of mind when you are in the impersonal self has innate value which is the highest value of which we are aware, of which you are capable of achieving in your third density at this particular stage of your development. Indeed, in a more and more refined way, this is all any particle of consciousness has to offer—its birthright. That birthright is nothing less than a single and original Thought before which there was no thought. That Thought, that Creator of all that there is, is love, guided only by free will. Examine yourself at this moment. What in you is of value? In your heart, you know. There is that within you that is utterly priceless. It is surrounded by a great deal of illusion, and you are seeking to pierce the veil of that illusion.

As to virtues, we find that the list is long and well-known. Much can be quoted from holy books about virtue. The virtues always include patience, hope, charity, spiritual seeking, politeness to others, a cheerful attitude, and so forth and so on. The list of seeming virtues is endless. But, like a skin disease, which also seems endless when one is a—we scan—teenager, so these virtues come and go. They are only skin deep. It is not that the list is wrong, it is that the culture which you now enjoy and experience believes in inculcating virtue from the outside inward, working from a list of rules: do this, but don't do that, and while you're at it, don't do that either, and there is a third and a fourth and fifth thing and so forth. This is not true of virtue, although there is the potential always for significant polarization in one who desires so utterly to bring pleasure to those around it that it is willing to assume the various postures which are designed to be most appropriate and acceptable.

True virtue is a natural overflowing and outpouring of that contact with love which you keep fresh by meditation, prayer, contemplation and the analysis of your thoughts, each in degree to which each aids you personally. Virtue is, in essence, a state of being rather than a process of doing. As with value, the one who is virtuous is first the sufferer, for it is painful to relinquish the amount of control over one's incarnational experience necessary to allow the principle of seeking to work.

The principle of seeking is, to the best of our knowledge, infallible. There are no occasions when it does not work. The time frames may change from experience to experience, but if you seek, you will find. And if you seek the truth, you find yourself surrendering more and more of that which you may have considered very special about yourself in order to get on with the seeking of something called love, something that is impersonal, and yet something that, once touched, seems worth more than all the precious booty one can imagine, whether that treasure be fame, fortune, power, success or knowledge.

In the light of the tabernacle which you once established, near the fire of your own holy ground, much is burned away that you would cherish. That which must be relinquished is different for each unique seeker. It is not for us to describe stumbling blocks; we who describe them may put one before you. It is enough to say that the stumbling blocks are in the self, and when it is recognized that there is something that is keeping you from the opportunity for contact with intelligent infinity, there is value and virtue in the decision to surrendering whatever it may, whatever part of your personality it may be.

Each of you has seen transcendent beings, beings that were radiant, that glowed from within, and each has thought, "What a wonderful thing it must be to be so virtuous." The wonderful thing is, subjectively, that there is contact with love. That contact is so powerful that it creates value and manifests it in a clear channel. And what is that value, my friends? That value may be seen in the smile that lightens someone's day, a soft answer to a hard question, an insightful question to one who is muddled. What is value, my friends? Value is that which adds to someone or to someone's experience. What is the nature of addition? The nature of spiritual addition is that it is infinite. You do not have infinite powers as a mundane personality.

Thus, true value is the spiritual. You are a channel for it and it comes through you. Try to do the valuable thing on your own recognizance and you will find yourself in deep trouble, for each entity has designed situations, both of a general and a specific nature, which are for the sole purpose of learning a lesson you feel as your higher self before birth that you need to learn in a more fastidious or complete way. Any attempt to seek healing, the giving of love, the giving of any value at all, without first immersing the self within the greater self of the creation, is going to run into one of the situations which you have planned each of you for yourself, situations that will say, sometimes rather clearly, you are a limited being as long as you do not seek love.

What has virtue? The seeking of truth. What is the nature of truth? To use a sadly overused word, love. What has virtue? That which has virtue is that which is intended to manifest and to praise and bear witness to the Creator and the infinite love, the infinite joy and the infinite peace in which we are created and have our being.

We realize that there are those with children. To be of value to one's children is an especially challenging task. And yet, the rules hold true. When you, each of you, interact with the child, attempt to make even more room than usual for that great channel of love, for while you are channeling that love, you will know what to say, you will feel strongly about what will aid and what will discipline helpfully. Perhaps most fundamentally the aid of children that is of value to the greatest extent is that aid which involves familiarizing your child with your own understanding of your own nature. Let there be a place for meditation in your dwelling, and let meditation be an accepted part of the day, for this is the grounding for you and for all. The child learns first by example.

We do not suggest that your learning be made public, for indeed, each of us learns within. We only suggest that the process of going to your private place and meditating or contemplating or praying be made a normal and, from the parent's point of view, necessary portion of the daily activity. This will aid children greatly in grasping the process in their turn of becoming an impersonal channel for the infinitely personal compassion and wisdom of the one Creator.

We fear we have exceeded our time limit but hope we have given you enough to think about. It is indeed a tremendous pleasure to be able to speak to you and to be able to use this instrument, and we so appreciate your taking our suggestion and forming the group question, that this instrument may be in no danger whatsoever because of the question and answer format, which is not helpful for this instrument at this time. Rather than …

(Side one of tape ends.)

(Carla channeling)

Rather than closing, we are going to attempt to transfer this contact to the one known as Jim. It is an experiment and may not work. This instrument may prefer to work with those of Latwii to the exclusion of working with us. Therefore we offer this instrument the choice and would at this time offer the transfer to the one known as Jim. We leave this instrument. I am L/Leema.

(Jim channeling)

I am L/Leema, and we are happy to greet you through this instrument. Again we greet you in love and light. We have offered the opportunity of the transfer of our contact in order that we might attempt any further queries which any within this group might have left for the evening. May we serve in that capacity with another query?

Carla: If nobody else has one, while I'm pulling my cramp out of my big toe, I would ask one written by L. It's his number three, and I will read it to you whole and let you chop it up later or have it read in any way that you would like it reread.

The question reads: "Love is the paramount truth. This becomes clear in time and under various lights to all diligent students and seekers after truth. Consciousness is the essence of all things. This also comes to be literally felt as truth under various lights by all such also. Love expresses into a myriad hierarchy of consciousness which by sufficient analysis/devotion resolves into a single non-hierarchical consciousness. Are these statements correct?"

I am L/Leema, and L/Leema. We scan again the statements for their correctness. We find that with these particular statements, we view that which is the perception of a diligent seeker. The perception of any diligent seeker is correct in respect to that seeker. Each who seeks what may be called truth and finds any manifestation of that truth which may be called love will discover these portions of truth in a manner which is consummate with that seeker's nature. Each entity and portion of the Creator is an unique portion. Though all seek the same central truths, each approaches this truth from a somewhat different angle than does any other seeker. Therefore, though there will be many similarities in truths found by diligent seekers, there will always be those unique qualities that permit each seeker its identity. As this identity is developed to such an extent that it may become fully one with that which it seeks, it then may be given up in larger and larger portion in order that that unity may be fully realized, thus the great cycle of evolution completes itself within each portion of the one Creator. At the heart of all creation is that quality called love. It enables and ennobles each portion of the creation. All are moved by its power, yet each perceives it differently until there is no perception and only identity. Then all perceive as one.

May we answer in any further fashion, my sister?

Carla: No, thank you. There is more to the question which I will finish reading. I just couldn't stand to read the whole thing. The rest of the question reads: "Yogananda speaks of human consciousness/subconscious/superconscious/Christ consciousness/cosmic consciousness. Might this typology be useful in further explicating the above observations?"

I am L/Leema, and we find that this query opens a great field in which the seeker may quest for truth, for indeed each incarnation is experience spent in a tiny portion of an entity's beingness. That portion is what you call the conscious mind. This conscious mind moves about in what you may call an illusion, though most within your illusion feel the illusion to be quite, quite real. The conscious mind is but the tip of the mind of an entity viewed in its entirety. There is that which has been called a veil which separates the conscious mind from the greater portion of an entity's total beingness. A large portion of that being exists as a portion of an entity's mind complex and within this mind complex, then, will fall some of those descriptive terms given in the query.

The unconscious mind is as the roots of a tree. The branches are as the conscious mind traveling down the trunk into the roots. One may see the unconscious mind moving further and deeper into those portions of mind which are shared with other beings so that there is seen a group mind of an unconscious nature that you may term racial, and in some cases, planetary. These realms of mind are often given names such as superconscious experience, for within such realms are many beings, levels of creation or perception and experiences that one may have in connection with the evolutionary process ongoing in all that form this portion of mind.

As the complex of mind is followed to the limits of its creation—for all creation is a function of mind, consciously applied—there is then the opportunity for the entity or group of entities to make contact with the complex of spirit which then serves as a communicator or shuttle, as it has been called, with that which goes beyond all manifested form, beyond creation and the so-called conscious experience of creation, there is the infinity of that which is not made in any form, but which permeates all form and is, shall we say, the substance from which all which is made is made. This is the unity of infinite intelligence, the being of the one Creator without distortion of any kind.

Thus, those terms which were given in the query are terms which are generally applied to the ever-expanding process of the seeker's seeking wider and wider points from which to view the universe, its own being, and its being's movement through this universe.

May we answer further, my sister?

Carla: No, I thank you for L.

I am L/Leema, and we thank both the one known as L and you, my sister. Is there another query?

Carla: Well, I'll ask one last one. This one is just from Carla. I was really interested in the question tonight because I have been, ever since my friend, Don, died, feeling about as low as you can get, not only because of grieving, which is substantial and I expect will go on for some years, because we adored each other, but also because I feel so full of iniquity and sin. I can think of so many things, had I known that the man was so close to suicide, that I might have been able to get up the energy to do a little differently, even though I was under a lot of stress, if I had known how critical everything was. I keep going back and seeing one omission or commission after another that if I could take it back, I would give my life to do so. And so, I have never in my life felt so empty of virtue. And I wonder if you could comment on the subjective feeling of a person who attempts with all his heart to find value and to be virtuous as opposed to the objective or inner, shall we say, beyond the veiled reality of virtue and value.

I am L/Leema, and we feel that we have sufficient grasp of your query that we may comment within the boundaries of the Law of Confusion. As the small self which you are, seemingly, at this time moves in various patterns through the illusion, it is planned aforetimes that there will be the difficulties that will test certain, shall we say, characteristics, or as others may call them, virtues of the entity. These characteristics have been formed through great effort in many incarnational experiences. They may not be easily recognized by your peoples as obviously virtuous, for many are beyond the description of words commonly associated with virtuosity.

In the difficult experience, and by this we suggest that a challenge has been presented and the limitations of the small self have been stretched near to breaking, the entity has the opportunity to examine not only its performance or ability to meet the challenge which is a portion of the learning, but has the opportunity to view its own response to what it calls a failure, or what you have called the iniquity, the sin, that which has missed the mark. This is a greater portion of the learning, for within your illusion and within those small selves who populate your illusion, you find the challenges are infinite, yet the ability to meet such challenges is finite. It has limitations designed to form the very personality or small self which you seem to be. Limitations are merely the extent of manifestation of a certain character trait, thus they are not strictly or correctly defined as only a limitation.

Taken in sum, these various character traits, then, are the significant portion that is experiencing the incarnation in order to further develop or finely balance these energy patterns. For any such development or balancing process, the self must have a certain feeling of value or worth in order that there be the motivation or reason to continue learning. As your small self looks upon your so-called failures and makes its judgment, then it further biases the small self's view of itself in whatever direction, whether it be acceptance or lack of acceptance. Thus, a basic bias is offered an opportunity for further bias or further balance according to the needs of the entity in the total scope of its being.

May we answer further, my sister?

Carla: That in itself is a complete answer, but I would like to press forward with just one point which I just neglected to put into the first part. It was in my mind but I didn't got it out. During the period that I'm speaking of, which lasted about a year, I guess, before Don died, I had to make decisions many times. And I don't think I've ever prayed as hard in my life—ever. And each time I had to make the decision to do this or to do that, to sympathize or try to indicate, "No, this is not normal, this is abnormal; how can I help you get well?" that kind of thing, it seemed at the time that I had prayed it through, and that I had meditated, and that I was not running on my own steam but that I did have access to the higher self. And yet, all of those wise decisions all added up to an outcome which was, to my little self, vastly not to be desired. So is part of what you're saying, or what you were saying through me earlier about virtue, that it is liable to be unpopular and misunderstood, and seeming to miss the mark completely?

I am L/Leema, and we agree with this summary, shall we say, of our previous comments in response to your specific query, for that which has value to the total being may be that which is quite misunderstood by the small self which is, shall we say, bearing the weight of that which it does not and in some ways cannot understand. Such a burden increases the difficulty of any lesson. Yet at the same [time] such a burden increases the value or weight of the lesson when it is learned.

May we answer further, my sister?

Carla: No, thank you. Thank you very much.

I am L/Leema, and we are grateful to you, my sister. Is there another query?

(Pause)

I am L/Leema, and we thank you, each of you, for allowing our presence and humble words to be shared this evening. We are grateful beyond all words to be able to join a group such as this one which seeks the truth without pretense or presupposition that such truth is already possessed. We are with you at your request and shall at this time leave this instrument and this group, rejoicing in the love and the light of the one infinite Creator. We are L/Leema. Adonai vasu borragus.

Sunday Meditation
July 21, 1985

(Carla channeling)

I am Oxal. I greet you, my friends, in the love and in the light of the one infinite Creator in whose name we come this evening. We thank you for calling us to you and hope that our humble words may hold something that may be of value to you this evening, reminding you, as always, that we are, as you, full of mistakes, full of errors and without any pretension to infallibility. Therefore, we ask you to consult your own inner wisdom. There is that within you which recognizes truth and which knows the truths that you need at this particular moment. Take what you will and discard the rest without a backward glance, for our wish is only to aid you, not to teach you any dogma. We know the path and we know the journey. But the steps you take are your own. You cannot walk as others walk nor can you meet the difficulties that others meet or experience the joys that others experience. What is in common is the journey itself and the joy and peace that lies from the commitment of oneself to seeking the truth.

As the shadows lengthen and the evening comes into the windows of your domicile, so each of you sits, in some way broken. None of you is any longer whole; none of you is any longer confident that everything is perfect. And many of you count this to be a discomfort, perhaps even a weakness or a lack of faith. We ask you to consider the nature of transformation. We would use the example, simplistic though it is, of a cup which must be empty, emptied of all dregs and all substance before it may contain new drink. We ask you to consider a fresh-baked loaf of bread. It is useless until it is broken. In your young wholeness, my friends, you were full of something very valuable, the unexamined and totally trusted light and love of the Creator that blows about children and makes them so special to the adults about them. But there is no learning in this untouched condition. Does bread count it as cruelty to be broken that it may be eaten? We think not. Do you count it as cruel that life has fragmented your understanding and caused you to raise questions about yourself and others and the nature of the universe? Sometimes it is impossible for those within an illusion as dense as yours not to feel that it is cruel to be so broken by experience. And yet, brokenness is an utterly necessary prelude to transformation. Whole, untouched, you are finite. Broken, you become infinite, infinitely full of possibility, of newness, and of the potential for life, life that is new and vital.

It is as though the illusion which you now enjoy is a kind of threshing machine. It is inevitable that you shall come between the grinding wheels, and that you shall feel burst apart, sometimes slowly, sometimes all at once. These moments and times of your incarnational experience are the most pregnant with possibility for the acceleration of your spiritual evolution, for you have moved into an infinity when you are no longer closed.

What we say rings of the impractical and we realize that you seek not only that which is theoretical but that which may serve as an ethic that may inspire behavior which manifests that which you hold dear: service to others, love; there are many good qualities we could name for which you may be seeking inspiration. Your best quality is the willingness to be broken because that willingness is the willingness to learn, and, my friends, all things in your illusion teach the lessons of love. Each time you are broken, you are being offered a new way to come to a new understanding, if we may use that misnomer, of love. And by this we do not mean that which you call love, but rather that which you call Logos, that love which is creative and original, that love which is the Creator, for that love which is all of us, for we and you and all that there is are the Creator. Closed, you are the citizen of an illusion. It is as though your fullness were a prison. Each time you face adversity, you escape that prison and you are open to the transfiguration of another learning of love.

We do not say this simply because it is inevitable that experience shall cause discomfort and grief, although that is surely the nature of your illusion. We say this to attempt to inspire you to examine whatever faces you at this particular time, to find within it the seeds of love where there was none before within your heart. As always, the best adjunct to experience for the seeker is daily meditation. It does not have to be a full-time job, as this instrument would say. A very few minutes of seeking in silence that still, small voice, if we may quote from one of the holy works, is sufficient to put you in contact with the infinity that you can otherwise receive only from the harsh trials of experience. For there is that within you, as we have said, that will aid you in coming to a new knowledge, an expanded knowledge of your own nature and of the nature of love. Often there is great healing in such understanding, as that which no longer needed can fall away; as those bitter feelings disappear, for they are no longer needed; as dislike and prejudice disappears, for they are no longer needed. And then, once again, you become whole and you manifest to those about you that which has begun to come through you, that which is infinite, that which is love.

In the inevitable cycle of experience, you shall again be broken and the cycle turns again, offering you again and again the opportunity for new knowledge—or if you have refrained from learning the lesson given you previously, you may find yourself repeating one lesson again and again. Try as you may, you will not escape this lesson until it is learned. This is not a grim threat, my friends; this is the nature of your experience. It is our intent to give you encouragement so that you may welcome experience, so that you may, even in pain or grief or despair or loneliness welcome being broken, and look immediately for the love that you have not allowed into this moment.

We shall pause for a moment that you may do this exercise at this moment. Open yourself at this moment that love may sweep through you, sweep you clean and make you one with your experience. We pause. I am Oxal.

(Pause)

I am Oxal, and am again with this instrument. We would like to close through the one known as L1 if this instrument is not too fatigued. We shall offer the conditioning with the understanding that we do not wish to tax this instrument, and therefore the choice is certainly and always the instrument's. We shall leave this instrument. I am Oxal.

(L1 channeling)

I am Oxal. I am now with this instrument. My friends, it is our desire not to tax your patience with wordy sermons or dry discourses, but rather to share with those present that which we recognize to be an essential part of the process through which enlightenment is attained. Therefore, we thank those present for their patience and commend your dedication and perseverance and seeking. We are known to those present as Oxal. Adonai, my friends. Adonai vasu borragus.

(L1 channeling)

I am Latwii, and I greet you, my friends, in the love and light of the infinite Creator, and wish to offer our service at this point in attempting to answer any questions that those present might deem fit to pose. Are there any questions at this time?

Carla: Well, since nobody's jumped in, I'll go back to the venerable L2's list of ad hoc questions, if it's all right with you, Latwii. This is a short one for a change. Number five: "Is it true that the essence of love is compassion? How can there be explication of the ways whereby compassion steers between the twin distortions of being patronizingly maudlin, so to speak, on the one hand, and being too sternly judgmental on the other?"

I am Latwii. We are aware of your question. My brother, compassion is what may be described as the distortion of that which we term love. We would further observe that compassion is characterized by the distortion of judgment where compassion is quite often love given upon the establishment of certain prior conditions. If we might offer an example, the individual who passes an other self upon a thoroughfare might observe that the other self seems somewhat poorly attired or perhaps the physical vehicle of the other self does not appear to be well-nourished. This has the characteristic of an observation, however, rather than an outpouring of that which you term love. The viewer, however, when made aware that certain circumstances such as the loss of numerous loved ones, and the entirety of one's physical possessions resulted in the other self's dire appearance, might be overwhelmed with sudden feelings of that distortion of love which you term compassion.

As one might observe, the compassion or distorted love was only offered upon the basis of evaluation of appropriateness by the one extending that which you call compassion. The distortion of love that you refer to as compassion, then, may be characterized by that individual who offers such distorted love as falling within certain realms of appropriateness. And, indeed, it is the limitations which you, my brother, have suggested that are examples of the range within which such distorted love may be offered.

We would, in closing, observe that the offering of love to any other self for reasons resultant of judgment is still an extension of love and is therefore commendable. However, one who would be an adept must recognize that the extension of love is a form of service to one's other selves, and therefore does not require precondition.

May we answer you further?

Carla: Just for my own benefit, let me try to sum up what you said in a sentence or two. What you said was that compassion, since it's run through a person who feels it personally for another person, involves judgment, of necessity, since that's the way people's minds work. But compassion as an ideal has no precondition, but is given in total freedom. Therefore, we as human beings never quite reach the perfection of that distortion of love known as compassion. Is that what you're saying?

I am Latwii. My sister, we agree with your explanation with one variation. We would emphasize that the use of the word "love" rather than "compassion" in the latter portion of your statements would be more appropriate, for it is love, itself, which ideally should be given freely rather than the distortion of love known as compassion.

May we answer you further?

Carla: Yeah. The Live Aid concert brought a wave of what I would call compassion rather than love, that is, pity, and a desire to help a lot of people that were hungry that nobody knew. How does one make the step from compassion based on need to unconditional love, personal love, of strangers, billions of them, whom one does not know and can never know? Or is this even recommended?

I am Latwii. My sister, we would attempt to answer your question simply by extending the observation that the numerous strangers cited in your question are actually numerous other selves and for that reason one might observe that there is a reluctance on the part of the individual to love himself or herself through the extension of love to all other selves, in essence a reluctance to love oneself in totality. For this reason, we would offer the suggestion that to learn to accept and love oneself in its facets which are both attractive and unattractive is a step toward the loving of those same characteristics, both attractive and unattractive, in one's other selves. For to accept oneself is to learn to accept one's other self sufficiently that the extension of love to the degree which you described becomes possible. The recognition must occur that each other self is in essence identical to one's own self and the accomplishment of loving these numerous other selves is an extension of that recognition.

It is becoming difficult for this instrument to continue to maintain contact, and we would suggest that should further questions be desired, that another instrument offer to serve on this instrument's behalf. We are known to you as Latwii.

Sunday Meditation, July 21, 1985

(Jim channeling)

I am Latwii, and we are with this instrument whom we thank for offering a voice for us to utilize once again. Is there further query?

L1: Yes, Latwii. I'm disturbed as to the potential accuracy of what I was channeling. Would you make any corrections that are necessary through correction or repetition of the questions that were offered while I was channeling?

I am Latwii, and am aware of your query and your concern, my brother. We would not attempt to add or subtract from any concept which you utilized, and which we were able to utilize using your mind and its contents. We are most appreciative of each instrument's desire to be of service, for though our message is always and ever the same, there is much to be gained in variety of expression when we are able to utilize numerous instruments in speaking this one message. Therefore, we should not feel any concern to alter our message which was transmitted through your instrument but would simply thank you for your service and remind you that as you open yourself in service and give up your own small will that you may serve a greater will, that you then must needs accept that which proceeds through your instrument and allow its movement through your instrument in as free a manner as possible without the overconcern as to whether the task has been accomplished in one fashion or another. To put it more simply, my brother, do not be so judgmental upon your own abilities. We thank you for your service.

May we answer further, my brother?

L1: No. Thank you for your comfort.

I am Latwii, and we thank you, as always. Is there another query?

N: May I ask for some further explanation? Are you in essence saying, Latwii, that we have many problems within ourselves which we can't accept, and which is true, of course, but when we have problems with others which we seem to want to accept, yet can't rationalize love as an extension of the one infinite Creator, then this is again failings within our feelings for ourselves?

I am Latwii, and am aware of your query, my brother. We shall attempt clarification. When one sees any other being and has any of the range of emotions that are possible within your human condition, one may assume that the emotion is felt for the other self because that emotion has some impact or reference to the self. You are in essence a conglomeration or unit of learning, this is to say, you have your unique character, you have distortions of one sort or another that give you your strengths, your variety, and your uniqueness. You will feel in one manner or another about yourself or some portion of yourself according to the desire you have to learn in that area and your own conscious or subconscious assessment of your success in so learning. This process of learning and judging the self is one which is always ongoing, yet is usually not as conscious in the earlier portions of one's incarnation as it is in the latter portions. Therefore, as you become more and more aware of your own self and come to know that self, a portion of this awareness is gained by seeing your feelings for yourself reflected by others to you as your feelings for others. Thus, the mirroring effect of other selves shows you your attitude towards a portion of your own being. As you become more and more aware that this is the case, the process then is accelerated.

May we answer you further, my brother?

N: No, thank you. I think that was good.

I am Latwii, and we thank you, my brother. Is there another query? …

(Side one of tape ends.)

(Jim channeling)

I am Latwii, and we are with this instrument once again, now that the mechanical duties have been completed. May we again ask if there might be another query?

Carla: I am interested in the message tonight because it was sort of paradoxical, and I wondered if you could make your own comment on the subject. Having experienced what was to me definitely the biggest disaster of my life recently, I have felt more imprisoned by the situation than freed by the situation. And when I have been in the past much more unbroken and whole I have felt freer, whereas the message stated that when you are whole you are in prison. Could you offer comment on this basic theme to clarify Oxal's thoughts for me?

I am Latwii, and am aware of your query, my sister. We shall be honored to attempt clarification of this message which our brothers and sisters of Oxal were so inspiring in the presentation of this evening.

As you feel the feeling which you have described as wholeness, you are as the harvester who has plucked the fruit from the tree and enjoys the sweetness of the fruit which has taken long to produce. It is a milestone, shall we say, upon which you stand and which signifies a portion of a journey which has been completed. Yet, as all journeys of which we are aware in the seeking of truth are of an infinite nature, at some point there will be the setting out upon another portion of this journey of seeking. For as you have plucked the fruit of the previous journey and are nourished by it, there comes a time when the pilgrim, which each is, desires to move yet further upon the journey of seeking the truth. There is a price for each step. There is what often seems difficulties both small and large, both trivial and tragic, which will confront the doughty seeker.

If there were no such difficulties, if there were no price for the steps taken upon this journey, the lessons could not be learned, for there would be no weight against which to test and strengthen the spiritual muscle. For those who have gained much of the strength through many of the trials, further testing will require added weight and difficulty, shall we say. Within your illusion, such difficulties are not often seen for the great opportunity for growth which they offer. This is not surprising, my sister, for little within your illusion is seen for what it truly is. Much of sight rests upon the surface of things, the heart seldom seen. Yet it is our suggestion to you that within all such difficulties, the opportunity for learning and experiencing the love of the one Creator are infinite.

May we answer further, my sister?

Carla: No, thank you. That was very helpful.

I am Latwii, and we thank you, my sister. Is there another query?

(Pause)

I am Latwii, and we are honored to have been able to speak a few words this evening to this assembled group. We have enjoyed your vibrations and your queries. We thank you with a whole and joyful heart for requesting our humble presence. We also wish to remind each that we are but fallible seekers upon the same path of seeking which you now find your feet. Take that which we have given that has value in your own journey and leave behind that which has none. We are with you upon your request in your meditations to aid in their deepening and we are eager to join you again in your "Sunday night meetings," as they have come to be called. We thank you and we bless all and leave all in the love and in the light of the one infinite Creator. We are those of Latwii. Adonai. Adonai vasu borragus.

(Carla channeling)

I Yadda. I greet you in love and light of infinite Creator. We say to one known as J, "Howdy." We come as you call, but you must understand, we have to be very brief, for the seats become hard when the second side of the tape has been turned over, and we do not wish to make the seats of your couches and chairs any more hard for you.

We only wish to bring you a single thought, and to do that we ask you to come with us in your mind, to leave this room and move into the night sky, far and far away, farther than you can see, farther than your telescopes can see, until you are no more in space and time, until you are truly within the Creator. We ask you to feel the light that is so bright, that shines not from a single source, but everywhere, from everywhere and to everywhere at once. There is no night; there is no sky, there is no separation—"separ-ation"—we are learning to say our R's, are we not, aha?! We ask you now to rook—to look back at yourself and ask what lies before you.

What's your problem? We ask you! Detach yourself. Do you have a problem with your reputation? Forget it. Reputations are not important! Do you think ill of yourself? Forget it—what do you know? Do others think ill of you? Forget it—what do they know? Do you think that you are not as good as others think you are? Forget it—what do you know? Try to live in the light, my friends. Do not reach for it—allow it to fill you, for with every breath you are infused with that light, that love and that energy, and you are a powerful being.

So get on with it. With no fear, but with a will to serve, to love, and to be in the light. And that light is that which we leave you in, having no other possibility, for that is all that there is. The rest is confusion and dreaming. We wish you happy dreams and we wish you moments of wucidity—lucidity in which you see beyond your dream and beyond your darkness, beyond those few moments when you wear your funny costume of physical flesh and see the essential you which not only dwells in light, but is light.

We known to you as Yadda. That is not important, either. We, however, love you. Adonai. Adonai. We leave you in the love and in the light of the One Who Is All. ☥

L/L Research

Sunday Meditation
July 28, 1985

(L1 channeling)

I am Hatonn, and I greet you, my brothers and sisters, in the love and in the light of the infinite Creator. My friends, we are greatly pleased that you should take the time from your busy day to join your vibration with our own and to share with us that we may both benefit. It is our desire to come to you, not as a teacher, but rather as a brother or sister, who upon returning home, shares that which has recently been learned, those awarenesses which come upon one during one's day that he or she would offer to another self for examination and understanding. My friends, please understand that in this service, we necessarily learn from the sharing and therefore are quite grateful that you offer us the service of your time and attention.

It is our desire tonight to share with you some thoughts on the subject of eternity, for as your tuning has smoothed the path toward such a discussion, we desire to follow the flow of the river of consciousness and continue in the same channel.

My friends, eternity quite often is regarded in one of two fashions. It is either the vague and murky period somewhere in the distant future which we are often told we should somehow prepare for, yet recognize that it is sufficiently distant as to make such preparation lacking in immediacy.

The other perception of eternity is in itself almost a contradiction of itself, for we often regard it as a vague period of time, beginning in the quite immediate future, for which there is not sufficient time to make preparation, so we simply avoid thinking about it. In each of the two conceptions we manage to safely distance ourselves from any responsibility or effort. But, my friends, those here are seekers, and the seeker is aware that that which surrounds himself or herself is eternity, that that point within which one identified his location in time is perched quite deeply within that which we call eternity, rather than a safe distance before it.

So, my friends, we ask, is it not wiser to examine that with which we now occupy ourselves for eternity? Is it truly the wisest choice to spend our eternity in the pursuit of finite objectives, of petty quarrels, of insignificant pursuits? Are we wise to spend our eternity debating which vacation to take or how to invest our money? My friends, we offer these questions not to belittle those pursuits which are facets of your daily lives and those of your brothers, but rather to emphasize that it is quite tempting within the illusion to spend one's time and effort holding eternity at bay, to tell that quiet voice within that we will begin our efforts toward the development of ourselves just as soon as one more pursuit has been accomplished or perhaps later in the week when one is not so busy.

My friends, eternity does not begin now—eternity has been with you always. And we ask you to examine in your heart the wisdom of spending your eternity delaying your efforts to prepare yourselves for that eternity. We speak not in terms of eternal reward or eternal punishment, for, my friends, each of you is aware that those will be the result of your desire to reward or punish yourselves. We speak, rather, of your inner desire to return to that source, to once again reunite yourself with all of your other selves, to become again conscious of that which in the entirety of your brothers and sisters throughout your universe you will one day become.

My friends, if we may be forgiven for attempting to urge you to one decision over another, then we ask you to prepare yourselves for that journey. I am known to you as Hatonn. Adonai, my friends. Vasu borragus.

(Jim channeling)

I am Latwii, and we greet you, my friends, in the love and the light of our infinite Creator. We also are most privileged to be asked to join your group this evening. We hope, as always, that we might be of some small service by offering ourselves in an attempt to answer whatever queries may be of value to you. We would, however, preface this service by reminding each that we are but your fallible brothers and sisters. If any word we speak should confuse or annoy you in any way, please cast it aside. Take those that have value and use them as you will. With that disclaimer aside, we would ask if we might begin with the first query.

R: I wonder if you could answer without infringement who it was I saw last night?

I am Latwii. We are aware of your query, my brother. We find that you have had an experience of what would be called an unusual nature, one which is often desired in order that, shall we say, a certain form of reassurance might be had and might quiet the disturbed mind upon a certain point. Because this experience has the capability of answering this desire upon your part, and because this desire is a central portion of your own learning process, we must satisfy ourselves with this general response without giving more specific details that would do for you that which you seek to do for yourself.

May we answer further, my brother?

R: Not on that, Latwii, no. But I wonder if you could comment on the, I guess, the pros and cons of chemotherapy?

I am Latwii, and am aware of your query, my brother. This is a somewhat difficult query, for this technique of healing within your allopathic community is one which is usually utilized when the condition of the entity is quite, quite deteriorated. The disease, as you call it, among your peoples at this time known as the cancer is becoming more prevalent in various portions of the physical vehicle. Because of certain attitudes and ways of perceiving in a somewhat limited fashion, shall we say, diseases such as cancer proliferate among your peoples in order to provide learning devices or focuses for the attention. When the attention has been diverted for a long enough portion of what you call time, the teaching device, the disease, progresses in becoming more obvious that the one suffering the disease might notice and work with this catalyst for learning. When the condition has been allowed to progress to the point where it is feared that the physical vehicle shall fail and become unviable, it is often necessary if the incarnation is to be prolonged and further learning be available that what you would call drastic means be utilized.

Thus, in many cases, such a course of treatment would be seen as quite appropriate if the entity at the core of its being desired additional time to process the catalyst which had been placed before it. However, as you are aware, this particular course of treatment is one which has its own set of somewhat drastic, shall we say, side effects. In all types of healing treatment which do not take into account the lesson which has been symbolized in physical disorder there will be some side effect which is not desired. This must be weighed by any entity conscious of the evolutionary process which it is experiencing within its incarnation.

May we answer further, my brother?

R: I don't want to take up any more time. I really appreciate it, Latwii. It was most helpful. Thank you.

I am Latwii, and we thank you, my brother. Is there another query?

Carla: *(inaudible)* the last one of L2's. It's only four lines this time. "God," he defines God here as "the one Creator's power is so incomprehensibly infinite that in one text it is said, 'He tempts the true devotee with awesome powers experientially before admitting same back into mahapahanirvana.' Can this be further explicated?" Want it again?

I am Latwii, and we are unsure as to whether we have a complete grasp of this query but we shall make our best effort at focusing a response which lies within the boundaries drawn by this query.

The various philosophies that have been developed by the many cultures and groups within cultures of people upon your planet all speak in some manner of a God force, a Creator, a Logos, a primal force of some nature. All are aware, it would seem, that there is more to the daily life than what is usually experienced. It is felt by each on a subconscious level at least that there is some vitalizing force that moves through the life and which can be known in some fashion. The various religions and philosophies which have attempted to codify and explain this God force to individuals within the culture or religion have by the attempt to describe that which is indescribable often created distortions of understanding amongst these people who have adopted one or another philosophy as a path to that God force. Thus, each will describe this force and each entity's relationship to it in a slightly variant fashion. There will be numerous activities in many religions and philosophies that are seen as good and which promote this search and seeking for the truth or the God force. There will be, as well, many actions and thoughts which will be described as "bad" or "evil" and will be seen to prohibit this process.

Thus does each philosophy and religion seek to describe the path to the Creator for the seeker. Various enticements are offered, various prohibitions are put in place. Yet within each philosophy and religion, there exists enough of what you may call the truth that the seeker who is pure in heart and desire may travel a path within that religion or philosophy and find the goal which it seeks. This is true, my friends, for to the best of our understanding, there is no portion of any entity or of any part of creation which does not contain that which is sought. This is to say that all things, all entities, are the Creator and are that which each seeks.

That this is not obvious and clear to those within your illusion of reality is both a blessing and, while in the incarnation, would seem a curse. It is a blessing, my friends, that you operate in what has been called a veil or darkness, a forgetting of who you are, because in this state of thinking, the attempts that you make to seek the truth carry much more weight within your total beingness than would such attempts carry should it be obvious that all things are the one Creator. It would not be difficult to love without condition; it would not be difficult to give without stint; it would not be difficult to see the one Creator in all entities and experiences if there were no other thing to see.

Yet within your illusion it seems a curse to move in such darkness with such dimly lit pathways, for the errors seem to greatly outnumber the successes in finding any portion of truth and purpose in life. Yet, my friends, we say that because the one Creator exists in all entities, each experience of every entity is an experience of the Creator knowing Itself. Thus do each of you glorify the one Creator by presenting the gifts of your experiences, however small or large, to the one Creator. These experiences would not be available without your efforts.

May we answer further, my sister?

Carla: I'd like to pick on one phrase that L2 used because I think it's the heart of this question. And it is said that, "God tempts the seeker with awesome powers experientially before admitting same," which I assume to be, "before admitting the seeker," back into the state of bliss." Are, in your opinion, the powers of the one Creator a temptation? They certainly are awesome …

I …

Carla: … It strikes me that this is the heart of the question and there's something just … it's hard to put my finger on, but it seems wrong-headed somehow.

I am Latwii, and we ask your forgiveness for interrupting your query. We find we have caught this instrument's disease. We shall attempt to speak to this point. In our previous response, we attempted to cover this point in a general fashion by suggesting that the philosophies of those who move in darkness may be quite distorted, yet each is a portion of the one Creator. We may attempt clarification by suggesting that the query as stated suggests a Creator which exists apart from those who seek the one Creator. This is a premise which we do not accept, thus we did not speak in a direct fashion to it, for there is no external Creator that tempts any to seek it. There is one Creator which exists in all portions of creation which nurtures each of Its creations, and grants to each the free will to seek It in any fashion which it chooses.

May we answer further, my sister?

Carla: Could you say then that perhaps the temptations of which L2 speaks have more to do with blockages in the lower chakras which may cause a person to wish for power or success in the spiritual sense, possibly recognition, as opposed to desiring to find always the will of the higher self and the Creator?

I am Latwii, and we hope that we may be of service in this response by suggesting that the temptations spoken of in the query are more properly assigned to various philosophies and entities holding such points of view. The seeker has the will, the desire to seek. How this is used is a function of the seeker's point of view which in turn may be further affected by the philosophy or religion which it has adopted.

May we answer further, my sister?

Carla: No. I believe I see that what you're saying is that the question is so heavily biased that there's no real way to get at it. And I accept that. I thank you for L2.

I am Latwii, and we thank you and the one known as L2 for offering the service of this query. May we attempt another query?

N: Yes. I wonder if there's any authenticity to the newspaper report concerning *(inaudible)* extraterrestrial craft dogfight over *(inaudible)*?

I am Latwii, and am aware of your query, my brother. In matters of this nature, we find it more appropriate to leave the conclusions to those interested in such phenomena. We do not feel it appropriate to verify or nullify items of this nature, for they bear little fruit on the seeker's journey.

May we attempt another query, my brother?

Questioner: Latwii, is monogamy the ultimate form of relationship between a heterosexual mating couple?

I am Latwii, and am aware of your query, my brother. We find that the use of the adjective, "ultimate," befuddles somewhat the clarity of the query. We would perhaps be more comfortable and be of more service it we were allowed to substitute the phrase, "more efficient," for that particular adjective, for we believe that the heart of your query concerns the type of relationship which is most helpful to those within it as each pursues the evolutionary process of seeking the truth and discovering the nature of the self.

The pairing of the male and female entities within your illusion and beyond your illusion is seen as being the most efficient in that the nature of creation as we understand it is reproduced within such a couple. Yet, it must be remembered that these male and female forces, these positive and negatively charged forces, are found both in each biological entity, be that entity male or female. Yet, the male and female entities then, as they interact one with the other ...

(Side one of tape ends.)

(Jim channeling)

I am Latwii, and we are once again with this instrument. To continue. These male and female qualities, then, being expressed within this mated relationship allow the mirroring effect to occur with greater intensity and frequency. This mirroring effect is the effect that occurs when one sees within another self those characteristics that are loved and accepted and those that are not loved and not accepted. In truth, these are the characteristics of the self which are loved or not loved, and are those characteristics which outline the lessons and services that the entity has designed into the life pattern from the preincarnational state.

The intensity and frequency of this mirroring effect, then, is due to the natural attractions and interactions that are set in motion by the basic positive and negative forces of creation moving within the mated couple. That the relationship is one which is seen as a life-long relationship insures that the mirroring effect will be produced on a frequent basis. The frequency aids in the intensification of the opportunity to see the self within another and to work upon the self as one works upon the relationship with the other self.

Thus, the male qualities of radiance and reaching for that experience not yet held and the female qualities of magnetism, of awaiting the reaching and potentating the experience, are those qualities which continue to—we scan for the correct term—redound and rebound within the experience of each entity, echoing and reechoing the attraction of lessons, the catalyst of these lessons, and the opportunity to continue the lessons throughout the incarnation.

May we answer further, my brother?

Questioner: That was fine.

I am Latwii, and we thank you, my brother, for your query. Is there another query at this time?

L1: How is the instrument doing?

I am Latwii, and we find that the instrument t is available for a number of queries yet, having sufficient energy present.

May we ask if there might be a further query?

L1: Was I getting some communication from Yadda a little while ago?

I am Latwii, and am aware of your query, my brother. That you have discovered this fact is therefore that which allows our response. The one known as J was hopeful that he might once again hear from his favorite friends. The one known as Carla has been the sole instrument used by those of Yadda to date, and was itself hopeful that perhaps another might be able to "chew upon that rye bread." Thus, those of Yadda offered to your instrument the opportunity of tasting the rye.

May we answer further, my brother?

L1: No, I'll simply respond that I'd be willing to serve in that fashion when the time comes.

I am Latwii. We appreciate your offer of service, my brother, and those of Yadda are most appreciative as well.

Is there another query?

Carla: I don't know if you can remember this—speaking to the instrument—there was a question that I was supposed to ask and I have forgotten. If the instrument remembers it, would the instrument vocalize it and allow the channel to answer it?

I am Latwii, and if you do not mind our paraphrasing of the query which this instrument has fed into our awareness, we shall be happy to attempt this query.

The query concerned the proper density for holding that state of consciousness which has come to be known as the Christ consciousness. There is some difficulty with this query, for the term "Christ" within many of the cultures of your peoples is a term which is closely associated with an entity known as Jesus of Nazareth. This entity, the one known as Jesus, is one who through its own efforts at seeking the one Creator was one able to attain a state of consciousness that may be described as the Christ or Christed consciousness. This is a level of awareness and experience of being which is available to all portions of the one Creator in a more or less distorted fashion. The distortion is most usually a function of the density or vibratory frequency within which it has been attained. Thus, within your third-density illusion, though much is available to any attaining this crystal pure consciousness, there is by the very density itself some distortion that might be expected.

As the vibratory frequency becomes more filled with light, shall we say, or the energy of creation, to put it another way, the ability of an entity within such a vibratory frequency to experience the Christ consciousness is enhanced and therefore suffers less distortion. In some fashion, any entity achieving this Christ consciousness will have experienced unity with the one Creator and will be thus enspirited and inspired to be of further service to those about it, for each is seen as a portion of the one Creator to know that it is indeed loved and love itself. One who has known this facet of the one Creator, that is, love, then seeks to share that experience and power with those who call for it. Within your illusion, the lessons which all pursue in a unique fashion focus about the concept of love.

Therefore, the achievement of the Christ consciousness will have a strong coloration of this love portion or facet of the one Creator. Those within the next, shall we say, class or vibratory frequency learn lessons that focus upon wisdom, and thus will their experience of Christ consciousness be colored by the characteristic of wisdom. Those pursuing the balance of love and wisdom within the following vibratory frequency will, perforce, experience the Christ consciousness in that balanced fashion. And thus, each experiences the same level of consciousness, but from a different angle or facet, shall we say.

May we answer further, my sister?

Carla: No, thank you.

I am Latwii, and we thank you, my sister. Is there another query?

J: Yes, Latwii. I don't think Yadda is rye bread. I think he's crêpes with orange marmalade.

I am Latwii, and we enjoy your description of our brothers and sisters of Yadda, and we find that they are curling their tongues and smacking their lips at your menu.

May we be of service by answering a query?

Questioner: Latwii, the question came up this afternoon, I guess it was yesterday afternoon, about the sexual nature of the one known as Christ Jesus—the entity and the balancing of that sexual energy that he had, which I believe was recorded in Jane Roberts' *The Seth Material*. Can you speak a little bit about this balancing that the entity known as Christ experienced?

I am Latwii, and am aware of your query, my brother. Again, the entity known as Jesus was one who sought the love of the Father, as this entity put it, for this entity's experience was in the end one which equated love with the Creator and with all creation. The love of the sexual nature is an experience which when used in a conscious fashion may greatly accelerate the evolutionary progress within the conscious seeker, for that which enters the base energy center or chakra is what may be called prana or intelligent energy, also to be known as love, the creative force responsible for the creation itself. Thus, each individual receives this creative force through the base chakra, and by its own free will and its system of beliefs, will use that energy in any of an infinite number of ways.

Most who are not conscious of the seeking process utilize this energy in the sexual manner only, thereby insuring the reproduction of the species and the satisfying of the body's sexual urges. The one known as Jesus, as is necessary for any conscious seeker, was able to consciously move this energy received at the base chakra through each successive chakra or energy center, and with each move was able to step up the vibratory frequency of this energy and balance each chakra in turn, thereby regularizing and crystallizing its own being. Therefore, the intelligent energy or love of the Creator was free to move through this entity without diffraction or distortion in any way.

Thus, the white light of the Creator, this intelligent energy, moved through the crystallized being of the one known as Jesus in such a fashion that there was no color other than white, shall we say, which emanated from this entity's being or any chakra, as it was able to channel this intelligent energy in a pure fashion because of its conscious understanding and mastery of the evolutionary process at work in its own incarnation.

There was some experience of the physical sexual nature that served to trigger this entity's ability to achieve this channeling of intelligent energy in a pure fashion, but it was found by this entity that its own desires were such that it sought to refine this process of enhancing or stepping up the basal frequency in a conscious manner without the recourse to sexual intercourse, shall we say.

May we answer further, my brother?

Questioner: Am I to understand that this refractive process is what creates or is the process of desire, and that we have this balancing available to us also in order to achieve, let's say, a more balanced energizing. I don't know if I stated that correctly or not. Could Latwii speak on that?

I am Latwii, and am aware of your query, my brother. In general, we would agree with your summation. To hopefully clarify, we would also suggest that each distortion or imbalance that each entity contains in each chakra are the symbols of the lessons that each has encoded within the life experience. Thus, when the light of the Creator is diffracted into a certain color by a certain distortion, this is a process which points out to the entity within the incarnation that there is, shall we say, food for thought available, that there is a portion of the self awaiting discovery, there is experience to be had and balancing of this experience then to also be enjoyed.

May we answer further, my brother?

Questioner: I could probably keep you going all night, but I think that'll probably suffice for my questions at the moment.

I am Latwii. Is there another query?

(Pause)

I am Latwii. We find that we have, for the nonce, exhausted the queries. We thank each who has offered the gift of the query. We hope that our humble response has been of some service. Again, we remind each to take that which has value and to leave that which has none in the personal seeking of truth. We leave each of you at this time in the love and in the light of the one Creator Who Is All in All. We are those of Latwii. Adonai. Adonai vasu borragus.

(Carla channeling)

I Yadda. I greet in love and in light of infinite Creator. We so happy to be with Joe and his friends. And we bless each and are most grateful that we may speak with you ever so briefly, for we do not wish to make you sit too long. We are also confirm we were giving conditioning as best we could to one known as L1, and we find much luck with this instrument due to the lack, the lack of experience with the trance. We find we can use this instrument at a very right science level because of the instrument's ability to say, "Oh, what the heck, I go ahead and say whatever comes out because I have challenged."

You know, we have made fun many times of this instrument's challenging in the name of Christ. We say, "How about somebody else? There are many good people to challenge with. How about Mohammet; how about Buddha?" But this instrument is not Buddhist; this instrument is not Muslim. Therefore she challenge in name of Christ. We have come to understand this. Therefore, we no longer make fuss with this instrument when this instrument gives the challenge, for we are very happy that there is challenging, for it make this instrument free for us to use.

We leave you only a question, one we ask often. We shall phrase it not like question, but like situation. Here is your situation: Take away your job. Who are you? We gonna keep going here—aha! Take away your clothes; you are wearing sheets now—everybody look alike—aha?! Take away the haircuts, and any artificial means of decoration of the self. How much of you is left? All of you, of course. But who are you in there? We goin' find you. We take off shoes. We not goin' to leave anything but your inner self.

Now what are you going to do? Take away your body. You are only disembodied spirit. But you can turn on TV; you can do anything you wish. Now, there is no one to impress but yourself. Now. Where lie your interests? How would you spend your day? We suggest that most of you are still enough with this world that you would spend a lot of time with the television, the movie, the book, the record, and all the diversions that you so love. We of course are not mentioning things like the tennis because that is often a way of saying who you are, and it is false. We want you to go now through that period where you are tired now of watching that which is outside. Sooner or later, you gonna turn inside and you goin' to look around.

Now who are you? You got a lot of work to do. That work, my friends, can only be done with that which you do not have unless you meditate, for all that you attempt to do to be of service, all that you attempt to do by "rearning," by *learning*—we are sorry, that one hard for us—aha!—must go before you get the clear look at the limitation of the self that will go away unlamented when you do, indeed, lose this particular chemical body. But you are spiritual person; each is spirit, is soul, that which is ancient. Therefore, within meditation there is that which may put you in touch with who you are. And more than that, may give you tools to use, resources to use in the manifestation of the discovery of why you are. Can you love and serve without recourse to meditation and the contact with that which is infinite? You try—you get tired fast.

We thank you for asking us. We are through now, and so leave you in love and in light of infinite One. Listen, my friends, to the silence behind sound, for therein lies your consciousness in its whole reality. How many illusions shall you pierce within the next day or group of days this instrument call week or month? Attire yourself, my friends, not to your clothing first, not to your job first, never to the outer things first. But first to the silence and to the discipline of listening to that silence. For it will drum in your ears louder than all the birdsong, thunder, lightning, rain, hail, all the crickets and other insects, all the trains and planes, anything you can think of. There is nothing so deafening as the sudden tabernacling, shall we say, with the Creator that is you. And nothing is more beautiful than the soul that carries himself away from meditation and into the world. O, rejoice my friends, for you seek and you shall find.

We leave you. We are Yadda. Adonai. Adonai. Farewell. ☥

L/L Research

Sunday Meditation
August 4, 1985

(Carla channeling)

I am L/Leema, and greet you in the love and in the light of the one infinite Creator. We are most gratified this evening to be requested to join in meditation, and we are grateful for the work that one known as L1 has done. We feel that we are making progress in this conditioning and will continue when there is an opportunity such as this one by using this instrument to work with this channel and any other channel who may wish to experience the contact in the future, as you would say. We greet each of you and bless each of you and find great beauty in each of you and, again, we thank you that you allow us to share our limited suppositions and opinions with you.

The question before us is the point which occurs well into the spiritual journey. Therefore, we wish to state the question and then attempt to put [it] in context. It is our understanding that the query involves the balancing technique described by those known to you as Ra which involves accentuating of the distortion as the opening move towards the balance in the personality of that distortion.

To put this in context, we must look at your situation. You are shipwrecked on an island that spins in space. You cannot escape from this island during your incarnational experience and you are separated from other consciousness of the same or higher density by limitless light or space. You share this with each of those who are your companions upon your island home, the vast majority of which are not at all interested in balancing their distortions in the fullest sense, but rather are usually interested in accentuating pleasant distortions and eliminating or numbing uninteresting sensations and emotions.

Therefore, it must be assumed that this technique is of no use to most of those upon your planet. This does not mean that they who have no access to this technique will not learn, for the incarnational experience is very efficient and enough catalyst is given to each that the basic plan of the higher self is at least presented, if not realized. However, those within this domicile at this time have made a decision, the dimensions of which are immense. That decision is to seek the truth. Although there is no distance to this journey of seeking, the effort and the time which you spend in seeking actively and passively, that is, through action and through meditation is an accelerating force which causes your mental/emotional complex to experience in a more rapid and intense manner not only events, but the emotional overtones and undertones of the event.

Let us look at an analog that is very simple, an analog to a concept which does not seem simple, but complex. The analog is this: When a young boy or girl rides his bike, if he takes it very slowly, he will not have to lean as he goes around a corner and it is unlikely that any harm will come to him through miscalculation. This is the case of most upon your planet who have not chosen to accelerate their seeking. Now if this same boy or girl chooses to speed up his journey, he will run into several different problems, all related to his rate of speed. A bicycle going above a certain velocity cannot change its course without first leaning, not in the direction it wishes to go, but in the opposite direction; when one has achieved a certain velocity, one may not see a traffic problem, a bump in the road, and so forth and one may fall off one's bike and hurt oneself.

Now let us turn that simple analogy and look at what seems to be a complex question. When the seeker discovers catalyst affecting him, regardless of the conscious spiritual attitude of the seeker, the lower or deeper portions of the mind will cause certain reactions to bubble up as they had been programmed to do by this incarnational pattern of childhood or because of racial memory, planetary memory or cosmic memory. You will react to catalyst, my friends. The concept of indifference is not one we recommend as one which is helpful when one is faced with catalyst. Rather, we suggest a great deal of interest be given to what is occurring. Is the catalyst due to the attempt to go around the corner? Is the catalyst due, in other words, to a change, a transformation that one is attempting to achieve? Is the catalyst such that some change or transformation might be suggested? If this is the case, and it often is when catalyst is involved, the leaning as you go around the corner is the accentuation in a brief manner preparatory to making the change towards that which you do not want within yourself or within your mind.

For you must have a good grasp of what it is you are leaving as well as what it is you are seeking before you can plainly and efficiently make the transformation. It has been noted that the accentuation can get out of hand—a body can become sick, a mind can become diseased, an anger can become magnified, and all these things seem to blow up, to explode in such a way as to destroy the possibility of transformation.

Let us go back to the boy on the bike. When someone falls off of a bike, that entity picks up the bike, checks himself and the bike for damage, patches up what is necessary and renegotiates the turn. When the seeker in attempting to process catalyst falls off of the firm intention to "do good,"

shall we say, or to use a more accurate term, to follow a positive path, the seeker may well feel bruised, battered, injured and without any proper vehicle for making that transformation previously so eagerly sought. However, there is no moment within or without of the incarnational framework of your ongoing consciousness within which there does not lie the possibility for transformation, the possibility for polarization, the possibility to see love.

We do not mean to be simplistic. We realize that there are deep concerns within this group having to do with life and death. We realize that two within this group have died, and we realize that in both cases, the entities were in the process of making rapid spiritual progress. My friends, these entities are still making rapid spiritual progress due to the effort which knocked them off of their bicycles, spiritually speaking. You must remember that this is an illusion. You are looking at a shadow world. You feel as though you are full and the sky is empty, but in truth you are very empty compared to the fullness of the living ethers.

We shall leave this group, hoping that we may have been of some help and rejoicing with all our hearts that you have asked such a question. For we always hope to offer inspiration and we find that the concept of the infinite amount of hope which, as far as we know is the nature of spiritual reality, [is] a very inspiring message to offer you. We ask you to remember as you fall off, get back on, turn corners, accentuate the turning of the corner in order to make a more efficient turning, and so forth that you are the love in this island home; you are the light in this fragile Earth.

We thank you for your service; we thank you for allowing us to be of service. We are known to you as L/Leema. We leave you at an accentuated point at which it is darkest. And we wait with you for the dawning, rejoicing in the coming of the light and rejoicing with you that your love and your light, that which comes through you from the source of love and light, can and will renew the Earth. We leave you in the light. Adonai. Adonai.

(Jim channeling)

I am Latwii, and we greet you, my friends, in the love and light of our infinite Creator. We too thank you for inviting our presence this evening. We are overjoyed to be able to join your group and we look forward to any queries which might be presented for our mutual benefit. May we ask for the first query?

T: Yes, I have a question. I've been for the last month or so looking for a particular person, and one day at work I was meditating and I had actually spoken to Latwii and I laid my head back to meditate for awhile, and it seemed like two names that were actually younger brother and sister of the person I was trying to get ahold of, they just popped into my mind, I hadn't thought of those two names for a long time, and so I went inside and looked 'em up, and there was one of 'em. I called and got the phone number for the lady I was trying to get ahold of. Did you, you-all, have anything to do with that? That's my question.

I am Latwii, and we, my brother, are happy to say that we were merely witnesses to the coincidence of your seeking and finding that which you sought. The mind in its various portions and capacities contains a great deal more information than any here would easily believe, for indeed, you are one with all that occurs. Within your personal memory there were names which were retrieved and presented for the aid that they might give in your seeking. We observed this phenomenon, and our only part was, shall we say, was to deepen your meditation as requested in order that this information might become more easily accessible.

May we answer further, my brother?

T: No, thank you.

I am Latwii, and we thank you. Is there another query?

Carla: Well, that brings up an interesting query, at least it's interesting to me. My grandmother has a theory that we have little file clerks in our heads and when we can't think of something, we tell the clerk to go find it and then we forget about it because it doesn't do any good to worry about it. And in fifteen minutes or in two days or in two weeks, however long the file clerk takes, it will trot up to the front brain and tell it that it's found the information. Does something like that actually happen when we make a request to our brain for information that we can't immediately remember?

I am Latwii, and am aware of your query, my sister. Those who utilize the power of mind in a conscious fashion may describe and create their "fashion" and it shall be as effective as the image which was used to create it. Thus, if one imagines that there are clerks of one nature or another within the mind who may move to another portion of the mind and retrieve information needed from that portion and present it to the conscious mind in this fashion, then in this fashion will such a mind operate. There are many, many ways of utilizing the mind and its ability to recall that in which it was co-creator.

May we answer further, my sister?

Carla: Yes. I don't know computer language at all, but people have often spoken of the brain as a computer, and I see this request as kind of requesting the computer for data, and I guess what I should have said was that my question had to do with not whether there was a file clerk in there, but if there was a purposive searching that went on independent of the original intention to do the search, which was roughly equivalent to giving the computer a program that it would take an unknown amount of time to process but that it was going to process it.

I am Latwii, and believe that we now have a better grasp of the nature of your query. Please query further if we are mistaken. There are a number of ways to describe the process of which you speak, that is, the seeking of information by the conscious mind and the process by which the information is found and perhaps where it is found. The charging of a desire is the most important portion of the finding of the object of the desire. The experience of the entity provides it a framework within which it might move and continue to move as the framework accumulates what you would call experience through time.

All experience is recorded within the moment of its occurrence. Those partaking in the event will be the primary recorders, shall we say. They shall have the initial experience and shall be able to provide that experience to whatever mind seeks the experience for its own use. When the charge is put upon the desire to know a certain distortion of the truth, then this desire in a conscious fashion moves through the being or metaphysical portions of the entity so seeking. The charge matches that which is sought. Thus, if there are no resistances, shall we say, along the line of travel, the retrieval of the information is immediate, for the seeking is undertaken within one environment, that is, the fabric of your creation, the one Creator.

If there are, however, any forms, thought forms of interference or resistance along the line of travel—and this is usually the case in one degree or another—then the impulse must find its way through or around this resistance. There must be what you would call a gestation period during which the impulse is able to move through the resistance by a progress of what you might call osmosis or bleeding through. The resistances are usually a function of the program of catalyst, an emotional charge of one form or another which inhibits a free flow of information and necessitates a circuitous flow of information. Thus, the imperfect memory because of small emotional charges given to portions of learning as they are initially processed, usually within the younger years of an entity. Thus, dreams and intuitional hunches are often utilized by the deeper portions of the mind as means of circumnavigating these blockages or resistances to the free flow of information.

May we answer further, my sister?

Carla: Yeah. Just one question. One of the fringe religions, Scientology, has as its goal the clearing of such blockages, and it is considered the highest good for a person to achieve the state of clarity. On the other hand, I've noticed that naturally, without my attempting to do anything about it, that imperfect memory works all the time. I've found that I've blocked out almost every unfortunate thing that has happened to me that hasn't happened to me lately. And I go through a progressive way of kind of making my memories golden and just not remembering the rough parts and remembering the good parts. And I wonder, is it important to break through each and every blockage from childhood programming or whatever or is it healthy to accept the protective blocking of traumatic memory?

I am Latwii, and am aware of your query, my sister. We can suggest that as an entity becomes more consciously aware of the process of seeking that is underway in its own being that this choice then becomes more and more a conscious choice and is up to the entity to weigh the alternatives, shall we say. Each entity within your illusion seeks to learn certain lessons. Another way of stating this might be that each seeks to balance distortions or to develop a certain distortion or bias in attitude. It is not so much a case of breaking through a blockage as it is noting the nature of the blockage or resistance and determining the nature of the lesson that is held in this symbolic form. Thus, the process of seeking becomes more consciously undertaken and an entity may then determine that a certain action or attitude is more appropriate at this time than the one which it had been utilizing and the choice may be made to seek a transformation. The entity always has the opportunity for transformation, for such milestones are placed periodically throughout each incarnation. Yet one who seeks in a more conscious fashion may not only utilize those milestones so placed and utilize them more effectively, but may choose additional milestones or challenges, shall we say.

May we answer further, my sister?

Carla: Well, just one thing because I think this is probably only of interest to me. It is to be noted that due to the nature of imperfect memory, the only time that you find out about it is when somebody reminds you of something which you've forgotten, so usually you don't know that you don't remember stuff. So, I'm not sure exactly how you would know the nature of blockage or be able to work on it because you wouldn't even know what it is that you don't know—because you don't know it. If you see what I mean.

I am Latwii, and we believe we grasp the dilemma, and it is a dilemma which is most prevalent within your illusion, for each seeker is as one carrying a tiny light in the darkest of night, attempting to discover a path which will take it from where it is to where it wishes to be. The light illumines but the smallest portion of what lies about the entity. Thus there is much groping and bruising of the being, it would seem, as the path is sought. Yet the conscious desire to continue this journey tends to rekindle and enable the flame to burn somewhat brighter, that somewhat more of the surroundings might be known. Yet it is the desire to seek the truth that is consciously enhanced that most facilitates this seeking, for within such a darkly and dimly lit illusion there is a good deal of what you might call grace or support which …

(Side one of tape ends.)

(Jim channeling)

I am Latwii, and am once again with this instrument. As we were about to conclude, the seeker is most enabled by the conscious increase of the desire to seek the truth, for within such an illusion as that which you now inhabit, the grace of the one Creator which exists in all portions of the illusion is that which carries you beyond all true harm. Your desire to seek that one Creator is that which shall find its goal, for indeed, it contains that which it seeks.

May we answer further, my sister?

Carla: No, thank you.

I am Latwii and we thank you, my sister. Is there another query?

(Pause)

I am Latwii. We thank you each and every one for allowing our presence this evening. Our humble words are but poor attempts to describe that which is quite beyond description. The most carefully phrased query has the same response as the hum of your locusts for the One answers all in love. Our attempt at using words and concepts to in some fashion describe this love and its availability to you are but poor attempts. We thank you for seeking such with us. Upon such a journey it is of great comfort to travel with friends who seek as we seek. We are those of Latwii. Adonai, my friends. Adonai vasu borragus.

(Carla channeling)

I Yadda. I greet you in love and light of infinite One. We come say "Hi" to J. We not stay very long and wish only to encourage each, for there is a song which is beyond the ears, there is the poem which is beyond the language, and there is the life which is beyond death. Welcome to eternity; welcome to what this instrument call Kingdom of Heaven is here. Is now. And is the most powerful creative force in the universe. You think you can use it to fix up world? No, my friends, although a gentle spirit goes a long way. It is of you only in your heart as you gravitate more and more to the One whence you came. We leave you in that unity with much love in our hearts for you. We are with you if mentally requested, and we thank you for allowing to take your time. We known to you as those of Yadda. We say farewell in the One. In love and in light, farewell. ♣

Sunday Meditation
August 11, 1985

(Carla channeling)

I am L/Leema, and I greet you in the love and in the light of the one infinite Creator. It is a privilege and a blessing to be called to this meeting this evening and we share your path with you for a few short moments with utmost gratitude and in hopes that we may be of service to you as we discuss the question which you have put before us, that question being, "What is the nature of prejudice?"

The one whom you have often called the Ancient of Days, whom we prefer to call the Creator or the one original Thought, designed a universe with interest in the variety of consciousness which might precipitate from the giving of free will to various portions of the Logos or love. This variety was seen to be positive in nature and was intended further, in this particular Logos which your planet is influenced by, to offer endless opportunities for polarity, that is, the polarization in consciousness betwixt two conscious entities, thereby giving more variety of experience to the Creator. Therefore, from the same point of the one original Thought there is no possibility of prejudice.

Now let us comb through many densities, many eons of developmental time and space to that illusion which you now experience which is the fruit of all experience that has gone before. As your third-density experience nears its end, the polarity which it is possible for this population to develop has been more or less developed, and some of those polarities involve biases which among your peoples are called prejudicial.

We would like to make two points about prejudice. Firstly, there is an understanding of the word itself which separates the negative portion of prejudice from the positive portions of prejudice. The root of this particular word in your language—and we take this from this instrument's mind—is the Latin *judicare*, meaning to judge or discriminate. However, there is a prefix that is "pre-fixed," in other words, there is that which goes before the judgment or discrimination. Literally, the word means "to prejudge," to judge before you know the facts, to go into relationship with a stranger whom you have not previously known and whose heart and essence you cannot possibly begin to touch with a pre-formed and hardened opinion which takes on some of the negative qualities of that which you call among your peoples, will. The negative portion of prejudice, therefore, is simply that those who make judgments before they know the heart of any subject or consciousness are robbing themselves of an even greater variety of biases which might develop were one to attempt to walk in, as this instrument would say, the other man's shoes, to feel as he feels, to think as he thinks, to be in the situation in which this entity exists.

Since this is a limiting factor, and not a freeing factor, since prejudice imprisons the mind of the one who is prejudiced, it is a metaphysically unsound and counterproductive facet of one's character and it is not suggested that it be encouraged.

We would like to point out, however, that although in no ultimate terms can you judge or discriminate within the illusion in matters having to do with ultimate reality, nevertheless, it is clear that one who lives in an illusion such as yours will find his power of discrimination to be most helpful, for there are those who speak well and whose intentions are other than they speak. There are those who speak ill or who do not speak at all and whose intentions are pure and good. This has little or nothing to do with any prejudicial component such as race, creed, color, sex or age.

There is a further point which may be very helpful to those who wish to work with prejudice within themselves in order to become free of prejudice and become free to discriminate more freely and that is this. Prejudice is, to some extent, an instinct based upon the ultimate origin of the various races of your planetary sphere. Because more than one planetary sphere produced third-density candidates which have experienced third density upon this sphere, those of different planetary influences have fundamentally various archetypical minds, that is, part of their archetypical minds, that part connected with the racial consciousness, is in some cases subtly, in other cases widely different from race to race. The instinctive bias is that of the recognition of a difference. This is the fundamental instinctual and root reason for prejudice or prejudgment. It is not, however, valid in the sense that mind/body/spirit complexes are each the Creator, regardless of their planetary origins. Each, furthermore, has put in the span of third density's space/time attempting to learn the same lessons of love which each has attempted to learn. Therefore, the racial component becomes less and less as the entity becomes more and more consciously a child of the one infinite Creator.

To be prejudiced against any spirit which walks among you is possibly to be discriminating against one whom you would call a saint or angel if you but knew the heart of that person. We ask you therefore to forgive yourself for the inevitable prejudices that are involved in racial discrimination. We ask you further to clear your mind by progressive attempts during meditation of the prejudgment aspect having to do with discrimination. It is not appropriate when one is dealing with an infinite and eternal being that one should prejudge such a marvelous and miraculous piece and necessary portion of the one infinite Creator.

We would say one more thing about prejudice before we leave this instrument in order that we might answer a query. There are other prejudices or biases which have the same sort of limiting effect upon the self as racial prejudice. By this, we mean prejudice against certain types of music, certain types of written word, certain types of food, certain degrees of intelligence, certain accents, and so forth. These are the small change of prejudice. The damage done by this sort of prejudice is not as great as the damage done by racial prejudice due to the fact that you only hurting yourself and not other people. Since one seldom says to another human, "I cannot speak with you because you are too stupid," nor can music become insulted because one person will not listen to it, you are therefore limiting and damaging only yourself for the most part. However, it is well to think well enough of oneself to wish not to damage the self by these prejudices, but rather, again to listen once, taste once, see once, hear once, or feel once any new experience before one judges or discriminates.

Prejudice, my friends, is that which limits; it is therefore that which kills, for freedom is that which causes light. Without condemning yourself or any prejudice, therefore we ask you again to consider well the possible virtue of meditating upon any prejudice which you may entertain in order that the prejudgment may give way to true and valid discrimination.

We would leave this instrument at this time, being conscious of our tendency to give too long an answer when a short one has more pith and may be easier to digest. We are those of L/Leema and would now transfer, leaving you in love and light.

(Jim channeling)

I am L/Leema, and we are pleased to greet you through this instrument. We are happy that it has been able to discriminate our signal and to speak our thoughts. At this time we would offer ourselves in any further attempts to answer queries which those present may have value in the asking. May we be of such service, my friends?

Carla: I would like to ask for some help. I can't remember whether it was N or J that asked a question earlier—I guess it was N—about channeling the other Ra to find out what connection it might have with our Ra. It's not a valid metaphysical practice, but I was at a loss as to how to approach explaining that, even though I've come to know it through years of meditating. I wonder if you could be short and clear and pithy where I was totally lost?

I am L/Leema, and we shall attempt this, my sister. Without judging the efforts of any to serve the one Creator and those about it, we may suggest that some attempts at the vocal channeling are not quite what they appear at first to be. It may be that an entity who has a gift of being able to speak the thoughts of another is made aware of information which it feels is valuable. This information may also be of the channeled variety. This entity in some degree may feel that its service would be enhanced were it able to also offer the channeling of the information which it has come across and feels to be valuable. The desire to serve is at the heart of this effort. Yet, if it is not that entity's gift to channel this or that particular entity, it may be that within its own subconscious mind. The process then takes life and information seeming to come from the entity which it values is then produced. This, though not seeming to be as it is, that is, a product of one's subconscious mind, may however be of great value to that entity and perhaps others as well. Yet, for you, my sister, to attempt to channel that which was subconsciously fabricated would not be a service to this group anymore than another vocal channel's attempt to channel those of the Ra would be to others about it.

May we answer further, my sister?

Carla: No. It's basically N's question. N, *(inaudible)*?

N: No. I think I understood L/Leema's reply that it was a fabricated thought form from the individual's subconscious. Is that correct?

Carla: Yeah, that's what he said.

I am L/Leema. Is there a further response that we might give to either entity?

Carla: I'm satisfied.

N: Well, then who is it that's coming from the subconscious that's not Ra?

I am L/Leema, and am aware of your query, my brother. As you know from your own experience, in attempting to become what has been called the vocal channel or instrument, there is a great leeway or possibility of doubt for one serving as an instrument in that it is not provable to any entity that one is actually channeling another entity when the vocal channeling is attempted. This is in order that one's free will shall always remain intact and that no seemingly superior entities will be unquestionably listened to, shall we say. The channel of whom you speak is one desiring to serve and we do not wish in any way to denigrate that service. Yet it is a common error, shall we say, that entities with a great desire to serve others as vocal channels will when made aware of information of a channeled variety which they value then attempt to reproduce this in their own experience and thereby be of further service. But it is usually the case that instruments have abilities that match or vibrations of seeking that match those discarnate entities who then transmit information through them. When an instrument seeks to choose who it shall channel, then the surrender of the will which is necessary in this channeling process is not completely given. In such an instance there are two possibilities which explain the source of the entity then channeled.

Firstly, there are those of the negative polarization who are happy to mimic positive contacts and slowly lead astray those listening to their words, for the mimicking is continued only so long as is necessary to maintain the contact. Inevitably, there is information given which tends to detune the instrument and the group that may have gathered about it to support it in its service. In such a manner then, negative entities are able to remove the positive light of groups who become so detuned.

The second possible source of such information is more benign, and that is the subconscious fabrication which the instrument may undertake on a somewhat conscious, yet very likely more unconscious level of determination. In such an instance the information given remains within the realm of knowledge of the instrument who serves as channel.

May we answer further, my brother?

N: If a question is not educated, the channels on that level, when you mentioned knowledge, are limited?

I am L/Leema. We believe we grasp your query. Please question further if we are mistaken. We spoke in the second instance of the possibility of information being subconsciously fabricated by an instrument whose desire is to serve others by channeling information from an entity belonging to another group. When this occurs, that is, the subconscious fabrication of information, this information then will remain within the realm of whatever level of metaphysical understanding the channel has achieved.

May we answer further, my brother?

J: Okay. I'm new at this game, so who will I channel?

I am L/Leema, and this query is upon another topic, for within this group there are a number of entities who have become regulars, shall we say, to this group. As you or any new instrument would then undertake to serve as a channel for this group's contacts, you then would be available for the channeling of whatever entity was at that time working with this group. The newer instruments in this group are usually introduced to the vocal channeling phenomenon by those of Laitos and Hatonn, for they are of the love vibration which is much broader in its broadcast beam than are those of Latwii, those of Oxal, or our own social memory complex. For we inhabit the density of light and must therefore transmit a narrower and more difficult beam to receive.

If you are desirous of pursuing the path of the vocal channel within this group and if you give over your will that a contact can be made through your instrument, you will channel whatever entity is working this group at the time you are channeling. It is not likely that you will choose what entity you desire to channel because you admire or appreciate one entity's information over another's. The vocal channel desires to serve in whatever capacity is available to it; when it has tuned this desire and has challenged any contact, then it may speak freely, without fear of fabrication of any kind.

May we answer further, my brother?

J: No. But I'm glad you told me that I won't channel some weirdo out there—and that's not a question. Thank you.

I am L/Leema. Is there another query that we might attempt?

N: Yes, as an addendum to J's question, the Yadda that Carla channels, is that Yadda Dishihity, the same as Mark Prover's? Yadda, and do all, shall we say, does Yadda transmit to other channels at this time, and does L/Leema and Latwii also transmit to other channels? At the same time?

I am L/Leema, and am aware of your query, my brother. The ones known as Yadda to this group are the ones which you have become familiar with in your studies and in your listening to the tapes which contain this entity's words as they were transcribed and delivered through the one known as Mark. It is occasionally the case that a group of entities such as Yadda or even ourselves or any within the Confederation will be able to make contact and maintain contact with a number of groups such as this one. The number is not important. The groups so contacted are contacted because their call or desire to serve and to learn matches a certain group's vibratory identification, shall we say.

It is seldom the case that such contacts are able to be maintained by those of the Confederation over a very long period of time as you measure time, for each group and each instrument will undergo the testing and the temptations by those of a negative orientation who desire to remove the light that is metaphysically created by such a contact between the Confederation and any group of your planet. This is a balancing phenomenon that must accompany any such contact, for where there is the opportunity for light to radiate to those of your planet, there must also be the opportunity for the darkness to have its sway as well. In this way, the free will of each instrument is maintained and enhanced as the continuous choice is made to tune and challenge all such contacts and further serve the one Creator by purifying the desire of the self and the group.

Thus, it is often the case that groups or instruments will be unaware of the necessity of tuning and challenging, and will then receive a temptation from the negative entity or entities to focus on information that is of a more transient nature, such as the date and nature of various disasters and information of a specific nature regarding inventions, discoveries, means of making great wealth available that the group might be glorified above the message that it has previously been privileged to offer to others. Thus, contact is often lost and continuous channeling of one entity by a number of groups is therefore not a frequent phenomenon.

May we answer you further, my brother?

N: Thank you very much. I have a problem that's been bothering me, not for great wealth or truth or anything else, other than the fact that it's for my own particular awareness, and I'd ask Latwii about it …

(Side one of tape ends.)

N: … but there was a question asked of Latwii about an intergalactic battle that occurred over in Africa, and I'm not really interested in the date, other than the fact than just some sort of confirmation that the two hundred people saw it, that it did occur. And if it did occur, why would the Confederation allow this sort of scene to occur to sort of put a, shall we say, negative light on the UFOs, or was it a negative implant? You see, it didn't occur in our regular newspapers. And, the reason that it was allowed to occur was the germane point.

I am L/Leema, and we feel we have a grasp of your query, my brother. As we investigate this issue, we see there has been a great deal of misunderstanding generated by those who were witness to this event, and this misunderstanding was further amplified by those who chose to report it in the manner in which it was finally received and read by those of this group. The occurrence itself must remain somewhat within the realms of mystery, for it was a display that was meant to have a limited impact, shall we say.

Those witness to this display interpreted it in a manner which matched their expectations, or—to return to our topic for the evening—in a manner which matched their prejudicial points of view, for when craft of a seeming extraterrestrial origin are observed within the skies, and there are a number of such craft maneuvering in a manner which is quite eccentric, it is easy to assume that there is a battle being fought. It is as the child observing an incident which is beyond its scope and of necessity needing to describe this incident in terms which it understands, yet in such a description great distortions enter in. We may suggest that this is the case with the incident of which you speak. Therefore, the ones reporting this incident, shall we say, jumped upon the bandwagon, and were only too happy to amplify the description, and we are somewhat surprised that there was not a body count given.

May we answer further, my brother?

N: Thank you very much. I did feel that there should not have been an intergalactic battle, so to speak, between the three ships that they mentioned, and that was my premise for repeating the question that wasn't answered earlier. But thank you very much.

I am L/Leema, and am honored to be able to serve in even a small capacity. Is there another query?

C: Yes. Earlier I was picking up your conditioning, and after a period of time of experiencing it I was starting to drift off, and after it occurred, one of our second-density creatures came over and more or less grounded me down. How was this creature able, if it was the case, that it felt that I needed it to come over and help keep me in place?

I am L/Leema, and we apologize, my brother, for giving our conditioning vibration in such a large dose, for we are yet new to contact with those of your peoples and tend to step up our voltage somewhat overmuch with initial contacts. This was the case this evening and we were happy to find a small creature who could easily be influenced to infringe upon your aura and thus call you back to, shall we say, the land of the conscious.

May we answer further, my brother?

C: Whenever I get a conditioning, and I know it's warm tonight, but the experience was done, it was, well, say heavy-handedly, the energy is felt as heat. Is that the case always? Is it always experienced as heat when it's, say, overdone?

I am L/Leema, and this is usually the case, my brother, for the one such as yourself who chooses to serve as the vocal instrument does so in manner much like a wire which carries one of your electrical impulses. When the impulse is of too great a voltage for the capacity of the wire to conduct, there is usually the overheating. This is quite literally the case with you this evening and is usually to be associated with any instrument who has been given too great a dose of the conditioning vibration.

May we answer further, my brother?

C: Well, the conditioning initially was to me an extremely pleasant sort of state. I guess I got too much into the experience of feeling it as opposed to really—I guess I was—analyzing's the main [thrust]. But yet I want to again get back into being a vocal channel. I'm very interested in doing—in actually channeling yourself, but there is a hesitancy because I do tend to go further into a trance than need be for channeling. What do I need to do to keep this from occurring?

I am L/Leema. With practice, this tendency towards trance may be alleviated by the suggestion to yourself with each experience that you shall remain conscious and able to cease the process at any point. We shall, as always, be most happy to work with you, and to offer our conditioning in doses which are determined to be of the proper quantity. We will attempt, if this is your desire, to offer that conditioning which is well short of any amount that would aid in trance and then work our way toward the optimum level of conditioning that would facilitate the clearest possible transmission of our thoughts through your instrument.

May we answer further, my brother?

C: No, thank you for working with me tonight.

I am L/Leema, and we are honored to do so, my brother. And we thank you for your open-hearted sharing of your own self with us. Is there another query?

(Pause)

I am L/Leema. We thank you, my friends, for inviting our presence this evening. We are honored to share our words with you. We are honored to take those thoughts which have some value in your seeking and to fashion them as best we can into those concepts known as words. Yet we realize how far short any word falls in its ability to describe that which is beyond description. We hope that each of you will look and listen with not only the mind but the heart and your very soul as well and see beyond the word to the great field of love which lies behind all manifestation. It is this love that we attempt to share, the great variety of ways that equals the many words we speak through these instruments.

Please look at the words as messengers. They cannot contain that which sends them forth and which gives them life; yet they can point a direction. The direction is toward the heart of love within each of you and within all creation. Look there within your own being and about you as [you] move through your daily lives for the inspirations that will carry you onward. We move with you in this great journey of seeking the truth and the one Creator that is all truth. We leave you now and look forward to joining again in such a gathering. We are L/Leema. Adonai, my friends. Adonai vasu borragus.

(Carla channeling)

I Yadda. I greet you in love and light of infinite Creator. We thank the entity known as J for asking for our presence, and we thank each for the patience at the end of long session to allow us come among you at this time. We identify ourselves to you formally. We are Yadda Di-shi-hi-ty. We been trying to lose the last of that name, but it keep catching up with us. Aheh heh! So, we go ahead and use the whole thing.

Now, we got to say a few good words or we don't have any reason to be here. So, we going to give you a few cosmic words here—and practice our "R's" too.

Now, we want to talk to you about food and anything else that you love. This instrument loves food; other people love money; other people love power, but we always ask you the same question: Who are you? Love.

Let's look at food. There is a banquet before you, and you eat and eat and you are just so happy because your stomach is so full, and you have eaten until you can eat no more, but you know you gonna get hungry again. Now those who want money, they usually get money because that's what they want. But you know what? They never get enough. The more money, the more they want money more. It is the same with power; it is the same with those things that you love that are part of the mundane world.

What are you going to do to get yourself a meal that sticks with you or money that does not spend? We suggest that there is food which shall cause you to hunger no more, that there are riches so great that the wise man sells all that he has to get the riches of wisdom. There are those who love power but finally discover power that does not corrupt or go away within themselves. That is the power to surrender to the inner self. You got a whole kingdom there that will give you food and money and power. It will not stand on this Earth, as you call it; however, you are not here for very long at a time, are you? And you need to store up that which will not become corrupt nor will it go away. Therefore, we ask you to look within in the meditation for that sustenance that does not fail you.

We would say in closing that we begin to understand this instrument's love of the one she call Jesus because he fed all the people with bread and fish. But you know, the one known as Buddha would say, "Go hungry if you want to; it does not matter—you can eat in your next lifetime." This instrument likes food too much to like that kind of thinking. Aha?!

So. We shall leave you in joy that we are able to share with you. How fortunate we are and we thank you for asking as to our origin. It is good to know to whom you are speaking. We are one of the good guys, as far as we know. We ask that if anything which we may have said is not that which would have been said by good guys, you ignore us completely and get on with your life. On that note, we shall leave you in the utmost wimitwess—we gonna have to do that again—*limitless* love and light of the one infinite Creator. We are those of Yadda. Adonai. Adonai.

L/L Research

Sunday Meditation
August 18, 1985

(Carla channeling)

I am Hatonn, and we greet you, my friends, in the love and the light of our infinite Creator. We ask your patience as we found the necessity of once again answering the challenge due to the instrument's movement which then caused the need for his own reestablishment of his ritual. We are most honored to be able to join each of you this evening. The request has been made that the topic concern the accentuation of the positive path in the seeker's life as the result of the recognition of the bi-polarities, the positive and the negative.

Each within your illusion is undertaking this very process. The nature and efficiency of the process is a function of the conscious recognition of this process. One can move upon this positive path in an unconscious sense. Yet, the movement is only possible up to a certain point. This point, however, may we reassure you, is quite sufficient for one to be, shall we say, graduated to the fourth density of understanding. Yet, one may enhance this journey and enhance the harvestability, shall we say, therefore, by becoming more consciously aware of the working of this process of accentuating positive perceptions and attitudes and the falling away of the more dark and dimly lit or negative choices.

Within your illusion are provided an infinite number of means by which you may continue this process. Indeed, your entire illusion is, may we use the term, training ground, an opportunity in each instance for you to make positive or negative choices and thereby enhance your evolutionary progress. Whether the choices are conscious or unconscious, there will be progress in direct proportion to the purity of the choices, that is to say, progress is made by choosing a polarization, be it positive or negative, and following that choice in as frequent and pure a manner as possible.

Each entity moves through the daily round of activities. Each entity has basic attitudes or points of viewing these experiences which color each experience in a repeating fashion as each experience symbolizes the perceptions and the emotional colorization that follow each perception, so that each experience is colored in an unique fashion by each seeker.

The point of viewing the experience determines whether it is seen in this or that fashion, whether it is basically positive or basically negative in the entity's perception. Each experience, in truth, contains the one Creator in full, balanced and perfect. This Creator may be seen in a positive or negative fashion. These positive and negative perceptions may then be further distorted into any number and variety of forms. Whether the form is one that works upon the mental level, the emotional level, the physical level, or the spiritual level or any combination of these levels is a function of how the seeker perceives the experience.

To give an example. An entity may wish to further the support of the family by enhancing the amount of money, as you call it, that is available for use. This desire to provide sustenance to the loved ones is a basic lesson of love, for the entity who has taken the responsibility of supporting in a material sense those that are close and loved is one who then is sharing a form of love. The desire, then, to be of service to others forms the foundation for action for this entity. This entity, then, as it attempts to improve its market position with, as you call it, the job or the occupation, fuels the desire by a desire that is at its base that of serving others. The entity then may engage in any number of activities upon the job that are designed to increase its income of money. This then may be realized in the entity's life pattern or experience in any number of ways, for at the base of the action is the desire to serve others by providing material sustenance, further then translated or distorted by the entity's perception to mean money or income that is then seen possible of obtaining from the job or through the occupation.

Now, what shall actually occur to this entity in this focus of its experience may or may not take the form that the entity images. For if it does not image with a consciously honed and precise mind or mental frame of reference, that which answers the desire may take a variety of forms. It may be that support or sustenance is challenged through the emotional complex in order that it then be, as you would say, of good cheer or greater cheer, and in such a fashion provide a form of nourishment that does indeed nourish those about it at a central portion of the being but does so in a form which is a great variance from that which was consciously sought because the conscious seeking was of an unfocused nature.

This is a general and quite simplistic example of the process whereby one consciously seeks and obtains some distortion of that seeking as a function of the purity and clarity and intensity of the seeking which motivates the action. In each life experience, one takes whatever focus of understanding one has concerning the process of seeking the truth—or accentuating the positive in this case—and sees through that focus any experience that may come before the entity in its daily round of activity. Whatever degree of understanding one has achieved through searching resources, meditating and seeking within for the truth of any resource's information and then forming this focus of understanding will determine the clarity with which any experience is seen through this focus.

Thus, as one fuels the desire to know the truth and accentuate the positive, as it has been termed this evening, one has done the fundamental requirement or step; one has laid the basic foundation for realizing whatever finer focus may be necessary in order to achieve the desire. One may then take this desire and further refine or tune the focus in order that that which is desired might be realized in a closer and closer approximation of image so that what is received more closely resembles that which [is] desired and sought.

This is a self-propelling or motivating process. Once one has become consciously aware that such a process is being undergone and is a portion of one's experience and being, the seeking to understand more clearly how this process functions is that fuel which will allow one to refine the process according to the intensity and the efficiency, shall we say, of one's seeking. Whatever resources are sought and utilized is then taken in a distilled form by the conscious seeker into the meditation in order that the truer portions of the information may, shall we say, percolate or resonate through the mind down into the roots of mind where the truth of all being resides and attract to it some portion of truth that resonates in a frequency with the information so sought and rises then through the unconscious mind through the intuition and in various symbolic forms becomes available to the conscious mind in order that the conscious mind might be informed of that which it has requested.

As the conscious mind seeks in a more and more efficient manner, fueled by the continuing great desire to know the truth, the information gotten by this search, then, through meditation is passed through deeper levels of the unconscious mind and attracts that which resonates in frequency with it, further accelerating the conscious recognition of the process of evolution that is being experienced in the day-to-day activities of the more and more conscious seeker of truth. Thereby is the focus through which the seeker views each experience expanded and expanded upon each level of understanding through the emotional colorization, the mental analysis, the physical symbolic experience, and the spiritual basis for each other perception.

The focus, then, is seen to include more of each experience as being seen as a distortion of the Creator by the seeker, whether the distortion be towards love, wisdom or unity, those three portions that are available to all seekers in each experience.

To sum this lengthy discourse, and one which we hope has not been overly complex, we may use an analogy further utilizing the concept of the school with the grades that represent the levels of understanding or densities of experience. In your third-density illusion, each experience is a question—each experience is the same question. There is only one question on this test which you call life. It is reflected in each experience. The question is, "Do you see love in this experience?" In some degree the seeker will see love in each experience; in some degree the seeker will not. As the seeker is able to answer each experience question with an answer that approaches one hundred percent "Yes," the seeker is polarizing in the positive sense. We may report that the good news of the test is that fifty-one percent is passing. When the seeker is able to answer each answer to a level of fifty-one percent of experiencing and seeing love, the seeker is then of a polarized enough nature to move into the fourth-density grade in the octave of creation that you now experience. The seeker, then, has achieved the minimum polarization that will allow it to withstand the greater intensity of energy available within the fourth-density class.

Without at least the ability to see love in fifty-one percent of one's perceptions and experiences, the energy available in the fourth-density class would be too much for the circuit of the seeker who had not yet sufficiently regularized or polarized its being in order that its circuits not be blown, shall we say, as the greater intensity of light became the reality for the seeker.

We remind each that our words are but humble attempts to describe and share that which is quite beyond description, yet may be shared in some form where there is desire to know and desire to share. We, therefore, thank each of you for providing the desire to know, and we remind each that our words are but our fallible attempts to be of the service which you desire. We shall leave this instrument at this time in order that our brothers and sisters of Latwii may offer their service of attempting queries which those present may find the value in requesting. We are those of Hatonn and we leave you now in the love and in the light of the one infinite Creator. Adonai, my friends. Adonai vasu borragus.

(Jim channeling)

I am Latwii, and we are honored as well to join your group in the name of the one infinite Creator whose love and light illumine all experience. May we begin with the first query, since our brothers and sisters of Hatonn have given our preface?

(Pause)

I am Latwii, and we are most surprised, my friends. It is not often that we join this group without queries having been placed before us. We are aware that the beginning message this evening was one which might somewhat boggle the mind and we hope that our brothers and sisters of Hatonn have not overtaxed the understanding and patience of this group. We are happy to pass on to the one known as J the greetings of his friends of Yadda. We are aware that these of Yadda would have been happy to greet the one known as J in person if there had been the presence of an instrument capable of channeling these vibrations which are of a somewhat unusual nature. Nevertheless, Yadda says, "Hi." We also greet each of you and thank you for even this small portion of your time.

J: Wait—I have a question.

Ah—we are pleased. May we hear the query, my brother?

J: If one thinks in the negative, does it distort the aura?

I am Latwii, and would be happy to attempt this query, my brother. In short, yes, but we must qualify that response, for whatever manner one uses to perceive, there is a corresponding distortion to the aura, for the aura may be seen as a reflection of one's mental, emotional, physical and spiritual being. Therefore, any thought within one's being is reflected in a corresponding fashion in one's aura.

May we answer further, my brother?

J: So. A person is physically, mentally and spiritually, and if he thinks negatively, all three are distorted?

I am Latwii, and am aware of your query, my brother. This again is true, but must be qualified. The effect moves through all of the energy complexes, the physical, the intellectual, the emotional for its duration, and the spiritual, for the entity is one being undergoing experience upon each level. Each experience, each perception of experience will then be reflected in all portions of one's being. The mental and the physical, when the mental becomes unbalanced, are the energy centers most affected by one's thinking. If one perceives in a negative or unharmonious or unbalanced manner in a certain area of experience for a long enough portion of time, the mental negative frame or focus will be translated or transferred to the physical body in the form of what you would call a disease, for it reflects the disharmony of the mind and serves therefore as a teaching tool that the mind might see a reflection of its thinking and serve then to balance that thinking and remove the disharmony and the corresponding disease.

May we answer further, my brother?

J: If someone were to think negatively and then two hours later found out that he was thinking negatively, can he correct it?

I am Latwii, and am aware of your query …

J: Wait a minute—could I go a little further, please?

We would be happy to have you do so, my brother.

J: Okay. Can he correct the disease and disharmony also or is the damage done?

I am Latwii, and am aware of your query, my brother. The ability to correct a disharmony which has taken the form of a physical disease is in direct proportion to the intensity of the thought and the length of time of the thinking of this thought, for time often intensifies the form which thought takes. The ability to correct the disharmonious thought and its corresponding diseased physical form is then a function of the intensity of the balancing action which the entity has been able to successfully undertake. Where love was not seen and was not shared, there must be the ability to see and share love in a form or intensity which balances the movement away from love which then became the distortion of the mental and then the physical nature.

May we answer further, my brother?

J: Well, I get very angry at myself sometimes. And I enjoy the anger, but then I know that I've done something wrong. Does that still mean that I can correct that anger?

I am Latwii, and may respond by saying most emphatically yes, that there is no thought or action that cannot be balanced, for all experience is undertaken within the realm of the one Creator which contains as much love in the positive form as there is the seeming lack of love in the negative form. Because you experience your life within the form of creation, there is as much potential for you to utilize the positive expression of that form as there is the opportunity and potential to experience the negative of that love.

May we answer further, my brother?

J: Thank you. So, to simplify, you accentuate the positive and eliminate the negative. Thank you.

I am Latwii, and we could not have put it better. And we thank you. Is there another query?

D: I've been reading a book lately—I'm reading it through a second time on and in that book, they point out that a lot of times the way that we deal with others and treat others depends on the way that we speak to ourselves and treat ourselves and that there are mental voices in our heads. We learn from our parents a way of dealing with ourselves—am I making any sense? Anyway, the question that I have is when we catch ourselves talking to ourselves in a less than kind or loving manner, do you have any advice on how we can turn that around and become kinder to ourselves and thus to …

(Side one of tape ends.)

I am Latwii, and am once again with this instrument. We may begin by suggesting that to the seeker all about it is a symbol of its seeking. Within your culture it is logical that the parental experience, that is, being the child with the mother and father, would be utilized as a basic means of talking to the self, shall we say, and of dealing with the world about the self, for the mother and father are the two greatest formative forces within the entity in its early life and thereby form the foundation stones upon which the entity shall form its point of viewing itself and the world about it. When the entity finds itself talking to itself or behaving in a manner which is less than loving, the entity may use this experience as catalyst for growth, food for thought, the focus for meditation, for each viewing of the self in a less than loving manner is a symbolic representation of a basic attitude or experience which the entity has programmed into its life pattern in cooperation with, most especially, the parents and others about it in order that there might be the balancing or biasing of the being in a certain fashion that lends to an overall balance of the total being or soul or spirit of an entity. This lesson or program emerges in symbolic form throughout the entity's life experience.

Each time an entity in any single experience views itself or another in a manner which is less than loving, that experience can be used to achieve the balancing of love. In the meditation there may be the focus upon what is mentally known. However much the entity analyzed the seeing of the self in a negative fashion and has thought upon this subject, these distillations of thought may then be taken to the meditation and further focused upon in order that the unconscious mind may respond in a fashion which our brothers and sisters of Hatonn spoke upon earlier, and give the conscious mind some form or symbol of that which it seeks. These symbols from the unconscious mind may become apparent to the conscious mind by intuitional inspirations, a hunch, what is frequently called the "aha" experience, as an answer to a long-asked query finally surfaces, or through dreams as the symbols are given again and again, thus accounting for what you would call the repeating dream.

As the conscious mind becomes more aware of why it sees a portion of the self in a negative fashion, this understanding then releases the necessity for seeing in this fashion, for the entity has achieved some degree of the lesson that it programmed in the form of the understanding which it has now achieved, the product of experience, analysis and meditation allowing the intuition to bring a portion of that which is sought.

We apologize for the length of this query's response, for the query was one of depth and we felt the necessity of responding in depth in as well. May we respond in any further or simpler fashion, my sister?

D: No. *(Inaudible)* Thank you.

I am Latwii, and we thank you, my sister. Is there another query?

(Pause)

I am Latwii, and we had thought that perhaps if we waited for a long enough time once again we would have another opportunity to answer a query but we find that we have well and truly exhausted the queries for the evening. We thank you, each of you, my friends, for your request for our presence and the special gifts of your queries. We shall be with you in your meditations and any request. We leave you now in the love and the light of the one infinite Creator. We are those of Latwii. Adonai. Adonai, my friends. ♣

L/L Research

L/L Research is a subsidiary of Rock Creek Research & Development Laboratories, Inc.

P.O. Box 5195
Louisville, KY 40255-0195

www.llresearch.org

Rock Creek is a non-profit corporation dedicated to discovering and sharing information which may aid in the spiritual evolution of humankind.

ABOUT THE CONTENTS OF THIS TRANSCRIPT: This telepathic channeling has been taken from transcriptions of the weekly study and meditation meetings of the Rock Creek Research & Development Laboratories and L/L Research. It is offered in the hope that it may be useful to you. As the Confederation entities always make a point of saying, please use your discrimination and judgment in assessing this material. If something rings true to you, fine. If something does not resonate, please leave it behind, for neither we nor those of the Confederation would wish to be a stumbling block for any.

CAVEAT: This transcript is being published by L/L Research in a not yet final form. It has, however, been edited and any obvious errors have been corrected. When it is in a final form, this caveat will be removed.

© 2009 L/L Research

Sunday Meditation
September 15, 1985

(Carla channeling)

I Yadda. I greet you in love and in the light of infinite Creator. We so privileged to be here with you and we thank you for asking for us. We have just a few words to say for there is much *(inaudible)* one of our comrades, J. We only come to bless you and to be blessed, for in serving we are served. We do not leave you; we are with you if summon us mentally, we shall come. However, we shall relinquish this instrument without further ado. Farewell. I am Yadda. We leave you in the love and in the light of the One.

(Carla channeling)

I am L/Leema. I greet you, as do my brothers and sisters of Yadda, in the love and in the light of the one infinite Creator in whose good fellowship we all *(inaudible)* learn and progress.

We shall begin our discourse upon what you call stress by using information which this instrument has in her mind already. It comes from what you call Zen Buddhism. The story is this.

Once upon a time there was an old man. He sat in his room and prayed. When he was hungry, he went into the market and begged with his bowl. He went back to his room and prayed. In the course of time a young woman who knew the habits of this hermit was with child. She did not want the baby and so she stated that the young one had been begotten upon her by the hermit. She then left the baby with the hermit. The hermit then got up, took care of the child, nursed it, fed it, and worked very hard as a coolie for two years. The child prospered.

One day the woman who had lied about her child saw the child in the market place with the old man. The child pleased her sight and so she went back and claimed her child. The old man gave her the child and then returned to his prayers.

Stress is due to an emotional tension regarding the outcome of events which are seen within the framework of your space and time and as experienced within this incarnation. There are those who have nothing about which to worry who can worry, fret and distress themselves into an early decline. There are others who one would think would be extremely stressed but who exhibit a marvelous lack of tension from within. The trick is, my friends, to be aware that all things are as they are for a reason and that you are where you should be at this moment. The spiritual tense is the present tense. The unspiritual tense is tension. We do not suggest that you forget your history or cease having hopes for the future. We suggest rather a detachment born during meditation from the crying little needs or large needs which fill your days and nights.

You will notice that the old hermit in the story had no money [and left] each day to its own hunger. He was quite aware that bread cannot be kept longer than a day. And in a spiritual sense this is quite so. If you have been inspired yesterday, by today the world will have moved in upon that inspiration. That is what the world is for, my friends. It is intended to encroach in any way or form that it can upon your peace of mind in order to test your peace of mind, for those who seek the truth are constantly at risk, constantly dying and being reborn. This is not a comfortable state. Entities normally resist change, and yet change occurs continually.

In the garden of your life we suggest most emphatically that you make yourself a comfortable [spot] upon this [crannied seat] when you have come to your meditation. This seat is within your mind. It does not have to be physically present. In the quiet of this arbor, you can plant all that you want to, the glory of flowers and trees, the sweet singing of the birds, the gentle lifting of the breeze and the energy and power of love here in your garden. It is to this garden that you return for your solitude. You can have this garden if you are in prison or in chains, or as is more likely, bound by your desire for outcomes, to living a life that is less full to living a life that is most principled.

Let us introduce a concept here. This is important. You will fail, not just once but frequently, to avoid stress. The habit among your peoples is great, especially within your own country, as you call the arbitrary division of the creation. Do not feel cast down when you fail, for each moment is here. Each moment is a moment in which you have not failed. Hanging on to those things which trouble you about yourself or about others causes you to forget the electric present moment. This moment is infinite. If you can become one with the present just for a little while in your garden in meditation, you shall awake cleansed, refreshed and more ready than before to recognize the trains of thought that shall bring you stress.

Meditation is an excellent means of gaining knowledge of the self. One of the great things that it begins to show you is the thought patterns, complex but predictable, which will result in the stressing of mental nervousness and physical nervousness. Much illness which is unnecessary is caused by this same stress. We say it is unnecessary; nevertheless, it is not mistaken, for when you are uncomfortable, you begin to pay attention. Once you begin to pay attention to your thought patterns, it shall be ever and ever more easy to refrain from hanging like a terrier onto the hem of the garment of your worry. In the present moment, there is naught about which to worry.

We would pause while we use some of your space/time for offering our vibration to those within this room. If you wish to [be] made aware of our presence, please mentally request it and we shall be with you. The purpose of our being with you and the purpose of any Confederation entity's being with you is to strengthen your ability to meditate and to soften the blow of the utter and complete solitude of each person's life within the illusion which you now live. It is an illusion, my friends, but this does not make the solitude of the spiritual search any the less. We shall pause. I am L/Leema.

(Pause)

(Carla channeling)

I am L/Leema, and am again with this instrument. We thank you for the opportunity to share your life experience at this time. We feel that it would be appropriate at this time to transfer this contact to the one known as Jim. Therefore, we leave this instrument in love and in light. I am L/Leema.

(Jim channeling)

I am L/Leema, and we greet you again through this instrument. We are hopeful that we might be able to continue our development of our use [of] this instrument, and would do so by attempting to answer any queries which those present this evening might have value in the requesting. May we then ask if we may attempt a query?

J: I'd like to ask a question. You mentioned detachment. That's very easy to say and harder to do.

I am L/Leema, and we thank you for this opportunity to clarify our statement, my brother. The detachment that we spoke of is a goal which each may envision for any area within the life experience where one finds great emotion, for the emotions and the desire that accompanies each for thus and such an outcome in whatever area is to propel an entity that it might gain experience. You have heard it said that experience is a great teacher. As you move through your incarnation, you will find that you have great attachment and emotional coloration in various areas. These are then your areas in which learning and service to others are most probable, for you have biased before the incarnation your thinking in order to allow learning and service to occur during the incarnation.

The emotions, therefore, signal the areas and the intensity in each area where you may focus your attention and profitably seek a balance to each emotion so that in your experience you will gradually develop a range of responses in these areas that will hopefully provide you with a broader perspective in each area. Where there has been intense emotion, then the pendulum, shall we say, is brought to swing in the opposite direction by slow degrees in order that what was previously unacceptable might become acceptable; that which was seemingly unforgivable, might become forgivable; that which is not seen as the Creator might then be seen as the Creator; where love did not seem apparent, then it will be seen to be ever-present.

When this has been accomplished—and we agree it is a great task, my brother—then one will find that instead of the emotional charge in these areas, there will be, rather, a detached point of view which simply sees through the illusion to the Creator.

May we answer further, my brother?

J: Lord have mercy! Reincarnation emotional coloring? I don't know what-all that is about. How would I know what my incarnation is? How do I find out about my emotional coloring?

I am L/Leema, and we are grateful to be allowed further clarification, my brother. There are many techniques. The ancient dictum, shall we say, is that one should know oneself. As you move through your daily round of activity and you pause at the end of each day, you may assess the events which you have experienced. You will find what you call the positives and the negatives, those things which you liked and those things which you did not. You will find after repeating this assessment of each day over a period of your time that patterns emerge. Soon you will be able to predict what shall please you and what shall not. It is in these areas, where you find an emotion of any kind, that you may assume lie the lessons that shall allow you to progress upon your own spiritual journey. Your life, then, shall become your laboratory in which you experience the catalysts of various emotions. Then you shall retire, if it is your desire, at the end of each day to a quiet place in your meditation and assess the day's laboratory work by proceeding in this manner. In a growingly dedicated fashion, if we might use poor terms, you shall continue to build your progression as you become more and more aware of those lessons which you have programmed within your life pattern.

May we answer further, my brother?

J: You mean I should come home at night and assess what I did during the day, and what about being with my wife and kids and all their problems? How does one concentrate on oneself?

I am L/Leema. We are aware of your query, my brother. You may do as you will, my brother, for there are no mistakes in any incarnational pattern. You have asked how one may become aware of the incarnational programming, the lessons, the services. To be constantly aware and to learn in a conscious fashion does indeed require a great deal of desire, a great deal of your time, and a great deal of your effort. Most upon your planetary surface progress in their evolutionary patterns in an unconscious fashion, shall we say, for either they have not the awareness that such can be accomplished or they have not the desire to follow it. It will take effort to make room in the daily round of activities, to assess these activities and to use them as the food for your spiritual journey. Whether you do this in a conscious fashion or not, you shall still proceed upon that same path, perhaps at a reduced speed, shall we say. Yet you shall proceed.

May we answer further, my brother?

J: No, thank you. I disagree with you and I agree with you but I do like the idea about detachment. Thank you, sir.

I am L/Leema, and we thank you, my brother. Is there another query?

N: I have a query. I would like for you to differentiate with reference to the spirit as concerned with the difference between trance and meditative channeling.

I am L/Leema, and we feel that we may best respond to this query by suggesting that the meditative type of channeling, which is the conscious channel and which is utilized in the meditation, is of a dual consciousness variety. The ones serving as instruments are aware of both their own experience and consciousness and aware that there is a stream of thoughts moving through their minds. As the thoughts are spoken, the channeling occurs. It is a product of our thoughts combined with the thoughts and concepts of the instrument that we are able to blend into our messages, shall we say, all tailored to meet, hopefully, the queries and needs of the ones requesting the information. Thus, we speak within boundaries determined by the questions, the use of words, and the experience of each instrument.

In the trance type of contact, the one serving as instrument plays a much more neutral, shall we say, role, for though words are used, words and concepts quite beyond the instrument's experience and vocabulary might be transmitted, for the instrument in the trance type of channeling is much more the machine, shall we say, much as your telephone allows two entities to speak in a relatively clear fashion by its use. Thus, the information which one might derive from the trance type of channeling is potentially more precise in its ability to convey concepts.

May we answer further, my brother?

N: Thank you very much. But I was wondering if in trance if the instrument's spirit was sort of displaced?

I am L/Leema. Upon this point we may suggest that in the trance type of channeling there is a greater need for the entity's, as you have called it, spirit, or mind/body/spirit complex as it has been called by those of Ra, to step aside for the duration of the contact. This is what allows the more neutral participation, shall we say, in that the one serving as instrument does not lend its own personal coloration to the contact or the information, for that coloration is not present.

May we answer further, my brother?

N: Many of those have gone through the brotherhood and have come to feel that they channel their spirit guides, of which there are seven. I wonder if you would address the consideration for [seven.] Number one, as it occurs throughout our exposure as well as the consideration for their feeling that they have to be in a trance in order to channel their spirit guides and yet they have no memory?

I am L/Leema, and we find there are various areas in which your query moves. The number seven is not one which we find is universal among your peoples, for each entity being of a unique nature will draw unto it various guides and friends and teachers, both seen and unseen, throughout the incarnational experience as needed. In order to make a contact with or be influenced by the guides, friends and teachers, one may utilize a great variety of techniques as well. It is more, shall we say, the "in" thing to do among your peoples at this time to make the more mundane type of two person contact in which words are utilized, this possible through trance or meditation or contemplation, also through automatic writing.

However, though these techniques may be somewhat more showy and more popular for that reason, one may make contact with these, shall we say, angelic presences by other means as well. To simply speak one's thoughts to such beings while in a meditative or contemplative state, or even within the daily round of activities during such activities, one may communicate effectively and one then may observe one's own immediate feelings in order to become aware of the concept or feeling tone which may then be communicated back from such presences so that the, as it has been called, still, small voice within might further be strengthened. For indeed, as one seeks upon the evolutionary path from any source, friend or guide, seen or unseen, one seeks with the Creator and the Creator within is that source which offers the guidance which is most helpful to any upon the path of seeking.

May we answer further, my brother?

N: May I ask one other question? There is an ancient science of vibration *(inaudible)*. Is there any possibility of your explaining that or at least addressing some area where it might be interpreted?

I am L/Leema, and your query again is one which covers an area that has been long studied by the peoples of various cultures of your planet, for all of creation, all of the patterns of illusion is held together by the vibration of light. As the seeker becomes more and more consciously aware of the nature and purpose of its own life and the greater life in which it moves, it comes to see this pattern of illusion in a less and less distorted fashion. The study of vibrations, of sound, of color and of the very heart of creation itself is a study of the, shall we say, mechanics of the illusion that can be quite helpful when one attempts to make analogies between the nature of vibration in any particular area and the qualities of one's own thinking, for the type of thoughts which an entity entertains is that which reflects the entity's current vibratory …

(Side one of tape ends.)

(Jim channeling)

I am L/Leema, and am once again with this instrument. To continue. These thought patterns then reflect the entity's current position within its own preincarnatively chosen evolutionary path.

The science of vibration, then, may be seen by such a conscious seeker to be directly analogous to the various energy centers or chakras within the entity's physical vehicle, for each center vibrates at a given frequency utilizing the catalyst of the daily round of activity in an increasingly sanctified manner. Thus, any catalyst may move from lower to higher chakras or may be held or blocked at any chakra according to the pattern of thought common to the entity.

May we answer further, my brother?

N: If we could measure these vibrations, could we not increase or raise our own individual vibrations if we try it?

I am L/Leema, and am aware of your query, my brother. One need not measure by any machine these vibrations in order to raise them. The conscious attention in contemplation, prayer and meditation given to these vibratory patterns of thought is that which is most effective in unblocking those centers at which such patterns may be held or blocked, and thereby allowing the raising of that serpent within, which has been called the kundalini, in order that it might find its full height at the crown of the skull and at that energy center location.

May we answer further, my brother?

N: Where does the consideration for this ancient science lie? Interpretation of *(inaudible)*. Is it available to us in America?

I am L/Leema, and if we have understood your query correctly, my brother, there are writings and teachers representing this study available to all who seek it.

May we answer further, my brother?

N: Thank you very much. I haven't been able to locate any. *(Inaudible)*.

I am L/Leema, and we thank you, my brother. Is there another query?

Carla: I'd like to follow up on J's question. It tells in the Bible and I've learned that in every situation to be content and I recognize that as a conscious way of avoiding stress—just to accept what is. However, I've been experiencing for some time an unconscious, totally unconscious, stress that sort of bubbles up in the unconscious mind, and losing some sleep and so forth, it has to do with breathing and so forth. But, the question is, when the source of the stress is in the unconscious, what tool can be used from the conscious mind's data, I suppose you could say, to more effectively keep the unconscious stresses from becoming real emergencies on the conscious level?

I am L/Leema, and am aware of your query. We wish to state that the unconscious or subconscious mind is the source of all emotional colorations which one may interpret as stress throughout each portion of the incarnation. It is the subconscious mind that contains the preincarnational programming that will determine how one will see any event and how one will color that event with the mind and the emotions. Therefore, whatever intensity of emotion comes into the conscious mind from the subconscious mind, the tools are the same for working upon such catalyst. The meditation, prayer, fasting, contemplation, working with dreams and writing their meaning and relating such to the conscious life are tools which you have utilized as many have utilized in working with such catalyst.

When it occurs in a seeker's life that the catalyst grows in intensity to the point at which the seeker feels his mental and physical well-being might be in jeopardy, there is the increased need to fuel these tried and proven techniques by increased desire, which may be called will, and by increasing also the faith that the further exercise of will will bear fruit, for within your illusion nothing within the life pattern is clear and easy to discern in the metaphysical sense. You live within and move within an illusion. Things are not as they seem. You progress in ways unseen.

The will and the faith to continue to attempt to move in a loving fashion and in a fashion which is of service to others is that which is most important. The strengthening of the will and the faith is done in darkness, thus work can be done, for if it were clearly seen that you yourself are the Creator, that all that comes before your sight and experience is the Creator, and that all emotional responses are the Creator, then it would be easily seen that all is well, for all is One, and little experience could be gained in such clear seeing. Thus, you enter incarnation after incarnation in order to gain experience that becomes your harvest as you journey homeward to the Creator.

May we answer further, my sister?

Carla: No, thank you.

I am L/Leema, and we thank you, my sister. Is there another query?

J: May I ask if the answer to the last question implies that the only limitations we really have are those we have put on ourselves?

I am L/Leema, and this is most emphatically correct, my brother. It is the placement of limitations in each incarnation by your own free choice which allows you to experience and to gain a greater knowledge of yourself and the creation and the Creator through such experience. The limitation of the viewpoint is the source of all distortion, and distortion is a means by which experience is gained.

May we answer further, my brother?

J: Then you would imply from that if we eliminate our own limitations, then we have virtually [complete] command of almost any area that we desire through the thought process? Including the elimination of karma?

I am L/Leema, and this is also correct, my brother. Yet within each entity's incarnational pattern there are set certain limitations or distortions or lessons or services, for all are opportunities to experience the same thing, that is, the one Creator.

May we answer further, my brother?

J: But if we eliminate the consideration for boundaries, can we not review our lessons and learn them much more rapidly?

I am L/Leema, and though the statement is largely correct upon its surface, we feel there is the possibility of misperception in that it sounds quite easy to say that one is attempting to remove the boundaries of limitation. To approach from this angle is somewhat misleading, for this very process and activity is that which you undertake constantly in your daily round of activities by whatever technique you use or by no technique at all, this being the unconscious progression.

May we answer further, my brother?

J: No, thank you.

I am L/Leema, and we thank you, my brother. Is there another query?

N: How is the instrument doing?

I am L/Leema, and we scan this instrument and find that it is available for two or three more queries of the normal length. May we ask if you might have such a query, my brother?

N: I'd like to ask a question that Yadda D. said in the book, *(inaudible)* and also on some of his tapes, that before you enter a psychic *(inaudible)* you should know a lot about mathematics. How do you explain that?

I am L/Leema, and without being fully aware of the context in which this statement was made, we find that we are somewhat limited in our ability to respond. It is useful for some entities, depending upon the type of studies within the psychic or paranormal field, to be aware of the language of mathematics, for the illusion which you inhabit and your progression through it may have what may be called geographical, geometrical and mathematical relationships. Each portion of the illusion is purposeful, in short. Therefore one may gain an insight into the workings of the illusion, the creation, and paths through it by studying the language of mathematics. Yet at the heart of any such study, one must move beyond the mechanical and the outer teachings in order to find that source within that speaks all languages.

May we answer further, my brother?

N: No, thank you.

I am L/Leema, and once again we thank you, my brother. Is there another query?

(Pause)

I am L/Leema, and we thank each of you for requesting our presence this evening, and for allowing us the great honor of speaking our humble thoughts to you. We remind each that we are but fallible seekers of the same truth which is within each of you. Do not take our words too seriously, my friends. Use those which have value in your own seeking. Leave all else behind. We shall be with you at your requests and leave you in the love and in the light of the one infinite Creator. We are known to you as those of L/Leema. Adonai. Adonai vasu borragus. ☙

L/L Research

L/L Research is a subsidiary of Rock Creek Research & Development Laboratories, Inc.

P.O. Box 5195
Louisville, KY 40255-0195

www.llresearch.org

Rock Creek is a non-profit corporation dedicated to discovering and sharing information which may aid in the spiritual evolution of humankind.

ABOUT THE CONTENTS OF THIS TRANSCRIPT: This telepathic channeling has been taken from transcriptions of the weekly study and meditation meetings of the Rock Creek Research & Development Laboratories and L/L Research. It is offered in the hope that it may be useful to you. As the Confederation entities always make a point of saying, please use your discrimination and judgment in assessing this material. If something rings true to you, fine. If something does not resonate, please leave it behind, for neither we nor those of the Confederation would wish to be a stumbling block for any.

CAVEAT: This transcript is being published by L/L Research in a not yet final form. It has, however, been edited and any obvious errors have been corrected. When it is in a final form, this caveat will be removed.

© 2009 L/L Research

Sunday Meditation
September 22, 1985

(Carla channeling)

I am L/Leema. I greet you in the love and in the light of the one infinite Creator, one terrible in majesty and full of the power of the Creator, Creator of Creator, love of love, light of light. Before we begin, we would say to this group that we approve and encourage the time of silent meditation before the beginning of words, for how can one tune one's instrument to seek for the truth or to perceive it except by going within into the silence and finally into the silence that speaks that ears that hear and hearts that understand? We have been asked to speak this evening upon the subject of despair, its form, its function, and its use. We would divide our speaking into three categories—the despair of the mind, the despair of the body and the despair of the spirit.

The despair of the mind is an empty thing, full of no virtue except that of self-destruction. Within the mind there are limitations which have been given to the self by the self. Some of these limitations are those called limitations of intelligence. One of the burdens of increased intelligence is an increased capacity for despair.

And what, my friends, is that of which the mind despairs? The mind despairs of its very limitations. In truth there are no limitations—there are only challenges, lessons and glory. Yes, my friends, we say glory, for the stronger the despair, the more glorious the battle which may be waged to outlast the feelings of helplessness, doom and foreboding, uselessness, boredom and disinterest that altogether add up to the definition of despair. The despair of the mind is that which is not, standing in the face of that which is. Therefore the state of mental despair is folly and almost always unproductive. However, the dynamic of despair—that is, midnight as opposed to noon—is available to everyone, every spirit that lives in mind and body in your illusion at some time within the incarnation. Therefore, although it is useless, it is a common experience. In the grand scheme, the very uselessness of despair is that which limits man's ability to feel it. It is, rather, a dynamic against which one plays out one's incarnation, the other dynamic being pure joy. It is between those two poles that one may analyze one's true position with regard to the learning of the one great original Thought of love.

Therefore, that which is useless is rather a constant, an undertone within the life experience, always available, in which the mind knows nothing. Mental joy is the opposing dynamic in which the mind knows all. These are the limits within your illusion of that which we call love.

The despair of the body is a reflection of the despair of the mind. When an entity is in possession of mental despair and has not moved from that dynamic into a productive mode of thinking, analyzing, feeling and acting, that despair becomes incorporated within the body complex. Thence comes disease and ultimately death. Therefore, the wages of continued despair are the death of the body and therefore the death of the intelligence which informs the body. There you have form and function, form, as always, following function.

Spiritual despair, on the other hand, is an absolute necessity. It is, rather than being a zero, a moving dynamic within that which informs the growth and evolution of spirit. It is only metaphysical despair, that is, the recognition that one knows nothing, that one has lost control of everything, and that one is faced with complete darkness of soul which forces that great sliver or portion of the one Creator which is your consciousness to turn, transform, and begin the new; not having left behind that which is old in the soul, but adding unto it, accreting more wisdom, more compassion, and more and more of a feeling of unity which one can receive only when one has become desperate enough to release oneself from the expectation of any knowledge whatsoever.

There is a way in which one may use mental despair and its reflection in the physical body complex to best effect. That is to transmute mental despair into what this instrument would call the dark night of the soul or spiritual despair. One cannot analyze despair and rise transformed. One cannot act out despair by illness and rise transformed. One can, however, seek the grace and comfort that is your birthright in transmuting that which is lower into that which is higher. For as you know, my friends, one portion of the creation is a holograph for all else in the creation, thus mental despair may, as alchemists [would] change lead to gold, be changed into the dark night of the soul, burnished and shining. This spiritual despair then may transform itself into great revolutions and positive and forward changes within the spirit.

The spirit is always the same. It is not a portion of your illusion. However, your perception of the spirit can only grow. All that you have learned before is still yours and all that is ahead of you shall be learned because of turning from despair. It is rare that one enters into or graduates from any initiation without the impetus, the pain, and the challenge of spiritual despair. Therefore, if your soul is in agony, rejoice, for it is from this point that all good comes. Despair is the great opportunity to endure, to show strength, to indicate faith, and to exercise the will, not just the will to think but the will to do.

We thank you for asking this question in order that we may share what humble thoughts we may have with you. We realize that our style of speaking, reflecting as it does our density, may be less warming than others of your contacts. We are as we are, and we thank you for calling us from the very depths of our beings. We thank you also for being who you are, for you are all joys to us. We would leave this instrument and speak through the one known as Jim. I am L/Leema.

(Jim channeling)

I am L/Leema, and we greet you again through this instrument. At this time it would be a further privilege to attempt to answer further queries which any may have value in the asking. May we begin with a query?

Carla: Is there anything which you would like to say through the instrument known as Jim which the instrument known as Carla was of a frame of mind not to pick up on the subject of despair?

I am L/Leema, and, my sister, we appreciate your concern and care that your message has been delivered with accuracy and the proper scope. It is your particular hallmark as an instrument, however, to open your channel without qualification. Therefore, we are most satisfied with the information which it was our privilege to provide on the subject of despair.

Is there another query?

Carla: When people do something like find something negative within something which does not seem to others to be negative, what is occurring within that person?

I am L/Leema. My sister, each who pursues the path of the seeker, whether this path is pursued consciously or unconsciously, will construct a point from which to view the life as it is lived. This is the viewpoint, the conglomeration of beliefs and knowledge which one has gained by whatever means and which forms a lens, as you may call it. Through this lens, all that the entity comes in contact with must move in order for the entity to perceive it and to know that it exists and to know one or another characteristic about anything.

Thus, the point of viewing may be seen to be constructed of the experience of the mind, and the lens which is this construction has the various distortions of personal opinion or experience or expectation which in some way allows and refuses to allow the light or essence of the experience to pass through. Any experience will be seen according to the personal point of view. Each entity being an unique portion of the one Creator contains the ability to view all experience in an unique fashion. Not only is it unique but it is changing as the entity gains in experience.

Therefore, according to the individual point of view, a thing or idea or offering or person or any thing will be seen in a more or less distorted yet always unique manner. If one then encounters a new experience, the experience will for the moment seem beyond the grasp, the perception, until the mind of the entity attempts to grasp that which is new with that which is old, that which is the perception, and will attempt to hold the concept with the perception in order that its nature may be assayed. Each seeks and sees uniquely. One can never know how another will see the self or the offering of the self. One is not responsible for other's points of view but only for shaping the point of view of the self. Thus does each seek and find some portion of the one infinite Creator.

May we answer further, my sister?

Carla: No, thank you.

I am L/Leema, and we thank you, my sister. Is there another query?

Carla: I'd like to know your views on the transformations from the sexual on a simple red-ray basis to sacramental sex, with any comments you may have on that subject.

I am L/Leema, and, my sister, we must apologize for our hesitancy and seeming lack of words, but the field of study which you have queried about is one which is large. Many volumes could not contain its scope. The manner of seeking the one Creator by the use of the transformational potentials within the sexual energy exchange is a study which requires the discipline and intent and purity that any study concerning one's evolutionary path would require. The basic concept is that through the sexual energy exchange, a levering factor may be utilized to propel the consciousness of an entity or entities through the routes of mind that the shuttle of the spirit may be activated and allow the fully experienced presence of the one infinite Creator.

The means by which this transformation of red-ray sexual energy into the indigo-ray energy center and out the crown chakra is quite beyond simple description and must remain hidden except by the careful experience and analysis of the seeker who travels this path. Then there are avenues of information that are available.

May we answer further, my sister?

Carla: Well, yes, just on one specific thing. The reason that I thought of it was that you said earlier that the despair of the body was a reflection of the despair of the mind, and I have read before in the Ra material that the body in general is a reflection of the mind. In the seeking of sacramental sex, it seems that the body is informing the mind, rather than vice versa, and I thought that was kind of interesting. If you can comment at all on that, I'd appreciate it.

I am L/Leema, and we will attempt comment that does not overly confuse. The body, in its function of providing the physical orgasm, serves as a trigger for the levering effect which we mentioned previously. The trigger, then being pulled, will allow further work according to the degree of success of the seeker in previous use of mental catalyst and physical catalyst in the process of its own inner balancing or accepting of lessons presented in the daily round of activities. Thus, prepared by such disciplined meditative balancing, the mind and body may rest in their accepted distortions and the greater work of wind and fire may then proceed through the purified intentions of the entities so utilizing the sexual energy transfer.

May we answer further, my sister?

Carla: Well, just to clarify whether that would mean that sex itself then partakes, without transformation, that is, in red ray of earth and water—those being the other two elements?

I am L/Leema. This is basically correct, my sister, for within the illusion that is yours, experience is drawn, magnetically speaking, through the female nature of earth and water, that desires and lessons through desires may be manifested into your physical reality, be then mentally perceived and processed as catalyst. This work having been accomplished to a sufficient degree, the mind and body in their female functions draw the processed catalyst through the lower energy centers and out through the crown chakra in a reaching or yearning for the light of the wind and fire qualities of the spirit.

May we answer further, my sister?

Carla: Are wind and fire, then, male? And earth and water, female? Or does each element have both aspects?

I am L/Leema, and we find your former assumption to be more nearly correct.

May we answer further, my sister?

Carla: No, thank you.

We thank you for the privilege of responding to these queries and ask if there is a further query?

(Pause)

I am L/Leema. We thank each of you for inviting our presence. We hope that our humble words have provided the information which might become your food for further thought. We encourage the discarding of any portion of our information which does not have this value. The great treasures that you seek are available within your own being, our words merely signposts along the way. We leave you now, rejoicing for the opportunity to speak with each. We are L/Leema. Adonai, my friends. Adonai vasu borragus.

(Carla channeling)

I Yadda. I greet you in love and light of the one infinite Creator. We have a time tonight to get a word in edgewise. We keep saying to this instrument at beginning, "I Yadda." She keeps saying, "Go away—wait until the end." So we waited, and this is the end, my friends. Heh?! So we only stay for a moment.

We would share a thought with you concerning that which had been discussed earlier than this point in your space/time, and that is why mathematics useful in the learning of the path to the One. Is simple and obvious but not so obvious, I suppose, because we are having to explain. But we are glad to do so and wish to especially say hehro—hello to the one known as J. We are so happy to be with him, even during the time he not in this domicile and not speaking through an instrument but only as a presence.

If one says "What is mathematics?" perhaps the first [thoughtless] answer is, "Two plus two is four." Ah, yes, my friends, but two times two is four also. Now let us look at "twos." Interesting. If you double the size of a vibrating string, it will emit the same note one octave lower. If you take in half this same vibrating string, it [is] one octave higher, yet still the same note. Each of you can sing many notes, each of your beings can vibrate in many ways. Do you choose to be lower or higher? [It] is that simple.

We thank the one known as J for the calling of us. We are always …

(Side one of tape ends.)

(Carla channeling)

… therefore we do not leave you, we only stop the words from coming through the mouth of this girl. We are full of joy and we hope you may find joy, for it is your friend and your companion whether it walk unseen and unknown beside you or whether you reach out and take it by the hand. Therefore, reach out, my friends. Reach in also for that dynamic which will raise your octave instead of wohwering—lowering it—we sorry for our pronunciation, we having a difficult time this night. We leave you however in utmost joy and hope that we have been intelligible. We leave you, as always, in love and in light of One, the One Is All. Adonai. Adonai. I Yadda. ☙

Sunday Meditation
September 29, 1985

(Carla channeling)

I Yadda. I greet you in love and light of infinite Creator, and am pleased that you have called us to you this evening. It is most pleasant for us to be present. Hah! Therefore we greet you in much devotion. We are going slowly with this instrument, for this instrument is low in its vital energies and therefore we wish to be careful.

We speak only briefly, and that is to ask, "What prosperity is?" We are aware that it is something that all peoples upon your sphere wish. They wish to be prosperous, to have that which will buy that which you want to buy. There is a rumor going around that prosperity is unhappy or anti-spiritual. That is a misperception. There is another rumor going around that prosperity is all that one needs for the life experience. That is a misconception also. Look for yourself at the riches of your world. They come in different forms and they are equal one thing and that is energy. We ask each of you to practice releasing the fear of prosperity or the hunger for prosperity and rest in the knowledge that prosperity is infinite and that you shall be infinitely prospered regardless of outer circumstance.

There are so many walls built up one brick at a time between people and nations and continents and forces due to greed. The hunger for prosperity is inappropriate because it will take your attention away from the Creator. The Creator will prosper you—you shall not be left alone. Furthermore, the earthly vessel of your body is but that a pot made of clay. It is that which is within that is important. Therefore, we ask you to think what is true prosperity. When do you feel that you have enough? We say to you, consider that you may feel that you have enough when you look within, not outside the self, for your prosperity is infinite and all that you need shall be attracted to you. In fact, we give you fair warning, my friends, be careful what you seek—for you shall receive it.

We go now. We leave you in love and light of infinite One. We are known to you as Yadda. Adonai. Adonai. Adonai.

(Carla channeling)

I am Hatonn, and I greet you, my friends, in the love and in the light of our infinite Creator. It is blessing for us to be able to share your life experiences at this moment and we most humbly thank you that you have allowed us to share some few thoughts with you. We find that this instrument is excited about our contact, and we are pleased that this is so for we had been working with this instrument word by word in an attempt to further improve this instrument's ability as an instrument. The concept cluster approach is the one we often use due to the fact that it is more comforting to an instrument to know a little of what is ahead so that the instrument does not feel like a perfect fool. However, we can use an instrument more accurately if we are able to feed the instrument one word at a time. And this we shall do this evening.

We would like to tell you a story, and we should appreciate the opportunity to move backwards and forwards between the two channels within the group.

Once upon a time, as all stories begin, there was a little girl who had a beautiful doll. The doll had beautiful blue eyes that opened and closed and lovely yellow hair that felt like silk and looked like true hair. The hair could even grow and be styled and many clothes came with the doll and this child spent many happy hours dressing and undressing the doll, speaking to it, making up stories with it and so forth until the doll became the child's companion.

As mothers often will, the child's mother thought very little about the movement of the child's mind from that which was tangible to that which was intangible in her child's playing with the doll. But one day she realized that the child spoke to the doll and listened to it with equal sense of reality for both.

We shall transfer.

(Jim channeling)

(Inaudible) … concerned the mother for she wished to know that her young daughter was maturing at the normal pace and in a normal manner, for she wished the best for her daughter. She wished to see her daughter develop into one who could move through the world in a successful manner. These thoughts and attitudes flooded her mind all at once and she became concerned that her daughter, in carrying on with the doll as if it were human, might be developing an abnormal behavior which could be deleterious to her further development. Yet, in her concern, she was quite unsure as to how to deal with the situation, for her young daughter seemed quite absorbed in the roles and playing of them with the doll and was quite content and happy while doing so. This seemed of benefit both to mother and child in her mind, yet it was the unusualness that concerned the mother.

The mother approached the young daughter. She asked what it was that she talked to her doll about and how it was that the young daughter seemed to be able to hear what the doll replied.

We shall transfer.

(Carla channeling)

"Whatever am I do?" she said to her cat.

"Meow," said the cat.

"I know," said the mother, "that's what I'm really worried about, my daughter's not being like other children."

"Meow," said the cat.

"I love you, too," said the mother, "and I thank you but I really am worried about my child. What shall I do?"

The cat followed, interested in the conversation. She stood looking at the beautiful trees in her yard and looked about and finally settled down to the sidewalk, for it was Fall and it was time for the leaves to fall and for [someone] to remove them from their natural resting place. "Could it be that I do not need to talk to my child?" The trees whispered, the leaves rattled …*(inaudible)*… "No," she said …

(Several minutes inaudible.)

… and in the giving up of the daily rush of thoughts, ideas and actions. This does not have to be a long, drawn-out procedure which will put you to sleep and which will certainly impart to those about you the knowledge that religiousness is boring. It needs only be done in joy and moment by moment. Yes, you may sit down to meditate and that will help those about you to see that that is a normal and important part of the daily round. But it is that which you gain in the silence that will teach and be shared with those about you without your conscious knowledge.

My friends, you do not know what you do, and yet that which you do is perfect. You are, however, as seekers asking to become more and more responsible on deeper levels of knowing what you do, knowing where the roots of your consciousness are, and in what soil they grow. You are finally responsible as conscious and seeking beings for watering the roots of the tree of your consciousness that it may take in more and more and bring up more and more to consciousness from the unconscious roots so that it may blossom within your life and share its beauty with those about you.

This is a story about a child talking to a doll because the mother talked to the cat. This is also a story about each and every one of you and the little things that limn and etch your indelible character and quality upon the consciousnesses of others. Be graceful, then, in your ways, my friends, and let your smile be sweet and your words soft. For all wish to be peaceful and to be poor in heart and humble. All wish to be kindly affectioned one to another. Yet it is not possible for you as humans to do these things consistently. It is beyond human telling. It is not, however, beyond that which may be called grace but which we choose to call contact with the source of your being and all beings, that one great original Thought of love. Love is what you seek; love is what you will find, for all things are love. No matter how distorted and seemingly ugly, there is love there; there is love everywhere. Seek and know love, my friends. It is your gift to those about you and most of all your gift to yourself and to the Creator within and without you.

We would attempt to contact the one known as N at this time that we may bid you goodbye. We would now transfer to the one known as N. I am Hatonn.

(N channeling)

I am Hatonn. I greet you in the love and light, light and love of the one infinite Creator. Sometimes light appears in the darkness for all to see. It is difficult … Transfer please.

(Carla channeling)

I am Hatonn. We thank the one known as N for the openness to contact and we assure this instrument that it will become easier and easier to sustain the concentration necessary to reproduce our concepts.

My friends, we leave you in one creation. It is an infinite creation. The finite eye shall never see its end, for there is no limit to the creation. Therefore, it being infinite, it is also One. You are an unique and perfect portion of that great consciousness. How we thank you that we have been privileged to share our thoughts with you. We ask you please to recognize our fallibility and to discard anything which we may have said which does not appear to be helpful, accurate or true. As always, we ask that you use your discrimination in those things which we tell you, for we ourselves are only a few steps ahead in our evolutionary progress, and we share with you that which we feel we have come to know. There is far more for us to learn also.

My friends, the trees outside your dwelling rustle, the leaves turn, awaiting the chill of fall, and squirrels go chattering along the branches of the trees, storing away their food for the winter. How peaceful and beautiful are the sounds of this evening as we hear through this instrument's ears and how full of love is this room and those who dwell within it [at] this time. We are known to you as those of Hatonn. We leave you in the love and in the light of our infinite Creator. Adonai, my friends. Adonai vasu borragus.

(Jim channeling)

I am Latwii, and I greet you, my friends, in the love and in the light of our infinite Creator. We thank you once again for inviting our presence to your joining in the seeking for truth. We, as always, are overjoyed to be with you. We hope that our few humble words may provide a service to you in the answering of those queries which you may have the value in the asking. May we then begin with the first query?

Carla: Well, I'll jump in if nobody wants to. We sell books through the mail and we have some wholesale book sellers that order our books. We've never put a price on the books, but several of the booksellers are giving us less for the book than it costs us to print it and mail it and the situation will worsen as our costs go up in the next month or so, our prices having gone up from the printer. We have decided, at least tentatively, that we will continue to offer the book for whatever donation seems appropriate to the person, sending it through personal mail, but we've decided to tell the book shops what it costs us to make the book. We are concerned that we may have somehow broken the magic of total freedom from thinking about money, and I wonder if you can comment on that?

I am Latwii, and am aware of your query, my sister. We may speak in general terms in this instance only, for it is a process of the exercise of your own free will which is being experienced and we would not influence that in one direction or another by suggesting that a decision in process is affecting what you have called your magical natures in one way or another.

You are aware of the principles which are in motion and in your efforts to be of service it will be necessary for the further application of these principles. We speak in general of those concepts which were touched upon by those of Yadda at the beginning of this meeting. There is the need to balance various desires and fears, the desire to serve with the fear of not being of service, the desire to be financially successful enough to serve with the fear of having too few finances to continue. As you move through your incarnational patterns, you will find the constant need to balance these types of concerns in various ways, for the question posed by those of Yadda is most pertinent to each who seeks the truth, that is, what is prosperity? How does one define …

(Side one of tape ends.)

(Jim channeling)

I am Latwii, and we are once again with this instrument. What truly nourishes one's being? The answers to these queries are, as you know, of a philosophical nature, one which does not lend itself to proof. Thus, in your own seeking, you will continue to discover those clarifications in your own understanding that will allow you to make decisions in any area that concerns the giving and the receiving of the one energy which binds all in this creation.

May we answer further, my sister?

Carla: No, thank you.

I am Latwii, and we thank you, as always, my sister. Is there another query?

Carla: The only question I can think of, I can't think of. The instrument and I were talking about sometime during this week, and a question came up, and we said we ought to ask about that. If the instrument can remember the question, would the instrument state the question and then answer it?

I am Latwii, and am aware of your query in its form of desire but we are afraid that you have called upon a well which has run dry when asking this particular instrument to remember upon this occasion the query of which you speak. We search this instrument's mind and are bumping into this instrument doing the same. We excuse ourselves and must also apologize to you, my sister, for we are unable to retrieve this query.

May we ask if there might be another?

Carla: What is the probability that within our lifetime, say before 2020, physics will have been rethought and refurbished and a new paradigm found which includes the physics of consciousness?

I am Latwii, and am aware of your query, my sister. We suggest that in your current culture and period of time there are those who have done a great portion of this work and who are in the process of sharing the blending of the current level of discovery of physics, as you call it, with the newer metaphysics, as many call it. The widely accepted ideas within the field of scientific thought as regards the nature of creation and its functioning is also in the process of slow change, as all thought and concepts change with new minds to hold them and old minds with new room develop.

The level of thinking of a culture is a reflection of the mass mind in its movement both consciously and subconsciously. Thus, as each individual within your culture and all cultures of this planet continues the process of learning the self, the life, and the environment about the self, these increased perceptions will feed the unconscious mind with a, shall we say, impulse that may be described as a desire. This desire serves to open pathways to the greater portion of each entity and each culture's being. These pathways then allow an interchange of information so that one feeds the other, the conscious mind feeding desire, the subconscious mind feeding that which is desired. When this process reaches a certain point or critical mass, there is an acceleration which becomes quite rapid. That point is the point of which we feel you speak and it is difficult to determine precisely when that point might be reached by a societal complex, but it is a point which we can note is being more rapidly approached from the various avenues of individual and small group process.

May we answer further, my sister?

Carla: No. I'll have to read that over, but thank you.

I am Latwii, and we again thank you, my sister. Is there another query?

(Pause)

I am Latwii, and as it seems that we have exhausted the queries for this evening, we shall thank each for inviting our presence and offering us the gifts of seeking our humble words and allowing us to serve in our small way. We also wish each to remember that we are but your brothers and sisters, quite fallible in our own seeking, yet quite desirous of sharing that which we feel we have found. We are those of Latwii. We leave you now in the love and in the light of our one infinite Creator. Adonai, my friends. Adonai vasu borragus. ☙

Sunday Meditation
October 6, 1985

(Carla channeling)

I am Hatonn. I greet you, my friends, in the love and in the light of our infinite Creator. It is with a great deal of pleasure that we welcome to the circle the ones known as B and G which have never been far from us, as all is One. Yet we are so pleased that we are able to blend our vibrations with those lifestreams at this time. We will be overshadowed by those of Laitos who does not desire to speak but who wishes to greet each and to aid in the deepening of the meditative state. We encourage each to picture the room in the domicile in which you are sitting as a circle of light of which you are all part and to feel the energy spinning in a clockwise fashion, spiraling ever upward, ever gaining in strength as each of you melts into oneness in the circle of light and the glory of light.

We are using word by word communication with this instrument, therefore there may be pauses at times. We apologize for any inconvenience but are attempting to train this instrument for more precise communication.

Picture if you will … We must pause. We are sorry for the delay, however the instrument was distracted by the "putty tat."

Picture if you will a mountain stream gushing forth from a living spring, ever fresh, ever beautiful, moving and singing along its bed and refreshing all that lives therein. Such is the living wellspring of your spirits, my friends. Where can one go to find such a wellspring, such a fountainhead? Can one go into the city and find it there amidst the crowds and the cries of those who barter and sell, and the angers and disappointments of those who have come in second in a trade, and [the] vainglory and folly of those who believe they have won in the trade? It would take a special person to find sanctuary and nourishment in a city.

Shall you then go to the country, and live through the ancient cycles of time and space, watching the trees and the foliage, the flowers and shrubs change their colors in the fall and become bleak and austere statues of dignity in your winter, only to bloom again with blossom in springtime and open their faces to the sun in the spate of full summer? My friends, it may seem to be a far more desirable haunt, and yet the wellspring of spiritual life is not easily found from without, even under such beautiful circumstances.

Can you go then into the ocean, away from all land into the simplicity of waves and sky and stars? My friends, the difficulty with picturing a better and better and better environment is that into such an environment you bring yourself. The self that is you is always with you and the wellspring and fountainhead of your spirit is within you. Therefore, into each environment you project those opinions and biases, those pains and pleasures of your own experience that make you what you are. That which is outer cannot do the job of bringing to birth that within you which is to come in your search for the truth.

The small entity known as a cat which plays about your feet at this time is a living example of the perfect environment into which is projected a self incapable of using large portions of *(inaudible)*. To this cat, the room is warm, the food bowl and the water bowl are full, and all would seem to be perfect, and the cat plays and is happy. But where shall it go that its spirit may progress? If you are seeking to survive, my friends, find the correct environment. If you are seeking to grow, know that the only environment that matters is within you. You are the wellspring of your evolution in spirit; you are the fountainhead of your birth into that new portion of yourself which you wish to be lifted up in love to the light that shines from the one great original Thought.

You do not carry this within you as if you were a basket and it the precious cargo. No, my friends, you are far more like the pipe through which is funneled the clear precious water of the fountainhead, the wellspring of that clear mountain lake, full of living water. Things do not come from you as much as through you, for in whatever you may do, you are a channel. There is no situation in which you are not channeling and being used as an instrument either by yourself, by other entities, or by circumstances themselves. The great choice to make, then, in the desire to speed up the spiritual evolution is the choice to allow that through you which you desire to be spent through you. And never, if possible, to accept circumstance or environment as a reason for ignoring the opportunity for finding love that may flow through you that you may become a light to lighten the darkness of those about you who are seeking just such light.

Personalities have often been confused with pure channels. The pure channel is an impersonality, clear and exquisitely pure. If you would be a channel for love, open yourself inside to that spring of living water in which your soul may bathe and become clean and shining pure and from which and through which a great light may shine in a dark world.

Before we leave this instrument, we would like to pause in order that you may feel the considerable spiraling energy that the combination of all of you and us create at this time. Allow it to whirl you ever upward as your seeking flies toward the Creator as toward a giant sun. I am Hatonn.

(Pause)

I am Hatonn, and am again with this instrument. It is with great reluctance that we leave you, but we feel we have said what is called upon, and we know how you relish the silence. Therefore, those of Laitos greet and send love to each as do we. We are known to you as Hatonn. Please know that in all your meditations we are most happy to be with you that we may aid you in deepening your meditation and that you may aid us in providing another opportunity for service to the one Creator that is expressed in each of you infinitely. We leave you in the love and in the light of the One Who Is All. Adonai, my friends. Adonai vasu borragus.

(Jim channeling)

I am Latwii, and I greet you, my friends, in the love and the light of our infinite Creator. We are overjoyed to be able to join you this evening. As always, we hope that our humble words will be of some small service to you. We would attempt to be of this service by answering those queries which you may have brought with you this evening. May we then begin with the first query?

T: I have a question regarding what I have read about what has been referred to as a soul mate, a person's—I'm not sure, I don't understand what's involved in that. Could you comment at all on if this indeed exists, and is it fair for a person to expect to meet a soul mate in a particular life?

I am Latwii, and we feel we have the grasp of your query, my brother. The concept of that called the "soul mate" is one which is not well understood among your peoples, for it is commonly associated with a kind of cosmic romance, shall we say. There are, however, many friends, shall we call them, that have for great portions of what you call time and incarnational experiences traveled through these experiences together. There has been a bonding of desire to be of service in a certain fashion amongst these kinds of entities and, indeed, those who so join are not unusual, for there will be such groupings found widely scattered upon your planetary surface at this time.

Those who have shared of the soul stuff, shall we say, the essence of being, seek then together to express this beingness in the incarnational experiences and serve thus as teachers, each to the other. The experiences within the incarnation then that can be had are of a somewhat more rich and pure and intense nature, for it is not just the power or momentum of one incarnation that affects any individual within the present incarnation, but is rather the momentum generated by many, many such experiences and lessons that have been shared over great periods of time. We would add, however, that there are also those entities who have found that what you might call the mated kind of relationship is a further refinement of this general grouping that allows further intensification of the learning process and the sharing of service to others as well.

Thus, the soul mates who have chosen to experience an incarnation from time to time as the biological mates does have its place, and is that which is experienced from time to time and in various incarnations, yet is not that which is as frequently experienced as is the general grouping of entities who have chosen once again to locate themselves in time and space as one group.

May we answer further, my brother?

T: No, that was sufficient. Thank you.

I am Latwii, and we thank you, my brother. Is there another query?

Carla: Just to follow up on that. I've often thought that the group of people who got together when Eftspan was formed had some special closeness to each other that was impossible to express except that we were all really tight with each other without trying. Is that what you meant by the group incarnating together by choice?

I am Latwii, and, my sister, since this supposition is known by those present, we can confirm that this is an example of that grouping of which we spoke.

May we answer further, my sister?

Carla: Yes. Then would such a group be more properly considered soul mates than the concept of soul mate of cosmic romance?

I am Latwii, and this again is correct, my sister, for it is the most prevalent type of incarnational pattern for those who have long sought the ways of the One.

May we answer further, my sister?

Carla: Yes. What, then, would you term the couple that decides to return in several incarnations as a biological male and biological female to seek for truth together?

I am Latwii, and am aware of your query, my sister. The terms are also numerous which have been used to describe this kind of relationship or phenomenon. Again, the terms soul mate are the most widely used. You are also aware of the terms, star-crossed lovers. There are many ways and terms to describe the relationship that exists between two who have found their beingness and their desires to seek the Creator so much as one that they have indeed grown in many ways to become one being by pursuing the dual nature of the one Creator, that is, the male and the female, the light and the dark, the radiant and the magnetic. The terminology is at heart quite unimportant, for in the hearts of these beings there are no words to describe the yearning which draws each to the other.

May we answer further, my sister?

Carla: I don't think so. I just wondered what a more apt term would be. I'm aware of the phenomenon, having experienced it myself with Don, but I never had felt that any of the terms used really had it down and I wondered if there was a more precise description that could be invented, maybe. If not, you don't have to answer anymore.

I am Latwii, and we apologize for our lack of ability to find words within your language which would properly express this phenomenon. May we direct our humble attempts towards another query?

Carla: Earlier, Jim and I were considering talking to a discarnate entity; it's something that I'm aware is possible. And my concern was that by such continued conversation the discarnate entity might be tied in some way to the Earth plane. Could you comment?

I am Latwii, and feel that we may comment thusly. The purpose of such a communication is the guiding force which will determine that which results from such communication. The desire to express the love for such an entity and to, shall we say, complete that which may yet be incomplete would be acceptable for those involved. The intention to utilize the communication for any kind of personal gain, shall we say, then would distort the effort in such a fashion as to perhaps add weight where once there had been lightness.

May we answer further, my sister?

Carla: No. Thank you.

I am Latwii, and we thank you, my sister. Is there another query?

Carla: Yeah. I'm kinda interested in what T asked in the first place. Is there for every man a woman, the way people sometimes say, or are some those who chose to incarnate to be solitary? Or to flit from flower to flower?

I am Latwii, and am aware of your query, my sister. The assumptions that you have made are somewhat limiting, and we would hope that we may answer your query without confusion. The experience of one biological sexual orientation or the other during an incarnation is chosen for certain reasons by each of you and all upon your planet with the understanding that one so choosing includes both natures in the total beingness and wishes to express one of these natures during an incarnation in order that certain lessons and services might be more available according to the desires of this entity. Thus, for each man there may be many women, as you call them, and many men, as you call them, that have had the mated relationship at one time or incarnation or another. Yet there may also be, as we mentioned previously, those paired entities who have more often than others chosen to incarnate as polar opposite biological entities for the intensification of learning and serving that is made possible by such continued shared incarnational patterns.

May we answer further, my sister?

Carla: No. I think I heard a definite maybe in there. I'll be satisfied with that. Thank you.

I am Latwii, and we thank you, my sister. Is there another query?

Carla: I guess I just have one more question, and this is just a teeny one. But that is, are the cats excited because of the energy in the room? They often play like this during meditations, I've noticed.

I am Latwii, and we have noticed that from time to time, according to the harmony of the group gathered, the energies thus produced have this exciting effect upon those creatures which you have called the cats. We are aware that there is little that can be done in this regard other than removing these small entities from the room in which you work. However, we appreciate their response and playfulness.

May we answer further, my sister?

Carla: No, thank you.

I am Latwii, and again we thank you, my sister. Is there another query?

(Pause)

I am Latwii. As it appears that we have exhausted the queries for this evening, we shall thank each for allowing us the honor and opportunity to join your meditation and your seeking for that which we and you call the truth. We are but your humble brothers and sisters who wish only to serve. Please take that which we have offered that may be of value and leave that which is not. We are those of Latwii. Adonai, my friends. Adonai vasu borragus. ✺

L/L Research

L/L Research is a subsidiary of Rock Creek Research & Development Laboratories, Inc.

P.O. Box 5195
Louisville, KY 40255-0195

www.llresearch.org

Rock Creek is a non-profit corporation dedicated to discovering and sharing information which may aid in the spiritual evolution of humankind.

ABOUT THE CONTENTS OF THIS TRANSCRIPT: This telepathic channeling has been taken from transcriptions of the weekly study and meditation meetings of the Rock Creek Research & Development Laboratories and L/L Research. It is offered in the hope that it may be useful to you. As the Confederation entities always make a point of saying, please use your discrimination and judgment in assessing this material. If something rings true to you, fine. If something does not resonate, please leave it behind, for neither we nor those of the Confederation would wish to be a stumbling block for any.

CAVEAT: This transcript is being published by L/L Research in a not yet final form. It has, however, been edited and any obvious errors have been corrected. When it is in a final form, this caveat will be removed.

© 2009 L/L Research

Sunday Meditation
October 13, 1985

(Carla channeling)

I am L/Leema. I greet you in the love and in the light of the one infinite Creator. We give thanks that we may join with you at this time and share our vibrational complexes with yours as we flow together through time and space for this present moment.

You question us concerning houses. We shall answer you in two parts, the first a brief one. The placement of spiritual dwellings matters little except in specialized instances. Those specialized instances are those in which the dwelling place is attempting to attune itself to the incoming energy patterns that meet and greet the shell of your planetary sphere. As research in this area has been competently done, we shall mention only that in your particular geographical area, the ley line which is closest to your location lies approximately 35 to 60 miles south of you and moves roughly along your waterway towards the location you call Cincinnati. Please note the very specialized nature wherein this information would be applicable and informational.

The second part of your query is not so easily answered, yet we shall attempt to be brief insofar as accuracy and brevity concur. There is one architect. This architect has been called the Creator, and from the Creator flow many ideas, many shapes, many possibilities, many inspirations concerning houses. When it is given to a group of individuals who wish to act in love, to draw from that one architect a certain type of dwelling, the dwelling may be built. Some shapes are more easily attuned vibrationally for magical work than others. However, all shapes in general have equal potential, for it is not the builder of the house but the architect to whom praise may be given, and that architect—that is, the one original Thought—works not through board and clay and stone but in the heart and spirit of those who build. We encourage entities of loving heart and will to put forth effort in that which may seem to be advantageous.

However, we must send out a stern caveat. It is the love for the architect that invests the house with excellence of vibration. With this love, any shaped and placed dwelling shall be magical; without this same love, the most carefully designed and placed house shall be one which is dead in a spiritual sense. Love for the architect, my friends, brings with it a sense of unity, of love, one for another, and of praise. When there are quarrelsome and divisive entities building an house, that house shall be a house of shame. When the humblest dwelling is put up with loving hands and adoring hearts, so that dwelling shall be full of love.

We can give no encouragement or discouragement to any plan for becoming those who dwell within a house, for you already dwell within a house, my friends, and that house is your physical vehicle. Have you caused it to dwell in holy places by the purity of your thoughts and the love within your heart? Or have you made your body dead by pursuing with it endless divisiveness? Your civilization encourages the latter path, and thus you see more and more the diseases that come from the hard heart and a divisive will. So it shall be upon the metaphysical plane for any structure that is builded by man. We can say no more than this—build in love, in unity, and praise to the architect who is no man, but the very Creator.

We thank you for allowing us to share our imperfect thoughts with you and ask you always to remember that we are finite entities capable of erroneous statement. Therefore, take unto yourselves that which is good to you. That which is bad to you, leave. We are those of L/Leema. It is our enormous pleasure to serve you this evening. We leave you as we greeted you in the hands of the great architect, the great principle of love and builded light and that which is inaccessible, that of which we are merely the echo. We leave you in the mystery of the one infinite Creator. Adonai. We are L/Leema.

(Pause)

We are those of L/Leema, and greet you once again in love and light. This instrument has made an error. This instrument lost the next concept which was that we were leaving this instrument but would continue the contact. We now leave this instrument. We are those of L/Leema.

(Jim channeling)

I am L/Leema, and greet you again in the love and the light of the One. We are pleased that we have been able to make a contact so easily with this instrument who is in the process of learning our vibration and manner of contact. We would at this time be pleased to attempt any other queries which those present may find value in the asking. May we attempt such a query?

N: Yes. Thank you very much for the philosophical answer. Of course, I did realize that any house would be satisfactory, but we were wondering primarily about the location in the knobs of southern Indiana since it would be accessible to the Louisville area and was primarily wondering about the energy sources for that particular area, which would not be forty to sixty miles south, but rather, almost due west or perhaps a little west-northwest.

I am L/Leema. We feel the query which you have asked about may best be answered by again suggesting that it is only for the most fine of the magical, as you would call it, workings that an exact location that would harmonize with your planet's lines of force would be necessary. These workings are usually accomplished by those who make but small contact with the peoples and cultures of your planet. The desire to be of service to a larger group of people, as you may put it, and to interact with these people is that force which is most important in the establishing and constructing of any structure to so further that service, be that structure physical, mental or spiritual.

May we answer further, my brother?

N: No, thank you very much. It was primarily to be of service to more mind/body/spirit complexes so that the harvest might be increased that we thought that there might be one area that might be a little better than others. But if it's primarily the individual, then, thank you very much.

I am L/Leema, and we thank you, my brother. Is there another query?

L: May I ask one of a more personal nature? I'm having a little trouble staying in contact with the group tonight. Am I experiencing something unusual?

I am L/Leema. As we observe your vibrations, my brother, we can only note that there has been some slight difficulty in your readjusting to this atmosphere, having been absent for a portion of your time. The other factor which has sway at this moment and which accentuates the rustiness, shall we say, is that which we feel would best be pondered by your own efforts for a period of time, perhaps at a later time, in order that you at this time may set aside the concern and become as much as possible a functioning portion of this particular group.

May we answer further, my brother?

L: No, thank you very much.

I am L/Leema, and we thank you, my brother. Is there another query?

Carla: Well, I'd like to follow up on L's, because I can feel a difference in the vibration this evening, and I always do when L/Leema comes through. It is a quieter and deeper state of meditation, and I was wondering whether, in sensitive people, this degree of meditative state might not encourage the leaving of the body by the spirit? If that's so, what can be done to keep us in the body besides holding hands?

I am L/Leema. Your query presupposes a situation which we find is correct in general, that is, that this group this evening has the opportunity to delve into those deeper levels of meditations because of the vibration which we use to steady our contact with this group. The more sensitive, as you call it, entities within the group will notice this factor first and most profoundly, and it is also possible for such a sensitive entity having any predisposed concern of a mental origin [to] be somewhat distracted by the combination of the concern and the deeper potential for deeper meditation.

May we answer further, my sister?

Carla: Yes. Given that it is desirable to remain within the body, is there a tool which one may use to remain in the meditative state and enjoy the deeper state and yet be assured of remaining in the body and not rolling out?

I am L/Leema. There are many such tools, my sister, for those who are practiced at the "rolling out" of the body, as you have put it. However, for those present who have not such practice, we suggest the simple holding of the hands, for such auric infringement will of necessity cause the enlivener of the entity, the mind/body/spirit complex, to remain with its physical vehicle.

May we answer further, my sister?

Carla: No. Thank you.

I am L/Leema, and we thank you, my sister, and greet the next query.

A: Can a cat serve the same purpose as a hand?

I am L/Leema, and we find this is in large part correct, for the auric infringement of the second-density creature works also upon the third-density physical vehicle by the very nature of the enlivened touch, shall we say.

May we answer further, my sister?

A: No, thank you.

I am L/Leema, and we thank you. Is there another query?

N: Yes. I wonder if you would perhaps define and explain the various stages between light meditation, deep meditation, through deep meditation, trance, as far as the spirit or shall we say the individual's remaining with the vehicle or the displacement of that spirit through astral projection or whatever, as well as the instrument's ability to remember through the various stages through trance?

I am L/Leema, and am aware of your query, my brother, which covers much ground. We shall attempt to respond by asking that you picture the mind as a tree. In the conscious mind one is existing as upon the outer limbs and branches of [the] tree of mind. The winds of conversation, the thought and action, blow and gust and the limbs move about in response. As one quiets the mind by removing the attention from the outer world of winds, one moves down the branches to the trunk of the tree of mind.

The trunk may represent the deeper levels of meditation, which may be likened unto the waves of the brain which have been described as the alpha waves, which correspond also to the lighter levels of dozing or sleep but with the attention focused and alert. The mind may further be quieted and focused upon fewer and fewer points until the point of unity of focus is achieved.

This moves further down the trunk of the tree and as the tree then moves into the ground with its system of roots, so may the conscious mind be passed from, and the attention of the mind/body/spirit complex be able to perceive below the conscious mind into the roots of mind in a fashion which uncovers awareness of experience not consciously known to the entity.

This movement is that which roughly corresponds to the movement from the conscious meditation to the more trance-like state of awareness in which portions of the subconscious mind become available to the focused attention of the mind/body/spirit complex. As various of the roots of the tree of mind are explored by the focused attention, there is a deepening and enrichment of the trance state. The ability of an entity to remember consciously that which occurs while in the deeper levels of the trance state is a function of that entity's ability to achieve this trance state consciously as a function of the exercise of will and the practice of this ability. Many entities in the dream state enter the roots of the tree of mind and yet remember little of the experiences gathered there upon awakening, for there has been little conscious effort made to train the self to retain that which is experienced. The practice, whether in trance or in dreams, of remembering those experiences which occurred within the roots of the tree of mind is gained by the repetition of such experience.

May we answer further, my brother?

N: Yes. Then you're equating trance with sleep. During trance and with sleep, is the spirit complex displaced from the vehicle or is it only connected by the cord, or exactly what? I'm asking for several reasons. One is that when Mark Provost channeled Yadda, he seemed to be in a deep trance, or at least they keep referring to the fact that he's in a deep trance. But yet when someone in the room holds their hand up, Yadda seemed to be able to recognize them. And of course, I always thought deep trance mediums or instruments or whatever were totally oblivious to outside influences of a physical nature.

I am L/Leema, and your query is based upon some slight misunderstanding of the nature of the deeper levels of trance. There is the possibility that some entities who serve as the trance medium may wish to remain with the physical vehicle as it is given over in its use on some occasions to those who would speak through it, those entities not having physical vehicles of their own of that nature. The medium who chooses to remain with the vehicle is one who is usually learning another facet of the service that it performs as a trance medium and is not present because of any need to perform a function at that moment other than the learning of a certain lesson.

This level of trance of which we now speak is a level that is of the deeper nature and is of the nature utilized by the one who was known as Mark. This entity, however, did not choose to remain with its vehicle and gave over its use completely to others or individualized portions of others. This then allowed those known as Yadda to enter the vehicle and use it in a fashion which resembled its use by the one known as Mark. This enabled those of Yadda to utilize the optical apparatus as well as other portions of the physical vehicle, and thus enabled vision, sight and recognition to occur. It is much as you would use another entity's coat.

Most who serve as trance mediums do not work in these deeper levels of trance, for much can be accomplished in levels which do not require the complete giving over of the physical vehicle and its exit in so doing. These types of trance may allow, therefore, the one serving as …

(Side one of tape ends.)

(Jim channeling)

I am L/Leema, and am once again with this instrument, and we shall continue. These entities, therefore, remain with the physical vehicle and serve as what may be called an interpreter in order that the patterns of energy in the form of various visions may be translated and transmitted into the third-density illusion. This is the more normal level of trance, yet it still resides in the roots of the tree of mind and beneath the veil, shall we say, which separates the conscious and subconscious minds and the conscious meditation from the trance level of awareness.

May we answer further, my brother?

N: Yes, thank you very much. Then there is a differential in memory, as well as understanding, in the deeper trance as compared to the meditative or some level in between?

I am L/Leema, and am unsure as to whether we have a firm grasp upon your query, but shall attempt response. Please requestion if we have not properly grasped your query. The deeper levels of meditation and the deeper levels of trance provide a greater challenge for any entity to remember to bring back and to put together that which was experienced at those levels. Again, the practice and repetition is that which allows a greater remembering.

May we answer further, my brother?

N: Yes, thank you, if the instrument's not too tired, I have another query.

Please continue.

N: In those trance mediums who channel their spirit guides and so forth, there are some that can produce ectoplasm, or it is said that they can produce ectoplasm. How does this occur? And what level is usually necessary for channeling spirit guides?

I am L/Leema, and to take the latter query first, the entities known as spirit guides may be contacted in a variety of manners and levels of awareness, from the conscious waking state to the light meditation to trance and sleep.

Those who are able to produce the substance known as ectoplasm are those who have over a long portion of your time and in many cases in previous incarnations have been able to produce this substance by the application of the desire to be of service and the practice of the trance state. The substance itself is a materialization of that which would seem in your reality to be immaterial. It is the stepping down of the vibratory frequency of a certain form of light which is awakened in the heart chakra of the entity serving as trance medium. The connection then having been made between this third-density illusion and the finer levels or inner planes of this illusion and the lower levels of the fourth-density illusion then allow a contact to be made in what frequently is experienced as a shape or form which assumes a recognizable shape, most usually that of an entity resembling your third-density physical vehicle.

May we answer further, my brother?

N: Then these materializations are actual ectoplasm and are not thought-form considerations, I would assume? And I also understand from what you've said that it is—you have to have been doing this during prior incarnations in order to rechannel the material? It's not easily learned, in other words? Or developed?

I am L/Leema, and may affirm that much practice is necessary in order for this service to be performed. It is not impossible that it can be learned within one incarnational period of time, yet it is more likely to have been experienced in a series of incarnations. The form of the ectoplasmic material is a function of the thought of the one contacted, thus it is a thought form in that respect. The one so materializing is able to take the ectoplasm and form it according to its desire which is in turn a function of the desire and experience of those present in the third-density illusion who call for this service.

May we answer further, my brother?

N: And as you said, this does emanate from the heart chakra?

I am L/Leema, and this was indeed our statement, though this instrument is somewhat doubtful.

May we answer further, my brother?

N: Only one more query. I know the instrument must be getting tired. I have found it very difficult to completely clear the mind in meditation, in other words to go into the silence. Is there any sort of way that we can—any sort of gimmicks or so forth, that we can either hook up with universal mind or in some way quiet our own mind?

I am L/Leema, and many are the ways that have been devised by those such as yourself seeking to quiet the ever-rambunctious mind in its constant meanderings. The most frequently used technique is to use a mediator, shall we say, that is, a phrase or word or note or a single thought that will put the attention of the mind, through repetition, upon one thought or focus with the eventual goal of the removing even of that one focus in order that a more complete unity of self with all might be experienced.

This general type of technique attempts to strike a bargain or compromise, shall we say, for a time with the conscious mind, as the conscious mind is most normally functioning and therefore most usually comfortable with the activities of action and reaction and will in some cases be more easily quieted if it is given one simple activity to repeat time and again, like a child in the corner, shall we say, in order that after a variable length of time it may even be persuaded to become completely quiet and enjoy its new environment of silence and those experiences which emanate from the infinite inner silence.

May we answer further, my brother?

N: Well, just one clarification. The redundancy of one simple object will then focus on total quietness? Is that the basic conception?

I am L/Leema, and this is the hoped for result. As you are aware, there are varying degrees of success with various entities and upon various occasions for any entity.

May we answer further, my brother?

N: Thank you very much for all your answers.

I am L/Leema, and we thank you, my brother. Is there another query?

(Pause)

I am L/Leema, and we thank each for those queries offered this evening. Our words are but halting and humble attempts to reflect the greater portion of what we have found to be true in our own seeking. We realize that we may have spoken much which was not of value to one but we offer any that is of value to any so seeking, and we thank each for the invitation to join your group in whatever capacity. We shall leave this group at this time, rejoicing, as always, in that same love and light which shines upon all. We are L/Leema. Adonai, my friends. Adonai. ✣

www.ingramcontent.com/pod-product-compliance
Lightning Source LLC
Chambersburg PA
CBHW080420230426
43662CB00015B/2166